SOFTWARE
ENGINEERING
SELECTED READINGS

Edited by
Eric J. Braude
Boston University,
Metropolitan College

IEEE
*Networking
the World*™

The Institute of Electrical and Electronics Engineers, Inc.

2000 EDUCATIONAL ACTIVITIES BOARD (EAB)

Dr. Lyle D. Feisel
Vice President, Educational Activities

Printed in the United States of America

ISBN 0-7803-4817-6

Editorial Production Administration - Jill R. Bagley

Published by the Institute of Electrical and Electronics Engineers, Inc.
445 Hoes Lane, PO Box 1331, Piscataway, NJ 08855-1331.

http://www.ieee.org/organizations/eab/

ABOUT THE EDITOR

Dr. Eric J. Braude holds a master's degree in computer science from the University of Miami and a Ph.D. in mathematics from Columbia University. From 1978 to 1990, he held research, management, and engineering positions in industry and government. He was chairman of the Boston University Metropolitan College Computer Science Department form 1990 to 1995, where he is currently on the faculty. Dr. Braude teaches software engineers at the graduate level, and advises corporations on object-oriented methods and tool design. He is the author of several papers on object-oriented simulation including, "The Algebra of Calculus" (Houghton Mifflin, 1990), "Designing and Analyzing Object-Oriented Systems" (IEEE, 1997), and "Object-Oriented Analysis, Design and Testing (IEEE, 1998).

CONTENTS

PREFACE

The extent and complexity of software increased rapidly during the last decades of the 20th century. As a result, there is a widespread demand for improvement in the application development process.

This collection of papers describes tools, techniques, experimental results, ideas, and hints for each of the software engineering phases. Improvement in software engineering is ultimately a social process, in which teams develop collective confidence in tools, methods, languages and procedures, one at a time. Software engineering is now mature enough to progress beyond simplistic prescriptions. For example, the question is not so much whether or not engineers believe in code inspection, but whether particular code inspection techniques pay off in particular circumstances.

The debates about whether or not silver bullets exist are behind us: they don't. Before us, however, is the work of implementing known, useful development methods: methods that we owe it to our users to implement, and for which this collection of papers provides some guidance.

Eric J. Braude
Editor

CHAPTER 1
PROCESS

There are many ways of going about developing software products: each of these ways is a "process." A process has to be readily understandable to the development team using it, believed by them to be effective, and adaptable to varying circumstances. In addition to team processes, engineers also require individual processes for creating software.

In the papers that follow, Jacobson, Booch, and Rumbaugh describe the Unified Process, containing an amalgam of processes and techniques that each of them developed in prior years. Diaz and Sligo explain how Motorola used the Software Engineering Institute's Capability Maturity Model to improve its software development process. Fitzgerald and O'Kane report on a corporate process improvement effort, identifying "critical success factors" which are particularly useful in moving organizations to higher levels of process competence. Moore describes efforts by the IEEE Software Engineering Standards Committee to "unify and integrate its collection of software standards." Watts Humphrey presents the Personal Software Process™ (PSP), targeted to individual the software engineer. Ferguson *et al* recount results of applying the PSP in three case studies. Brown and Wallnau describe Component-Based Software Engineering, distilling key points from a group discussion of this subject. Yang et al present a process based on Jacobson's Objectory process, and utilizing the Unified Modeling Language.

Feature

Reprinted from IEEE Software,
May/June 1999, pp. 96-102.

The following article is the introductory chapter from The Unified Development Process *by Ivar Jacobson, Grady Booch, and James Rumbaugh. These "three amigos" have been influential in creating a standardized object-oriented analysis and design notation, UML. This offering describes the three amigos' vision of a standardized software development process.*
—Steve McConnell, editor-in-chief

The Unified Process

Ivar Jacobson, Grady Booch, and James Rumbaugh, Rational Software

oday, the trend in software is toward bigger, more complex systems. This is due in part to the fact that computers become more powerful every year, leading users to expect more from them. This trend has also been influenced by the expanding use of the Internet for exchanging all kinds of information—from plain text to formatted text to pictures to diagrams to multimedia. Our appetite for ever-more sophisticated software grows as we learn from one product release to the next how the product could be improved. We want software that is better adapted to our needs, but that, in turn, merely makes the software more complex. In short, we want more.

We also want it faster. Time to market is another important driver.

Getting there, however, is difficult. Our demands for powerful, complex software have not been matched with how software is developed. Today, most people develop software using the same methods that were used as long as 25 years ago. This is a problem. Unless we update our methods, we will not be able to accomplish our goal of developing the complex software needed today.

The software problem boils down to the difficulty developers face in pulling together the many strands of a large software undertaking. The software development community needs a controlled way of working. It needs a process that integrates the many facets of software development. It needs a common approach, a process that

3

♦ provides guidance to the order of a team's activities,

♦ directs the tasks of individual developers and the team as a whole,

♦ specifies what artifacts should be developed, and

♦ offers criteria for monitoring and measuring a project's products and activities.

The presence of a well-defined and well-managed process is a key discriminator between hyperproductive projects and unsuccessful ones. The Unified Software Development Process—the outcome of more than 30 years of experience—is a solution to the software problem.

THE UNIFIED PROCESS IN A NUTSHELL

First and foremost the Unified Process is a software development process. A software development process is the set of activities needed to transform a user's requirements into a software system (see Figure 1). However, the Unified Process is more than a single process; it is a generic process framework that can be specialized for a very large class of software systems, for different application areas, different types of organizations, different competence levels, and different project sizes.

The Unified Process is component-based, which means that the software system being built is made up of software components interconnected via well-defined interfaces.

The Unified Process uses the Unified Modeling Language when preparing all blueprints of the software system. In fact, UML is an integral part of the Unified Process—they were developed hand in hand.

However, the real distinguishing aspects of the Unified Process are captured in the three key words—use-case driven, architecture-centric, and iterative and incremental. This is what makes the Unified Process unique.

THE UNIFIED PROCESS IS USE-CASE DRIVEN

A software system is brought into existence to serve its users. Therefore, to build a successful system we must know what its prospective users want and need.

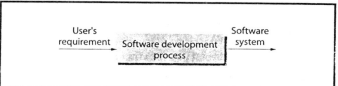

FIGURE 1. A software development process.

The term *user* refers not only to human users but to other systems. In this sense, the term user represents someone or something (such as another system outside the proposed system) that interacts with the system being developed. An example of an interaction is a human who uses an automatic teller machine. He or she inserts the plastic card, replies to questions called up by the machine on its viewing screen, and receives a sum of cash. In response to the user's card and answers, the system performs a sequence of actions that provide the user with a result of value, namely the cash withdrawal.

An interaction of this sort is a *use case*. A use case is a piece of functionality in the system that gives a user a result of value. Use cases capture functional requirements. All the use cases together make up the *use-case model,* which describes the complete functionality of the system. This model replaces the traditional functional specification of the system. A functional specification can be said to answer the question, What is the system supposed to do? The use case strategy can be characterized by adding three words to the end of this question: for each user? These three words have a very important implication. They force us to think in terms of value to users and not just in terms of functions that might be good to have.

However, use cases are not just a tool for specifying the requirements of a system. They also drive its design, implementation, and test; that is, they drive the development process. Based on the use-case model, developers create a series of design and implementation models that realize the use cases. The developers review each successive model for conformance to the use-case model. The testers test the implementation to ensure that the components of the implementation model correctly implement the use cases. In this way, the use cases not only initiate the development process but bind it together. *Use-case driven* means that the development process follows a flow—it proceeds through a series of workflows that derive from the use cases. Use cases are specified, use cases are designed, and at

Feature ···

the end use cases are the source from which the testers construct the test cases.

While it is true that use cases drive the process, they are not selected in isolation. They are developed in tandem with the system architecture. That is, the

The architecture must be designed to allow the system to evolve, not only through its initial development but through future generations.

use cases drive the system architecture and the system architecture influences the selection of the use cases. Therefore, both the system architecture and the use cases mature as the life cycle continues.

THE UNIFIED PROCESS IS ARCHITECTURE-CENTRIC

The role of software architecture is similar in nature to the role architecture plays in building construction. The building is looked at from various viewpoints: structure, services, heat conduction, plumbing, electricity, and so on. This allows a builder to see a complete picture before construction begins. Similarly, architecture in a software system is described as different views of the system being built.

The software architecture concept embodies the most significant static and dynamic aspects of the system. The architecture grows out of the needs of the enterprise, as sensed by users and other stakeholders, and as reflected in the use cases. However, it is also influenced by many other factors: the platform the software is to run on (such as computer architecture, operating system, database management system, and protocols for network communication), the reusable building blocks available (such as a framework for graphical user interfaces), deployment considerations, legacy systems, and nonfunctional requirements (such as performance and reliability). Architecture is a view of the whole design with the important characteristics made more visible by leaving details aside. Since what is significant depends in part on judgment, which, in turn, comes with experience, the value of the architecture depends on the people assigned to the task. However, process helps the architect to focus on the right goals, such as understandability, resilience to future changes, and reuse.

How are use cases and architecture related? Every product has both function and form. One or the other is not enough. These two forces must be balanced to get a successful product. In this case function corresponds to use cases and form to architecture. There needs to be interplay between use cases and architecture. It is a "chicken and egg" problem. On the one hand, the use cases must, when realized, fit in the architecture. On the other hand, the architecture must allow room for realizations of all the required use cases, now and in the future. In reality, both the architecture and the use cases must evolve in parallel.

Thus the architects cast the system in a form. It is that form, the architecture, that must be designed so as to allow the system to evolve, not only through its initial development but through future generations. To find such a form, the architects must work from a general understanding of the key functions, that is, the key use cases, of the system. These key use cases may amount to only 5 percent to 10 percent of all the use cases, but they are the significant ones, the ones that constitute the core system functions. Here is the process in simplified terms:

♦ The architect creates a rough outline of the architecture, starting with the part of the architecture that is not specific to the use cases (such as platform). Although this part of the architecture is use-case independent, the architect must have a general understanding of the use cases prior to the creation of the architectural outline.

♦ Next, the architect works with a subset of the identified use cases, the ones that represent the key functions of the system under development. Each selected use case is specified in detail and realized in terms of subsystems, classes, and components.

♦ As the use cases are specified and they mature, more of the architecture is discovered. This, in turn, leads to the maturation of more use cases.

This process continues until the architecture is deemed stable.

THE UNIFIED PROCESS IS ITERATIVE AND INCREMENTAL

Developing a commercial software product is a large undertaking that may continue over several months to possibly a year or more. It is practical to divide the work into smaller slices or mini-projects.

5

Each mini-project is an *iteration* that results in an *increment*. Iterations refer to steps in the workflow, and increments, to growth in the product. To be most effective, the iterations must be controlled; that is they must be selected and carried out in a planned way. This is why they are mini-projects.

Developers base the selection of what is to be implemented in an iteration upon two factors. First, the iteration deals with a group of use cases that together extend the usability of the product as developed so far. Second, the iteration deals with the most important risks. Successive iterations build on the development artifacts from the state at which they were left at the end of the previous iteration. It is a mini-project, so from the use cases it continues through the consequent development work—analysis, design, implementation, and test—that realizes in the form of executable code the use cases being developed in the iteration. Of course, an increment is not necessarily additive. Especially in the early phases of the life cycle, developers may be replacing a superficial design with a more detailed or sophisticated one. In later phases increments are typically additive.

In every iteration, the developers identify and specify the relevant use cases, create a design using the chosen architecture as a guide, implement the design in components, and verify that the components satisfy the use cases. If an iteration meets its goals—and it usually does—development proceeds with the next iteration. When an iteration does not meet its goals, the developers must revisit their previous decisions and try a new approach.

To achieve the greatest economy in development, a project team will try to select only the iterations required to reach the project goal. It will try to sequence the iterations in a logical order. A successful project will proceed along a straight course with only small deviations from the course the developers initially planned. Of course, to the extent that unforeseen problems add iterations or alter the sequence of iterations, the development process will take more effort and time. Minimizing unforeseen problems is one of the goals of risk reduction.

There are many benefits to a controlled iterative process:

♦ Controlled iteration reduces the cost risk to the expenditures on a single increment. If the developers need to repeat the iteration, the organization loses only the misdirected effort of one iteration, not the value of the entire product.

♦ Controlled iteration reduces the risk of not getting the product to market on the planned schedule. By identifying risks early in development, the time spent resolving them occurs early in the schedule when people are less rushed than they are late in the schedule. In the "traditional" approach, where difficult problems are first revealed by system test, the time required to resolve them usually exceeds the time remaining in the schedule and nearly always forces a delay of delivery.

♦ Controlled iteration speeds up the tempo of the whole development effort because developers work more efficiently toward results in clear, short focus rather than in a long, ever-sliding schedule.

♦ Controlled iteration acknowledges a reality often ignored—that user needs and the corresponding requirements cannot be fully defined up front. They are typically refined in successive iterations. This mode of operation makes it easier to adapt to changing requirements.

These concepts—use-case driven, architecture-centric, and iterative and incremental develop-

> **By identifying risks early in development, time spent resolving occurs early when people are less rushed.**

ment—are equally important. Architecture provides the structure in which to guide the work in the iterations, whereas use cases define the goals and drive the work of each iteration. Removing one of the three key ideas would severely reduce the value of the Unified Process. It is like a three-legged stool. Without one of its legs, the stool will fall over.

Now that we have introduced the three key concepts, it is time to take a look at the whole process, its life cycle, artifacts, workflows, phases, and iterations.

THE LIFE OF THE UNIFIED PROCESS

The Unified Process repeats over a series of cycles making up the life of a system. Each cycle concludes with a product release to customers.

Each cycle consists of four phases: inception, elaboration, construction, and transition. Each phase is further subdivided into iterations, as discussed earlier. See Figure 2 (on the next page).

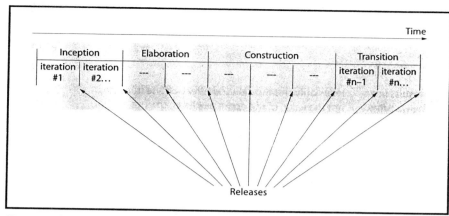

FIGURE 2. A cycle with its phases and its iterations.

The product

Each cycle results in a new release of the system, and each release is a product ready for delivery. It consists of a body of source code embodied in components that can be compiled and executed, plus manuals and associated deliverables. However, the finished product also has to accommodate the needs, not just of the users, but of all the stakeholders, that is, all the people who will work with the product. The software product ought to be more than the machine code that executes.

The finished product includes the requirements, use cases, nonfunctional requirements, and test cases. It includes the architecture and the visual models—artifacts modeled by the Unified Modeling Language. In fact, it includes all the elements we have been talking about in this chapter, because it is these things that enable the stakeholders—customers, users, analysts, designers, implementers, testers, and management—to specify, design, implement, test, and use a system. Moreover, it is these things that enable the stakeholders to use and modify the system from generation to generation.

Even if executable components are the most important artifacts from the users' perspective, they alone are not enough. This is because the environment mutates. Operating systems, database systems, and the underlying machines advance. As the mission becomes better understood, the requirements themselves may change. In fact, it is one of the constants of software development that the requirements change. Eventually developers must undertake a new cycle, and managers must finance it. To carry out the next cycle efficiently, the developers need all the representations of the software product (Figure 3):

♦ A use-case model with all the use cases and their relationships to users.
♦ An analysis model, which has two purposes: to refine the use cases in more detail and to make an initial allocation of the behavior of the system to a set of objects that provides the behavior.

♦ A design model that defines (a) the static structure of the system as subsystems, classes, and interfaces and (b) the use cases realized as collaborations among the subsystems, classes, and interfaces.

♦ An implementation model, which includes components (representing source code) and the mapping of the classes to components.

♦ A deployment model, which defines the physical nodes of computers and the mapping of the components to those nodes.

♦ A test model, which describes the test cases that verify the use cases.

♦ And, of course, a representation of the architecture.

The system may also have a domain model or a business model that describes the business context of the system.

All these models are related. Together, they represent the system as a whole. Elements in one model have trace dependencies backwards and forwards with the help of links to other models. For instance, a use case (in the use-case model) can be traced to a use-case realization (in the design model) to a test case (in the test model). Traceability facilitates understanding and change.

Phases within a cycle

Each cycle takes place over time. This time, in turn, is divided into four phases, as shown in Figure 4. Through a sequence of models, stakeholders visualize what goes on in these phases. Within each phase managers or developers may break the work down still further—into iterations and the ensuing increments. Each phase terminates in a *milestone*. We define each milestone by the availability of a set of artifacts; that is, certain models or documents have been brought to a prescribed state.

The milestones serve many purposes. The most critical is that managers have to make certain crucial decisions before work can proceed to the next phase. Milestones also enable management, as well as the developers themselves, to monitor the progress of the work as it passes these four key points. Finally, by keeping track of the time and effort spent on each

7

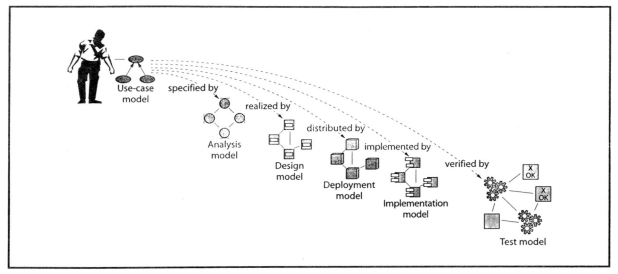

FIGURE 3. There are dependencies between many of the models of the Unified Process. As an example, the dependencies between the use-case model and the other models are indicated.

phase, we develop a body of data. This data is useful in estimating time and staff requirements for other projects, projecting staff needs over project time, and controlling progress against these projections.

Figure 4 lists the workflows—requirements, analysis, design, implementation, and test—in the left-hand column. The curves approximate (they should not be taken too literally) the extent to which the workflows are carried out in each phase. Recall that each phase usually is subdivided into iterations, or mini-projects. A typical iteration goes through all the five workflows as shown for an iteration in the elaboration phase in Figure 4.

During the inception phase, a good idea is developed into a vision of the end product and the business case for the product is presented. Essentially, this phase answers the following questions:

♦ What is the system primarily going to do for each of its major users?

♦ What could an architecture for that system look like?

♦ What is the plan and what will it cost to develop the product?

A simplified use-case model that contains the most critical use cases answers the first question. At

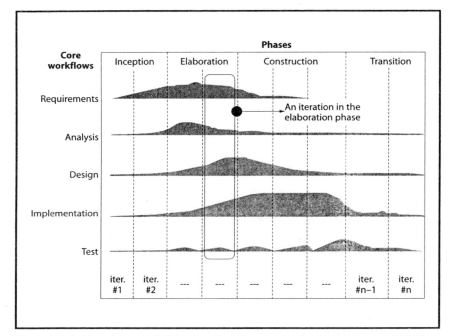

FIGURE 4. The five workflows—requirements, analysis, design, implementation, and test—take place over the four phases: inception, elaboration, construction, and transition.

this stage the architecture is tentative. It is typically just an outline containing the most crucial subsystems. In this phase, the most important risks are identified and prioritized, the elaboration phase is planned in detail, and the whole project is roughly estimated.

During the elaboration phase, most of the product's use cases are specified in detail and the system

architecture is designed. The relationship between the architecture of a system and the system itself is paramount. A simple way to put it is that the architecture is analogous to a skeleton covered with skin but with very little muscle, the software, between the bone and the skin—just enough muscle to allow the skeleton to make basic movements. The system is the whole body with skeleton, skin, and muscle.

Therefore, the architecture is expressed as views of all the models of the system, which together represent the whole system. This implies that there are architectural views of the use-case model, the analysis model, the design model, the implementation model, and the deployment model. The view of the implementation model includes components to prove that the architecture is executable. During this phase of development the most critical use cases identified during the elaboration phase are realized. The result of this phase is an architecture baseline.

At the end of the elaboration phase, the project manager is in a position to plan the activities and estimate the resources required to complete the project. Here the key question is, Are the use cases, architecture, and plans stable enough, and are the risks under sufficient control to be able to commit to the whole development work in a contract?

During the construction phase the product is built—muscle, the completed software, is added to the skeleton, the architecture. In this phase, the architecture baseline grows to become the full-fledged system. The vision evolves into a product ready for transfer to the user community. During this phase of development, the bulk of the required resources is expended. The architecture of the system is stable, however, because the developers may discover better ways of structuring the system, they may suggest minor architectural changes to the architects. At the end of this phase, the product contains all the use cases that management and the customer agreed to develop for this release. It may not be entirely free of defects, however. More defects will be discovered and fixed during the transition phase. The milestone question is, Does the product meet users' needs sufficiently for some customers to take early delivery?

The transition phase covers the period during which the product moves into beta release. In the beta release a small number of experienced users try the product and report defects and deficiencies. Developers then correct the reported problems and incorporate some of the suggested improvements into a general release for the larger user community.

The transition phase involves activities such as manufacturing, training customer personnel, providing help-line assistance, and correcting defects found after delivery. The maintenance team often divides these defects into two categories: those with sufficient effect on operations to justify an immediate delta release and those that can be corrected in the next regular release.

The Unified Process is component based. It uses the new visual modeling standard, UML, and relies on three key ideas—use cases, architecture, and iterative and incremental development. To make these ideas work, a multifaceted process is required, one that takes into consideration cycles, phases, workflows, risk mitigation, quality control, project management, and configuration control. The Unified Process has established a framework that integrates all those different facets. This framework also works as an umbrella under which tool vendors and developers can build tools to support the automation of the process, to support the individual workflows, to build all the different models, and to integrate the work across the life cycle and across all models. ❖

Adapted from Chapter 1 of The Unified Software Development Process, *by Ivar Jacobson, Grady Booch, and James Rumbaugh, ISBN: 0-201-57169-2. Reprinted by permission of Addison Wesley Longman, One Jacob Way, Reading, MA 01867. All rights reserved. Contact Addison Wesley Longman at (781) 944-3700, http://www.awl.com/cseng/.*

9

feature

Reprinted from IEEE Software,
Sept./Oct. 1997, pp. 75-81.

How Software Process Improvement Helped Motorola

MICHAEL DIAZ AND JOSEPH SLIGO
Motorola SSTG

Many organizations are using or considering the Capability Maturity Model as a vehicle for software process improvement. But does the CMM provide real benefits? The authors offer metrics and data that show the results of Motorola's CMM usage.

In many companies, the Capability Maturity Model[1] plays a major role in defining software process improvement. Frequently, organizations contemplating software process improvement (SPI) seek assurances that tangible benefits will result from such activities. Pockets of data across industry[2] show that CMM-based process improvement is making a difference in those organizations committed to improvement. Raytheon yielded a twofold increase in its productivity and a return ratio of 7.7 to 1 on its improvement expenditures, for a 1990 savings of $4.48 million from a $0.58 million investment. Over a period of four and a half years, from mid-1988 to the end of 1992, the company eliminated $15.8 million in rework costs.

SEI CMM Level	Number of Projects	Quality (In-Process Defects/ MAELOC*)	Cycle Time (X factor)	Productivity (Relative)
1	3	n/a	1.0	n/a
2	9	890	3.2	1.0
3	5	411	2.7	0.8
4	8	205	5.0	2.3
5	9	126	7.8	2.8

TABLE 1
MOTOROLA GED PROJECT PERFORMANCE BY SEI CMM LEVEL.

*Million assembly-equivalent lines of code

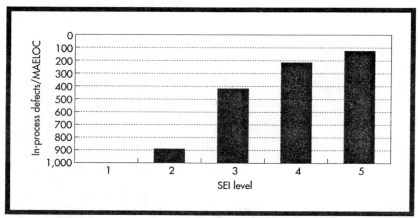

Figure 1. Quality by SEI level, with quality defined by the scarcity of in-process defects.

Hughes Aircraft has computed a 5-to-1 return ratio for its process improvement initiatives, based on changes in its cost–performance index. This has generated an annual savings of about $2 million above Hughes' process improvement expenditures. Tinker Air Force Base recently computed a 5-to-1 return on investment for its process improvement initiatives, which generated a savings of $3.8 million from a $0.64 million investment. Other sources confirm this trend.[3,4]

Motorola has long been a champion of the SEI's CMM as a vehicle for furthering software process improvement. In November 1995, the company's Government Electronics Division was independently assessed at SEI level 4. The assessment further rated GED's policies and procedures at SEI level 5, without verifying project implementation of the level 5 key process areas. Motorola GED employs about 1,500 engineers to design and build a wide variety of government electronic systems. Approximately 350 GED engineers participate directly in software development. Our organization's long history of support for process improvement was, we found, to prove key in reaping benefits from the CMM process. In effect, we supplemented the SEI's model with several of our own programs.

The cycle time, quality, and productivity metrics we use are based on current measures from approximately 34 programs, which are at various stages in the software life cycle. Motorola GED plans to reevaluate this project performance analysis when all projects are completed.

PROCESS METRICS

At Motorola GED, each project performs a quarterly SEI self-assessment. The project evaluates each key process area (KPA) activity as a score between 1 and 10, which is then rolled into an average score for each KPA. Any KPA average score that falls below 7 is considered a weakness. The SEI level for the project is defined as the level at which all associated KPAs are considered strengths, that is, all KPA average scores must equal 7 or more.

GED uses quality, cycle time, and productivity to evaluate development programs because our customers value these attributes. In addition, Motorola has always valued quality in all its products and processes: its Six Sigma Quality focus has been a corporate initiative for several years. Six Sigma is a quality process that looks at reject rates as low as a few per million opportunities. This process originally started in the manufacturing arena and has been expanded to software at Motorola.

Recently, Motorola corporate has been championing the 10X cycle-time initiative, which seeks to have all business elements achieve a 10-fold reduction in product cycle time to accelerate the introduction of new products. Productivity is directly related to our ability to win new programs from our traditional US Department of Defense customer and drives our profitability in emerging commercial products. Table 1 summarizes the Motorola GED improvement trends for quality, cycle time, and productivity by SEI level. Motorola obtained performance data in these areas for each program from its internal metrics, and categorized them by SEI level as determined by each project's internal self assessment. The projects involved in the analysis are at various stages of development.

A more detailed examination of each

12

metric follows, beginning with the empirical methodology by which the metric was derived. Specific improvement results are not entirely attributable to increasing SEI maturity levels, because Motorola GED has put into place significant cycle time and quality initiatives above and beyond the SEI CMM.

Quality. A problem detected in the same phase it was introduced is defined as an *error*; a *defect* is a problem that escapes detection in the phase it was introduced. The *quality* metric is defined as defects per million earned assembly-equivalent lines of code (defects/MEAELOC). AELOC, the *assembly-equivalent lines of code*, equals delivered source instructions × the Capers Jones Expansion Factor.[5] The *earned* AELOC, or EAELOC, is defined as AELOC × percent complete, which equals the budgeted cost of work performed/budget at complete.

Results. Figure 1 examines the quality of each project categorized by the project's internal SEI self-assessment. Since most of these programs are still active, we derived the normalization factor by using the EAELOC.

Analysis. Project results show that each level of the CMM improves quality by a factor of about 2. The improvement in quality is expected for projects that transition from level 2 to 3 due to the Peer Review KPA found in level 3. Peer reviews have been widely recognized in the industry for being the single most important factor in detecting and preventing defects in software products. Quality is also expected to improve for projects transitioning from level 3 to 4 due to the Quantitative Process Management and Software Quality Management KPAs. Using quality metric data such as phase containment effectiveness (the ratio of problems inserted and detected within a phase to the summation of all problems introduced in that phase) will let projects modify their processes when the observed metric falls below the organizational control limits.

For example, if the peer review

process detects 75 of every 100 problems introduced during detailed design, the phase containment effectiveness would be 75 percent. You can estimate the number of problems introduced by using historical defect density data from similar projects and tracking problems found early in the development cycle. (A method to predict problems throughout the development cycle is given elsewhere.[6]) The Motorola GED control limit is at 85 percent phase containment effectiveness. Projects below this threshold perform causal analysis to improve their peer review and testing processes. We attribute the improvement from level 4 to level 5 to the Defect Prevention and Process Change Management KPAs. Projects operating at this level perform Pareto analysis on the root cause of their problems and perform causal analysis to determine the process changes needed to prevent similar problems from occurring in the future.

You can more readily achieve large improvements in defect density when the number of defects is large, as would be expected in lower–maturity-level projects. At higher maturity levels, it becomes increasingly difficult to dramatically reduce the defect density.

Cycle time. We define the X factor or cycle-time metric as the amount of calendar time for the baseline project to develop a product divided by the cycle time for the new project. For example, if the

baseline project took six months to complete, and the new project took two months to complete, then the new project's X factor would be 3. Motorola's goal is to achieve an X factor of 10 for new projects within five years.

The project we used as our baseline was a similar project completed at Motorola GED prior to 1992. Each project at GED tracks its cycle time by selecting a program with a similar target domain and by tracking its progress against that baseline program. The cycle-time ratio of the current program over the baseline program is known as the program's X factor. Many times the completion of a program is not entirely under the contractor's control, especially with government funding curve slowdowns. In addition, government contracts typically involve a qualification test cycle that is not normally seen in the commercial world. To more accurately reflect the potential cycle time from a commercial viewpoint, cycle time is measured with respect to a project's first increment. This should eliminate the effect of qualification testing and government funding changes on a project and more accurately compare Motorola GED with the rest of the commercially oriented company.

Results. Figure 2 shows the cycle-time improvements with respect to SEI level. Because the X factor is derived by dividing an older, baseline project's completion time by the current project's com-

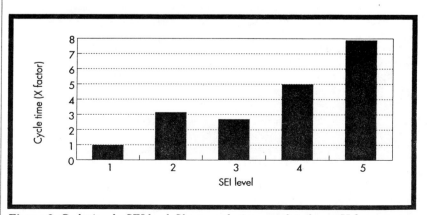

***Figure 2.** Cycle time by SEI level. Shorter cycle times result in larger X factors.*

13

feature

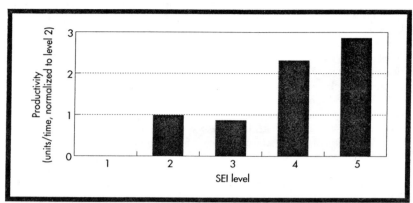

Figure 3. *Relative productivity by SEI level, normalized to the productivity of an average level 2 project. We define productivity as the number of assembly-equivalent lines of code produced, divided by the time required to produce them.*

pletion time, the shorter the current project the larger the X factor.

Analysis. Analysis of the data shows a 3.2 X factor for projects transitioning from level 1 to 2, a surprising decrease in cycle time for projects that move from level 2 to 3, an increase from 2.7X to 5.0X for projects that move from level 3 to 4, and an increase from 5.0X to 7.8X for projects that move from level 4 to 5. The decrease in cycle-time X factor for projects moving from level 2 to 3 may indicate a weak correlation between schedule performance and maturity level that has been seen in other CMM benefit surveys. Elsewhere, we have noted a weak schedule performance index correlation to maturity levels above level 1.[4] At least one other survey, however, does not evince such a correlation.[3]

The upward trend in cycle time above level 3 tends to corroborate the underlying assumption that higher-maturity projects have a better schedule performance index.

Motorola's 10X initiative is separate and in addition to the SEI CMM level 5 initiative. A major component of the 10X initiative is the implementation of a life cycle called incremental development. The idea is to complete a thread of functionality that will test all the system interfaces and demonstrate some functionality that has meaning to the customer.

Because the effort to progress from level 2 to level 3 involves a significant number of KPAs and process changes, it is expected that such a project may also have trouble absorbing a new life cycle such as incremental development.

Because many of the projects used as a basis for this analysis are still in development, further analysis with final schedule performance data is required to corroborate the preliminary findings. Another attribute that seems to correlate with increasing SEI maturity level is the decrease in variability of schedule and cost performance. The performance to plan variability decreases with higher maturity levels.

Productivity. We define *productivity* as the amount of work produced divided by the time to produce that work. This may be measured in source lines of code per hour or a similar measure. Each project at Motorola GED tracks its productivity by measuring AELOC produced and the number of hours needed to produce that code.

Results. For proprietary reasons, we do not show the actual number of lines of code per hour. Figure 3 does, however, show the relative productivity between projects at different levels of maturity. The data is normalized to the productivity of an average level 2 project.

Analysis. Factors other than process maturity affect productivity, most importantly technology changes. For example, the data shown includes projects that may have started before some form of automated code generation became available. In addition, the amount of code reuse on a project can greatly affect that project's productivity. As projects increase their level of maturity, the organization is better able to effectively reuse software source code. Likewise, software code that is reused from a high-maturity-level project requires less rework and is more easily understood. These factors act as multipliers in the productivity of high-maturity-level projects.

Projects experience an unexpected decrease in productivity when moving from level 2 to level 3. This appears to be a side effect of asking project staff to do too many new things all at once at level 3. When instituting a level 3 system, new processes are rolled out that greatly affect the way individual project members perform their tasks. This "new process rollout" does not have as great an impact at higher maturity levels. As with any adoption of new technology, we expect that an absorption cycle will be needed before the full benefits can be observed. At levels 4 and 5, each project quantitatively measures its own performance and can effectively change its processes while maintaining productivity.

Yet simply measuring performance does not ensure that productivity can be maintained. First, when you analyze and select any new process improvement, you should do so with the overall goal of at least maintaining productivity if not increasing it. Second, you must then monitor the actual productivity impact of the process improvement you implement. Real-time adjustments to the process improvement may be needed to keep the project working efficiently.

IMPLEMENTATION STRATEGIES

SPI implementation at Motorola GED began in 1989, when GED was assessed at level 2 of the Process Maturity

14

Model. At this time, we had already met most of the level 2 KPAs by doing what our government contracts required. Yet, while each project performed certain level 2 activities as required, there was no real organizational focus on software engineering processes.

While at level 2, GED's chief software engineers began focusing on process improvement. A high-level standard policy and procedure further defined GED processes for software engineering, as did the publication of the *Software Quality Management Manual*. This manual laid out steps to follow in a typical "waterfall" software development, where requirements analysis led to design, which in turn led to code and testing. At this time a software functional team was created to attempt to unify software engineers from various parts of the organization into a cohesive team. Peer review concepts were also introduced. These activities led to a level 3 assessment of Motorola GED in 1992.

Working groups. Starting in 1992 and continuing through 1994, the engineering organization created a process improvement working group, made up of senior practitioners. In addition, an initial software engineering improvement working group was formed with eight senior task leaders responsible for software development. This group had hands-on leadership from the engineering department manager, which proved critical to its success. It created the burden code metrics tool, which collected the amount and type of effort expended on each project. The group also defined and applied process and quality metrics that were useful for each project. At the end of this period, GED staff created the *Handbook for Quantitative Management of Software Process and Quality*, based on this group's work. These activities resulted in GED being assessed at level 4 of the Process Maturity Model, based on the PMM, with goals added from the CMM.

Since 1994, GED has maintained a defect prevention working group that looks at quality data from around the organization to identify systemic causes of poor quality. This group also created the *Defect Prevention Handbook*, which projects can use to perform their own defect prevention activities. The chief software engineer group was expanded to ensure that all new projects could begin operating at level 5; each project performs a self-assessment of CMM activities to identify areas that need work. During this period, the level 5 metrics tool was created and released to help projects integrate metrics collection from various sources in their level 4 and level 5 activities. In addition, GED expanded the working group from a single team of eight members to approximately four teams, each with a dozen software leaders. The chief software engineers also created handbooks for process change management and technology change management.

Throughout these activities, senior management sponsorship proved critical to the success of the process improvement efforts. This meant not only taking an active interest in the progress of various process improvement initiatives, but also providing funding and time to do the work, and rewarding those who contributed. Ongoing activities include

♦ continuing review and improvement of existing handbooks;
♦ maintenance of the process improvement request system;
♦ weekly meetings of the working groups to address process, technology, and people issues;
♦ meetings of chief software engineers and all new-project staffs to ensure that level 5 principles are followed; and
♦ ongoing integration of development and management tools.

Optimizing implementation. From the data gleaned during these activities, we found that several strategies provide optimal results.

♦ Focus on improving new projects. It is extremely difficult to change projects, especially at a low maturity level, once they have started.
♦ Adopt a top-down focus before immersing yourself in CMM details; start by assessing the intent of each KPA so that you can determine how it fits into your environment.
♦ Emphasize productivity, quality, and cycle time. Avoid process for its own sake.
♦ Management commitment is needed from all levels; commitment from upper management won't be enough unless individual project leaders and managers are also determined to succeed.
♦ Practitioners and task leaders, not outside process experts, should be used to define processes.
♦ Managers must be convinced of process improvement's value; it's not free, but in the long run it more than pays for itself.
♦ The customer must be kept informed about the process, especially when process changes occur.
♦ Copying process documents from other organizations usually does not work well; the process must match your organization.
♦ Overcoming resistance to change is probably the most difficult rung to climb on the SEI CMM ladder.

Process change takes time, talent, and a commitment that many organizations are uncomfortable with. Based on our experience, we believe the investment is worth it.

> **Practitioners and task leaders, not outside process experts, should define process.**

ECONOMIC BENEFITS

To evaluate how much we saved, we must first calculate how much we expended on SPI efforts, then evaluate how much the errors and defects caught or eliminated by these processes would have cost us.

The process improvement effort consisted of the following to support the base

feature

of 350 software developers:

- ♦ four full-time chief software engineers = 48 staff-months;
- ♦ task leaders of the software engineering improvement working group = 34 projects × 1 hour/week = 10.5 staff-months;
- ♦ prephase kickoffs and post-mortems: 34 projects × 1 hour per phase × 7 phases = 1.5 staff-months;
- ♦ software development planning: 34 projects × 5 days = 1 staff-month; and
- ♦ defect prevention working group: 8 members × 1 hour per week = 2.5 staff-months.

The total of all process improvement activities was approximately a 1.5 percent investment of our base staffing.

From a quality perspective, the defect injection rate decreases by roughly half each time a project advances a CMM level. Therefore, an SEI level 2 project has a defect injection rate eight times greater than an SEI level 5 program. The cost of rework is therefore at least eight times greater at level 2. Assuming that each defect requires an average of 16 hours' rework and analysis, and that the cost of rework is approximately $100 an hour, a typical 500,000-AELOC (about 100,000 SLOC) project can anticipate the following savings:

- ♦ At level 5, 63 defects (based upon 126 defects per MAELOC) would expend $100,800 on rework.
- ♦ At level 2, 445 defects (based upon 890 defects per MAELOC) would expend $712,000 on rework.

A typical 100,000-SLOC project would span 18 months and employ approximately 20 software engineers. If we allocate the 1.5-percent process improvement cost into each specific project, this would amount to 1.5 percent × 20 people × 18 months × 167 hours × $100/hr = $90,180 investment.

The resulting return on investment would be ($712,000 − $100,800) = $611,200 for a $90,180 investment, or a total return of 677 percent.

Unfortunately, given the government nature of our contracts, Motorola GED does not realize all these savings as profits. The true cost–benefit occurs when projects finish earlier, allowing us to apply more engineering resources to the acquisition and development of new business.

Each level of SEI CMM maturity reduces defect density by a factor of 2. Cycle time and, to a lesser extent, productivity improve with each maturity level except level 3, when cycle time and productivity both decrease. From this, we can conclude that achieving level 3 involves significant new process introduction, which can negatively affect these two metrics until the project absorbs and learns to tailor the processes. From the data presented here, it would appear that setting a goal of SEI level 3 for an organization is the least beneficial point to shoot for.

The effort to transition from level 2 to level 3 is probably the most difficult because of the many KPAs associated with level 3 and the impact that process maturity plays in SPI. Lower-maturity organizations find it much more difficult to change and implement SPI for a variety of reasons.

- ♦ Keying process changes to metric analysis data is not addressed until CMM levels 4 and 5. Such data is critical to improving the effectiveness of SPI efforts.
- ♦ Lower-maturity organizations focus on defining their core processes, not on improvement.
- ♦ Lower-maturity organizations are just starting to improve their software processes. This requires significant effort, especially in the beginning. Staff skepticism can also be an obstacle. Before they buy into a new SPI initiative, most software engineers will wait to see if it truly has management support and staying power.

These factors suggest that the SEI CMM could be improved by addressing some aspects of all KPAs even at the lower maturity levels. For example, some aspects of defect prevention and process improvement can be performed at the lower maturity levels. The ISO Spice model is an example of such a graduated approach.

Process improvements take time to institutionalize and require a commitment from management to succeed. Achieving higher levels of process maturity requires an investment of time and money in process improvements, including tool integration to aid in the collection and interpretation of quantitative data.

Given the costs they incur, process improvement activities must be undertaken with a view to return on investment. You could easily set up a high–SEI-maturity organization that would suffer slowed delivery times and reduced productivity if process were followed for process's sake. Thus, in addition to the traditional SEI CMM emphasis, we must tailor our processes and focus on cycle time.   ♦

REFERENCES

1. M. Paulk et al., "Capability Maturity Model Version 1.1," *IEEE Software*, July 1993, pp. 18-27.
2. J.G. Brodman and D. Johnson, "Return on Investment from Software Process Improvement as Measured by U.S. Industry," *Crosstalk*, Apr. 1996, pp. 23-28.
3. J.D. Herbsleb and D.R. Goldenson, "A Systematic Survey of CMM Experience and Results," *Proc. ICSE 18*, IEEE Computer Soc. Press, Los Alamitos, Calif., 1996, pp. 323-330.
4. P. Lawlis, R. Flowe, and J. Thordahl, "A Correlational Study of the CMM and Software Development Performance," *Crosstalk*, Sept. 1995, pp. 21-25.
5. C. Jones, *Applied Software Measurement*, McGraw Hill, New York, 1991, 1996.
6. F. Arkell and J. Sligo, "Software Problem Prediction and Quality Management," *Proc. 7th Int'l Conf. Applications of Software Measurement*, Software Quality Engineering, Jacksonville, Fla., Oct. 1996.

16

Michael Diaz is the manager of Security/Integrity and Quality for the Motorola Information Security Division. His areas of focus are software process improvement, metrics, security countermeasures, and risk man-agement. Diaz was the chief software engineer for Motorola GED from 1994 to 1996. Diaz's previous experience includes 15 years of software technical leadership in requirements management, systems engineering, security architectures, and secure key management systems at Motorola. Diaz has been awarded membership in Motorola's Scientific Advisory Board Association, the highest technical association within Motorola.

Diaz received a BSEE and an MS in computer engineering from Boston University. He is a member of the IEEE Computer Society and the Society for Hispanic Engineers (SHPE).

Joseph Sligo is the chief software engineer for Motorola ASD, responsible for all aspects of software development in an organization of 350 software engineers. His areas of focus include software process improvement and project management. Sligo's previous experience includes 15 years of software technical leadership for GPS receivers, spaceborne advanced digital communications transponders, and position determining systems. Sligo has been awarded membership in Motorola's Scientific Advisory Board Association, the highest technical association within Motorola. His experience includes work on Omega navigation receivers and instrument landing systems with the Ohio University Avionics Research Center.

Sligo received a BSEE from Ohio University.

Address questions about this article to Diaz at Motorola GED, 8201 E. McDowell Rd., Scottsdale, AZ 85252; p17114@email.mot.com; or to Sligo at the same address; p16628@email.mot.com.

Reprinted from IEEE Software,
May/June 1999, pp. 37-45.

Studying a software process improvement effort over
time reveals the factors associated with its success. This
case study shows how Motorola's Cellular Infrastructure
Group progressed to CMM level 4, and examines what is
needed to optimize its software development process.

A Longitudinal Study of Software Process Improvement

Brian Fitzgerald, University College Cork, Ireland
Tom O'Kane, Motorola

Given the extent to which software underpins all our everyday activities, software development has become a critical issue for modern organizations, and indeed for all of society. The "software crisis," a term first coined more than 30 years ago, continues unabated, however—software still takes too long to develop, costs too much, and does not work very well when eventually delivered. Some argue that this is because the software process in many organizations is undisciplined, chaotic, and completely unpredictable.[1] In other organizational areas, increased process maturity has led to concomitant improvements in efficiency. Therefore, increasing software process maturity is an obvious and logical step in addressing the software crisis. The most comprehensive and effectively realized model of process maturity is the Capability Maturity Model from the Software Engineering Institute.[1]

While the CMM was initially applied to government and military software development, its use is now spreading to all industry sectors. However, a large-scale comprehensive study of organizations that have undergone CMM evaluation reveals that only two percent of organizations have achieved level 4 or 5; nearly 62 percent are at level 1.[2] Also, the process of achieving level 3 takes four years on average,[2] which shows that progression through CMM maturity levels is both time-consuming and difficult.

FROM THE TRENCHES: Wolfgang B. Strigel, editor • wstrigel@spc.ca

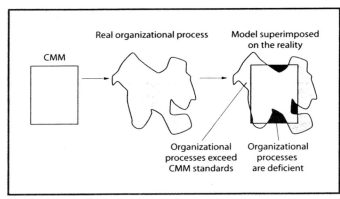

FIGURE 1. Application of CMM to the organizational reality of an organizational process.

This case study examines how Motorola's Cellular Infrastructure Group at Cork, Ireland achieved each of the CMM maturity levels up to level 4 between 1993 and 1997. CMM assessment findings, particularly the critical success factors, are a rich source of information for the organization. We identify and discuss in detail the CSFs that CIG's CMM assessment team associated with the achievement of each maturity level, as well as those CSFs that were not achieved—these represent opportunities for further improvement. Given the ever-increasing interest in software process improvement in general, and the CMM in particular, the lessons learned by the Motorola organization are likely to be of significant interest to others.

DEFINING AND ACHIEVING SUCCESS

The CMM is a five-layer model describing an evolutionary path from ad hoc, chaotic processes to mature, disciplined software processes. The five maturity levels describe successive foundations for continuous process improvement and define an ordinal scale for measuring the maturity of an organization's software process. The CMM consists of 18 key process areas categorized across the five maturity levels. These KPAs can be split further into management, organizational, and engineering categories (see Table 1).

The CSF method, first applied to the information systems field in 1979,[3] defines specific things that must go right for a business to flourish and maintain its competitive edge. The concept has been widely applied in the IS field,[4] but not so much in the specific area of software development. Some notable examples of CSF research in software development include studies of strategic information systems development,[5] executive information systems development,[6] and the development of IBM's OS400 system.[7] The latter is perhaps the most rele-

vant to our work; the 13 CSFs identified in that study overlap quite well with the CSFs we identified at the Cork facility (listed in Table 1).

However, while these previous studies identify a number of CSFs, some of which are broadly similar, none addresses the achievement of a particular measurable standard of success. In our study, the CSFs identified are closely coupled to the achievement of CMM maturity levels. We also extend the application of the CSF concept to software process improvement.

The relationship between KPAs and CSFs requires elaboration. While Motorola satisfied the relevant KPAs to achieve each CMM level, KPAs actually represent a binary concept in that just exceeding the threshold level on each factor is "better" (at least in CMM terms) than scoring very well on several KPAs but failing to reach the threshold on one. Thus, no strong incentive exists for an organization to greatly exceed any KPA. We believe, however, that the focus should always be on improving the software process, not merely achieving a score, as richness in any aspect of process improvement is rendered somewhat sterile by reverting to a single score. The CMM assessment team at Motorola noted this richness, and therefore successful process improvement can be viewed in terms of CSFs rather than KPAs. CSFs can be seen as situated exemplars that help push out the boundaries of process improvement, which cannot be realized by merely achieving a threshold level on a set of KPAs.

Figure 1 depicts this issue graphically. Illustrating how the CMM model is superimposed onto the organizational reality lets us identify deficiencies in the organization's process. However, this is only within the frame of reference of the CMM and only to the degree to which the CMM itself is correct. This is, of course, how the CMM is supposed to be used.

In reality, however, this is a simplistic view. An organization may in fact be enacting processes identified by the CMM but far exceeding its boundaries. The organization may also be enacting processes not captured explicitly by the CMM, such as those for data security and disaster recovery. Even though the organization is following a process that is at variance with the CMM, it may be still correct as the CMM itself is not perfect. In Figure 1, the areas that are deficient in the organization's process, vis-à-vis the CMM, are represented with waved shading.

In effect, the totality of process in the real organization is much richer than that of the CMM. Unfortunately, some may have overlooked this and,

TABLE 1
KEY PROCESS AREAS AND CRITICAL SUCCESS FACTORS BY MATURITY LEVEL

CMM Level	KPA: Management	KPA: Organizational	KPA: Engineering	CSFs at Motorola, Cork
1. Initial	Ad-hoc processes			
2. Repeatable	Requirements management Software project planning Software project tracking and oversight Software subcontract management Software configuration management			**CSF1**: Dedicated project planning and tracking roles. **CSF2**: Formalized procedures for managing subcontractors. **CSF3**: Institutionalized software quality assurance program. **CSF4**: Software configuration management automated and intrinsic to the software life cycle
3. Defined	Integrated software management Intergroup coordination	Organization process focus Organization process definition Training program	Software product engineering Peer reviews	**CSF1**: Comprehensive process definition and tailoring technique. **CSF2**: Strong and pervasive culture for software process improvement. **CSF3**: Good training program with emphasis on leading-edge technologies. **CSF4**: Strong cooperation both within Motorola and with external organizations. **CSF5**: Peer review of all software products.
4. Managed	Quantitative process management		Software quality management	**CSF1**: Data-driven culture for management of products, projects, and subcontractors.
5. Optimized		Technology change management Process change management	Defect prevention	**CSF1**: Technology change program fully deployed across whole organization. **CSF2**: Organizational process improvement culture sufficiently proactive and involved in strategic goal setting. **CSF3**: Defect prevention program coordinated across the whole organization.

consequently, confine process improvement activity within the model's boundaries. Another more disquieting reason may be that commercial considerations force an organization to strictly confine itself to the model because it is pursuing a CMM score—it then takes a minimalist approach instead of fully engaging in software process improvement. In effect the CMM is regarded as the reality, which of course is wrong since all models are wrong to a greater or lesser degree.

APPLYING THE CSF CONCEPT

Motorola, a major mobile telecommunications systems provider, has over 300 engineers creating large, complex, expensive switching and communications infrastructure systems in Cork, Ireland. Clients are typically very large telecommunications providers who use these systems to support their mobile phone networks. Users (individuals who make mobile telephone calls) take the underlying system completely for granted and expect total reliability. With several significant and reputable competitors in the marketplace, Motorola systems must be reliable. Also, the telecommunications technology area is constantly evolving, with new products and services continually offered. Systems are constantly being adapted to incorporate interfaces to these new developments.

The systems themselves are developed using common languages such as C and C++. Technical

personnel, who typically have a background in engineering or computer science, work in a formalized development environment where the design, implementation, and testing phases are clearly differentiated. All projects follow a methodology tailored precisely to the development process, and Motorola uses special test laboratory facilities to test each system function rigorously. Given the system requirements and the competitive marketplace, errors and downtime must be kept to a minimum. When errors do occur, all fixes undergo rigorous testing before a system is released to customers.

The development process is explicitly documented, and is evolving as the company follows its program for continuous process improvement, which it expects will ultimately lead to an improved CMM rating. Motorola places much emphasis on satisfying the concepts of the CMM and has created a specialist group—the Software Engineering Process Group—at the Cork facility to ensure compliance with the CMM criteria. The SEPG collects and analyzes metrics on the development process and posts this information on internal notice boards for developers to read.

The pioneers of the CSF method state that its application requires a thorough understanding of "the industry, the specific company, and the job being performed."[8] Our research took place longitudinally over a five-year period, and one of us manages software process improvement at the Cork facility. Our overall research strategy was based on *action research*,[9] a method that merges research and practice while accepting that pragmatic organizational realities take precedence over the artifices of any research method. The method consists of a spiral of planning, acting, observing, and reflecting cycles, which is compatible with a software process improvement program as the same steps are essentially followed. Thus, the method was ideally suited to the research objective.

Critical success factors: CMM level 2

CMM level 1 is the default for all organizations—it doesn't have to be achieved as such. The software process at this level is characterized as chaotic and ad hoc, and any successes are primarily due to the heroic efforts of talented individuals. Thus, the first significant level of the CMM, in that it represents a

> **Maintaining the integrity of all software work products is essential for any software organization.**

hurdle to be achieved, is level 2, the *repeatable* level. The KPAs of CMM level 2 (see Table 1) focus on bringing discipline and basic management control to the software process. Project management is institutionalized and projects begin to meet cost and schedule deadlines and satisfy requirements.

The CIG at Cork has a long track record in software process improvement and was initially assessed at CMM level 2 prior to 1993, based on an internal self-assessment.

CSF 1: Dedicated project planning and tracking roles. Producing software is an expensive business. Making optimal use of available resources, both human and computer, is vital if software development is to make economic sense. Project planning and tracking are therefore essential.

At CIG, full-time project planning and tracking personnel are assigned to each project and work as part of the software product engineering team. Starting with the requirements group's estimates for all feature deliverables, they estimate project risks based on historical data from previous projects, then factor in other known-overhead activities such as training, software process work, and holidays. Finally, they allocate engineering team resources and compile a work breakdown structure for the project. Once the project plan is in place, they track progress using such techniques as earned-value analysis. Their principal aim is to ensure the project budget is maintained. Regular project meetings are convened to assess progress, and progress reports and a history of the project are maintained. These then provide feedback for the engineering teams.

CSF 2: Formalized procedures for managing subcontractors. Selecting and managing software subcontractors requires great care and discipline—failure to do so effectively has the potential to create havoc and put the software organization in a vulnerable position.

CIG has formalized a set of solid and proven procedures to deal with the selection, verification, tracking, and performance measurement of software subcontractors. A dedicated subcontract manager ensures that the software produced by subcontractors at least matches the quality of the software produced by CIG itself in terms of defect densities, timeliness of delivery, and quality of development processes. All subcontractors must pass a formal and rigorous assessment to qualify for selection, and once selected their performance is closely moni-

22

tored to ensure quality standards are maintained.

CSF 3: Institutionalized software quality assurance. It is essential to ensure the software organization's processes, procedures, and standards are complied with if previous project successes are to be repeated. This is usually achieved through compliance audits where the auditor maintains an independent, objective view of the software work products and activities.

At Cork, the software quality department ensures software product quality by auditing all work products for compliance with the defined software process. The quality department has sign-off responsibility for all customer deliverables, conducts regular reviews with the project groups, and is the conduit for customer feedback reports and customer satisfaction indices.

CSF 4: Software configuration management is an intrinsic, automated part of the software life cycle. Maintaining the integrity of all software work products is essential for any software organization. CIG staff assigned to SCM use specialized tools for integrated file management. Automated SCM is a key feature deployed throughout CIG and affects all aspects of the software life cycle. The primary task is to ensure that version control is exercised over all the components that make up the final software deliverable plus any other artifacts developed by the organization.

Critical success factors: CMM level 3

CMM level 3 ("defined") extends the scope of process improvement to organizational issues. An appropriate infrastructure must be established to ensure that both software engineering processes and the related management processes are fully institutionalized. CIG developed a technique to explicitly define the software process and established sound management practices to enhance it.

CSF 1: Comprehensive process definition and tailoring. Having a defined process is absolutely essential for progressing to higher levels of process maturity. However, in practice, this can be a cumbersome and difficult task. Prompt (PROcess MaPping and Tailoring) is a method developed by Tom O'Kane for defining software process maps at Motorola. It is based on a simple but rigorous set of symbols and rules, and allows for a concise graphical depiction of the software process (see the boxed text, "The Prompt Notation," on pp. 43-44 for more details). The technique was developed at Cork but is now in widespread use throughout Motorola, and its use has spread to other companies.

The Prompt technique makes possible a high level of accuracy and permits tailoring the process to the contingencies of each project. The process map can reflect the process as actually applied rather than documenting what it should be. Prompt maps are also task-oriented—rather than describing jobs performed by individuals, they provide a holistic, graphical representation of the entire software workflow.

CSF 2: Strong and pervasive culture for software process improvement. At CIG, ownership of the software process, plus the responsibility for its maturation and continuous improvement, pervades all organizational levels. While the software process improvement effort focuses on facilitating and managing change in the organization, the overriding belief at CIG is that process ownership and develop-

Process ownership and development are best placed with those closest to the process.

ment are best placed with those closest to the process, who experience its bottlenecks and inefficiencies. Ownership of the software processes therefore does not reside with the process management function, which is responsible for providing the necessary resources and support infrastructure to enable the process to evolve in a controlled manner. To realize benefits such as cycle-time reduction, those managing the improvement program need to create awareness among the general engineering community of the need to change.

CSF 3: Good training program with emphasis on leading-edge technologies. Motorola regards employee training as critical. At CIG this is driven through the development of individual training plans for each employee. New employees receive intensive training on both the technical and nontechnical aspects of their positions. Thereafter each employee receives a minimum of five days of training per year. The training department develops the annual training plan for the facility based on individual training plans. It also maintains an extensive suite of Web-based and PC-based self-directed

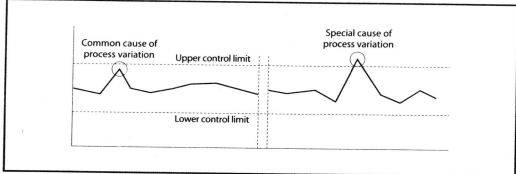

FIGURE 2. Common and special causes of process variation, represented graphically.

learning programs. All employees are encouraged to conduct workshops, both to share their knowledge and to improve their own presentation skills.

CSF 4: Strong cooperation within Motorola and with external organizations. Developing external contacts, participating in other engineering groups' activities, and maintaining links with parent organizations in the US help employees gain a greater awareness of the business context within the organization. This is seen as vitally important at Motorola. In addition to cooperation between the various functional groups at CIG, employees also have a great deal of contact with external organizations. These include the parent organization in the US, subcontractor companies, other Motorola sites around the world, educational institutions, professional societies, and many others. Cooperation occurs at both individual and organizational levels.

CSF 5: Peer review of all software products. Motorola has found formal inspections to be the most efficient and cost-effective means of removing defects from software products. At CIG, all software products and artifacts undergo peer review. The organization has adopted the formal inspection methodology developed by Michael Fagan and has evolved and tailored this process to suit the precise contingencies of Motorola's development process. The peer review process, always considered strong at Motorola, has formed a foundation for subsequent achievement of higher levels, as it has catalyzed the collection of a huge amount of data for level 4 analysis.

Critical success factors: CMM level 4

CMM level 4, the managed level, focuses on establishing quantitative goals for both the software process and software products. At Motorola, individual managers are responsible for developing metrics (for example, requirements estimation accuracy) to indicate their group's performance levels. The company also devotes resources to the full-time collec-

tion and analysis of data. Much effort is invested in measuring the performance of key process indicators and ensuring they remain within acceptable levels.

Thus the software process is under quantitative control, and *special causes* that represent deviations outside the control limits are identified and isolated (Figure 2). A special cause is a source of variation that is intermittent, unpredictable, or unstable; it is signaled by a point beyond the control limit.[10] *Common causes*, also shown in Figure 2 and discussed later, are signaled by points that approach but do not exceed the control limit.

For example, in C code inspections, scatter plots may reveal that the optimum inspection rate is 150 lines of code per hour. If inspection occurs at a rate (faster or slower) beyond the limits of acceptable process variation, inspection effectiveness falls dramatically, to an unacceptable level. Subsequent investigation could reveal that the team started late and was then in a hurry to finish or, alternatively, got bogged down in actually solving a problem rather than concentrating on fault-finding.

CSF 1: Data-driven culture for management of products, projects, and subcontractors. A strong data-driven culture exists at CIG. Metrics are collected during all phases of the software life cycle; hence a very rich and organizationally diverse set of raw data is available for analysis and refinement. These metrics are formally presented and reviewed monthly at internal quality and operations reviews, but the information is also made available to the wider engineering community through notice boards, the Internet, and individual group feedback sessions. The assessment team also noted the potential for increased leverage of Internet technology to further enhance Motorola's metrics collection activities.

Critical success factors: CMM level 5

At CMM level 5, the KPAs focus on continuous and measurable process improvement to optimize the software process. At Motorola, special empha-

24

THE PROMPT NOTATION

Prompt, which derives its name from Process Mapping and Tailoring, is a notation composed of four basic symbols—rectangles, triangles, circles, and dots—and a simple rule set. Prompt maps describe the actions of human beings in a field of work. They are not prescriptive—they do not attempt to describe how tasks are performed or who performs them, but instead facilitate and time-order such descriptions.

Prompt maps consist of the following:

♦ *Entry/exit criteria*: rectangles labeled Entry or Exit Criteria, containing the entry or exit criteria text. These provide the control signals that either start or end a process. Every Prompt map begins with a single Entry Criteria node describing the criteria to be satisfied before the first action can be started, and terminates with a single Exit Criteria node describing the criteria to be satisfied for the process to be fully completed.

♦ *Input/output criteria*: a rectangle with an arc leading from or to it and containing the input/output criteria text. Input criteria are artifacts required by an action point but satisfied by some other independent process; output criteria are artifacts used by some other independent process.

♦ *Action points*: a triangle containing an exclamation mark. These represent processes or other Prompt maps (submaps). Activities are collected into actions that are highly cohesive and

loosely coupled. For example, the activities High-Level Design, Low-Level Design, and Code are sequential—coding cannot start if low-level design has not started, and low-level design cannot completely finish until high-level design has finished (Figure A).

♦ *Option Points*: a circle containing a question mark. These represent junctions where a human decision must be made. The decision is strictly Boolean; when a decision is made, only one of the two exit paths is followed. The selected action following an option point cannot conclude until the action immediately preceding the option point is complete.

♦ *Parallel Processing Points*: a dot/period on the arc between two nodes. These represent the instigation of independent, concurrent processing. A maximum of three exit paths may follow from a single parallel processing point. Activities following a parallel processing point cannot conclude until the action immediately preceding the parallel processing point is complete.

♦ *Document/Map References*: a dashed line perpendicular to the map. These point to a library reference, Internet URL, online documentation, or another Prompt map. Where a documentation reference emanates from an action point, the documentation is specific to that activity. Where the reference emanates from the arc between two nodes, the documentation is nonspecific but applies to the general process from this point on. Other Prompt maps (submaps) can only be referenced from an action point and obey the same rules as any other Prompt map.

Prompt maps are living artifacts and not intended to be definitive; they are strictly linear, flowing from left to right. They describe what has to be done, and the referenced procedures provide specific instructions on how to perform the work, including specific conditions, roles and responsibilities, iterations, recursions, and metric data to be collected or produced.

Prompt maps are typically Web-based, and the example in Figure B shows a process initiated by a Document Change Request. The first activity is to prepare the document change notification (DCN) using a DCN template, retrievable directly by

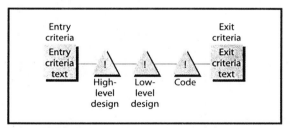

FIGURE A. Sequential ordering of action points indicates their dependent relationships.

Continued on the next page

sis is placed on measuring and analyzing variations in software process performance to assess the common causes of problems and to effect prevention measures. The concern here is to go beyond the elimination of special causes, the focus at level 4, and to identify and eliminate the *common causes* of problems and defects to achieve a more uniform pattern of performance (represented by a flatter profile in Figure 2).

A common cause is a source of variation that is always present—it is part of the random variation inherent in the process itself and is indicated by the measure approaching the acceptable control limit (see Figure 2). Its origin can usually be traced to an element of the system

that only management can correct.[10] To continue the code inspection rate example above, suppose that code inspection rates for a particular module commonly approach the acceptable upper limit. This could indicate that the module is overly complex or defect-prone and is thus a candidate for reengineering. The decision to proceed with such reengineering work would require management intervention.

Identifying and addressing common causes requires a two-pronged approach: first, continuous incremental improvement to the existing software process; and second, proactive efforts to introduce radical and innovative process changes through the deployment of new technologies.

clicking on the Prompt map component. A Web-based DCN process document that describes the DCN process is also available, retrievable directly from the Prompt map. The Retrieval and Update Process Document is a general document that describes the overall process from this point onward. After starting the DCN process, the user will begin the document retrieval process but will not be able to complete it until the Prepare DCN process is complete.

After beginning the retrieval process, the user needs to decide whether this is a design document,

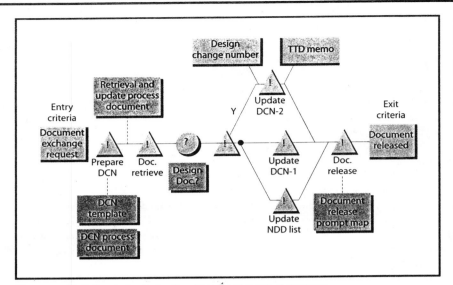

FIGURE B. A Prompt map for the document request process.

and can use tailoring criteria available online to make this decision. If it is a design document, the user can commence updating DCN-2 but will be unable to complete this process until the document retrieval process is complete and the design change number is available. At some point during this activity a Technical Tracing Department (TTD) memo will be made available to other processes. If the document wasn't a design document, the user needs to update DCN-1 and, at the same time, update the Non-Design Document (NDD) list. Neither of these activities can be completed until the Doc Retrieve process is completed. Regardless of the update path chosen, the user will at some point be able to commence the document release process, described by its own Prompt map. The entry and exit criteria for this submap are coherent with this process path. The document request process will eventually complete when the exit criteria are met.

In summary, the objective of the Prompt map is to specify a logical perspective for the activity domain by identifying actions, decisions, parallelisms, input/output artifacts, and overall entry/exit criteria. The terms used in this example are purposefully vague because humans and human processes use fuzzy logic, and attempts to eliminate the fuzz typically result in something inordinately complicated.

Motorola uses the Prompt notation widely in both Europe and the US. The Motorola Cellular Support Centers, which support Motorola's cellular customer base worldwide, aligned their processes using Prompt and thereby reduced many thousands of pages of documentation to a set of 21 maps that are Web-based and totally interactive. Now, as the worldwide Customer Network Resolution Centers, they serve Motorola's cellular customers with greatly enhanced service management facilities.

CSF 1: Technology change management program deployed across the whole organization. The CMM assessment team reported that while they were fully satisfied with the technology change management program developed at CIG, the evidence of its deployment had been drawn from only a single project type. While this evidence was good, Motorola wished to achieve deployment across all projects. This encapsulates the differences between KPAs and CSFs in that the KPA threshold had already been achieved in this case; however, Motorola viewed the CSF as a stronger basis for software process optimization.

We should note that the technology base at Cork is fairly stable; significant technological shifts are comparatively rare. Also, the decision to make a rad-

ical change such as using a new technology is more likely to be made at the higher group or sector levels and then passed down to the individual organizations for implementation.

CSF 2: Defect prevention program coordinated and deployed across the whole organization. The CMM assessment team noted that while many facets of the defect prevention program were in place at CIG, the group needed a more coordinated approach to organizing and deploying the program. This conclusion stemmed from the observation that while vast amounts of metric data were collected and analyzed, these activities were essentially reactive in nature. The defect prevention program needed to be more proactive, focusing on the prevention of faults in subsequent releases of software based on data collected and statistically analyzed for the level 4 KPAs.

CSF 3: The organizational process improvement culture is proactive and involved in strategic process goal-setting. Again, the CMM assessment team found that while CIG had a strong process improvement culture, it was essentially reactive. It recommended that the organization identify more strategic opportunities for process improvement, set goals to realize those opportunities, plan ahead to reach those goals, and monitor progress towards their achievement. The net effect on the software process would be reduced statistical variation over a given period of time.

While CIG was addressing some of the level 5 KPAs, it was not achieving all the identified level 5 CSFs to the required level. It therefore shifted its focus to establishing these level 5 CSFs, as this would contribute significantly both to achieving level 5 and to ensuring optimization of its software process in the future.

We see the future for high-maturity organizations in terms of CSFs rather than KPAs. KPA achievement is somewhat simplistic and sterile in that it largely represents the achievement of a specific binary threshold, and there is no real incentive for an organization to hugely exceed any KPA. Also, because lower-level KPAs may be easier to achieve than some of the more abstract higher-level ones, software process improvement will progress at a diminishing rate as it proceeds to higher levels, perhaps to the discouragement of some organizations. However, as more organizations achieve CMM level 5, the future of the CMM will need to be considered.

Motorola found it more useful to concentrate on those critical success factors that reflect the richness of their process improvement program. These represent the tailoring of the process improvement program to the contingencies of the organization's development process. CSFs help push out the boundaries of process improvement and thereby form a richer base for continuing and future software process improvement. Some view creativity and software process maturity as mutually exclusive. Motorola rejects that view, and sees the coupling of their software process improvement program with CSFs as providing a basic infrastructure upon which creativity can be meaningfully nurtured.   ❖

REFERENCES

1. M. Paulk et al., "Capability Maturity Model for Software, version 1.1," *IEEE Software*, July 1993, pp. 18-27.
2. D. Zubrow, *The Software Community Process Maturity Profile,* Software Eng. Inst., Pittsburgh, Pa., 1997.
3. J.F. Rockart, "Chief Executives Define Their Own Data Needs,"
   Harvard Business Rev., Vol. 57, No. 2, 1979, pp. 81-93.
4. T. Butler and B. Fitzgerald, "A Review and Application of the CSF Concept for Research on the IS Development Process," *Information Systems—The Next Generation,* L. Brooks and C. Kimble, eds., McGraw-Hill, London, pp. 231-247.
5. H. Krcmar and L.C. Lucas, "Success Factors for Strategic Information Systems," *Information and Management,* Vol. 21, 1991, pp. 137-145.
6. J. Nandakumar, "Design for Success?: Critical Success Factors in Executive Information Systems Development," *European J. Information Systems,* Vol. 5, 1996, pp. 62-72.
7. D.D. Phan, D.R. Vogel, and J.F. Nunamaker, Jr., "Empirical Studies in Software Development Projects: Field Survey and OS/400 Study," *Information and Management,* Vol. 28, 1995, pp. 271-280.
8. C.V. Bullen and J.R. Rockart, "A Primer on Critical Success Factors," *The Rise of Managerial Computing,* J.F. Rockart and C.V. Bullen, eds., Sloan School of Management, Massachusetts Inst. of Technology, Cambridge, Mass., 1986, pp. 383-423.
9. F. Lau, "A Review on the Use of Action Research in Information System Studies," *Information Systems and Qualitative Research,* A. Lee, J. Liebenau, and J. DeGross, eds., Chapman & Hall, London, 1997, pp. 31-68.
10. M. Brassard, *The Memory Jogger. A Pocket Guide for Continuous Improvement,* Goal/QPC, Salem, N.H., 1994.

●   ●   ●

About the Authors

Brian Fitzgerald is senior researcher at the Executive Systems Research Centre at University College Cork, Ireland. He is actively involved in applied research projects in the areas of systems development approaches, foundations of the IS field, and executive information systems. He has more than 15 years of experience in the IS field, having worked in industry prior to taking up an academic position. He has published in *The Information Systems Journal, Information and Management, INFOR, the Journal of Information Technology,* and the *International Journal of Information Management,* among others. He is an associate editor for *The Information Systems Journal.*

Fitzgerald holds a PhD from the University of London.

Tom O'Kane is a senior staff engineer with Motorola, Cork, Ireland. He has over six years of experience in software process improvement and over 10 years of experience of software development in Motorola and with other US multinationals. At Motorola, his prime responsibility is managing the Cork software process improvement program utilizing the SEI CMM as the improvement framework. He works closely with other Motorola facilities both in Europe and the US, where he has acted as an internal process consultant. He regularly gives guest lectures on software process improvement and has written several internal publications on various aspects of it. He chaired the third Motorola European Software Engineering Symposium and was the first person to be presented with the General Managers Quality Award for Excellence for his work on process mapping.

Readers may contact Fitzgerald at the Executive Systems Research Centre, Room 321, O'Rahilly Building, University College, Cork, Ireland; e-mail bf@ucc.ie.

Reprinted from IEEE Software,
Nov./Dec. 1999, pp. 51-57.

The IEEE Software Engineering Standards Committee has taken
deliberate steps to unify and integrate its collection of software
engineering standards. Encouraging results are apparent in its
latest publication, which is organized around a single
architecture for the SESC collection.

An Integrated Collection of Software Engineering Standards

James W. Moore, The Mitre Corporation

ver the years, there has been broad interest in creating software engineering standards. One authoritative survey discovered approximately 315 standards, guides, handbooks, and other prescriptive documents maintained by 46 different organizations (see the "Sources of Software Engineering Standards" sidebar).[1] Nevertheless, uptake of the available standards has been somewhat disappointing. Hopeful users report difficulty in finding the standards that suit their particular situation among the numerous ones available. They also report that detailed differences between standards make it difficult to apply them in unison. For example, in an area of overlap between two standards, each might emphasize a different approach or use different terminology.

We need an approach to managing a standards collection that emphasizes integrating the various standards. Since 1991, those of us working on the IEEE Computer Society's Software Engineering Standards Committee have undertaken efforts to manage the standards collection to promote consistency. Although the col-

SOURCES OF SOFTWARE ENGINEERING STANDARDS

Software engineering standards concern the responsible practice of software engineering. They often deal with processes, but sometimes they deal with generic product characteristics or supporting resources. The subjects of the standards include phrases familiar to large-scale software developers—configuration management, quality assurance, verification, validation, and so forth. The standards generally do not deal with specific programming languages or technologies. The disciplines provided by the standards generally transcend the lifetimes of specific technologies.

Three organizations are generally regarded as the source of international standards—the International Organization for Standardization, the International Electrotechnical Commission, and the International Telecommunications Union. Two of those organizations cooperate in a Joint Technical Committee, ISO/IEC JTC1, responsible for information technology. A subcommittee, ISO/IEC JTC1/SC7, is responsible for standards related to software engineering and software systems engineering. SC7 currently manages a collection of about two dozen standards, the most popular being *ISO/IEC 12207, Software Life Cycle Processes*. Other

technical committees and subcommittees of ISO and IEC make standards in related areas—for example, *ISO TC176 (Quality Management)*, *IEC TC56 (Dependability)*, and *IEC SC65A (Functional Safety)*.

Standards-making in the US is not rigidly delegated as it is in many other countries. Over 500 organizations in the US make standards of some kind. Two organizations mentioned in this article are the Electronic Industries Alliance and the Institute for Electrical and Electronic Engineers. EIA has played an important role in "demilitarizing" the standards for complex software development that were originally written for use in the defense industry.

The Software Engineering Standards Committee of the IEEE Computer Society manages the world's most comprehensive collection of software engineering standards (nearly 50), developed since 1979. SESC serves as a developer of these standards, but also as an integrator of specifications and standards developed by other organizations. It has adopted, sometimes with changes, standards developed by organizations such as ISO/IEC JTC1/SC7 and the Project Management Institute.

lection has doubled in size, we have substantially improved its degree of integration. The process is not yet complete but significant progress has been made, culminating in the publication of the 1999 four-volume edition of SESC standards—packaged along the lines of the integrating principles for the collection.

This article explains the principles of the SESC collection and describes our progress toward integrating the various standards within it.

BUYER AND SELLER BENEFITS

To some, the value of using software engineering standards might be obvious—they contribute to disciplined practice, hence they improve product quality. Although these reasons validly account for using standards in the software engineering craft, they do not characterize the unique contribution of standards to the profession. For this, we must look at the value of standards to those buying and selling software engineering goods and services.

Many goods and services can be confidently purchased after simple examination or after studying the supplier's product literature. The complexity of software products, however, induces a need for a more thorough analysis. Whether purchased as a completed product or as a contracted development, the purchasing or acceptance decision is complicated

because important characteristics may be effectively hidden from examination until unusual circumstances or changing patterns of usage reveal them.

Standards can provide assistance and can protect the buyer by

♦ providing a vocabulary for communication between the buyer and seller;
♦ providing objective criteria for otherwise vague claims regarding the product's nature;
♦ defining methods for characterizing elusive characteristics, such as reliability; and
♦ assuring the seller that specific quality assurance practices were applied.

The benefit of standards in protecting the seller is probably underappreciated in the software engineering community. From this viewpoint, standards are important, not because they represent best practice, but because they represent good enough practice. Courts generally view the application of standards as important evidence that engineers perform their work with appropriate diligence and responsibility. If sued for negligence or reckless conduct, an engineer can cite the standards used when he or she conducted the work to demonstrate that it was performed in accordance with codified professional practices.

By providing important benefits for both the buyer and the seller, software engineering standards support the emergence of a software engineering profession characterized by consensually validated

norms for responsible conduct. With such clear benefits, you would expect a nearly universal application of software engineering standards. Unfortunately, this is difficult due to the vast amount of available and occasionally inconsistent information.

VISION 2000 ARCHITECTURE

Early in the 1990s, the SESC established a planning committee to initiate the long-range efforts needed to integrate its collection. The committee studied customer needs[2] and surveyed existing standards,[3] concluding that there was no shortage of available advice for the practice of software engineering. However, there existed no clear way for users to select the advice appropriate to their needs. Furthermore, the individually optimized nature of each standard presented obstacles to selecting and applying them together. The software engineering community needed an integrated collection of standards that could be applied in unison and from which users could easily select appropriate standards.

With this information, we were ready to develop an integrating architecture for the SESC collection, termed Vision 2000.[4] The most recently published edition of the SESC collection[5] reflects the Vision 2000 architecture, which comprises three important organizing criteria (see Figure 1). The concept of the first organizing criterion, *normative levels*, is that different standards should provide different levels of advice—sometimes detailed, sometimes general—for different uses. The second organizing criterion, *objects of software engineering*, recognizes that software engineering standards address four different objects: customer, process, product, and resource. The third organizing criterion is *relationships to other disciplines*. The SESC software engineering collection is positioned within the context of other standards selected from software engineering, quality management, and various systems engineering disciplines.

Normative levels

We borrowed the concept of normative levels from other successful standards collections. The top layer includes standards for terminology and other key concepts. Such standards are generally nonprescriptive; they simply provide definitions, taxonomies, or other reference material that can be used in other standards in the collection. The IEEE software engineering vocabulary, *IEEE Std. 610.12*, falls under this category.

The next layer is also nonprescriptive, occupied by one or a few documents that serve as an overall guide to the remainder of the collection. The document explains the collection's architecture and the key relationships among the standards within it. We decided to fill this layer by authorizing and endorsing a textbook rather than writing a standard.[6]

The third layer contains standards providing policies or principles to a user. Principles are useful because it is difficult to write detailed standards covering the entire conceivable range of usage. In a specific situation, if the details don't seem applicable, a user can apply the principles instead. In the case of the SESC collection, there are currently no principles documents dealing with resources and products. However, portions of *IEEE/EIA 12207* fill this role for the standards dealing with customers and processes.

The fourth layer, element standards, is the one most familiar to standards users. It contains documents with conformance requirements in various important areas. Most of the SESC collection's standards are grouped into this layer.

The fifth layer makes provisions for application

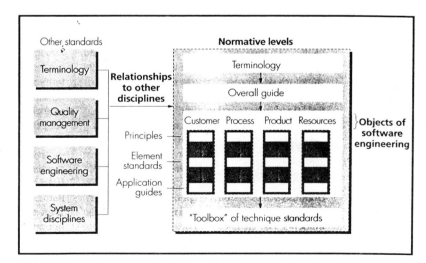

FIGURE 1. The Software Engineering Standards Committee's architecture for its standards collection. The main organizing criteria are normative levels, objects of software engineering, and relationships to other disciplines.

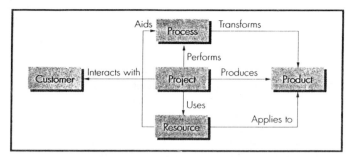

FIGURE 2. The objects of software engineering, suggesting a categorization of standards in the subject areas of customer, process, product, and resource.

guides. Sometimes, users need supplementary documents to describe how to apply an element standard within particular situations. These documents are often guides but can be standards deriving their conformance requirements from the appropriate element standards. For example, we have an element standard on a software quality assurance plan and an application guide describing the overall discipline of SQA planning.

The bottom layer is viewed as a toolbox of detailed techniques. The standards in this layer are "subroutines" that any of the other standards can invoke to provide requirements in a specific area. An example from the SESC collection is *IEEE Std. 1044* regarding the classification of software anomalies.

Objects of software engineering

The objects of software engineering result from the abstract model of software engineering depicted in Figure 2. This model centers on the software engineering project as the focal point for applying software engineering standards. In this view, a project uses resources in performing processes to produce products for a customer. The model is instructive in providing four major subject areas that can be treated by standards: customer, process, product, and resource. We organized the four volumes of the 1999 standards edition according to the four objects.

Relationships to other disciplines

Software engineering does not exist in isolation from other disciplines. Its purpose is to apply the principles of mathematics, engineering, and computer science to various application domains. In addition, it inherits principles from more general disciplines such as systems engineering, quality management, and project management. Its work is also influenced by cross-cutting disciplines such as dependability, safety, and security.

Particularly in this time of emphasis on process improvement, we cannot afford for our standards to be inconsistent with closely related standards from other disciplines. It would be a tragedy if the stan-

dards for the best practices of software engineering were capriciously incompatible with, say, the standards for quality management.

Therefore, where the relationship is strong, and where suitable standards exist, we have selected a few key standards from other disciplines as targets for integration. For example, *ISO 9000-3* provides a bridge between software engineering and the famous *ISO 9000* series of quality management standards, and the Project Management Institute's *Guide to the Project Management Body of Knowledge* (PMBOK) describes general project management principles that SESC standards adapted to the subject of software project management (http://www.pmi.org/publictn/pmboktoc.htm).

By adopting or otherwise recognizing key standards from related disciplines, we avoid the need to reinvent key principles.

AN UMBRELLA STANDARD: IEEE/EIA 12207

Not all integrating standards of the SESC collection are borrowed from other disciplines. *IEEE/EIA 12207, Software Life Cycle Processes*, is an umbrella for all of the customer and process standards in the SESC collection.

ISO/IEC 12207

IEEE/EIA 12207 is an adoption of a 1995 ISO/IEC standard with the same name and number. The international standard establishes a common framework for software throughout its life cycle from conception through retirement, and it addresses the organizational context of those software processes both from the system's technical viewpoint and from the enterprise's business viewpoint. The standard is widely regarded as providing a basis for world trade in software services; adoption of the standard is completed or underway in most of the world's major countries.

The *ISO/IEC 12207* standard improved over past standards in similar areas. Most importantly, it is defined at the process rather than the procedure level. Rather than provide the step-by-step requirements characteristic of a procedure, it describes continuing responsibilities that must be achieved and maintained during the life of the process. The standard addresses the functions to be performed rather than the organizations that will execute them. (For example, the standard describes a quality assurance process; this does not imply that a conforming enterprise must es-

32

tablish a quality assurance department.) The standard describes software development, maintenance, and operation within the context of the system, thus effectively establishing the minimum system context essential to software processes.

Three categories describe the *ISO/IEC 12207* processes:

♦ *Primary processes* are executed by parties who initiate or perform major roles in the software life cycle. They include both business (acquisition and supply) and technical roles (development, operation, and maintenance).

♦ *Supporting processes* contribute to the execution of other processes as an integral part with distinct goals. They include documentation, configuration management, quality assurance, verification, validation, joint review, audit, and problem resolution.

♦ *Organizational processes* inherently exist outside the individual project's scope, but the project employs instances of them. They include management, infrastructure, improvement, and training.

IEEE/EIA 12207

IEEE/EIA 12207.0 adds a foreword and some annexes to the text of the international standard. Two additional guidance parts were added to the standard: *IEEE/EIA 12207.1* provides guidance on the data produced by the life cycle processes and is cross-referenced to the provisions of *12207.0*, and *IEEE/EIA 12207*.2 provides guidance on implementing processes by quoting the complete text of *12207.0* and interspersing guidance notes.

12207.1 describes data but not documents. It describes 84 different information items, which the user selects and packages into documents appropriate for the project. Forty of the information items have specific content (but not format) requirements, while the other 44 information items are classified as one of seven different kinds of data that have generic content requirements. A *12207.1* user might apply it as a guide, meaning that it is presumed simply to offer good advice. On the other hand, *12207.1* also contains optional conformance provisions that permit users to cite the standard if they want to make strong claims regarding the nature of the data that their processes produce. The user can claim that one or more documents conform to *12207.1* by providing a mapping from the documents to the selected information items. The mapping must demonstrate that the document satisfies generic and specific content requirements; captures the data required by the cross-referenced provisions of *12207.0*; and achieves some general requirements for the treatment of data.

12207.1 also provides cross-references to other IEEE standards that might be helpful in implementing the provisions concerning data. For instance, a user might choose to adopt *IEEE Std. 1016, Software Design Descriptions*, to detail the data provisions related to the information item for software item description. Working in the other direction, the SESC has supplemented each of the referenced IEEE standards with a content map describing the extent to which the standard satisfies the data provisions of *12207.1*. Within

> **The standard addresses the functions to be performed rather than the organizations that will execute them.**

the next few years, the SESC will revise the content of each standard so that it directly implements the relevant provisions of *12207.1*.

IEEE/EIA 12207 also plays an important role in the principles layer of the SESC architecture. The IEEE/EIA adoption of *12207* supplemented each of the 17 processes with a statement of objectives. In unusual cases, in which the more detailed *12207* requirements are unsuitable for adoption, an organization can instead choose to adopt the processes at the objectives level.

In overall terms, we have adopted policy designating *12207* as a strategic, integrating standard for its collection. All of the relevant standards of the SESC collection will be revised to improve their fit with *12207*; in particular, many of them will detail the processes of the *12207* framework. From the user's viewpoint, *IEEE/EIA 12207* will serve as a single entry point to all the process standards of the IEEE software engineering collection.

We are also using *IEEE/EIA 12207* as the baseline to articulate new processes. For example, *IEEE Std. 1517, Software Reuse Processes*, adds three reuse-specific processes to those of *12207*, and the planned *IEEE 1540* standard (still under development) will add a software risk management process.

SESC Four-Volume Edition

All of the SESC standards are available for individual purchase from the IEEE (http://standards.

ieee.org/catalog). Every few years, we have gathered our standards and collectively published them in a volume similar in size to a major city's phone directory. With total page count approaching 2,400, the 1999 edition needed a new approach.

The four objects of the Vision 2000 architecture suggested a four-volume packaging, with each volume containing the standards pertaining to customer, product, process, or resource. We bundled the standards from the terminology layer into the customer volume and the standards from the technique layer into the resource volume. We made the guide to the collection available at a discounted price when purchased with the four-volume edition. We also omitted from the edition a few large standards intended for specific audiences, making them available for purchase separately.

Of course, it wasn't practical to publish multiple copies of standards that legitimately fit into more than one category. So, each standard had to be force-fitted into a single category for publication purposes. Our rationale for these decisions is explained below.

The customer volume

Because *IEEE/EIA 12207* is the umbrella standard for both process and customer interaction, its placement was one of the toughest decisions in designing the edition. We decided to place all three parts of the standard into the customer volume so that the volume would be self-contained from the software acquirer's point of view. Those who desire a more detailed standard for software acquisition can also find *IEEE Std. 1062* in this volume.

Another key decision involved treating systems engineers as part of the customer set for software engineering. Certainly, *IEEE/EIA 12207* takes this view when it treats software requirements as derived from an essential systems context. So, all of the standards involving the system context of software development are in this volume:

♦ *IEEE Std. 1220, Systems Engineering Process,*
♦ *IEEE Std. 1228, Software Safety Plans,*
♦ *IEEE Std. 1233, Systems Requirements Specification,* and
♦ *IEEE Std. 1362, Concept of Operations.*

To complete its self-contained nature, this volume includes the vocabulary standard from the terminology layer of the collection, *IEEE Std. 610.12.*

The process volume

Although we placed *IEEE/EIA 12207* in the edition's customer volume, we placed another impor-

tant umbrella process standard in the process volume; *IEEE Std. 1074* addresses the process architect and provides building blocks for constructing processes that meet the requirements of *12207* or other standards.

You'll find standards in this volume that provide additional details on many of the technical processes and activities of *12207*:

♦ *IEEE Std. 730, Software Quality Assurance Plans,*
♦ *IEEE Std. 828, Software Configuration Management Plans,*
♦ *IEEE Std. 1008, Software Unit Testing,*
♦ *IEEE Std. 1012, Software Verification and Validation,*
♦ *IEEE Std. 1028, Software Reviews,* and
♦ *IEEE Std. 1219, Software Maintenance.*

IEEE/EIA 12207 treats management as a process, so *IEEE Std. 1058, Software Project Management Plans,* is included, along with *IEEE Std. 1490,* the *PMBOK Guide,* which provides a broader treatment of project management issues.

Some of the tough calls in placing standards into the volumes relate to the practice in some SESC standards of expressing process requirements in terms of the content of a plan to be developed. In each case, we evaluated the standard to determine if its emphasis was truly on the process or the plan's content. As a result, we included *IEEE Std. 730* and *IEEE Std. 828* in this volume, but placed *IEEE Std. 829, Software Test Documentation,* in the resource volume. *IEEE Std. 1045, Productivity Metrics,* is in this volume, because it offers means for measuring the performance of software processes.

Generally, you'll find standards related to system engineering processes elsewhere—many of them in the customer volume. *IEEE Std. 830* regarding software requirements specifications is in the resource volume.

Some developers, particularly those in the defense community, might be interested in using *EIA/IEEE J-Std-016* to guide their software development process. We decided to omit this standard from the four-volume edition for several reasons: it is currently being revised; it is already standalone and users do not need the other material from this volume; and it is large and would have significantly increased the volume's price. *EIA/IEEE J-Std-016* is available for separate purchase from either the IEEE or EIA.

The product volume

The trend in software engineering over the past 15 years or so has been to focus on evaluating and improving processes. Nevertheless, we should not forget that the purpose of any engineering effort is to create a product. This volume includes standards useful for software product evaluation.

Unfortunately, unlike the customer and process volumes, there is no standard providing principles to serve as a unifying umbrella for the others. The closest candidate would be *IEEE Std. 1061*, which provides a methodology for software quality metrics. *IEEE Std. 982.1* is a dictionary of metrics that can be applied to measure software reliability and related characteristics.

IEEE Std. 1465 is an adoption of *ISO/IEC 12119* and provides quality requirements for software packages—that is, prepackaged software products. Because user documentation is an important component of a software product, *IEEE Std. 1063* is included in this volume, although other documentation standards appear elsewhere.

All standards focusing on the processes for ensuring product quality appear elsewhere in the edition.

The resource volume

The term resource is deliberately broad, encompassing anything that might be used or consumed while executing a software process or creating a software product. Accordingly, we included a wide variety of standards in this volume. It is perhaps not surprising, therefore, that there is no umbrella standard to provide general principles in this area.

This volume contains the so-called "IDEF" notational standards—("Integrated Definition," a modeling language, combining graphics and text, used to analyze and define system functions and requirements). The volume contains both *IEEE Std 1320.1*, specifying IDEF0, and *1320.2*, specifying IDEF1X97 (IDEFObject). The basic interoperability data model is a series of standards (*IEEE Std. 1420.1* and its supplements) providing a data model for describing and interchanging reusable software components. The volume includes these standards and their guide, *IEEE Std. 1430*.

In addition, it has standards for CASE tools: *IEEE Std. 1462* considers tool evaluation and selection and *IEEE Std. 1348* considers organizational adoption. A standard on CASE tool interconnections, *IEEE Std. 1175*, was omitted because of its size and because its audience is primarily tool developers.

Some environments do not utilize CASE tools when transferring engineering data. Instead, they apply documentation conventions to move data among the various processes and phases of a software project. The resource volume holds standards

appropriate for this purpose:

♦ *IEEE Std. 830, Software Requirements Specifications,*
♦ *IEEE Std. 829, Software Test Documentation,* and
♦ *IEEE Std. 1016, Software Design Descriptions.*

Finally, the standard in the SESC architecture's techniques layer is included in this volume. *IEEE Std. 1044* (and an accompanying guide) describes the classification of software anomalies for a variety of purposes.

The level of integration among the IEEE software engineering standards is not yet perfect. As each individual standard is revised, on a cycle of roughly five years, it will be modified to fit more smoothly with IEEE/EIA 12207 and with the other standards in the collection. Of course, the IEEE collection continues to grow as additional subjects are treated. We also cooperate with the appropriate international standards committee to encourage the evolution of ISO/IEC 12207 in a direction consistent with the needs of SESC's users. ❖

REFERENCES

1. S. Magee and L.L. Tripp, *Guide to Software Engineering Standards and Specifications*, Artech House, Boston, 1997.
2. SESC Long Range Planning Group, *Master Plan for Software Engineering Standards, Version 1.0*, Dec. 1993; http://computer.org/standard/sesc/MasterPlan (current Oct. 1999).
3. SESC Business Planning Group, *Survey of Existing and In-Work Software Engineering Standards, Version 1.2*, Dec. 1996; http://computer.org/standard/sesc/survey0.htm (current Oct. 1999).
4. SESC Business Planning Group, *Vision 2000 Strategy Statement, Version 0.9*, Aug. 1995; http://computer.org/standard/sesc/strategy.htm (current Oct. 1999).
5. Institute of Electrical and Electronics Engineers, *Software Engineering, 1999*, Vols. 1–4, IEEE Press, Piscataway, N.J., 1999.
6. J.W. Moore, *Software Engineering Standards: A User's Road Map*, IEEE Computer Soc. Press, Los Alamitos, Calif., 1997.

● ● ●

About the Author

James W. Moore is the standards coordinator for the WC3 Center of The Mitre Corporation. He serves as a member of the Management Board of the IEEE Software Engineering Standards Committee, as a member of the IEEE Standards Board Review Committee, and as the head of the US delegation to ISO/IEC JTC1/SC7 (Software Engineering). He received his BS in mathematics from the University of North Carolina and his MS in systems and information science from Syracuse University. The IEEE Computer Society has recognized him as a charter member of their Golden Core and has given him the Meritorious Service Award. Contact him at The Mitre Corporation, 1820 Dolly Madison Blvd., W534, McLean, VA 22102; james.w.moore@ieee.org.

feature

Reprinted from IEEE Software,
Nov./Dec. 1996, pp. 77-88.

Using A Defined and Measured Personal Software Process

Improved software processes lead to improved product quality. The Personal Software Process is a framework of techniques to help engineers improve their performance — and that of their organizations — through a step-by-step, disciplined approach to measuring and analyzing their work. This article explains how the PSP is taught and how it applies to different software-engineering tasks. The author reports some promising early results.

WATTS S. HUMPHREY
Software Engineering Institute

F ewer code defects, better estimating and planning, enhanced productivity — software engineers can enjoy these benefits by learning and using the disciplines of the Personal Software Process. As a learning vehicle for introducing process concepts, the PSP framework gives engineers measurement and analysis tools to help them understand their own skills and improve personal performance. Moreover, the PSP gives engineers the process understanding they need to help improve organizational performance. Up to a point, process improvement can be driven by senior management and process staffs. Beyond Level 3 of the Software Engineering Institute's Capability Maturity Model, however, improvement requires that engineers apply process principles on an individual basis.[1]

In fact, it was because of the difficulties small engineering groups had in applying CMM principles that I developed the PSP. Large and small organizations alike can benefit from CMM practices, and I focused the original PSP research on demonstrating how individuals and small teams could apply process-improvement methods.

In this article, I describe the PSP and experiences with teaching it to date. Thus far, the PSP is introduced in a one-semester graduate-level course where engineers develop 10

TABLE 1
PSP EXERCISES

**Program
NumberBrief Description**

1A	Using a linked list, write a program to calculate the mean and standard deviation of a set of data.
2A	Write a program to count program LOC.
3A	Enhance program 2A to count total program LOC and LOC of functions or objects.
4A	Using a linked list, write a program to calculate the linear regression parameters (straight line fit).
5A	Write a program to perform a numerical integration.
6A	Enhance program 4A to calculate the linear regression parameters and the prediction interval.
7A	Using a linked list, write a program to calculate the correlation of two sets of data.
8A	Write a program to sort a linked list.
9A	Using a linked list, write a program to do a chi-squared test for a normal distribution.
10A	Using a linked list, write a program to calculate the three-parameter multiple regression parameters and the prediction interval.
1B	Write a program to store and retrieve numbers in a file.
2B	Enhance program 1B to modify records in a file.
3B	Enhance program 2B to handle common user errors.
4B	Enhance program 3B to handle further user error types.
5B	Enhance program 4B to handle arrays of real numbers.
6B	Enhance program 5B to calculate the linear regression parameters from a file.
7B	Enhance program 6B to calculate the linear regression parameters and the prediction interval.
8B	Enhance program 5B to sort a file.
9B	Write a program to do a chi-squared test for a normal distribution from data stored in a file.

Reports

R1	LOC counting standard: Count logical LOC in the language you use to develop the PSP exercises.
R2	Coding standard: Provide one logical LOC per physical LOC.
R3	Defect analysis report: Analyze the defects for programs 1A through 3A.
R4	Midterm analysis report of process improvement.
R5	Final report of process and quality improvement and lessons learned.

module-sized programs and write five analysis reports. Early results are encouraging — while individual performance varies widely, data on 104 students and engineers show reductions of 58 percent in the average number of defects injected (and found in development) per 1,000 lines of code (KLOC), and reductions of 71.9 percent in the average number of defects per KLOC found in test. Estimating and planning accuracy are also improved, as is productivity — the average improvement in LOC developed per hour is 20.8 percent.

You can apply PSP principles to almost any software-engineering task because its structure is simple and independent of technology — it prescribes no specific languages, tools, or design methods.

PSP OVERVIEW

A software process is a sequence of steps required to develop or maintain software. The PSP is supported with a textbook and an introductory course.[2] It uses a family of seven steps tailored to

develop module-sized programs of 50 to 5,000 LOC. Each step has a set of associated scripts, forms, and templates. During the course, engineers use the processes to complete the programming and report exercises shown in Table 1. As engineers learn to measure their work, analyze these measures, and set and meet improvement goals, they see the benefits of using defined methods and are motivated to consistently use them. The 10 PSP exercise programs are small: the first eight average 100 LOC and the last two average 200 and 300 LOC, respectively. Completing these programs, however, takes a good deal of work. While a knowledgeable instructor can substantially assist the students, the principal learning vehicle is the experience the students gain in doing the exercises.

When properly taught, the PSP
♦ demonstrates personal process principles,
♦ assists engineers in making accurate plans,
♦ determines the steps engineers can take to improve product quality,
♦ establishes benchmarks to measure personal process improvement, and
♦ determines the impact of process changes on an engineer's performance.

The PSP introduces process concepts in a series of steps. Each PSP step, shown in Figure 1, includes all the elements of prior steps together with one or two additions. Introducing these concepts one by one helps the engineers learn disciplined personal methods.

Personal Measurement (PSP0) is where the PSP starts. In this first step, engineers learn how to apply the PSP forms and scripts to their personal work. They do this by measuring development time and defects (both injected and removed). This lets engineers gather real, practical data and gives them benchmarks against which they measure progress while learning and practicing the PSP. PSP0 has three phases: plan-

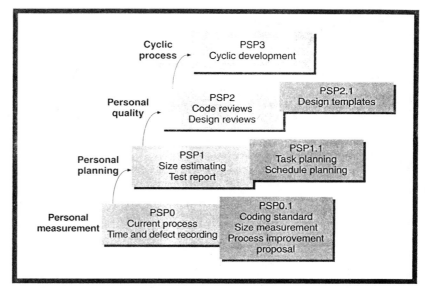

Figure 1. PSP process evolution.

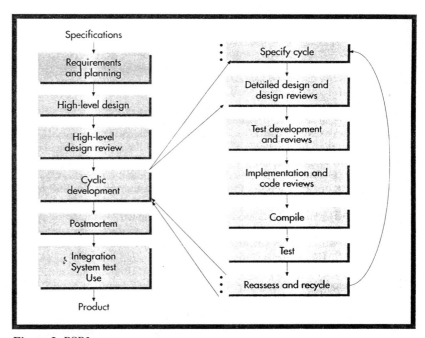

Figure 2. PSP3 process.

ning, development (which includes design, code, compile, and test), and postmortem. PSP0.1 adds a coding standard, size measurement, and the Process Improvement Proposal form. The PIP form lets engineers record problems, issues, and ideas to use later in improving their processes. They also see how forms help them to gather and use process data.

Personal Planning (PSP1) introduces the PROBE method. Engineers use PROBE to estimate the sizes and development times for new programs based on their personal data.[2] PROBE uses linear regression to calculate estimating parameters, and it generates prediction intervals to indicate size and time estimate quality. Schedule and task planning are added in PSP1.1. By introducing planning early, the engineers gather enough data from the 10 PSP exercises to experience the benefits of the PSP statistical estimating and planning methods.

Personal Quality (PSP2) introduces defect management. With defect data from the PSP exercises, engineers construct and use checklists for design and code review. They learn why it's important to focus on quality from the start and how to efficiently review their programs. From their own data, they see how checklists can help them effectively review design and code as well as how to develop and modify these checklists as their personal skills and practices evolve. PSP2.1 introduces design specification and analysis techniques, along with defect prevention, process analyses, and process benchmarks. By measuring the time tasks take and the number of defects they inject and remove in each process phase, engineers learn to evaluate and improve their personal performance.

Scaling Up (PSP3) is the final PSP step. Figure 2 illustrates how engineers can couple multiple PSP2.1 processes in a cyclic fashion to scale up to developing

modules with as many as several thousand LOC. At this PSP level, engineers also explore design-verification methods as well as process-definition principles and methods.

PSP/CMM relationship. The CMM is an organization-focused process-improvement framework.[1,3] While the CMM enables and facilitates good work, it does not guarantee it. The engineers

must also use effective personal practices.

This is where the PSP comes in, with its bottom-up approach to process improvement. PSP demonstrates process improvement principles for *individual engineers* so they see how to efficiently produce quality products. To be fully effective, engineers need the support of a disciplined and efficient environment, which means that the PSP will

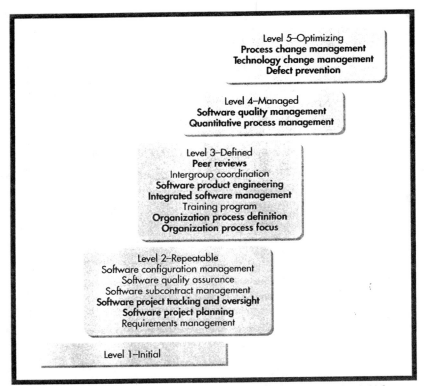

Figure 3. PSP elements in the Capability Maturity Model, highlighted in bold face.

be most effective in software organizations near or above CMM Level 2.

The PSP and the CMM are mutually supportive. The CMM provides the orderly support environment engineers need to do superior work, and the PSP equips engineers to do high-quality work and participate in organizational process improvement. As Figure 3 shows, the PSP demonstrates the goals of 12 of the 18 CMM key process areas. The PSP demonstrates only those that can be accommodated with individual, classroom-sized exercises.

PSP development. In the initial PSP experiments, I wrote 61 Pascal and C++ programs using a personal process as near to meeting the goals of CMM Level 5 as I could devise. I also applied these same principles to personal financial work, technical writing, and process development. This work showed me that a defined and measured personal process could help me do better work and that programming development is a compelling vehicle for introducing personal process management. A more complex process than other personal activities, software development poten-

tially includes many useful measures that can provide engineers an objective evaluation of their work and the quality of their products.

After the initial experiments, I needed to demonstrate that the PSP methods could be effectively applied by other software engineers, so I had two graduate students write several programs using an early PSP version. Because this early PSP was introduced all at once in one step, the students had difficulty. They tried some parts of the PSP and ignored others, which meant they did not understand the overall process and could not measure its effect on their personal performance. This experiment convinced me that process introduction was important; thus, the seven-step strategy evolved.

Early industrial PSP experiments corroborated the importance of process introduction. Various groups were willing to experiment with the PSP but until these methods were introduced in an orderly phased way no engineer consistently used the PSP. In one group, for example, project engineers defined personal and team processes and committed to use them. Although a few gath-

ered some process data and tried several methods, no one consistently used the full process. The problem appeared to be the pressure the engineers felt to complete their projects. Management had told them that using the PSP was more important than meeting the project schedules, but they still felt pressured and were unwilling to use unfamiliar methods.

Learning new software methods involves trial and error, but when faced with deadlines engineers are reluctant to experiment. While they might intellectually agree that a new practice is an improvement, they are reluctant to take a chance and generally fall back on familiar practices.

I was thus faced with a catch-22. Without data, I couldn't convince engineers to use the PSP. And unless engineers used the PSP, I couldn't get data. Clearly, to obtain industrial experience, I needed to first convince engineers that the PSP methods would help them do better work, so I decided to introduce the PSP with a graduate university course. By introducing PSP methods one at a time and with one or two exercises for each, this course would give engineers the data to demonstrate how well the PSP worked, without the pressure of project schedules.

PSP METHODS

Among the software-engineering methods PSP introduces are data gathering, size and resource estimating, defect management, yield management, cost of quality, and productivity analysis. I discuss these methods here with some examples that merge data for several PSP classes and for multiple programming languages. As you can see from the statistical analysis box on page 81, it makes sense to pool the PSP data in this manner.

The analysis of variance test was applied to data for 88 engineers from eight PSP classes. Program sizes, development times, and numbers of defects found were all separately tested. The results are shown in Table A. Since $F_{(80, 7)}$ at 5 percent is 3.29, the null hypothesis cannot be rejected in any of the program 1 cases. For the analyses in this article, the various class data are thus treated as a single set.

Data for program 10, the last PSP exercise, was similarly examined. Here, the population examined was 57 engineers from five courses. The smaller population was used because two of the eight courses only completed nine of the exercises and one course had not completed at the time of the analysis. As Table A shows, the analysis of variance test showed that the null hypothesis could not be rejected. In this case, $F_{(52, 4)}$ at 5 percent is 5.63. Again, for this article, data from all the PSP classes are thus pooled for the analyses.

The analysis of variance test also examined potential performance differences caused by six different programming languages used in the PSP classes to date. Only three had substantial use, however: C was used by 46 engineers, C++ by 21, and Ada by 8. The other languages were Fortran, Visual Basic, and Pascal. Only data on C, C++, and Ada were tested. As Table A shows, the variances among individuals were substantially greater than those among languages, so the null hypothesis cannot be rejected and the data for all languages are pooled. Here, $F_{(72, 2)}$ at 5 percent is 19.5.

The Wilcoxon matched-pairs signed-rank test examined the significance of the changes in the engineers' performance between programs 1 and 10. The comparison was made for one class of 14 engineers for total defects found per KLOC, defects per KLOC found in compiling, and defects per KLOC found in testing. The T values obtained in these cases were 5, 1, and 0 respectively. For N=13 and 0.005 significance in the one tailed test, T should be less than 9. In all cases, these improvements thus had a significance of better than 0.005. A repeated measures test has also been run on these same parameters and all the changes were found to be significant.

Table A
Analysis of Variance — F Values

Measure	Program 1	Program 10	Ratio of Variances Languages
Program size	2.09	2.37	0.450
Development time	1.20	1.87	1.460
Number of defects	0.65	3.31	0.042

Gathering data. The PSP measures were defined with the Goal-Question-Metric paradigm.[4] These are the time the engineer spends in each process phase, the defects introduced and found in each phase, and the developed product sizes in LOC. These data, gathered in every process phase and summarized at project completion, provide the engineers a family of process quality measures:

♦ size and time estimating error,
♦ cost-performance index,
♦ defects injected and removed per hour,
♦ process yield,
♦ appraisal and failure cost of quality, and
♦ the appraisal to failure ratio.

Estimating and planning. PROBE is a proxy-based estimating method I developed for the PSP that lets engineers use their personal data to judge a new program's size and required development time. Size proxies, which in the PSP are objects and functions, help engineers visualize the probable size of new program components. Other proxies —

function points, book chapters, screens, or reports — are also possible.

The PSP estimating strategy has engineers make detailed size and resource estimates. Although individual estimates generally have considerable error, the objective is to learn to make unbiased estimates. By coupling a defined estimating process with historical data, engineers make more consistent, unbiased estimates. When engineers estimate a new development in multiple parts, and when they make about as many overestimates as underestimates, their total project estimates are more accurate. The estimating measure is the percentage by which the final size or development time differs from the original estimates.

Overall, engineers' estimating ability improved moderately during the PSP course. At the beginning, only 30.8 percent of 104 engineers estimated within 20 percent of the correct program size. For program 10, 42.3 percent did. For time estimates, 32.7 percent of these 104 engineers estimated within 20 percent of the correct development time for program 1 and 49.0 percent did for program 10.

In general, individual estimating errors varied widely. Some engineers master estimating skill more quickly than others, so it was no surprise that some engineers improved considerably while others did not. Even though 10 exercises can help engineers understand estimating methods, they generally need more experience both to build an adequate personal estimating database and to gain estimating proficiency. These data suggest, however, that by using PROBE most engineers can improve their ability to estimate both program size and development time.

Planning accuracy is measured by the *cost-performance index*, the ratio of planned to actual development cost. For the PSP course, engineers track the cumulative value of their personal CPI through the last six exercises.

Managing defects. In the PSP, all defects are counted, including those found in compiling, testing, and desk checking. When engineers do inspections, the defects they find are also counted. The reason to count all defects

TABLE 2
PSP DEFECT TYPES

Type Number	Type Name	Description
10	Documentation	comments, messages
20	Syntax	spelling, punctuation, typos, instruction formats
30	Build, package	change management, library, version control
40	Assignment	declaration, duplicate names, scope, limits
50	Interface	procedure calls and references, I/O, user formats
60	Checking	error messages, inadequate checks
70	Data	structure, content
80	Function	logic, pointers, loops, recursion, computation, function defects
90	System	configuration, timing, memory
100	Environment	design, compile, test, or other support-system problems

is best understood by analogy with filter design in electrical engineering. If you examine only the noise output, you cannot obtain the information needed to design a better filter. Finding software defects is like filtering noise from electrical signals — the removal process must be designed to find each defect type. Logically, therefore, engineers should understand the defects they inject before they can adjust their processes to find them.

A key PSP tenet is that defect management is a software engineer's personal responsibility. If you introduce a defect, it is your responsibility to find and fix it. If the defects are not managed like this, they are more expensive to find and fix later on.[1]

As engineers learn to track and analyze defects in the PSP exercises, they gather data on the *phases* when the defects were injected and removed, the *defect types*, the *fix times*, and *defect descriptions*. Phases are planning, design, design review, code, code review, compile, and test. The defect types, shown in Table 2, are based on Ram Chillarege's work at IBM Research.[5] The fix time is the total time from initial defect detection until the defect is fixed and the fix verified.

Defect trends for 104 engineers are shown in Figure 4. These are the engineers in the PSP classes for whom I have data and who have completed the 10 programming exercises. (Other engineers met these criteria but reported

either incomplete or obviously incorrect results.) Of the 104 engineers, 80 took the PSP in university courses and 24 in industrial courses. Of the 80 university students, 16 were working engineers taking a night course and 28 were working engineers earning a graduate degree by returning to school full-time. Thus more than half of the engineers in this sample had worked in software organizations.

The top line in Figure 4 shows the average of the total number of defects found for each of the exercises. With program 1, the average is 116.4 defects per KLOC with a standard deviation of 76.9. By program 10, the average number of defects had declined to 48.9, and the standard deviation narrowed to 35.5.

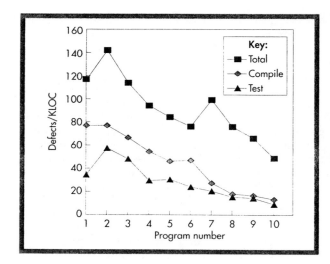

Figure 4. Defects per KLOC trend.

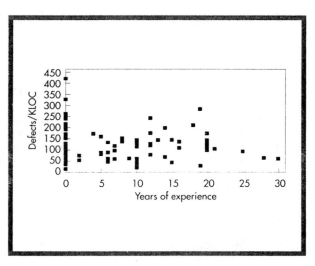

Figure 5. Defects versus experience, program 1.

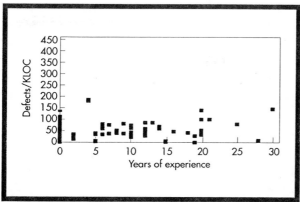

Figure 6. Defects versus experience, program 10.

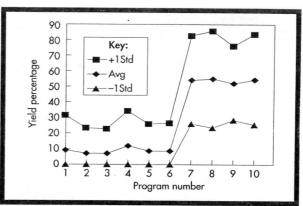

Figure 7. Yield versus program number.

The middle line in Figure 4 shows fewer defects found in compiling, from an average of 75.5 to 12.7 per KLOC, which is an improvement of about six times. The standard deviation narrowed from 58.7 to 12.7. For defects found in testing, the bottom line in Figure 4 shows reduced average defect levels, from 33.8 to 9.5 per KLOC, and reduced standard deviation, from 33.8 to 12.0.

Almost half (41) of these 104 engineers completed questionnaires, and the demographic data shows a modest relationship between defects per KLOC and years of engineering experience. While there is considerable variation in the defect rates for program 1, Figure 5 shows that the engineers with more than 20 years experience had somewhat lower defect rates than many less-experienced engineers, some of whom had low rates while many did not. As shown in Figure 6, the relationship between defect rates and experience does not hold for program 10. In fact, it appears that the less-experienced engineers learned the PSP methods better than their more experienced peers. Plots of defect levels versus both total LOC written and LOC written in the previous 12 months show no significant relationships.

Managing yield. Yield is the principal PSP quality measure. Total process yield is the percentage of defects found and fixed before the engineer starts to compile and test the program. Although software quality involves more than defects, the PSP focuses on defect detection and prevention because finding and fixing defects absorbs most of the development time and expense. When they start PSP training, engineers spend about 30 percent of their time compiling and testing programs, which probably mirrors their actual work practice. When engineers release actual modules for integration and system test, software organizations devote another 30 to 50 percent of development time in those phases,[6] almost exclusively to find and fix defects. Thus, despite other important quality issues, defect management will receive priority, at least until defect detection and repair costs are reduced.

If engineers want to find fewer defects in test, they must find them in code reviews. If they're going to review the code anyway, why not review it before compiling? This saves time they would have spent in compiling, and the compiler will act as a quality check on the code reviews. With few exceptions, however, engineers must first be convinced by their own data before they will do thorough design and code reviews prior to compiling.

In PSP, engineers must review their code before the first compile. Engineers often think the compiler's efficiency at finding syntax errors means they needn't bother finding them in reviews. However, some syntax defects will not be detected, not because the compilers are defective, but because some percentage of erroneous keystrokes will produce "valid" syntax that is not what the engineer intended. These defects cannot be found by the compiler and can be difficult to find in test. PSP data indicates that 9.4 percent of C++ syntax defects escape the compiler. If these defects are not found before compiling,

they can take 10 or more times as long to find in unit test and, if not found in unit test, can take many hours to find in integration test, system test, or system operation.

The satisfaction that comes from doing a quality job is another reason to review code before compiling. Engineers like finding defects in code review, and they get great satisfaction from a clean first compile. Conversely, when they find few defects in code review, they feel they wasted their time. My personal experience also suggests that projects whose products have many defects in compile tend to have many defects in test. These projects also tend to be late and over budget.

Evidence shows that the more defects you find in compile, the more you are likely to find in test. Data on 844 PSP programs from 88 engineers show a correlation of 0.711 with a significance of better than 0.005 between the numbers of defects found in compile and those found in test. Thus, the fewer defects you find in compile, the fewer you are likely to have in test.

Reduced numbers of test defects imply a higher quality-shipped product. While it could be argued that finding few defects in test indicates poor testing, limited data show high correlation between the numbers of defects found in test and the numbers of defects later found by users. Martin Marietta, for example, has found a correlation of 0.911.[7]

Figure 7 shows the yield trends for our 104 engineers. Here, the sharp jump in yield with program 7 results from the introduction of design and code reviews at that point.

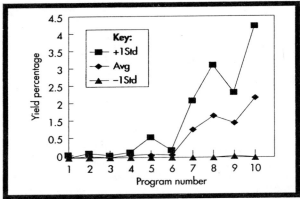

Figure 8. A/FR versus program number.

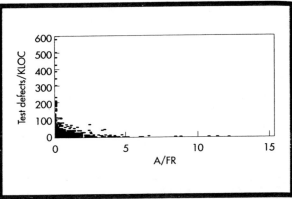

Figure 9. Test defects per KLOC versus A/FR.

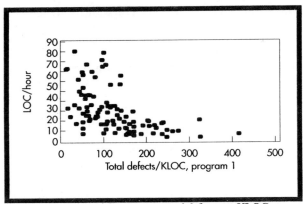

Figure 10. LOC per hour versus total defects per KLOC.

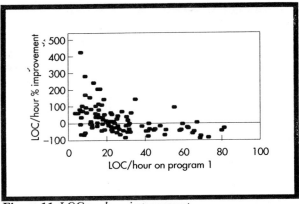

Figure 11. LOC per hour improvement.

Controlling cost of quality. To manage process quality, the PSP uses three cost-of-quality measures:

♦ appraisal costs: development time spent in design and code reviews,

♦ failure costs: time spent in compile and test, and

♦ prevention costs: time spent preventing defects before they occur. Prevention costs include prototyping and formal specification, methods not explicitly practiced with the PSP processes.

Another cost-of-quality measure is the ratio of the appraisal COQ to the failure COQ, known as the appraisal-to-failure-ratio. The A/FR is calculated by dividing the appraisal COQ by the failure COQ, or the ratio of design and code review time to compile and test time. The A/FR measures the relative effort spent in early defect removal. While the yield objective is to reduce the number of defects found in compile and test, the A/FR objective is to improve yield.

Figure 8 shows the improvement in A/FR for the same 104 engineers. Notably, A/FR increases with exercise 7 when design and code reviews are first introduced. Figure 9 shows data on A/FR and test defects for the 1,821 programs for which I have data. Here, A/FR values above 3 are associated with relatively few test defects while A/FRs below 2 are associated with relatively many test defects. PSP's suggested strategy is that engineers initially strive for A/FR values above 2. If they continue to find test defects, they should seek higher A/FR values. Once they consistently find few or no test defects, they should work to reduce A/FR while maintaining a high process yield.

Achieving higher product quality is the reason to increase A/FR. Once the quality objective is met, A/FR reductions will increase productivity. Since engineers generally cannot determine product quality during development, the A/FR measure is a useful guide to personal practice. By striving to increase their A/FR, engineers think more positively about review time. This helps them reduce compile and test time, and it reduces defects found in test.

The difference in time the engineers spend in compile and test shows how effective the A/FR measure can be. In one class, 75 percent of the engineers spent more than 20 percent of their time compiling and testing program 1. On program 10, only 8 percent did. Similarly, with program 1, no engineer spent less than 10 percent of the time compiling and testing, while with program 10, 67 percent did.

Understanding productivity. PSP-trained engineers learn to relate productivity and quality. They recognize that it makes no sense to compare the productivity of one programming process that found no test defects with one that had many. Defect-filled code will likely require many hours in integration and system test. Conversely, once engineers

44

learn to produce defect-free (or nearly so) programs, their projects will likely be more productive.

Figure 10 shows the LOC/hour rate achieved with PSP program 1 by the 104 engineers. From these data, higher defect content appears associated with lower LOC/hour rates (productivity). Note, however, that low defect content by itself did not guarantee high productivity. This relationship is even more pronounced with program 10: Those engineers who injected the most defects had the lowest LOC/hour development rates.

Figure 11 shows the improvement in LOC/hour for the group of 104 engineers. Engineers with the highest LOC/hour rates on program 1 usually had no improvement. Although the productivity of this group improved by an average of 20.84 percent, it is clear that many engineers who had high LOC/hour rates for program 1 had lower rates for program 10. This suggests two conclusions:

♦ Because many inexperienced engineers initially have higher defect rates and lower LOC/hour rates, the PSP disciplines will most likely increase their LOC/hour rates. They will then see the PSP as helping them to work faster and will probably continue using PSP methods.

♦ Some experienced engineers start with low defect rates and high LOC/hour rates. When these engineers add the PSP estimating and planning tasks, follow defined coding standards, review their programs, and track and report their results, their LOC/hour rates will often drop. These engineers will then see the PSP as slowing them down; if they do not appreciate the benefits of these planning and quality-management practices, they will probably stop using the PSP.

Engineers do not normally do several major tasks featured in the PSP, so it is not surprising that, when these tasks are added, some engineers end up with lower LOC/hour rates. Writing module-sized programs is a little like running a four-minute mile. When engineers can produce 40-plus LOC per hour, where will improvement come from? This focus on maximizing engineers' personal rates, however, leads to suboptimization. The PSP management and planning methods take time, but these are the very methods that make software engineers effective organizational team members. By taking the time to follow disciplined personal methods, they produce higher quality programs. When their programs have fewer defects, they require less time in integration and system test. The engineers' more disciplined work thus prepares them to develop high-quality large programs.

OTHER PSP ISSUES

Software design, process scale-up, and process definition are also addressed in the PSP.

Design. PSP's principal design focus is preventing design defects. The PSP approach is to use design-completion criteria, rather than advocating specific design methods. PSP research shows that defects result mainly from oversights, misunderstandings, and simple goofs, not complicated logic designs. Many defects are caused by improperly represented designs, incomplete designs, or no design at all. Moreover, poor design representation can cause engineers to design during implementation, which can be a significant source of error. By establishing design completion criteria, therefore, the PSP helps engineers produce reviewable designs that can be implemented with minimum error.

PSP data also show that engineers inject about 3.5 times as many defects

RESOURCES FOR EDUCATORS AND TRAINERS

The following materials are available from Addison-Wesley Publishing Company, Reading, Mass:

♦ Instructor's Guide for *A Discipline for Software Engineering*. This is free to people who teach or plan to teach a PSP course with this textbook. It contains the course outline, lecture suggestions, data presentation guidelines, grading criteria, instructions for the instructors' spreadsheets, and copies of the homework assignment kits.

♦ Instructor's Diskette for *A Discipline for Software Engineering*. This diskette is free to PSP instructors. It contains 701 lecture overheads for the 15 course lectures, spreadsheets for analyzing and graphing student data, and spreadsheet instructions.

♦ Support Diskette for *A Discipline for Software Engineering*. This contains a spreadsheet for each student to use to enter and graph exercise data, a summary spreadsheet to simplify exercise reporting, and the assignment kits.

Additional material and information can be obtained electronically from Addison-Wesley via Internet at gopher aw.com or via the World Wide Web at http://www.aw.com/cseng/. Look under book and author.

The SEI offers industrial PSP courses:

♦ PSP Instructor Training
♦ Intro to PSP
♦ Advanced PSP
♦ PSP for Managers

The SEI provides additional information on PSP publications and industrial courses on the World Wide Web at SEI http://www.sei.cmu.edu.

per hour during coding as they do during design. When engineers can save implementation time by producing better designs, they inject fewer defects and increase their productivity.

Although the PSP does not define generalized design completion criteria, it does offer an approach through four design templates that help engineers determine when their design is complete. The template structure is based on Dennis de Champeaux's[8] proposed object definition framework:

- *Internal-static.* Contains a static picture of the object, such as its logical design. For this, the PSP provides a logic-specification template.

- *Internal-dynamic.* The object's dynamic characteristics concerning its behavior. The dynamic behavior of an object can be described by treating it as a

> # A principle PSP objective is to extend to larger programs the productivity experienced in small programs.

state machine. For this, the PSP provides a state-specification template. Other possibly important dynamic characteristics are response times and interrupt behavior.

- *External-static.* The static relationship of this object to other objects. For this, the PSP provides a function-specification template, which includes the inheritance class structure.

- *External-dynamic.* The interactions of this object with other entities. An example would be the call-return behavior of each of the object's methods. For this, the PSP provides an operational scenario template.[2]

Scale-up. The PSP's objective is to extend to larger programs the productivity engineers typically experience with small program development. The final PSP step, PSP3, follows the spiral-like process shown in Figure 2. After subdividing the large program into smaller elements, each element is developed with a PSP2.1-like process. These elements are then progressively integrated into the completed product.

Process definition. In helping engineers learn to apply process principles, the PSP shows them how to define new processes, how to plan a process-definition task, and how long such work typically takes. In the middle of the course, engineers are assigned the task of defining a process for analyzing process data and writing a report on their findings. They enact this process and submit the report they produce, their process definition, and work data.

At course end, the engineers update the midterm process to fix previously encountered problems and extend the process to include the more sophisticated analyses required for a second report. From these exercises, they see that process definition is straightforward and applicable to many tasks besides program development, including requirements definition, system test, program enhancement, and documentation development.

TRANSITIONING THE PSP INTO PRACTICE

Our focus now at the SEI is on transitioning the PSP into general practice through academic and industrial introduction.

Academic introduction. The initial PSP course was aimed at first-year graduate

software engineers largely because I believed the students would have the required programming language proficiency and software development competence. The one-semester course is designed for 15 90-minute lectures. The standard PSP course assigns the 10 A-series programs listed in Table 1; the B series is optional. Because the full A-series course takes about 150 to 200 hours of an engineer's time, the 15-week class schedule represents a heavy workload. The time could be extended, depending on the academic schedule and whether or not other materials are introduced. It is essential, however, that engineers understand at the outset the amount of work involved.

The primary learning mechanism is the engineer's experience in completing the exercises. Frequent discussion of overall class data is necessary, but no individual engineer's data are shown to anyone except that engineer.

We are also experimenting with the PSP concepts in the undergraduate software-engineering curriculum. If the PSP were taught during their earliest courses, engineers would have the maximum opportunity to practice and perfect these methods before they started professional work. Based on the PSP experience, inexperienced engineers are more likely to find that the PSP discipline improves their performance, and they are then more likely to continue using these methods.

College juniors and seniors have completed the current PSP course with apparent success. PSP concepts are within the intellectual grasp of most college freshmen, however, so an undergraduate course textbook (now in test) is being prepared.[9]

Industrial introduction. Introducing the PSP into industrial organizations appears to be most successful in a course format. Individual self-study has been tried, but only about one in five to

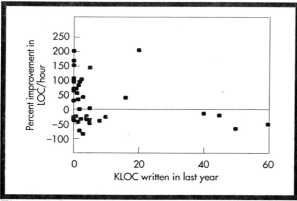

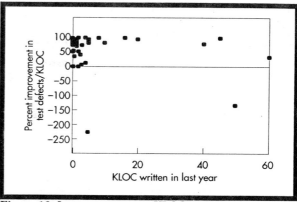

Figure 12. Improvement versus KLOC written in last year.   *Figure 13. Improvement versus KLOC written in last year.*

10 of the engineers who start such a course actually completes it. One industrial group of three engineers and a manager has taken the course as a team, with success. At latest report, this group is now starting to use the PSP on their project.

Another successful approach is to introduce the PSP from the top down in a course taught to the top management team, then to the engineers who work for them. In the one case that has been tried, two laboratory technical directors and the laboratory management team took the first course. Courses are next being given to a class that includes project engineers and leaders. Because the managers understood the work involved, they could convince their teams to take the PSP course. With their PSP background, the managers also appreciated the methods their people would be using and will be better equipped to lead their teams after PSP training.

Currently, the SEI offers several types of PSP training (see the box on p. 85). The SEI is also working with several corporations to determine the PSP's impact on organizational performance and is gathering data on engineers' backgrounds, the tools and methods used, and organizational performance. In addition, various techniques are being explored to determine how PSP affects different organizational quality and productivity indicators. It will likely take several years to complete these studies.

LANGUAGE FLUENCY AND IMPROVEMENT

Is some of the PSP improvement due to the programming fluency the engineers gain while completing the programming exercises? To find out, the SEI developed a questionnaire that

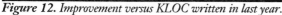

Another successful approach is to introduce PSP from the top down.

asked the engineers to estimate how many LOC they had developed in the preceding 12 months. Figure 12 compares the change in LOC/hour versus the LOC the engineers claimed to have written in the past year. Although it is unlikely that many engineers knew precisely the number of LOC they had written in the last year, it is likely that those who had written little or no code would give low numbers. From Figure 12, it does not appear that recent programming experience is a major factor in the PSP learning process.

Similarly, Figure 13 shows the improvement in test defects versus the LOC written in the last year. Again, the relationship appears insignificant and also suggests that the large improvement in PSP student performance cannot be explained by the increased language fluency gained by completing the exercises.

When more questionnaire data are gathered we will refine our statistical analyses of these questions.

PSP data show that engineers can substantially improve their performance by using a defined and measured personal process. By defining their tasks, measuring their work, and striving to produce the highest quality products, engineers find that their work is more predictable and their products have fewer defects. Results from the PSP work done to date show the following:

♦ The PSP is effectively taught in a university graduate course. With adequate management support, this same course format works in industry. In all cases, the key to learning the material is that the engineers do the course exercises and periodically analyze their exercise data. The PSP is a self-learning experience that provides engineers an appreciation of data gathering and process management.

♦ The improvement in average defect levels for engineers who complete the PSP course is 58.0 percent for total defects per KLOC and 71.9 percent for defects per KLOC found in test.

♦ With extensive PSP data supporting their estimates, engineers can better justify their plans and explain to their managers the logic behind their cost and schedule estimates. This in turn helps them make realistic commitments to, and negotiate them with, their management.

The PSP is a promising discipline, but many questions remain to be studied. Early indications are that improved PSP performance will result in improved engineering practices. This has not yet been demonstrated in industrial practice however and will be the next challenge.   ♦

ACKNOWLEDGMENTS

I thank Howie Dow for his early work in teaching and demonstrating the PSP with his first class. Nazism Madjahavi's early support and encouragement helped me formulate the PSP and structure the course and textbook. Iraj Hirmanpour and the faculty of the Aviation Computer Science Department at Embry-Riddle Aeronautical University have made the PSP the required first course for all graduate software-engineering students, and they are assisting me in developing and testing the PSP course for freshmen. Girish Seshagiri and Pat Ferguson at the AIS Corporation have given me helpful feedback from their early experiences in introducing and using the PSP.

I also thank those who reviewed this article: Alan Christie, Suzanne Couturiaux, Howie Dow, Andy Huber, John Leary, Julia Mullaney, Jim Over, Bob Park, Lauren Quinn, Erik Riedel, Neal Reizer, Glenn Rosander, Dan Roy, Jim Rozum, Larry Votta, and Dave Zubrow. I also appreciate the help and advice that Will Hayes and Jim Herbsleb gave me with the statistical issues.

This work is supported by the US Department of Defense.

REFERENCES

1. W.S. Humphrey, *Managing the Software Process*, Addison-Wesley, Reading, Mass., 1989.
2. W.S. Humphrey, *A Discipline for Software Engineering*, Addison-Wesley, Reading, Mass., 1995.
3. M.C. Paulk et al., *The Capability Maturity Model: Guidelines for Improving the Software Process*, Addison-Wesley, Reading Mass., 1995.
4. V. Basili and D.M. Weiss, "A Methodology for Collecting Valid Software Engineering Data," *IEEE Trans. Software Engineering*, Nov. 1984, pp. 728-738.
5. R. Chillarege et al., "Orthogonal Defect Classification — A Concept for In-Process Measurements," *IEEE Trans. Software Eng.*, Nov. 1992, pp. 943-956.
6. B.W. Boehm, *Software Engineering Economics*, Prentice-Hall, Englewood Cliffs, N.J., 1981.
7. J. Henry et al., "Improving Software Maintenance at Martin Marietta," *IEEE Software*, July 1994, pp. 67-75.
8. D. de Champeaux, D. Lea, and P. Faure, *Object-Oriented System Development*, Addison-Wesley, Reading, Mass., 1993.
9. W.S. Humphrey, *Introduction to the Personal Software Process*, Addison-Wesley, Reading, Mass., to appear.

Watts S. Humphrey founded the Software Process Program of the Software Engineering Institute and is currently an SEI fellow. The process program provides leadership in establishing advanced software-engineering processes, metrics, methods, and quality programs for the US government. Humphrey worked at IBM for more than 25 years, where his assignments included responsibility for commercial software development, managing the Endicott, N.Y., development laboratory, and directing IBM's programming quality and process work. In 1991, he served on the Board of Examiners for the Malcolm Baldrige National Quality Award. He has been issued five US patents and has authored four books.

Humphrey received a BS in physics from the University of Chicago, an MS in physics from the Illinois Institute of Technology, and an MBA from the University of Chicago. He is an IEEE fellow and a member of the ACM.

Address questions about this article to Humphrey at SEI, Carnegie Mellon University, Pittsburgh, PA 15213-3890; watts@sei.cmu.edu.

Reprinted from IEEE Computer,
May 1997, pp. 24-31.

Results of Applying the Personal Software Process

Too often, software developers follow inefficient methods and procedures. The Personal Software Process, developed by Watts Humphrey at the Software Engineering Institute, provides software engineers with a methodology for consistently and efficiently developing high-quality products. The value of PSP has been shown in three case studies.

Pat Ferguson
Advanced
Information
Services

*Watts S.
Humphrey*
Software
Engineering
Institute

*Soheil
Khajenoori*
Embry-Riddle
Aeronautical
University

Susan Macke
Motorola

*Annette
Matvya*
Union Switch
& Signal

I n most professions, competent work requires the disciplined use of established practices. It is not a matter of creativity versus discipline, but one of bringing discipline to the work so that creativity can happen. The use of plans and procedures brings order and efficiency to any job and allows workers to concentrate on producing a superior product. A disciplined effort, too, removes waste, error, and inefficiency, freeing financial resources for better uses.

Sadly, software professionals today often do not plan or track their work, and software quality is rarely measured. This is not surprising as software engineers are generally not taught planning, tracking, or quality measurement. When software organizations do plan, it is only at the project level, and few software organizations measure the quality of their work.

The Personal Software Process is a defined and measured framework that helps software engineers plan and track their work and produce high-quality products. PSP shows engineers how to manage the quality of their products and how to make commitments they can meet. It also provides them with the data to justify their plans. PSP can be applied to many parts of the software development process, including small-program development, requirements definition, document writing, systems tests, and maintenance and enhancement of large software systems.

PSP has been shown to substantially improve the estimating and planning ability of engineers while significantly reducing the defects in their products. PSP is introduced with a course, and during the course productivity improvements average around 20 percent and product quality, as measured by defects, generally improves by five times or more. While PSP is new, a growing number of engineers use it and find it helpful.

PERSONAL SOFTWARE PROCESS

In his work at the Software Engineering Institute at Carnegie Mellon University, Watts Humphrey began

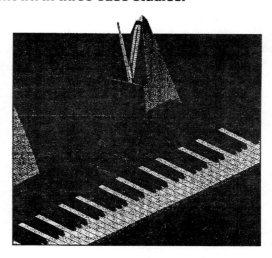

developing PSP in 1989. The program came about when groups began asking SEI how to apply its Capability Maturity Model to small projects. CMM, also a product of SEI, helps software organizations improve their development and maintenance capabilities by assessing their work according to five maturity levels and 18 key process areas. The CMM is widely used in both the public and private sectors to guide the evaluation and improvement of software organizations.[1,3]

CMM and PSP are thus mutually supportive, with CMM addressing management practices and PSP defining a disciplined way for engineers to do their work. With PSP, engineers practice 12 of CMM's 18 key process areas. PSP training can also help accelerate an organization's CMM process improvement program.

PSP is a process framework and set of methods that help engineers be more disciplined in their work. It shows them how to estimate and plan their projects, measure and track their work, and improve the quality of the products they produce.

0018-9162/97/$10.00 © 1997 IEEE

PSP consists of a series of scripts that define tasks, of forms for recording data, and of standards that govern such things as coding practices, size counting, and the assignment of defect types. When engineers follow PSP, they first plan their work and document the plan. As they do their work, they record their times and track and report every defect they find. At the end of the project, the engineers do a postmortem analysis and complete a project plan summary report.

For larger projects, PSP's task and schedule templates guide engineers through the steps of developing a schedule. This helps the engineers think through in advance how they will do the work, and thus they go down fewer blind alleys, make few mistakes, and follow an overall strategy for attacking the work.

PSP's quality improvements result from three key aspects: First, by tracking all defects, engineers are sensitized to the mistakes they personally make and therefore become more careful in their work. Second, when they analyze their defect data, they gain a clearer understanding of the cost of removing defects and thus apply the most effective ways of finding and fixing them. And third, PSP introduces a number of quality practices that have proven effective in preventing defects and in efficiently finding and fixing them.

Training is key

Successful application of PSP requires training. PSP can be studied in a one-semester graduate-level university course, which includes a PSP textbook and 10 programming and five analysis exercises.[4] PSP is now being taught at more than 20 universities in the US and at institutions in Europe, South America, and Australia. Some universities, too, now offer an introductory freshman course that is designed to start engineers off on the right track.[5] Finally, a condensed version of the university course, also with 10 programming and five analysis exercises, is available for industrial software groups.

Both university and industry PSP courses work through seven process levels while the engineers develop 10 module-sized programs. Each process level introduces several elements of PSP, accompanied by applicable scripts, forms, and templates. New levels build on material taught in preceding levels, allowing engineers to practice what they learn and to see the benefits of PSP procedures before moving on to the next level.

Seven process levels

Figure 1 shows the seven process levels. Each new level introduces new elements and more complicated material until the engineers reach the highest level, PSP 3. The Team Software Process (TSP), now in development at SEI, extends the PSP approach to the software team environment.

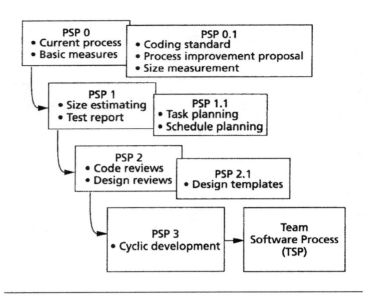

Figure 1. PSP process evolution.

- *PSP 0.* In the first level, engineers essentially follow their current practices, learning some basic PSP techniques. This level covers how to record development time and how to log each compile-and-test defect. These measurements are used in process analysis and planning and as a benchmark for assessing improvement.
- *PSP 0.1.* This level adds size measurement and the *process improvement proposal,* a form that engineers use to record the process problems they encounter as well as their ideas for addressing them. These problems can make processes very inefficient, but because many amount to minor details, engineers tend to forget them without the use of a form.
- *PSP 1.* In this level, engineers are introduced to the PROBE method, which uses historical data to estimate size and determine the accuracy of the estimate. PROBE is a regression-based size-estimating method developed specifically for PSP.
- *PSP 1.1.* This level adds resource and schedule estimating and *earned-value tracking.* Engineers often have trouble tracking their work because they do tasks in an order different from their plan. Earned-value tracking allows them to weight the relative importance of each task and to judge their progress as they finish some tasks early and others late.
- *PSP 2.* This level introduces design and code reviews, as well as quality measurement and evaluation. Using defect data from their earlier exercises, engineers also develop personal design and code review checklists.

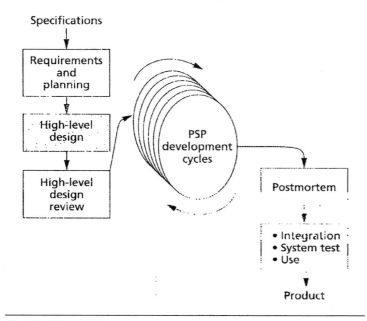

Figure 2. PSP 3 process.

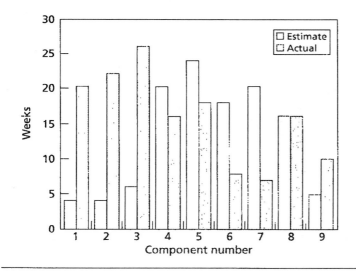

Figure 3. AIS Project A schedule estimates.

- *PSP 2.1.* In this level, engineers learn design specification techniques and ways to prevent defects.
- *PSP 3.* In this highest process level, software engineers become fully conversant in PSP. This level covers design verification techniques and methods for adapting PSP to engineers' working environments.

By applying the techniques and procedures learned during the course, engineers see how to apply PSP to large-scale software development. Figure 2 shows the spiral-like strategy of PSP level 3 for developing program modules of up to several thousand lines of code. This cyclic process builds on several well-known software engineering principles: First, by using abstraction and modular design concepts, engineers are better able to produce clean designs and to capitalize on reusable parts. Second, this cyclic development strategy follows the common practice of building large programs through a family of progressively enhanced versions. Finally, the process incorporates the divide-and-conquer strategy of Barry Boehm's spiral model for minimizing risks by attacking complex problems a step at a time.[6]

SEI's data on 104 engineers shows that, on average, PSP training reduces size-estimating errors by 25.8 percent and time-estimating errors by 40 percent. Lines of code written per hour increases on average by 20.8 percent, and the portion of engineers' development time spent compiling is reduced by 81.7 percent. Testing time is reduced by 43.3 percent, total defects by 59.8 percent, and test defects by 73.2 percent.[7,8]

CASE STUDY OVERVIEW

Because PSP was only experimentally introduced in 1994 and has been undergoing further development and introduction to the industry over the past two years, relatively little data on its use and effectiveness are available.[4,9] This problem is compounded by the time required to introduce PSP into a workplace and by the length of many software development efforts. Furthermore, pre-PSP data are often unavailable.

Nevertheless, three industrial software groups have used PSP and have collected data to show its effectiveness. They are Advanced Information Services, Inc., Motorola Paging Products Group, and Union Switch & Signal Inc. Each has trained several groups of engineers and measured the results of several projects that used PSP methods. In all cases, the projects were part of the companies' normal operations and not designed for this study.

The three companies offered a variety of situations useful for demonstrating the versatility of PSP. The projects at Motorola and US&S involved software maintenance and enhancement, while those at AIS involved new product development and enhancement. Among the companies, application areas included commercial data processing, internal manufacturing support, communications product support, and real-time process control. Work was done in C or C++.

Company sizes ranged from less than a hundred employees to thousands in a large international corporation. Most projects involved one to three engi-

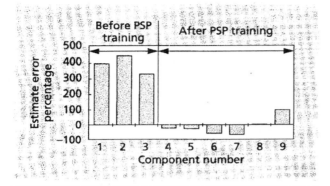

Figure 4. AIS schedule estimating error.

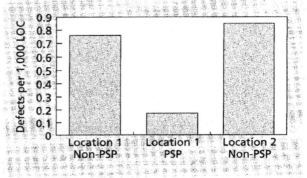

Figure 5. AIS acceptance test quality.

neers, but one of the AIS projects used two groups—one in the US and the other in India—of three to five engineers. While most of the projects were for commercial clients, one program was developed for an agency of the US government.

Advanced Information Services

AIS is located in Peoria, Illinois, with a subsidiary in Madras, India. The company offers software development, consulting services, Internet services, and process training. AIS engineers develop custom business applications for clients or do contract work at client sites.

AIS first introduced PSP with a pilot course in the spring of 1994. The course was given outside regular work hours with instructors who had not been trained in PSP, so it was perhaps not surprising that only half the engineers completed the course. As a result, AIS sent one engineer to SEI for PSP instructor training, put the course on company time, and tried various formats to shorten course time. Since then, AIS has presented five PSP courses, and essentially all the engineers have completed the work. The improvements during the course have been similar to SEI's general findings.

Project A. One of AIS's first applications of PSP was in 1995 when engineers in Peoria (working with another team in Madras) developed software for a Fortune 50 client. The Peoria components of Project A ranged from about 500 to 2,200 lines of code. By April 1995 the engineers had completed components 1, 2, and 3, but the project was not meeting its internal target dates or its external commitments. Project A had to be replanned and new delivery dates negotiated with the client.

At this point, management decided to train the Peoria engineers in PSP, and they subsequently used PSP methods to plan and develop components 4 through 9. Figure 3 shows the schedule performance

for all nine components, and Figure 4 shows the schedule estimating errors. Before PSP training, schedule estimating error averaged 394 percent; afterward the average was −10.4 percent.

Quality also improved after PSP training. Figure 5 shows that in acceptance tests, the software of the Peoria engineers had 0.76 defects per 1,000 lines of code before PSP training and 0.17 defects per 1,000 lines of code after training, a 78 percent improvement. The Madras engineers, who had not received PSP training, had 0.85 acceptance-test defects per 1,000 lines of code. PSP also improved productivity. Figure 6 shows that the PSP-trained engineers wrote 7.99 lines of code per hour before training and 8.58 lines of code per hour after training, an improvement of 7.4 percent. The untrained Madras engineers wrote only 6.4 lines of code per hour. Since this product has not yet been installed, there is no usage data.

Projects B, C, and D. Project B, an application enhancement effort by three PSP-trained engineers in 1996, is similar to Projects C and D, which were com-

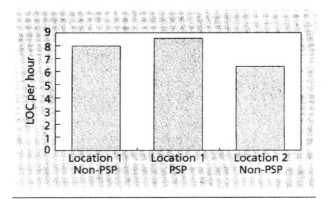

Figure 6. AIS productivity.

Table 1. Summary of AIS project data.					
Project	PSP staff	Non-PSP staff	Product size	Delivery: Planned/ actual (months)	Acceptance test defects	Usage defects
B	3	0	24 requirements	7/5	1	0
C	0	3	19 requirements	2/5	11	1
D	0	3	30 requirements	10/19	6	14
E	1	0	2,255 LOC	6/6	0	0
F	1	0	1,400 LOC	2/2	0	0
G	2	1	6.196 LOC	2/2	0	3

pleted in 1995 and 1996, respectively, by AIS engineers not trained in PSP. All projects were of similar size, used the same platform, language, and database tools, and required three engineers. Of the three projects, Project C's engineers had the most experience. Table 1 shows results for these projects.

In acceptance tests, Project C had 11 defects, Project D had six, but Project B had only one. After several months of use, customers found one defect in Project C, 14 in Project D, but none in Project B. Because data on lines of code are not available, Figure 7 shows the acceptance and use defect data for these products normalized by the number of requirements. While the requirement count is only a crude size measure, it is the only data available. Project C was scheduled for two months, but took five to reach the acceptance test stage; Project D was scheduled for 10 months, but took 19; Project B, however, was scheduled for seven months, but took five.

Projects E, F, and G. AIS undertook three other projects using PSP-trained engineers. Projects E and F, with 2,255 and 1,400 lines of code, respectively, both used one PSP-trained engineer. Project G, with 6,196 lines of code, required three engineers, two of whom were trained in PSP. Both Projects E and F were completed

on time, with no defects found during customer acceptance and after several months of use. Project G was also completed on time, but the customer reported three defects. Table 1 and Figure 7 show data for all three projects.

Project E is noteworthy because it was a cost-plus government contract (the government paid for actual development costs plus a percentage for profit) and was completed on schedule and substantially under budget. During the project, the engineer provided the client and AIS management with his weekly PSP task and schedule planning templates, allowing them to easily track project status. The development manager reported that these and other PSP practices sharply reduced the need for management supervision.

In addition to quality and productivity, PSP can help shorten project schedules. Table 2 shows system test time for the seven AIS projects discussed plus three newer projects. Before PSP training, system testing took as much as several months. For example, Project C's three testing cycles took several weeks. However, after PSP training, system test time was only a few days. The only exception was Project A2, whose system test took 1.5 months because it had to be tested with Project A1.

AIS plans for PSP

All engineers and managers at the AIS subsidiary in India have now completed PSP training. In the US, 58 percent of engineers and managers have completed training, and all should be fully trained by the end of this year. AIS now trains all new engineers in PSP before they are assigned a project. They expect this to reduce the disruption of training in the middle of a project and result in more general use of PSP.

MOTOROLA PAGING PRODUCTS GROUP

The North American Paging Subscriber Division of the Motorola Paging Products Group, located in Boynton Beach, Florida, develops and manufactures one-way numeric and alphanumeric pagers. Using simulcast broadcast techniques, these products provide digital message service. The embedded code in a pager provides message handling, user-friendly

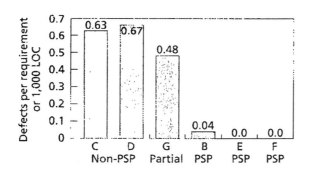

Figure 7. AIS project defects.

prompts, and automatic message reception.

Three Motorola managers and two professors from Embry-Riddle Aeronautical University introduced PSP at the company. So far, Motorola has presented three PSP classes, training 40 engineers and 22 managers. The Motorola Paging Products Group has initiated a program to make all Motorola divisions aware of and literate in PSP.

Motorola's management has strongly supported PSP. The company commits eight hours per week for training and another four hours for process improvement. To build PSP team spirit, they give trained engineers customized sports shirts with a PSP logo, hold discussion lunches, and provide a graduation party where a certificate is presented in the presence of colleagues and family members. Engineers who complete the course receive financial rewards and join a user group that meets once a month.

These efforts have resulted in a high level of participation in PSP training and continued use of PSP methods. A Motorola post-training survey of 12 engineers showed that most would continue using PSP. Another survey six months after the pilot course showed that more than 80 percent of the engineers used PSP methods in their work and that 77 percent of the engineers used PSP methods in nonsoftware tasks.

Motorola project results

Engineers at Motorola first used PSP in a project that changed five lines of code in a large program supporting a manufacturing area. Although coding time was slightly more than planned, integration and test time were reduced by 60 percent. The project took 44 percent less time than planned and was completed on time.

One defect was found in code review (which took two minutes to fix), but no defects were found during system testing, and none have been found in over five months of operation—which is unusual. This was critical for Motorola because the manufacturing station was required to work on the software, and any testing and debugging interrupts production, costing several thousand dollars per hour in lost manufacturing capacity.

A second project involved adding menus to existing product-test software. This project achieved early removal of more than 80 percent of defects. Only 20 percent of development time was spent in testing, and 56 percent of development time came before coding.

A third project using PSP at Motorola was a crash effort of one engineer to add 3,894 lines of code to the 9,150 lines of code in a pager-support system. By using PSP planning and tracking methods, this engineer precisely tracked his status every day. He fell one day behind schedule on three occasions, but was able to quickly recover. He was able to find 80 percent of

defects before the first test, and he completed system testing one week early. No defects have since been found in more than four months of product use.

So far, PSP-trained engineers at Motorola have completed 18 projects. As shown in Table 3, several of these products have been used for many months, and only one defect has been found in one of them. Unfortunately, detailed usage data were not gathered on the products labeled "NA," but there is no record of any defect reports for any of them. In the case of the single defect report, Motorola was unable to deter-

Table 2. AIS system test time improvement.

Project	Size	System test time
Non-PSP Projects		
A1	15,800 LOC	1.5 months
C	19 requirements	3 test cycles
D	30 requirements	2 months
H	30 requirements	2 months
PSP Projects		
A2	11,700 LOC	1.5 months
B	24 requirements	5 days
E	2,300 LOC	2 days
F	1,400 LOC	4 days
G	6,200 LOC	4 days
I	13,300 LOC	2 days

Table 3. Motorola operational defect data for PSP projects.

Project number	Size (LOC)	Months used	Total defects	Test defects	Use defects
1	463	18	13	5	0
2	4,565	NA	69	10	0
3	1,571	NA	47	8	0
4	3,381	NA	69	22	0
5	5	9	0	0	0
6	22	5	2	0	0
7	1	18	1	0	0
8	2,081	10	34	0	1
9	114	8	15	2	0
10	364	NA	29	2	0
11	7	5	0	0	0
12	620	3	12	2	0
13	720	NA	9	2	0
14	3,894	NA	20	2	0
15	2,075	NA	79	27	0
16	1,270	NA	20	1	0
17	467	NA	17	3	0
18	3,494	8	139	50	0
Total	25,114	NA	575	136	1

Table 4. US&S usage data.				
Product	Lines of code	Months of use	Defects in test	Defects in use
M45	193	9.0	1	0
M10	453	7.0	2	0
M77	6,133	4.0	25	0
M54	477	3.5	8	0
M53	1,160	1.0	21	0
Total	8,415	NA	57	0

mine whether this was a latent problem with the prior code or a newly injected defect with this project.

UNION SWITCH & SIGNAL

Union Switch & Signal manufactures a wide range of hardware products for the railroad and transit industries. It also develops and installs software-intensive process-control systems for real-time control of railroad and transit operations. The Automation and Information Systems business unit of the US&S Engineering Division is located in Pittsburgh and has approximately 100 software managers and engineers developing software and hardware for railroad and transit control centers.

US&S has given three PSP classes to nine managers and 25 engineers. The managers' class was held during regular work hours, but managers had to complete homework assignments on their own time. This turned out to be too heavy a workload, and only about half the managers completed all the work. Subsequently, the engineers' classes have been given during work hours, and a full day is provided to complete each of the 10 programming exercises. This has proved adequate as long as the managers track the engineers' progress and encourage them to finish the work. To date, 72 percent of the engineers have completed the course assignments.

At US&S, PSP-trained engineers have completed five projects. All were maintenance and enhancement releases for a large railroad information and control system, and each project required only one engineer. Using PSP techniques, the engineers completed their projects on schedule, and no defects have been found in any project during installation or customer use.

Data on these five projects are shown in Table 4. As of the time of this writing, no defects have been found in any of these products.

The effective use of PSP depends on proper training. The three companies described here followed course plans similar to, though shorter than, the standard 15-week academic course, with one lecture given each week. Since its third class, AIS has offered

a two-week course, with a lecture given in the morning and with the remainder of the day devoted to completing the exercises. The engineers use a third week for additional work. Either strategy can be effective as long as management uses qualified instructors, provides sufficient time for the engineers to complete the exercises, and monitors the training.

In both courses, engineers require about 125 hours to do the work. In the most successful classes, management has provided a full working day for each lecture and assignment, and the engineers have been willing to spend some personal time studying. Unfortunately, it has been found that some engineers fail to do the assignments, even when work time is provided. Because the exercises are critical for learning PSP, it is important that managers treat PSP training as part of the engineers' jobs and monitor their progress.

After learning PSP, engineers require some discipline to continue following PSP methods and procedures. Management needs to constantly stress the importance of quality goals, of thorough planning, and of effective tracking. A US&S manager, for example, strongly supports PSP and holds weekly meetings with his project team to review status, plans, and data. Another manager, however, has not emphasized the importance of PSP, and his engineers have essentially reverted to their old practices.

With proper training and with continuing management interest, PSP is an effective methodology for efficiently developing quality software. Although extensive data are not yet available, the case studies here show that PSP can improve planning and scheduling, reduce development time, and produce better software. Of the PSP projects reported to date, all have been delivered on or ahead of schedule and only one has had any customer-reported defects. PSP also has been found to accelerate an organization's CMM process improvement efforts.

As the effectiveness of PSP becomes evident, interest in the program is growing. SEI continues to introduce PSP to the industry, offering presentations, training, and on-site consultations. The institute has also developed several training programs complementary to PSP. One is designed for managers who supervise PSP-trained engineers. Another, the Team Software Process, now in early development, extends PSP beyond the individual engineer to the software development team.

These efforts—for management, engineers, and software teams—will help companies consistently and efficiently produce high-quality products. At a time of growing competition, when engineers are under increasing pressure to quickly produce error-free products, software companies can little afford to ignore better ways of doing their work. ❖

Acknowledgments

We thank the many people who have participated in this work, as well as our associates who reviewed and commented on this article. From AIS, we particularly thank Girish Seshagiri, Vikas Khanna, Gloria Leman, Srikanth Nallapareddy, Bob Pauwels, and Prasad Perini. From Motorola, we especially thank John Wirth, John Pange, Efrain Nieto, Kamran Nili, Jeff New, and Jed Coxon. At ERAU, Iraj Hirmanpour was a great help. From US&S, we recognize the help of Julia Mullaney, Nadine Bounds, Bob Elder, Linda Falcione, Ron Morton, and John Staub. From SEI, we thank Andy Huber, Dan Roy, and Bill Peterson.

This work was supported by the US Department of Defense.

References

1. D.R. Goldenson and J.D. Herbsleb, *After the Appraisal: A Systematic Survey of Process Improvement, Its Benefits, and Factors that Influence Success,* Tech. Report CMU/SEI-95-TR-009, Software Eng. Inst., Pittsburgh, 1995.
2. W. Hayes and D. Zubrow, *Moving On Up: Data and Experience Doing CMM-Based Process Improvement,* Tech. Report CMU/SEI-95-TR-008, Software Eng. Inst., Pittsburgh, 1995.
3. M.C. Paulk et al., *The Capability Maturity Model: Guidelines for Improving the Software Process,* Addison-Wesley, Reading, Mass., 1995.
4. W.S. Humphrey, *A Discipline for Software Engineering,* Addison-Wesley, Reading, Mass., 1995.
5. W.S. Humphrey, *Introduction to the Personal Software Process,* Addison-Wesley, Reading, Mass., 1997.
6. B.W. Boehm, "A Spiral Model of Software Development and Enhancement, " *Computer,* May 1988, pp. 61–72.
7. W.S. Humphrey, "A Personal Commitment to Quality," *Am. Programmer,* Apr. 1995, pp. 2–12.
8. W.S. Humphrey, "Using a Defined and Measured Personal Software Process," *IEEE Software,* May 1996, pp. 77–88.
9. W.S. Humphrey, "The Power of Personal Data," *Software Process Improvement and Practice,* Vol. 1, Issue 2, Dec. 1995, pp. 69–81.

Pat Ferguson has worked as a software engineer, as a project manager, and most recently as the development manager at Advanced Information Services, Inc. She currently serves on the steering committees of the Chicago Software Process Improvement Network and the Heartland SPIN. Ferguson received a BS in mathematics and an MS in computer science, both from Bradley University. She is a member of the IEEE Computer Society.

Watts S. Humphrey founded the Software Process Program at the Software Engineering Institute at Carnegie Mellon University. He is a fellow of the institute and is a research scientist on its staff. He has written many technical papers and six books, most recently A Discipline for Software Engineering *(Addison-Wesley, 1995),* Managing Technical People *(Addison-Wesley, 1996), and* Introduction to the Personal Software Process *(Addison-Wesley, 1997). He holds five US patents. Humphrey received a BS in physics from the University of Chicago, an MS in physics from the Illinois Institute of Technology, and an MBA from the University of Chicago. He is a member of ACM and a fellow of IEEE.*

Soheil Khajenoori is a professor and director of the Master of Software Engineering Program at Embry-Riddle Aeronautical University. He is currently working with Motorola Paging Products Group and McDonnell Douglas Space Division on the PSP. Khajenoori currently teaches courses on PSP, software requirements engineering, and software architecture and design. Khajenoori's research interests are in the areas of software development methodologies, software metrics, and software process engineering and improvement. Khajenoori received a PhD in computer engineering from the University of Central Florida. He is a member of IEEE.

Susan Macke is a manager at Motorola, leading the decoder and software engineering teams for the North American Paging Subscriber Division. Macke received a BS in computer science and operations research and processes from Lebanon Valley College.

Annette Matvya has 20 years of experience in software engineering at Union Switch & Signal Inc. and is currently a member of that company's Software Engineering Process Group. She has completed the personal software process course and is currently involved in implementing PSP at US&S. Matvya graduated from the University of Pittsburgh with a BS in computer science.

Further information on SEI's PSP offerings and activities can be found at http://www.sei.cmu.edu/technology/psp.

Contact Ferguson at patf@pjstar.com, Humphrey at watts@sei.cmu.edu, Khajenoori at soheil@db.erau.edu, Macke at Susan_Macke-FMS010@email.mot.com, and Matvya at almatvya@switch.com.

Reprinted from IEEE Software,
Sept./Oct. 1998, pp. 37-46.

As organizations adopt component-based software engineering, it becomes essential to clearly define its characteristics, advantages, and organizational implications. This report presents key discussion points from a workshop on CBSE and provides a useful synthesis of participants' diverse perspectives and experiences.

The Current State of CBSE

Alan W. Brown, Sterling Software
Kurt C. Wallnau, Software Engineering Institute

omponent-based software engineering is generating tremendous interest not just in the software community but in numerous industry sectors. Recent technology advances such as the Web, JavaBeans, ActiveX, and others spur this interest.

But CBSE goes well beyond these technology enablers, as shown by the diverse perspectives brought to a recent workshop on CBSE, held in conjunction with the 20th International Conference on Software Engineering. This diversity also characterized a related ICSE panel discussion, "CBSE: Can it Change the Way of Software Development?" which generated active debate from a large audience. The discussion ranged from the theory of software reuse to the reality of commercial software markets, from available tools to future programming language mechanisms, and from practical testing to rigorous formal specification.

In both the ICSE panel and the CBSE workshop, divergent perspectives at times threatened to blur CBSE's conceptual outlines. Does this diversity imply that we are exploring the same basic CBSE concepts from many different points of view? Or are we exploring fundamentally different or unrelated concepts that we capriciously label CBSE?

Focus

The workshop results suggest the former: CBSE is a coherent engineering practice, and we are making good progress in identifying its core concepts as well as different perspectives on them. We found that such diversity, far from diffusing the concept of CBSE, often works like stereoscopic vision, adding depth of field to our perception.

For example, while most participants agreed that components act as replacement units in component-based systems, "replacement unit" has different meanings depending on which of two major perspectives is adopted. One, CBSE with off-the-shelf components, views components as commercial off-the-shelf commodities. In this context, CBSE requires industrial standardization on a small number of component frameworks. The other, CBSE with abstract components, views components as application-specific core business assets, which emphasizes component-based design approaches rather than standard component infrastructures or component marketplaces. Although this illustration exaggerates each perspective's tendencies (both influence any large system development effort), it does reflect real differences that conditioned much of the workshop discussion.

This article focuses on the workshop's closing session, which synthesized the major themes from panel discussions. Organized as a facilitated, large-group brainstorming session, it sought to bring into focus the different perspectives on CBSE and identify the major results participants could take away from the panel discussions. The discussion ranged from the conceptual (what is CBSE?) to the skeptical (why will it work now if it didn't before?) to the practical (what will it mean to organizations if CBSE does work?).

What Is CBSE?

Predictably, some discussion focused on definition of terms—notably the term "component." Just as predictably, these definitions only sketched the contours of this complex concept. Fortunately, the workshop had access to several established definitions, and to their credit the participants used these as a basis for exploring additional characteristics of components rather than arguing for or against the validity of any particular definition.

The following definitions of "software component" typify those emerging in the software industry.

1. A component is a nontrivial, nearly independent, and replaceable part of a system that fulfills a clear function in the context of a well-defined architecture. A component conforms to and provides the physical realization of a set of interfaces. (Philippe Krutchen, Rational Software)

2. A runtime software component is a dynamically bindable package of one or more programs

managed as a unit and accessed through documented interfaces that can be discovered at runtime. (Gartner Group)

3. A software component is a unit of composition with contractually specified interfaces and explicit context dependencies only. A software component can be deployed independently and is subject to third-party composition. (Clemens Szyperski, *Component Software*[1])

4. A business component represents the software implementation of an "autonomous" business concept or business process. It consists of the software artifacts necessary to express, implement, and deploy the concept as a reusable element of a larger business system. (Wojtek Kozaczynski, SSA)

These definitions seem to describe approximately the same concept, but close inspection reveals sufficient differences to make them nonsubstitutable. For example, definitions 1 and (especially) 4 underscore the large-grained nature of components; we might infer this from definition 2, but not from definition 3. Definitions 1 and 3 emphasize the need to accommodate context dependencies, but only definition 3 requires explicit description of context dependencies. We might infer explicit context dependencies from definition 4, but not from definition 2. Similarly, the notion of component autonomy varies—it may refer to a component's ability to be deployed independently, or execute independently, and so forth.

Each definition has its merits, but rather than debate these in detail, workshop participants noted the importance of two additional component characteristics:

♦ the relationship between components and object technology, and
♦ the relationship between components and software architecture.

Object technology is neither necessary nor sufficient for CBSE

Curiously, this strong statement—as obvious as it may seem to some—passed without vigorous contention. Instead, workshop participants acknowledged it to be a natural consequence of the panel presentations and discussions—even though most available technologies for component-based development clearly are object-oriented. JavaBeans and Enterprise JavaBeans exemplify component-based technology. The Object Management Group's

Unified Modeling Language—itself an outgrowth of object-oriented analysis and object-oriented design—actively addresses component concepts. It therefore seems strange to assert CBSE's independence from object technology. How can we justify this apparent incongruity?

To state the conclusion first, participants agreed that OT was a useful and convenient starting point for CBSE, but

♦ by itself, OT did not express the full range of abstractions needed by CBSE; and
♦ it is possible to realize CBSE without employing OT.

Thus, OT is neither necessary nor sufficient. Moreover, CBSE might induce substantial changes in approach to system design, project management, and organizational style—changes that go well beyond those implied by a large and growing base of industry experience with OT.

We see that OT is insufficient for CBSE when we consider the component's role as replacement unit. The definitions above each address at least one characteristic related to replaceability: explicitly specifying context. Concretely, this might be imple-

CBSE is a coherent engineering practice, but we still haven't fully identified just what it is.

mented via a "uses" clause on a specification, that is, a declaration of required system resources. This suggestion causes some contention because a "uses" clause implies that the interface describes an implementation rather than an abstraction of possible implementations. OT does not typically support this concept—and there are strong arguments why it should not. However, these lose force when applied to design-level abstractions, especially when attempting to compose using existing components.

To illustrate OT's non-necessity, we ironically draw on workshop participants' experiences in attempting to use OT to implement CBSE. Put bluntly, some practitioners are seeking ways to insulate their approaches to CBSE from OT. Why? Because the OT technology market—in particular, distributed OT such as Java, Corba, and ActiveX—is far too unstable and contentious and will, many feel, continue to be so. The workshop discussion tended to treat distributed OT as infrastructure "plumbing" and components as larger-grained abstractions and implementations applicable to diverse infrastructures.

FOCUS

COMPONENTS AND TRANSACTIONS

DAVID CHAPPELL, Chappell & Associates

Business computing depends on transactions. A transaction groups two or more changes into a single unit, then ensures that either all or none of the changes occur. New technologies combine components and transactions, the two most visible being the Microsoft Transaction Server (MTS) and Enterprise JavaBeans (EJB), the latter from a vendor consortium led by Sun Microsystems.

Applications that need support for transactions generally need other services, too; in particular, they often must scale to handle many simultaneous clients. Along with supporting transactions, then, transaction processing (TP) monitors commonly support scalability by allowing effective sharing of resources such as threads, memory, and database connections. To best understand how the advent of components affects TP monitors, let's look at exactly how MTS and EJB provide transaction and scalability services.

To control when a transaction begins and ends, the client may be required to inform the TP monitor of the transaction's boundaries. This is a common solution in non-component-oriented TP monitors, and both MTS and EJB support it. However, MTS and EJB also allow for directly configuring the components' transactional requirements—usually a better solution. It permits using the same component binary in different transactions and facilitates the black-box style of reuse typical of component software. It also frees the client from having to demarcate transactions.

TRANSACTIONS IN MTS

In MTS, every component has a *transaction attribute*. This tells the TP monitor (that is, MTS itself) whether to start a transaction when the first method is invoked in a new instance of this component. MTS defines four possible values for this attribute:

♦ *Requires New*: Begin a new transaction upon the first method call to a new component.

♦ *Required*: Begin a new transaction only if the component's caller isn't currently part of a transaction. Otherwise, any work this component performs will become part of the caller's existing transaction.

♦ *Supported*: MTS never starts a new transaction for this component. If a transaction is in progress for the caller, any work this component performs will become part of it. If no transaction is in progress, this component's work will not be done inside a transaction.

♦ *Not Supported*: MTS never starts a new transaction for this component. Even if the caller has a transaction in progress, the new component will not join it—it just doesn't participate in transactions.

To end a transaction, MTS allows a component to explicitly indicate when its work is completed and whether it wants that work to be committed or aborted. To do this, the component calls either `SetComplete` to commit the transaction or `SetAbort`

Continued on the next page

Questioning whether components can be separated from infrastructure led to the following discussion on their relationship.

Components are inseparable from architecture

If one motivation for CBSE is to improve system flexibility through a compositional style of development, we might then ask what makes composition possible. It must exceed our ability to describe abstractions via abstract interfaces—otherwise we would not need CBSE. Instead, the degree to which we are able to "plug in" components—the operative phrase in compositional development—relates directly to the degree to which components adhere to some set of predefined constraints or conventions.

The most prominent component technologies— Enterprise JavaBeans, ActiveX, and Corba (assuming the Object Management Group adopts a component model)—all impose constraints on components. For example, the ability of a component infrastructure to inquire into a component's interfaces requires that the component implement some service or obey some convention as defined by its underlying component infrastructure.

Some participants suggested that components should implement two interface types: a functional one that reflects the component's role in the system, and an extrafunctional one that reflects the component model imposed by some underlying component framework. The latter interface expresses the architectural constraints that enable composability and other desirable properties of component-based systems. Therefore, our understanding of what makes a component a component is inextricably linked to our understanding of the archi-

to abort it. If this component is the only one involved in the transaction, MTS will commit or abort the transaction then. If several MTS components are participating in a transaction, each can call `SetComplete` or `SetAbort` when it completes its work. The transaction doesn't end until the root component—the one created directly by the client—calls either method. If the root and every other component in this transaction call `SetComplete`, the transaction is committed. If any component called `SetAbort`, the transaction is aborted and the work performed by all its components is rolled back.

TRANSACTIONS IN EJB

EJB, like MTS, permits setting a transaction attribute on components. The attribute's primary values—`TX_REQUIRES_NEW`, `TX_REQUIRED`, `TX_SUPPORTS`, or `TX_NOT_SUPPORTED`—closely mirror those defined by MTS. As in MTS, an EJB-based TP monitor uses this transaction attribute to determine whether to begin a new transaction when a method is invoked on a component.

Unlike MTS, every method call a client makes on an EJB component using this style of transaction demarcation is its own transaction. Although this method can invoke other methods in the same or other EJB components, all of which may be part of this transaction, the transaction ends when the client's call returns. EJB does allow a component to call `setRollbackOnly`, analogous to MTS's `SetAbort` call, to roll back the transaction. If any component involved in a transaction invokes this method, work performed by all components will be rolled back. Otherwise, EJB will commit the transaction before returning the method's results to the client.

SUPPORTING SCALABILITY

MTS and EJB define similar services to help developers create scalable applications, including thread management and client authorization. The most interesting distinction, however, is in how each manages a component's state. MTS does not permit a component to maintain its state across a transaction boundary—calling `SetComplete` or `SetAbort` causes that state to be destroyed. This improves resource sharing, since a component can't hang onto anything for very long. It also decreases the possibility that applications will rely on an in-memory state that doesn't match what's in the database after a transaction aborts. But each component must refresh its state after each transaction, which can exact a performance penalty.

EJB, by contrast, allows components to maintain their state across transaction boundaries. This is more natural for developers steeped in the object paradigm, and can avoid the performance penalty of frequently recreating a component's state. However, it also requires that developers diligently ensure effective resource sharing and application correctness.

We're sure to hear much debate about whether MTS or EJB provides better support for creating transactional, component-based applications. Both technologies, however, assertively address the key issues by providing a component-oriented style of transaction demarcation, supporting scalability, and permitting direct management of a component's state.

David Chappell is principal of Chappell & Associates, an education and consulting firm. Readers may contact him at david@chappellassoc.com.

---

tectural constraints imposed on components by a component framework-cum-object model.

After some discussion, participants decided that although components and architecture seem to go hand in hand, the "two interface" suggestion unduly emphasizes the role of the component framework in software architecture. Indeed, as noted, some participants sought a clean separation between the software architecture and component framework. A more general definition avoids this problem but still preserves a component–architecture duality by recognizing three different views of architecture:

♦ *Runtime.* This includes frameworks and models that provide runtime services for component-based systems.

♦ *Design-time.* This includes the application-specific view of components, such as functional interfaces and component dependencies.

♦ *Compose-time.* This includes all the elements needed to assemble a system from components, including generators and other build-time services; a component framework may provide some of these services.

These additional characteristics that emerged from the discussion suggest that components are complex design-level entities, that is, both abstractions and implementations. Does this complexity help us solve enterprise-level problems? To answer this, we must explore the motivations behind CBSE.

WHY CBSE NOW?

Over the past decade, many people have attempted to improve software development practices by improving design techniques, developing more

Focus

expressive notations for capturing a system's intended functionality, and encouraging reuse of pre-developed system pieces rather than building from scratch. Each approach has had some notable success in improving the quality, flexibility, and maintainability of application systems, helping many organizations develop complex, mission-critical applications deployed on a wide range of platforms.

Despite this success, any organization developing, deploying, and maintaining large-scale software-intensive systems still faces tremendous problems. Furthermore, in recent years, the requirements, tactics, and expectations of application developers have changed significantly. With this context in mind, workshop participants examined the question "why CBSE now?" and discussed various CBSE solutions.

Two important aspects of the question "why CBSE now?" quickly emerged in the discussion. First, several underlying technologies have matured that permit building components and assembling applications from sets of those components. Second, the business and organizational context within which applications are developed, deployed, and maintained has changed.

Maturing component technologies

Several participants stated that CBSE is happening now and emphasized that system development methods have changed greatly in the past few years. Development environments such as Visual Basic and languages such as C++ and Java dominate new application development. These languages, and the supporting tools, make it possible to share and distribute application pieces through approaches such as Visual Basic Controls (VBXs), ActiveX controls, class libraries, and JavaBeans. As these technologies have matured, so has understanding about how to develop pieces of applica-

The gulf between hype and reality makes it difficult to compare Microsoft's and the OMG's technologies. The OMG has adopted many standards for which no implementations exist; Microsoft has announced technology that it may not deliver for years. To be fair, then, we should ignore future promises and examine what is generally available and in use today.

For the OMG, "generally available and in use today" means:

♦ Corba IDL for defining component interfaces;

♦ the basic Corba client–component model;

♦ IIOP, the interoperability standard that allows different Corba vendors to work together;

♦ Life Cycle Service, to define how component instances are instantiated;

♦ Naming Service, to define how component instances are shared;

♦ Security Service, to define how clients and component instances work together securely; and

♦ Transaction Service, to define how distributed transactions are controlled.

For Microsoft, "generally available and in use today" means:

♦ Microsoft IDL for defining component interfaces;

♦ the basic COM client/component model;

♦ DCOM for distributing components across a network;

♦ Microsoft Transaction Service (MTS) to provide a secure runtime environment, transaction management, and scalability;

♦ DTC for distributed transaction coordination; and

♦ Microsoft Message Queue for asynchronous messaging.

Although OMG seems to be winning the bullet race (seven to six), Microsoft's MTS product is equivalent to several OMG specifications.

THE RESULTS

Because OMG standards can be implemented on many platforms, customers are not locked into a particular operating system or hardware. However, OMG creates no reference implementations and depends on vendors for actual delivery; this leaves a huge lag between what OMG has standardized and what vendors are actually delivering. It also means that portability between vendors is often more promise than reality.

Microsoft creates implementations; this leaves no doubt about exactly what has been implemented. And Microsoft's control over not only the component-oriented middleware but the underlying operating system permits great efficiencies. On the other hand, component systems based on Microsoft technology cannot easily be ported to other platforms.

If you are designing component-oriented commerce systems, remember that components aren't enough. You also need an infrastructure to support your components. Both the OMG and Microsoft are working hard to convince you that they can and should provide that infrastructure.

Roger Sessions is president of ObjectWatch and consults on distributed component middle-tier technologies. His most recent book is COM and DCOM: Microsoft's Vision for Distributed Objects. *He writes the* ObjectWatch Newsletter, *available at http://www. objectwatch.com.*

---

tions following these approaches. Component-oriented development no longer seems foreign to many application developers.

Each of these approaches relies on some underlying services to provide the communication and coordination necessary to piece together applications. The infrastructure acts as the "plumbing" that allows communication among components. To communicate, components must share an understanding of how to use the infrastructure. This could be as simple as a set of naming standards for operations, a standard place to put information about the components, or a conventional way to use other components via the infrastructure (sometimes referred to as a *component model*). This infrastructure may also allow components using the infrastructure to do so effectively and efficiently through services to

♦ find out what components are currently connected to the infrastructure,

♦ make reference to other components via some meaningful naming scheme,

♦ guarantee once-only delivery of messages between components,

♦ manage transactions consisting of multiple interactions among components, or

♦ allow secure communication between components.

Among the component infrastructure technologies that have been developed, three have become somewhat standardized: the OMG's Corba, Sun's JavaBeans and Enterprise JavaBeans, and Microsoft's Component Object Model and Distributed COM. Participants discussed these infrastructure technologies and related examples of their use in various operational contexts.

Tools and environments supporting each of these technologies are widely available and used, providing many benefits. However, some participants pointed out the many challenges of using these tools to develop larger applications, manage multiple versions of components, and integrate components developed by different people using different technologies.

Evolving business and organizational context

Far from concentrating exclusively on technology issues, workshop participants broadened the discussion to consider the business and organizational context within which CBSE evolved and must operate, and some important recent developments.

> ## CBSE has broad implications for how we acquire, build, and evolve software systems.

First, the style and architecture of the applications being developed has shifted. Centralized mainframe-based applications accessed via terminals over proprietary networks have given way to distributed, multitiered applications remotely accessible from a variety of client machines over intranets and the Internet. Building such applications requires tools and techniques that support new development methods and approaches. Organizations that once handled a few large projects now typically manage many smaller projects whose results must be shared.

Second, organizations have invested significant financial and intellectual resources in the applications they have built over the past two decades. This has left fewer resources for developing new applications from scratch, making it essential to leverage and reuse the existing investment across a range of operations and in developing new applications quickly and reliably. To achieve this, developers require greater support and guidance for decomposing applications into meaningful pieces and for assembling new applications from a mixture of new and existing pieces.

Third, organizations began to realize the strategic implications for their business practices of the software-intensive systems that support their organization. Some found themselves locked into proprietary software solutions, at significant cost. Typically this arose from two sources.

Those who attempted to develop large parts of their software infrastructure (both systems and application software) on their own often found themselves responsible for a growing—and very expensive—software maintenance backlog. This put them at a disadvantage against more agile organizations that could quickly respond to customer and market changes by updating or replacing their computer infrastructure.

Other organizations found that they had relied too much on a single product from a single vendor. The resultant "vendor lock-in" made it difficult to take advantage of a free market of computing suppliers, left important decisions about computing infrastructure in the hands of third parties, and often significantly reduced the ease with which information could be shared among partner organizations. Complete, packaged applications proved difficult to customize readily as specific organizational needs arose.

Organizations therefore began to look for an appropriate balance, an approach that did not require writing everything from scratch each time, and that provided a flexible system that could evolve as needed to meet changing business needs.

Finally, and perhaps most importantly, the business environment in which organizations operate has changed drastically. To succeed, an organization must maintain some stability and predictability in its market, in the technology supporting its core businesses, and in its internal structure. Unfortunately, the rate of change in all these areas rises inexorably, making the ability to manage complexity and adapt rapidly to change an important differentiator among competitors.

The solution to these problems seemed to lie in a software development approach that addresses each of these requirements. As stated in the workshop, the goals of CBSE include the ability to

♦ embrace opportunities offered by new technologies in software system delivery and deployment;

♦ encourage reuse of core functionality across applications;

♦ enable flexible upgrade and replacement of system pieces whether developed in-house, supplied by third parties, or purchased off-the-shelf; and

♦ encapsulate organizational best practices such that they can be adapted as business conditions change.

CBSE AT WORK

Workshop participants experienced with CBSE development projects were quick to point out that CBSE involves much more than simply using object request brokers, setting up a library of useful code, or acquiring Visual Basic controls over the Internet.

These tactical approaches must be supplemented with strategic thinking and planning for successful adoption of CBSE. In particular, CBSE has broad implications for building, acquiring, assembling, and evolving systems, raising some important concerns.

We can distinguish two classes of concerns based on whether components are

♦ used as a design philosophy independent from any concern for reusing existing components, or

♦ seen as off-the-shelf building blocks used to design and implement a component-based system. For this discussion, we denote these as CBSE with abstract components and CBSE with off-the-shelf components, respectively.

CBSE with abstract components

This approach involves radically rethinking the relationship between design, requirements, and components. Fundamentally, it requires new methods for software development, new processes, and powerful tools to automate generation and management of components and interfaces. These CBSE-oriented methods and tools, currently under development, provide an interface-based design focus that concentrates on a solution's basic component architecture.

In participants' experience, this approach stabilizes system design at the interface level, concentrates attention on collaborations among interfaces as the basis for understanding a system architecture, and enables reuse and replacement of implementations that conform to the interface specifications. Several emerging CBSE methods[2-4] are being tracked or applied in current projects, but participants emphasized the need for further experience with these.

Some pointed out one important consequence of this revolution in design approaches: a dramatic change in software engineers' primary roles and required skills. Some organizations moving toward CBSE find they must rethink how they organize teams to concentrate on component provisioning within a well-defined component architecture. Finding people who can operate in this environment is proving to be a major challenge, and the lack of appropriate skills within an organization could severely hamper CBSE's adoption.

Wojtek Kozaczynski pointed out the major day-to-day challenge for organizations moving to CBSE: managing component-based applications as they are deployed, and maintained, and continue to evolve. Multiple components will provide similar functionality, many versions of the same component will emerge, multiple configurations of component sets will be in use, and so on.

Traditional configuration management and version control techniques provide an important starting point to manage some of these issues. As monolithic development and deployment approaches yield to component-oriented methods, however, new management methods and tools will prove essential. In particular, high composeability in a product line setting amounts to mass customization, which introduces tremendous configuration management challenges and support challenges. Many opportunities for new tools and techniques exist in this area.

CBSE with off-the-shelf components

This approach moves organizations from application development to application assembly. Constructing an application now involves the use of predeveloped pieces, perhaps developed at different times, by different groups of people, and with many different uses in mind. One scenario highlighted in detail at the workshop illustrates the implications of such a change: black-box assembly of commercial off-the-shelf components.

An organization assembling COTS components to create a command-and-control application for the US government found it had limited access to the components' internal design, predefined options for customizing the components' behavior, no ability to influence the release cycle of new component versions, and total reliance on the long-term viability, integrity, and ability of the packages' maintainers. This affected many aspects of the design, assembly, testing, deployment, and maintenance of the system.

In such cases, the development effort becomes one of gradual discovery about the components, their capabilities, their internal assumptions, and the incompatibilities that arise when they are used in concert.[5] As happened in this example, the architecture of a COTS-based system often degenerates into a series of contingency and risk mitigation strategies based on this discovered information. The workshop concluded that a growing emphasis on outsourcing of systems and increased use of COTS components will demand many improvements in how such components are documented, assembled, adapted, and customized.

> We can expect dramatic change in engineers' primary roles and required skills.

As software technology becomes a core part of business enterprises in all market sectors, customers demand more flexible enterprise systems. This demand coincides with a maturing software technology infrastructure for building distributed enterprise systems. CBSE is a new style of software system development emerging from this growing demand and maturing technology. While CBSE is still evolving, and perspectives vary on what it is all about, there is little doubt that something is happening, that we are calling that something CBSE, and that its outlines are becoming clearer all the time. ❖

ACKNOWLEDGMENTS

We thank the ICSE workshop organizers, and Mikio Aoyama in particular, for the excellent workshop arrangements. Thanks also to Wojtek Kozaczynski for his detailed recording of the summary session, and to Wojtek Kozaczynski, Philippe Kruchten, Chris Dellarocas, David Carney, and Mikio Aoyama for their comments on this summary.

REFERENCES

1. C. Szyperski, *Component Software: Beyond Object-Oriented Programming*, Addison Wesley Longman, Reading, Mass., 1998.
2. D. D'Souza and A.C. Wills, *Objects, Components, and Frameworks with UML: The Catalysis Approach*, Addison Wesley Longman, Reading, Mass., 1998.
3. P. Coad, *Java Design: Building Better Applications and Applets*, Prentice Hall, Upper Saddle River, N.J., 1997.
4. P. Allen and S. Frost, *Component Based Development for Enterprise Systems: Applying the Select Approach*, Cambridge University Press, New York, 1997.
5. D. Garlan et al., "Architectural Mismatch: Why Reuse Is So Hard," *IEEE Software*, Nov. 1995, pp. 17-26.

About the Authors

Alan W. Brown is Director of Research for Sterling Software's Applications Development Division. His responsibilities include coordinating research activities across the organization and advising on the future of component-based software development products. Prior to this, Alan spent five years at the Software Engineering Institute at Carnegie Mellon University, where he led the CASE Environments Project that advised US Government agencies and contractors on the application and integration of CASE technologies.

Brown's primary research interests include component-based development, software engineering environments, and CASE tools. Among his many publications in these areas are *Principles of CASE Tool Integration*, *Object-Oriented Databases and their Application to Software Engineering*, and *Software Engineering Environments*. He obtained a BSc in computational science from University of Hull and a PhD in computing science from University of Newcastle upon Tyne.

Kurt C. Wallnau is a senior technical staff member at the Software Engineering Institute (SEI), where he leads the COTS-Based Systems project. His current interests include the role of product evaluation in system design and the movement from COTS-based to component-based systems. Prior to joining SEI, Wallnau was System Architect of a DoD program focused on designing systems for the use of COTS software.

Wallnau received a BS in computer science from Villanova University.

Address questions about this article to Brown at Sterling Software, Applications Development Division, 5800 Tennyson Parkway, MS/142, Plano, TX 75024; Alan_Brown@sterling.com.

Reprinted from IEEE Software
Engineering Conference, Feb.
1998, pp. 211-218.

A UML-based Object-Oriented Framework Development Methodology

Young Jong Yang, Soon Yong Kim, Gui Ja Choi

Software Engineering Department

ETRI Computer & Software Technology Laboratory

Daejon, Korea 305-333

yjyang@seri.re.kr

Eun Sook Cho, Chul Jin Kim, Soo Dong Kim

Dept. of Computer Science

Soongsil University

Seoul, Korea 156-743

sdkim@computing.soongsil.ac.kr

Abstract

Recently, object-oriented (OO) frameworks have been known to be highly effective [Fay97] and practical for software reuse; as shown in San Francisco project, a large-scaled industry project for framework development [IBM97]. However, systematic development process and detailed instructions for building OO frameworks have not been studied enough. In addition, it has not been clearly defined how to apply OMG's Unified Modeling Language(UML) in building OO frameworks.

In this paper, we propose a practical OO development process that extends UML notations and semantics. The proposed process consists of four typical software development phases; analysis, design, implementation and testing, and each phase is defined as a logical sequence of development tasks. In order to help the seamless migration from one task to subsequent tasks, we provide instructions for carrying out tasks. Since the proposed process is based on UML diagrams and the basic Objectory process, we believe that OO frameworks can be more efficiently developed by utilizing the proposed process, and higher quality OO frameworks can be produced. In order to show the applicability and effectiveness of the process, we present a case study of Electronic Commerce application.

1. Introduction

As the size and complexity of system are increasing, the development cost is sharply increasing. Therefore, effective reuse technology becomes more important. Reuse of software has been one of the main goals of software development for decades. However, the early approaches, e.g. function and procedure libraries, only provided reuse of small, building-block components.

With an emergence of the object-oriented paradigm, an important enabling technology for reuse of larger components became available and resulted in the definition of object-oriented framework. An object-oriented framework is defined as a set of classes that embodies an abstract design for solutions to a family of related problems [Joh88]. A running application can be developed by extending framework classes or by plugging application-specific objects into designated slots. To develop such OO frameworks, it is desirable to have a systematic framework development methodology.

Traditional object-oriented design methods such as OMT [Rum91] or UML [RAT97] only deal with the design of specific applications, but do not deal with the analysis and design of framework. Recently, much concern of framework focuses on analysis and design method, but current framework methods only provide outline of framework analysis and design. They do not provide stepwise development process and concrete analysis and design guidelines. Therefore, we define a framework development process, and propose concrete analysis and design techniques.

Section 2 of the paper gives an overview of object-oriented framework and related works of framework development methods. Section 3 explains the development process and analysis/design method and guidelines for OO framework. Section 4 presents a case study of the methodology applied to Electronic Commerce domain.

2. Related Work

2.1. Overview of Object-Oriented Framework

211

Object-oriented framework is often characterized as a set of abstract and concrete classes that collaborates, and it provides the skeleton of an implementation for an application. The concrete classes in the framework are intended to be invisible to the framework user. An abstract class is either intended to be invisible to the framework user or intended to be sub-classed by the framework user. The latter classes are also referred to as hot-spots [Pre94].

Frameworks are categorized variously according to a basis point. According to domain dependency, frameworks are classified into *vertical* and *horizontal* frameworks. A framework dependent on specific domain is referred to as *vertical framework*. A framework independent on specific domain is referred to as *horizontal framework*. Also, some authors categorize frameworks into white box and black box framework. In a white box (inheritance-based) framework, the framework user is supposed to customize the framework behavior through sub-classing of framework classes. On the other hand, a black box framework requires deep understanding of the fixed and variant aspects of the domain [Rob96].

2.2. Existing Framework Development Methods

2.2.1. Designing a Framework by Stepwise Generalization

When they design a framework, their main concern is to recognize things that should be kept flexible. These are called the hot spots of the framework [Pre94]. In order to identify variant parts, some of questions are proposed as follows:

1) Which concepts of the problem domain exist in variants and should be treated uniformly?

2) Is it possible to find a concrete concept that can be generalized?

3) Which parts of the system might change?

4) Where might a user want to hook custom code into the framework?

The author suggests a two-phase design method to build an initial version of a framework; the first phase is called problem generalization and the second phase is called framework design [Kos97].

Problem generalization starts from the specification of a representative application of the intended framework, and generalizes it in a sequence of steps into the most general form. During the second phase the generalization levels of the previous phase are considered in reverse order leading to an implementation for each level.

The one of limitations of this method is that essential tasks to problem generalization or framework design are not defined concretely. Also, concrete guidelines to identify hot spot are not described in this method.

2.2.2. Development Process based on Application Experiences

This method is a pragmatic framework development approach [Wil93]. First develop n, say two, applications in the problem domain. Identify the common features in both applications and extract these into a framework. To evaluate whether the extracted features are the right ones, redevelop the two applications based on the framework.

The advantage of this method is that the framework development is easy, because we extract commonalties from pre-built applications through building applications previously. Whereas it requires much of time to build framework in the case of complex or large domain, and it is difficult to evaluate whether extracted commonalties are right ones.

2.2.3. Development Process based on Domain Analysis

The first activity is to analyze the problem domain to identify and understand well-known abstractions in the domain [Wil93].

Analyzing the domain requires analyzing existing applications and the analysis of existing applications will also take a large portion of the budget. After the abstractions have been identified, develop the framework together with a test application, then modify the framework if necessary. Next, develop a second application based on the framework. Identifying commonalties through domain analysis, we can extract well-defined abstract concept, whereas this method requires much of time and budget because of domain analysis.

3. UML-based Object-Oriented Framework Development Process

3.1. Overview of Process

As given in Figure 1, framework development process consists of four phases (e.g. analysis, design, implementation, testing), and tasks for each phase are defined.

Analysis phase consists of making framework requirement specification (FRS) through extracting common functionality from a set of similar application requirement specifications (ARSs) and identifying frameworks. Design phase consists of identifying classes and hot spots in frameworks, determining black box, white box, or hybrid box approach to design framework, and documenting frameworks.

Framework development process is applied repeatedly and incrementally. As depicted in Figure 1, framework grows by adding new functions within each development cycle. Each cycle tackles a relatively small set of

212

68

framework requirements, proceeding through analysis, design, implementation, and testing in Figure 1. The framework grows incrementally as each cycle is completed. Also, tasks in each phase are iterated.

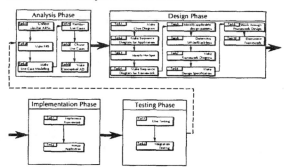

Figure 1.   Framework Development Process

3.2. Analysis Phase

Analysis phase consists of six phases whose tasks and workflow among tasks are depicted in Figure 2.

3.2.1. Collecting Similar Application Requirement

Specifications(ARSs)

This task is to extract commonalties among several applications, and it is divided into two cases.

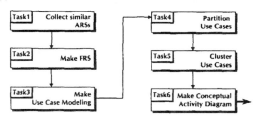

Figure 2.   Analysis Phase

If there exist application requirement specifications for a specific domain, we collect only a set of ARSs. If there are no existing ARSs or incomplete ARSs, we perform walkthroughs of current workflow for domain through user interviews, and we make ARS based on functional requirements identified by user interviews.

3.2.2. Making Framework Requirement

Specification(FRS)

We extract only functional requirements from a set of ARSs because a framework focuses on functional requirements. We identify what is general and what is

specific from the **extracted** functional requirements. Functional requirements specified commonly in all ARSs become general part, and they are marked with 'G'(e.g. G: Order Product). Functional requirements specified in a few ARSs become specific part, and they are marked with 'S'(e.g. S: Trace Delivery). We make FRS based on general parts('G'-added functional requirements). Through this task, we can identify potential hot spots. The contents of FRS consist of the name of functional requirement, overview, and workflow.

3.2.3. Making Use Case Modeling

This task is also divided into two cases. If there exist ARSs and FRS, we perform use case modeling for FRS. If there are no existing ARSs or incomplete ARSs, we apply use case modeling with ARSs. The latter is depicted in Figure 3.

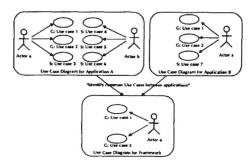

Figure 3.   Use Case Modeling for ARSs

To make a use case model, we should initially identify actors. To identify actor, we extract noun, subject, or application module name which occurs event in system environment or requests task in FRS by using UML use case notation. And then, we identify use cases by listing all events from the outside environment to which we want to react. Then, we define links between actors and use cases or between use cases, and write use case description for each use case.

In case of making use case modeling for each application, we add 'G' into common use cases and add 'S' into specific use cases. We make use case diagram for framework based on common use cases extracted from use case diagrams for ARSs.

3.2.4. Partitioning Use Cases

In this task, we determine the layers of uses cases based on the degree of generality and specialty for each use case. Layer is divided into three layers, which are foundation layer, common business layer, and core business layer (Figure 4). Foundation layer consists of frameworks that provide system services. Common

213

business layer consists of frameworks that provide business objects used in various domains. Core business layer consists of frameworks that provide common functions for a specific domain. After determining layers, we assign each use case into each layer. Use cases contained in foundation layer are independent in business domain, and they become horizontal frameworks.

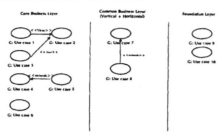

Figure 4.   Partitioning Use Cases into Layers

3.2.5. Clustering Use Cases

This task is to identify frameworks. We should cluster related use cases into each layer. The criteria for clustering use cases is as following:

1) Use cases that have independent functionality are not contained in any cluster.

2) Use cases that have "extends" relationship are contained in the same cluster.

3) Use cases that have "uses" relationship are contained in the same cluster.

Through above criteria, each cluster becomes one framework. After we integrate use case descriptions for each use case, we make use case description for each framework, and refine use case diagram for each framework.

3.2.6. Making Conceptual Activity Diagram

First of all, we map each use case in a framework into one activity.

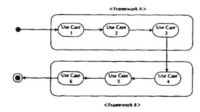

Figure 5.   Conceptual Activity Diagram for

Framework

Identifying event flow described in use case description, we can define sequence between activities. As given in Figure 5, we can express workflow between use cases as well as workflow between frameworks in a conceptual activity diagram. If use cases are very abstract, we decompose use case into concrete use cases.

3.3. Design Phase

Design phase of framework consists of ten tasks, and they are iterated (Figure 6).

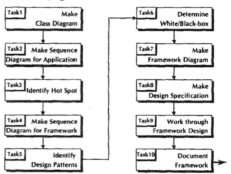

Figure 6.   Design Phase

3.3.1. Making Class Diagram

We identify candidate classes from each ARS through listing noun or subject in ARS. Next, we should identify candidate relationships between classes through listing verb or verb phrase described in ARS and FRS. And then, we identify attributes, which correspond to nouns followed by possessive phrases and identify candidate operations through extracting actions or functions in candidate relationships. We make class diagram based on identified classes, relationships, attributes, and candidate operations.

3.3.2. Making Sequence Diagram for Application

The purpose of making sequence diagram for each ARS is to extract operations for classes in ARS. To make sequence diagram, we should arrange classes based on scenarios described in use case descriptions. Next, we should identify messages between classes. To do it, correspond event flows described in scenarios to messages. After identifying messages, we should map receiving messages to a class into member functions of it.

3.3.3. Identifying Hot Spot

First of all, we should extract classes, which have common attributes and operations from class diagrams, and identify hot spot for ARSs. Next, we define common abstract class for these classes and represent relationship

214

70

between common class and subclasses that have common attributes and operations as inheritance. After result, common attributes and operations are moved in abstract class. This process is described in Figure 7.

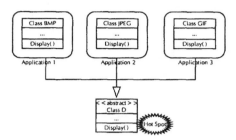

Figure 7.   Identifying Hot Spot

After defining abstract class, we should define function signatures for functions in abstract classes because some of functions can be implemented differently according to application, on the other hand, other functions can be implemented uniformly in all applications.

Function signatures are classified into virtual (e.g.V:foo( )), concrete (e.g. C:foo( )) and abstract (e.g. A:foo( )). Virtual function has only function signatures in abstract class and its body is implemented differently in each application. Concrete function is mapped into functions implemented fixedly in all application classes. Abstract function has a few implementations as well as a few calling virtual functions in function body. Signatures for functions are reflected on class diagram.

3.3.4. Making Sequence Diagram for Framework

To make sequence diagram for framework, we arrange classes in a framework, application that uses framework, or other frameworks which use it. Next, we should identify messages through event flows described in use case description for framework. We map each of messages into classes in framework, application, or other framework.

The purpose of making sequence diagram for framework is to identify applicable design patterns and identify control flows between classes in framework.

3.3.5. Identifying Applicable Design Patterns

We identify applicable design patterns in sequence diagram for framework in previous task. We make mapping table for identified patterns, with matching classes in class diagram with the role of classes based on defined patterns ([Gam95],[Rog97]).

3.3.6. Determining White box/Black box Approach

Now, we should consider white box, black box, or black and white box approach into framework design through class diagram. We can select different approaches according to hot spots.

White box approach is as following: When hot spots conform to core business layer (or vertical layer) or there are a number of subclasses inherited by abstract class, we should design framework with white box approach.

A case of designing framework with black box approach is as following: Above all, we should design classes that have fixed implementations with black box approach. That is, concrete classes contained in framework should be designed with black box. Also, when hot spot is contained in horizontal layer, it should be designed with black box approach. In the third case, if there are a few of subclasses inherited from abstract classes, they are designed with black box.

A case of designing framework with black and white box approach is as following: When hot spot is contained in common business layer, fixed parts should be designed with black box approach, and variant parts should be designed with white box approach.

3.3.7. Making Framework Diagram

The purpose of this task is to define framework interfaces for each framework and assign control flows between classes in a framework. After grouping relevant classes in a framework, we should assign control flows into classes based on messages in sequence diagram for framework.

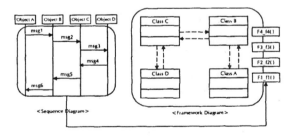

Figure 8.   Defining Framework Interface

And then, we should define framework interfaces for framework designed with black box or black and white box approach. A criterion of defining framework interface is a scenario for use case contained in framework. That is, we define framework interface as a wrapping method of message flows described in sequence diagram (Figure 8).

After making framework diagram for each framework, we should define relationships between frameworks. The relationships (e.g. association or aggregation) are identified with sequence diagram and clustered frameworks.

3.3.8. Making Design Specification

215

71

This task is to make design specification for classes existed in a framework with pseudo code format. A format of pseudo code is based on Java language syntax. A framework is represented by 'Package' and abstract class is represented by 'Interface' or 'Abstract Class'. In the case of declaring abstract class with 'Interface', the abstract class has only virtual functions. In the case of declaring abstract class with 'Abstract Class', the abstract class has one more concrete functions and virtual functions as well as attributes. Additionally, concrete classes are depicted in 'Class' and prefix 'F_' is added in framework interface(e.g. F1_find( )).

3.3.9. Reviewing Framework Design

This task is a process of refining tasks in framework design repeatedly, with reviewing the mapping among class diagram, sequence diagram, and framework diagram. That is, it reviews consistency between diagrams.

3.3.10. Documenting Framework

Documenting framework provides formal framework and user manual of framework usage to application developers. Especially, in the case of white box approach, extension points (e.g. hot spots) which application developers extend in specific application should be documented. The contents of framework document are as following:

1) Framework Name: Describe framework name.

2) Framework Type: Describe whether a framework is a vertical, mixed, or not, or whether a framework is a black box, black and white box, or not.

3) Functional Requirements: Describe functional requirements provided in framework (Use Case Unit).

4) Structures: Describe framework diagram.

5) Applied Design Pattern: Describe design pattern applied in framework.

6) Participants: Describe classes contained in framework.

7) Collaborations: Describe sequence diagram for framework.

8) Design Specification: Describe pseudo code for framework.

9) Usage: Describe using method of framework. That is, using method is described according to in the case of black box, white box, and black and white box. In the case of black and white box and white box, extension point should be described.

3.4. Implementation Phase

Implementation phase consists of two tasks (Figure 9). First task is to implement classes and interfaces of framework. Implementing framework interface is to implement control flows between classes contained in a

framework. Second task is to build specific application by using implemented framework. This task applies framework to specific application and implements hook method through sub-classing hot spot in the case of white box approach and through composing object into framework.

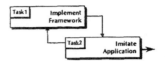

Figure 9.   Implementation Phase

3.5. Testing Phase

Unit testing is processed in testing phase above all (Figure 10). Unit testing is executed in two types. One is to test classes in framework. The other is to test framework itself. Unit testing for class is to test interfaces of classes, and unit testing for framework is to test whether message passing between classes is executed correctly or not.

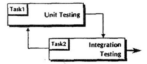

Figure 10.   Testing Phase

After executing unit testing, integration testing is processed. Integration testing is to test whether message passing between frameworks is executed correctly or not, with integrating frameworks.

4. Case Study and Assessment

In this section, we propose a case study for EC (Electronic Commerce) domain applied with proposed framework development process and describe assessment between proposed process and existing development process.

4.1. Case Study

Many of Web applications for EC domain have been established. Therefore, we collected similar application requirement specifications and extracted common functions from them. Common functions are 'Enter order', 'Validate user', 'Cancel order', 'Enter payment', 'Validate payment', etc. Use case diagram for these functions is described in Figure 11.

After partitioning use cases into layers, a result of clustering use cases is depicted in Figure 12.

216

72

Because clustered use cases became a framework unit, there are three frameworks for EC domain.

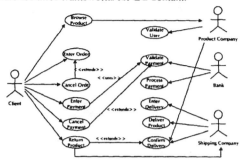

Figure 11.   Use Case Modeling for EC Domain

Sequence of among frameworks and workflow of among use cases in a framework are described through conceptual activity diagram (Figure 12).

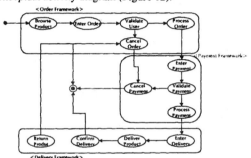

Figure 12.   Conceptual Activity Diagram

Common abstract classes identified in application class diagrams are 'Product' class, 'Payment' class, and 'Delivery' class. 'Product' class is a hot spot of 'Order Framework', 'Payment' class is a hot spot of 'Payment Framework', and 'Delivery' class is a hot spot of 'Delivery' Framework. Class diagram for frameworks based on identified classes is given in Figure 13.

The result of determining white box, black and white box, black box approach is as following: 'Product' class is designed with white box approach because there are many of classes inherited by 'Product' class according to application. 'Payment' class is designed with black box, because there are standard classes accepted payment method in EC applications. 'Delivery' class also is designed with black box, because there are a few of classes inherited by 'Delivery' class.

Therefore, in 'Order Framework', application developers should implement hot spots through sub-classing from abstract class('Product' class). In a 'Payment Framework' and 'Delivery Framework',

application developers only deliver object reference into framework interface because hot spot is implemented in framework.

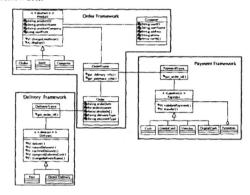

Figure 13.   Class Diagram for EC Domain

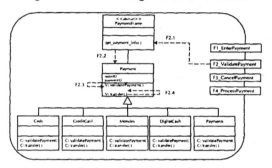

Figure 14.   Framework Diagram for Payment

Framework

This is executed through dynamic binding. Because 'Order Framework' implements hot spot with white box and fixed part with black box, this becomes black and white box framework. On the other hand, 'Payment Framework' and 'Delivery Framework' become black box framework, because all classes are implemented in framework.

The result of making framework diagram is depicted in Figure 14. Figure 14 describes framework diagram and framework interface for 'Payment Framework'.

4.2. Assessment

We propose a comparison and assessment of between proposed framework development process and other development processes.   Existing methods describe development phase, task, or guidelines roughly. On the other hand, we defined concrete development phases, tasks, and workflow between tasks in framework

217

development process as well as concrete guidelines for each task. As described in Table 1, existing methods only provide partial tasks for framework development and don't describe the task of a framework interface definition and documentation. However, our process provides almost tasks for framework development. Especially, we proposed the method of identifying hot spots, extracting frameworks, and defining framework interfaces. These methods are not described in existing methods.

Also, current methods do not apply specific notations to framework development. On the other hand, we applied not only UML notations and semantics to framework development but also produced new framework diagram notation to apply for framework development.

5. Concluding Remarks

In this paper, we proposed a practical OO framework development process that is based on UML notations and semantics. We defined development phases and tasks for each phase. We defined essential tasks for framework development and applied UML notations to each task. Each task is given a set of instructions on how to carry out the task. In order to help the seamless migration from one task to subsequent tasks, we provided instructions for task migration. Since the proposed process is based on UML diagrams and the basic Objectory process, we believe that OO frameworks can be more efficiently developed by utilizing the proposed process, and higher quality OO frameworks can be produced.

Table 1. Comparison of among Framework Development Processes

Methods \ Contents	Stepwise Generalization	Based on Applciation experience	Based on Domain Analysis	Proposed Process
Development process definition	Partially	Partially	Partially	Yes
Framework Identification	Partially	Partially	Partially	Yes
Hot Spot Identification	Partially	Partially	Partially	Partially
Black/White box Identification	Partially	No	No	Partially
Design Pattern Identification	Partially	No	No	Yes
Framework Inteface	No	No	No	Yes
Framework Document	No	No	No	Yes

6. [References]

[Joh88] R.E. Johnson, B. Foote, "Designing Reusable Classes," Journal of Object-Oriented Programming, Vol. 1, No. 2, June 1988.

[Joh92] R.E. Johnson, "Documenting Frameworks with Patterns," Proceedings of the 7th Conference on OOPSLApplications, Vancouver, Canada, 1992.

[Gam95] E. Gamma, R. Helm, R. Johnson, J.O. Vlissides, *Design Patterns: Elements of Reusable Object-Oriented Software*, Addison-Wesley, 1995.

[Rob96] D. Roberts, R. Johnson, "Evolving Frameworks: A Pattern Language for Developing Object-Oriented Frameworks," Proceedings of the Third Conference on Pattern Languages and Programming, Montecillio, Illinois, 1996.

[Rum91] J. Rumbaugh, M. Blaha, W. Premerlani, F. Eddy, W. Lorensen, *Object-Oriented Modeling and Design*, Prentice-Hall, 1991.

[Kos97] K. Koskimies, H. Mössenböck, "Designing a Framework by Stepwise Generalization", 1997.

[Pre94] W. Pree, "Meta Patterns – A means for capturing the essential of reusable object-oriented design," Proceedings of the 8th European Conference on Object-Oriented Programming, Bologna, Italy, 1994.

[Spa96] S. Sparks, K. Benner, C. Faris, "Managing Object-Oriented Framework Reuse," *IEEE Computer*, pp.53-61, September 1996.

[Wil93] D. A. Wilson, S. D. Wilson, "Writing Frameworks – Capturing Your Expertise About a Problem Domain," Tutorial notes, The 8th Conference on Object-Oriented Programming Systems, Languages and Applications, Washington, 1993.

[RAT97] Rational Software Corp., *Unified Modeling Language(UML) Summary*, 1997.

[Rog97] G. F. Rogers, *Framework-based Software Development in C++*, Prentice-Hall, 1997.

[IBM97] IBM Corp., "San Francisco Project Technical Summary," http://www.ibm.com/Java/Sanfrancisco/prd_summary.html, 1997.

[Fay97] M. E. Fayad and D. C. Schmidt, "Object-Oriented Application Frameworks," Communication of the ACM, Vol. 40, No. 10, October 1997.

CHAPTER 2
PROJECT MANAGEMENT

Software project management consists mainly of controlling schedule, cost, quality and scope. Project managers ensure that team members properly define and execute all required tasks. Controlling a program requires defining and collecting measures of its health (metrics). A key part of project management is identifying and handling risks to successful completion. Web development, an area of growing importance, requires the same discipline as all other software development, but presents novel challenges as well.

In the papers that follow, Myers discusses project communication. Tackett and van Doren provide case studies of successful projects, providing useful results about what does and does not work. They apply states as an organizing principle to deal with multiple engineers engaging simultaneously in multiple tasks. Nesi relates a manager's understanding of object-orientation to project success. Williams, Walker and Dorofee recount lessons learned from the Software Engineering Institute's Risk Program. Hall and Fenton discuss metrics, as do Grable and Divis. Software engineering for Web applications is discussed by Aoyama, and, separately, by Wiegers.

Reprinted from IEEE Computer,
May 1999, pp. 110-111.

Early Communication Key to Software Project Success

Ware Myers

I n *Cultivating Successful Software Development* (Prentice Hall, 1997), Scott Donaldson and Stanley Siegel note that "The software industry has unequivocally demonstrated that customer/seller faulty communication underlies a majority of software systems development problems." At least part of this communications breakdown stems from customers' lack of comprehension regarding their role in the development process. Developers must help customers realize that software development is an inherently complex and uncertain activity that can only succeed through close cooperation.

DEFINING PROJECT SCOPE

Before development can begin, developers must find out which of a customer's business activities fall within the scope of a particular system. Clearly, the customer must define the project's scope, although they may seek assistance from consultants or the developer's own software specialists.

No matter how the customer accom-

Editor: Barry Boehm, Computer Science Department, University of Southern California, Los Angeles, CA 90089; boehm@sunset.usc.edu

The customer and developer need to nail down specifics up front to make projects flow more smoothly.

plishes this task, it will delay the start of bulk feature development. Make customers be aware that, in a modern software organization, bulk feature development is nearly the last step, begun only after the completion of concept definition, COTS evaluation, prototyping, requirements specification, analysis, architecture, risk identification, critical feature development, and high-level design.

If you begin bulk feature development before you've blocked off what you are going to work on, you will pay for it later—with time, money, or both.

Inception

Because the first phases of development are upstream activities that affect all that follows, they're vital to overall project success. It's foolish, for example, to proceed with a software project if it proves technically infeasible or fails to make business sense. Although it's obvious that meeting those two qualifications is the main work of the inception phase, the software landscape is littered with countless projects whose sponsors were distracted from this priority by an unattainable vision. Unfortunately, experience shows that a naive customer can always find a developer to help them spend millions of dollars on a poorly thought-out project. The software organization must capture enough of the entire requirements to help identify those risks so serious they might jeopardize the project's success. Beyond this, the customer and developer must collaborate to prototype and outline enough of the architecture to establish that such a system is possible.

These two tasks interact. You must have an architecture from which to build the structure in which you will seek critical risks. Then, if you find such risks, you can modify the architecture to avoid them. You may even need to narrow the project's scope so that a formidable risk falls outside the proposed system's boundaries.

Although such feedback loops add to development complexity, you must carry risk mitigation and architecture far enough to establish that the system is doable. Do you have the resources? Will the system reduce costs or return revenues beyond what it will cost to build? Can you deliver a product fast enough to fill a time-sensitive market niche? Inception terminates when customer, developer, and other key stakeholders—such as users and maintainers—agree on the system's objectives.

Given the delays involved, you don't want to prolong this phase. If the customer does not pay the developer directly for this work, the latter must load the cost onto its construction or main-build bids. Because the software facilitates the customer's business or mission, the customer should assign at least one of its senior executives to become the project's subject-matter expert. This person can then provide a reality check when the proposals wander into overly optimistic territory.

Elaboration

The next phase carries requirement capture, architecture development, and risk management to the point at which the developer can make a detailed bid. The size estimate during this phase still contains a large error margin, yet it is the key input for estimating the time, effort, and cost of building the software. If the size value is uncertain, the estimate is uncertain to a similar degree.

In an ideal world, elaboration would conclude only after specifying and validating all pertinent requirements. Further, the developer would ensure the feasibility of the architecture to the point, if necessary, of implementing executables of any questionable system parts. Customer and developer would assess the risks of these parts to ensure they could be completed with the available resources.

In the real world, elaboration is seldom carried this far. The architecture is generally incomplete, the size variance still large, and the risks not entirely mitigated. These uncertainties typically carry over into the construction phase.

LIVING WITH UNCERTAINTY

It follows that a developer cannot realistically convert this uncertain construction estimate into a fixed price and schedule bid. Given these uncertainties, what he ought to do is choose one of two alternatives:

- Submit a range bid. For example, the schedule may stretch from 12 to 18 months, with the most likely period 15 months; the effort may run from 42 person-months to 81 person-months, with the most likely figure 63 person-months; the price may run from $400,000 to $850,000, with the most likely price $630,000.
- Submit a fixed-schedule, -effort, and -price bid with the proviso that it be renegotiated periodically as the

developers narrow the size range and work out the risks.

Customers prefer fixed prices and schedules. That leaves knowledgeable developers no recourse except to pursue a third alternative. Given some knowledge of probability, statistics, and simulation—and software tools to do the

The customer must define the project's scope, although they may seek assistance from consultants or the developer.

computations—a developer can submit a fixed bid that carries a high probability of success. To achieve that high probability, however, the bid must be high enough to absorb these uncertainties.

Such a high bid, regrettably, is not what the customer wants.

MITIGATING DISASTER

Unfortunately for all concerned, there are developers that don't know about probability, statistics, and simulation—or much about project estimation in general.

Such a developer will invariably submit a low bid because it does not appreciate the uncertainties confronting it. The customer, focused on the bottom line, chooses the low bid, blissfully unaware of the likely consequences. Generally, when the time and effort set forth in this low bid have nearly run out, the project will still be far from complete.

In 1995, for example, the Los Angeles County Welfare Department weighed an $86 million low bid against the next higher bid of $147 million. "The difference was so substantial, it looked bizarre," one county supervisor commented during a 1998 hearing convened to add $52 million to the project (Nicholas Riccardi, "County Computer Contractor Assailed," *Los Angeles Times*, Dec. 21, 1998).

Barry Boehm's most recent Management column ("Making RAD Work for Your Project," Mar. 1999, pp. 113-114)

contains a strategy that avoids the mistake of throwing more money at an ailing project. Boehm's "schedule-as-independent-variable" approach advises reducing the amount of work to what current schedule or effort estimates can support. One way to do so is to reduce the work amount in the first release, deferring to a later release any work that exceeds what can be accomplished with the available resources. Removing nonessential, bells-and-whistles features is also an option. The US Department of Defense's cost-as-independent-variable initiative works similarly in the cost domain.

Software development is complicated, uncertain, and expensive. Only if all parties are knowledgeable and cooperative can these challenges be overcome.

The first requirement, knowledge, can be achieved when both customer and developer comprehend the realities of software development. They must be willing to do work up front and deal with inescapable uncertainties regarding risks, architecture, and size.

Acknowledging these realities provides the basis for the second requirement, cooperation. The customer knows its business or mission and knows what part of its operations it wants the software to facilitate or enhance. The software developer, on the other hand, knows about software: how it's built, how it works, what its limits are.

Early in development, there is an interface between mission and software that extends through inception and elaboration and into construction. If, during this time, the two parties can devise a structure for the project that synthesizes customer needs with developer capabilities, the project is more likely to succeed. ❖

Ware Myers is a freelance writer and contributing editor for IEEE Software *magazine. Contact him at 1271 N. College, Claremont, CA 91711; 73153.1762@ compuserve.com.*

Reprinted from IEEE Software,
May/June 1999, pp. 24-29.

Can you develop a bug-free mission-critical system on time?
This author's customized approach delivered a highly
sensitive missile warning system to Cheyenne Mountain
within budget and meeting all the customer requirements.

Process Control for Error-Free Software: A Software Success Story

Buford D. Tackett and Buddy Van Doren, ITT Industries

FROM THE TRENCHES: Wolfgang B. Strigel, editor • wstrigel@spc.ca

oftware development projects typically sail through much of their life cycle and miss the early warnings of the high-risk issues that eventually break or damage them.[1] To reduce the risk of producing a poor-quality, late product, we created the State-Based Development Process, an approach based on systematic design and peer review.

A small team at ITT Industries used this development process to create a critical system under high schedule and operational pressure for the North American Aerospace Defense Command, a binational command involving the US and Canada that provides missile and air attack warnings and defense against air attacks. The approach was a powerful synthesis of people, process, and technology that yielded tangible improvements in software engineering.

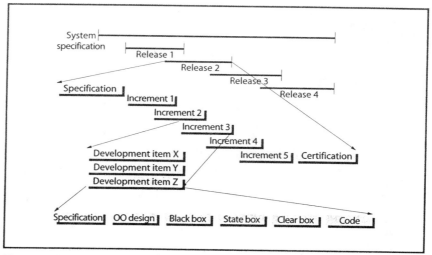

FIGURE 1. The evolutionary, incremental approach to developing software.

DEEP INSIDE THE MOUNTAIN

Completed in 1966, the Cheyenne Mountain Operations Center is a 15-building complex that houses NORAD, the US Space Command, and the Air Force Space Command. The complex is actually inside the mountain, 1,750 feet below its surface. In 1981, the Pentagon started the Cheyenne Mountain Upgrade, a $968 million, six-year project to update the facility's computer systems. By 1994, the project was a decade late and $1 billion over budget.

In the shadow of this quintessential "runaway" software project,[1] NORAD and the Airforce Space Command undertook another software project to develop an automated tracking and monitoring system (Atams) in April 1995, as highlighted in *Scientific American*.[2] The existing system forced a team of technicians to scan more than 20 monitors for a variety of complex alerts and warnings. Atams needed to control an "entire network with two monitors and a simple, consistent interface."[2] The first fully operational phase of Atams had to be deployed within one year.

The Air Force boldly decided to waive its standard approach and allow the development team to use a new process derived from the Harlan Mills Cleanroom methodology.[3] Implementing a system robust enough for this command and control environment was not easy, since it consisted of two "hot/shadow" configurations in Colorado and Nebraska, processing over 50 real-time messages and over 35 real-time, interactive status displays to the NORAD crews.

Amazingly, Atams was deployed on time and within budget, to the user's delight. The State-Based Process used to develop the Atams project was central to this success.

THE STATE-BASED PROCESS

We designed the State-Based Process to improve productivity, quality, process, and overall risk management to produce a software-intensive, operational product. Our approach was evolutionary and incremental; each increment was fully executable,

testable, and demonstrable to the user for observation and approval. This addressed a common problem in software projects: the user is rarely involved in product development.

In our approach, each incremental release delivers functionality, and work on increments overlaps. A software item under development is treated as a development item, or DI, undergoing a series of state-to-state transitions with a prescribed set of operations acting on it within each state. Each DI within an increment proceeds through the process as a separately tracked entity (although dependencies that exist between DI's will influence the sequence and progression through the process). Figure 1 illustrates this approach.

We first identified what we believed were the major states through which a DI must transition. Then we identified the operations within each state needed to transform the DI into the form necessary to transition to the next state. We realized, however, that the State-Based process must be simple enough to be captured graphically on a single page, so that the team could reference it without a large, complex document. Most likely the team would not successfully use the process otherwise.

The resulting process thus uses a state transition diagram to describe the states through which each DI must pass to reach its final state. In this case, a DI transitions through 12 states, beginning with State 1, Specification Review, and ending with State 12, Certification. State 13 is the software's operational state. Figure 2 gives an overview of the State-Based Process.

We developed a process guide to detail the process and management activities that must occur within each state and each transition. As a DI enters a state, the process guidelines define what activities

Focus

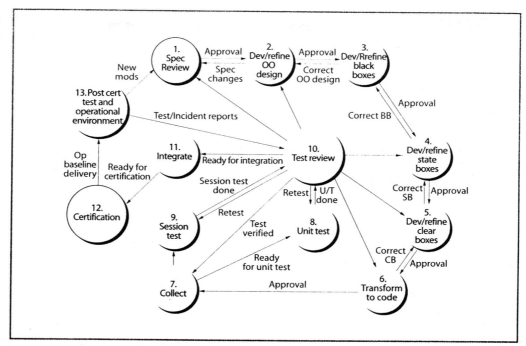

FIGURE 2. A summary view of the State-Based Process.

must be performed on it and what must be achieved to transition it to the next state.

Team walkthroughs constitute the major activity in which the DI's state is examined and verified, and transition decisions are made. Our objective was to "design a little" and then verify the correctness of the changes. When the lead engineer for a DI finished the design changes, he then delivered those changes to a team of reviewers and announced the walkthrough time and place. The reviewers individually inspected the changes and brought their findings to the walkthrough, which the lead developer always chaired. The process guide describes the roles of the lead engineer and the reviewers for each DI throughout its life cycle. The reviewers and the lead engineer formed a development team that had technical and emotional ownership of the DI. Defects were the responsibility of the entire team, not the lead developer's alone.

Walkthroughs

Walkthroughs were the heart of the process; they provided clear and organized project management. We recognized from the beginning, however, that it was important to maximize the effectiveness of a walkthrough and minimize its overhead. We faced a constant battle to get the developers to schedule and conduct enough walkthroughs to keep the size of the review material reasonable. They tended to go too long between reviews and include too much in each review. In other words, there was a constant

creep from "design a little" to "design a lot." Management needed to mitigate this and ensure the process itself didn't create obstacles that encourage developers to delay the walkthrough process. For this reason, we kept the roles and requirements for the walkthrough simple.

Each walkthrough had a well-defined list of entry and exit requirements. In most cases, the exit requirements consisted of walkthrough minutes, an approval to proceed, and the actual software development item products. Developers produced the minutes using a template from the Process Guide, and included metrics collection, decisions, and action items for every defect noted during the walkthrough. The approval to proceed determined whether or not a transition was made out of the current state and to which state the object proceeded. The process allowed customization so that certain states could be skipped or, if significant problems were encountered, the approval to proceed could direct the process to return to an earlier state.

Within each state, the guidelines outlined an initial, intermediate, and final walkthrough. Multiple walkthroughs were held within a state before the approval to proceed directed a state transition. Figure 3 shows this internal state walkthrough process.

The lead developer was responsible for producing the announcement and minutes for each walkthrough. Templates for both were provided online. The lead distributed the announcement along with

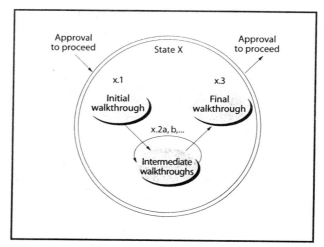

FIGURE 3. Internal state walkthrough process.

the documents required for the review. After the minutes were produced, team members received an e-mail message that included a file name and location of the minutes and the names of everyone who had action items.

The minutes consisted of three major areas: metrics, general comments, and action items. The action items were the main reason for the walkthrough, since its objective was to uncover every defect and ensure they are corrected. When problems were uncovered, each defect had an action item with a named individual given responsibility for completing it. Action items were tracked to closure via the walkthrough itself. The lead developer was responsible for reviewing all previous action items at the beginning of the next walkthrough. Outstanding action items could prevent approval to proceed or, by explicit decision, be carried forward to the next walkthrough, with annotation in the minutes.

Inspections

Each walkthrough included a dialogue focused on the results of each reviewer's individual inspection of the DI. Inspection was essential preparation for the walkthrough: the success of the walkthrough depended on the reviewers' professional and conscientious examination of the DI. If a reviewer had not had sufficient time to inspect the materials, we postponed the walkthrough. The objective was not to simply check a box on a form, but to uncover every defect. Reviewers were assigned at the start of the process and remained the same throughout; this developed a team ownership that was evident when we uncovered defects—the attitude was, "how did *we* miss that?" We never had a problem with pride of authorship or damaged egos.

The process also yielded an exciting technical benefit: it raised junior developers' expertise level. When an experienced developer reviewed a junior developer's work, after several walkthroughs the junior developer began to pick up on the expert advice. He began to ask the same kinds of questions in other walkthroughs in which he was the reviewer.

Metrics

Metrics were collected throughout the process to assess status; they included walkthrough duration, number of participants, external inspection time, pre- and post-walkthrough overhead, and major and minor defects or issues uncovered. We defined major defects as those that could negatively

affect the operational system. Minor defects included every other problem. At the end of each walkthrough, both schedule status and technical status of the DI were also assessed. This status was a major input for management briefings.

Additionally, our metrics captured the return on investment in terms of the resources required to conduct walkthroughs and the number of defects uncovered. At the beginning of each walkthrough, every reviewer was polled on the amount of time they spent on inspections. The lead developer had the authority to cancel any walkthrough if insufficient review time had been spent.

State notes

A set of state notes associated with each state assisted the lead developer and team as they proceeded through the process. The notes were continually revised. Referencing the state notes as they entered a state gave the developers valuable insight into past lessons learned, suggestions, questions to ask, hints, critical items to check, and any other information collected during previous activity in this state. The team was responsible for identifying items to be added to the state notes, with the lead developer taking the update action.

KEYS TO SUCCESS

The Atams development team used the State-Based Process with great success, and it continues to undergo refinement and improvement. The State-Based Process was designed to allow management and users the ability to see inside the product during development. Both management and the development team would be reluctant to develop software without it. Management was especially

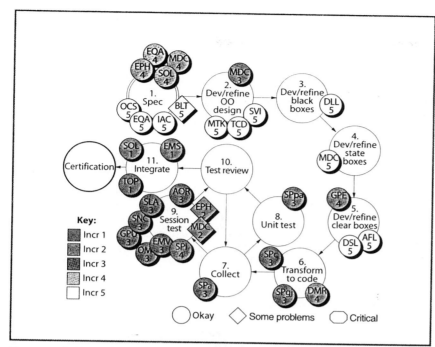

FIGURE 4. Management status view of a development item.

pleased that they could query any developer about the status of his work and receive a clear answer on the state he was in, the state he was moving toward, and the schedule status.

User involvement

The users were heavily involved throughout the life-cycle development. Eliciting requirements is one of the most difficult tasks in developing systems, and arriving at a true requirement set is challenging because it is difficult to express in human language the behavior of a computer. Codification of human thought into software, even using modern tools such as use cases, is fraught with difficulty and prone to error.

We depended on continuous, face-to-face user involvement from the specifications state through the design state. The incremental approach allowed us to gain user feedback early and often. We frequently asked the users' opinions on interface and functionality to ensure we fulfilled the system requirements. In the project's first few weeks, we developed user interfaces using a display builder tool. In an early walkthrough, 12 operational crew members voted on screen display colors. They participated in our walkthroughs daily until the screens were exactly what they wanted. We were not afraid of their input throughout the project—we asked for it repeatedly. No one saw this as a late requirements change, because it allowed us to produce a high-quality product. When we delivered the software,

the users were not surprised by anything because they had been an essential part of the development team.

Management benefits

Project management was greatly improved because the managers could track the developers' progress and see "inside" the software product. A major objective driving our process definition approach was to reduce overall risk by wedding the management process directly to the technical process.

Figure 4 shows a typical management briefing slide from the Atams project, showing the status and progress of the development items within the increments for Release 3.0. Each DI is represented by a bubble. The bubble's color indicates the DI's increment number and the shape indicates its development status—a circle is "okay," a diamond is "some problems," and an octagon is "critical." This overview permits assessing and tracking the entire project status.

The process offered a number of benefits to the project manager:

♦ It gives managers and developers an easily understood one-page graphic representation of project and item status.

♦ It provides concise, definable states with clear entry and exit criteria, activity steps, procedures, and methodologies.

♦ It provides natural points and clear guidance for valuable capture of metrics.

♦ It promotes team ownership.

♦ It facilitates continuous process improvement.

♦ It increases product quality.

Quality assurance and process improvement

We designed the State-Based Process to engage every team member in quality assurance and process improvement activities and to make them a natural part of their development paradigm. We believe that the only way to ensure quality in the end product is to build QA activities into the process from beginning to end, and we achieved this through the discipline of inspections and walkthroughs.

Additionally, process improvement becomes the responsibility of every member of the development team. The Atams team owned the process and were quick to change it when they discovered a weakness. The process guidelines helped formalize the process improvement activities in several ways.

♦ When defects were discovered, team members considered whether the defect resulted from a process weakness. If so, they discussed process improvement inputs and annotated them as action items in the walkthrough minutes.

♦ The team updated state notes from inputs gathered in the walkthroughs and annotated them as an action item in the minutes.

♦ The weekly team meetings permitted discussions of how to improve the process. This input was also captured as an action item in the meeting minutes.

RESULTS

The State-Based Process was used throughout the Atams project with great success, in terms of both productivity and quality. Our typical walkthrough involved five to six people, lasted almost one hour, required over two hours of external inspection, and took almost one hour of pre-walkthrough overhead and 48 minutes of post-walkthrough overhead. The average return on investment per walkthrough was 2.5 major defects found and more than 6 minor defects uncovered. This equates to just over one hour of staff time per defect when considering all the costs for both major and minor defects—a small price to pay for the return. Another way to look at it is that 748 defects did not live to traumatize the test or operational environment. Since only one defect survived into the first operational release, technically speaking, we uncovered 748 of the 749 defects before compilation.

These numbers are actually rather conservative, since the defect count should be much higher—we estimate approximately three times higher, because in many cases multiple defects were counted as one. For example, problems detected in a particular scenario diagram were usually tagged as one defect. Also, an undetected error in the design or specifications could have resulted in multiple defects later. Of the four operational incident reports written for Atams, only one applied to the over 37,000 hand-developed lines of code.

Many other factors beyond the scope of this article contributed to the eventual success of Atams. For example, the tools we used were a major force multiplier. But the people factor really deserves one final comment. The Atams project was a challenge from the beginning, mostly due to schedule constraints. We are convinced that we would not have succeeded without the process, but it also took dedication by an enthusiastic staff. We believe that team ownership of the process was key to their enthusiasm, since a significant part of their commitment went to improving the process.

The State-Based Process does not require "super-programmers." Our experience showed that the process brought out the best in each programmer. They felt empowered by the process, not hampered by it. We didn't have to fight the process or the team to get the indicators and insight we needed. In fact, we empowered them to do it for us. ❖

REFERENCES

1. B.W. Boehm, "Software Risk Management: Principles and Practices," *IEEE Software*, Jan. 1991, pp. 32-41.
2. W.W. Gibbs, "Command and Control: Inside a Hollowed-Out Mountain, Software Fiascoes—and a Signal Success," *Scientific American*, Aug. 1997, pp. 33-34.
3. H.D. Mills et al., "Cleanroom Software Engineering," *IEEE Software*, Sept. 1987, pp. 19-24.

About the Authors

Buford D. Tackett is a senior systems engineer at ITT Industries, System Division, and was program director for Atams. He is a retired Air Force Lt. Colonel and the former White House Director of Technical Plans for the National Security Council during the Bush Administration. He holds a BS in computer science from Kansas State University, an MS in software engineering from Auburn University, and is a doctoral candidate in management.

Buddy Van Doren is a senior systems engineer for ITT Industries, System Division, where he is in charge of implementing knowledge management practices. He has spent more than 32 years in the development and maintenance of information systems for commercial and defense applications. He holds an MS in electrical engineering from the University of California at Berkeley.

Readers may contact Tackett at ITT Industries, System Division, 4450 E. Fountain Blvd, Colorado Springs, CO 80935-5012; e-mail bdtackett@csprings.com.

From the Trenches

Reprinted from IEEE Software,
July/Aug. 1998, pp. 50-60.

Although OO development methods and models have been in use for several years, management techniques optimized for OO development have not kept pace. The author participated in several OO projects and, based on those experiences and the lessons learned from them, developed a management process tailored to OO development.

MANAGING OO PROJECTS BETTER

Paolo Nesi, University of Florence

ver the past decade, the object-oriented paradigm has gained a large following, and in many cases[1] has replaced traditional software development approaches with OO equivalents.[2,3] New schemes have been proposed for modeling the development life cycle as well.[4] Unfortunately, many of these approaches focus on modeling the system development around a single task or team, rather than considering how to build a specifically object-oriented system in terms of planning, team structure, and project management.

Thus, the definition of these new OO development methodologies has yet to be supported by a comparable effort in defining methods and strategies for managing OO projects, or for modeling the life cycle at both the system and the task and subtask levels. OO project management also requires integration in effort planning and process prediction. Traditional models fall short in this regard, too, because they take an almost entirely bottom-up approach and base their project plans on the mechanisms of allocating and deallocating people.

Table 1								
Significant Statistics For Studied Projects								
Project	**OS**	**Language**	**Tools and Libraries**	**Number of Classes**	**SC_{LOC}**	**Person-Months**	**People**	**Teams**
TOOMS	Unix	C++	Lex/Yacc, CommonView	204	16568	41.5	16	6
ICOOMM	Windows NT	C++	MFC	193	10870	20	6	3
QV	Unix	C++	XLIB, Motif	65	3900	7	4	2
LIOO	Linux	C++	Lex/Yacc, XVGAlib	165	16020	30	11	5
TAC++	Unix	C, C++	Lex/Yacc, QV, XLIB	62	2300 for C, 4340 for C++	13.5	5	2

As a first step toward alleviating these short-comings, I outline several lessons learned while deriving a more efficient model for managing OO projects. Summaries of these lessons, which represent the experiences of myself and my colleagues in managing several small- and medium-size OO projects over the last seven years, appear in italics throughout the sections that follow.

PROJECT PROFILES

Table 1 shows the profiles, in chronological order, of some of the projects from which I drew the lessons described in this article:

♦ TOOMS (Tool Object-Oriented Machine State), a CASE tool to specify, verify, test, and assess real-time systems;

♦ ICOOMM (Industrial Control Object-Oriented Milling Machines), a computerized numerical control for milling machines;

♦ QV (Q View), a library providing uniform OO support for Motif and X;

♦ LIOO (Lectern Interactive Object-Oriented), a lectern and editor for music scores; and

♦ TAC++ (Tool for Analysis of C++), a tool for developing and assessing C/C++ projects.

Each profile lists the project's pertinent data, including the number of system classes, SC_{LOC}, effort in person-months, number of non-project-management people involved, and number of different teams. SC_{LOC}, or OO system complexity based on lines of code, is an evolution of the LOC metric that also considers class attributes, class definition, and method interfaces.[5]

Most of these projects were carried out by het-erogeneous teams that included staff members from the University of Florence, the Centro Sviluppo Tecnologicao (CESVIT) research center, and various companies. Although the project partners were in separate locations, to improve the homogeneity of results the various heterogeneous task and subtask teams assigned to a particular project worked in one place. Doing so let them use the same "quality manual," a reference document containing all guidelines for project development as prescribed by the company's general criteria. The teams performed most of the work using C++, but implemented some projects in TROL (Tempo Reale Object-oriented Language), a formal language and model similar to object-oriented SDL, ObjecTime, and others.[1]

TEAM STRUCTURE AND ORGANIZATION

A project manager coordinates the subsystem managers and directs the overall project. When the project manager adopts the well-known waterfall life cycle, a clear division is present between the phases of analysis (requirement analysis and detailed analysis), design (structural design and detailed design), coding (class implementation), test, and so on. The team organization usually replicates this division. Different groups work on the same project in different phases, and communicate via a few meetings and documents. These groups may use different notations and methods. Even if an integrated quality and methodological model unifies these notations, misunderstandings may still occur between the many people tasked with drafting and interpreting the project's documents. Thus a mis-

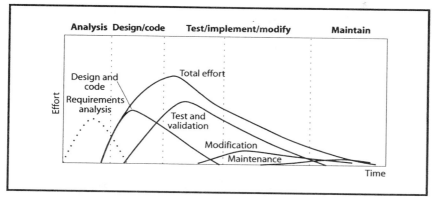

FIGURE 1. Putnam's resource allocation model, which shows project effort as a function of time.

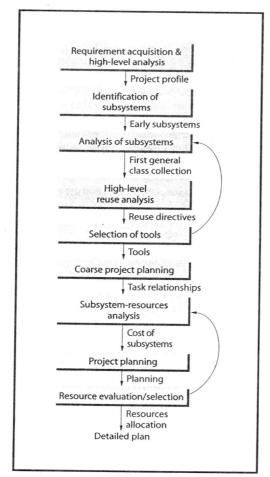

FIGURE 2. Project start-up structure with the most important products of each phase.

match between consecutive phases may develop,[6] which causes teams to work on wrong or unrequired functionalities. Although several integrated approaches to reduce these problems have been tried, their results have been limited by the persistence of different interpretations and viewpoints within groups and between groups.

In many cases, project managers adopt Larry Putnam's resource allocation model,[7] shown in Figure 1. As the project evolves, the dynamic allocation of people may lead to an increase in the number of subsystems and in the team's size. Typically, management allocates people dynamically, passing them from one phase to the next to satisfy incoming deadlines. Although training new people would avoid this reshuffling, it is often a costly and self-defeating alternative because it usually entails the support of skilled people needed elsewhere on the project.

♦ In our experience, the hierarchical organization of a team can be successfully applied to OO projects. But the project plan, the development life cycle, and the roles of the project manager and subsystem managers must be revised as described in the following lessons.

PROJECT START-UP

As Figure 2 shows, the project start-up consists of several phases typically performed sequentially or only partially overlapped.

We typically perform the requirements acquisition and high-level analysis, also called user needs analysis and feasibility study, to

♦ evaluate commercial issues such as benefits and risks;

♦ analyze the technological risks;

♦ examine the requirements with respect to industry trends and general goals;

♦ define ultimate targets in terms of end users, environments, platforms, and so on;

♦ define the quality profile of the final product; and

♦ define project timing, the most important milestones, and the critical path.

The project manager and subsystem managers identify the main subsystems according to a structural decomposition. The subsystems are, in most cases, comprised of multiple classes, many of which are used by other subsystems. This occurs because in classical OO analysis methodologies, you usually model the problem domain and not a specific system or subsystem.[2]

Typically at this stage, you strive to model exactly that part of the domain needed for the system you're building, and no more, unless reuse considerations prompt you to undertake extra work. On the other hand, during project start-up you usually have limited knowledge of the problem's scope, and thus it is best to manage as much of the problem domain as you can. A too-restrictive modeling performed during the early phases of system development typically results in hierarchies having too many complex leaf classes. The presence of too many leaf classes is frequently due to the lack of specialization. In turn, the lack of specialization is frequently due to a poor analysis of the system domain. This occurs, for example, when the application's problem domain has been neglected in favor of a limited analysis of the application under development. All applications start small and grow throughout their service life. To start with a restricted analysis frequently leads to an insufficient class hierarchy. During the analysis the focus should be on those classes used in several tasks. These are usually the most important ones for the domain under analysis or are fundamental to the system. They include repositors, model symbols, graphic components, and so on.

In the first part of subsystem analysis, each subsystem manager must identify the most important classes of the assigned subsystems. Then, classes identified by all subsystem managers are organized in the unique domain model. In OO projects, a subsystem can be

- a subtree or tree,
- a number of independent classes, or
- a classical subsystem, identified by a structural composition-decomposition process.
- *We re-extracted the main subsystems from the general collection of classes by identifying branches related to the most important classes, usually called key classes. We reassigned these new versions of subsystems to subsystem managers. The two-phase process I describe regularizes the identification of sub-*

systems, improving efficiency by avoiding class duplication and reducing the dependencies among subsystems (and thus among subsystem teams). Each subsystem or subtask should have from 15 to 30 classes to be manageable, depending on the role these classes play in the system. A larger number usually means that team members must learn a lot about the system, while too few classes may lead to people working on the same class too frequently. A subsystem can include

- *several small classes (basic objects, part of other classes);*

Lack of specialization is frequently due to poor analysis of the system domain.

- *a number of so-called "key classes" (such as the root class for persistent objects, a class implementing the list) and,*
- *among these key classes, a few very important classes, called engine classes. These are more complex than the other key classes and cannot always be decomposed because their complexity derives mainly from their functional and behavioral aspects.*

Instances of engine classes usually control the most important parts of the application, such as the database manager, the state machine editor, the window manager, the event manager, or the interpreter. For such classes, the effort—defined as the hours spent executing a particular task—may be as much as five times greater than that for normal key classes. The start-up phase continues with reuse analysis, in which the project manager and the subsystem managers identify sources of existing subsystem parts, classes, or clusters that can be profitably reused in the current project. For each potential reuse source, the cost of adaptation must be evaluated before proceeding.

Next, the subsystem managers and project manager identify suitable tools for system development. These decisions may lead to reiterating from the subsystems analysis step.

The subsequent coarse-grained project plan includes

1. analyzing the overall system,
2. defining subsystems (tasks) and subtasks,
3. examining dependencies among tasks,
4. planning time-to-market, and
5. identifying milestones and other target dates.

Determining how many staff-hours are needed to develop each subsystem and its corresponding subtasks cannot be done yet because the assess-

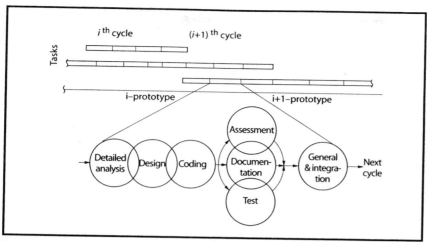

FIGURE 3. The macrocycle of the task and subtask development life cycle, and the microcycle—a simplified version of the spiral model integrated with a modified version of the fountain model.

prototype for progress control. Each cycle can involve several tasks and includes, at the system level, general assessment and risk analysis.

Working from the project plan, management selects and allocates project staff, based on the skill and experience of available personnel. In our teams, the typical efficiency was from 2.2 to 4 SC_{LOC} points per hour, including analysis, design, coding, documentation, test, and assessment phases.

ment effort must be performed later. During the subsystsem-resource analysis, the effort for developing each subsystem and the corresponding subtasks is evaluated in terms of human resources.

♦ *The number of identified key classes multiplied by a factor, K, gives an approximate measure of the final dimension of each system or subsystem in terms of classes. We found that K is equal to 2 for subsystems without a user interface and communication with devices, and 4 for subsystems that include the relationships with a complex user interface. We use the hypothesis for the number of system classes to predict the effort needed for each task by considering the typical person-hours needed to analyze, design, and implement a class. In the projects mentioned, this mean factor is 15 to 40 hours per class; differences depend on team efficiency and application complexity. We used the number of class attributes and methods as a more precise predictive measure of class complexity.*

You can now prepare the detailed project plan, considering at least the temporal constraints identified in the requirements acquisition and high-level analysis phases, as well as the number of people needed for each subsystem and subtask. The plan must also consider the nature of the life cycle adopted. In the case of OOP, the classic life cycles are evolutionary and typically prototype-oriented, such as the spiral or fountain models.[4,6] The fountain model leads to an unpredictable number of cycles at the system level because it is too rule-free to produce repeatable results. This makes it difficult to predict the duration of the analysis, design, implementation, and other phases.

♦ *At the system level, we used a spiral-oriented project schedule: two or three cycles of from six to eight months each that produce a milestone and*

SYSTEM DEVELOPMENT

After project start-up, the system development phase begins by activating tasks and subtasks according to the project plan and the preanalysis performed during start-up.

Task life cycle

The spiral model is too complex and complete to be applied at the subsystem level, while the fountain model is difficult to control. The adopted microcycle, shown in Figure 3, consists of a simplified version of the spiral model integrated with a modified version of the fountain model. According to the fountain model, the first three steps can be locally iterated by restarting from the first step when strictly necessary to achieve the cycle objectives. Unlike the fountain model, the last steps are performed simultaneously and only once.

Figure 3 shows that, as in the spiral model, a task or subtask is typically completed in one or more cycles, each with a duration of two to four weeks depending on fixed subgoals and milestones. Given the team members' typical productivity, you can obtain the number of cycles required by considering that a task or subtask must contain from 15 to 30 classes to be manageable. For example, it requires three cycles of two weeks each, with a two-person team—a total of 480 hours—to produce from 12 to 32 classes for C++. Less time will be needed if you are producing key classes, because fewer classes must be considered if the subsystem includes key classes. Task and subtask teams consist of two to three people, including the subsystem manager. The develop-

TABLE 2		
IMPOSED LIMITS FOR CLASS PARAMETERS		
Parameter	**Mean Values**	**Maximum Values**
Class complexity	200	1800
Class complexity, inherited	150	1200
Class complexity, local	50	600
Number of class attributes	9, 27	15, 45
Number of inherited class attributes	6, 18	10, 30
Number of local class attributes	3, 9	5, 15
Number of class methods	36, 90	44, 144
Number of inherited class methods	24, 60	36, 96
Number of local class methods	12, 30	18, 48
Number of superclasses	2	5, 6
Number of subclasses	5	30, 90

ment process is a sequence of partially overlapping steps. We found it advantageous to use an analysis and design methodology very similar to Grady Booch's,[2] because it meshes well with the management and lifecycle models we selected. After the design phase, the same team performs testing, documenting, and assessment simultaneously. Because consecutive microcycles partially overlap, team members have different roles in different contexts.

♦ *We observed that the effort spent in documenting and assessing depends quite linearly on the number of classes, while testing depends on time for testing classes and their relationships. The first factor is linear and the second takes a time that depends more than quadratically on the number of classes, since interactions among classes exploiting relationships of is-part-of and is-referred-by are frequently made concrete with several method calls. A small number of classes per subsystem lets you work in the first part of the cost evolution curve, where the cost of testing relationships is much lower than that for testing class relationships. This also depends on the number of relationships established among classes (another parameter that must be maintained under control along the development process). Moreover, we reduced testing, assessing, and documenting time by improving these processes.*

Test activity

Typically, the test activity can last anywhere from as long as the first three phases combined to less time than it takes to complete the first phase. We reduced the time for testing by preparing test scripts of test cases and procedures directly in the analysis phases and, in some cases, by using an automatic tool for regression testing based on Capture and Playback.[8] This approach is based on two distinct phases: the capture and the playback. During capture, the system collects each computer-user and external-device interaction. The histories of these interactions are stored in sequential form in a script file. The histories are reposed during playback to the computer interfaces, simulating the presence of real entities: users, other machines, sensors, and so on. After each simulated stimulus, the computer's responses can be tested to verify that the applica-

tion answers correctly according to its predetermined behavior.

In subsequent cycles, regression testing is performed automatically for those parts that are mainly unchanged.

Documentation activity

Documentation usually takes much more time than other activities. Suitable CASE tools for analysis and design can generate a draft version of documentation, in which details related to the implementation must be added manually.

♦ *The team member who serves as main designer of the classes is the best choice for performing this work. The subsystem manager also must help prepare the documentation that describes the task status and evolution, and the decisions carried out in the task cycle. This part of the documentation helps the project manager understand and discuss the project's status at a higher level.*

Assessment activity and related mechanisms

Evolutionary development lets you produce something that can be automatically measured right from the early phases of the project, when class definitions are available. We used the class structure's attributes and method interfaces to apply predictive metrics for estimating development, maintenance, and other task effort.[5,9] We analyzed values and corresponding trends of a few metrics and indicators for each task and subtask class: complexity (as it relates to class effort, maintainability, and so on), verifiability index, reuse index, efficiency, and so on.[10,11]

As Table 2 shows, for classes we imposed specific profiles, such as number of attributes, number of methods, class complexity, inherited class complexity, and class interface complexity. When two values appear in a cell, they refer to classes not involved and involved in the GUI, respectively. Data for these met-

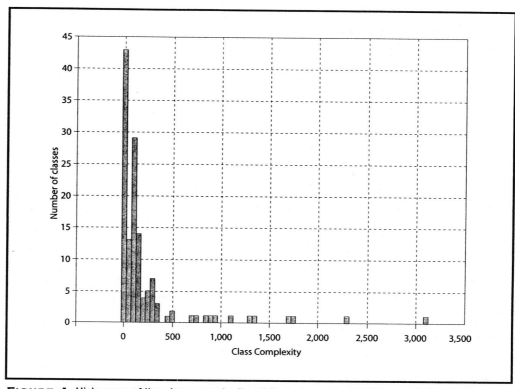

FIGURE 4. Histogram of the class complexity attribute for project LIOO near the midpoint of the process's development. The typical histogram must present an exponential trend, while in this case a couple of classes exhibited a class complexity greater than 1800.

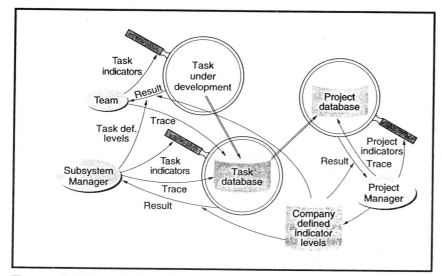

FIGURE 5. Task and project levels in a sample assessment. Only one task is reported.

rics has been evaluated using a definition developed in my work with colleagues.[5,11]

We define these profiles using the typical histograms obtained for that metric in other projects, as shown in Figure 4. When a class grows beyond its imposed limits it must be carefully analyzed and, if possible, corrected. We accomplish this by, for example, splitting the class or moving the code closer to its parents.[11] Doing so maintains the class's quality and ensures control of the staff effort devoted to the class.

Assessment, the shortest activity of those performed in parallel, is done by a team member skilled in OO analysis, with the

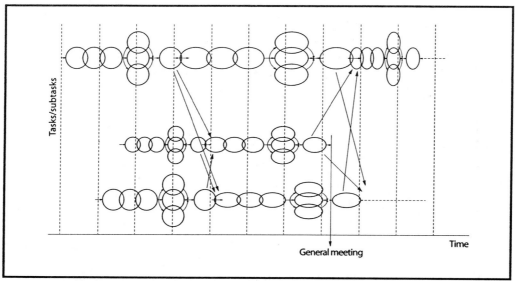

FIGURE 6. Relationships and integrations among project tasks and subtasks. The dotted lines indicate the intervals for periodic meetings to discuss integration among classes and clusters by different teams.

help of the subsystem manager. As Figure 5 shows, the assessment checks that the process satisfies company metrics and indicators for controlled software development. The subsystem managers must include in the documentation and the project database any strategies for correcting deviations from the plan.[5] For our assessments we used a suitable tool for measuring selected metrics and comparing the imposed profiles with the current ones.

♦ *Continuous metrication must be associated with a continuous revalidation of the indicators adopted to adjust weights and threshold values, and for tuning the organization's metric suite. We collected non-automatically measurable data by filling in an electronic questionnaire daily with, for example, the effort of each class (for detailed analysis, design, coding, and other tasks), the modification of class hierarchy, the effort for the other activities, and a brief description of the work. Real and measured values let us identify the model.*

Generalization and integration activity

This phase partially overlaps the next microcycle. To accomplish generalization and integration, the subsystem manager must first identify the detailed goals of the next microcycle. These goals may be best defined once the subsystem manager finishes the current phase and begins full-time work on the next microcycle.

♦ *During this phase each subsystem manager may meet with other subsystem managers and the project manager, depending on task relationships, to*

1. identify new detailed requirements for generalizing classes and clusters developed so that they can be used in the whole system;

2. provide other teams with the current version of software developed in the corresponding task or subtask, along with its documentation, test, and assessment reports;

3. discuss with the project manager how to correct problems identified by the assessment activity.

As regards point 2, the other task and subtask teams will use the results produced starting from their next detailed analysis phase, as shown by the arrows in Figure 6.

Task relationships

The dotted lines in Figure 6 show that, about every two to four weeks, depending on the length of the microcycle, project task and subtask teams hold periodic meetings to exchange information. In these meetings, only the choices made in the analysis and design phases are discussed, with the intent of improving integration among classes and clusters implemented by different teams. Thus, the periodic meetings address the general aspects of analysis and design, while restricted meetings between the team and its subsystem manager address

From the Trenches

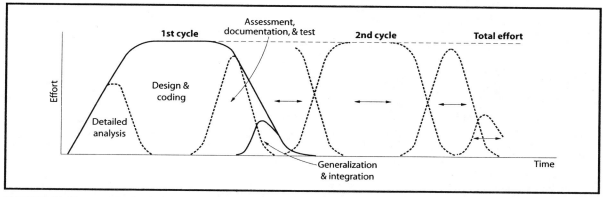

FIGURE 7. The model adopted for task and subtask effort as a function of time. The dashed line represents general effort.

more detailed and technical problems.

♦ *Periodic meetings avoid class duplication and facilitate the adoption of uniform notations in the project database's quality manual for the selection of class, method, and attribute names; for compiling documentation; for preparing test scripts; and so on. To improve control and uniformity, plan general meetings with all team members and subsystem managers*

♦ *when an important task is completed,*

♦ *when an important change to the project structure and management is needed, or*

♦ *for discussing prototypes of the whole system or time-consuming milestones and deliverables.*

At general meetings, everyone explains what they are doing and are going to do, then comments on issues raised by the others. Such meetings improve the code's uniformity and quality because they let all points of view be taken into account. They also have a strongly positive affect on morale and motivation. General meetings can even help reduce the fuzzy thinking of programmers who sometimes get distracted by a trivial task that could be safely neglected, even if doing so caused inconsequential errors in the finished product.

Team people

Traditional project and subsystem managers typically lack the training and expertise to manage OO projects. This shortcoming becomes more pronounced when using our approach, which requires management participation in several meetings that address technical problems.

♦ *As shown, the roles of the project manager and subsystem managers are quite different than in traditional projects where, during the development,* they only supervise the work of all groups, defining documents' structure, instruments, and planning. According to our model, the project manager can profitably manage the project only if he or she directly knows how the problem domain has been covered in terms of classes and class relationships. Moreover, the subsystem manager must participate actively in the task and subtask development by analyzing details and designing and implementing specific parts, or parts related to other tasks.

Effort planning

Models such as the Putnam Resource Allocation model, Jensen's model, and COCOMO are mainly suitable for single-team projects.[12] Although some versions of these models can be applied to multi-team projects, they entail considerable dynamic allocation of human resources during the design and coding phases at the task level, as Figure 1 shows. At the subsystem level, this means it is difficult to predict costs, especially if you use traditional development models. With OO methodologies, on the other hand, effort is shifted from the design phase to that of analysis. System development starts by using a bottom-up approach and then reverts to a top-down one.[4] Doing so moves the peak of the effort curve to the analysis phase, but the problems related to dynamic allocation persist because the traditional effort allocation method remains. This problem becomes more severe when you use the Putnam model for each cycle of the spiral development life cycle, because it calls for the allocation and deallocation phases to be performed at each cycle, with a consequent increase in overhead costs.

Using the alternative approach shown in Figure 7, we report the effort for a task or subtask as a func-

tion of time. I constructed this idealized diagram by observing what happens when our micro life cycle is applied across several OO projects. The graph includes the first cycle's detailed analysis phase, when human resources are allocated. The subsystem analysis starts with the allocation of the subsystem manager and continues until all other team members have been assigned. The design and coding phases follow the analysis and are performed by the same team, with a constant number of people. Each cycle overlaps the next, with team members constantly allocated to the task (represented by the dashed line in Figure 7), but performing different duties depending on the cycle.

♦ *Because no clear separation exists between the life-cycle phases of OO methodologies, allocating a constant number of people to the task team is consistent with the OO approach, letting the same people who perform the analysis work on all other phases. This leads to a reduction of effort and less risk of misunderstanding. The lack of clear separation stems mainly from the impossibility, in many cases, of separating the development phases—for example, whether to include or exclude object and class specialization and relationship identification from the analysis phase. All these relationships have a strong impact on cluster identification and on the general domain analysis. Some methodologies are more flexible while others are much too rigid in this regard. Further, during each single cycle there are periods in which one team member still works on the analysis while the others proceed to the other phases. The project manager must try to distribute the project staff's efforts uniformly throughout the project or at least along the single tasks. Uniformity of effort also guarantees consistent quality and efficiency, improves controllability and effort predictability, and avoids the extra training required by dynamic allocation.*

When the team needs more effort to perform a cycle, project management lengthens the phases as depicted in the second microcycle of Figure 7. This does not conflict with the schedule if the *total* effort needed to develop a task (represented as the area under the curve) remains the same. The effort predicted for each task, and that of the whole project, can be adjusted after each task cycle in relation to the trend of normalized indicators,[5,9] such as

♦ the increment of task classes per time unit,
♦ the increment of class complexity per time unit,
♦ the increment of task complexity per time unit,
♦ the relative difference between the number of classes and the predicted number, and
♦ the ratio between internal and external class complexity.

Development teams of more than four people result in decreasing productivity.

If project management predicts insufficient effort for the planned trend, more effort is allocated by, for example, increasing the next cycle's duration. If this is infeasible because of task deadlines or other factors, project management divides the task into two subtasks under a single subsystem manager. In this case, dynamic allocation takes place in the analysis phase.

Task division can, however, generate mismatches. To reduce such problems, project management can perform the real division into subtasks after the detailed analysis. In some cases, task division is infeasible or too expensive because it would affect too many related classes. In such cases, the team can be increased to at most four people, some minor classes can be reassigned to related subsystems, or both. Larger teams would result in decreasing productivity and increasing cohesion among subsystems.

♦ *Using our microcycle approach requires more effort from the project manager than that needed to manage traditional projects: we obtained a value of nearly 210 hours per year for a project of four person-years. This value must be scaled for larger projects, which contain a higher number of subtasks, and thus require additional meetings and greater technical involvement by the project manager.*

I have found traditional methods inadequate for managing OO projects, for several reasons:

♦ There is a sizeable gap between OO software development methodologies and diffuse managing approaches.
♦ The life cycles usually adopted focus too much on single-task projects and structured or functional methodologies.
♦ Managers lack prior experience in the adoption of OO indicators for controlling system development at both project and task levels.
♦ Organizations share a deeply ingrained tradi-

tion of allocating and deallocating human resources among different projects.

♦ Project and subsystem managers lack the technical expertise necessary to profitably manage OO projects. Thus, to be effective, the OO approach I've proposed must be introduced throughout the whole organization.

My project experiences and those of my colleagues have enabled us to create and fine-tune a stable OO management and development model that addresses these shortcomings. Our method is now being used by several organizations that manage internal and multipartner Esprit projects. On these projects, the method has predicted final effort with errors lower than 10 percent, satisfying the project organizations' early-defined quality and company requirements. We obtained these results by facilitating strong collaboration among team members and increasing gratification and motivation according to the lessons and guidelines I've described. Other, longer-term benefits have resulted from our approach as well. For example, some team members have exhibited a growing capability to manage projects after they participated in a project using our method, which distributes management tasks more evenly across the team hierarchy. ❖

ACKNOWLEDGMENTS

I thank the following project managers and subsystem managers. For project TOOMS: U. Paternostro of the Department of Systems and Informatics; M. Traversi and M. Campanai of CESVIT; F. Fioravanti, M. Bruno, and C. Guidoccio of DSI. For project TAC++: A. Borri of CESVIT and T. Querci of DSI; S. Perlini. For project ICOOMM: M. Perfetti and F. Butera of ELEXA. For the QV/MOOVI project: T. Querci; L. Masini, M. Caciolli, and L. Fabiani. For project LIOO: F. Bellini, N. Baldini, S. Macchi, A. Mengoni, and A. Bennati. For the projects of series MICROTelephone: M. Traversi, G. Conedera, D. Angeli, C. Rogai, and M. Riformetti of OTE S.r.l. For project INDEX-DSP: M. Montanelli and P. Ticciati of SED S.r.l. A warm thanks to the many developers who have worked and are working on these and other projects with me.

REFERENCES

1. G. Bucci, M. Campanai, and P. Nesi, "Tools for Specifying Real-Time Systems," *J. Real-Time Systems*, Mar. 1995, pp. 117-172.
2. G. Booch, *Object-Oriented Design with Applications*, Addison Wesley Longman, Reading, Mass., 1994.
3. R.J. Wirfs-Brock, B. Wilkerson, and L. Wiener, *Designing Object Oriented Software*, Prentice Hall, Upper Saddle River, N.J., 1990.
4. B. Henderson-Sellers and J. M. Edwards, "The Object Oriented Systems Life Cycle," *Comm. ACM*, Sept. 1990, pp. 143-159.
5. P. Nesi and T. Querci, "Effort Estimation and Prediction of Object-Oriented Systems," *J. Systems and Software*, to appear, 1998.
6. B.W. Boehm, "A Spiral Model of Software Development and Enhancement," *IEEE Software*, Sept. 1988, pp. 61-72.
7. L. H. Putnam, "A General Empirical Solution to the Macro Software Sizing and Estimation Problem," *IEEE Trans. Software Eng.*, July 1978, pp. 345-361.
8. P. Nesi and A. Serra, "A Non-Invasive Object-Oriented Tool for Software Testing," *Software Quality J.*, Vol. 4, No. 3, 1995, pp. 155-174.
9. W. Li and S. Henry, "Object-Oriented Metrics that Predict Maintainability," *J. Systems Software*, Vol. 23, No. 2, 1993, pp. 111-122.
10. P. Nesi and M. Campanai, "Metric Framework for Object-Oriented Real-Time Systems Specification Languages," *J. Systems and Software*, Vol. 34, No. 1, 1996, pp. 43-65.
11. F. Fioravanti, P. Nesi, and S. Perlini, "Assessment of System Evolution Through Characterization," *Proc. IEEE Int'l. Conf. Software Eng.*, IEEE CS Press, Los Alamitos, Calif., Apr. 1998, pp. 456-459.
12. S. D. Conte, H. E. Dunsmore, and V. Y. Shen, *Software Engineering Metrics and Models*, Benjamin/Cummings, Menlo Park, Calif., 1986.

About the Author

Paolo Nesi is an assistant professor of information technology and a researcher with the Department of Systems and Informatics of the University of Florence. His research interests include OO technology, real-time systems, quality, testing, formal languages, physical models, and parallel architectures. He holds the scientific responsibility for high-performance computer networking at CESVIT, a high-tech agency for technology transfer. He also belongs to the editorial board of the *Journal of Real-Time Imaging*.

Nesi received a Laurea in electronic engineering from the University of Florence and a PhD in electronics and informatics from the University of Padoa, Italy. He is a member of IEEE, the International Association for Pattern Recognition, Taboo (the Italian association for promoting object technologies), and AIIA (the Italian association on artificial intelligence).

Address questions about this article to Nesi at Department of Systems and Informatics, Faculty of Engineering, University of Florence, Via S. Marta 3, 50139 Florence, Italy; nesi@dsi.unifi.it; http://www.dsi.unifi.it.

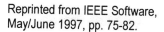
Reprinted from IEEE Software,
May/June 1997, pp. 75-82.

Putting Risk Management into Practice

RAY C. WILLIAMS, JULIE A. WALKER,
and AUDREY J. DOROFEE, *Software Engineering Institute*

*The authors use an
SEI-designed road map
as a guide to discussing
effective and ineffective
risk management
methods based on six
years' experience with
software-intensive
DoD programs. These
programs followed
the SEI approach of
continuous and team risk
management, selecting
processes and methods
that would best fit their
work cultures.*

Your life is going along fine when suddenly you're given the responsibility for risk management in a major software-intensive development program—one in which software content amounts to more than half the development costs. You have a team of capable system and software engineers to work with, but none of you will manage risk full-time. In general, people are eyeing you either with confidence (though you've never before functioned in this role) or with cynicism, believing that nothing you do will make a difference. To top it off, your organization has no established risk management activity, so you can't simply follow procedure.

Where can you turn for guidance? Your first stop is the closest technical library, where you find a wealth of books and articles on risk management in general, and a few directed specifically at software. You breathe a sigh of relief: Surely there's a plan in here somewhere. But after traveling some distance down your new reading list you realize you've found plenty of theorizing and scant practical experience. You begin to wonder: What actually happened when programs like mine put this theory into practice? How did they come up with the risks they intended to manage? Which of the things they tried worked well? Which ones bombed?

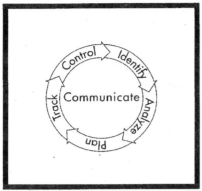

Figure 1. The SEI Risk Management Paradigm.

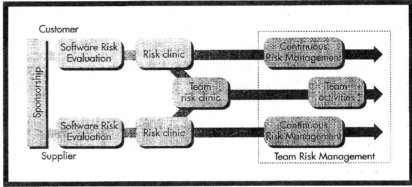

Figure 2. The risk management road map.

This article is about practical experience: lessons we learned working in the Software Engineering Institute's Risk Program with Department of Defense programs, at the customer and supplier levels (the program office and contractor project levels, respectively), for the past six years. These programs followed the SEI approach of continuous and team risk management, selecting processes and methods that would best fit their work cultures. Before evaluating their effectiveness, a little background.

THE SEI APPROACH TO RISK MANAGEMENT

The SEI established the Risk Program in 1990 to improve the risk management in DoD programs involving software-intensive systems. Although at that time risk management had been extensively addressed in other disciplines, little had been written about software risk management. The notable exceptions—the *IEEE Tutorial on Software Risk Management*[1] and Robert Charette's *Software Engineering Risk Analysis and Management*[2]—served as important guides as we began working with organizations to design risk management processes that they could successfully install and improve upon in their own work cultures. Our mission was and

is to identify risk management processes and methods that are practical and can be integrated into standard software project management processes.

Figure 1 shows the Risk Management Paradigm,[3] an elaboration of the classic "plan-do-check-act" cycle of project management that captured the initial SEI view of risk management. The paradigm differs from the classic cycle mainly in the "identify" step, in which risks are recorded for later analysis, and in the central hub, "communicate," in which issues and concerns that could affect the program's success are shared across all working levels.

CHARTING NEW TERRITORY

Although the Risk Management Paradigm continues to be useful as an overall guide to our work, we found that programs needed a more specific road map. Figure 2 shows the road map we now use for a complete installation of SEI risk management in a program that includes a customer and supplier organization.

The road map places SEI risk management focus activities—software risk evaluation, continuous risk management, and team risk management—in an appropriate sequence for the typical program. The road map is symmetrical: For

risk management to be successful, the customer and the supplier must continuously and independently manage their lists of risks. Although some risks will be managed jointly by the customer and the supplier, most remain with the organization that identified the risk.

Sponsorship. As Figure 2 shows, we emphasize sponsorship: For a risk management effort to succeed, your program must have the commitment of a suitably powerful individual—typically, the customer program manager. The sponsor must be visibly involved throughout the program's life cycle. (One of the surest ways for the sponsor to demonstrate continued support is simply to ask for the latest status of identified risks on a regular basis!)

Focus activities. The software risk evaluation is the risk program's initiating event. SRE generates a list of risk statements (typically 100 or more), evaluates them for probability and impact, classifies and ranks them in priority order, and lays out mitigation strategies for them. These risk statements are identified through a series of interviews using the SEI *Taxonomy of Software Development Risk* and *Taxonomy-Based Questionnaire*.[4] The SRE provides only a snapshot of the program risks; the ultimate challenge is to manage the risks as they arise through-

out the program's life cycle using continuous risk management (CRM) and team risk management (TRM).

The first step to that end is a *risk clinic*, conducted individually with the members of the customer and supplier work groups. In this extended workshop, the group's key leaders determine the best way to adapt and install methods and tools to support each phase of the SEI Risk Management Paradigm. CRM then continues the refinement of this risk management process.

The *team risk clinic* is similar to the work-group risk clinic, except that it establishes methods and tools for interorganizational risk management: between customer and supplier, and—beyond even that—among all organizations on which the program's success depends, such as users, subcontractors, and vendors. In this larger team environment ("team activities" in Figure 2) perspectives may be different, but it is a basic tenet of TRM that those committed to program success must understand all relevant perspectives and manage risks accordingly.

A TYPICAL INSTALLATION

Figure 3 shows one view of a typical SEI Risk Paradigm implementation. The risk management activities (shown in boxes) are carried out continuously. The risk and mitigation plan database serves as the information clearinghouse to support these risk management activities.

We'll use Figure 3 as a guide to show what we've found to be effective and ineffective in risk management. We begin at "identify new risks" and work our way around, concluding with a description of the database.

Identify new risks: *It's harder to ignore if it's written down.* The first step to successful risk management is to write down the risks and make them visible to all; the first step in making that happen is to define what a risk is in the first place.

According to the 1991 *American Heritage Dictionary*, risk is "the possibility of suffering harm or loss; danger." For programs with software-intensive systems under development, the harm or loss could be in the form of

- ♦ diminished quality of the product,
- ♦ increased costs,
- ♦ delayed completion, or
- ♦ total program failure.

Unfortunately, this definition alone does not necessarily help you find mitigation approaches for risks (that is, Where do you start? What do you do next?).

♦ Effective: Groups working with the SEI use a risk statement construct as a model for consistency. Risk statements are made up of a condition and at least one consequence of the condition. The condition is something perceived to be true today (it could be a problem, something neutral, or even a good thing) from which undesirable outcomes are expected. This model then becomes the benchmark for all new risks.

♦ Effective: An SRE is an effective one-time method of identifying risks. Nothing is more successful in getting managers interested in risks than a large list of 100 or more analyzed and priority-ordered risk statements. When such a list is shown to the entire work group in priority order, with an estimate of the risk exposure associated with each state-

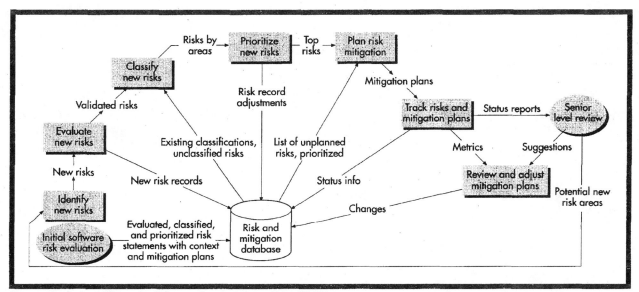

Figure 3. *A typical framework for a risk management installation.*

Risk ID	Risk statement	Priority	Probability	Impact	Assigned to	Status	Red flag
9	Potential slip in module translation schedule; will impact rest of system coding.	1	H	H	Smith	Mitigate	RED
99	Allocation of development hardware to sites doesn't match needs; delivery of modules from sited will be delayed.	2	H	H	Smith	Mitigate	RED
91	Display performance requirements not quantified; won't know if we'll pass acceptance testing.	3	H	H	Jones	Mitigate	
10	Integration Lab Time may not be sufficient, integration and test will be delayed or cut short.	4	H	M	Brown	Mitigate	
89	Contract authorities from different countries have different program objectives; may cause conflicts in priorities.	5	M	H	Jones	Mitigate	
1	Potential slip in module translation schedule; will impact rest of system coding.	6	H	H	Smith	Mitigate	
94	System impact of YYY display/timing/interface problems is not known; planned fix schedule may not have taken all issues into account.	7	H	M	Brown	Mitigate	
88	Government furnished equipment does not work; test schedule may be in jeopardy if GFE not repaired or replaced by the time testing begins.	8	H	M	Smith	Mitigate	
96	Potential slip in module translation schedule; will impact rest of system coding.		M	M			
13	Compiler bugs require vendor fixes (which may not come quickly enough); could delay coding.		L	M			
...							
87	New coders don't all have tool documentation; impacts their schedules to go looking for answers.		L	L			

Figure 4. A risk spreadsheet can help work groups summarize risk information for a number of risks. It shows the probability and impact of individual risks using a simple high (H), medium (M), low (L) rating system to establish the top n list. The "Red flag" category indicates that the mitigation plan is not working and action is required.

ment, people want to do something. Once it is on paper, a manager feels obligated to take action.

♦ Ineffective: Early on, some work groups used vaguely worded issues that were too easy to dismiss as impossible to prevent (such as, "We'll probably exceed our budget"). Others depended upon managers to recognize and articulate all possible problems. These managers may only foresee what their experiences have conditioned them to look for.

Evaluate new risks: *Qualitative or quantitative?* Some say you cannot adequately manage a risk if you cannot quantify its probability and impact. However, insistence on quantification can lead to a "paralysis of analysis" and a breakdown in communication about risk. There are of course cases when you can assess the probability of a future event and estimate its cost, but those instances are rare. Most of the risks we have helped groups identify were related to unstable requirements or personnel issues. None of the groups we've worked with had to quantify risk probability and impact— even for all of the top *n* risks—to effectively manage them.

♦ Effective: Work groups that use "quick and dirty" estimates (such as high, medium, or low impact) or categories such as "I really need to look at this now," "keep an eye on it," or "ignore it—it's not significant enough to justify doing anything." Unless the risk has a significant impact on the program (such as a year's delay in delivery), early quantification of impact and probability is unnecessary. For example, one group filtered out the top six risks for precise analysis during risk planning. Other risks were managed without further analysis.

♦ Ineffective: One group spent a day with four key individuals making a detailed quantitative assessment of probability and impact for one risk that had a worst-case impact of five days' work by one person and a 10 percent probability of occurrence. The group spent as many resources evaluating the risk as would have been spent if the risk had materialized.

Classify new risks: *The many faces of risk.* Risks come in all shapes and sizes. Typically, they are more complex than an individual risk statement and often encompass several. For example, with a single risk, a configuration manager might see an aspect that affects configuration management, a software engineer might see an aspect that affects component quality, and a project manager might see an aspect that affects the customer. Three different risk statements emerge, pointing to different aspects of the same risk. Classifying or grouping risk statements into categories based on shared characteristics can help you find global risks that can be solved together (three for the price of one).

♦ Effective: One project classified risks according to the system component it affected. They found a group of risk statements identified by different individuals over time that related to their compiler. Analysis of these risks led to the renegotiation of the vendor contract to significantly reduce *all* the risks at the same time.

♦ Ineffective: Separate mitigation teams on a project developed and put into place their own contingency plans, workarounds, and special tools to reduce the project's risk with respect to a support tool. They never sought or found a common solution and therefore wasted resources.

Classification around a common

ID	ABC 23	Risk Information Sheet	Identified 3/2/95

Priority	6	**Statement**
Probability	High	With our lack of experience in X Windows software, we may not be able to complete the GUI code on time and it may not be the quality of code we need.
Impact	High	

		Origin G. Smith	**Class** Personnel Experience	**Assigned to:** S. Jones
Timeframe	Near			

Context
The graphical user interface is an important part of the system and we do not have anyone trained in the X Window system. We all have been studying it, but it is complex and only one person in the group has any graphic/user interface experience and that was with a completely different type of system and interface requirements. There are other personnel within the company who have relevant experience and training, but they may not be available in time to support this project.

Mitigation Strategy
1. Update coding estimates and schedules to reflect the need for increased training and for hiring an expert in X Windows (changes due 5/1/95).
2. Coordinate with customer and get approval for changing schedule (approve by 6/1/95).
3. Identify an available expert from other projects in this division (hired by 6/15/95).
4. Bring in outside training source for current programmers (training complete by 7/30/95).

Contingency Plan and Trigger
Plan: Subcontract GUI development to LMN Corp. and accept the increase in our cost, $25,000. LMN has a level of effort contract with ABC Headquarters and can support with 1 week notice.
Trigger: If internal expert is not on board and training not completed by 7/30/95.

Status	**Status Date**
GUI code delivered on time, required quality.	1/30/96
GUI code has been delivered for testing on shedule.	11/13/95
Code 50% complete and 1 week ahead of schedule.	9/15/95
Personnel completed 2 week training; will monitor progress and quality of work.	7/15/95
Brown from project XYZ will be available on 6/5/95 to provide quality assurance, mentoring, and critical path programs.	6/1/95
Customer approved revised schedule milestones.	5/3/95
Revised estimates and schedule complete; indicates a worst-case 3 week slip if we get the addtitional expert.	4/23/95

Approval J.Q. Jones, ABC Project Manager	**Closing Date** 2/15/96	**Closing Rationale** Code delivered on time, Acceptance test excellent. Risk is gone.

Figure 5. A risk information sheet can help you document and monitor risk mitigation plans.

structure for all projects can provide an added bonus for the organization. It allows categorization, analysis, and retrieval of risk information from across projects, letting you identify common risks, successful (and unsuccessful) mitigation strategies, and organization-wide trends.

Prioritizing new risks: *Which risk first?* Your organization should deal with the most important risks first and decide how many of these it has the resources to mitigate. In general, groups new to risk management have trouble dealing with more than 10 risks. More experienced groups can better judge how much effort to spend on each risk and can thus deal with more.

♦ Effective: A work group created a prioritized list of risks with the top eight risks clearly identified and the remaining risks ordered according to the most recent evaluation of their probability and impact. They periodically reordered the top risks by voting or by using pairwise comparison techniques based on group consensus about the most important criterion at the time (such as quality or cost). An example of such a list is shown in Figure 4.

♦ Ineffective: A work group's weekly reprioritization of the top n risks resulted in constant thrashing, and some risks moved on and off the priority list. With limited mitigation resources, action on risks started and stopped in direct response to the changes in priority.

Plan risk mitigation: *You can't fix everything!* Not every risk can be mitigated; every condition has many possible consequences and each will create a risk that *could* be mitigated. Which are really important? You must identify critical risks and watch them for significant changes. You must identify which risks can be accepted (that is, you can live with them if they do become problems) and which risks can be assigned to someone who is better able to manage them.

♦ Effective: The Planning Flowchart[5] is a decisionmaking structure that helps a work group decide which risks on their list

they must mitigate and which can be handled by less resource-intensive means. The chart has a three-stage decision flow that assigns responsibility for the risk, determines an approach for dealing with it, and defines the mitigation plan's scope.

♦ Ineffective: A work group tried to plan most of the 100-plus risk statements from the SRE, including those with only minor probability and impact. The effort to develop plans for 50 minor risks was greater than the impact to the program if most had materialized.

To mitigate a risk, the goal (such as eliminate the risk or reduce its impact by 50 percent) and constraints (can you

delay delivery to ensure quality?) must be known. With these in mind, you can use problem solving and analytical techniques to develop strategies and guide your actions.

♦ Effective: Resolution can be a single action item (such as put everyone through training) or a complex, long-range prototyping effort. Mitigation plans can be action item lists or the equivalent of task plans. Figure 5 shows a risk information sheet,[5] which is one way to effectively document and monitor mitigation plans.

♦ Ineffective: Work groups making plans or agreements without any docu-

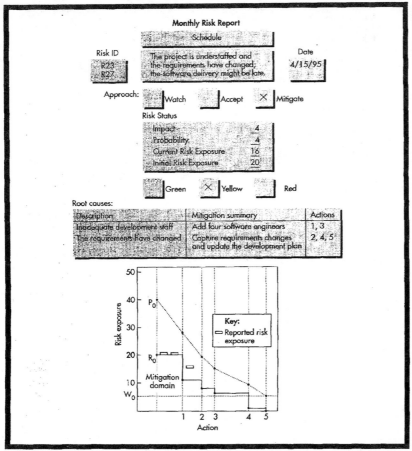

Monthly Risk Report

	Schedule	
Risk ID R23 R27	The project is understaffed and the requirements have changed; the software delivery might be late.	Date 4/15/95

Approach: ☐ Watch ☐ Accept ☒ Mitigate

Risk Status

Impact	4
Probability	4
Current Risk Exposure	16
Initial Risk Exposure	20

☐ Green ☒ Yellow ☐ Red

Root causes:

Description	Mitigation summary	Actions
Inadequate development staff	Add four software engineers	1, 3
The requirements have changed	Capture requirements changes and update the development plan	2, 4, 5

Figure 6. *The Mitigation Status Report uses colors—red, yellow, and green—to indicate the current success of mitigation actions. Green indicates the plan is working, yellow indicates the reported risk exposure is higher than expected (expectations are represented by the R_o step function) given completion of actions thus far, and red indicates that the current plan is not working as intended.*

mentation or follow-up.

Track risks and mitigation plans: *How do you know when the risk is gone?* Managers need good metrics to make good decisions about risks. Measures, indicators, triggers, and so on can help you watch for significant changes in the risk and its mitigation plan. If you have a clear mitigation goal, you should be able to determine when the mitigation effort is not

working. You can then either try something else or accept the risk.

♦ Effective: Work groups have found that spreadsheets summarize the project's risks well. Figure 4, for example, uses simple tracking metrics for each risk: subjective estimates of the current probability and impact and a "red" status indicating extreme criticality. However, for important risks you may need backup data, such as that shown in Figure 5.

♦ Effective: Complex tracking reports may be needed for critical risks. One effective portrayal of risk exposure vs. time is the Mitigation Status Report,[5] developed by one of our clients to monitor mitigation progress on critical risk. As Figure 6 shows, the reported "risk exposure" (probability × impact) remains below the "problem" threshold (line P_o) as mitigation actions are taken, but above the "watch only" (line W_o) threshold. Thus, you would continue to act upon this risk.

♦ Ineffective: One work group used verbal reports and no documentation—not even meeting minutes. By the end of the week they could not remember what they had done or which risks were still open.

Review and adjust mitigation plans: *Are you sure you can close it?* Closing a risk because you took an action, any action, is not controlling the risk—it is abdicating to the first thing that comes along. Controlling a risk means

♦ altering your mitigation strategy when it becomes ineffective,

♦ taking action on a risk that becomes important enough to require mitigation,

♦ taking a preplanned contingency action,

♦ dropping to a watch-only mode at a specific threshold, or

♦ closing the risk when it no longer exists.

So what if it seems that you really can put this risk behind you? There's information in what you've done that is useful for others—and the opportunity to mitigate the risk that you just might be wrong.

♦ Effective: Several work groups retained risk information in their database after the risks were closed. This information will be a tremendous benefit to the organization on future projects. One group also documented lessons learned: When a risk was closed, they captured a record documenting the rationale for closing, successful and unsuccessful actions, assumptions that were proven wrong, mitigation costs, and project savings or return on investment.

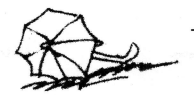

♦ Ineffective: One work group closed risks as soon as any mitigation activity was completed, without verifying the effect. One of these "closed" risks was identified as a new risk within a month. At that point, the potential impact to the program was even greater than before but circumstances had changed such that they could no longer prevent the problem. They thus lost their chance to mitigate the risk.

Risk and mitigation plan database: *Information is only useful if it's accessible and easy to understand.* You don't have to use electronic databases to implement and support risk management, but it is far more effective. Compared to paper-based risk-documentation systems, risk databases do require extra effort and time to set up. However, the database quickly repays the initial investment. Even better, using an existing database that conforms to a corporate standard supports corporate lessons learned. Papers will not be lost, nor will updates be forgotten. Managers can get immediate insight into how their projects stand with respect to risks ("How many critical risks have we mitigated? Which are left? Are we still identifying requirements risks when we've already started coding?").

♦ Effective: A work group captured all risk data and integrated it with other types of data, such as problem and safety reports. A variety of different reports (weekly summaries, complete information on each risk, condensed risk information for senior management, trending reports) presented the risk data in a meaningful way to various audiences. Having the data online and accessible to all personnel let them enter new risks as soon as they were identified.

♦ Ineffective: One program's access to their database was restricted to a single person who did all of the data entry and report generation. The ensuing information bottleneck resulted in a database that was hopelessly out of date, and risk communication broke down.

Signs of success. When you have effective risk management in place, you can focus your planning on avoiding future problems rather than solving current ones. You can routinely apply lessons learned to avoid crises in the future rather than fixing blame. You can evaluate activities in work plans for their effect on overall project risk, as well as on schedule and cost. You can structure important meeting agendas to discuss risks and their effects before discussing the specifics of technical approach and current status.

Above all else, you can achieve a free flow of information at and between all program levels, coordinated by a centralized system to capture the risks identified and the information about how they are analyzed, planned, tracked, and controlled. You can achieve this when risk is no longer treated as a four-letter word, but rather is used in your organization as a rallying perspective to arouse creative efforts.

With effective risk management, people recognize and deal with potential problems daily, before they occur, and produce the finest product they can within budget and schedule constraints. People, work groups, and projects throughout the program understand that they are building just one end product and have a shared vision of a successful outcome.

As shown in these examples, the SEI Risk Program has accumulated a rich store of lessons learned over the past six years. Even an effort that was not totally effective for a pilot project was a "win" for the organization and the software community because it provided experience for us to build on for the future.

Open communication about risks is central to the SEI Risk Management Paradigm and to the work of the software community as a whole. Each group's approach to risk and mitigation holds valuable lessons for us all.

At the SEI, we will continue to collect, develop, and refine processes, methods, and tools for managing risks, and we will continue to share them to help change software practice. But making these products practical requires the help of the entire community. Only by sharing experiences and best practices of risk management and participating enthusiastically in experimental risk management approaches can we develop the most effective methods for managing risk in our projects. ♦

ACKNOWLEDGMENTS

The authors extend special appreciation to the client personnel throughout the Risk Program's collaboration projects, whose support and participation contributed significantly to the successful development of the risk management processes, methods, and tools and provided the basis for this paper.

REFERENCES

1. B.W. Boehm, *IEEE Tutorial on Software Risk Management*, IEEE Computer Soc. Press, Los Alamitos, Calif., 1989.

2. R.N. Charette, *Software Engineering Risk Analysis and Management*, McGraw-Hill, New York, 1989.

3. R.L. Van Scoy, *Software Development Risk: Opportunity, Not Problem*, CMU/SEI-92-TR-30, ADA258743, SEI, Carnegie Mellon Univ., Pittsburgh, 1992, p. 9.

4. M. Carr et al., *Taxonomy-Based Risk Identification*, CMU/SEI-93-TR-6, ADA266992, SEI, Carnegie Mellon Univ., Pittsburgh, 1993.

5. A. Dorofee et al., *Continuous Risk Management Guidebook*, SEI, Carnegie Mellon Univ., Pittsburgh, 1996.

Ray C. Williams is a senior member of the technical staff in the SEI's Risk Program, where he leads the development of team risk management methods and tools. His interests are organization theory and executive decisionmaking. Before joining the SEI, he was a software project manager in the steel industry.

Williams received a BS in electrical engineering from Carnegie Mellon University and an MBA from the University of Pittsburgh.

Audrey J. Dorofee is a senior member of the technical staff in SEI's Risk Program, where she leads the development of continuous risk management methods and tools. Her interests include risk and project management. Before joining SEI, she was an engineer with several NASA programs.

Dorofee received a BS and an MS in computer science from Florida Institute of Technology and the University of Houston, respectively. She is a member of the IEEE and ACM.

Julie A. Walker is a member of the technical staff in SEI's Risk Program. Her responsibilities include developing risk management practices and supporting the risk management work with the program's collaboration partners. Her interests include decision and risk analysis.

Walker received a BS in mathematics from Clarkson University and an MS in systems engineering from the University of Virginia. She is a member of the Society for Risk Analysis.

Readers can address questions about this article to Williams at Software Engineering Institute, Carnegie Mellon University, 5000 Forbes Avenue, Pittsburgh, PA 15213-3890; rcw@sei.cmu.edu.

Reprinted from IEEE Software,
Mar./Apr. 1997, pp. 55-65.

Implementing Effective Software Metrics Programs

TRACY HALL, *University of Westminster*
NORMAN FENTON, *City University*

Increasingly, organizations are foregoing an ad hoc approach to metrics in favor of complete metrics programs. The authors identify consensus requirements for metric program success and examine how programs in two organizations measured up.

Until relatively recently, software measurement in the Western world has been a rather *ad hoc* affair focused on measuring individual, product-based software attributes. This rather one-dimensional approach to software measurement is now changing. Increasingly, organizations are integrating complete software metrics programs into their software development processes. That is, they are habitually using a balanced range of product and process measures in their micro and macro decision making systems.

There are several reasons that partially explain the recent move toward complete metrics programs. Not only has the process improvement bandwagon raised a general awareness of metrics, but to reach higher Capability Maturity Model levels, organizations must incorporate metrics into their development process. Moreover, there now appears to be consensus about the need for

0740-7459/97/$10.00 © 1997 IEEE

TABLE 1
ORGANIZATIONAL DETAIL

Characteristic	Embedded Systems	Information Systems
General profile	Engineering company	Large public-sector organization (in the process of transferring into the private sector)
Applications	Defense-related Embedded control software 90% of applications are safety-critical	Online data processing systems
Development environment	Variety of advanced approaches, including formal methods and code, analyzing tools	State-of-art in using new methods Keen on using project management methods and tools
Quality framework	Strong (on the surface), but suboptimal use of reviews and inspections AQAP certified (defense quality certificate)	Well-used framework Consistent use of basic quality controls In the process of seeking software quality certification
Management framework	Very complex staff structure Steep hierarchy Low morale score Two-year pay freeze High staff attrition rate	Simple staff structure Flattish hierarchy Average morale score Stable staff group

metrics programs within improvement initiatives.[1] However, perhaps the most important positive push for metrics programs was the publication of Robert Grady and Deborah Caswell's 1987 book, *Software Metrics: Establishing a Company Wide Program.*[2] The book—and its 1992 revision[3]—describes the Hewlett-Packard software metrics program. Grady and Caswell identify many important, and usually neglected, organizational issues surrounding software measurement. In particular, they proposed, along with other commentators,[3-5] various criteria for achieving a successful metrics program. After studying this and other research, we identified a consensus on requirements for metric program success.

♦ *Incremental implementation.* Implementing a metrics program over time holds significantly less risk than a "big bang" approach.

♦ *Transparency.* The metrics program must be obvious to practitioners. Practitioners must understand what data is being collected, why it is being collected, and how it is being used.

♦ *Usefulness.* The usefulness of metrics data should be obvious to all practitioners. If usefulness is not transparent (or, worse, if the data is not actually useful), practitioners will collect data

without enthusiasm and the data will probably lack validity.

♦ *Developer participation.* Developers should participate in designing the metrics program. With high levels of developer participation, buy-in is more likely, as is the implementation of a more incisive metrics program.

♦ *Metrics integrity.* Practitioners should have confidence in the collected data. They should believe it is sensible to collect, accurately collected, and not being "fiddled."

♦ *Feedback.* When practitioners get feedback on the data they collect, it gives them a clear indication that the data is being used rather than going into a black hole. This makes practitioners more likely to view the program positively. Commentators suggest several feedback mechanisms including newsletters, newsgroups, and graphical posters.

♦ *Automated data collection.* This should be done wherever possible. Minimizing extra work for developers also minimizes developer resistance to metrics. It also means that the data collected is more likely to be valid.

♦ *Practitioner training.* Case studies show that a metrics program that has a base of trained practitioners is more likely to be successful. Appropriate training must be targeted at all levels in

a company and should range from awareness raising to training in statistical analysis techniques.

♦ *Gurus and champions.* Organizations can increase practitioners' initial enthusiasm by bringing in an external metrics guru (Hewlett-Packard, for example, brought in Barry Boehm; Contel brought in Dieter Rombach). Organizations should also appoint internal metrics champions to help with the difficult and arduous task of sustaining a metrics program.[6]

♦ *Dedicated metrics team.* Responsibility for the metrics program should be assigned to specific individuals.

♦ *Goal-oriented approach.* It is very important that companies collect data for a specific purpose. Usually the data will be for monitoring the attainment of an improvement goal. Unsuccessful or ineffective programs collect data for no specific reason and find they have no use for the data they have collected. The Goal-Question-Metric model[7] has been highly popular among companies implementing a goal-oriented approach to measurement.

On the last two factors, the broader software engineering community does not entirely agree. Although there is consensus on the need for some kind of dedicated metrics team, there is no clear agreement on how

Organization	Staff Directly Affected by Metrics Program	Number Responding to Questionnaire			Response Rate (%)
		Total	Manager	Developer	
Embedded systems	24	20	10	10	83
Information systems	125	103	48	55	82

TABLE 2
RELEVANT STAFF AND RESPONSE RATE

centralized it should be, nor whether metrics should be the team's sole activity. Questions have also been raised about the GQM approach.[8] For example, Hetzel highlights the fact that GQM encourages organizations to use data that is likely to be difficult to collect.[9] This directly contradicts other advice on metrics programs, which encourages organizations to use available or easily collected data.

Notwithstanding these minor doubts, the factors above appear to be commonsense advice on implementing a metrics program. However, these factors are apparently proposed on the basis of either anecdotal evidence or single program experiences.

We spent six months conducting an independent study of these factors at work in two organizations. Here, we present quantitative data that describes practitioner experiences of metrication. This data generally supports—but occasionally contradicts—existing anecdotal evidence about metrics programs.

Although both of our case study programs were structurally similar, one was judged to be successful (by the organization and by us), and the other was judged as not yet successful (by the organization's metrics group and by us). Despite the fact that anecdotal evidence suggests that most metrics programs are unsuccessful, with a few notable exceptions (such as a 1993 study by Ross Jeffery and Mike Berry[10]), only successful programs are typically reported.

Our ultimate aim in this article,

which follows on our earlier work,[11] is to present the critical success and failure factors associated with the two metrics programs. In particular, we report on each organization's metrics implementation strategy, quantify the extent to which they implemented various metrics, and detail the ongoing management of the metrics programs.

THE STUDY

Our case study involved two organizations which, for reasons of commercial confidentiality, we refer to as Embedded Systems (ES) and Information Systems (IS). Both organizations
♦ have more than 10,000 employees, are more than 20 years old, and have complex internal bureaucracies;
♦ have a large software development function, with more than 400 software staff; •
♦ are fully dependent on in-house software systems to support or enhance their main (nonsoftware) products;
♦ have a progressive approach toward new development methods and tools;
♦ have mature quality programs and usually consider the software they produce to be high quality; and
♦ have had a metrics program for between two and three years.
Some metricating success or failure factors may result from organization-specific issues; Table 1 gives the organizational context of each metrics program.

Phase one: fact finding. At each organi-

zation, we started with a few fact-finding interviews with middle managers who had a high level of corporate responsibility for the metrics program. We designed this fact-finding phase to identify the context, framework, and content of the "officially" implemented metrics program. Managers commonly have an inaccurate picture of what is really happening "on the ground." Thus, we designed this phase to establish what state the organization believed its metrics program to be in. In particular, we found out about the organization (such as number of employees in various activities), applications developed, development environment, metrics collected and how they were used, and implementation and management of metrics. We used the results of phase one as a baseline for phase two.

Phase two: data collection. In phase two we wanted to find out what was really happening in the metrics program. We managed to get serious input from nearly all the relevant staff by distributing detailed questionnaires to all managers and developers affected by metrics.

The aims of the questionnaire were to
♦ identify which metrics were really being collected (as opposed to the ones managers believed were being collected),
♦ find out how the metrics program was initially implemented and subsequently managed,
♦ establish the contributions that individuals and groups made to metrics, and

TABLE 3
IMPLEMENTATION FACTORS

Implementation Factors	ES	IS
Consensus recommendations		
Incremental implementation	✓	✗
Well-planned metrics framework	✓	✗
Use of existing metrics materials	✓	✗
Involvement of developers during implementation	✓	✗
Measurement process transparent to developers	✓	✗
Usefulness of metrics data	✓	✗
Feedback to developers	✓	✗
Ensure that the data is seen to have integrity	✓	✗
Measurement data is used and seen to be used	✓	✗
Commitment from project managers secured	✓	✗
Use automated data collection tools	✓	✗
Constantly improving the measurement program	✓	✗
Internal metrics champions used to manage the program	✓	✗
Use of external metrics gurus	✗	✗
Provision of training for practitioner	✗	✗
Other Recommendations		
Implement at a level local to the developers	✓	✗
Implement a central metrics function	✗	✓
Metrics responsibility devolved to the development teams	✓	✗
Incremental determination of the metrics set	✓	✗
Collecting data that is easy to collect	✗	✗

Key: ✓ shows that the recommendation is followed; ✗ shows that it is not

♦ solicit views and experiences of the success and value of metrics.

As Table 2 shows, we had an overall response rate of 83 percent. Thus, almost everyone affected by the metrics programs at both organizations contributed to this study: 24 practitioners at ES and 125 at IS. (ES implemented metrics in only one critical department whereas IS implemented metrics throughout software development.)

Our high response rate can likely be attributed to several factors.

♦ *Topicality.* Although both metrics programs were maturing, neither was long established. Thus, metrics was still a hot issue in both organizations, and practitioners had a lot they wanted to say about it.

♦ *Desire for evaluation and improvement:* In both organizations, metrics program managers fully and publicly supported our study. Because they had not formally evaluated the metrics programs themselves, they were keen to find out their practitioners' views. Developers also seemed keen to contribute, perhaps thinking their contribution might improve the metrics program.

♦ *Independence of the study:* Practitioners were confident that their views could not be used against them by management, and, thus, we suspect, were more open and honest in their contributions.

Because of our high response rate, we're confident that our results are an accurate representation of each organization's metrics program. However, this was not a controlled experiment and does not assess each factor's impact on metrics program success. Moreover, although it would be wrong to generalize results from a case study to the industry as a whole,[12] we believe our results offer many interesting insights that are relevant and applicable to other metricating organizations.

STUDY RESULTS

At both organizations, metric program managers agreed that good metrics implementation was important. Still, as Table 3 shows, they ignored experts' key recommendations discussed above, although ES adhered to more of the proposed success factors than IS did. And, indeed, ES's metrics program was the successful one. Now the details.

Introducing metrics. No comprehensive international survey has quantified the industrial penetration of metrics since the Drummond-Tyler study.[13] Indeed, influential software commentators disagree about the extent to which metrics have penetrated the software industry. For example, Capers Jones claims an encouraging industry-wide use of measures such as function points,[14] while Bill Hetzel is much less optimistic.[9]

Measurement was initially introduced at ES only because they were given external funding to field test the Application of Metrics in Industry (ami) approach to metrication.[1] Ami combines CMM with the Goal-Question-Metric method. With it, you use the SEI CMM questionnaire to establish process maturity, then use GQM to identify metrics that are appropriate for your organization's maturity level.

Although not particularly motivated at the start, ES quickly discovered the value of metrics and implemented the

MARCH/APRIL 1997

program reasonably well. Metrics were implemented initially only in one development team, which meant that the metrics program was very close to the developers and could be tightly controlled by the managers.

Metrics implementation at IS was weak. The initial motivation for implementing metrics was that senior managers wanted to monitor productivity. Other studies have shown that weak motivations like this are commonplace, although the relationship between weak motivations and program failure is not clear.

IS set up a centralized metrics group to introduce metrics across the whole development function. There was no discernible use of metrication aids, nor was metrics use piloted. The implementation strategy seemed to consist solely of the metrics group instructing the development departments to start collecting specified metrics.

Developer involvement. Although managers were very involved in metrics design in both organizations, IS had little developer input into the design process. Interestingly, managers at both organizations thought developers were more involved in metrics design than developers said they were: 60 percent of managers—compared to 20 percent of developers—thought metrics design at ES was a joint effort, while 27 percent of managers and 4 percent of developers at IS thought the same.

Goal clarity. We asked practitioners to rank five software development goals according to their organization's priorities and their own. A score of 1 was awarded for the most important goal and 5 for the least important goal. Table 4 shows practitioner perception of the organization's goals. Clearly, neither ES nor IS was good at communicating development goals to their employees.

These poor results are surprising considering that ES was actively using GQM (though the model does not address the method of identifying and disseminating goals). There was, however, much less disagreement when practitioners were asked to rank their own personal goals (and not everyone ranked low costs as their least important goal).

Usefulness. As Table 5 shows, practitioners were generally positive about the usefulness of metrics, although the practitioners at ES were more positive than those at IS (90 percent of ES practitioners and 59 percent of IS prac-

TABLE 4
RANKING SOFTWARE GOALS

Embedded Systems				Information Systems			
Perceived Organizational Goals	Mean Scores			Perceived Organizational Goals	Mean Scores		
	Overall	Managers	Developers		Overall	Managers	Developers
Low costs	2.5	2.2	2.8	User satisfaction	2.6	2.6	2.6
Conformance	2.9	2.6	3.2	Speed	2.9	2.9	2.8
Speed	3.0	3.0	3.0	Reliability	3.0	3.0	3.0
Reliability	3.1	3.6	2.6	Conformance	3.1	3.2	3.1
User satisfaction	3.5	3.6	3.4	Low costs	3.4	3.3	3.5

TABLE 5
USEFULNESS OF METRICS

Metrics Usefulness	Embedded Systems			Information Systems		
	Overall	Managers	Developers	Overall	Managers	Developers
Very useful	30	40	20	15	22	9
Quite useful	60	60	60	44	50	41
Not very useful	10	0	20	25	18	30
Not useful at all	0	0	0	10	9	11
Don't know	0	0	0	7	1	10

TABLE 6
METRICS EFFICACY AND INTEGRITY

	Embedded Systems			Information Systems		
	Overall (%)	Managers (%)	Developers (%)	Overall (%)	Managers (%)	Developers (%)
1. *Is the data collected accurately?*						
Accurate	40	60	20	18	31	8
Not accurate	10	10	10	41	39	43
Don't know	50	30	70	41	29	50
2. *Metrics feedback?*						
Feedback is provided	30	50	10	18	25	11
Feedback is not provided	15	20	10	53	56	50
Don't know	55	30	80	29	19	39
3. *Is the right data collected?*						
Yes	40	60	20	11	13	10
No	10	0	20	46	48	44
Don't know	50	40	60	43	39	44
4. *Is the data manipulated?*						
Often	20	20	20	27	29	26
Occasionally	40	30	50	50	58	41
Never	5	10	0	1	0	2
Don't know	35	40	30	22	13	31
5. *Who manipulates the data?*						
Developers	5	0	10	15	21	9
Managers	35	40	30	40	42	39
Neither	5	10	0	2	2	2
Both	20	20	20	22	24	20
Don't know	35	30	40	20	10	30

titioners thought metrics were very useful or quite useful).

Table 6 shows practitioner confidence in each organization's metrics program. Once again, the metrics program at ES was received much more positively than the metrics program at IS. However, as the table also shows, most practitioners at both organizations were convinced that the metrics data was manipulated. Follow-up research suggests the practitioners were convinced that data was "massaged" (usually by managers) to make a situation look better than it actually was.

We also found a clear difference in metrics feedback between ES and IS. At ES, 30 percent of practitioners said feedback was provided, compared with only 18 percent at IS. Still, uncertainty reigned: 55 percent of ES practitioners and 29 percent of those at IS said they didn't know if their organization provided feedback or not.

Overall results. The approach adopted by each organization gives us a particu-lar insight into GQM, which forces an incremental approach to identifying a metrics set. GQM thus complimented ES's incremental implementation strategy and helped it avoid problems, such as lack of transparency and developer buy-in.

IS used neither GQM nor data that was easily available. They had many problems with their metrics program. IS's approach to identifying a metrics set lacked a clear strategy. Whether GQM is being used or not, an organization must provide its practitioners a clear use for the data they collect. IS did not do this. Further, there must be a clear link between the metrics and improvement goals. If this relationship is not obvious, practitioners lack motivation to put effort into metrics collection. The validity of the data collected is thus compromised.

Our results also gave us interesting insight into the nature of metrics feedback. Practitioners at ES were reasonably satisfied with metrics feedback whereas practitioners at IS were not at all satisfied. At ES, only 15 percent said they did not get feedback, as opposed to 53 percent of IS respondents. This surprised program managers at both organizations.

Before our study, IS managers felt confident that formal feedback mechanisms were in place (although they had not properly evaluated the effectiveness of these mechanisms). Since the study, managers at IS have taken steps to improve metrics feedback.

Managers at ES were surprised at how relatively satisfied practitioners seemed to be with feedback, as they had few formal feedback mechanisms. They did, however, use metrics on a day-to-day basis and regularly discussed results informally. ES also operated an open-house policy for metrics data. Thus, although metrics results were not formally distributed or displayed, practitioners did have access to the data. On the other hand, the program may have been an even greater success if ES had provided more formal feedback.

Finally, many practitioners marked

MARCH/APRIL 1997

"Don't Know" when asked about aspects of metrication. Even at ES, where the metrics program was well established and apparently successful, many practitioners did not know, for example, whether metrics data was accurate or if the right data was collected. Practitioner ignorance was a weak spot in both programs. However, practitioners had strong views on some aspects of metrication, indicating better communication and higher practitioner interest. On metric usefulness, for example, few practitioners responded with "don't know."

EMERGING CRITERIA

In addition to the expert recommendations discussed so far, there are other, broader ways to assess a metrics program. Among the most important we identified were metrics collection effort, metrics selection, practitioner awareness, and practitioner attitude.

Choosing metrics. Table 7 quantifies the extent to which each organization collected various metrics data. The table lists a subset of the measures con-

tained in the official metrics programs. IS's metrics list included several other measures and was considerably longer than the ES list.

We determined the most frequently used metrics in each organization based upon the activity levels in Table 7. For ES, the core metrics were
♦ resource estimates,
♦ lines of code,
♦ design review data, and
♦ code complexity data.
For IS, the core metrics were
♦ resource estimates,

TABLE 7
METRICS PENETRATION LEVELS

| | Total | | | | Manager | | | | Developer | | | |
| | Question One | | Question Two | | Question One | | Question Two | | Question One | | Question Two | |
	ES	IS	ES	IS	ES	IS	ES	IS	ES	IS	ES	IS
Function points†	-	86	-	15	-	87	-	19	-	85	-	11
Metrics for size estimates*	85	50	40	11	90	57	60	13	80	44	20	9
Metrics for cost estimates*	90	80	30	26	90	85	50	56	90	76	10	7
Metrics for effort estimates*	70	65	35	27	90	77	60	42	50	54	10	13
Analysis inspection data	40	35	10	8	50	41	20	13	30	30	0	4
Design review data	75	39	25	8	80	44	50	10	70	34	0	6
Design effort data	40	31	20	9	50	40	30	11	30	23	10	7
Code interface data	65	16	20	5	60	13	30	4	70	19	10	6
Code complexity data	70	7	20	0	90	8	30	0	50	6	10	0
Lines of code data	80	43	25	12	100	52	40	19	60	35	10	7
Coding effort data	45	20	10	12	70	49	20	19	20	26	0	6
Code inspection data	30	29	15	7	40	38	20	10	20	22	10	4
Fault rates	25	14	10	2	20	15	10	4	30	13	10	0
Defect densities	20	15	10	3	30	23	20	4	10	9	0	2
Change data	60	28	20	5	70	32	30	6	50	24	10	4
Testing effort data	40	31	10	7	60	49	20	13	20	15	0	2
Test review data	65	25	20	6	70	34	30	11	60	17	10	2

Key: Each entry represents the percentage of respondents answering "yes" to the following questions:
Question One: *Does your organization collect the following metrics data?*
Question Two: *Do you know, from personal involvement, that the following metrics data is collected?*

† = IS practitioners were very keen on function points, so we asked them separately about function point penetration.
* = We asked only about fairly general metrics in order to avoid fragmenting the results.

- function points, and
- lines of code.

Although ES was generally more active in its metrics activity, both orga-

> **Data cannot be used to motivate productivity if people do not know it is being collected.**

nizations favored a typical set of core metrics, dominated by size and effort metrics—primarily used for resource estimation and productivity measurement—rather than quality metrics. This result supports other research and runs contrary to the advice of all commentators. Overemphasis on cost-oriented data is probably another common fault of many metrics programs.

Collection effort. There is little explicit discussion in the literature about what constitutes a reasonable overhead for a metrics program, although 7 percent overall has been suggested as an average effort overhead.[15] In our study, neither program appeared to have a large effort overhead. At ES, 90 percent of practitioners said they spent less than 3 percent of their time on metrics-related activity, with the remaining 10 percent spending between 3 and 14 percent. At IS, 79 percent spent less than 3 percent, 16 percent spent between 3 and 14 percent, and 4 percent spent between 14 and 29 percent of their time on metrics activities. The fact that practitioners at ES spent less time collecting metrics data than practitioners at IS was probably because ES used automated tools.

Ironically, IS was not as effective at metricating as ES, and yet spent more effort on its metrics program. Part of this was because IS was collecting more metrics data. It is also likely that some of the IS metrics were not needed or used.

As Table 7 shows, managers at both organizations were more personally involved in metrics collection than developers, although ES had a higher overall participation level than IS. Also, while ES had a successful metrics program, there was minimal developer involvement in data collection. This is because the ES program was deliberately driven by managers and used automated data collection. The metrics program at IS seemed generally inactive, with few managers or developers directly participating in metrics collection. Indeed only 19 percent of IS managers and 7 percent of its developers said they knew from personal involvement that LOC data was collected. (IS's program did not use any special-purpose automated metrics collection tools and was largely paper-based.)

These results suggest that it is important for practitioners to know what is going on in the metrics program, but that personal involvement in collection is not very important. This finding supports other experiential reports[4,16] in which using automated tools and keeping practitioners informed seem like necessary prerequisites to metrics success.

Table 7 also shows that although ES had the most active metrics program, it lacked clarity and goal orientation in two areas.

- *Poor transparency.* Although 70 percent of ES managers said that coding effort data was collected, only 20 percent of developers knew this and no developers claimed to be involved in collecting this data. It is difficult to understand how accurate data can be collected over the life cycle without developer participation (although they may not have realized that time sheets are used for collecting coding effort data). It is also difficult to understand the purpose of collecting such data if developers do not know that it is required. It cannot be used to motivate productivity if people do not know it is being collected.

- *Poor goal-metric coupling.* Although 90 percent of managers said code complexity data was collected, only 50 percent of developers realized this and very few managers or developers were involved in collecting it. The main purpose of collecting complexity data is to control complexity. If developers do not know that complexity data is being collected, they are unlikely to take reducing complexity seriously. It also makes collecting complexity data ineffective.

Practitioner awareness. We analyzed metrics activity in terms of what practitioners knew about the measurement and how involved they were in collecting the data. Our rationale was that, although there may be an *official* metrics program in place, unless practitioners are aware of that program and see themselves as involved in it, the organization has not created the necessary measurement culture and the program is likely to be ineffective. Indeed, many of the metrics cited by both organizations as part of their "official" metrics program were so little known about and used that it is difficult to accept that they were an actual part of the metrics programs.

As Table 7 shows, ES had consistently more metrics activity than IS among both managers and developers. Although the official metrics program at IS contained many measures, awareness of these measures was generally low. Although there was a higher general level of awareness at ES, the awareness gap between managers and developers was lower at IS (an average 13-percent difference between managers' and developers' metrics awareness levels at IS and a 20 percent difference at ES). LOC metrics are a good illustration of this awareness gap: 100 percent of managers and 60 percent of developers at ES knew that lines of code data was collected (an awareness gap of 40 percentage points) compared with 52 percent of managers and 35 percent of developers at IS (an awareness gap of

112

17 percentage points).

Generally, practitioners at both organizations exhibited poor awareness of what was happening to review and inspection data. Both organizations used reviews and inspections regularly; the review process can be a rich source of metrics data. As Table 7 shows, the use of this data was not obvious to managers or developers at either organization, thus suggesting that the data was being used suboptimally. This is probably a common metrication weakness and is another example of organizations not heeding the published experiential advice.

Practitioner attitude. One of the most important factors in metrics program success is practitioner attitude: If you fail to generate positive feelings toward the program, you seriously undermine your likelihood of success. As Table 5 shows, in general, ES practitioners were more positive about metrics use than those at IS.

A significant influence on attitude towards metrics was job seniority. In both organizations, managers were much more positive than developers about metrics use, introduction, and management. Furthermore, the more senior managers were, the more enthusiastic they were about using metrics. At IS, for example, 87 percent of senior managers were positive about metrics compared to 72 percent of middle managers and 45 percent of junior analysts and programmers.

However, we also found that developers were more positive about metrics than conventional wisdom has led us to believe (Tom DeMarco suspected this was this case.[5]) It is generally thought, especially by managers, that developers are unenthusiastic about quality mechanisms like metrics and cannot see their value. Our results actually show that 80 percent of ES developers and 50 percent of IS developers were positive about metrics use.

It has been said that when develop-ers are asked their opinion about software quality mechanisms, they say such things are useful, but when they're asked to participate they find many reasons why their work must be exempt. This could explain the positive attitudes toward metrics that we found in this study. If this is the case—and developers are only positive about metrics in the abstract—then organizations need to work toward realizing this positive potential. In any case, the relationship between positive perceptions and negative action warrants more research.

Table 5 supports our view that practitioners' perceptions of metrics are strongly influenced by the reality of their metrics program rather than vice versa. If this were not the case, we would expect a stronger alignment between developer and manager views between the organizations. In fact, the table shows that practitioner perceptions varied significantly, even though within each organization the perception patterns of managers and developers were very similar. This has important implications for managers: it means that what practitioners think about metrics and how they respond to them is within managers' control. Too frequently, managers assume that developers will be negative about metrics *per se*. Our results suggest that developer attitudes are built upon experience.

The integrity of metrics data also seems to have a powerful influence on practitioner attitudes, as Table 6 shows. Managers at both organizations were significantly more convinced than developers that

♦ the data collected was accurate,
♦ enough metrics feedback was provided, and
♦ the right metrics data was collected.

Such a manager/developer perception gap is troublesome. For an effective metrics program, it is important that the metrics data not only has integrity, but that developers believe that it has. Our study has not yet examined the integrity of the ES and IS metrics data, so we do not know whether the data has integrity or not. We do know, however, that many practitioners affected by metrics do not believe that the data has integrity. This perception will probably do more damage than if the data has no integrity but practitioners believe that it does. As Tables 5 and 6 show, ES developers were less negative overall about the integrity of metrics data and more positive about using metrics.

There are two probable explanations for the manager/developer perception gap that we observed. First, managers probably have more access to metrics information and data. So, for example, they probably have more feedback and are probably in a better position to judge data accuracy. Second, managers in both organizations were more actively involved in setting up and managing the metrics programs. Consequently, they are less likely to criticize something they were instrumental in setting up. This gap may be compounded by the fact that no metrics evaluations had taken place at either organization and so managers may have been unaware of the problems our study uncovered.

> **What practitioners think about metrics and how they respond to them is within the managers' control.**

EPILOGUE

These case studies form part of a continuing longitudinal study into the quality and measurement programs in several major UK organizations. As

such, we continue to monitor the ES and IS metrics programs.

Our results were taken very seriously by the metrics managers at IS. Since we conducted the study two years ago, IS has either rectified, or is in the process of rectifying, many of the weaknesses we identified in its metrics programs. The program has radically improved, both because of our findings and because IS has since been taken over by a company with a more established quality and measurement regime. In particular, the IS program has been improved in the following ways:

♦ Metrics responsibility has been devolved to individual development teams and is thus much more local to developers.

♦ The centralized metrics group now acts in a more advisory rather than managerial role.

♦ Managers have made a big effort to improve transparency and feedback within the program.

♦ The actual metrics set has also been revised and is now smaller and more goal-focused, addressing the basic areas of effort, size, change, defects, and duration.

The metrics program at ES continues to be carefully managed and improved in an incremental way. The metrics set has been refined and some metrics are no longer collected. The program is viewed by ES senior managers as so successful that it is now in the process of being rolled out to all other software teams in the organization.

Neither organization has divulged to us metrics data about software quality. Thus, even at this stage, it is impossible for us to report on how the quality of software produced by ES compares to that produced by IS.

Our study confirmed that the success of a metrics program depends upon a carefully planned implementation strategy. We also found that the consensus "success" factors in the literature are generally correct, but that the advice is not always heeded. Success seems particularly linked to an organization's willingness to

♦ do background research on other metrics programs and use advice given in the published experiential reports,

♦ involve developers in metrics program design and inform them on the program's development and progress,

♦ use an incremental approach to implementation and run a pilot of the metrics program, and

♦ acknowledge developer concerns about metrics data use.

Also, in our study both metrics programs could have benefited from earlier and regular evaluations.

In contemplating the two programs, we suspect that one of the most important but intangible success factors is the approach and attitude of metrics program managers. The successful program was managed with a tenacious commitment to see metrics work. In contrast, the unsuccessful program seemed half-hearted, despite the fact that it was ambitious and expensive to implement. Indeed, at the outset, the odds were probably stacked against the successful organization: it had a weaker quality framework and lower staff morale. This suggests that organizations implementing metrics not only need to make use of the good practices, but must manage those programs with a certain amount of gusto. ♦

REFERENCES

1. *Metric Users Handbook*, ami Consortium, South Bank Univ., London, 1992.
2. R.B. Grady and D.L. Caswell, *Software Metrics: Establishing a Company-Wide Program*, Prentice Hall, Englewood Cliffs, N.J., 1987.
3. R.B. Grady, *Practical Software Metrics for Project Management and Process Improvement*, Prentice Hall, Englewood Cliffs, N.J., 1992.
4. S.L. Pfleeger, "Lessons Learned in Building a Corporate Metrics Program," *IEEE Software*, May 1993, pp. 67-74.
5. T. DeMarco, *Controlling Software Projects*, Prentice Hall, Englewood Cliffs, N.J., 1982.
6. G. Cox, "Sustaining a Metrics Program in Industry," *Software Reliability and Metrics*, N.E. Fenton and B. Littlewood, eds., Elsevier, New York, 1991, pp. 1-15.
7. V.R. Basili and H.D. Rombach, "The TAME Project: Towards Improvement-Oriented Software Environments," *IEEE Trans. Software Eng.*, Vol. 14, No. 6, 1988, pp. 758-773.
8. R. Bache and M. Neil, "Introducing Metrics into Industry: A Perspective on GQM," *Software Quality, Assurance and Measurement: A Worldwide Perspective*, N.E. Fenton et al., eds., Int'l Thompson Computer Press, London, 1995.
9. W.C. Hetzel, *Making Software Measurement Work: Building an Effective Software Measurement Programme,"* QED, Wellesley, Mass., 1993.
10. R. Jefferey and M. Berry, "A Framework for Evaluation and Prediction of Metrics Program Success," *1st Int'l Software Metrics Symp.*, IEEE Computer Soc. Press, Los Alamitos, Calif., 1993, pp. 28-39.
11. T. Hall and N.E. Fenton, "Implementing Software Metrics—The Critical Success Factors," *Software Quality J.*, Jan. 1994, pp. 195-208.
12. B. Kitchenham, L. Pickard, and S.L. Pfleeger, "Case Studies for Method and Tool Evaluation," *IEEE Software*, July 1995, pp. 52-63.
13. E. Drummond-Tyler, *Software Metrics: An International Survey of Industrial Practice*, Esprit 2 Project Metkit Sema Group, South Bank Univ., London, 1989.
14. C. Jones, *Applied Software Measurement*, McGraw-Hill, New York, 1991.
15. D.H. Rombach, V.R. Basili, and R.W. Selby, *Experimental Software Engineering Issues*, Springer Verlag, Berlin, 1993.
16. M.K. Daskalantonakis, "A Practical View of Software Management and Implementation Experiences within Motorola," *IEEE Trans. Software Eng.*, Vol. 18, No. 11, 1992, pp. 998-1009.

114

Tracy Hall is a senior lecturer in software engineering at the University of Westminster, UK. Her research interests center around quality and measurement in software engineering.

Hall received a BA and MSc from Teesside University and is studying for a doctorate at City University, London.

Norman Fenton is a chartered engineer and a professor of computing science at the Centre for Software Reliability, City University, London. His research interests are in software metrics, safety-critical systems, and formal development methods.

Reprinted from IEEE Software,
Mar./Apr. 1999, pp. 21-29.

Experience Report

An organized, comprehensive metrics program can bring order to the chaos of small-project management and form the foundation for a concerted process improvement effort. The authors describe their experience in applying metrics to one such US Army organization.

Metrics for Small Projects: Experiences at the SED

Ross Grable, US Army Missile Command

Jacquelyn Jernigan, Casey Pogue, and Dale Divis, Tennessee Applied Physical Sciences, Inc.

The Software Engineering Directorate of the Research, Development, and Engineering Center at the US Army Missile Command designs, builds, and maintains small embedded applications. These projects consist of 10,000 to 50,000 lines of source code. Some SED projects also address larger systems in their sustainment phase, which often require modifications or enhancements to only a small percentage of the overall code per build.

Organizations such as the SED that produce and maintain many small embedded application software packages can benefit from a well-organized metrics program. Since the SED's emergence in 1984, software metrics have played an increasing role in the organization's development process. Before undertaking a concerted effort to coordinate its software metrics process, the SED had inaccurate, inconsistent data reported with no validation of usefulness or relevance. There was little respect or insight into the value of the metrics or measuring process, and virtually no return on the investment of time spent in data collection.

Although earlier attempts were unsuccessful, the SED has established an organization-wide metrics program that has been functioning successfully for over a year.

FROM THE TRENCHES: Wolfgang B. Strigel, editor • wstrigel@spc.ca

Most IEEE Software *submissions are experience stories from academia or from fairly large companies. Articles from small companies are very rare, especially when it comes to experience reports on process improvement. This article is one of the few that describes attempts to introduce some process improvements in small companies.*

Although the results are based on limited sample sets, they demonstrate that even in the smallest of development organizations a sensible approach to metrics can yield useful results. In this case, the results were helpful because the experiments were highly goal-oriented. The goals had a practical purpose and allowed the companies to learn something they could use for future improvements.

Provided metrics are collected with clear goals in mind, whether in large companies with sophisticated processes or in small ad hoc development environments, the results can give valuable insight into the success of improvement work. One lesson I learned from this article is that the mere existence of measurements leads to communication and discussion of results, which in turn enables teams to become more aware of key success factors in their work. Even if this was the only outcome, I believe it shows it is worth it to start taking some measurements.

—Wolfgang Strigel, From the Trenches editor

METRICS AT THE SED

In the SED's earlier days, development teams periodically performed panic collections of each day's code output for approximately 50 ongoing projects. The data collected was inconsistent, unreliable, and incomplete. After these early efforts, tactical missile projects began using standardized metrics for management briefings.[1] These metrics consisted of the number of people on the project, progress of the development phase, use of the target computer resources, analysis of schedule risk, resolution of trouble reports, number of delivered software projects, and supportability of software maintenance. Cooperation, completeness, and accuracy problems plagued the collection effort even though project leads presented some useful information in the quarterly progress review meetings. Scattered experiments performed on special pilot projects measured the complexity of, and effort devoted to, software developed in-house. However, the SED still lacked a coordinated effort to collect and analyze metrics data throughout the organization. Only with concerted effort and upper-management involvement did a useful software metrics program emerge.

These early attempts at metric collection, although they fostered no great revelations, taught the organization important lessons:

♦ Most project engineers routinely collected some kind of tracking data, yet resisted the imposition of centralized data collection.

♦ Project personnel expressed concern that the data collected would be used to assess individuals negatively.

♦ Project leaders expressed concern about the time taken from software development activities to collect metrics.

♦ Project leaders expressed concern about how the collected data would reflect poorly on their projects when compared to the data from other projects.

♦ Management and policy makers appreciated and used simple presentations of analysis results, such as pie charts or red-amber-green traffic-signal graphics.

♦ Measurement of an activity, initially at least, caused improvement in the activity, as predicted by the Hawthorne Effect.

♦ Variations in metric definitions made it difficult to get consistent measurements.

♦ Software cost models produced good estimates for experienced engineers, even when there were no grounds for validation.

Software Engineering Evaluation System

In 1990, the SED developed a method of gathering metrics for validation and verification, called the Software Engineering Evaluation System. The SEES metric set consists of the number of people on the project, hours worked on the project, product items, planning, preparation, and defects. SEES records these metrics for software requirements, requirements traceability, software design and code, test plans, test descriptions, test witnessing, and functional- and physical-configuration audits. The SED provided training in SEES data collection and the reporting process for project leads involved with verification and validation of software, and developed a database for maintaining these metrics. The SED completed formal documentation of the SEES process in 1994.[2] Since then, a software group of the US National Aeronautics and Space Administration has also adopted this procedure for maintaining verification and validation metrics.

Metrics Working Group

The SED published an organization metrics policy in 1994 that established a Metrics Working Group

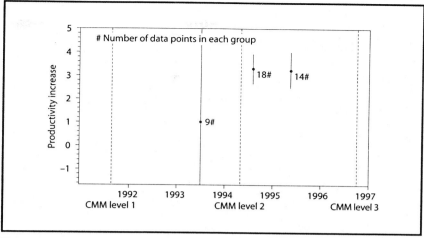

FIGURE 1. Annual productivity at the Software Engineering Directorate. The SED's productivity increased by a factor of approximately three between 1993 and 1994.

and laid the guidelines for collection and analysis of organization-wide metrics. This policy, still in use today, provides process audits and support funding. It requires that the information gathered be excluded from individual performance evaluations. This stipulation opened the door for integration of the metrics processes and procedures into the operational structure of the whole organization. The SED rewrote the standard operating procedures to include periodic collection and reporting of software metrics.

Overseeing the metrics initiative for the organization was the Metrics Working Group, which acts as a software metrics information center. Today the working group participates in professional metrics standards groups and leads research in metrics effectiveness. It maintains the metrics definitions for the organization, collects data from projects, and provides data analysis to management and project leads. Training provides SED personnel with an understanding of metrics policies and explains metrics definitions. The working group is also responsible for acquiring and maintaining the organization's metrics database.

The Metrics Working Group evaluated the SED's software-producing efficiency and calibrated a cost model for use in estimating future project costs.[3,4] This task began with the bulk collection of a standard dataset for internal software development projects. The set included lines of code, engineering hours, calendar months, and the number of defects discovered in peer reviews and testing.

The collection process consisted of project leads completing a metrics form that contains the needed information. Scheduled interviews with each project leader answered questions about the data. The data collected demonstrated the diversity of the organization's projects: they varied significantly in size, effort, duration, and languages used. This data formed a baseline for the organization, one that helps indicate trends and areas of process improvement.

The analysis in the following sections lists projects anonymously and shows data for the organization as a whole, not by individual projects. The projects are listed anonymously to promote the honesty of reporting the data. Managers must get data on specific projects through the project leader, not

from the Metrics Working Group. Giving the project leads authority over their own data alleviated some of their concerns about project comparisons.

Along with these tasks, there have been various experimental data-collection projects. Typical data in these acquisitions include software science metrics, function points, feature points, state entropy, cyclomatic complexity, coupling and cohesion metrics, and cleanroom metrics.

ANALYSIS

The SED actively applies the SEI's Capability Maturity Model,[5] which claims to increase the efficiency and productivity of an organization. The following analysis indicates that this claim is valid.

Efficiency analysis

The main goal of our efficiency analysis is to show productivity increases at the SED since the start of its software improvement efforts. Data collection began in January 1990, but data generated prior to 1993 is so sparse and unreliable that it was inadequate for establishing a baseline. Therefore, the efficiency analysis uses 1993 data to normalize each year's productivity mean. Figure 1 shows the productivity ratio, which is defined as each year's average productivity divided by 1993's average productivity. The data indicates that the SED's productivity increased by a factor of approximately three between 1993 and 1994. The productivity of SED projects completed in 1995 showed no significant change from the 1994 results. The large increase in productivity between 1993 and 1994 was primarily the result of appreciable software training during that interval. However, that very large productivity

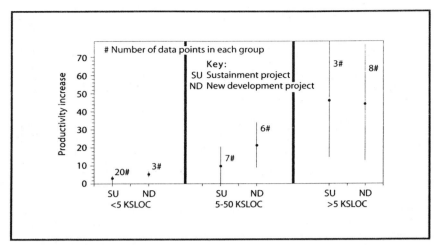

FIGURE 2. Average productivity for each project size category at the SED.

increase would not be expected year after year.

The productivity analysis partitioned the metrics data by size to investigate what effect project size would have on productivity. The analysis also divided the data between sustainment builds and new-development builds. Figure 2 shows the average productivity computed for each size category. The data indicates that the new-development builds are more efficient than the sustainment builds for the "very small" (less than 5,000 lines of code) and "small" (5,000 to 50,000 lines of code) size categories. The data also suggests that, for the SED, productivity increases for larger projects. This finding contradicts some experiments that show that productivity decreases for larger projects,[6] and provides an example for why organizations should gather and analyze their own data. Not all organizations should follow the standard assumptions made by most software professionals. They should measure, analyze, and develop calibration models from their own software projects.

The statistical analysis included the use of small sampling theory since, in most datasets, the number of data points in a group numbered less than 30. The small sample numbers clearly contributed to the relatively large one-standard-deviation error shown in all the figures provided. In addition, the large differences in the characteristics of these small projects also contribute strongly to the large statistical deviations. In future work, we hope that sufficient numbers of projects in each year will allow the splitting of projects into subgroups that share similar characteristics. This may allow observation of statistical differences in productivity for different project categories.

Other factors that contributed significantly to errors in the calculations include the following.

♦ Project leaders obtained much of the data from recordings made by people and not by unbiased machines. When people record data measurements on work they themselves performed, they often provide numbers in their favor or inaccurate values.

♦ Developers used several different languages to generate project code. Even though methods were used to normalize use of the various languages, large uncertainties persist.

♦ No one evaluated the education and experience levels of the contributors, even though there is general agreement that experience and education can exert a marked positive influence on productivity.

♦ Although project members recorded software error information, they did not use it to calculate the productivity values shown. This is important because a project may have relatively high lines of source code per effort value but also have a relatively high error rate. Thus, the effective productivity may not be high and certainly could be reduced.

Because of the diverse software being developed at the SED, the small number of builds with available data, and other limitations, determining conclusive results from this organizational analysis is difficult. However, we have identified several trends. Primarily, the analysis shows the importance of collecting accurate data and investigating trends in that data.

Cost model analysis

The cost model analysis investigated relationships between the metrics used in the cost models. This analysis computed linear and rank correlation coefficients and used nonlinear curve fits. The only metric pair with a "high" correlation coefficient was size (lines of code) and effort (0.80). However, this correlation does not appear in every project. Moreover, this relationship is not as strong in the sustainment builds (0.61) as in the new-development builds (0.84). This is because sustainment has much greater variability in requirements than new development.

A study of one project that measured individual code modules showed no correlation between effort and lines of code. This was, in large part, due to variations in module complexity. The project consisted of complex, tight hydraulic control loops and simple user interfaces. Nevertheless, a cost model based on estimated lines of code accurately

TABLE 1		
SOFTWARE EQUATIONS DERIVED FROM SED DATA		
	Effort*	**Schedule****
New-development projects	PM* = (2.22 KSLOC)$^{0.55}$	TDEV = (9.28 PM)$^{0.154}$
Sustainment projects	PM = (7.48 KSLOC)$^{0.302}$	TDEV = (2.28 PM)$^{0.428}$
All projects	PM = (5.39 KSLOC)$^{0.368}$	TDEV = (4.14 PM)$^{0.316}$
"Very small" projects	PM = (6.64 KSLOC)$^{0.0723}$	TDEV = (3.64 PM)$^{0.169}$

*Computed as person-months needed to generate 1,000 lines of source code.
**Total development time, measured in person-months.

predicted project effort and schedule to within 10 percent. The number of actual lines of code was also within 10 percent of the estimated number.

Was the estimate a self-fulfilling prophecy? We think not, but will never know for sure. Verification of the reason behind the results requires more data than was available.

Barry Boehm's Constructive Cost Model[7] (Cocomo) is one of the most popular software development cost-estimation models. However, the coefficients given in the Cocomo textbook are not valid for all organizations. Using the collected data, we calibrated the SED cost model analogous to the Cocomo basic model. The top graph in Figure 3 shows the effort versus the size of all SED projects. We measured effort in person-months, with each PM defined as 152 person-hours. The graph also shows the best nonlinear fit computed from the data, and the results obtained from the Cocomo basic organic model.

Table 1 lists the equations computed from several different data groups. The effort equation shows the relationship between the thousands of lines of codes (KSLOC) and the project person-months to generate the value of the KSLOC. The schedule or time-of-development equation (TDEV) shows the relationship between the total person-months and the total duration to complete the project. Significantly, the effort equations in the basic Cocomo model contain an exponent greater than one. When the exponential coefficient is greater than one, the model assumes that larger projects cost more per line of code than do smaller ones. Yet the effort equations from the SED data produced exponents less than one. The Cocomo model's "diseconomy of scale" did not appear in our calibrated coefficients. With an exponent less than one (as for the SED projects), the model predicts that larger projects cost less per line of code than do small projects.

Figure 3 shows how data clusters near the origin, then spreads out as the project's size grows. Therefore, the analysis also calibrated the Cocomo

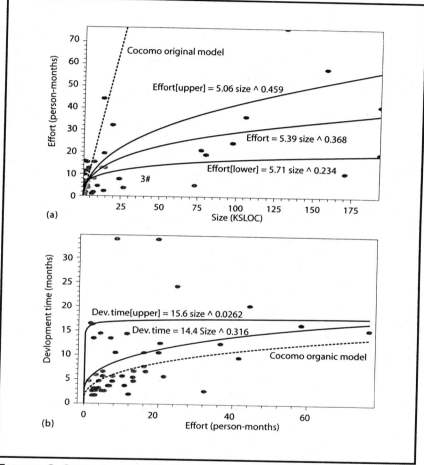

FIGURE 3. Comparing project data with the Cocomo organic model. The top graph (a) shows the effort in person-months vs. size for all SED projects; the bottom graph (b) shows the data related between development time and effort for all SED projects.

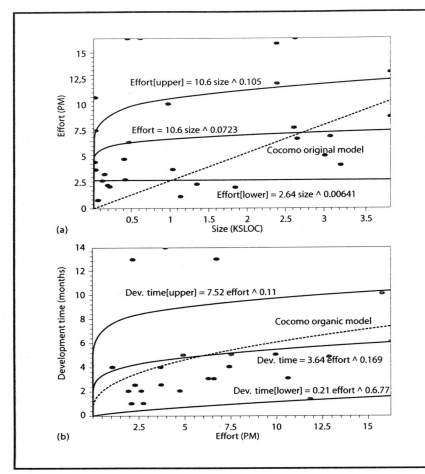

Effort[upper] = 10.6 size ^ 0.105

Effort = 10.6 size ^ 0.0723

Cocomo original model

Effort[lower] = 2.64 size ^ 0.00641

(a)

Dev. time[upper] = 7.52 effort ^ 0.11

Cocomo organic model

Dev. time = 3.64 effort ^ 0.169

Dev. time[lower] = 0.21 effort ^ 0.6.77

(b)

FIGURE 4. Comparing the very small project data with the Cocomo organic model. The top graph (a) shows the effort in person-months vs. size for all SED projects; the bottom graph (b) shows the correlation between development time and effort for all SED projects.

basic model for the "very small" projects (less than 5,000 lines of source code). Figure 4 shows the curves for the very small data.

The cost model analysis also computed upper- and lower-bound values for the calibrated cost model coefficients. In theory, these upper- and lower-bound coefficients should provide one standard deviation about the calibrated cost model. The upper- and lower-bound curves for the small projects contained approximately 53 percent of the SED builds. These curves also have exponents less than one.

The Cocomo basic schedule model estimated the SED builds much closer than did the effort model. The exponent for these curves was very close to the Cocomo model. The bottom graphs in Figures 3 and 4 show the SED duration in months as a function of effort hours. The upper and lower bounds of the small projects for the schedule data

contain approximately 87 percent of the SED builds.

The cost estimation analysis shows the importance of calibrating cost models. Using coefficients calibrated with data from other organizations can lead to large errors in software estimation. Textbook cost models give software practitioners a place to start; however, once data is available, analysts should compute new coefficients for their projects or organization. Metrics analysts should also update the cost model coefficients periodically to incorporate the most recent data collected.

CURRENT COLLECTION PROCEDURES

In February 1996, the SED implemented a standard procedure for the periodic collection and analysis of current-build metrics. The main goal of the SED Metrics Working Group in establishing this procedure was to make it minimally intrusive to project personnel while it gathered the needed data with more accuracy and consistency than previous attempts. Before initiating the organization-wide collection procedures, the Metrics Working Group held detailed discussions on several topics, including

- metrics to collect,
- definitions of metrics,
- design of the metrics collection form,
- metric collection time period,
- person responsible for data collection, and
- analysis procedures.

The working group decided to begin with four basic metrics: effort, schedule, defects, and size, as recommended by the Software Engineering Institute.[8] Substantial discussion and planning went into the design of the metrics collection form, incorporating suggestions from project personnel that would work for all SED projects. At first, the forms were confusing and complicated: they consisted of several sheets, with separate sheets for each metric and a different sheet for each project classification. Based on suggestions from project leaders, the final collection form consisted of one page, with all four metrics and their definitions listed on the form's back.

The effort metric consists of hours directly charged to the project for 15 activities. Of these activities, 10 deal directly with the software development process, including requirement definition, design, code, and test. Four categories address project support activities, but are not directly involved with software development or sustainment; these include management and software quality assurance. An "other" category includes activities performed on the project that may not fit any of the previous categories.

The schedule metric consists of the planned date and actual date for 10 milestones, chosen to represent the main events in the software development process. A project's staff can tailor its process to have fewer milestones, in accordance with the SED procedures.

The defect metric represents the number of new and closed defects. The metric divides defects into three classes depending on the severity of the defect. Several projects use peer inspection reports for recording defects. Project leads can attach the peer inspection reports to the metrics collection sheet, which helps reduce their paperwork.

The size metric consists of the language, number of lines of source code developed or modified, and number of document pages generated. The sustainment builds also record the total lines of code in the system.

We decided to collect metrics biweekly for two reasons: government employees report their hours biweekly, and it is less intrusive than weekly collection but frequent enough to ensure the data's consistency and correctness. Project leaders collect and submit the forms to the working group, ensuring collection of all project data and helping to guarantee the data's accuracy.

The SED consists of approximately 300 government and contract personnel. Approximately 130 of

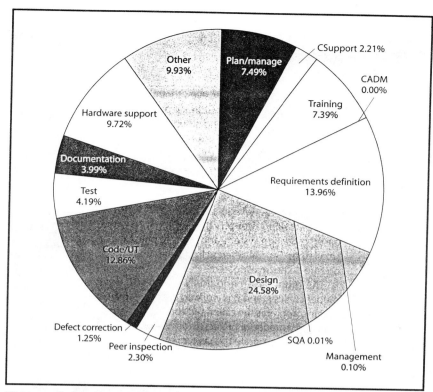

FIGURE 5. Sample monthly metrics report for an SED project.

these are software personnel who work on the 22 projects currently participating in the metrics collection program. Thus, within a two-week period, project leaders typically record 5,700 personnel hours on the metrics collection sheets. The number of hours collected varies, since project personnel are always changing and new projects begin as others end.

The Metrics Working Group generates monthly metrics reports for each project and sends them to the project leads. The reports consist of comparisons between actual and estimated values, percentages of effort hours spent in each category, and the number of defects open. Figure 5 contains a sample pie chart that shows the percentages of effort hours expended in each category. The pie chart summarizes the distribution of effort by activity in concise and easy-to-read form.

Other simple charts of size, defects, and schedule metrics also aid project leaders in managing their projects. These simple charts may also alert the leaders to potential problems early in the software development process and provide time for corrective action. The monthly metrics reports are still evolving; they change as project leads realize the management benefits this data provides.

Taking advantage of SED-funded training for several of its members, the Metrics Working Group began using a sophisticated database tool to manage the data. However, even though the database had some powerful features, it proved difficult to learn and use. The working group discovered that simple, inexpensive database tools and spreadsheets could adequately produce the needed results.

FUTURE PLANS

The working group is developing a network-based collection system, and plans to phase it in in small steps. Several different implementation methods are being investigated.

The group also periodically updates the cost model analysis, and it is working on a spreadsheet that incorporates the calibrated coefficients into an estimation model for project leader use. This spreadsheet will incorporate the percentage data for each effort category from completed projects to help project leads estimate hours in each effort category. Calibrating the cost models for the organization, providing training, and providing metrics tools will help increase the accuracy of software project estimation.

The Metrics Working Group continues to research new metrics and models, investigating different ways of measuring complexity. Several other areas are also being investigated as the SED begins plans for reaching CMM level 4.

Upper management's involvement and the publication of an organizational metrics policy contributed to the success of the present metrics collection program at the SED. The organization learned many lessons in the process of establishing measured feedback for its processes, including the following:

♦ A successful metrics program must have support from the highest management.

♦ Training is essential for the correct collection and analysis of data, and for management to be able to appropriately apply metrics. All managers and engineers need training in the collection and use of the data.

♦ Although metrics use does lead to better organizational performance, it requires an up-front investment of 3 to 8 percent of the project's overall cost, which must be paid at the beginning of the metrics program. This cost drops to less than 1 percent after project personnel become familiar with the program.

♦ Experiments to validate and analyze the metrics are an essential process component. Analysis of the data can validate assumptions or show that typical software process assumptions do not apply to a particular organization or project.

♦ Periodic calibration of cost models helps ensure accurate cost estimation.

♦ The metrics analysis techniques used should be statistically sound to ensure the accuracy of conclusions drawn from data analysis.

♦ A metrics collection program should be initiated with a small set of metrics that will show the benefits of collecting data. The metrics collection form should have a simple and easily understood design; a complicated form will only discourage software personnel from collecting data.

♦ Establish a metrics feedback procedure for engineers and managers to learn how to use the metrics and to help them understand the use and benefits of the measurement system.

♦ Inexpensive commercial database and spreadsheet tools are all that an organization needs to track metric data and provide meaningful reports.

The SED continues to learn important lessons from the metrics process. Our organization monitors its process improvement program's progress using the baseline established from collected data. The metrics program continues to expand as SED personnel experience the benefits of collecting and analyzing software metric data. ❖

REFERENCES

1. "Methodology for the Management of Software Acquisition," Software Engineering Directorate, Research, Development, and Engineering Center of the US Army Missile Command, Redstone Arsenal, Ala., 1991.
2. "Software Engineering Evaluation System (SEES), Volume I, SEES Executive Summary," Software Engineering Directorate, Research, Development, and Engineering Center of the US Army Missile Command, SED-SES-IES-001, Redstone Arsenal, Ala., 1994.
3. J.G. Jernigan and D.H. Divis, "Metric Analysis of Historical Data for the Software Engineering Directorate," Tennessee Applied Physical Sciences, TAPS-22-1995, Sept. 1995.
4. J.G. Jernigan, C.R. Pogue, and D.H. Divis, "Software Metric Analysis for the Software Engineering Directorate 1996," Tennessee Applied Physical Sciences, TAPS-24-1996, Sept. 1996.
5. M.C. Paulk et al., "Capability Maturity Model for Software, Version 1.1," Software Eng. Inst., Carnegie Mellon Univ., CMU/SEI-93-TR-24 or ESC-TR-93-177, Pittsburgh, 1993.
6. L.H. Putnam and W. Myers, Measures for Excellence: Reliable Software on Time, Within Budget, Yourdon Press, Englewood Cliffs, N.J., 1992.
7. B.W. Boehm, Software Engineering Economics, Prentice-Hall, Upper Saddle River, N.J., 1981.
8. A.D. Carleton et al., "Software Measurement for DoD Systems: Recommendations for Initial Core Measures," Software Eng. Inst., Carnegie Mellon Univ., CMU/SEI-92-TR-19 or ESC-TR-92-019, Pittsburgh, 1992.

About the Authors

D. Ross Grable is on the computer science faculty at the Clinch Valley College of the University of Virginia. His research interests are software and system metrics, software project management, and information system measurement techniques. He has worked with the Army Aviation and Missile Command as a senior scientist and consultant, and has also worked as a programmer, analyst, and project manager on many aerospace and military software-intensive real-time systems projects.

Ross received a BS in mathematics and physics, and an MS and a PhD in computer science from the University of Alabama Huntsville. He is a member of IEEE and the IEEE Computer Society.

Jacquelyn G. Jernigan is a weapon system analyst at Lockheed Martin Missile and Space in Huntsville, Alabama. Previously she was a senior software engineer at Tennessee Applied Physical Sciences. She has performed systems and radar analysis and developed analysis tools and radar simulations for government agencies for seven years. Her recent work includes metric analysis for the Software Engineering Directorate of the US Army Missile Command. Her current research interests include software metrics, process improvement, and system performance.

Jernigan received a BS in electrical engineering from the University of Alabama, Huntsville. She is a member of the IEEE Computer Society.

Casey R. Pogue is a computer scientist at Tennessee Applied Physical Sciences. He has developed accounting tools for small businesses and worked in computer services support. His current work includes metric analysis, Ada Compiler evaluation, and code analysis for the Software Engineering Directorate of the US Army Missile Command. His current research interests include software metrics and compiler optimization.

Pogue received a BS in computer science from Middle Tennessee State University.

Dale H. Divis is president of Tennessee Applied Physical Sciences. He has performed physics and mathematical modeling research for government agencies, and has evaluated data from physical experiments with unique statistical methods. Currently, he is involved with the statistical evaluation of software metrics data.

Divis received a BA in physics with minors in mathematics and chemistry from Rutgers and a MS in physics from Texas Christian University. He is a member of the American Physical Society.

Readers may contact Divis at Tennessee Applied Physical Sciences, Inc., P.O. Box 994, Fayetteville, TN 37334-0994, e-mail mld@vallnet.com.

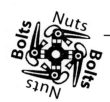

Reprinted from IEEE Software,
Nov./Dec. 1998, pp. 56-65.

The accelerated pace of software development and the geographically distributed nature of many development teams demand new process models. The author describes the Agile Software Process, a model that tackles these challenges and that is already in use at Fujitsu.

WEB-BASED AGILE SOFTWARE DEVELOPMENT

Mikio Aoyama, Niigata Institute of Technology

The Internet changed software development's top priority from *what* to *when*. Reduced time-to-market has become the competitive edge that leading companies strive for. Thus, reducing the development cycle is now one of software engineering's most important missions. The market demands that we deliver software ever more quickly, but also with richer functionality and higher quality. Further, today's time-sensitive business climate requires that we quickly accommodate requirements changes during development and, after development, be equally adept at delivering the upgrades caused by software's rapid software evolution and the customer's ever-increasing requirements.

On the other hand, many software development organizations have become dispersed, with more than 50 percent of their developers spread across multiple teams at geographically distributed sites. Thus, the friction of distributed—and therefore often delayed—communication actually works to slow software development.

To meet the sometimes conflicting demands of delivering software products faster

127

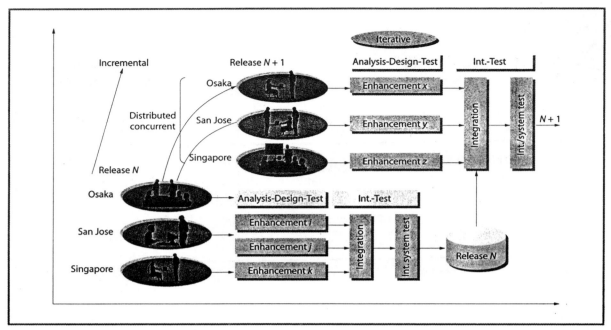

FIGURE 1. A process model of the ASP system. The software process is segmented so that teams can work on different releases concurrently.

while simultaneously facilitating their widely distributed development, I propose a fundamental redesign of the software development process, which I call the Agile Software Process.[1,2] ASP aims to develop software quickly while maintaining the flexibility needed to respond to changing requirements.

However, because ASP is more complex and vulnerable to disruption than are conventional software process models, it must operate within a specially tailored software engineering environment to function smoothly. Among various management techniques that I and my colleagues at Fujitsu developed, two methods—the time-based process enaction model and just-in-time process management—play a central role in managing ASP.

These methods are embedded into a process-centered software engineering environment called Prime, and a Web-based information-sharing environment, the Wide-Area Information Network. Together with other software engineering tools, Prime and WAIN form the network-centric Agile Software Engineering Environment.

We have used ASEE to develop large-scale communications software systems at Fujitsu for several years. Our experiences with the development and application of ASEE follow.

THE AGILE SOFTWARE PROCESS

Agility in software development means not only quick delivery of software products but also quick adaptation to changing requirements. To be agile, the process must be flexible enough to adapt smoothly to changes in requirements and delivery schedule. Conventional software process models, such as the waterfall model, are monolithic and slow, focusing as they do on a single long cycle time. Further, conventional process management is based on the volume of requirements. The greater the requirements' functionality, the longer the project's time-to-delivery and the lower the process's flexibility and productivity. Conventional management principles also lead to various scheduling problems, such as achieving on-time delivery, because it is hard to estimate the exact volume of work involved at the project planning stage.

To address these issues, ASP alters traditional management principles as follows:

♦ the process architecture shifts from monolithic to modular, and

♦ the process dynamics shift from volume-based to time-based.

Figure 1 shows the ASP model's modular and time-based nature.[2] The example depicted in the figure assumes that the development organization consists of several small development teams spread across multiple sites. From an architectural viewpoint, ASP consists of two parts:

♦ the upper-stream process, which covers the analysis to implementation phases, and

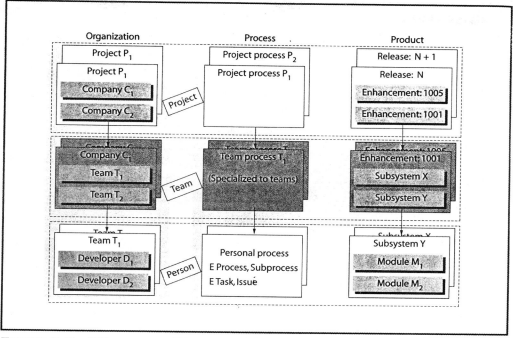

FIGURE 2. The ASP management hierarchy, distributed horizontally across the organization, and vertically down through the project, team, and personal levels.

♦ the lower-stream process, which covers the integration testing and system testing phases.

Typically, the upper-stream process consists of several concurrent software processes assigned across multiple teams. When each team completes its upper-stream process, it checks in the products to be integrated into a whole system, say Release *N*. Then, the Release *N* integrated software goes through the lower-stream process of integration testing and system testing.

ASP's agility stems from its macroprocess architecture. Although the unit software process is based on the waterfall model, ASP's entire architecture is incremental and iterative. Thus, the unit process has been redesigned to accommodate concurrent development. Each team iterates the two-part, upper- and lower-stream release cycle. ASP is time-based in that requirements are divided or integrated into units of incremental releases, called "enhancements," which have a fixed time for development. The development of an enhancement must be completed within a single release. Thus, enhancement allocation, which assigns enhancement work to a particular team, is a critical task whose success depends on the development teams' expertise and capabilities.

The software process is divided at the middle, so that the lower-stream process for Release *N* overlaps the upper-stream process for the next release, *N*+1. This enables each development team to work seamlessly and concurrently on multiple releases.

MANAGING IN REAL TIME

Managing ASP is a real-time activity. It requires the timely management of ASP's dynamic behavior to apply its software process over multiple releases. I have identified two key principles of time-managing the ASP:

♦ a time-based process enaction mechanism, and

♦ just-in-time process management.

The time-based process enaction mechanism mandates that all of a project's development processes have a fixed development cycle time, such as six months. As Figure 1 shows, each development process overlaps at the middle. Thus, the delivery cycle time would be three months.

Just-in-time process management mandates that the right information be provided to the right people at the right time—a shorter cycle time requires such precise and systematic process management. For example, we must support people at different levels of the organization—the individual developer, the team leader, and the project manager—so that each can track, at the appropriate level of abstraction, the processes and products upon which they are working.

To design ASP's just-in-time management, I analyzed our software process and products extensively, then set up a JIT management reference model. As Figure 2 shows, the model has three levels of management hierarchy—person, team, and

project—that function across the organization, process, and product.

I developed the concept of management levels because each management level requires different information and methods. I also found it necessary to define the relationships among the organization, the process, and the product so that we can coherently manage the process and product together within the organization. Further, management must be able to move easily up and down the levels of abstraction, which required us to establish the relationships between the different management levels. For example, project leaders must be able to browse through progress reports for the project and teams, while team leaders must be able to browse reports for their team and individual developers.

To succeed at JIT management, we emphasized helping the individual developer improve his or her quality of work because, as Watts Humprhey observed when defining his Personal Software Process,[3] software's quality depends on the individual developer's performance.

AGILE SOFTWARE ENGINEERING ENVIRONMENT

To manage the Agile Software Process, I developed an integrated software engineering environment, which I call the Agile Software Engineering Environment. I based ASEE's design on the following concepts.

♦ *Support for just-in-time management of both process and product.* ASEE supports the management model shown in Figure 2. Conventional software engineering environments, such as process-centered software engineering environments, focus on process control, while CASE environments focus on products. However, the process and product are two sides of the same coin. For a project to succeed, we must provide integrated support for both process and product. For example, we provide the design team with both a design process and design documents, and we provide the testing team with both test progress reports and quality information such as the number of bugs.

♦ *A network-centric architecture.* ASEE is network-centric because it is designed for distributed multi-team development. Collaboration over the extranet is critical to distributed development.

♦ *Support for the individual developer.* ASEE supports each individual's work by providing a personal viewpoint so that each project member can understand the role he or she plays on the team and the project. The environment provides support at the planning stage by letting team members view their own status and that of their co-workers, such as which modules or enhancements each individual is working on. Further, like conventional PSEEs, the ASEE also supports the management viewpoint of project progress, showing who is responsible for each project and enhancement.

Because distributed-computing technologies change so rapidly, I developed a reference model of the ASEE architecture. To be successful, the ASEE must evolve to incorporate the best technologies and practices. Thus, over the years, we have developed several tools that have been integrated into the ASEE. A reference model is indispensable to the planning and design of such tools, and helps us incorporate them into the ASEE.

Further, the reference model separates concerns so that different layers can evolve independently. As Figure 3 shows, the model breaks down into three layers. Each layer relates directly to one of the three major issues that the environment's architecture addresses: collaboration, information sharing, and distributed computing. The management model shown in Figure 2 is embedded into these three layers.

1. *Collaboration.* The top layer provides, through ASP, a collaboration mechanism for multiple teams.

2. *Information.* The middle layer supports the

As Humphrey observed, software's quality depends on the individual developer.

distribution of product information across the Internet.

3. *Operations.* The bottom layer is a computing and communication infrastructure that extends across the corporate extranet and connects multiple subsidiary companies and software houses.

The collaboration layer is implemented as a process-centered software engineering environment named Prime; the information layer is implemented as a Web-based distributed repository named WAIN. The operations layer is implemented across a common client–server platform that consists of standardized hardware and software. For the client, we use PCs running Windows; for the server,

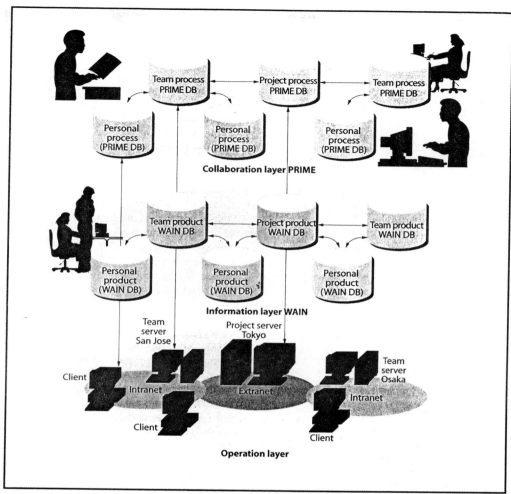

FIGURE 3. The Agile Software Engineering Environment's framework. Each layer of the framework relates directly to one of the three major issues that this architecture addresses: collaboration, information sharing, and distributed computing.

we use Unix workstations.

Based on the management mode and framework required to support the ASP management model, we developed ASEE's Web-based client–server software architecture, shown in Figure 4. The architecture consists of three layers: the client, the team server, and the project server. Individual developers and the team leader can access the client. The team server functions at the project level and can be accessed by the team leader and the project leader. The project server functions at the enhancement level and can be accessed by the project leader and upper-level managers.

ASEE is implemented using a federated multidatabase system in which every client's and server's database is built using the same schema structure. Thus, the collection and distribution of information across clients and servers occurs via the transmis-

sion of database replicas. Because all clients and servers share the same schema structure, it's possible to retrieve multiple databases using only SQL operations. Currently, we use Unix machines for our server platforms and Microsoft Windows machines for our client platforms.

Prime for the collaboration layer

Figure 5 shows the three layers of Prime's distributed hierarchical architecture. Prime

♦ provides just-in-time guidance of the individual developer's software process, as defined in a tree-structured YAC-II Process Description Language chart executed on the developer's workstation;

♦ supports planning and execution of the software process;

♦ supports, through its interlinked networks, the collection of statistics at appropriate levels of

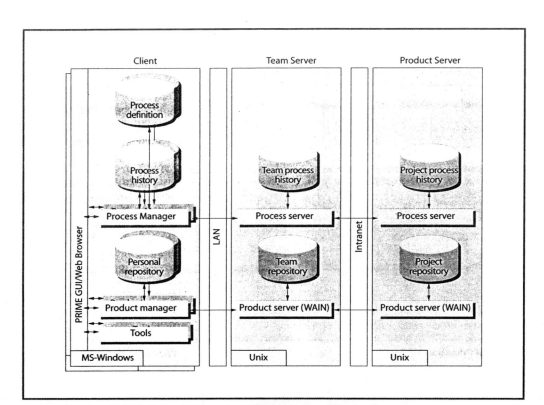

FIGURE 4. The Agile Software Engineering Environment's architecture.

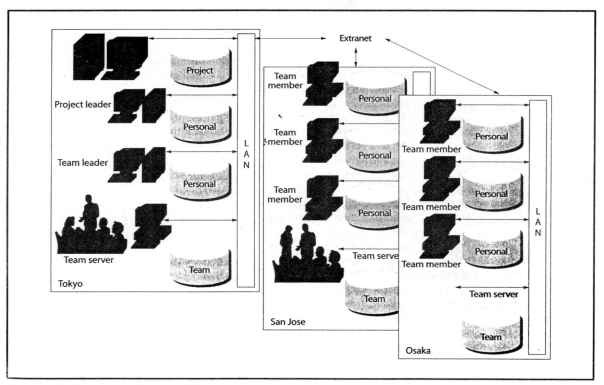

FIGURE 5. Prime's operational architecture.

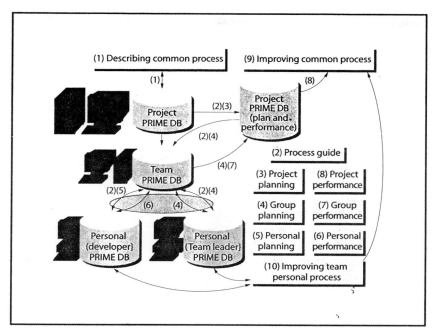

FIGURE 6. An overview of Prime's workflow.

process and organization;

♦ enables statistics visualization from multiple viewpoints at appropriate levels of process and organization; and

♦ controls security.

Figure 6 shows an overview of Prime's workflow; Figure 7 shows a screen view of Prime. The upper-left subwindow shows a list of base processes. The upper-right subwindow shows planning support. The progress of multiple teams and individual developers appear in the screen's left- and right-bottom subwindows, respectively. Prime tracks this data because it's critical to the software process's efficiency to visualize the dynamic behavior of multiple teams at the different levels of the organization's structure: project, teams, and individuals.

As an example of using Prime, Figure 8 shows three Progress and Bug charts from Project X: the large chart on the left provides an overview of the project, while the two smaller charts on the right track the performance of Teams A and B. The Progress and Bug chart, originally proposed by Joichi Abe and colleagues,[4] shows along the vertical axis of a single chart both the number of residual test cases (in a decreasing curve) and the number of bugs identified and fixed (in increasing curves). The vertical axis shows the number of test cases—some 3,000 for Project X—and the number of bugs is normalized to balance the chart. The horizontal axis shows the date. Because the number of bugs identified depends on testing progress, both progress and number of bugs must be viewable in

a single chart. Thus, we introduced an extended Progress and Bugs chart into ASEE. Prime automatically collects test results through the extranet from the distributed team servers, then generates the daily Progress and Bugs charts at the team and project levels, as shown in Figure 8. The charts reveal that the progress and quality at the project level appear good, but that Team A is in trouble because the number of bugs it has uncovered exceeds the expected maximum value.

WAIN for the information layer

The middle layer of the ASEE provides a platform for the WAIN, which allows sharing of information over the Internet. From our experience developing CASE environments, we identified two major issues in WAIN's development.

♦ *Semistructured design information.* Conventional product management systems focus on either source code or well-structured design information such as dataflow diagrams and state transition diagrams. However, a huge volume of design information is not well-structured, but semistructured at best or unstructured at worst.[5] ASEE aims to manage consistently throughout the software process not only well-structured information, but also semistructured and unstructured information. The Web and e-mail systems are particularly suitable for such management.

♦ *Information sharing over the Internet.* To effectively share design information, we must first classify it, then identify which parts should be shared. Further, because design documents are stored in various formats and structures, we must encapsulate those documents' physical structure to ensure their portability. In addition to functioning as a supernetwork for file sharing across geographically distributed locations, the Web's hypertext structure helps us dynamically represent the relationship among information entities.

WAIN is designed to manage the structured, semistructured, and unstructured design documents posted to the corporate extranet.[5] Figure 9 shows WAIN's architecture. I first implemented WAIN with Gopher, then later ported it to the Web.

133

Working in conjunction with Prime, WAIN

♦ encapsulates the structure of various design documents and provides uniform access methods to them;

♦ supports the creation, editing, retrieval, and change control of design documents;

♦ enables developers to navigate across the distributed repositories; and

♦ controls security.

To manage all three kinds of data in WAIN, I developed the categorization criteria shown in Figure 10. Data falls into one of three categories according to a document's logical and temporal characteristics: structured, semistructured, or unstructured. For each document a given project generates, we define a mapping from the data category to the storage system. Figure 11 shows a WAIN screen.

LESSONS LEARNED

Since 1993, the Agile Software Engineering Environment has been used in a large-scale communications software project at Fujitsu. Prior to implementing the ASEE, we used a mainframe-based software engineering environment. However, in conjunction with the development of ASEE, we moved to a client–server environment. The ASEE itself has evolved since then. Because we set six-month intervals for our development cycle times, and three-month intervals for our delivery cycle times, we have delivered ASEE releases every three months for more than four years. In that time, we have learned some major lessons from ASEE's application.

♦ *Moving from a volume-based to a time-based perspective.* ASEE supports time-based management. Thus, time is a new and critical parameter in ASEE-based development. For example, previously, we needed a few hours to collect data from the dis-

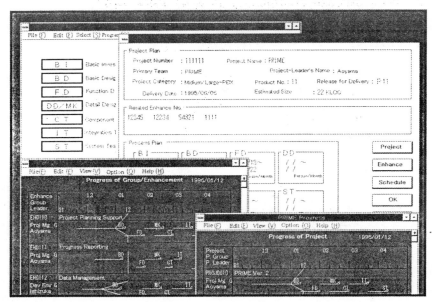

FIGURE 7. A screen from the Prime process-centered software engineering environment.

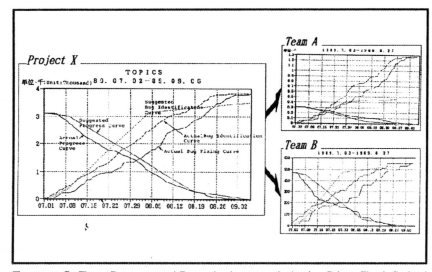

FIGURE 8. Three Progress and Bugs charts generated using Prime. The left chart presents an overview of the entire project, while the right two charts focus on the performance of Teams A and B.

tributed teams. Further, each team needed time simply to input the data. This delay meant that the data collected did not represent the team's current status and, because it was gathered asynchronously, sometimes lacked integrity. Such data flaws can cause critical problems in tasks such as the daily build,[6] in which staff must have access to accurate bug information each day. Thus, for ASEE to function properly and avoid these problems, we had to make it a real-time system by re-architecting the

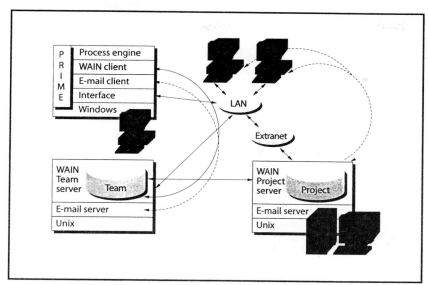

FIGURE 9. WAIN's operational architecture.

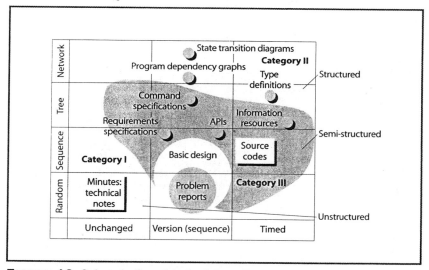

FIGURE 10. Categorization of design information.

processes under a specific level. Thus, we set up the management levels so that developers can avoid inflexible process enactment at the level of individual processes. The level structure also separates the concerns of the different management levels as they follow their preferred development methods. Drawing on an analogy from mechanical engineering, we call this the backlash mechanism because it allows for a limited freedom that avoids unnecessary friction and constraints. ASEE users adopted this concept readily.

♦ *Moving from point-contact to phase-contact.* Although an integrated, conventional software engineering environment supports only specific points of development work, a PSEE must support the everyday life of software development. Thus, usability is a critical issue in PSEE design. Significantly, the largest number of change requests submitted by ASEE users concerned usability issues.

♦ *Shifting from the manager's to the developer's viewpoint.* People often regard PSEE as a management tool. However, using the PSEE as a management tool sometimes runs afoul of the for-the-sake-of-management syndrome, which causes developers to view it as an unwelcome burden that interferes with their "real" work. To avoid this reaction, we designed ASEE to provide support for the developer's viewpoint as well, so that it helps both developers and managers.

♦ *Enhancing security.* ASEE has been used by multiple companies over the extranet. Because some information is sensitive, we provided a high-security version of ASEE that protects some information.

♦ *Moving to the Web.* WAIN's initial implementation was Gopher-based. However, after Web technology became popular we integrated ASEE into the Web, which is particularly suited to managing design documents because they are not well structured. However, our work in this regard is not finished: we have yet to add various support features specific to

software engineering environment from the time viewpoint.

♦ *Moving from enforcement to empowerment.* I believe that the mission of a process-centered software engineering environment is not the enforcement of methods but the empowerment of individuals. Many PSEEs and groupware packages force people to follow a specific order of processes or tasks.[7-9] We found, however, that software developers work back and forth across multiple processes and tasks.[10] Rigorous ordering at the detailed process level interferes with this pattern, causing inflexibility and loss of productivity. We observed that to be optimally effective, developers needed to iterate certain micro-

135

software engineering documents, such as configuration management and tool integration.

The ASEE, which supports the ASP over the Internet, provides just-in-time management of the software development process by providing the right process and product information to the right people at the right time. Because time-to-market offers a competitive edge, I believe that agility will become an increasingly important aspect of software engineering environments. Thus, we must re-architect our software engineering environments from a time-sensitive viewpoint. Further, ASEE is network-centric and promotes a virtual software factory of multiple teams geographically distributed over the Internet.

Since 1996, I have been involved with the Software Continuous Acquisition and Life-Cycle Support consortium sponsored by the Information Technology Promotion Agency in Japan. Unlike the CALS projects in other countries, Japan's CALS is a purely commercial initiative. Its fundamental philosophy is open and global. It strives to integrate best practices and tools over the Internet so that people can collaborate to quickly deliver products across companies and across countries.

Software organizations have discovered that speed is a strong weapon. To remain competitive, developers must work in real time; their processes must be agile. The Internet has proven the perfect environment for such development, allowing teams to collaborate around the clock, around the world. Thus, Web-based agile software engineering has become an emerging discipline.[11]

ACKNOWLEDGMENTS
I thank Kiyoo Nakamura and Carl K. Chang for their continuous encouragement. Thanks also to many of my colleagues at Fujitsu for their participation in the development of ASEE.

REFERENCES
1. M. Aoyama, "Concurrent-Development Process Model," *IEEE Software*, July 1993, pp. 46-55.
2. M. Aoyama, "Agile Software Process and Its Experience," *Proc. 20th ICSE*, IEEE Computer Soc. Press, Los Alamitos, Calif., Apr. 1998, pp. 3-12.
3. W.S. Humphrey, *Introduction to the Personal Software Process*, Addison Wesley Longman, Reading, Mass., 1997.
4. M. Aoyama, "Sharing and Managing the Design Information in a Distributed Concurrent Development of Large-Scale Software Systems," *Proc. IEEE COMPSAC '96*, IEEE Computer Soc. Press, Los Alamitos, Calif., Aug. 1996, pp. 168-175.
5. J. Abe et al., "An Investigation of the Nature of the PB Curves of Software Projects," *Trans. Information Processing Soc. of Japan*, Vol. 20, No. 4, July 1979, pp. 306-313.
6. M.A. Cusumano and R.W. Selby, *Microsoft Secrets*, The Free Press, New York, 1995.

FIGURE 11. Sample screen from WAIN, the wide area information network.

7. *Software Process Modelling and Technology*, A. Finkelstein et al. (eds.), John Wiley and Sons, New York, 1994.
8. P.K. Garg and M. Jazayeri, *Process-Centered Software Engineering Environments*, IEEE Computer Soc. Press, Los Alamitos, Calif., 1995.
9. L.J. Osterweil, "Software Processes Are Software Too," *Proc. 9th ICSE*, IEEE Computer Soc. Press, Los Alamitos, Calif., Mar. 1987, pp. 2-13.
10. D.E. Perry et al., "People, Organizations, and Process Improvement," *IEEE Software*, July 1994, pp. 36-45.
11. *Proc. Workshop on Software Eng. over the Internet*, F. Maurer (ed.), http://sern.cpsc.ucalgary.ca/~maurer/ICSE98WS/ICSE98WS.html.

About the Author

Mikio Aoyama is a professor at the Department of Information and Electronics Engineering, Niigata Institute of Technology. Previously, he worked at Fujitsu from 1980 to 1995. His current research interests include component-based software engineering, OO methodology, and process engineering.

Aoyama received a BS and an MS in electronics from Okayama University He is a member of the IEEE Computer Society, ACM, Information Processing Society of Japan, and the Institute of Electronics, Information, and Communications Engineers, Japan.

Address questions about this article to Aoyama at mikio@iee.niit.ac.jp.

From the Trenches

Reprinted from IEEE Software,
July/Aug. 1999, pp. 78-86.

Process engineering is sometimes seen as a luxury relevant only to large projects with long time frames. The author describes the successful application of structured software process improvement methods to a fast-moving Web development group. Beneficial results were achieved within five months.

Software Process Improvement in Web Time

Karl Wiegers, Process Impact

FROM THE TRENCHES: Wolfgang B. Strigel, editor • wstrigel@spc.ca

Much of the software process improvement literature describes how large corporations and government contractors have changed their software development and management processes over long periods of time. Commercial application developers and Web development groups sometimes conclude that process improvement doesn't apply to, and isn't feasible for, their time scales, product types, and cultures.

Not so! This article relates the five-month process improvement experience of a team of about 25 people doing Web development at a major corporation. We tackled several aspects of project management, change control, requirements engineering, and quality practices. The tangible and cultural benefits we achieved have the potential to help this group meet its commitments to deliver Web applications ("sitelets") in the very public eye: the company's 41,000-page Web site averages more than one million hits per day.

The software practice areas the group chose to improve are neither novel nor profound. Indeed, that is a significant message. Even a group that undertakes fast-paced Web projects can benefit from the application of traditional software process improvement approaches. Like any other project, Web projects have users, requirements, schedules, resources, and quality goals. Superior technical and management processes can yield superior results in the world of Web time, just as in any other software development setting.

137

0740-7459/99/$10.00 © 1999 IEEE

From the Trenches

Software process improvement has come a long way since the concept was developed in the 1980s. The Software Engineering Institute defined an excellent SPI framework with the Capability Maturity Model. However, the model was initially conceived for aerospace and military contractors who ran large projects with big budgets. The costs associated with CMM assessments and subsequent improvement activities were prohibitive for smaller, commercial software development organizations.

As Karl Wiegers mentions in this article, the term process is often regarded as synonymous with unconstructive overhead. This is especially true in corporate cultures with small teams that develop commercial products, including Internet applications. These companies have very little room for overhead activities that do not directly contribute to the next product release. Competitive forces dictate deadlines and all resources are allocated more than 100 percent to meet the next release date. To suggest the establishment of a formal Software Engineering Process Group would not be a winning proposition.

Wiegers' article is particularly important because it shows how the basic concepts of SPI can be successful in these environments, provided they are used in a sensible way. His observations match my own experience that once the team size of small companies grows beyond a certain threshold, the companies experience the same needs and pains as do large aerospace projects, only at a smaller scale.

The trick for successful SPI in small and fast-moving companies (or teams) is to be sensitive to their culture and to tailor SPI initiatives to their essential needs and their available resources. We may be tempted to invent yet another SPI model for companies living in "Web time" but one of this article's most significant contributions is to show that this is not necessary (see Wiegers' "Read My Lips: No New Models!" in the Sept./Oct. 1998 issue). CMM concepts can be tailored to meet the needs of many different development situations.

—Wolfgang Strigel, From the Trenches Editor

THE GROUP

The Web development group at Eastman Kodak Company began several years ago with just a few people developing simple sites. They soon experienced rapid growth in team size, application size and complexity, and the number of new sitelets requested by business units. The group came to include a software architecture team of about a dozen highly experienced and talented developers and a "customer experience" team with about 10 young, creative visual designers and several human factors specialists.

Unfortunately, development and management processes did not evolve in parallel with work demands. Practices that worked well for a few people doing small projects were not adequate for the larger teams, more complex projects, and backlog of requests that came about over time. This led to the group's internal commitment to focus some energy on process improvement. Their goals included

◆ managing the huge influx of new work;
◆ developing a foundation of common practices to help new team members quickly become effective;
◆ maintaining the high quality of work while improving productivity; and
◆ exchanging knowledge effectively among group members.

Each project is assigned a multifunctional team, to avoid the expectation that everyone be a fully proficient generalist. A typical project team might include a project leader, a technical lead, a design lead, a business unit representative, a software developer, a database expert, and a human factors expert. One consequence of this structure is that each team member works on several projects at once, with the accompanying challenge of setting priorities and the inefficiency caused by frequent task switching and many communication interfaces.

Some development infrastructure and process was already in place in this group, including a recommended Web site creation process. However, there was considerable variation in the ways different individuals performed common activities, and many holes remained in the development, management, and quality practices being used.

OUR APPROACH

The software architecture team was responsible for developing the software behind each Web sitelet. As their customers' quantity and quality expectations increased, the software architecture team members realized that their current approaches were not adequate to the influx of work. A brainstorming ses-

Project: _____   Date: _____
Estimated Completion Date for All Activities: _____
Goals:
Measures of Success:
Scope of Organizational Impact:
Staffing and Participants:

Name   Role   Time Commitment
_____   _____   _____

Tracking and Reporting Process:
Dependencies, Risks, and Constraints:

Action Item Number: __   Owner: _____   Due Date: _____
Description of Activity:
Deliverable(s):
Resources Needed:

FIGURE 1. Process improvement action plan template.

sion pointed to several areas for possible action: peer reviews, testing, problem tracking, requirements gathering, and project planning. Additional hot spots soon became clear, including shortcomings in the Web site creation process and the need to prioritize the many incoming requests for new work. As an internal Kodak consultant, I joined the software architecture team as a full-time process improvement leader and worked with them hands-on for five months to address these and other issues.

Team members were honest about acknowledging their problems, an essential precondition for effective process improvement. While they had the usual concerns about "process" adding unconstructive overhead to their work, they appreciated the prospect of some increased structure. The structure we eventually provided ranged from more focused post-project review meetings to templates for documenting project plans and requirements.

As with most development groups, many of our problems related to the key process areas found at level 2 of the Capability Maturity Model for Software.[1] However, we chose not to pursue a pure CMM approach. We were not concerned about specifically satisfying the criteria to achieve CMM level 2, although we certainly wanted to enjoy the level 2 results of predictability and stability. We would have been foolish had we not used the CMM as a guide for addressing our problem areas; it would have been equally inappropriate to apply the CMM dogmatically.[2] While my understanding of the CMM helped direct our activities, we never even discussed the CMM during the five months I worked on this process improvement project.

We focused on a few improvement areas at a time, with two or three group members collaborating with me in a small working group for each area.

We wrote an action plan for each improvement initiative using the template illustrated in Figure 1. The action plans identified goals for the improvement activity, measures of success, the participants, and up to 10 individual action items. Every action item identified an individual as the owner, a target date for completion, deliverables to produce, and resources needed.

A simple, focused improvement action plan makes it easy to know what tasks must be executed and provides a way to track progress. If you need a full-blown project management tool to manage your tactical action plans, they are scoped too large.

The methods for delivering process documentation to the group must match the culture. As this was a Web development group, publishing the process documents on our group's intranet was an obvious choice. We published the more complex procedures in Adobe Portable Document Format (PDF) so that users could print a complete, formatted copy. The procedures were also broken into hierarchically sensible components and published in HTML format. Templates to help team members create project documents, such as project plans and requirements specifications, were published as Microsoft Word documents.

The specific improvements we undertook in each process area are summarized in Table 1. While I cannot claim that every improved practice is being applied religiously by every member of the team on every project, each technique has been used enough times to demonstrate success and to lay the foundation for future benefits. Whether the group can sustain these improvements in the face of continued growth and time pressures will depend on management commitment and the education of new team members.

139

TABLE 1	
IMPROVEMENT AREAS PURSUED AND APPROACHES USED	
Improvement Area	**Approaches Used**
Project management	Project plan template
	Project prioritization model
Post-project reviews	Post-project review process description
	Collection of lessons learned
Risk management	Risk documentation template
	Informal team risk analysis
	Risk management action plan
Change control	Change control process description
	Change control tool
Requirements engineering	One-day requirements training class
	Requirements specification template
	Workshops to elicit use cases
Development life cycle	Defined life cycle for Web site creation process
	Procedures, checklists, templates, examples of deliverables
Peer reviews	Half-day peer review training class
	Peer review process description and work aids

PROJECT MANAGEMENT

As the number and size of our projects increased, we realized we needed improvements in our project management practices. Many small software groups equate a project plan with a work breakdown structure or a schedule of major tasks. To succeed, though, even small, fast-paced projects need more detail in their plans. The trick is to develop plans that are just detailed enough to make sure you have a thorough understanding of your project and thereby the ability to control it.

Project plan template

We began by defining a standard template for our project plans. Document templates remind the author to think about aspects of the project that might otherwise be overlooked; they also provide sections in which to capture the myriad bits of information necessary for effective project execution. We started with IEEE Standard 1058.1, a template for software project management planning, and adapted it to fit our needs.[3] (The current version is IEEE Std 1058-1998.[4]) Templates should always be tailored to your specific circumstances.

One of the first people to try out the template on a real project came to me one day, somewhat discouraged. "I wrote the plan, but I didn't know what to put in many of the sections," she lamented. She was concerned not because the template contained a lot of sections that weren't important to her project, but

because the sections *were* important and she simply did not have the information. The project plan template was well received because it provided a valuable framework for discussions among project stakeholders and helped elicit the necessary information.

One section of the project plan template clarifies the roles and responsibilities of the various project participants. Confusion about such roles emerged as a problem at two post-project reviews. For example, on one project, various participants from the customer experience team thought several different people were the prime point of contact from the software architecture team. Clarifying roles and responsibilities enhanced the group's culture by helping diverse people collaborate more effectively on these multidisciplinary projects.

Prioritizing projects

Software process improvement research usually addresses the planning and tracking of large projects. The Kodak Web group, along with many software maintenance groups, faces a different challenge: how to deal with a large number of new project requests. At one point, our queue contained more than 150 requests for new or enhanced projects. We decided to develop a project prioritization model by adapting some principles from Quality Function Deployment.[5] With this model, we hoped to identify the most appropriate projects to undertake using the limited resources available, chosen from the many worthy pro-

jects that our customers had requested.

We identified a dozen factors that indicate how favorable a proposed project would be for us to undertake. The factors include

♦ immediacy of the need,
♦ level of technology risk,
♦ extent to which the project could exploit our current Web development capabilities,
♦ business value,
♦ alignment with known demographics of our current Web site visitors, and
♦ degree of user interface complexity.

We assigned a relative weight to each factor; the weights totaled 100. Then we defined a rating scale for each "favorability factor," whereby each proposed project could receive a score on each factor. By multiplying factor score times factor weight and summing the results, we could generate an overall favorability score for each candidate project.

We calibrated the model using several completed projects. We adjusted the factors, their weights, and the rating scales until the model yielded results consistent with our after-the-fact assessment of how appropriate each of those projects really was. The model had to generate a significant range of scores so we could distinguish the great project candidates from less desirable ones.

A model like this could be useful for any organization confronted by a large number of projects.

Once calibrated, the model did help us get a better handle on the projects that were most appropriate for us to undertake and helped us manage the large request backlog with confidence that company resources were being invested in the best way. The model was well received by most of our group's stakeholders, including multiple business units, managers, and practitioners. A model like this could be useful for any organization confronted by a large number of projects, all of which are important. Identify your own success drivers, calibrate the model based on work already completed, and use the output from the model as a part—but only a part—of the decision-making process.

POST-PROJECT REVIEWS

The Kodak Web team had previously conducted post-project reviews, but we wanted to make them more structured. Post-project reviews provide an opportunity to look back at a completed project (or from a mid-project checkpoint) and capture the lessons learned.[6] We defined a post-project review process that included a summary of things that went well, a frank exploration of things that could have gone better, and a list of any experiences that surprised us.

Our post-project reviews took the form of facilitated workshops that included the project participants from both the software architecture and customer experience teams. The facilitator emphasized collaboration, steering the participants away from any blaming behaviors. The participants really contributed constructively to these post-project reviews. From the raw data collected during the workshop, we extracted perhaps a dozen lessons learned, which we organized into categories and collected on one of our process Web pages. We tried to write the lessons learned in a neutral tone, so the reader couldn't tell if we learned the lesson because the project went extremely well or because we made a mistake. Future project managers can review these lessons to remind them of practices they should incorporate into their plans, and risks they may need to control. The project team also uses the post-project review results to develop an action plan addressing the key issues revealed by the review.

The insights gained by reflecting on recently completed projects can be of great value in a rapidly evolving environment like Web development. The post-project reviews were well received because all project participants knew that things had not gone perfectly, and they were willing to put their issues on the table and learn from them. Issues raised during the post-project reviews meshed nicely with those generated by the other process improvement activities.

RISK MANAGEMENT

Although it has been identified as a software industry best practice,[7] formal risk management is not regularly practiced on many small development projects. In addition to managing the tactical risks facing individual projects, we felt it was important to take a look at the strategic risks threatening the success of the group's activities as a whole.

The software architecture team identified more than 45 strategic risk items. Many of these pertained to the security and reliability of the Web delivery in-

141

frastructure, critical for a heavily trafficked site engaged in e-commerce. As an example, one risk factor was that there might be security shortcomings that could allow users to access off-limits directories on the Web server. Several risk factors related to the leading-edge Web technologies the group was using. Others had to do with organizational, business unit, and management issues, in part reflecting the growing pains of this young development organization.

We applied conventional risk management principles, estimating the probability that each risk could materialize into an actual problem and the impact if it did. This analysis helped us to prioritize the identified risks. Again, we wrote an action plan to begin mitigating risks selected from the top of the priority list. Unfortunately, monitoring the risk management actions did not float to the top of the busy group manager's priority list. To help make risk management succeed, assign a risk officer other than the project or group manager to coordinate risk management activities, and incorporate risk tracking into your routine project status tracking.

CHANGE CONTROL

Small software teams often use an informal approach for making changes to their products. The person who has an idea or who found a bug tells the programmer, who makes the change. This method does not scale up well. Change control and problem tracking constitute another software industry best practice.[7] Despite the malleability of Web site software and data content, discipline is needed to effectively manage changes to Web products. We needed to manage five kinds of changes:

♦ requests for new projects,
♦ changes to the requirements for projects currently under development,
♦ problem reports concerning current systems or the Web infrastructure,
♦ enhancements to current systems, and
♦ content changes in current systems.

Practitioners sometimes think that simply installing a problem-tracking tool constitutes a complete change control system. However, a change control system includes both a documented process and clear procedures for the activities to be performed, and tools to automate some of these activities.

We collected requirements for the change control system from several stakeholders who would use it or be affected by it. Requesting voice-of-the-customer input is a way to foster buy-in to the process changes you propose. Those affected become part of the solution, rather than being victims of the improvement initiative. This is particularly important with processes such as change control that redefine the interface through which your customers and other stakeholders interact with the software group.

We established a formal mechanism for collecting and evaluating the requests for new projects that came in from business units every week.

Based on these requirements and on previous experience, we wrote a change control procedure, had several stakeholders review it, and published it on our internal process Web page. The principal initial benefit was that we established a formal mechanism for collecting and evaluating the requests for new projects that came in from business units every week. For a few weeks, the two people who managed the resulting project queue also piloted the change control function using paper forms. During that time, we explored commercial problem-tracking tools that might meet our need for a Unix-based server and Web-based user interface. The feedback from this pilot helped us improve the process before we committed to selecting, installing, and customizing a specific tool.

The community was receptive to using this change control process to reduce the chaos of the change backlog, with its uncertain change request status and unclear decision making. Any development organization of any size can apply formal change control in this way. One success factor for implementing change control is to minimize the process overhead of submitting and evaluating change requests. Another is to make sure the change process, and the people who practice it, are responsive to submitted requests. If a process doesn't work, people will work around it.

REQUIREMENTS ENGINEERING

While the group had built a series of successful Web sites based on informal requirements collected from business units, such a casual approach breaks

From the
Trenches

down with larger and more complex projects. Although some people hold that documenting the project requirements imposes excessive process overhead on small projects, the costs associated with reworking a software product because of poorly understood requirements can be substantial. We took several actions to improve our requirements engineering processes, specifically requirements elicitation and specification. We began by adapting the IEEE software requirements specification template (IEEE Std 830)[3,4] to meet the nature and scale of our projects. For example, we added a section on internationalization requirements, an important aspect of many Web projects.

Accumulated pain from the current state of affairs motivated team members to pursue better processes.

The entire Web development team attended a one-day training class on requirements development and management. This helped the participants reach a common understanding about requirements concepts and practices, such as the application of use cases for eliciting requirements, and dialog maps for modeling user interfaces.

Several project leaders began applying the use case method. An initial attempt floundered because too many people attended the workshops that captured and defined the use cases. When we reduced the workshop size from 12 people to six, progress accelerated nicely. Two business unit participants stated that the use case approach helped them to clarify the scope of their project and to understand the actions a prospective Web surfer would be able to perform at their new sitelet. Months later, the Web group manager indicated that the increased emphasis on gathering requirements was a major factor in the group's successful completion of several new projects.

DEVELOPMENT LIFE CYCLE

Millions of people are now amateur Web site developers. While a code-and-fix life cycle can work for the individual assembling a few simple pages, building complex Web sites involves an intimate collaboration among programmers, database experts, visual design specialists, and content providers. A well-defined but flexible development life cycle can help.

Our group's existing Web site creation process was thinly documented, lacked a supporting infra-structure, did not relate to how projects really were performed, and was not practiced in a consistent way. Several post-project reviews revealed problems that an improved development life-cycle process could solve. This is another example where traditional software process approaches can benefit a Web development team when the scope of the team's projects exceeds its ability to deliver through informal collaboration.

First, we surveyed the team about the shortcomings of the current process. Based on the responses, several team members then outlined a rational sequence of phases through which our projects should progress. For each phase, we allocated activities, identified the major deliverables, and defined entry and exit criteria. We generated lists of activities and deliverables by combining the contents of the current life cycle, elements from similar models found within Kodak, and the actual experiences of what people really did on their projects.

We recognized that some activities bridge two life-cycle phases. Web projects include development of both content and the enabling software. The site design has to take place before the software architecture design can be completed. We incorporated this time offset in allocating activities and deliverables to each phase. For example, Phase 2 includes development of user interface navigation design and the preliminary software functional specification. The functional specification is completed and baselined in Phase 3, after the interface design is completed. Life-cycle models that artificially constrain multiple-phase activities to a single phase do not reflect the way people actually work.

We documented the improved Web site creation life cycle on our intranet, with descriptions of each activity and deliverable. Both the customer experience and software architecture teams responded favorably to the improved life-cycle process, because it represented a more realistic approach to executing their projects. We are now supporting this framework by developing procedures and checklists to facilitate performance of the key activities and by collecting templates and examples of the deliverables.

Early experience suggests that project leaders who feel their management-imposed schedule deadlines are unrealistic may be tempted to hide behind the more extensive documentation demands of this new life-cycle process as a justification for not meeting deadlines. Not surprisingly, this approach does not sit well with upper managers. We need to evolve the culture to a state in which new processes

143

are seen as enablers, not obstacles, and as structures, not straitjackets. This will take time.

PEER REVIEWS

The group wished to begin holding peer reviews and inspections of software work products, another industry best practice,[7] both for the quality benefits of finding defects early and for the increase in information exchange among team members. We began by sending the software architecture team to a half-day class on software technical reviews. Two members of the team then worked with me to develop a suitable peer review process, which included both formal (inspection) and informal review procedures. We published the process documents on our intranet, along with forms for capturing review results and checklists of common defect types found in various work products.

Although the team members were receptive, peer reviews were not one of our great successes. The consensus was that reviews would not become a regular practice until they were incorporated into project plans and schedules. Therefore, we included reviews as key activities to be performed at various checkpoints in our new Web site creation life cycle.

I think it is quite difficult to establish a culture of technical peer reviews. Asking someone else to tell you what's wrong with your work is a learned behavior, not an instinct. To help make a review program succeed, train the whole team, focus your limited review time on high-risk items, and publicly recognize those team members who routinely solicit a little help from their friends.

WHAT WE LEARNED

Five months after beginning our process improvement activities, we surveyed the members of the customer experience and software architecture teams to gauge their reaction to the program. The responses were strongly favorable. We could not quantify the results, but the improvement areas of change control, life-cycle definition, project prioritization, requirements engineering, and project planning were perceived to have yielded the most benefit. Many respondents mentioned the value of reducing the chaos level through improved project management

and resource planning. No one indicated that any of the improvement efforts were a waste of time.

The respondents agreed that having a dedicated process improvement leader on staff was highly beneficial. Several participants felt our change initiative had proceeded a little too quickly for comfort, even though new processes were phased in gradually over five months. This points to the limits that any group, even one with highly capable and receptive members like this one, has in accepting and internalizing new ways of working.

Several factors converged to make this process improvement activity successful:

♦ Accumulated pain from the current state of affairs motivated team members to pursue better processes.

♦ Management demonstrated initial commitment by bringing a process improvement leader into the group and by clearly stating expectations about the importance of making appropriate changes.

♦ The team leaders got involved hands-on in the improvement activities.

♦ Many practitioners participated in devising, reviewing, piloting, and critiquing suggested new procedures and document templates.

♦ We had access to a corporate repository of software engineering "good practices" that included

> **To help make a review program succeed, train the whole team, focus review on high-risk items, and publicly recognize team members who routinely solicit a little help from their friends.**

sample procedures, templates, and work product examples across the entire range of software engineering and management practice areas.[8] If you don't have such resources available, start with the *IEEE Software Engineering Standards Collection*.[3,4] Another useful product is EssentialSET from the Software Productivity Centre (www.spc.ca), which contains more than 50 sample documents covering the gamut of software project development and management activities.

♦ Perhaps most significantly, practitioners from both the software architecture team and the customer experience team were willing to try new ways of working, despite their tremendous workloads and schedule pressures.

If I were to undertake a similar enterprise again, I would engage middle management earlier to pro-

vide more "pull" for the improvement initiative. This lack of early engagement did not pose a problem in our case, but management must continue to set strong expectations if the practices we launched are to be institutionalized into routine application. This may also help turn action plans into useful actions.

One of the leaders of our group succinctly expressed an ideal attitude toward process improvement. She said, "Our processes give us the ability to select the right projects and complete them on schedule." She recognized that successful software groups of any kind prosper because of intelligently chosen processes, not in spite of them. Structured software process improvement is a valuable means to improve the results from project teams working at the frantic pace of Internet time, as well as for more traditional software development projects. This group's experience demonstrates that even a team dealing with leading-edge technologies, rapid projects, and heavy business pressures can—indeed must—improve the methods it uses to manage and implement software projects. ❖

ACKNOWLEDGMENTS

None of the improvement efforts we undertook would have borne fruit without the commitment of the Web development group's leadership team, LuAnne Cenci, Lee Corkran, Alan Dray, and Deborah Patrie.

REFERENCES

1. Software Eng. Inst., *The Capability Maturity Model: Guidelines for Improving the Software Process*, Addison Wesley Longman, Reading, Mass., 1995.
2. K. Wiegers, "Software Process Improvement: Ten Traps to Avoid." *Software Development*, May 1996, pp. 51-58.
3. *IEEE Software Eng. Standards Collection*, 1997 ed., IEEE Computer Soc. Press, Los Alamitos, Calif., 1997.
4. *IEEE Software Eng. Standards Collection*, 1999 ed., IEEE Computer Soc. Press, Los Alamitos, Calif., 1999.
5. W.J. Pardee, *To Satisfy & Delight Your Customer*, Dorset House, New York, 1996.
6. B. Collier, T. DeMarco, and P. Feary, "A Defined Process for Project Postmortem Review," *IEEE Software*, July 1996, pp. 65-72.
7. N. Brown, "Industrial-Strength Management Strategies," *IEEE Software*, July 1996, pp. 94-103.
8. K. Wiegers, "Improve Your Process with Online 'Good Practices,'" *Software Development*, Dec. 1998, pp. 45-50.

About the Author

Karl E. Wiegers is principal consultant with Process Impact, a software process consulting and education company in Rochester, New York. Previously, he spent 18 years at Eastman Kodak Company, where he held positions as a photographic research scientist, software developer, software manager, and software process and quality improvement leader. Wiegers authored *Creating a Software Engineering Culture* and the forthcoming *Software Requirements: A Pragmatic Approach*, as well as 120 articles on software development and management, chemistry, and military history.

Wiegers holds a BS in chemistry from Boise State College and MS and PhD degrees in organic chemistry from the University of Illinois. He is a member of the IEEE, IEEE Computer Society, and ACM.

Readers may contact Wiegers at www.processimpact.com; e-mail, kwiegers@acm.org.

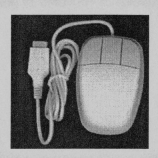

CHAPTER 3
REQUIREMENTS

Defects in software products are very often the result of requirements errors. Although requirements documents are often impenetrable and poorly maintained, there is no escaping them. Indeed, without them we can neither tell what we are intended to build and test for, nor fully describe the product itself.

In the papers that follow, Manion, Keepence, and Harper describe a way to organize requirements according to the viewpoints of the principle stakeholders. They factor in both the cost of implementing each requirement, as well as its value. Regnell shows how the use case model for requirements can be combined with software reliability engineering so as to integrate reliability techniques early in the process. Lee and Xue present a way in which use cases can be extended to cover non-functional requirements. Bach recounts experiences which suggest practical limits of detail in requirements specification.

> Although requirements reuse has many potential benefits, a lack of accepted methodology for sorting through a domain's myriad requirement specifications makes the task daunting. The authors' VODRD method relies on stakeholder viewpoints to organize user requirements. Here, they describe their method and its application in a mission planning system for the European Space Agency.

Reprinted from IEEE Software, Jan./Feb. 1998, pp. 95-102.

USING VIEWPOINTS TO DEFINE DOMAIN REQUIREMENTS

Mike Mannion and **Barry Keepence,** Napier University
David Harper, Vega Space Systems Engineering GmbH

For all the promise of reuse—shorter time-to-market, reduced costs, and increased productivity and quality—it is rarely applied to requirements. The reasons are clear. To reuse requirements, you must analyze your domain and find where requirements overlap. It sounds simple until you realize that each domain has multiple systems and multiple users, all of which generate requirements specifications that must be compared and contrasted to find where the reuse potential lies.

We have developed a method to make the analysis of user requirements across a domain easier. The viewpoint-oriented domain requirements definition method, or VODRD, analyzes user requirements from an individual stakeholder's perspective. Although functionality often differs across user requirements specifications, stakeholders and their viewpoints are more stable, making requirements comparison tractable.

Researcher's CORNER

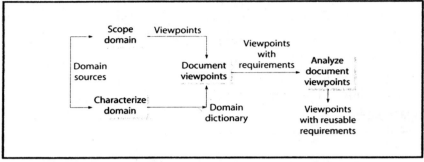

Figure 1. The VODRD method is an iterative one: the four steps are shown in boxes.

specific requirements. For the first stage, Daniel Jackson and Michael Jackson offer a framework for helping to identify common problem classes.[2] For the second stage, Ruben Prieto-Diaz uses information science methods to construct a domain vocabulary, taxonomy, and classification scheme.[3] The emphasis of these approaches is on reusing concepts across domains. For an organization developing applications in a single domain, however, there is little practical advice about how to get started.

To use VODRD, you analyze existing system user-requirements specifications (URSs) to identify the domain's stakeholders and establish a domain dictionary. You then assign the requirements of each domain system to the appropriate viewpoint. Next, you compare requirements within each viewpoint and identify which are reusable. To make this step effective, you must maintain links between requirements. Because there are more intra-viewpoint links than inter-viewpoint links, merging requirements is much easier.

We used the VODRD method to build a URS for a mission planning system, part of the European Space Operations Centre's new generation of spacecraft control systems. To analyze the domain, we used the URSs of four existing spacecraft mission-planning systems, each of which had 100 to 200 requirements. We also had access to developers who worked on these systems, and to people procuring future systems.

The completed domain URS had 539 requirements and took three staff members about five person-months to produce. Because of the complexity, computer-aided support is essential for domain requirements definition. We used MS Access to create a simple database of domain requirements with facilities for defining viewpoints and for adding, editing, linking, merging, and extracting requirements within viewpoints.

The VODRD method can be used for any set of applications within any domain. The method assumes that an organization uses natural language to specify requirements. However, the method can be modified to suit an organization's needs. The success of VODRD will depend on the quantity, quality, and availability of domain experts and existing requirements specifications.

DEFINING DOMAIN REQUIREMENTS

Several approaches to domain requirements definition have been proposed. Will Tracz, Lou Coglianese, and Patrick Young[1] suggest there are two stages: define the domain's scope and define/refine domain-specific requirements.

Defining difficulties

Domain requirements definition produces a domain URS. This specification is typically a natural-language document written in a standard format and containing numerous atomic requirements (requirements expressed in one sentence with one "shall"). The specification must describe the domain systems' commonality and discriminants (any feature that differentiates one system from another).

Defining domain requirements is a difficult process for several reasons. First, you need a domain expert. Typically, their availability is limited, their daily rate is high, and you cannot charge that rate to any revenue-earning project. In some domains, you need several experts because no one person has experience on each system within a particular domain. Second, many applications are large and/or complex and building a detailed domain picture requires considerable time. Finally, without an effective method for comparing and contrasting domain systems, the effectiveness of experts and computer-aided support is limited.

Finding such a method is problematic because requirements specifications can be written in different ways. Many standards' guidelines suggest you simply break down requirements into functional and nonfunctional categories, which often results in individual specifications looking quite different. In addition, although natural language is typically used, the style of expression can differ. For example, you might express requirements as top-down, bottom-up, or as a set of scenarios.

Defining challenges

To construct a domain URS, you must find a way to compare the individual requirements of all systems so you can associate them. You must also modify and maintain these associations. This is difficult, since the catalog of requirements typically evolves over a period of days, weeks, and sometimes months as the domain expert's understanding increases. Word processors are inadequate to handle these problems. What we need is a controlled database environment and a relatively static organizing principle.

150

VIEWPOINTS

Viewpoints are often used to elicit, analyze, and specify software requirements in a single system.[4-6] VODRD's use of viewpoints to define domain requirements has several advantages.

♦ Viewpoints are likely to remain consistent across domain systems, giving you greater confidence in understanding and comparing requirements.

♦ Viewpoints let you better use the domain expert's time: system analysts with limited domain expertise can conduct the initial domain investigation, after which the domain expert can modify and clarify the analysts' work.

♦ Viewpoint documentation can accommodate requirements overlap and domain inconsistencies.

♦ Methods of single-system development are now emerging[7] that partition requirements into viewpoints and evolve a design while maintaining the viewpoint infrastructure.

THE VODRD METHOD

As Figure 1 shows, VODRD is an *iterative* method consisting of four steps: scope the domain, characterize the domain, document the viewpoints, and analyze the viewpoints. The outputs from this method are a domain dictionary, domain viewpoints, and a catalog of reusable requirements collected within viewpoints. These outputs can serve as inputs to the rest of the domain engineering process. The sidebar, "Domain Engineering: An Overview," offers a brief overview of this process.

Scope the domain

In the first step, you identify the stakeholders in the domain. By stakeholders we mean the people or systems with an interest in, influence over, or specialist knowledge of the application domain, such as end users, an external database system, software engineers, quality assurance people, or a managing director. Influential factors such as company policy, industry standards, or national laws are attributed to the representative stakeholder's viewpoint.

Each stakeholder has a viewpoint on a domain system. In principle, stakeholder viewpoints are defined as the set of system services required by stakeholders to do their duties, along with any constraints one stakeholder might place on the services provided to another. Thus, in practice, you must allocate to a particular viewpoint all those requirements relevant to providing the desired service and expressing its constraints.

Interviewing staff and analyzing documents are the best means of understanding the domain. You can draw upon several sources of knowledge, including the set of stakeholders identified from context diagrams,

---

DOMAIN ENGINEERING: AN OVERVIEW

A promising approach to dealing with software's supply–demand problem is to divide the development of software products into two life cycles: *domain engineering* to create reusable assets and *systems engineering* to use those assets to build systems.

Domain engineering encompasses four phases:
♦ domain requirements definition, which produces a domain user requirements specification;
♦ domain analysis, which produces a domain system requirements specification;
♦ domain design, which produces a domain system design specification; and
♦ implementation, which produces domain code components.

The VODRD method is concerned with the first phase: it compares and contrasts user requirement specifications from previous projects in the domain to create a domain-wide user requirements specification.

---

documentation from previous systems, knowledge gained from work on previous systems, and new customer requirements.

Because you want to make visible all stakeholder concerns, viewpoint identification is important, but can be difficult. For example, two telephone companies using a satellite may have similar but slightly different demands. Whether their needs are expressed by one or two viewpoints depends on the significance of their differences. However, you must find a balance between sufficient diversity and viewpoint overload. Too many viewpoints can create an unmanageable amount of information; too few can make comparing separate concerns difficult. The difficulty in finding this balance is compounded as the number and complexity of requirements increase. Typically, new viewpoints are introduced to simplify through abstraction and then associated with other viewpoints. You can add a viewpoint when a stakeholder appears in only one system or when a new stakeholder emerges. Once all stakeholders agree on the set of viewpoints, you can begin documentation.

Characterize the domain

In this step, domain sources are analyzed to establish a set of domain entities in a domain dictionary. Domain entities will be nouns; they can be real-world objects or more abstract entities that are generally recognized within the domain. Examples from the Spacecraft MPS domain are flight dynamics system, mission planning cycle, requester, and operational request. The resulting domain dictionary is the foundation for a data dictionary.

Although you can have a systems analyst create your domain dictionary, you should have it reviewed and modified by a domain expert. For example, even in a tightly coupled domain, it is common for differ-

Viewpoint	Name
Rationale	Justification for inclusion
Associations	Viewpoint name or set of requirements
Requirement	Number in document
Definition	Statement of requirement
Rationale	Justification for inclusion
Associations	<requirement link>

Figure 2. The viewpoint template includes a name, rationale, and viewpoint association.

Viewpoint	Flight Dynamics System
Rationale	External system
Associations	None
Requirement	ERS1-FDS-01
Definition	The MPS shall take Flight Prediction files from the flight dynamics system and modify the plan to allow the operations [OP_a, OP_b, OP_c] to occur
Rationale	To ensure accurate plans
Associations	ERS1-SEC-01
Requirement	CLUSTER-FDS-01
Definition	The MPS will use the Flight Dynamics Prediction files to define windows in the plan for the operations [OP_a, OP_b, OP_c, OP_d]
Rationale	To produce accurate plans
Associations	CLUSTER-SEC-01

Note: [OP_a, OP_b, OP_c, OP_d] are variables whose definition and value appear in the domain dictionary.

Figure 3. This part of the Flight Dynamic Systems viewpoint shows two similar requirements from two different systems: ERS-1 and Cluster.

ent terms to be used for the same element. A "short-term plan" in one system may be termed a "detailed plan" or even a "daily plan" in another. A domain expert knows that it is possible to standardize on one entity (short-term plan). This entity then becomes part of the domain dictionary, along with information about its attributes, its synonyms, and its relationships with other entities.

Document viewpoints

In this step, you consider each existing system in turn, and allocate a list of atomic requirements for each viewpoint. You must allocate all requirements in every existing system to at least one viewpoint. When this is complete, you can analyze the viewpoint documentation.

As Figure 2 shows, each viewpoint has a name, rationale, and association. The rationale explains the stakeholder's role, thus setting the context for requirements in this viewpoint. The rationale can also include a trace-back to knowledge sources, a statement on standards and quality issues, and a domain expert's comments.

Because many requirements in single systems are interconnected, you can only effectively compare them if you maintain the associations or links be-

tween viewpoints and requirements. Such relationships are depicted by a label and a viewpoint name or set of requirement identifiers. The label describes the relationship between one or more requirements in the same or another viewpoint. It can be any string, such as "applies_to," "depends_on," "opposite_to," and so on. You can use these links to aid your memory when requirements change and during detailed user requirements specification analysis, which results in the system requirements specification. Formalizing these links will help support the automated management of inconsistency.

A potential problem arises when a single requirement can be allocated to more than one viewpoint. Great care is needed to update each copy of the requirement if it changes or is linked to another requirement. The issue is more easily managed in a modern database tool, which can allow each viewpoint to see the one copy of the requirement.

As the number of requirements increases and new requirements are added, it becomes more difficult to know which requirements to link to and where to find them. It is impractical to consider every requirement. It helps to group and label requirements within viewpoints; for example, PLN-xxx indicates all requirements related to the planning algorithm. Practical tool support is required to link effectively, as we briefly describe later.

Analyze viewpoint documentation

Different systems requirements that share the same viewpoint should be compared on a one-to-one basis. The output is a viewpoint that contains reusable requirements. Whether or not to merge requirements will depend on each requirement's links. If both requirements have the same constraint, then the constraint itself may be reusable. In some cases you might be justified in relaxing the constraints to make the requirement reusable. When partitioning domain requirements into viewpoints, there are more intra-viewpoint links than inter-viewpoint links, making merging considerations much easier. You can leave conflicting requirements in the viewpoint. For single systems, conflict analysis within or between viewpoints is difficult. In domain modeling, modeling the conflict is important, but resolving it is not.

TABLE 1
AMPI VIEWPOINTS

Viewpoint	Explanation
MPS designer	
Flight dynamics system	generates orbital events and dynamics-related commands and parameters for a specified spacecraft
Ground station	this sends and receives the signals from the satellite
Space operations centre (end user)	someone who has bought space on the satellite (such as the weather organization)
Space operations centre (spacecraft engineer)	person responsible for the control of the satellite
AMPI system designer	
Mission information base	a repository, shared with the MCS, containing information about the operations of a satellite
MPS end user (planner)	person who can browse and edit plans generated by the MPS software
MPS end user (operator)	person who can browse plans generated by the MPS software;
MCS	
Mission support staff	people responsible for configuration management and change control of MPS software and mission plans.
Security	
Simulator	

In practice, system requirements that belong to a particular viewpoint are only as good as their sources. Sometimes the domain expert must carefully assess cases of inconsistency and omission and consider whether or not to change requirements or add them. An earlier article we wrote offers further details about writing reusable requirements.[8]

A VIEWPOINT CASE STUDY

A spacecraft mission control system monitors and controls a satellite by transmitting an operations sequence to the satellite and monitoring the telemetry the satellite sends back. The operations are carried in mission plans, based upon requests from customers (such as weather forecasters) and operations staff (spacecraft control engineers). Mission plans are generated by a mission planning system and edited by end users before being sent to mission control. Each MPS takes about 10 person-years to develop.

Because the complexity of spacecraft platforms and payloads is increasing and budgets face growing constraints, mission control systems must be developed and operated with greater performance and efficiency. In response to these pressures, systems are being developed that are easily customized across a range of missions. To this end, a European Space Operations Centre program is designing an Advanced Mission Planning Infrastructure (AMPI), a reusable and reconfigurable model that will help designers generate spacecraft MPSs based on their mission specifications. Our case study was part of this program.

The AMPI will have two types of users: the design-

ers of MPSs and those systems' end users. We worked on a project that used the VODRD method to build the AMPI requirements specification for the end users. We drew upon many sources, including

◆ the user requirements specification for four previous MPSs (Cluster, ISO, ERS-1, ERS-2),
◆ members of the staff who built these systems,
◆ the intended AMPI users, and
◆ the mission operations division of ESOC.

We developed each user requirements specification according to the European Space Agency's PSS-05 software engineering standard; each had 100 to 300 user requirements. Requirements were numbered, atomic, and written in natural language supplemented by drawings.

Initial steps

When we scoped the domain, we identified 13 viewpoints, as Table 1 shows. Our next step was to characterize the domain dictionary by entering a set of domain entities. These entities included dynamics system, mission planning cycle, operational requester, and scientific community.

Document viewpoint

We then allocated a list of atomic requirements for each viewpoint. Figure 3 shows part of the Flight Dynamics System viewpoint, which had two similar requirements from two different systems: ERS-1 and Cluster. Both requirements are linked to requirements of the Security viewpoint, as Figure 4 shows.

Figure 5 shows an association between the viewpoints of an MPS planner and an operator. The significant difference between the two is that the planner has

Security	
Rationale	This role is played by the Procurer, who is responsible for the mission's success
Associations	None
Requirement	ERS1-SEC-01
Definition	The MPS shall display a warning if the flight dynamics data is two days from expiration
Rationale	To ensure that flight dynamics data is up-to date
Associations	None
Requirement	CLUSTER-SEC-01
Definition	The MPS shall display a warning if the flight dynamics data is less than three days from expiration
Rationale	To ensure that flight dynamics data is up-to-date
Associations	None

Figure 4. Requirements in the Security viewpoint, shown here, are linked to those of the Flight Dynamic Systems shown in Figure 3.

Viewpoint	MPS End User (Planner)
Rationale	Interacts with MPS software such that can generate and edit plans
Associations	• Viewpoint: MPS End User (Operator) "All requirements in Operator apply to Planner"
Requirement	ERS2-PLN-01
Definition	The Planner will perform planning and replanning through the MPS.
Rationale	The MPS should be the sole source of planning and replanning activity
Associations	None

Figure 5. MPS End User (Planner) viewpoint and operator association.

Viewpoint	Flight Dynamics System
Rationale	External system
Associations	None
Requirement	AMPI-FDS-01
Definition	The MPS shall use the Flight Dynamics Prediction files to define windows in the plan for the operations OP_a / OP_b / OP_c / OP_d
Rationale	To ensure accurate plans (source: ERS1-FDS-01, CLUSTER-FDS-01)
Associations	AMPI-SEC-01

Figure 6. The revised Flight Dynamics System viewpoint.

a full set of browse/edit planning privileges, whereas the operator has read-only. Thus, all requirements that apply to the operator also apply to the planner.

Analyze viewpoint documentation

Figures 6 and 7 show the result of the rationalized Flight Dynamics System and Security viewpoints in Figure 1 and Figure 2. In both cases, we identified a parameterized reusable requirement and merged the rationale for inclusion and links to other viewpoints. The reusable requirement in each viewpoint now has a unique identifier. In the revised MPS End User (Planner) viewpoint (shown in Figure 5), we made only one change: the requirement identifiers were prefixed by "AMPI." Table 2 shows the profile of requirements allocated to each viewpoint.

Findings

Of the 539 requirements only 68—12 percent—were new (undocumented). Of the 471 existing requirements, 348—66 percent—emanated from the user requirements specifications for Cluster, ISO, ERS-1, and ERS-2. Of these requirements, 170 were common to more than one user requirements specification; the rest originated from one specification as follows:

- ◆ 18 from ERS-1
- ◆ 20 from ISO
- ◆ 16 from Cluster
- ◆ 124 from ERS-2

The 123 existing requirements not emanating from the previous projects came from other existing material, which shows how important it is to use a variety of sources for domain model definition.

The total effort to produce the AMPI user requirements specification was 713 person-hours. Of this, 263 person-hours were spent looking at previous documentation and talking to staff, and 450 person-hours were spent creating, writing, and reviewing the new document.

DISCUSSION

Between them, the four existing specifications we used contain around 500 user requirements. That we wrote 348 of them into the domain's user requirements specification confirms our belief that this domain has significant reuse potential, even if the organization's cultural and managerial strength is insufficient to fully exploit them.

The number of requirements related to the MPS Designer viewpoint was quite high and made cross-checking and comparison difficult, although we alleviated much of this difficulty by using database tool support. We created a simple database (using MS Access) with facilities for adding, editing, and linking viewpoints; and for adding, editing, merging, and searching for requirements within viewpoints. Our tool could have been improved by increasing its ability to navigate between related requirements, but we did not explore that option on this project.

One important assumption of our method is that existing specifications contain numbered atomic requirements. In our case study, all existing documentation in ESOC's development environment satisfied this assumption. However, legacy system documentation not written in this way would require additional effort to isolate requirements for reuse.

Regarding effort, the staff involved in our study had about nine person-years' domain experience between them and had some exposure to the previous mission planning systems. In general, the success of any domain engineering method is constrained by the differences in content, structure, and level of detail provided by system documents, as well as by the commitment and skill of the systems analysts and domain experts. Finally, it is essential to have computer-aided support, particularly when you identify domain entities, and identify and populate viewpoints.

Defining domain requirements is the first stage of the domain engineering lifecycle; the number, size, and complexity of the systems being compared make it a difficult stage indeed. Methods for easing this difficulty must be sensitive to numerous contextual factors, including the organization's software processes, existing software base, business objectives, and the domain's maturity.[9]

VODRD is a lightweight method for domain requirements definition. Although the form and structure of user requirements specifications may differ, viewpoints are somewhat static and make comparing requirements tractable. VODRD permits a user-centered approach to domain modeling that helps you build systems that users want. Our approach is flexible because the work can be distributed evenly among staff and performed successfully, which addresses a key issue in domain engineering: the resources needed to carry it out. Although our results using VODRD in this case study are promising, more studies are needed to validate the approach. ❖

Viewpoint	Security
Rationale	External system
Requirement	AMPI-SEC-01
Definition	The MPS shall display a warning if the flight dynamics data is FDD-EXPIRY-DAYS] days from expiration
Rationale	To ensure that the flight dynamics data is up to date (source: ERS1-SEC-01, CLUSTER-SEC-01)
Associations	None

Figure 7. The revised Security viewpoint.

TABLE 2
PROFILE OF REQUIREMENTS PER VIEWPOINT

Viewpoint	Requirements
MPS designer	135
Flight dynamics system	23
Ground station	5
Spacecraft operations centre (end user)	36
Spacecraft operations centre (spacecraft engineer)	25
AMPI system software designer	61
Mission information base	10
MPS end user (planner)	71
MPS end user (operator)	87
Mission control system	41
Mission support staff	11
Security	33
Simulator	1
Total	539

ACKNOWLEDGMENTS

Our case study is based on work by a consortium that includes Vega Space Systems Engineering GmbH, Darmstadt, Germany, and Space Applications Services, Zaventem, Belgium, for the Operations Centre of the European Space Agency, Darmstadt, Germany. The opinions and conclusions we draw are our own and not those of the European Space Agency. We thank all the reviewers of this paper for their helpful comments. Their astute observations contributed considerably to the development of our ideas.

REFERENCES
1. W. Tracz, L. Coglianese, and P. Young, "A Domain-Specific Software Architecture Engineering Process Outline," ACM Software Eng. Notes, Apr. 1998, pp. 40-49.
2. D. Jackson and M. Jackson, "Problem Decomposition for Reuse," Software Eng. J., Jan. 1996, Vol. 11, No. 1, pp. 19-30.
3. R. Prieto-Diaz, "Domain Analysis: An Introduction," ACM Sigsoft Software Eng. Notes, Vol. 15, No. 2, 1990, pp.47-54.
4. G. Mullery, "CORE : A Method for Controlled Requirements Expression," Proc. 4th Int'l Conf. Soft. Eng.(ICSE-4), IEEE Comp. Soc. Press, Los Alamitos, Calif., 1979, pp.126-135.
5. J.C.S.D.P. Leite, and P.A. Freeman, "Requirements Validation Through Viewpoint Resolution," IEEE Trans. Software Eng., Vol.

Researcher's
CORNER

17, No. 12, 1991, pp. 1253-1269.

6. M. Ainsworth, S. Riddle, and P.J.L. Wallis, "Formal Validation of Viewpoint Specification," *Software Eng. J.*, Jan. 1996, Vol. 11, No. 1, pp. 58-66.
7. G. Kontonya and L. Sommerville, "Requirements Engineering with Viewpoints," *Software Eng. J.*, Vol. 11, No. 1, Jan. 1996, pp. 5-18.
8. M. Mannion, B. Keepence, and S. Smith, "SMARTRe Requirements: Writing Reusable Requirements," *Proc. 1995 Int'l Symp. and Workshop Systems Eng. Computer-Based Systems*, IEEE Comp. Soc. Press, Los Alamitos, Calif., 1995, pp. 27-34.
9. S. Wartik and R. Prieto-Diaz, "Criteria for Comparing Reuse-oriented Domain Analysis approaches," *Int'l J. Software Eng. and Knowledge Eng.*, Vol. 2, No. 3, 1992, pp. 403-431.

Address questions about this article to Mannion at the Department of Mechanical, Manufacturing and Systems Engineering, Napier University, 10 Colinton Road, Edinburgh, Scotland, EH10 5DT; m.mannion@napier.ac.uk.

About the Authors

Michael Mannion is a senior lecturer in systems engineering at Napier University, Edinburgh. His research interests are in system requirements engineering, software reuse, and artificial intelligence. He previously worked for GEC Marconi Radar and Praxis Systems. He is chair of the BCS Special Interest Group on Software Reuse.
Mannion received a BSc in computer science from Brunel University, London, and a PhD in artificial intelligence from Bristol University. He is a member of the BCS and the IEEE.

Barry Keepence is a lecturer in systems engineering at Napier University. His research interests are in system requirements engineering and software reuse. He was previously a systems engineer in the European space industry working on ground and control systems. He is a member of the British National Space Centre Software Steering Committee.
Keepence received a BSc in electronics and a PhD in robotics from the University of Wales, Cardiff.

David Harper is a project manager and consultant for Vega Group Plc, a British company specializing in spacecraft operations and systems engineering consultancy. He is currently based in Vega's German office in Darmstadt, Hessen, where he divides his time between a variety of projects in spacecraft operations and equipment emulation for maintenance training. Previously, he spent three years at Imperial College, London, working in the computing department's functional programming section.
Harper received a BSc in computer science from Imperial College.

156

Reprinted from IEEE Software,
Sept./Oct. 1997, pp. 67-74.

A Cost–Value Approach for Prioritizing Requirements

JOACHIM KARLSSON
Focal Point AB

KEVIN RYAN
University of Limerick

Deciding which requirements really matter is a difficult task and one increasingly demanded because of time and budget constraints. The authors developed a cost–value approach for prioritizing requirements and applied it to two commercial projects.

Developing software systems that meet stakeholders' needs and expectations is the ultimate goal of any software provider seeking a competitive edge. To achieve this, you must effectively and accurately manage your stakeholders' system requirements: the features, functions, and attributes they need in their software system.[1] Once you agree on these requirements, you can use them as a focal point for the development process and produce a software system that meets the expectations of both customers and users. However, in real-world software development, there are usually more requirements than you can implement given stakeholders' time and resource constraints. Thus, project managers face a dilemma: How do you select a subset of the customers' requirements and still produce a system that meets their needs?

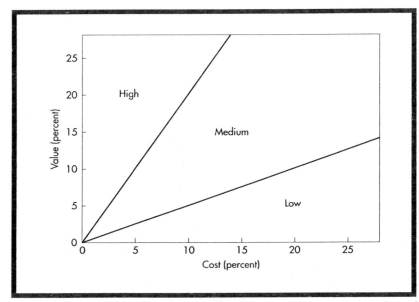

Figure 1. *Using AHP, you can calculate each candidate requirement's relative value and implementation cost and plot them on a cost-value diagram, such as the one shown here.*

Most software organizations carry out this selection process informally, and quite frequently produce software systems that developers, customers, and users view as suboptimal. Without techniques to make these crucial choices, this outcome is hardly surprising. Indeed, despite the recent rapid and welcome growth in requirements engineering research, managers still don't have simple, effective, and industrially proven techniques for prioritizing requirements. A recent survey[2] shows that few companies know how to establish and communicate requirements priorities; another[3] identified prioritization as a key but neglected issue in requirements engineering research.

Clear, unambiguous knowledge about requirement priorities helps you focus the development process and more effectively and efficiently manage projects. It can also help you

♦ make acceptable tradeoffs among sometimes conflicting goals such as quality, cost, and time-to-market;[4] and

♦ allocate resources based on the requirement's importance to the project as a whole.

Finally, when time-to-market is particularly important, knowing how to rank your requirements can help you plan releases by indicating which functions are critical and which can be added (and in what order) over successive releases.

We have developed an analytical tool

for prioritizing requirements based on a cost–value approach. This tool can help you rank candidate requirements in two dimensions: according to their value to customer and users, and according to their estimated cost of implementation. Our method has been successfully applied in two commercial telecommunications software development projects.

A COST–VALUE APPROACH

A process for prioritizing software requirements must, on one hand, be simple and fast, and, on the other, yield accurate and trustworthy results. If both of these conditions are not met, the process is unlikely to be used in commercial software systems development. The prioritizing process also must hold stakeholder satisfaction as both the ultimate goal and the guiding theme. Shoji Shiba and his colleagues argue that there are three main factors in stakeholder satisfaction: quality, cost, and delivery.[5] For a software system to succeed, quality must be maximized, cost minimized, and time-to-delivery be as short as possible. Our cost-value approach prioritizes requirements according to their relative value and cost. Based on this information, software managers can make decisions such as which requirements to be excluded from the first release to keep the time-to-market at minimum.

We interpret *quality* in relation to a candidate requirement's potential contribution to customer satisfaction with the resulting system. *Cost* is the cost of successfully implementing the candidate requirement. In practice, software developers often calculate costs purely in terms of money. However, we found that prioritizing based on relative rather than absolute assignments is faster, more accurate, and more trustworthy.[6]

Why pairwise? To investigate candidate requirements, we use the Analytic Hierarchy Process,[7] which compares requirements pairwise according to their relative value and cost. The pairwise comparison approach includes much redundancy and is thus less sensitive to judgmental errors common to techniques using absolute assignments. The AHP actually indicates inconsistencies by calculating a consistency ratio of judgmental errors. The smaller the consistency ratio, the fewer the inconsistencies, and thus the more reliable the results. The box "The Analytic Hierarchy Process" on page 69 describes the AHP in more detail.

Process. There are five steps to prioritizing requirements using the cost–value approach.

1. Requirements engineers carefully review candidate requirements for completeness and to ensure that they are stated in an unambiguous way.

2. Customers and users (or suitable substitutes) apply AHP's pairwise comparison method to assess the relative value of the candidate requirements.

3. Experienced software engineers use AHP's pairwise comparison to estimate the relative cost of implementing each candidate requirement.

4. A software engineer uses AHP to calculate each candidate requirement's relative value and implementation cost, and plots these on a cost–value diagram. As Figure 1 shows, value is depicted on the *y* axis and estimated cost on the *x* axis.

5. The stakeholders use the cost–value diagram as a conceptual map for analyzing and discussing the candidate

THE ANALYTIC HIERARCHY PROCESS

To make decisions, you identify, analyze, and make trade-offs between different alternatives to achieve an objective. The more efficient the means for analyzing and evaluating the alternatives, the more likely you'll be satisfied with the outcome. To help you make decisions, the Analytic Hierachy Process compares alternatives in a stepwise fashion and measures their contribution to your objective.[1]

AHP in action. Using AHP for decision making involves four steps. We'll assume here that you want to evaluate candidate requirements using the criterion of value.

Step 1. *Set up the n requirements in the rows and columns of an* $n \times n$ *matrix.* We'll assume here that you have four candidate requirements: Req1, Req2, Req3, and Req4, and you want to know their relative value. Insert the *n* requirements into the rows and columns of a matrix of order *n* (in this case we have a 4×4 matrix).

Step 2. *Perform pairwise comparisons of all the requirements according to the criterion.* The fundamental scale used for this purpose is shown in Table A.[1] For each pair of requirements (starting with Req1 and Req2, for example) insert their determined relative intensity of value in the position (Req1, Req2) where the row of Req1 meets the column of Req2. In position (Req2, Req1) insert the reciprocal value, and in all positions in the main diagonal insert a "1." Continue to perform pairwise comparisons of Req1–Req3, Req1–Req4, Req2–Req3, and so on. For a matrix of order *n*, $n \cdot (n-1)/2$ comparisons are required. Thus, in this example, six pairwise comparisons are required; they might look like this:

	Req1	Req2	Req3	Req4
Req1	1	1/3	2	4
Req2	3	1	5	3
Req3	1/2	1/5	1	1/3
Req4	1/4	1/3	3	1

Step 3. *Use averaging over normalized columns to estimate the eigenvalues of the matrix* (which represent the criterion distribution). Thomas Saaty proposes a simple method for this, known as averaging over normalized columns.[1] First, calculate the sum of the *n* columns in the comparison matrix. Next, divide each element in the matrix by the sum of the column the element is a member of, and calculate the sums of each row:

	Req1	Req2	Req3	Req4	*Sum*
Req1	0.21	0.18	0.18	0.48	*1.05*
Req2	0.63	0.54	0.45	0.36	*1.98*
Req3	0.11	0.11	0.09	0.04	*0.34*
Req4	0.05	0.18	0.27	0.12	*0.62*

Then normalize the sum of the rows (divide each row sum with the number of requirements). The result of this computation is referred to as the *priority matrix* and is an estimation of the eigenvalues of the matrix.

$$\frac{1}{4} \cdot \begin{pmatrix} 1.05 \\ 1.98 \\ 0.34 \\ 0.62 \end{pmatrix} = \begin{pmatrix} 0.26 \\ 0.50 \\ 0.09 \\ 0.16 \end{pmatrix}$$

Step 4. *Assign each requirement its relative value based on the estimated eigenvalues.* From the resulting eigenvalues of the comparison matrix, the following information can be extracted:

- Req1 contains 26 percent of the requirements' total value,
- Req2 contains 50 percent,
- Req3 contains 9 percent, and
- Req4 contains 16 percent.

Result consistency. If we were able to determine precisely the relative value of all requirements, the eigenvalues would be perfectly consistent. For instance, if we determine that Req1 is much more valuable than Req2, Req2 is somewhat more valuable than Req3, and Req3 is slightly more valuable than Req1, an inconsistency has occurred and the result's accuracy is decreased. The redundancy of the pairwise comparisons makes the AHP much less sensitive to judgment errors; it also lets you measure judgment errors by calculating the consistency index of the comparison matrix, and then calculating the consistency ratio.

Consistency index. The consistency index (CI) is a first indicator of result accuracy of the pairwise comparisons. You calculate it as $CI = (\lambda \max - n)/(n-1)$. $\lambda \max$ denotes the maximum principal eigenvalue of the comparison matrix. The closer the value of $\lambda \max$ is to *n* (the number of requirements), the smaller the judgmental errors and thus the more consistent the result. To estimate $\lambda \max$, you first multiply the comparison matrix by the priority vector:

$$\begin{pmatrix} 1 & 1/3 & 2 & 4 \\ 3 & 1 & 5 & 3 \\ 1/2 & 1/5 & 1 & 1/3 \\ 1/4 & 1/3 & 3 & 1 \end{pmatrix} \cdot \begin{pmatrix} 0.26 \\ 0.50 \\ 0.09 \\ 0.16 \end{pmatrix} = \begin{pmatrix} 1.22 \\ 2.18 \\ 0.37 \\ 0.64 \end{pmatrix}$$

Then you divide the first element of the resulting vector by the first element in the priority vector, the second element of the resulting vector by the second element in the priority vector, and so on:

$$\begin{pmatrix} 1.22 / 0.26 \\ 2.18 / 0.50 \\ 0.37 / 0.09 \\ 0.64 / 0.16 \end{pmatrix} = \begin{pmatrix} 4.66 \\ 4.40 \\ 4.29 \\ 4.13 \end{pmatrix}$$

To calculate $\lambda \max$, average over the elements in the resulting vector:

$$\lambda \max = \frac{4.66 + 4.40 + 4.29 + 4.13}{4} = 4.37$$

Now the consistency index can be calculated:

$$CI = \frac{\lambda \max - n}{n - 1} = \frac{4.37 - 4}{4 - 1} = 0.12$$

To find out if the resulting consistency index (CI = 0.12) is acceptable, you must calculate the consistency ratio.

Consistency ratio. The consistency indices of randomly generated reciprocal matrices from the scale 1 to 9 are called the random indices, RI.[1] The ratio of CI to RI for the same-order matrix is called the consistency ratio (CR), which defines the accuracy of the pairwise comparisons. The RI for matrices of order n are given below. The first row shows the order of the matrix, and the second the corresponding RI value.

1	2	3	4	5	6	7	8	9	10	11	12	13	14	15
0.00	0.00	0.58	0.90	1.12	1.24	1.32	1.41	1.45	1.49	1.51	1.48	1.56	1.57	1.59

According to Table A, the RI for matrices of order 4 is 0.90. Thus, the consistency ratio for our example is

$$CR = \frac{CI}{RI} = \frac{0.12}{0.90} = 0.14 \ .$$

As a general rule, a consistency ratio of 0.10 or less is considered acceptable.[1] This means that our result here is less than ideal. In practice, however, consistency ratios exceeding 0.10 occur frequently.

REFERENCES

1. T.L. Saaty, *The Analytic Hierarchy Process*, McGraw-Hill, New York, 1980.

TABLE A
SCALE FOR PAIRWISE COMPARISONS

Relative intensity	Definition	Explanation
1	Of equal value	Two requirements are of equal value
3	Slightly more value	Experience slightly favors one requirement over another
5	Essential or strong value	Experience strongly favors one requirement over another
7	Very strong value	A requirement is strongly favored and its dominance is demonstrated in practice
9	Extreme value	The evidence favoring one over another is of the highest possible order of affirmation
2, 4, 6, 8	Intermediate values between two adjacent judgments	When compromise is needed
Reciprocals	If requirement i has one of the above numbers assigned to it when compared with requirement j, then j has the reciprocal value when compared with i.	

requirements. Based on this discussion, software managers prioritize the requirements and decide which will actually be implemented. They can also use the information to develop strategies for release planning.

CASE STUDY 1: THE RAN PROJECT

Since 1992, Ericsson Radio Systems AB and the Department of Computer and Information Science at Linköping University have been involved in a joint research program to identify, apply, and evaluate ways to improve the early phases of the software engineering process. As part of this collaboration, in January 1994 we were invited in to use the industry-as-laboratory approach,[8] performing in-depth case studies in an industrial environment. For the first study, we selected Ericsson's Radio Access Network project.

The goal of the RAN project was to identify and specify requirements for a system that would give managers information about mobile telephony system operation.[9] The project started small, with a staff of five, but as a result of our study it grew considerably and is now an umbrella for a portfolio of both research and development projects.

First steps. We identified 14 high-level requirements (services) that covered the main system functionality. These high-level requirements were intended to give managers information about issues such as capacity, coverage, and quality in a mobile communications system. Once we'd defined the 14 requirements, the project members reviewed and agreed on them. The prioritizing technique in use at that time was to rank-order the requirements on an ordinal scale ranging from 1 to 3, where 1 denotes highest priority. In practice, the requirements belonging to category 1 were then implemented and the rest discarded or postponed to future releases. Because we'd used this technique before and found it far from optimal,[6] we decided to prioritize RAN requirements

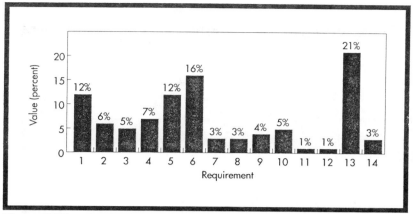

Figure 2. The value distribution of the 14 requirements in the RAN project.

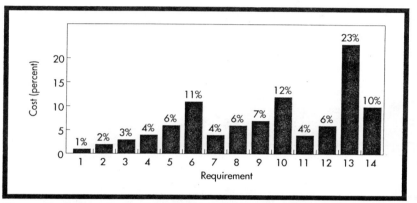

Figure 3. Estimated cost of requirements implementation in the RAN project. Requirements 6, 10, 13, and 14 constitute 56 percent of the total implementation costs.

using the cost–value approach.

We asked a group of experienced project members to represent customers' views and carefully instructed them on prioritizing requirements, making pairwise comparisons, choosing the scale to be used, and deciding how many comparisons would be needed. We also explained the importance of carrying out the pairwise comparisons carefully.

To begin, the project manager explained each candidate requirement and discussed it with project participants. He did this to make the requirements more clear and reduce subsequent misinterpretations. We distributed sheets outlining the 91 unique pairs of requirements, including the fundamental scale (as shown in Table A in "The Analytic Hierarchy Process" on page 70). Participants then performed pairwise comparisons of the candidate requirements, first according to value and later, in a separate session, according to the estimated

implementation cost.

We let the participants work with the requirement pairs in any order they chose, allowing for retraction during the comparison process. The session was not moderated and participants worked at their own pace. Discussions were allowed, though in fact there were very few. Completing the cost–value approach took about an hour. When all 14 requirements had been pairwise compared, we calculated the value distribution and the cost distribution, as well as the consistency indices and ratios of the pairwise comparisons. There were some judgmental errors, since the consistency ratios for both value and cost were computed as 0.18. Based on the resulting distributions, we outlined the candidate requirements in a cost–value diagram and presented the results to the project members.

Requirements' value. Each requirement's determined value is relative and based on

feature

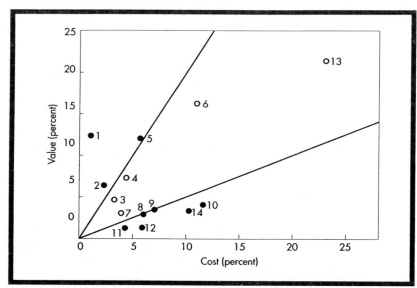

Figure 4. *Cost–value diagram for the RAN project requirements. By not implementing the requirements that contribute little to stakeholder satisfaction, such as 10, 11, and 12, you can significantly reduce the cost and duration of development.*

a ratio scale. This means that a requirement whose determined value is 0.10 is twice as valuable as a requirement with a determined value of 0.05. Moreover, the sum of all requirements value measures is always 1. Thus, a requirement with a determined value of 0.10 represents 10 percent of the total value of the requirements set. Figure 2 shows the value distribution of the 14 requirements in the RAN project. As the figure shows, the value of individual requirements can vary by orders of magnitude. The four most valuable requirements—1, 5, 6, and 13—constitute 61 percent of the total value; the four least valuable requirements—7, 8, 11, and 12—contribute a mere 8 percent. At the extremes, requirement 13 is about 20 times as valuable as requirement number 11.

Requirements' cost. A requirement's estimated cost is also relative and based on a ratio scale; the sum of all costs is again 1. Figure 3 shows the estimated cost of RAN's 14 requirements, which can again vary by orders of magnitude. The four most expensive requirements—6, 10, 13, and 14—constitute 56 percent of the total cost; the four least expensive re-

quirements—1, 2, 3, and 11—account for only 10 percent. Looking again at the extreme values, requirement number 13 is about 20 times as expensive to implement as requirement number 1.

Requirements cost–value analysis. Figure 4 shows the cost–value diagram of the 14 requirements. For discussion purposes, we divide cost–value diagrams into three distinct areas:

♦ requirements with a high ratio of value to cost (a value–cost ratio exceeding 2),

♦ requirements with medium ratio of value to cost (a value–cost ratio between 0.5 and 2), and

♦ requirements with a low ratio of value to cost (a value–cost ratio lower than 0.5).

As such, we infer that requirements 1, 2, and 5 fall into the high ratio category; requirements 3, 4, 6, 7, and 13 into the medium ratio category; and requirements 8, 9, 10, 11, 12, and 14 into the low ratio category. Based on these categories, the software managers were able to effectively and accurately prioritize their requirements.

The cost–value diagram clearly facilitates requirements selection. If, hypothetically, you chose to implement all requirements except numbers 10, 11, and 12, the software system's value for its customers would be 94 percent of the possible maximum, while the cost would be reduced to 78 percent of the cost for implementing all requirements. In general, by not implementing the requirements that contribute little to stakeholder satisfaction, you can significantly reduce the cost and duration of development.

CASE STUDY 2: THE PMR PROJECT

Encouraged by the apparent usefulness and effectiveness of the cost–value approach in the RAN project, we undertook a second case study. We picked a project that was developing a fourth release: the Performance Management Traffic Recording project. PMR is a software system that enables recording and analysis of mobile telecommunications traffic. The project began in 1992 with a full-time staff of 15 people, and has delivered 10 releases of varying sizes thus far.

At the time we joined the project, the system's third release was installed and running at customer sites. Many new requirements had emerged that had to be taken into account in planning the next release. We divided these new requirements into three categories: those demanding traditional defect correction, those requiring performance enhancement, and those suggesting added functionality. We decided to prioritize only the last category because both the project managers and the customers agreed that all defects had to be corrected and performance had to be enhanced. However, the exact functions to be added were up for negotiation.

The 11 high-level functional requirements dealt with issues such as presentation, sorting, and structuring new types of information. To prioritize these requirements each project member had to complete 55 pairwise comparisons for each criterion using the cost–value approach; this required slightly over 30 minutes. This rate is in line with the effort on the RAN project.

Requirements' value. Figure 5 shows the value distribution of the 11 requirements in the PMR project. Once again, the three most valuable requirements carry most of the value: requirements 4, 5, and 6 account for 63 percent.

Requirements' cost. Figure 6 shows the cost distribution of the 11 requirements. The three most expensive requirements—4, 5, and 9—account for 57 percent of implementation costs.

Requirements' cost–value analysis. Figure 7 shows the candidate requirements in the PMR project in a cost–value diagram. Of the 11 candidate requirements in the PMR project, two fall into the high ratio, six into the medium ratio, and three into the low ratio category. This illustrates how the management task of release planning, for example, is aided by the cost–value diagram. If the requirements with high and medium ratios were selected for implementation, 95 percent of the value would be obtained at 75 percent of the cost. Again, this suggests that you can deliver a software system with substantial customer satisfaction at a significant reduction in cost.

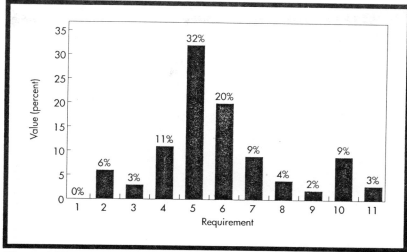

Figure 5. *The requirements' value in the PMR project. Requirements 4, 5, and 6 account for 63 percent of the value.*

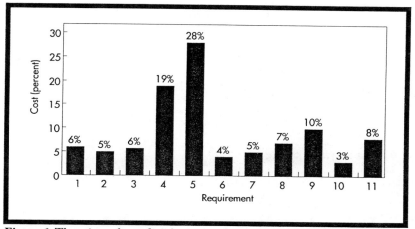

Figure 6. *The estimated cost of implementing the 11 requirements in the PMR project.*

Software engineering has been criticized for lacking the trade-off analysis that is always part of multidisciplinary systems engineering.[10] We believe the cost–value approach is a useful first step in filling this need. In some respects, our approach is similar to that of the Quality Attribute Requirements and Conflict Consultant tool within Barry Boehm's Win-Win system.[11] However, because of the mathematical basis of AHP, our approach yields more concrete results and could be a useful complement within the Win-Win environment. Similarly, recent work in the field of software architecture provides mathematical analyses of the quantitative design space,[12] such as spectrum analysis and contribution analysis. The cost–value approach is

an important addition to these approaches as well, as it is more visible, more robust, and easier to use.

There are still a number of problems to be overcome if our approach is to be easily adopted by practitioners. Although our initial users found the cost–value approach intuitive and more useful than traditional approaches, they also found carrying out all the required pairwise comparisons tedious. They sometimes got distracted and had to backtrack to check the consistency of earlier pairwise comparisons.

We have identified several additional issues to be resolved. First, the method takes no account of interdependencies between requirements, leaving software managers to deal with them. For example, to imple-

ment a low-cost, high-value requirement, you might have to implement a high-cost, low-value one as well. This situation did not arise in our case studies, where the requirement sets were quite small. With a larger number of requirements, this could be a major consideration. We are continuing to work on these issues. A more detailed account of this work, including our experience with a prototype tool, will be published in *Requirements Engineering Journal*, Vol. 2, No. 1 (Springer-Verlag, 1997). More requirements will also raise the problem of complexity, since the number of pairwise comparisons is of $O(n^2)$. Thus, we are now developing adequate tools to support the pairwise comparison process, to minimize the number of comparisons required, and to cater to the interdependen-

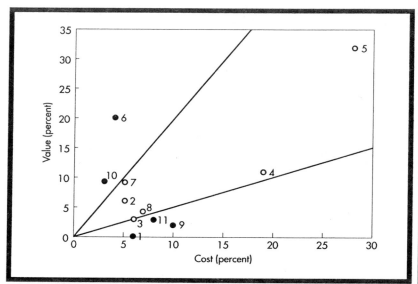

Figure 7. *Cost–value diagram depicting the PMR project requirements.*

cies that will inevitably arise. This tool will also be capable of storing information about the pairwise comparisons such as the people responsible, their rationale, and their assumptions.

Our cost–value method is based on a well-established analytical technique and, with reasonable effort, provides a clear indication of the relative costs and values of all candidate requirements. The case studies have shown that, even in its present form, the cost–value approach is useful for prioritizing requirements. It may also be especially applicable as an aid for requirements selection, since we have found that both the value and cost of requirements can vary by orders of magnitude. Such differences are effectively visualized through cost–value diagrams, which let management take action to maximize stakeholder satisfaction. The diagrams can also be used to prioritize requirements over several release cycles.

Communications between customers, users, and project managers are always likely to be difficult. A clear understanding of the choices involved in requirements selection can greatly assist this communication. We believe that our cost–value approach lays the foundation for a clear, sound, and usable method for determining requirements priorities. ◆

ACKNOWLEDGMENTS

This work was supported by Ericsson Radio Systems AB and The Swedish National Board for Industrial and Technical Development, project number 9303280-2. We also thank the anonymous reviewers for providing valuable comments, and Lena Bjerlöw, Stefan Olsson, and Kristian Sandahl for commenting on a draft of this article.

REFERENCES

1. A. Davis, *Software Requirements: Objects, Functions and States*, Prentice Hall Int'l, Englewood Cliffs, N.J., 1993.
2. M. Lubars, C. Potts, and C. Richter, "A Review of the State of the Practice in Requirements Modeling," *Proc. IEEE Int'l Symp. Req. Eng.*, IEEE Computer Soc. Press, Los Alamitos, Calif., 1993, pp. 2-14.
3. J. Siddiqi and M.C. Shekaran, "Requirements Engineering: The Emerging Wisdom," *IEEE Software*, Mar. 1996, pp. 15-19.
4. B. Curtis, H. Krasner, and N. Iscoe, "A Field Study of the Software Design Process for Large Systems," *Comm. ACM*, Dec. 1988, pp. 1268-1287.
5. S. Shiba, A. Graham, and D. Walden, *A New American TQM: Four Practical Revolutions in Management*, Productivity Press, Portland, Ore., 1993.
6. J. Karlsson, "Software Requirements Prioritizing," *Proc. 2nd IEEE Int'l Conf. Req. Eng.*, IEEE Computer Soc. Press, Los Alamitos, Calif., 1996, pp. 110-116.
7. T.L. Saaty, *The Analytic Hierarchy Process*, McGraw-Hill, New York, 1980.
8. C. Potts, "Software Engineering Research Revisited," *IEEE Software*, Sept. 1993, pp. 19-28.
9. J. Karlsson, *Towards a Strategy for Software Requirements Selection*, Dept. of Computer and Information Science, Linköping Univ., Linköping, Sweden, Licentiate thesis 513, 1995.
10. S.J. Andriole and P.A. Freeman, "Software Systems Engineering: The Case for a New Discipline," *Software Eng. J.*, May 1993, pp. 165-179.
11. B.W. Boehm and H. In, "Identifying Quality-Requirements Conflicts," *IEEE Software*, Mar. 1996, pp. 25-35.
12. T. Asada et al., "The Quantified Design Space," *Software Architecture*, M. Shaw and D. Garlan, eds., Prentice Hall, Englewood Cliffs, N.J., 1996, pp.116-128.

Joachim Karlsson is cofounder and managing director of Focal Point AB in Linköping, Sweden, and is affiliated with Linköping University. He consults, lectures, and conducts research on software process, software quality, and requirements engineering.

Karlsson received his MSc and Licentiate degree in computer science from Linköping University, Sweden. He is a member of IEEE.

Kevin Ryan is a professor of information technology at the University of Limerick in Limerick, Ireland. His main research interest is requirements engineering. He has lectured and done research on software topics in universities and in industry in Ireland, the US, Africa, and Sweden and has been involved in major Esprit projects on software methods and tools.

Ryan received his BA, BAI engineering, and PhD in computer science from Trinity College, Dublin. He is a member of the IEEE Computer Society, ACM, and the Irish and British computer societies.

Address questions about this article to Karlsson at Focal Point AB, Teknikringen 1E, 58330 Linköping, Sweden; joachim.karlsson@focalpoint.se; or Ryan at kevin.ryan@ul.ie.

164

Reprinted from IEEE ISSRE 98,
September 1998, pp. 70-79.

Derivation of an Integrated Operational Profile and Use Case Model

Per Runeson and Björn Regnell
Department of Communications Systems
Lund University, P.O. Box 118
SE-221 00 Lund, Sweden
e-mail: (per.runeson, bjorn.regnell)@tts.lth.se

Abstract

Requirements engineering and software reliability engineering both involve model building related to the usage of the intended system; requirements models and test case models respectively are built. Use case modelling for requirements engineering and operational profile testing for software reliability engineering are techniques which are evolving into software engineering practice. In this paper, approaches towards integration of the use case model and the operational profile model are proposed. By integrating the derivation of the models, effort may be saved in both development and maintenance of software artifacts. Two integration approaches are presented, transformation and extension. It is concluded that the use case model structure can be transformed into an operational profile model adding the profile information. As a next step, the use case model can be extended to include the information necessary for the operational profile. Through both approaches, modelling and maintenance effort as well as risks for inconsistencies can be reduced. A positive spin-off effect is that quantitative information on usage frequencies is available in the requirements, enabling planning and prioritizing based on that information.

1. Introduction

Bringing the software development under control is a common goal for requirements engineering (RE) and software reliability engineering (SRE). Requirements engineers strive for capturing as much as possible of the requirements on the software, before it is being built. Thereby late and expensive changes are reduced. Software reliability engineers strive for quantifying and improving the quality of the software, in particular the reliability. Thereby disappointing experiences on insufficient operational reliability, with belonging costs are reduced.

However, the strive for reduced costs by taking problems upfront is not the only common denominator for RE and SRE. In both areas a large share of the job is collecting information and building models, both of which take the user's viewpoint. There are opportunities for coordinating tasks for RE and SRE, which leads to reduction of total modelling effort.

Use cases are means for requirements engineering to capture the requirements on a system [1, 2]. Use cases define usage scenarios for different users of the system, thereby defining the external requirements on system capabilities.

The operational profile is an external user-oriented test model which specifies the intended usage of the system in terms of events and their invocation probabilities [3, 4]. A similar approach is presented as statistical usage testing in the Cleanroom methodology [5, 6, 7]. Test cases are generated from the operational profile, thus enabling estimation of the operational software reliability already during system test.

Positive results are reported on the application of both methods. Use cases and scenarios have gained acceptance, both in research and industry, for their ability to support analysis, documentation and validation of requirements [8, 9, 10, 11]. Operational profile testing is reported to save effort during system test and to reduce the operational failures [4]. In this paper we present an integrated approach which provides both use cases for the requirements specification and the operational profile for testing from the same information collection and modelling. A use case based requirements specification has a structure very similar to an operational profile model. Many concepts can be mapped upon each others. We propose a mapping scheme for transformation of a requirements model into a test model. This approach can be further elaborated towards making a single integrated model that fulfils both purposes: requirements and test model. In both cases, effort can be saved in the derivation of the model and in the second approach, also in the maintenance of the model during development and in future maintenance of the system.

The paper is structured as follows. Chapter 2 gives a brief overview of the use case based requirements and Chapter 3 provides and introduction to operational profile testing. In Chapter 4 two approaches to integration are presented and evaluated, the *transformation* and *extension* approaches. A summary is given in Chapter 5.

A subset of a telephone system, a Private Branch eXchange (PBX), which is used in an educational environment, is used throughout the paper as an example [12]. The PBX is a commercial switch with its control processor "short-circuited" and connected to a UNIX workstation running the control software. The PBX provides basic telephony to the connected subscribers, see Figure 1. In its basic version, its only feature is to make a call from one caller to a callee. During a project course, the students implement extended services to the control software, such as charging, and call forwarding.

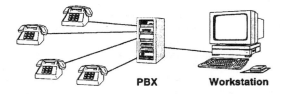

PBX   **Workstation**

Figure 1.   Example PBX system

2. Use Case Based Requirements

2.1. Background

The elicitation, analysis and documentation of requirements on software systems is a crucial and non-trivial task. The concepts of use cases and scenarios has gained widespread acceptance in object-oriented methods [1, 13, 14] and in the field of requirements engineering [15, 16, 17]. A strong motivation for applying use cases is their support for the modelling of functional requirements in a way that is understandable to users and customers. This ability is embodied in the main idea behind use case modelling, which is to elicit and document requirements by defining and discussing specific contexts of system usage as they are anticipated by the users.

2.2. Method

In [18, 19] a method for use case modelling is presented. This method is an extension of the use case modelling part of the OOSE approach [1]. The major activities are summarized below:

- Elicit actors and their goals.
- Define use cases based on the actors and their goals.
- Elicit scenarios for each use case.
- Describe the events in the scenarios.

The main concepts in the these activities are briefly described in the following. Users can be of different types, called **actors**. A user is thus an instance of an actor. An actor represents a set of users that have some common characteristics with respect to why and how they use the target system. In the PBX system, two actors can be identified, *subscriber* and *operator*. Each actor has a set of **goals**, reflecting such common characteristics. Goals are objectives that users have when using the services of a target system. Thus, goals are used to categorize users into actors. Figure 2a shows the goals of the two actors in the PBX example.

A **service** is a package of functional entities (features) offered to the users in order to satisfy one or more goals that the users have. Figure 2b includes the services of our PBX example system.

A **use case** represents a usage situation where one or more services of the target system are used by one or more actors with the aim to accomplish one or more goals. Figure 2c shows use cases of the PBX example, and their relation to actors, goals, and services.

A **scenario**[1] is a specific realisation of a use case described as a finite sequence of events. A scenario may either model a successful or an unsuccessful accomplishment of one or more goals. A use case may cover an unlimited number of scenarios as it may include alternatives and repetitions. A scenario, however, is a specific and bound realisation of a use case, with all choices determined to one specific path. Figure 3a shows a number of scenarios identified for the use case *normal call*.

When describing the events of each scenario it is useful to define a **data model**, **messages** of the system and **system actions**. The latter mean system intrinsic events which are atomic in the sense that there is no communication between the target system and the users that participate in the use case. The data and messages for the PBX example are shown in Figure 3b and 3c respectively, and the system actions can be seen in the example scenario described in Figure 4.

---

1. Some authors use the terms scenarios and use cases as synonyms, but here we distinguish between them, to differentiate between type level and instance level.

a) Actors and goals.

Actors	Goals
Subscriber	GS1 To achieve communication with another subscriber
	GS2 To cease communication with another subscriber
	GS3 To achieve reachability at another destination
	GS4 To cease reachability at another destination
Operator	GO1 To maintain markings information representing call duration
	GO2 To achieve a printout of the number of markings for each subscriber
	GO3 To achieve a resetting of the number of markings for each subscriber

b) Services.

Service	Description
NCC	Normal Call with Charging
CFU	Call Forward Unconditional
RMR	Read Markings and Reset

c) Uses cases.

Use Cases	Actors	Goals	Services
Normal Call	Subscriber	GS1, GS2, GO1	NCC
Activate CFU	Subscriber	GS3	CFU
Deactivate CFU	Subscriber	GS4	CFU
Invoke CFU	Subscriber	GS1, GS2, GS3	CFU
Read Markings	Operator	GO2	RMR
Reset Markings	Operator	GO3	RMR

Figure 2. Actors, goals, services and use cases in the PBX example.

a) Scenarios for use case "Normal Call".

Scenario	Description
Reply	Call to idle subscriber that replies
Busy Subscriber	Call to busy subscriber
No Reply	Call to idle subscriber that does not reply
Non-Existent	Call to non-existent subscriber
Timeout	Subscriber waits too long after offhook

b) Data model.

```
toneType =
  (dialTone, ringSignal, ringTone,
   busyTone, errorTone, infoTone);
maxNumberOfSubscribers: Natural;
SubscriberType: record (
    state: (idle, busy, off);
    telNumber: TelNbrType;
    CFU_active: Boolean;
    CFU_number: TelNbrType;
    markings: Natural;
    talkingTo: SubscriberType);
SubscriberSet:
    Set (1..maxNumberOfSubscribers)
    Of
      SubscriberType;
```

c) Messages.

Message	Description
offHook	From Subscriber when lifting receiver
onHook	From Subscriber when hanging up the receiver
number(telNbrType)	From Subscriber when dialling a Number
activateCFU(telNbrType)	From Subscriber when activating CFU
deactivateCFU	From Subscriber when deactivating CFU
startTone(toneType)	To Subscriber when a tone is given
stopTone(toneType)	To Subscriber when a tone is stopped
readMarkings	From Operator when issuing a reading of markings
resetMarkings	From Operator when issuing a reset of markings
markings(markingListType)	To Operator when reporting the markings

Figure 3. Data, messages and a subset of the scenarios for the PBX example.

Figure 4. Use Case "Normal Call" Scenario "Reply"

Actor(s)	Caller, Callee: Subscriber	
Pre-condition(s): Caller.state = idle		
	Events	Constraints
1.	Caller to System: offHook	Caller.state = busy
2.	System to Caller: start-Tone(dialTone)	
3.	Caller to System: number(X)	
4.	System to Caller: stop-Tone(dialTone)	
5.	System action: number analysis	Callee.telNumber = X; Callee.state = idle
6.	System to Callee: start-Tone(ringSignal)	Callee.state = busy
	System to Caller: start-Tone(ringTone)	
7.	Callee to System: offhook	
8.	System to Callee: stop-Tone(ringSignal)	
	System to Caller: stop-Tone(dialTone)	
9.	System action: connect Caller and Callee	Caller.talkingTo = Callee; Callee.talkingTo = Caller;
10.	Callee to System: onHook	
	Caller to System: onHook	
11.	System action: disconnects Caller and Callee	Caller.talkingTo = nil; Calle.talkingTo = nil;
12.	System action: updates marking info	Caller.markings is incremented based on the time between 9–11;
Post-condition(s): Caller.state = idle; Callee.state = idle;		

2.3. Results

Use cases and scenarios are gaining increased attention in requirements engineering research and industrial application. In [8], an industrial case study reports that use cases facilitates all stakeholders to participate in the requirements process with good results in revealing defects. In [11], a survey of industrial application of use cases and scenarios identifies a number of perceived benefits.

Potential problems applying use cases and scenarios are to choose the appropriate level of detail and degree of completeness for the use cases.

In [10], it is concluded that there is an industrial need to base system tests on use cases and scenarios. The studied projects, however, rarely satisfied this demand, as most projects lacked a systematic approach for defining test cases based on use cases. In the this paper we investigate if such an approach can be based on operational profile testing.

3. Operational Profiles

3.1. Background

Software reliability is defined as "the probability for failure-free operation of a program for a specified time under a specified set of operating conditions" [20]. The reliability is hence not only depending on the number of faults in the software, but on how the software is used, hence exposing the faults as failures. In order to predict the operational reliability during test, the test cases executed has to resemble the operational usage, thus constituting a sample from the future operation. For this purpose a model of the future operation is built: the operational profile.

The operational profile consists of the structure of the usage and the probabilities for different uses. Examples of structural elements of the operational profile are different types of customers, different types of users, modes in which the system can operate, functions and operations which can be invoked by the user. The probabilities for activation of users, services etc. are connected to each structural element, constituting the operational profile.

From the operational profile, test cases are selected and executed. The test cases constitute a sample from the future operation, and hence the failure data collected during the test can be used for predicting the operational software reliability. In addition, the tests based on the operational profile has appeared to be efficient with respect to improved software reliability during testing [3, 4].

3.2. Method

In [4] a method for deriving an operational profile is presented. The method is summarized below in five steps:
- Develop a customer type list.
- Develop a user type list.
- List system modes.
- Develop a functional profile.
- Convert the functional profile to an operational profile.

For a more thorough description of the steps, refer to [4]. Here we illustrate the steps with the PBX example.

The **customer type list** collects the different types of customers that *acquire* the system. A customer type represents a set of customers which utilize the system in a similar manner. The example PBX can be sold to small companies with 4-8 employees and medium-sized companies with 9–50 employees. Hence there are two customer types, *small* and *medium.*

The **user type list** collects the different types of users that *use* the system. This list is not necessarily the same as the customer type list. For larger systems, it is generally not the same. In our example case, there are two user types, *subscribers* that make calls via the PBX and *operators* which maintains the charging information.

System modes represent a set of functions or operations that are grouped together in a way that is suitable for the application. The system modes need not to be orthogonal to each others; a function or operation can be member of different system modes. Criteria for defining system modes can be according to [4]: Relatedness of functions/operations to larger task, significant environmental conditions, operational architectural structure, criticality, customer or user, and user experience.

In our example, we define three system modes: *low-traffic subscriber use, high-traffic subscriber use* and *operator use.* The low-traffic and high-traffic system modes represent the same functions and operations but with different frequencies of use.

The first step in defining the **functional profile** is to create a function list. Functions are defined from the user's perspective and do not involve architectural or design factors. In the sample system there are four functions for the *low-traffic* and *high-traffic subscriber* system modes: *normal call,* and three functions for *call forward unconditional* (CFU), *activate, deactivate* and *invoke.* For the *operator* system mode there are two functions: *Read markings* and *reset markings.* The function list can be modified by taking environmental variables into account, for example different traffic levels. However this is already taken into account in the system modes in this example.

Now the profile is attached to the functions. We choose

an implicit form with **key input variables** for each function. The variables decide the variants of the functions. The different values of the variables are called **levels**. For the normal call function, the key input variable is the input, or lack of input from the callee. Different variants of the function are invoked depending on which input, or lack of input the called party gives. Five levels of the variable are identified: *reply, busy subscriber, no reply, non-existent* and *timeout.* Similarly the variables and levels can be identified for the other functions.

The functions and key input variables can be presented as an event tree for the user subscriber under the system mode low traffic, see Figure 5. Similarly is defined for the operator functions and the other system modes.

The **operational profile** segments for the customer types, user types and system modes are presented in Figure 6a. Note that all combinations are not possible between user types and system modes.

Finally the functions are mapped onto **operations**. For example, the *normal call* function can be built up by four operations, *number analysis, connect subscribers, disconnect subscribers* and *update markings.* It can be noted that operations may be involved in performing different functions. For example, the operations that are involved in the *normal call* function are also involved in the *invoke CFU.* The difference between the two functions is that in the *normal call,* the *number analysis* operation returns the identity of the callee, while in the *invoke CFU,* the *number analysis* returns the identity of the subscriber to which the CFU is directed. The resulting operations are listed in Figure 6b. The four subscriber functions result in six unique operations, of which four are shared by multiple functions.

There are key input variables for the operations as well, but this is not elaborated here. Nor is the functional profile mapped onto the operations, since the focus in this paper is

Figure 5.   Event tree for user "subscriber" under system mode "low traffic".

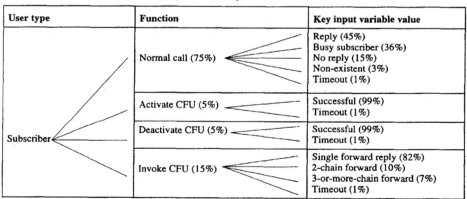

User type	Function	Key input variable value
Subscriber	Normal call (75%)	Reply (45%) Busy subscriber (36%) No reply (15%) Non-existent (3%) Timeout (1%)
	Activate CFU (5%)	Successful (99%) Timeout (1%)
	Deactivate CFU (5%)	Successful (99%) Timeout (1%)
	Invoke CFU (15%)	Single forward reply (82%) 2-chain forward (10%) 3-or-more-chain forward (7%) Timeout (1%)

a) Profile segments.

Customer type	User type	System mode
Small (75%)	Subscriber (95%)	Low-traffic sub-scriber (55%)
Medium (25%)	Operator (5%)	High-traffic sub-scriber (45%)
		Operator use (100%)

b) Functions and their mapping onto operations.

Function	Operations
Normal call	Number Analysis Connect Subscribers Disconnect Subscribers Update Markings
Activate CFU	CFU Activation
Deactivate CFU	CFU Deactivation
Invoke CFU	Number Analysis Connect Subscribers Disconnect Subscribers Update Markings

Figure 6. Operational profile parts.

on the structural parts, not on the profile parts.

3.3. Results

Application of operational profile testing is reported in [3, 4]. Firstly it provides measures of the software reliability which can be used for project and market planning. This is a substantial step forwards in the strive for having the software engineering process under control.

Secondly, it is reported to save effort during test. In [3] it is reported that test costs are saved with up to 56%. These figures has of course to be taken as is: a case study. Even if there was no saving at all in the general case, the operational profile testing moves effort upfront to earlier phases of the project which supports the approach of solving problems earlier, and thus cheaper.

Thirdly, the user perspective taken in the operational profile definition is beneficial since it affects the system design effort as well [21]. By looking at the system from outside-in, the customer and user viewpoints are taken. This helps prioritizing what are the requirements on the system, that fulfil the customer and user needs.

Problems encountered in operational profile testing are related to the usage information. For newly developed sys-

tems, the usage information may not be known in detail. However for evolving systems, usage information is available from earlier releases in operation.

These results from applying operational profile testing can be combined with use case modelling, giving coordination benefits, which is further elaborated in next chapter.

4. Derivation of Operational Profile from Use Cases

4.1. Introduction

A use case model and operational profile model has very much information in common. It can be observed in the examples in Chapter 2 and Chapter 3, that the structures of the models are very much the same. The operational profile model primarily adds the profile information i.e. the probabilities for use of different system capabilities. However the models originate from different disciplines and different terminology is used.

In the search for possibilities for integrating models from the two domains, we elaborate two different approaches, the *transformation* approach and the *extension* approach, see Figure 7.

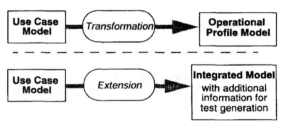

Figure 7. Two ways of integrating use case models with operational profile models.

4.2. Transformation approach

The transformation approach takes the information in the use case model and builds the operational profile model based on that information and additional information from other sources. In order to find the common parts in the two models, the concepts in the two domains are elaborated below.

The requirements model does not include quantitative aspects on usage frequencies, while the operational profile model does. This information has hence to be derived in addition to the use case information.

The **customer types** in the operational profile model address the customers, which acquire the system, and the probability information for different types of customers. If high-level goals are included in the use case model, customers might be found among the **actors**, otherwise others sources have to be consulted.

The **user types** in the operational profile generally correspond to the **actors** in the use case model. Both concepts refer to categories of objects, either human users or other systems, that interact with the system.

The **system mode** is a set of functions and operations that relate to each other. This corresponds in part to the **service** concept of the use case model. However the system mode may also cover profiling information, and that part cannot be found in the use case model.

The usage of **functions** in the operational profile model is described by **use cases** in the requirements model. The functions as well as the use cases are defined from the user's perspective, and do not consider architectural and design factors. Variants of functions in the operational profile are distinguished by **key input variables.** Depending on the value of the variable (the level), different alternatives of the function are chosen. The levels of the key input variables have their counterparts in the **scenarios** of the use case model, which are variants of a use case. A specific combination of key input variables gives a specific scenario, i.e. a realisation of a use case.

In the operational profile model, **operations** are tasks accomplished by the system in order to deliver a function to the user. A similar concept in the use case model are the **system actions**.

The mapping between concepts in an operational profile model and a use case model are summarized in Table 1.

Table 1. Mapping of terminology [a]

Operational profile model		Use case model
Customer type	≈	Actor
User type	=	Actor
System mode	≈	Service
Function	≈	Use case
Key input variable	≈	Scenario
Operation	=	System action

a. "≈" means that the concepts partially model the same information, "=" means that they actually model the same information.

4.3. Example on transformation approach

In this section we present an example on the transformation approach. Given the mapping scheme from Section 4.2, an operational profile model is derived from the use case model presented in Chapter 2. As in Chapter 3, we follow the steps proposed in [4], but now the information is collected from the use case model.

First the **customer type** list is derived. Since there are no high-level actors in the use case model, there is no information on customer types, so this information has to be collected elsewhere. Generally the different customer types are defined as a requirement written in plain text. In our example we have *small* (4–8 employees) and *medium-sized* (9–50 employees) enterprises as two different customer types.

The **user type** list can be derived directly from the list of **actors** in Figure 2a. The actors *subscriber* and *operator* are selected as user types.

Next, the **systems modes** are elaborated. The information can be taken in parts form the **services** in Figure 2b: *normal call with charging (NCC), call forward unconditional (CFU)* and *read markings and reset (RMR)*. In addition to this, we add the profile information. Among the subscribers, there are two different groups with respect to their usage frequencies Thus we add, *low-traffic* and *high-traffic* to the system modes for the subscriber services, defining in total four: *low-traffic CFU, low-traffic NCC, high-traffic CFU* and *high-traffic NCC*. The *operator use* is defined as a fifth system mode.

The list of **functions** is derived directly from the list of **use cases**, see Figure 2c. There are in total six functions, *normal call, activate CFU, deactivate CFU, invoke CFU, read markings* and *reset markings*.

The **key input variables** which define variants of the functions can be derived from the **scenarios** of the use case, see Figure 3a. For the normal call function, the key input variable is the input or lack of input given as response to the call. The levels of the variable are: *reply, busy subscriber, no reply, non-existent* and *timeout*.

The usage frequency information in the **functional profile** cannot be found in the use case model, but has to be derived from other sources, for example interviews or measurements on existing systems.

The functions are mapped onto **operations** which together constitute the function to the user. The **system actions** in the use case model constitute candidates for operations, see Figure 4. In the normal call use case, scenario reply, there are four system actions involved, *number analysis, connect subscribers, disconnect subscribers* and *update markings*. We define operations with the same names for the operational profile.

Finally, the functional profile is mapped onto the operations, defining the **operational profile**. A summary of the transformation is given in Table 2:

It can be concluded that the main part of the structural information for the transformation can be taken from the use case model. In some cases, the interpretations of the concepts differ, but the core of the information is valid. The profile information, i.e. probabilities and frequencies have to be taken from elsewhere. It can also be noticed that the operational model transformed from the use case

Table 2. Summary of information origin in the transformation approach.

Operational profile part	Information in use case model
Customer type	Partly
User type	Yes
System mode	Partly
Function	Yes
Key input variable	Yes
Functional profile	No
Operation	Yes
Operational profile	No

model can be slightly different from the one that was derived directly. In our example, the system modes are not exactly the same.

4.4. Extension approach

An alternative to transforming the use case model into an operational profile model is to extend the use case model with profile information. The resulting integrated model should then fit both the purpose of requirements specification and test specification. Given the two sets of models with different concepts and terminology presented in Chapter 2 and Chapter 3, an integrated model should be developed.

Basically the extension means that user frequencies and probabilities are added to the use case model. Additionally, the concepts of the operational profile model, which have no correspondence in the use case model or has a different interpretation must be added or tailored. The extension approach also means that concepts which are close to each other in the two models, have to be defined to be exactly the same. Below it is identified which concepts can be used exactly as is, and which have to be tailored or added to the integrated model. It shall not be seen as a complete proposal for an integrated model, but a basis for further definition work.

The **customer type** is not generally a part of the operational profile model, although sometimes modelled as **actors**, e.g. when defining high-level goals for the system. The information is beneficial for the understanding of the customer needs and is often provided in text in the requirements specification, hence it is added to the integrated model.

User types and **actors** are substantially the same in the two models, and can be integrated.

The **system modes** in the operational profile and the **service** concept in the use case model are integrated.

The usage of the **functions** in the operational profile are described by **use cases** and can be integrated. The functional profile information is added to the model.

Key input variables define alternatives in functions, while **scenarios** define alternative realizations of use cases. Given that usage of functions and use cases are integrated, these two can be integrated as well.

The **operations** of the operational profile model are the tasks that build up a function which correspond to **system actions** in the use case model. The operational profile is added to the model.

Table 3. Integrated use case and operational profile model

Operational profile model		Use case model	Integrated model
Customer type	≈	Actor	Customer actor
User type	=	Actor	Actor
System mode	≈	Service	Service
Function	≈	Use case	Use case
Key input variable	≈	Scenario	Scenario
Functional profile	–		Use case profile
Operation	=	System action	Operation
Operational profile	–		Operational profile

4.5. Analysis of approaches

The use case model and the operational profile model have similar structures and much information in common. It can hence be concluded that any form of coordination is beneficial with respect to effort spent on modelling, focus on test and testability already in the requirements and quantification of requirements for priority or other purposes.

The models have different terminology and notations used. However, also the purposes of the models differ. The purpose of the use case model is to provide understanding of customer needs while the purpose of the test model is to generate test cases to verify that requirements are fulfilled. The notations and terminology used can be mapped between the two domains, as elaborated above. The purpose conflict is more serious in the *transformation* approach than in the *extension* approach.

The two approaches to integration, *transformation* of the use case model into an operational profile model and *extension* of the use case model into an integrated model, have their advantages and disadvantages. The approaches are compared below, but in order to make a better evaluation, empirical studies have to be conducted.

The *extension* approach has advantages over the *trans-*

formation approach with respect to effort spent to derive the model. A single model is derived instead of two, which saves effort. Furthermore from a maintenance perspective, the extension approach is to prefer, since it reduces risks for inconsistencies between models. The consistency within a single model is easier to maintain. Furthermore the incentives for maintaining the integrated model are better since it is used both in requirements and test, not only for a single purpose.

The *transformation* approach has advantages over the *extension* approach when studying the fitness for purposes and level of detail. The extension approach always include compromises between needs for the different purposes. The purpose of the use case model is to bring best possible understanding of user and customer needs. The purpose of the test model is to generate test cases representative for the future operation. The main conflict concerns functions with low usage frequency, but high importance for the customer. These functions are given more attention in the requirements model and less attention in the test model.

The requirements model may be less detailed than the test model. On the other hand, if the extended model evolves during the development, the level of detail can be set for the requirements purposes in the beginning of the development, and evolve into more details, according to the test model needs.

The advantages and disadvantages are summarized in Table 4.

Table 4. Comparison between integration approaches.

	Transformation	Extension
Information	+ same information for both purposes	+ same information for both purposes
Structure	+ same structure for both purposes	+ same structure for both purposes
Derivation	– two models to derive	+ single model to derive
Maintenance	– two models to maintain. – risk for inconsistencies	+ single model to maintain + consistency within model
Fit for purpose	+ each model tailored for its purpose	– the model is a compromise between purposes
Level of detail	+ each model at appropriate level of detail	– the model is a compromise between levels of detail

5. Summary

This paper presents work which aims at integrating requirements engineering (RE) and software reliability engineering (SRE). Two different approaches are presented, the *transformation* and the *extension* approaches.

There are many advantages of an integration between RE and SRE. The SRE aspects are addressed earlier in the development cycle, enabling proactive rather than reactive actions. The quantitative aspects of the SRE usage modelling may help in the prioritizing of requirements. The connection between the requirements defined and their verification and validation is made closer. Finally, by utilizing the same sources for information, effort may be saved in the modelling tasks.

The transformation of a use case model to an operational profile model is one step towards integration of the two domains, which is evaluated in this paper. The model extension is another step which is supposed to save more effort, in particular in maintenance of software artifacts, but on the other hand may involve compromises between RE and SRE purposes for usage modelling.

The proposed approaches to integration have to be evaluated empirically in order to get more understanding on which approach is most preferable in different situations.

Acknowledgement

The authors would like to thank our colleague, Anders Wesslén for giving valuable comments on the paper. This work was financially supported by the National Board for Industrial and Technical Development, (NUTEK), Sweden, grant 1K1P-97-09690.

References

1 Jacobson, I. et al. *Object-Oriented Software Engineering – A Use Case Driven Approach*, Addison-Wesley Publishing Company and ACM Press, 1992.

2 Regnell, B., *Hierarchical Use Case Modelling for Requirements Engineering*, Technical Report 120, Dept. of Communication Systems, Lund University, Tech. Lic. dissertation, 1996.

3 Musa, J. D., "Operational Profiles in Software Reliability Engineering", *IEEE Software*, pp. 14–32, March 1993.

4 Lyu, M. R., (ed.), *Handbook of Software Reliability Engineering*, McGraw-Hill, 1995.

5 Linger, R., "Cleanroom Process Model", *IEEE Software*, pp. 50–58, March 1994.

6 Whittaker, J. A. and Thomason, M. G., "A Markov Chain Model for Statistical Software Testing", *IEEE Transactions on Software Engineering*, Vol. 20, No. 10, pp. 812–824, 1994.

7   Runeson, P. and Wohlin, C., "Statistical Usage Testing for Software Reliability Control" *Informatica*, Vol. 19, No. 2, pp. 195–207, 1995.

8   Gough, P., Fodemski, F., Higgins, S. and Ray, S., "Scenarios – an Industrial Case Study and Hypermedia Enhancements", *IEEE Second International Symposium on Requirements Engineering*, York, UK, pp. 10–17, March 1995.

9   Regnell, B. and Davidsson, Å., "From Requirements to Design with Use Cases – Experiences from Industrial Pilot Projects", *Proceedings of the Third International Workshop on Requirements Engineering: Foundations of Software Quality* (REFSQ'97), pp. 205–222, Presses Universitaires de Namur, 1997.

10 Jarke, M., et. al., "Scenario Use in European Software Organisations - Results from Site Visits and Questionnaires", Report of ESPRIT Project CREWS, no. 97-10, 1997.
    Available via e-mail: crewsrep@informatik.rwt-aachen.de.

11 Weidenhaupt, K., Pohl, K., Jarke, M. and Haumer, P., "Scenario Usage in System Development: A Report on Current Practice", Report of ESPRIT Project CREWS, no. 97-16, 1997.
    Available via e-mail: crewsrep@informatik.rwt-aachen.de.

12 Wohlin, C., "Meeting the Challenge of Large-Scale Software Development in an Educational Environment", *Proceedings 10th Conference on Software Engineering Education and Training*, Virginia Beach, Virginia, USA, pp. 40–52, 1997.

13 Rumbaugh, J., et al., *Object-Oriented Modeling and Design*, Prentice Hall, 1991.

14 Booch, G., *Object-Oriented Analysis and Design with Applications*, Second Edition, Benjamin/Cummings Publ., 1994.

15 Potts, C., Takahashi, K. and Anton, A., "Inquiry-Based Requirements Analysis", *IEEE Software*, pp. 21–32, March 1994.

16 Hsia, P., Samuel, J., Gao J. and Kung, D., "Formal Approach to Scenario Analysis", *IEEE Software*, pp. 33–41, March 1994.

17 Rolland, C., et. al. "A Proposal for a Scenario Classification Framework", Report of ESPRIT Project CREWS, no. 96-01, 1996.
    Available via e-mail: crewsrep@informatik.rwt-aachen.de.

18 Regnell, B., Kimbler, K. and Wesslén, A., "Improving the Use Case Driven Approach to Requirements Engineering", *IEEE Second International Symposium on Requirements Engineering*, York, UK, pp. 40–47, March 1995.

19 Regnell, B., Andersson, M. and Bergstrand, J., "A Hierarchical Use Case Model with Graphical Representation", *IEEE International Symposium and Workshop on Engineering of Computer-Based Systems*, Germany, pp. 270–277, March 1996.

20 "IEEE Standard Glossary of Software Engineering Terminology" IEEE 610.12, 1990.

21 Chruscielski, K. and Tian J., "An Operational Profile for the Cartridge Support Software", *Proceedings 8th International Symposium on Software Reliability Engineering*, Albuquerque, New Mexico, USA, pp. 203–212, 1997.

Because there is no systematic way in existing use-case approaches to handle nonfunctional requirements, the authors propose an approach to analyze and evaluate use cases with goals and to structure use-case models.

Reprinted from IEEE Software, July/Aug. 1999, pp. 92-101.

Analyzing User Requirements by Use Cases: A Goal-Driven Approach

Jonathan Lee and Nien-Lin Xue, National Central University

se-case approaches are increasingly attracting attention in requirements engineering because the user-centered concept is valuable in eliciting, analyzing, and documenting requirements.[1-5] One of the main goals of the requirements engineering process is to get agreement on the views of the involved users,[6] and use cases are a good way to elicit requirements from a user's point of view.

An important advantage of use-case-driven analysis is that it helps manage complexity, since it focuses on one specific usage aspect at a time. Use cases start from the very simple viewpoint that a system is built first and foremost for its users. The approach looks at the interactions of a single category of users at a time, considerably reducing the complexity of requirements determination.[7] However, current use-case approaches are somewhat limited in supporting use-case formalization,[4] and in structuring and managing large use-case models.[8]

175

The standard approaches to improving use cases have two main problems. Although quality issues are often crucial to the success of a software system, no systematic way exists to handle nonfunctional requirements. Also, although interactions between requirements are an important issue in the requirements-acquisition phase,[9,10] there have been no attempts to address them with use cases. Inspired by procedure logic (associating each process with a purpose),[11] we propose an approach to extend use cases with goals, called goal-driven use cases, or GDUC, to alleviate these problems. Our approach

♦ uses goals to structure use-case models and derive use cases,

♦ differentiates between soft and rigid goals to handle imprecise nonfunctional requirements,

♦ embeds goal information in the use cases, and

♦ analyzes interactions between requirements by investigating the relationship between goals and use cases.

We chose the meeting schedule problem as an example throughout this article to illustrate GDUC, because the research community has adopted it as a benchmark;[12] the requirements illustrate typical, real system problems; and it can help us address the main challenge of requirements analysis, which is to turn a vague and contradictory mission statement into a detailed specification.[9,12]

GOAL-DRIVEN USE CASES

The basic concepts of a use-case approach are *actor* and *use case*. An actor is a specific role played by a system user and represents a category of users that demonstrate similar behaviors when using the system. Use cases describe the way an actor uses the system. A use case has one basic course and several alternative courses. The basic course is the simplest course, the one in which a request is delivered without any difficulty. On the other hand, alternative courses describe variants of the basic course and the errors that can occur.

A use-case model specifies the relationships between use cases, as well as relationships between use cases and actors. Two powerful concepts, *extends* and *uses*, structure and relate use cases. An *extends* relation specifies how one use case may be embedded into another one, extending its functionality. A *uses* relation is used for refinement, extracting similar parts of two or more use cases. In this way, we can describe a similar part once instead

of showing a behavior in all use cases.

In Anne Dardenne and her colleagues' approach, goals determine the respective roles of agents in the system and provide a basis for defining which agents should best perform which actions.[13] A goal is a nonoperational objective while a constraint is an operational one; a goal cannot be achieved directly by the application of actions available to some agents. Instead, it is achieved by satisfying the constraints that make it operational. To satisfy these constraints, we may require appropriate restrictions on actions and objects.

> **Goals representing nonfunctional requirements are rarely accomplished or satisfied.**

According to John Mylopoulos and his colleagues, goals represent nonfunctional requirements, design decisions, and arguments in support of or against other goals.[14] Goals representing nonfunctional requirements are rarely accomplished or satisfied in a clear-cut sense. Instead, different design decisions contribute positively or negatively towards a particular goal. They also propose a labeling procedure to determining the degree to which a particular design supports a set of nonfunctional requirements.

In a nutshell, goal-based approaches focus on why systems are constructed and provide the motivation and rationale to justify software requirements. We conceived our approach based on the concept to extend use-case approaches with goals.

Our approach is for requirements engineers to structure and elicit users' requirements, and to analyze and evaluate relationships between requirements. We focus on how to structure and elicit users requirements with a three-step approach to constructing use cases:

1. Identify actors by investigating all possible types of users that interact with the system directly.

2. Identify goals based on a faceted classification scheme.

3. Build use-case models.

IDENTIFYING ACTORS

A person can play several roles and thereby represent several actors, such as computer-system operator or end user.[1] To identify a target system's use cases, we identify the system actors. A good starting

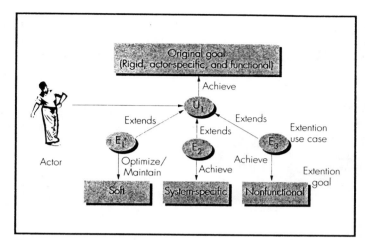

FIGURE 1. Deriving use cases with goals.

point is to check the system design and who it is supposed to help. For example, the meeting schedule system is mainly designed for an initiator to organize a meeting schedule, so the initiator is an actor. The actors who will use the system are primary actors. Each actor will perform one or more of the main system tasks. Besides these primary actors, secondary actors supervise and maintain the system.

In the meeting schedule system, we identified three actors: an initiator (to initiate a meeting, notify participants, and make decisions if conflicts occur), a participant (to register a meeting and indicate a preference for meeting dates, locations, or equipment), and an operator (to maintain and supervise the system). The initiator and participant are primary actors, whereas the operator is a secondary actor.

IDENTIFYING GOALS

To identify goals from domain descriptions and system requirements, we propose a faceted classification scheme based on our requirement classification scheme.[14] Each goal can be classified with three facets: competence, view, and content.

Competence

The first facet relates to whether a goal is completely or partially satisfied. A rigid goal, which must be completely satisfied, describes a target system's minimum requirement. A soft goal describes a desirable property for a target system and can be partially satisfied. For example, a meeting schedule that is convenient for all attendees completely satisfies its goal, *MaxConvenientSchedule*. However, if the schedule is only convenient to some of the attendees, it is only partially satisfied. A soft goal, therefore, is dependent on the rigid one. That is, a weak relationship exists between a rigid goal and its soft goals.

In our example, the rigid goal *Meeting-RequestSatisfied* has two related soft goals, *MaxNumberofParticipants* and *MaxConvenientSchedule*, which are weakly dependent on it, because the information about the number of meeting participants and the meeting's convenience will be meaningless if the meeting request is not satisfied.

View

This facet concerns whether a goal is actor-specific or system-specific. Actor-specific goals are an actor's objectives in using a system; system-specific goals are requirements on services that the system provides. For example, by examining the system description, we found that the initiator has three objectives for the meeting schedule system: to create a meeting, to make the meeting schedule as convenient as possible for the participants, and to maximize the number of meeting participants. Therefore, we identified three actor-specific goals: *MaxNumberofParticipants*, *MeetingRequestSatisfied*, and *MaxConvenientSchedule*.

On the other hand, a system-specific goal considers the properties the system needs to support services for all users as well as those necessary for system operation. Consider this partial system description for the meeting schedule system:

Dynamically replan a meeting to support as much flexibility as possible to take some external constraints into account after proposing a date and location, such as accommodating a more important meeting.

An initiator constructs a meeting, but the system can accommodate a more important meeting. Therefore, we can identify a system-specific goal: *SupportFlexibility*.

Content

We can classify requirements into functional and nonfunctional requirements based on their content.[15] The construction of functional requirements involves modeling the relevant internal states and behavior of both the component and its environment. Nonfunctional requirements usually define the constraints that the product needs to satisfy. Therefore, a goal can be further distinguished based on its content and can be either related to a system's functional aspects or associated with the system's nonfunctional aspect. We achieve a functional goal by performing a sequence of operations. A non-

177

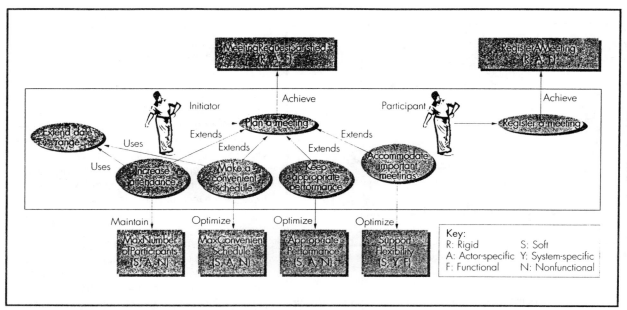

FIGURE 2. A goal-driven use-case model for a meeting schedule system.

functional goal is defined as constraints to qualify its related functional goal.

In our example, the initiator creates a meeting with a sequence of operations. Therefore, we can define *MeetingRequestSatisfied* as a functional goal. We can also view the goals *MaxNumberofParticipants* and *MaxConvenientSchedule* as constraints for a schedule to satisfy, or as nonfunctional goals.

BUILDING USE-CASE MODELS

In GDUC, we have extended Alistair Cockburn's work by considering several different types of goals to structure a use case and its extensions.[16] Essentially, each use case is viewed as a process associated with a goal that it must achieve, optimize, or maintain (see Figure 2). Building a use-case model involves three steps: identify original use cases to capture minimum requirements, identify extension use cases to construct a more complete model, and refine a use case model to enhance reusability.

Identifying original use cases

We first consider original use cases to guarantee that they can adapt the target system to the minimum requirements. Each original use case in our approach is associated with an actor to describe the process of achieving an original goal, which is rigid, actor-specific, and functional (see Figure 1). Building original use cases by investigating all original goals will make the use-case model satisfy at least all the actors' rigid and functional goals.

The basic course in an original use case is the simplest course—the one in which the goal is delivered without any difficulty. The alternative course encompasses the recovery or failure course, or both. The recovery course describes the process to recover the original goal, whereas the failure course describes what to do if the original goal is not recoverable.

In our example, the use case *plan a meeting* covers the case for an initiator to achieve the goal *MeetingRequestSatisfied*, which is rigid, actor-specific, and functional (see the boxed text, "Sample Use Case," p. 100). The use case starts when an initiator issues a meeting request to the system and lasts until a meeting schedule is generated or canceled. The basic course of *plan a meeting* describes steps to generate a meeting schedule to achieve the goal *MeetingRequestSatisfied*: (1) determining the date range, locations, meeting type, and potential attendees; (2) having participants input their personal agenda; (3) making a schedule based on the given information; and (4) informing all participants of the meeting.

The use case has several alternative courses that may change its flow. For example, there are different ways of recovering the goal *MeetingRequestSatisfied* when a strong schedule conflict exists.

Note that the problem statements do not indicate when to cancel a meeting, so we will need to elicit this information. The boxed text "Sample Use Case" includes an example of an alternative meeting plan.

Extension use cases

Original use cases are designed to satisfy original goals for modeling users' minimum require-

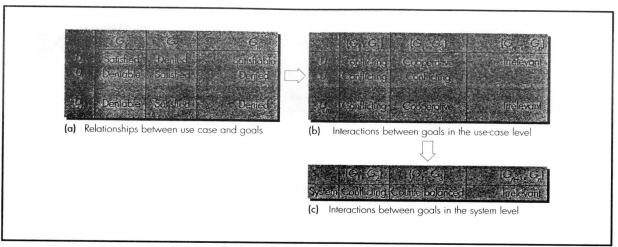

(a) Relationships between use case and goals

(b) Interactions between goals in the use-case level

(c) Interactions between goals in the system level

FIGURE 3. GDUC's three steps for requirements evaluation.

ments. To extend the model to take into account different types of goals, we create extension use cases.

Optimize or maintain a soft goal

By achieving a rigid goal, we can also satisfy all its related soft goals to some extent. To optimize or maintain the soft goals, we create extension use cases (see Figure 1, the use case E_1). Therefore, the basic course in an extension is to optimize or maintain its soft goal, whereas an alternative course describes what to do if it fails to optimize or maintain the goal.

In our example, satisfying the rigid goal *MeetingRequestSatisfied* does not guarantee that the meeting is convenient for all participants. To make the schedule as convenient as possible, we create an extension *make a convenient schedule*. If the basic course constraints are not satisfied, the alternative course is to recover the soft goal's optimization. For example, the system may extend the date range or ask participants to add dates to their preference sets.

An extension can also be used to maintain a soft goal. If the basic course of the use case *plan a meeting* goes successfully, all potential participants can attend the meeting. This completely satisfies the soft goal *MaxNumberofParticipants*. However, if an exception or conflict arises, a recovery course may impair the soft goal because some participants may withdraw from the meeting. To maintain the soft goal, we establish an extension *increase attendance*. This extension resolves the conflict by extending the date range or asking participants to remove dates from their exclusive sets. By doing so, it sustains the number of participants and maintains the soft goal.

Achieve a system-specific goal

An extension use case can be created to achieve a system-specific goal (see Figure 1, use case E_2). The original use case *plan a meeting* describes creating a meeting from a personal view, or the initiator's view. The extension use case *accommodate important meetings* extends it to take all actors into account—that is, to achieve a system-specific goal, *SupportFlexibility*.

Achieve a nonfunctional goal

To extend a use-case model to capture nonfunctional requirements, we add extension use cases to achieve a nonfunctional goal (see Figure 1, use case E_3). In this case, an extension use case serves as a constraint to qualify its original use case. In our example, the original use case *plan a meeting* ignores several meeting constraints: *AppropriatePerformance, MaxNumberofParticipants,* and *MaxConvenientSchedule*. The basic course of *make a convenient schedule* indicates the soft constraints on a meeting schedule. If the constraints are not satisfied, the alternative course is to recover the soft goal's optimization.

To summarize, an original goal is rigid, actor-specific, and functional, but an extension goal is achieved, optimized, or maintained by an extension use case. An extension goal is weakly dependent on its associated original goal. Satisfying an original goal does not always satisfy its associated extension goals, unless the extension goal is soft.

Refining use-case models

The use-case model as described thus far is sufficient to specify users requirements. However, to further enhance reusability, we need to elaborate the use-case model by looking for common fragments among different use cases and extracting the similar parts into an abstract use case, such as refining the use case model by *uses* relations.

Although both *extends* and *uses* add an addi-

179

tional subsequence into a base sequence, they are essentially different. In an *extends* relation, both extension and original use cases have their corresponding goals to achieve, optimize, or maintain. In a *uses* relationship, an abstract use case enhances reusability and does not have a goal associated with it.

We found that extending a meeting's date range is a common behavior of the use cases *increase attendance* and *make a convenient schedule*, and then this part of behavior is extracted into an abstract use case *extend date ranges* (see Figure 2).

GOAL EVALUATION

It is important for a good requirements-modeling approach to take real-world entities into account, although the results often contradict one another.[9] Figure 3 shows how GDUC evaluates interactions between goals in three steps:

♦ Analyze the relationships between use cases and goals by investigating the effects on the goals after performing use cases;

♦ Explore the interactions between goals in the use-case level; and

♦ Derive the interactions between goals in the system level.

Relationships between Use Cases and Goals

To better characterize the relationships between use cases and goals, we adopted the proposal from John Mylopoulos and his colleagues on nonfunctional requirements.[14] A goal can be either satisfied or denied, if the goal is completely achieved or ceased, respectively. However, a goal is either satisfiable and deniable if it can be partially satisfied or denied. In addition, a goal is independent if it will not be affected by performing a designated use case.

In GDUC, a use case is designed to achieve, optimize, or maintain its directly associated goals. However, goals not directly associated with the use case can also be affected or cause side effects.

Effects on associated goals

We can satisfy an original goal either by performing the basic course successfully or by recovering the goal from an alternative course (see Figure 4, arrow a). We can also deny the goal under the condition that it is ceased by performing an alternative course.

In GDUC, an extension goal can be either rigid or soft. For a rigid goal, its associated extension use case is designed to achieve and satisfy the goal. On the other hand, an extension use case can be designed to optimize or maintain a soft goal and make it satisfiable (see Figure 4, arrow b). For example, to completely satisfy the soft goal *MaxConvenientSchedule*, we need to successfully perform both use cases *plan a meeting* and *make a convenient schedule*. The role of the extension use case *make a convenient schedule* is to make the soft goal *MaxConvenientSchedule* satisfiable.

Side effects

By performing an original use case successfully, we can, to some extent, achieve the extension goals that are directly associated with specific extension use cases (see Figure 4, the arrow c). For example, if the use case *plan a meeting* is successfully performed, the extension goal *MaxConvenientSchedule* is satisfied to a degree.

Generally, an extension use case does not impair the original goal that is directly associated with its original use case, except that the extension is designed to achieve a system-specific goal (see Figure 4, arrow d). In this case, the original goal is denied. For example, the extension use case *accommodate important meetings* may cease the original goal *MeetingRequestSatisfied* under the condition that there is a more important meeting in conflict with it.

An extension use case may also achieve or impair an irrelevant goal associated with other extension use cases (see Figure 4, arrow e). For example, if the extension use case *increase attendance* extends the date range for maintaining its soft goal, another extension goal *MaxConvenientSchedule* may also be satisfiable. A typical example of impairing an irrelevant goal in the meeting schedule system is that performing the extension use case *keep an appropriate performance* may cease the activity to negotiate a convenient schedule. Therefore, the soft goal *MaxConvenientSchedule* is deniable.

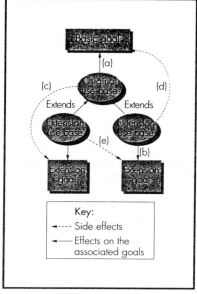

FIGURE 4. Relationships between use cases and goals.

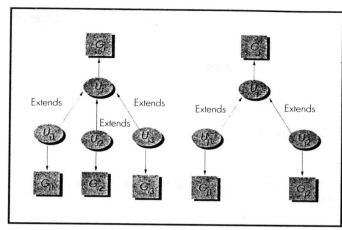

FIGURE 5. An illustration of a use-case model.

Interactions between goals in the use-case level

In GDUC, relationships between goals exist at two levels: use-case and system. The former is the relationships between goals and specific use cases, and the latter focuses on the overall system.

In the use-case level, two goals conflict with a use case if the satisfaction of one goal increases while the other decreases after the use case is performed. Barry Boehm and Hoh In's system QARCC identifies and diagnoses quality-attribute conflicts.[17] Their approach focuses on domain-independent conflicts involving high-level quality-attribute and architecture-strategy conflicts to achieve generality and scalability. For example, a layered architecture has a positive influence on portability, but has a negative influence on performance. In contrast, our approach deals with the conflicts between requirements.[15] On the other hand, two goals are said to cooperate with each other if both the satisfaction degrees of the goals are either increased (positively cooperative) or decreased (negatively cooperative). The third possibility is that the satisfaction degrees of goals remain unchanged. In this case, the goals are said to be irrelevant.

To obtain interactions between two goals, we need to look at relationships between the use case and those two goals. For example, if the relationships between a use case U_k and goals G_i and G_j are satisfiable and deniable respectively, it means that the satisfaction degree of G_i increases and that of G_j decreases after U_k is performed. G_i and G_j have a conflicting relationship with respect to U_k.

The predicates $cp_{u_k}(G_i,G_j)$ and $cf_{u_k}(G_i,G_j)$ are introduced to describe the relationship between goals G_i and G_j with respect to the use case U_k, where $cp_{u_k}(G_i,G_j)$ is true if G_i and G_j are cooperative with respect to the use case U_k, and $cf_{u_k}(G_i,G_j)$ is true if G_i and G_j are conflicting with respect to U_k. If the goals G_i and G_j are irrelevant with respect to U_k, the predicates $cp_{u_k}(G_i,G_j)$

and $cf_{u_k}(G_i,G_j)$ are both false.

The interactions between the use case *make a convenient schedule* and the goals *MaxConvenient Schedule* and *AppropriatePerformance* are satisfiable and deniable, respectively. Therefore, we can conclude that the two goals are conflicting with respect to the use case *make a convenient schedule*: $cf_{make\ a\ convenient\ schedule}$(MaxConvenientSchedule, Appropriate-Performance)=True.

Interactions between goals in the system level

Interactions between goals in the system level are mainly analyzed on the use-case models where related use cases are amalgamated together. We can derive interactions between goals in the system level based on use-case models and relationships between use cases in the use-case level.

The interaction between the goals G_i and G_j in the system level is denoted as $R_s(G_i,G_j)$, and is defined as a pair of predicates $< cp(G_i,G_j), cf(G_i,G_j) >$, where $cp(G_i,G_j)$ is true if G_i is cooperative with G_j, and $cf(G_i,G_j)$ is true if G_i is conflicting with G_j in the system level. There are four possible relationships between goals in the system level:

♦ $R_s(G_i,G_j) = < False,False >$: G_i and G_j are irrelevant
♦ $R_s(G_i,G_j) = < True,False >$: G_i and G_j are cooperative
♦ $R_s(G_i,G_j) = < False,True >$: G_i and G_j are conflicting
♦ $R_s(G_i,G_j) = < True,True >$: G_i and G_j are counterbalanced

We describe how to derive interactions between goals in the system level in Figure 5, where G_i and G_j are two original goals and U_i and U_j are their associated use cases, respectively. U_{i1} is an extension use case of U_i, and G_{i1} is its associated extension goal.

Interactions between original goals

We can derive the interactions between any two original goals in the system level by checking the relationships between those two goals with respect to their associated use cases. More specifically, the interactions between G_i and G_j are said to be cooperative if they cooperate with respect to use case U_i or U_j:

$$cp(G_i,G_j) = cp_{U_i}(G_i,G_j) \vee cp_{U_j}(G_i,G_j)$$

Similarly, the interaction between G_i and G_j conflicts if they conflict with the use case U_i or U_j:

$$cf(G_i,G_j) = cf_{U_i}(G_i,G_j) \vee cf_{U_j}(G_i,G_j)$$

181

By definition, a goal is always cooperative with itself. That is, $R_s(G_i, G_j) = <True, False>$ if $G_i = G_j$.

Interactions between original goals and extension goals

To explore the interaction between an original goal and an extension goal in the system level, we should also consider the original goal on which the extension goal is weakly dependent. In Figure 5, the extension goal G_{j1} is achieved (optimized or maintained) if G_j is satisfied. Thus, we should also consider the interaction between G_i and G_j while investigating the interaction between G_i and G_{j1}. More precisely, let $R_s(G_i, G_{j1}) = <cp(G_i, G_{j1}), cf(G_i, G_{j1})>$, where

$$cp(G_i, G_{j1}) = cp(G_i, G_j) \vee cp_{U_i}(G_i, G_{j1})$$
$$\vee cp_{U_{j1}}(G_i, G_{j1});$$
$$cf(G_i, G_{j1}) = cf(G_i, G_j) \vee cf_{U_i}(G_i, G_{j1})$$
$$\vee cf_{U_{j1}}(G_i, G_{j1})$$

We can determine the interaction between the original goal G_{MRS} (or *MeetingRequestSatisfied*) and the extension goal G_{MCS} (or *MaxConvenientSchedule*) by (1) the interaction between the goal G_{MRS} and the original goal G_{MRS} on which G_{MCS} is weakly dependent, (2) the interaction between G_{MRS} and G_{MCS} with respect to the use case *plan a meeting* (U_{PM}), and (3) the interaction between G_{MCS} and G_{MRS} with respect to the use case *make a convenient schedule* (U_{MCS}). That is, $R_s(G_{MRS}, G_{MCS}) = <cp(G_{MRS}, G_{MCS}), cf(G_{MRS}, G_{MCS})>$, where

$$cp(G_{MRS}, G_{MCS}) = cp(G_{MRS}, G_{MRS})$$
$$\vee cp_{U_{PM}}(G_{MRS}, G_{MCS})$$
$$\vee cp_{U_{MCS}}(G_{MRS}, G_{MCS})$$
$$= True;$$
$$cf(G_{MRS}, G_{MCS}) = cf(G_{MRS}, G_{MRS})$$
$$\vee cf_{U_{PM}}(G_{MRS}, G_{MCS})$$
$$\vee cf_{U_{MCS}}(G_{MRS}, G_{MCS})$$
$$= False$$

Therefore, the goal *MeetingRequestSatisfied* cooperates with the goal *MaxConvenientSchedule*.

Interactions between extension goals

The interaction between two extension goals, $R_s(G_{i1}, G_{j1})$ hinges on the system-level interaction be-tween G_{i1} and G_{j1}, the system-level interaction between G_i and G_j, the interaction between G_{i1} and G_{j1} with respect to U_{i1}, and the interaction between G_{i1} and G_{j1} with respect to U_{j1}. That is, $R_s(G_{i1}, G_{j1}) = <cp(G_{i1}, G_{j1}), cf(G_{i1}, G_{j1})>$, where

$$cp(G_{i1}, G_{j1}) = cp(G_i, G_{j1}) \vee cp(G_{i1}, G_j)$$
$$\vee cp_{U_{i1}}(G_{i1}, G_{j1}) \vee cp_{U_{j1}}(G_{i1}, G_{j1});$$
$$cf(G_{i1}, G_{j1}) = cf(G_i, G_{j1}) \vee cf(G_{i1}, G_j)$$
$$\vee cf_{U_{i1}}(G_{i1}, G_{j1}) \vee cf_{U_{j1}}(G_{i1}, G_{j1})$$

In our example, let $R_s(G_{MCS}, G_{AP}) = <cp(G_{MCS}, G_{AP}), cf(G_{MCS}, G_{AP})>$ be the interaction between the extension goals *MaxConvenientSchedule* (G_{MCS}) and *AppropriatePerformance* (G_{AP}) (G_{KAP} is an abbreviation for the use case *keep appropriate performance*):

$$cp(G_{MCS}, G_{AP}) = cp(G_{MCS}, G_{MRS})$$
$$\vee cp(G_{AP}, G_{MRS})$$
$$\vee cp_{U_{MCS}}(G_{MCS}, G_{AP})$$
$$\vee cp_{U_{KAP}}(G_{MCS}, G_{AP})$$
$$= False$$
$$cf(G_{MCS}, G_{AP}) = cf(G_{MCS}, G_{MRS})$$
$$\vee cf(G_{AP}, G_{MRS})$$
$$\vee cf_{U_{MCS}}(G_{MCS}, G_{AP})$$
$$\vee cp_{U_{KAP}}(G_{MCS}, G_{AP})$$
$$= True$$

Therefore, the goals *MaxConvenientSchedule* and *AppropriatePerformance* conflict.

We created GDUC based on the belief that goal information should be captured in the requirements-acquisition phase.[18] In GDUC, goals assist requirements acquisition and modeling in two roles: serving as a structuring mechanism and evaluating requirements.

Our approach offers several benefits:

♦ serving as a structuring mechanism to facilitate the derivation of use-case specifications;

♦ bridging the gap between the domain description and the system requirements—that is, the interactions between functional and non-functional requirements; and

♦ making easy the handling of soft requirements, and the analysis among conflicting requirements.

SAMPLE USE CASE: PLANNING A MEETING

Goal: Determine a meeting date and location (*MeetingRequest-Satisfied*: rigid, actor-specific, and functional).

BASIC COURSE

1. The initiator issues a meeting request.

2. The system automatically fills in the submission date. The initiator fills in the other fields, including the date range, meeting locations, meeting type, and all potential meeting attendants. The initiator also indicates attendees' importance levels.

3. The initiator notifies the potential attendants to input their data. Active participants should fill in the equipment they need. If an attendee is designated an important participant, he is required to fill in his preferred locations. The exclusive sets and preference sets should be contained in the date range.

4. After all participants input their data, the initiator asks the system to make a meeting schedule based on the given information. When making a schedule, the system should consider the proposed meeting date, the stated date range and none of the exclusive set, and find a meeting room available at the selected meeting date. The meeting room should support equipment requirements of all the active participants, and a lower bound should be fixed between the time the meeting date is determined and when the meeting is actually taking place.

5. The system lists all possible meeting schedules that satisfy the criteria. The initiator then chooses one of them and notifies all participants.

ALTERNATIVE COURSE

If a strong conflict occurs while generating a meeting, the system will notify the initiator and ask to

♦ notify a participant to remove a date from his exclusive set,

♦ propose a participant with low importance level to withdraw from the meeting,

♦ extend a date range, or

♦ cancel the meeting.

If none of the proposed locations can meet the equipment requirements while making a meeting schedule, the system should inform the initiator. The initiator can propose other locations or cancel the meeting. In the first case, the initiator first inputs some new locations and then restarts a new round of meeting scheduling. In the second case, the initiator cancels the meeting, and all participants should be informed of the cancellation.

---

the interactions can be utilized for object models to manage conflicting requirements. Additionally, as conflicting requirements are imprecise, we expect object models to possess the capability to model imprecise requirements. A fuzzy object-oriented modeling technique is needed for GDUC to model imprecise and conflicting requirements.

We will also investigate the issues of goal prioritizing using the Analytic Hierarchy Process[19] to support a more accurate requirements model for conflict resolution. The importance of users requirements may vary; some can be critical for the software system's success, while others may merely be adornments. Analyzing the importance of requirements will help construct a software system with high customer satisfaction.   ❖

ACKNOWLEDGMENTS
The research was supported by National Science Council (Taiwan) under grants NSC87-2213-E-008-024 and NSC88-2213-E-008-006.

REFERENCES

1. I. Jacobson, *Object-Oriented Software Engineering*, Addison Wesley Longman, Reading, Mass., 1992.

2. J. Rumbaugh, "Getting Started: Using Use Cases to Capture Requirements," *J. Object-Oriented Programming*, Vol. 7, No. 5, Sept. 1994, pp. 8–12.

3. T. Rowlett, "Building an Object Process around Use Cases," *J. Object-Oriented Programming*, Vol. 11, No. 1, Mar./Apr. 1998, pp. 53–58.

4. B. Dano, H. Briand, and F. Barbier, "Progressing towards Object-Oriented Requirements Specifications by Using the Use Case Concept," *Proc. Int'l Conf. Requirements Eng.*, IEEE Computer Soc. Press, Los Alamitos, Calif., 1996, pp. 450–456.

5. K.S. Rubin and A. Goldberg, "Object Behavior Analysis," *Comm. ACM*, Vol. 35, No. 9, Sept. 1992, pp. 48–62.

6. K. Pohl, "The Three Dimensions of Requirements Engineering: A Framework and Its Applications," *Information Systems*, Vol. 19, No. 3, 1994, pp. 243–258.

7. P.A. Muller, *Instant UML*, Wrox Press Ltd., Olton, Birmingham, UK, 1997.

8. B. Regnell, M. Andersson, and J. Bergstrand, "A Hierarchical Use Case Model with Graphical Representation," *Proc. IEEE Symp. and Workshop on Engineering of Computer-Based Systems*, IEEE Computer Soc. Press, Los Alamitos, Calif., 1996, pp. 270–277.

9. A. Borgida, S. Greenspan, and J. Mylopoulos, "Knowledge Representation as the Basis for Requirements Specification," *Computer*, Apr. 1985, pp. 82–91.

10. A. Finkelstein and R.C. Waters, "Summary of the Requirements Elicitation, Analysis and Formalization Track," *ACM Software Eng. Notes*, Vol. 14, No. 5, 1989, p. 40.

11. M.P. Georgeff and A.L. Lansky, "Procedural knowledge," *Proc. IEEE*, Vol. 74, No. 10, Oct. 1986, pp. 1383–1398.

12. C. Potts, K. Takahashi, and A.I. Anton, "Inquiry-Based Requirements Analysis," *IEEE Software*, Mar. 1994, pp. 21–32.

13. A. Dardenne, A. van Lamsweerde, and S. Fickas, "Goal-Directed Requirements Acquisition," *Science of Computer Programming*, Vol. 20, 1993, pp. 3–50.

14. J. Mylopoulos, L. Chung, and B. Nixon, "Representing and Using Nonfunctional Requirements: A Process-Oriented Approach," *IEEE Trans. Software Eng.*, Vol. 18, No. 6, 1992, pp. 483–497.

15. J. Lee and J.Y. Kuo, "New Approach to Requirements Trade-Off

We plan to continue research in two specific areas. Specifically, we will explore the possibility of extending object-oriented models to manage conflicting requirements. After we develop a use-case model with GDUC, we then move to the system-analysis model. As interactions between goals are analyzed in GDUC,

183

Analysis for Complex Systems," *IEEE Trans. Knowledge and Data Eng.*, Vol. 10, No. 4, July/Aug. 1998, pp. 551–562.

16. A. Cockburn, "Goals and Use Cases," *J. Object-Oriented Programming*, Vol. 10, No. 7, Sept. 1997, pp. 35–40.

17. B. Boehm and H. In, "Identifying Quality-Requirement Conflicts," *IEEE Software*, Mar. 1996, pp. 25–35.

18. A. van Lamsweerde, R. Darimont, and P. Massonet, *Goal-Directed Elaboration of Requirements for a Meeting Scheduler Problems and Lessons Learnt*, Tech. Report RR-94-10, Universite Catholique de Louvain, Louvain-la-Neuve, Belgium, 1994.

19. J. Karlsson and K. Ryan, "A Cost-Value Approach for Prioritizing Requirements," *IEEE Software*, Sept./Oct. 1997, pp. 67–74.

About the Authors

Jonathan Lee is a professor in the Department of Computer Science and Information Engineering at National Central University in Taiwan. His research interests include trade-off requirements, agent-based software engineering, and applications of fuzzy theory to software engineering. He received his PhD in computer science from Texas A&M University. He is a member of the IEEE Computer Society, ACM, and AAAI.

Nien-Lin Xue is a PhD student in the Department of Computer Science and Information Engineering at National Central University in Taiwan. His research interests include requirements engineering, object-oriented methodologies, and the applications of fuzzy logic to software engineering. He received his MS from National Central University and his BS from Soochow University. He is a member of the IEEE Computer Society. He can be reached at nien@se01.csie.ncu.edu.tw.

Readers may contact Lee at National Central University, Department of Computer Science and Information Engineering, Chungli 32054, Taiwan; e-mail yjlee@se01.csie.ncu.edu.tw.

CHAPTER 4
DESIGN

This section concerns ways in which the design of software can be created, expressed, and specified. The ideal design should be so thorough that it could be given to a programmer for coding, without further explanation. For many years, software designs oscillated among various notations and methodologies. As a result, designers communicated their designs only with difficulty. Recently, however, standard names and patterns for designs have emerged. In addition, focused software design areas and techniques such as real time systems and formal methods, are finding recognized followings in the design community.

In the papers that follow, Monroe et al discuss the reusability of architectures and designs using object-orientation, standardized style names, and design patterns. Vlaer and Babb describe the selection of development tools for user interfaces, using specific selection criteria. Digre present a way in which business objects can be organized, by isolating "enterprise domain semantics from specific technology bindings." Coplein provides a context for design patterns, elaborating on the relationship among architecture, object-orientation, and design patterns. Hedenetz recounts the increasing need for "fly-by-wire" applications (in automobiles, for example), and supports the increased reliability required with a real-time development framework. Rather than being event-driven in the traditional sense, this framework observes its environment on its own schedule, thereby increasing controllability. Finally, Luqi and Goguen discuss the "promises and problems" of formal methods, arguing for an increase in the use of domain-specific versions.

Reprinted from IEEE Software, January 1997, pp. 43-52.

Architectural Styles, Design Patterns, and Objects

ROBERT T. MONROE, ANDREW KOMPANEK, RALPH MELTON, and DAVID GARLAN
Carnegie Mellon University

Architectural styles, object-oriented design, and design patterns all hold promise as approaches that simplify software design and reuse by capturing and exploiting system design knowledge. This article explores the capabilities and roles of the various approaches, their strengths, and their limitations.

Software system builders increasingly recognize the importance of exploiting design knowledge in the engineering of new systems. Several distinct but related approaches hold promise.

One approach is to focus on the architectural level of system design—the gross structure of a system as a composition of interacting parts. Architectural designs illuminate such key issues as scaling and portability, the assignment of functionality to design elements, interaction protocols between elements, and global system properties such as processing rates, end-to-end capacities, and overall performance.[1] Architectural descriptions tend to be informal and idiosyncratic: box-and-line diagrams convey essential system structure, with accompanying prose explaining the meaning of the symbols. Nonetheless, they provide a critical staging point for determining whether a system can meet its essential requirements, and they guide implementers in constructing the system. More recently, architectural descriptions have been used for codifying and reusing design knowledge. Much of their power comes from use of idiomatic architectural terms, such as "client-server system," "layered system," or "blackboard organization."

0740 7459/97/ $10.00 © 1997 IEEE

These convey widespread if informal understanding of the descriptions and let engineers quickly communicate

> **Each approach has something to offer: a collection of representational models and mechanisms.**

their designs to others. Such architectural idioms represent what have been termed architectural styles.[2]

The object-oriented paradigm offers another approach to describing system designs. In its simplest form, object-oriented design lets us encapsulate data and behavior in discrete objects that provide explicit interfaces to other objects; groups of objects interact by passing messages among themselves. OOD has proven to be quite popular in practice, and sophisticated OOD methodologies offer significant leverage for designing software,[2-3] including ease of decomposing a system into its constituent elements and partitioning system functionality and responsibility among those elements. However, it is not by itself well suited to describing complex interactions between groups of objects. Likewise, although individual objects can often be reused in other implementations, capturing and reusing common design idioms involving multiple objects can be difficult.

Design patterns have become an increasingly popular choice for addressing OOD's limitations. Although the principles underlying design patterns are not inherently tied to OOD, much recent work in this area has focused on design patterns for composing objects.[4,5] Like architectural styles, design patterns provide guid-

ance for combining design elements in principled and proven ways.

Each of these often complementary approaches to capturing software design knowledge and software designs themselves has both benefits and drawbacks. To effectively use these approaches, we need to understand their terminologies, capabilities, similarities, and differences. Further, we need to understand the roles that each can play in successful software design.

WHAT IS SOFTWARE ARCHITECTURE DESIGN?

In practice, an architectural design fulfills two primary roles. First, it provides a level of abstraction at which software system designers can reason about system behavior: function, performance, reliability, and so on. By abstracting away from implementation details, a good architectural description makes a system design intellectually tractable and exposes the properties most crucial to its success. It is often the key technical document used to determine whether a proposed new system will meet its most critical requirements.

Second, an architectural design serves as the "conscience" for a system as it evolves. By characterizing the crucial system design assumptions, a good architectural design guides the process of system enhancement—indicating what aspects of the system can be easily changed without compromising system integrity. As with building blueprints, a well-documented architectural design makes explicit the software's "load-bearing walls,"[6] a fact that helps not only at design time but also throughout a system's life cycle. To satisfy its multiple roles over time, an architectural description must be simple enough to permit system-level reasoning and prediction; practically speaking, it should fit on a page or two. Consequently, it is usually hierarchical: atomic architectural elements at one level of abstraction

are often described by a more detailed architecture at a lower level.

Architectural descriptions are primarily concerned with the following basic issues:

- *System structure.* Architectural descriptions characterize a system's structure in terms of high-level computational elements and their interactions. That is, an architecture frames its design solution as a configuration of interacting components. It is specifically not about requirements (for example, abstract relationships between elements of a problem domain) nor implementation details (such as algorithms or data structures).

- *Rich abstractions for interaction.* Interactions between architectural components—often drawn as connecting lines—provide a rich vocabulary for system designers. Although interactions may be as simple as procedure calls or shared data variables, they often represent more complex forms. Examples include pipes (with conventions for handling end-of-file and blocking), client-server interactions (with rules about initialization, finalization, and exception handling), event-broadcast connections (with multiple receivers), and database accessing protocols (with protocols for transaction invocation).

- *Global properties.* Architectural designs typically describe overall system behavior. Thus the problems they address are usually system-level ones, such as end-to-end data rates and latencies, resilience of one part of the system to failure in another, or system-wide propagation of changes when one part of a system is modified (such as changing the platform on which the system runs).

ARCHITECTURAL STYLE

As with any design activity, a central question is how to leverage past experience to produce better designs. In current practice, architectural designs have been codified and reused primarily through informal transmission of architectural idioms. For example, a system architecture might be defined informally as a client-server system, a blackboard system, a pipeline, an interpreter, or a layered system. While these characterizations rarely have formal definitions, they convey much about a system's structure and underlying computational model.

An important class of architectural idioms constitutes what some researchers have termed architectural styles. An architectural style characterizes a family of systems that are related by shared structural and semantic properties.[2] An architectural style provides a specialized design language for a specific class of systems. Specifically, styles typically provide the following four things:

- A vocabulary of design elements: component and connector types such as pipes, filters, clients, servers, parsers, and databases.

- Design rules, or constraints, that determine which compositions of those elements are permitted. For example, the rules might prohibit cycles in a particular pipe-filter style, specify that a client-server organization must be an n-to-one relationship, or define a specific compositional pattern such as a pipelined decomposition of a compiler.

- Semantic interpretation, whereby compositions of design elements, suitably constrained by the design rules, have well-defined meanings.

- Analyses that can be performed on systems built in that style. Examples include schedulability analysis for a style oriented toward real-time processing, and deadlock detection for client-server message passing. An important special case of analysis is system generation: many styles support application generators (for example, parser generators), or lead to reuse of a certain shared implementation base (such as user interface frameworks and support for communication between distributed processes).

The use of architectural styles has a number of significant benefits. First, it promotes design reuse: routine solutions with well-understood properties can be reapplied to new problems with confidence. Second, it can lead to significant code reuse: often the invariant aspects of an architectural style lend themselves to shared implementations. For example, systems described in a pipe-filter style might reuse Unix operating system primitives to handle task scheduling, synchronization, and communication through pipes. Similarly, a client-server style can take advantage of existing RPC (remote procedure call) mechanisms and stub generation capabilities. Third, it is easier for others to understand a system's organization if conventionalized structures are used. For example, even without giving details, characterizing a system as a client-server organization immediately conveys a strong image of the kinds of pieces present and how they fit together. Fourth, use of standardized styles supports interoperability. Examples include CORBA object-oriented architectures, the OSI (Open Systems Interconnection) protocol stack, and event-based tool integration. Fifth, as we noted earlier, by constraining the design space, an architectural style often permits specialized, style-specific analyses. For example, we can analyze systems built in a pipe-filter style for throughput, latency, and freedom from deadlock, but this might not be meaningful for another system that uses a different style or an arbitrary, ad hoc architecture.

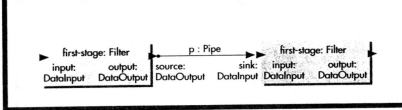

Figure 1. A simple system in the pipe-and-filter style is specified using an architectural notation.

```
Style pipe-and-filter
    Interface Type DataInput = (read → (data?x → DataInput
                                    [] end-of-data → close → √))
                                [] (close → √)
    Interface Type DataOutput = write → DataOutput [] close → √  ;


    Connector Pipe
       Role Source = DataOutput
       Role Sink = DataInput
       Glue = Buf<>
         where
           Buf<> = Source.write?x → Buf<x> [] Source.close → Closed<>
           Buf_s<x> = Source.write?y → Buf<y>s<x>
                    [] Source.close → Closed_s<x>
                    [] Sink.read → Sink.data!x → Buf_s
                    [] Sink.close → Killed
           Closed_s<x> = Sink.read → Sink.data!x → Closed_s
                       [] Sink.close → √
           Closed<> = Sink.read → Sink.end-of-data → Sink.close → √
           Killed = Source.write → Killed  [] Source.close → √

    Constraints
       ∀ c : Connectors  ● Type(c) = Pipe
       ∀ c : Components  ● Filter(c)
           where
               Filter(c:Component) = ∀ p : Ports(c) ● Type(p) = DataInput
                                                   ∨ Type(p) = DataOutput
    End Style
```

Figure 2. The system shown in Figure 1 is specified here using the Wright architecture description language.

OBJECT-ORIENTED DESIGN AND SOFTWARE ARCHITECTURE

The object-oriented design paradigm provides another abstraction for software design. In its simplest form, an OOD lets system designers encapsulate data and behavior in discrete objects that provide explicit interfaces to other objects. A message-passing abstraction is used as the glue that connects the objects and defines the communication channels in a design. Although OOD concepts can be used to address some architectural design issues, and doing so is popular among software developers, there are significant differences between the capabilities and benefits of object-oriented approaches to design and the approaches provided by an emerging class of software architecture design tools and notations. As the following examples illustrate, software architecture concepts allow an architect to describe multiple, rich interfaces to a component and to describe and encapsulate complex protocols of component interaction that are difficult to describe using traditional object-oriented concepts and notations.

To illustrate the different capabilities of style-based software architecture design and state-of-the-practice object-oriented design, consider the simple system presented in Figures 1 through 5. Figures 1 and 2 use common architectural notations (see the boxed text on architecture description languages on page 45) to present architectural views of the system. Figures 3 through 5 describe progressively more refined versions of the same system using the Object Modeling Technique OOD notation.[3]

In Figure 1, the system's architecture is described in a pipe-and-filter style that specifies the design vocabulary of components and connectors. In the pipe-and-filter style, all components are *filters* that transform a stream of data and provide specially typed input and output interfaces. All connectors in the style are *pipes* that describe a binary relationship between two filters and a data transfer protocol. Each pipe has two interfaces: a *source* that can only be attached to a filter's output interface, and a *sink* that can only be attached to a filter's input interface. Figure 2 provides a more formal definition of this style using the Wright notation.[7] The Wright style specification describes the semantics of the design elements that can be used in the style (pipes and filters), along with a set of constraints that specify how the design elements can be composed when building systems in the pipe-and-filter style. There is a direct correlation between the graphical notation and the formal specification of the design elements. Each design element in the graphical depiction of the system is typed, and the type corresponds to the

type and protocol specifications given in the Wright specification. Thus, the graphical diagram actually has a firm semantic grounding for specification and analysis.

The sample system has two primary components, labeled stage 1 and stage 2, each of which transforms a data stream and then sends it to the next component downstream. The components interact via the pipe protocol specified in Figure 2. For simplicity, Figures 1 and 2 show only two transformations and ignore system input and output.

We can make three observations about this architectural design, especially with respect to the OMT-based design of the same system in Figures 3 through 5. First, the protocol of interaction between the filters is rich, explicit, and well specified. The Wright specification in Figure 2 is associated with the pipe connector between two filters (and with all connectors of type pipe). This specification defines the protocol for transmitting data through a pipe, the ordering behavior of the pipe, and the various interfaces that the pipe can provide to its attached filters. Because a primary focus of software architecture is to describe interactions among components, this capability is important. Second, both the components and connectors—filters and pipes in this style—have multiple, well-defined interfaces. As a result, a pipe can limit the services that it provides to the filters on each end. Likewise, a filter can specify whether each of its interfaces will provide input or output, as well as the type of data passing through. In this example, the upstream filter can only write to the pipe, and the downstream filter can only read from the pipe, preventing inappropriate access to connector functionality (such as the upstream pipe reading from the pipe). Finally, because there is a rich notion of connector semantics built into the style definition, we can evaluate the

design to determine emergent systemwide properties such as freedom from deadlock (provided that the system contains no cycles), throughput rates, and potential system bottlenecks.

In contrast to the stylized architectural design shown in Figures 1 and 2, Figures 3 through 5 present different OODs of the same system in progressively more sophisticated descriptions. The first OMT diagram, in Figure 1, provides a simple class diagram that says each filter may be associated with other filters by a pipe association. Each pipe association has a source and a sink role to indicate directionality. The instance diagram in Figure 1 depicts the example system using this class structure.

The association between the first-stage and second-stage filters is not truly a first-class entity like the Filter class and

is therefore not capable of supporting an explicit, sophisticated protocol description like the pipe in the architectural example. Rather, this is a generic association, implying that the upstream filter can invoke any public method of the downstream filter. Although objects can be sophisticated entities in the OMT paradigm, the vocabulary for determining interactions between objects is relatively impoverished for use in architectural descriptions.

Any object that can send a message to another object can request that the target object invoke any of its public methods. There is effectively a single, flat interface provided by all objects to all objects. As a result, it is difficult for an architectural object to limit the services it can provide based on which aspects of the interface a requester is

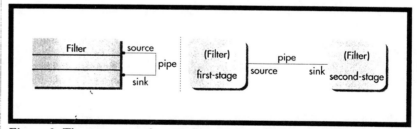

Figure 3. *The same system shown in Figure 1 is depicted here using a naive object-oriented notation (OMT).*

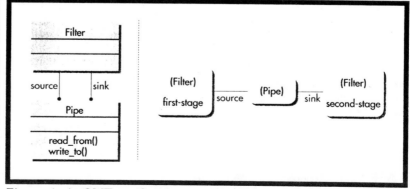

Figure 4. *An OMT specification is used to define the same system architecture shown in Figure 1. Pipe is now a first-class design entity.*

using and the type of connection between the two objects.

Finally, it is difficult to determine emergent system properties with an

The pattern approach lets us describe relatively complex protocols of interactions between objects.

impoverished vocabulary of connections and interface constraints. For example, the ability to invoke any method of an associated object at any time makes it difficult to determine dataflow characteristics and freedom from deadlock, which are both calculated relatively easily using the software architecture and architectural style constructs described earlier.

Figure 4 shows an attempt to address some of the issues raised by the design in Figure 3. It does so by making the pipe connector a first-class object. In this diagram, we use a pipe object to connect two filter objects. Using the OMT notation, it is now possible to add behavioral semantics to the Pipe class by associating dynamic and functional models with it. The Pipe class also introduces two new methods, read_from() and write_to(), that filters must call to send data on the pipe or read data from it.

One effect of placing a pipe entity between two filters is that the upstream filter no longer knows which downstream filter is receiving and processing its data. As a result, the upstream filter no longer has access to the downstream filter's methods. It can only access the pipe that connects them, ensuring a significant degree of independence from the downstream filter and transferring communication

responsibility to the pipe.

However, there is still a significant limitation to this design. Because the pipe object has to offer its full method interface to both of its attached filters, either filter can use the write_to() or read_from() methods. To maintain proper dataflow direction, however, we must be able to specify that the upstream filter, annotated by the source role, will use only the write_to() method, and that the downstream filter, annotated by the sink role, will use only the read_from() method. Unfortunately, the OMT notation does not let us formally specify these constraints. The directionality and well-defined pipe behavior are thus lost, along with the design analyses and assurances that go with them. It is certainly possible to create filters that abide by this protocol, but it is difficult to specify and enforce this constraint generally and explicitly using standard OOD notions.

Design patterns. An object-oriented approach to specifying an architectural pipe connector for use in pipe-and-filter style systems, along with rules for how a pipe can be properly instantiated in a design, apparently will require the cooperation of multiple objects. The emerging concept of *design patterns* addresses this issue.

Figure 5 presents a third and final revision of the simple pipe-and-filter architecture. This time, the pipe construct has been broken into three interacting objects:

♦ a pipe object controls dataflow and buffering,

♦ a source object attaches to the upstream filter and provides only a write_to() interface to the pipe, and

♦ a corresponding sink object attaches to the downstream filter and provides only a read_from() interface to the pipe.

This solution solves the problem of both filters having access to both read_from() and write_to() methods by

providing intermediary objects with limited interfaces.

By itself, however, this design does not completely mitigate the problem of access to inappropriate methods. It simply shifts the problem from the filter objects accessing inappropriate pipe methods to the source and sink objects improperly accessing pipe methods. Because the pipe, source, and sink methods are all encapsulated by the pipe-connector pattern, however, it is possible to describe a protocol by which the three objects agree to interact according to an appropriate pipe protocol; that is,

♦ the pipe object takes care of all queuing and buffering issues,

♦ only the source role may invoke the pipe's enqueue_data() method, and

♦ only the sink role may invoke the pipe's dequeue_data() method.

Further details of this protocol can also be encoded in the pattern and its objects.

The pattern approach lets us describe relatively complex protocols of interactions between objects that we want to encapsulate, but don't want to encapsulate within a single class. We could have described many of the constraints that the source and sink objects satisfy in the Filter class, but doing so would have added constraints to the class that may not be generally appropriate, and might have significantly decreased reusability. It would also have spread the interaction protocol among a wider variety of constructs, when we really want to be able to encapsulate it to clarify the design and ease the process of reasoning about the design. The need to use three different types of objects, interconnected with a pattern specification, significantly hinders the goal of simplicity. Although we could model a pipe connection using OMT and design patterns, much of the simplicity and elegance that came from specifying a simple type-annotated arrow with the architectural notation is lost when connectors are no longer first-class entities, as in the OOD paradigm.

Summary. As these examples illustrate, architectural designs involve abstractions that may not necessarily be best modeled as a system of objects, at least in the narrow sense of objects as encapsulated data types that interact through method invocation. This point is not limited to dataflow styles such as pipe-and-filter. We can easily make similar arguments about architectural design done in a layered style, a client-server–based style, a distributed-database style, or many other styles of architectural design.

Given that architectural styles can describe a broad range of different design families, it is tempting to view object-oriented design as a style of architectural design in which all components are objects and all connections are simple associations or aggregations (to use the OMT vocabulary). Indeed, it is possible to define object-based architectural styles that provide the typical primitive system construction facilities supported by many OOD toolsets. This view is quite reasonable for the subset of OOD that deals with architectural abstractions. There are, on the other hand, a number of design issues addressed directly by OOD that are generally considered outside the scope of architectural design. Examples include ways of modeling problem domains and requirements, and implementation issues such as designing data structures and algorithms. These concerns are relevant to software development and should probably be considered when a system architecture is being designed; it should not, however, be necessary to directly express and address all of them in an architectural description.

Architectural design is concerned with composing systems from components, and the interactions between these components. Such compositions provide an abstract view of a system, so that the designer can do system-level analyses and reason about system integrity constraints. Examples include throughput rates and freedom from deadlock. These distinctive aspects of architectural design highlight several

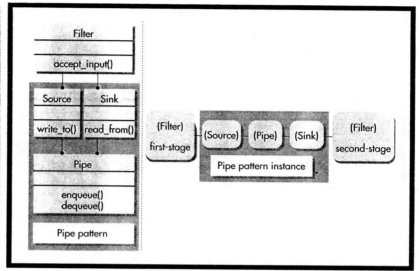

Figure 5. *In this OMT-based specification of the system shown in Figure 1, the pipe connector is represented as a design pattern. Connector interfaces (source and sink) are now first-class entities.*

important constrasts with object-oriented design. Although both are concerned with system structure in general, architectural design involves a richer collection of abstractions than is typically provided by OOD. These abstractions support the ability to describe new kinds of potentially complex system glue (or connectors). In addition to the pipe connector illustrated earlier, it is also possible to define n-ary connectors such as an event system, an RPC-based SQL query, or a two-phase-commit transaction protocol. Architectural abstractions also let a designer associate multiple interfaces with components and to express topological and other semantically based constraints over a design.

Thus neither architectural design nor object-oriented design subsumes the other. They are both appropriate at various times in the development process and they share some common notions and concepts. Just as you can specify an OO-based architectural style, you can use an OOD to implement or refine a sophisticated component or

connector in an architectural design. The fundamental issues that the two approaches address and the abstraction mechanisms that they provide, however, are not the same.

ARCHITECTURAL STYLES AND DESIGN PATTERNS

Two of the primary limitations of traditional OOD, as described in the previous examples, are the difficulty in specifying how groups of objects interact and in specifying and packaging related collections of objects for reuse. As Figure 5 shows, design patterns can mitigate these problems. The basic idea behind design patterns is that common idioms are found repeatedly in software designs and that these patterns should be made explicit, codified, and applied appropriately to similar problems. Several approaches to expressing these patterns have arisen over the past four or five years, most of which have focused on patterns for OOD.[4,5] The utility of

Primitive vocabulary:

Primitive vocabulary	Informal description	Interface constraints	Properties
Components:		(*ports* define typed component interfaces)	
Process	OS Process. Processes read input messages, send results to output interfaces.	at least 1 async-input port at least 1 async-output port at least 0 sync-caller ports	processing-cost, rate, input-message-type(s), output-message-type(s)
Resource	Component for which processes contend.	exactly 0 async ports at least 1 sync-callee port	resource-cost
Device	Send messages into the system at a predefined rate.	exactly 0 sync ports exactly 0 async-input ports at least 1 async-output port	output-rate, output-message-type
Connectors:		(*roles* define typed connector interfaces)	
async-msg-pass	Asynchronous message channel for typed messages.	exactly 1 async-input role exactly 1 async-output role	message-type
async-msg-pass-rendevous	Like async-msg-pass, but requires rendevous before sending message. N-ary connector.	at least 1 async-input role exactly 1 async-output role	message-type
sync-request	Binary synchronous request channel, typed messages.	exactly 1 sync-caller role exactly 1 sync-callee role	message-type

Design rules (list is a subset of all RTP/C style design rules):
- Async-msg-pass connectors may only connect (process, process) or (device, process) pairs of components.
- Sync-request connectors may only connect (process, resource) pairs of components.
- All processes must have an attached input interface.
- Each connector's input message type must match its output message type.
- ...

Style-based design analyses:

Analysis	Description
Message path typechecking	Insures only valid message types are passed along each message channel. Provides early detection of message type mismatch.
Rate calculation	Determines how often each process can be given control and resources.
Schedulability	Calculates whether this design could be scheduled on a uniprocessor with user-specified performance characteristics.
Repair heuristics	If the system cannot be scheduled, this analysis identifies bottlenecks and suggests likely repairs and improvements.

Figure 6. An informal specification of the Real-Time Producer/Consumer (RTP/C) style.

design patterns, however, extends beyond this. There are three fundamental requirements for specifying and reusing software design patterns: the design domain must be well understood, it must support the encapsulation of design elements, and it must have evolved a collection of well-known and proven design idioms. Pattern languages then let knowledgeable designers codify proven designs, design fragments, and frameworks for subsequent reuse.

Architectural styles relate closely to design patterns in two ways. First, architectural styles can be viewed as kinds of patterns[8]—or perhaps more accurately as pattern languages.[9] Describing an architectural style as a design pattern requires, however, a rather broad definition of the scope of design patterns. An architectural style is probably better thought of as a design language that provides architects with a vocabulary and framework with which they can build useful design patterns to solve specific problems—much as OMT provides a framework and notation for working with objects. Second, for a given style there may exist a set of idiomatic uses. These idioms act as microarchitectures, or architectural design patterns, designed to work within a specific architectural style. By providing a framework within which these patterns work, the designer using the pattern can leverage style's the broad descriptive and analytical capabilities along with proven mechanisms for addressing specific design challenges in the form of design patterns.

We see patterns and architectural styles as complementary mechanisms for encapsulating design expertise. An architectural style provides a collection of building-block design elements, rules and constraints for composing the building blocks, and tools for analyzing and manipulating designs created in the style. Styles generally provide guidance and analysis for building a broad class of architectures in a specific domain, whereas patterns focus on solving smaller, more specific problems within a given style (or perhaps multiple styles).

194

Shared-resource architectural pattern

Intent: Avoid deadlock when processes share common resources.

Motivation: System deadlock can occur when architectural components lock shared resources in an inappropriate order.

Applicability: Architectural designs done in the RTP/C style, where process components share resource components and freedom from deadlock is more important than run-time performance.

Structure:

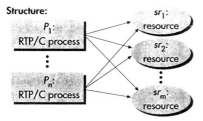

Participants: N RTP/C process components, each connected to m or fewer RTP/C resource components. All connectors used are RTP/C sync-request connectors from processors to resources.

Collaborations: In order to avoid deadlock, a process P_k can only send a request on resources sr_i (locking sr_i) if $i > j$, where s_j is the highest numbered resource currently held by P_k.

Consequences: Using the ordered access protocol to prevent deadlock will not generally lead to optimal resource access or allocation. Other protocols may lead to better average-case performance.

Message-Replicator architectural pattern

Intent: Send identical messages to a dynamically changing group of other components using a principled protocol.

Motivation: A component's output may need to be sent to a variable set of components. The set of receiving components may change as the system runs, and constraints on the order in which recipients receive the messages may be important (as in the case of a stock-quote and trading system).

Applicability: Architectural designs done in the RTP/C style where the set of applicable recipients for the output of a specific component may vary as the system runs.

Structure:

Participants: The Msg-replicator process is an RTP/C process component with a single input port and a variable array of output ports. There is a single async-msg-pass connector providing input and a set of async-msg-pass connectors that send output to the recipients.

Collaborations: When this pattern is instantiated the designer needs to select a protocol by which the messages will be sent to the outputs. Options include *sequentially*, whereby messages are written in a user-specified order to each output connector one at a time; *parallel*, whereby all messages are written to their output connectors concurrently; or a user-specified variation on one of these.

Consequences: The dynamic nature of this pattern can make some static analyses, such as dataflows and delivery guarantees, difficult or impossible to perform.

Figure 7. Two sample architectural design patterns in the RTP/C style.

It is also important to note that patterns need not be architectural. Indeed, many patterns in recent handbooks[4,5] deal with solutions to lower-level programming mechanisms, rather than system-structuring issues.

Pattern and style examples. To illustrate the scope and purpose of architectural styles, as well as how they relate to design patterns, consider the architectural style specification given in Figure 6. This style, described as the Real-Time Producer/Consumer style, is designed to assist architects putting together real-time multimedia systems running on uniprocessor computers.[10] Figure 6 provides an informal description of the RTP/C style, emphasizing the types of (primitive) design vocabulary used by designs constructed in the style, design rules and constraints that specify how the elements may be composed, and analyses that can be performed on the design. The RTP/C style definition describes a set of primitive building blocks and guidelines for putting together a fairly broad range of systems within a reasonably well understood domain.

Even with such a well-defined style, however, relatively concrete design patterns play an important role. The RTP/C primitive design elements and guidelines form a language that can be used to capture more detailed, concrete solutions to specific problems. This style provides a well-understood and well-defined vocabulary framework for composing individual design elements in principled ways that support real-time analyses. Figure 7 shows two simplified design patterns done in the RTP/C style—the forked-memory pattern and the message-replicator pattern. Along with a diagram, each pattern provides information describing its applicability, consequences of use, and so on. We have shown these patterns using the structure provided in a 1995 book by Erich Gamma and his colleagues.[4] This framework works well for architectural patterns as well as for OO patterns, with the primary difference being that architectural patterns address a more specific set of design issues (as described earlier under "What is software architecture?") than do OO patterns. Just as OMT and objects are used to show the design patterns in most OOD patterns handbooks, the vocabulary and rules of architectural style can be used to specify architectural design patterns.

It follows, then, that OMT and the design patterns notations from the OOD patterns handbooks can be used to specify architectural patterns also. In fact, several of the design patterns that Gamma and his colleagues describe appear to apply to architectural design.[8] Examples include the Facade pattern that provides a single interface to a collection of objects, the Observer pattern that specifies a mechanism for maintaining consistency among objects (or components), and the Strategy pattern that specifies how to separate algorithmic choices from interface decisions. None of the listed patterns are limited to being only architectural patterns. All have applicability at lower levels of design (such as detailed design or implementation code). In addition to the architectural patterns listed here, several patterns in the Gamma et al. book, for example, fail to address architectural issues. The Factory Method and Flyweight patterns. Both of these patterns, for instance, deal with lower-level implementation issues than architectures generally specify.

Thus, architectural design patterns and object-oriented design patterns are simply instances of the more general class of all design patterns. Unlike design patterns proper, however, an architectural style provides a language and framework for describing families of well-formed software architectures.

The role of style is to provide a language for expressing both architectural instances and patterns of common architectural design idioms. As a result, the constructs and concepts underlying architectural style are comparable to those underlying an OOD methodology like OMT, rather than a set of design patterns such as those given by Gamma and his colleagues.[4] A specific architectural style is better thought of as a language for building patterns than as an instance of a design pattern itself.

Architectures, architectural styles, objects, and design patterns capture complementary aspects of software design. Although the issues and aspects of software design addressed by these four approaches overlap somewhat, none completely subsumes the other. Each has something to offer in the way of a collection of representational models and mechanisms. ◆

ACKNOWLEDGMENTS

We thank Robert Allen for his helpful comments. This research was sponsored by the National Science Foundation under grant no. CCR-9357792 and a graduate research fellowship; by the Wright Laboratory, Aeronautical Systems Center, Air Force Materiel Command, USAF; by the Advanced Research Projects Agency under grant no. F33615-93-1-1330; and by Siemens Corporate Research.

REFERENCES

1. M. Shaw and D. Garlan, *Software Architecture: Perspectives on an Emerging Discipline*, Prentice-Hall, Englewood Cliffs, N.J., 1996.
2. G. Abowd, R. Allen, and D. Garlan, "Using Style to Give Meaning to Software Architecture," *Proc. SIGSOFT '93: Foundations Software Eng.*, ACM, New York, 1993. Also in *Software Eng. Notes*, Dec. 1993, pp. 9-20.
3. J. Rumbaugh et al., *Object-Oriented Modeling and Design*, Prentice-Hall, Englewood Cliffs, N.J., 1991.
4. E. Gamma et al., *Design Patterns: Elements of Reusable Object-Oriented Design*, Addison-Wesley, Reading, Mass., 1995.
5. W. Pree, *Design Patterns for Object-Oriented Software Development*, Addison-Wesley, Reading, Mass., 1995.
6. D. Perry and A. Wolf, "Foundations for the Study of Software Architecture," *ACM Software Eng. Notes*, Vol. 17, No. 4, Oct. 1992, pp. 40-52.
7. R. Allen and D. Garlan, "Formalizing Architectural Connection," *Proc. 16th Int'l Conf. Software Eng.*, IEEE Computer Soc. Press, Los Alamitos, Calif., 1994, pp. 71-80.
8. M. Shaw, "Some Patterns for Software Architecture," in *Pattern Languages of Program Design, Vol. 2*, J. Vlissides, J. Coplien, and N. Kerth, eds., Addison-Wesley, Reading, Mass., 1996, pp. 255-269.
9. N.L. Kerth, "Caterpillar's Fate: A Pattern Language for Transformations from Analysis to Design," in *Pattern Languages of Program Design*, J.O. Coplien and D.C. Schmidt, eds., Addison-Wesley, Reading, Mass., 1995.
10. K. Jeffay, "The Real-Time Producer/Consumer Paradigm: A Paradigm for the Construction of Efficient, Predictable Real-Time Systems," *Proc. 1993 ACM/SIGAPP Symp. Applied Computing*, ACM Press, New York, 1993, pp. 796-804.

Robert T. Monroe is a doctoral candidate in the Department of Computer Science at Carnegie Mellon University. He holds an MS in computer science from Carnegie Mellon and a BS from the University of Michigan. His research interests include software design tools, software architecture, and languages for expressing software design expertise. He is a member of the IEEE Computer Society and ACM.

Ralph Melton is a graduate student in the Department of Computer Science at Carnegie Mellon University. He holds a BS from Stanford University. His research interests include software architecture and the use of formal methods to describe design fragments and their composition.

Andrew Kompanek is a research programmer with the ABLE research group in Carnegie Mellon University's School of Computer Science. He recently received his BS in mathematics and computer science from Carnegie Mellon. His current work includes the design and development of visualization and automated layout tools for software architectures.

David Garlan is associate professor of computer science at Carnegie Mellon University, where he heads the ABLE Project. His research focuses on software architecture, the application of formal methods to the construction of reusable designs, and software development environments. He completed his PhD at Carnegie Mellon, and holds a BA from Amherst College and an MA from the University of Oxford, England. He is member of the IEEE Computer Society and ACM.

Address questions about this article to Robert Monroe, School of Computer Science, Carnegie Mellon University, 5000 Forbes Ave., Pittsburgh, PA 15213; bmonroe+@cs.cmu.edu.

196

Reprinted from IEEE Software,
July/Aug. 1997, pp. 29-39.

Choosing a User Interface Development Tool

LAURA A. VALAER, *Hughes Information Technology Systems*
ROBERT G. BABB II, *University of Denver*

Before you invest in a GUI development tool, you should know its benefits and drawbacks. The authors provide a checklist for choosing a tool that fits your needs. Usability, functionality, flexibility, portability, support, and cost are all part of the picture.

Software developers face many difficult decisions when building new applications, not the least of which is the design of the graphical user interface. The answer to one question—is it better to use a GUI development tool or build it manually?—is relatively straightforward. Today's tools offer several benefits that manual coding does not. Because these tools often provide a simple graphical interface for developing displays, nonprogrammers and human factors engineers can contribute their expertise. Also, if the schedule permits, a tool can be used to build prototypes throughout the development cycle; some tools even provide a test/prototype mode for testing displays without compiling and executing the entire application. And finally, end users can evaluate each prototype and provide feedback, increasing their satisfaction with the final product.

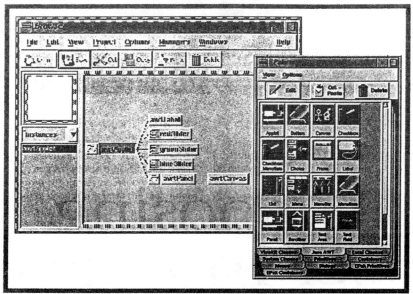

Figure 1. This example of Builder Xcessory illustrates the Java code generation capabilities of the tool. (Courtesy of Integrated Computer Solutions)

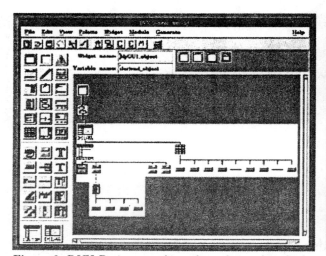

Figure 2. DVX-Designer combines the real-time data display capabilities of DataViews with the Motif GUI builder X-Designer. (Courtesy of DataViews Corp.)

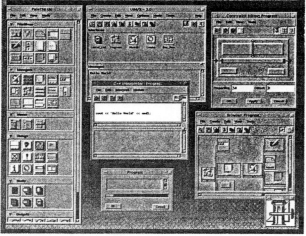

Figure 3. UIM/X is a popular GUI builder that is customized and redistributed by a number of other vendors. (Courtesy of Visual Edge Software)

Some tools offer the benefit of automatically generating at least part of the interface code. This is helpful because generated code is typically more consistent, and coding standards such as naming conventions and standard headers and comments are maintained automatically. Also, generated graphics code contains fewer bugs when it is isolated from the functional code, which must typically be manually edited. Moreover, tool-generated display designs, components, and even generated code can sometimes be reused. This not only saves development time but can provide a level of consistency across the different interfaces produced.

As with most software tools, using a GUI tool can have drawbacks. If a tool has a complicated interface and is difficult to use, the learning curve can be quite slow and can actually make the development process much less efficient. Developers may resist using the tool if it makes their work harder than it would have been to simply code the interface. Similarly, if the tool has poor performance, it can affect the interface development schedule. The functionality of the final product can be limited if a tool does not take advantage of all the hardware and native windowing platform capabilities, which often happens with multiplatform tools. They may only implement a set of display functionality that is common to all of the supported platforms.

Although a tool that generates code can be helpful, it can also hinder development if it is poorly implemented—for instance, if it cannot automatically regenerate the display code after functional code has been added. It is frustrating as

well as inefficient to manually cut and paste functional code back into the regenerated display stubs. Similarly, if the code generator is not well designed, the generated code may be extremely difficult to read and modify. It may also be inefficient and make integration with the rest of the application a difficult task.

Thus, the first decision you must make is whether or not to use a GUI tool, considering your specific application development environment. But once you are committed to using one, how do you pick among the tools available? The variety can be overwhelming.[1] Consider the benefits as well as drawbacks and keep in mind two goals: you want to simplify the development process, thus increasing productivity, and you want to create a better product. If a tool does not help you achieve these goals, it may not be a worthwhile investment. You start by selecting a category of tools, then you evaluate the different tools available in that category. Here we present a categorization scheme for current GUI tools and provide a checklist of criteria to be considered during that evaluation process. For information on other GUI tool evaluation techniques, see elsewhere.[2,3] Most of the criteria we use correspond to criteria commonly used in published evaluations of software tools.[4-6]

GUI TOOL CATEGORIES

To simplify the tool selection process, you can divide GUI tools into categories based on their most advertised functionality. Use the following categories to determine the types of tools most suitable to the given application.

♦ A *GUI builder*, sometimes referred to as an *interface development tool*,[5] provides a simple interface development environment. A developer can typically create and manipulate user interface displays in a "what you see is what you get" environment. Examples include Builder Xcessory, shown in Figure 1, and

X-Designer, an enhanced version of which is shown in Figure 2.

♦ A *user interface management system* provides the functionality of a GUI builder as well as the capability to define and execute the functionality of the displays from within the tool. A UIMS can also generate code to build a version of the interface that will execute independently of the tool. Examples include UIM/X, as shown in Figure 3, and TeleUSE, as shown in Figure 4.

♦ A *graphical user environment*, or *data visualization tool*, provides dynamic data representation and visualization. A developer can define and animate objects or scenes of objects. Using a drawing editor, the developer designs static displays

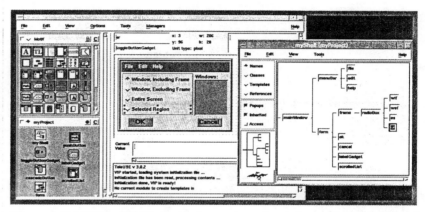

Figure 4. TeleUSE, *a UIMS, provides interactive tools to design and build Motif-based GUIs. (Courtesy of Aonix)*

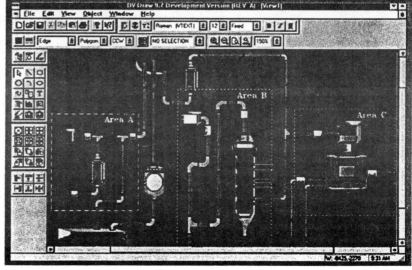

Figure 5. Using DataViews, developers can create graphical displays with the DV-Draw editor and add real-time dynamics via DV-Tools. (Courtesy of DataViews Corp.)

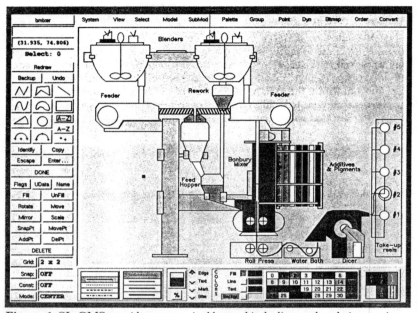

Figure 6. *SL-GMS provides a customizable graphical editor and real-time engine to drive display dynamics. (Courtesy of SL Corp.)*

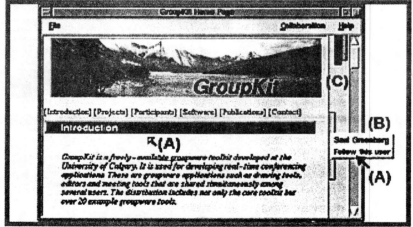

Figure 7. *GroupWeb is an application built in the free toolkit GroupKit. This example illustrates several groupware widgets: (a) multiple telepointers, (b) view-slaving controls, and (c) multiuser scrollbars that help people work together in real time over distance. (Courtesy of the Grouplab at the University of Calgary)*

♦ *Specialized widgets* provide functionality beyond the basic capabilities of a typical widget set, such as X/Motif. Individual widgets or libraries of widgets from different vendors can be integrated to provide developers with the necessary development tools. Examples include GroupKit, as shown in Figure 7, and INT Widgets, as shown in Figure 8.

♦ *Plotting and analysis tools* typically let the designer display technical data via a variety of generic and/or custom graphs or plots. Some tools also provide the ability to perform technical analysis on such data. PV-Wave, shown in Figure 9, is an example.

♦ *Three-dimensional visualization tools* make up a rather specialized category. They are generally most practical on hardware platforms that support the extensive calculations required in 3D graphics. Examples include AVS/Express, as shown in Figure 10, and IDL, as shown in Figure 11.

♦ A *cross-platform development tool* is essential if your application must be portable. A common "look-and-feel" across different platforms can be created using a layered Application Program Interface or a simulated API. Both add a layer of software between the application and the native windowing system. This layer provides a common programming interface across all the available platforms. A layered API makes calls directly to the native GUI library. A subset of functionality, that which is common to all the available platforms, is typically implemented. Examples of tools using the layered API approach are the XVT Development Solution for C and Development Solution for C++, as shown in Figure 12. A simulation API typically offers a superset of the functionality found on all the available platforms. Low-level graphics calls implement any function not found in a native GUI library. Open Interface Element, as shown in Figure 13, is an example of a tool based on the simulated API approach.

♦ *GUI porting tools* automatically port user interface code to a different platform. Native calls from the original

with standard or custom objects. Dynamic behavior can then be attached to the objects. This is a useful feature for real-time applications. Examples include DataViews, as shown in Figure 5, and SL-GMS, as shown in Figure 6.

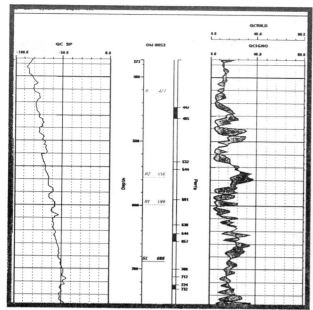

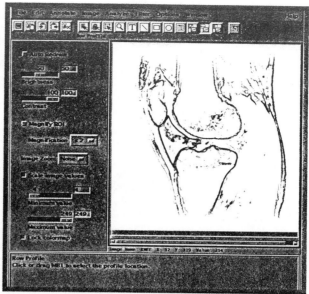

Figure 8. *This example, from the geoscience widget library, illustrates one of INT's tools for the oil exploration industry. A variety of general-purpose widgets are also available. (Courtesy of Interactive Network Technologies)*

Figure 9. *PV-WAVE lets users transform data into high-quality images for analysis and comparison. (Courtesy of Visual Numerics)*

platform are typically replaced with the native calls of the new platform. For example, Wind/U, shown in Figure 14, will port Visual C++ user interfaces by replacing Windows 95 or Windows NT calls with native platform calls, such as X/Motif.

♦ *Application development tools* provide miscellaneous capabilities beyond user interface design and development. The additional functionality of the tool may be useful in developing the rest of the application. Additional capabilities include distributed application communications, real-time system capabilities, database access, and expert system development. Examples include Galaxy, shown in Figure 15, and RTworks, shown in Figure 16.

Various tools have emerged in the realms of HTML home page creation,[7-8] virtual reality,[9] and Java programming.[10,11] A great deal of information is available today,[12] and each of these topics warrants an article in its own right. Although outside the scope of this work, they certainly provide an avenue for future research.

Examples. Many of these tools have functionalities that place them in more than one category. For example, DataViews is a graphical user environment tool that also provides some plotting and

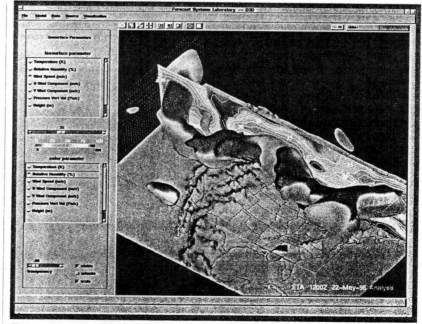

Figure 10. *AVS/Express provides the capability to prototype and construct applications. It includes technology for advanced imaging and data visualization. (Courtesy of Advanced Visual Systems and the Forecast Systems Lab at the National Oceanographic and Atmospheric Administration)*

graphing capabilities. IDL features technology for producing advanced imaging and 3D graphics, but also provides a basic GUI building capability. Similarly,

DVX-Designer is a GUI builder that also provides support for dynamic data visualization. Additionally, many of the tools referenced in this article provide

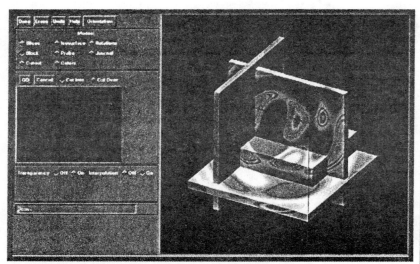

Figure 11. *IDL graphics routines provide features for developing GUIs with advanced image processing, 3D graphics, and volume visualization capabilities. (Courtesy of Research Systems)*

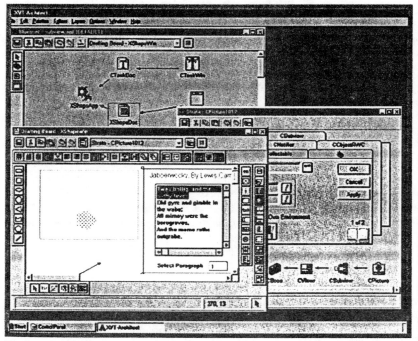

Figure 12. *XVT's development solutions for C and C++ help developers build portable user interfaces. DSC++ provides a visual tool for building displays and generates C++ interface code. (Courtesy of XVT Software)*

Java user interface development support. In cases where the interface requirements are characteristic of more than one category, you can choose tools from each category and review them for the additional features they provide, then finally pick the one most suitable for your particular application development environment.

To illustrate these ideas, we have chosen three examples from our experience.

♦ An online time accounting system required only basic widget functionality, so a GUI builder or UIMS would have been suitable. However, since the software needed to run on Windows 3.1, Macintosh, and Unix platforms while providing the native "look and feel" of each, we chose a cross-platform tool, XVT Development Solution for C++.

♦ A real-time monitoring and control system typically requires graphical displays for understandability. The dynamic characteristics of these displays help users perform their required activities more efficiently. Many of these systems are built using a graphical user environment. We have seen both Data-Views and SL-GMS used. These tools are available on various platforms and, in the case of real-time applications, the dynamic graphics capabilities may be more important than the ability to efficiently support standard interface look and feel. In cases where a standard look and feel is as important as the dynamic capabilities, DVX-Designer appears to be a good choice (we have not been involved in any projects that have chosen DVX-Designer). It has an additional drawing widget within which objects can be drawn and animated for graphical data visualization.

♦ A real-time monitoring and control system was developed in a PC environment with a completely different native windowing platform than the VAX on which it was eventually installed. We chose a GUI porting tool, Wind/U from Bristol, as an effective solution for this situation. This tool enabled us (the developers) to create an interface in a familiar environment and to maintain consistency with other parallel interface development efforts, while delivering the application on the required platform. Without the use of a porting tool in this situation, we would have had to purchase different products for each project and would have lost the advantage of cross-project training and expertise and any possible development reuse between projects.

EVALUATION CRITERIA

Once you have determined the most reasonable category, or categories, of GUI tools, you must choose a specific tool. It is important to evaluate actual copies of each candidate tool (Table 1 provides contact information for all the companies and products mentioned in this article). The following criteria can help you compare the candidates.

♦ *Usability.* A GUI tool should simplify the team's standard development process. A tool should be easy to install, learn, and use. One which does not possess these qualities will only frustrate the developers, leading to lower productivity. Look for a tool that provides appropriate levels of help and is suitable for the skills mix of the team.

♦ *Functionality.* The basic functionality of a chosen tool should match the requirements for the interface. Look for a tool that provides the necessary widgets or provides a convenient means for extending the widget set. A tool that automatically generates the required source code can be extremely useful and can increase productivity. Evaluate the languages, standards, and platforms supported by the tool.

♦ *Flexibility.* System requirements can evolve rapidly during design and development. A tool should be responsive to changing requirements in the application. Evaluate a candidate tool's support of different design methodologies, programming languages, hardware platforms, and support for multiple (human) languages. For example, depending on an application's requirements, it may be

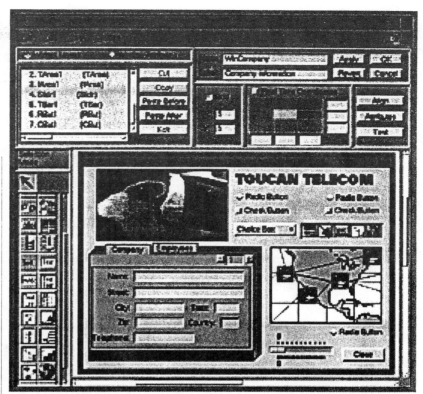

Figure 13. Open Interface Element is a cross-platform tool that provides developers with a superset of widgets. (Courtesy of Neuron Data)

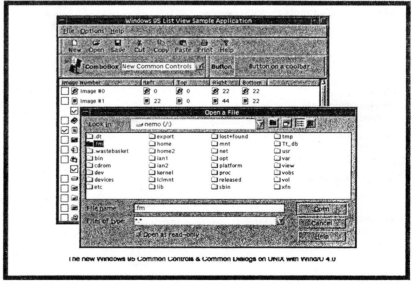

Figure 14. This example illustrates the new Windows 95 Common Controls and Dialogs on Unix with Wind/U 4.0. (Courtesy of Bristol Technology)

important to look at a tool's support for international application development.

♦ *Portability.* Current application requirements or long-term development goals may dictate reviewing a tool's support of interface portability. Evaluate what platforms are supported by the tool and how easy it is to port the interface between them. If an application is to be delivered on multiple platforms, the

TABLE 1
COMPANY AND PRODUCT INFORMATION

Category	Product	Contact Information	URL
GUI builders	Builder Xcessory	Integrated Computer Solutions Cambridge, Mass., USA +1-617-621-0060	http://www.ics.com/Products/BX40/ BX40Datasheet/Welcome.html
	X-Designer and DVX-Designer	DataViews Corp. Northampton, Mass., USA +1-413-586-4144	http://www.dvcorp.com/mktg/xd.html
UIMS	UIM/X	Visual Edge Software Ltd. St. Laurent, Quebec, Canada +1-514-332-6430	http://www.vedge.com/prods/ uimx.html
	TeleUSE	Aonix San Francisco, Calif., USA +1-415-543-0900	http://www.aonix.com/Products/ Teleuse/teleuse.html
Graphical user environment	DataViews	DataViews Corp. Northampton, Mass., USA +1-413-586-4144	http://www.dvcorp.com/mktg/ dv.html
	SL-GMS	SL Corp. Corte Madera, Calif., USA +1-415-927-1724	http://www.sl.com/
Specialized widgets	Groupkit	Saul Greenberg Univ. of Calgary, Alberta, Canada +1-403-220-6087	http://www.cpsc.ucalgary.ca/projects/ grouplab/projects/groupkit/groupkit. html
	INT Widgets	Interactive Network Technologies Houston, Texas, USA +1-713-975-7434	http://www.int.com/products
Plotting and analysis tools	PV-Wave	Visual Numerics Houston, Texas, USA +1-800-222-4675 or +1-713-784-3131	http://www.vni.com/products/wave/ newoverview.html
3D visualization tools	AVS/Express	Advanced Visual Systems Waltham, Mass., USA +1-617-890-4300	http://www.avs.com/products/xp-dev/ index.htm
	IDL	Research Systems Boulder, Colo., USA +1-303-786-9900	http://www.rsinc.com/idl/index.html
Cross-platform development tools — layered API approach	XVT development solutions for C and C++	XVT Software Boulder, Colo., USA +1-303-443-4223	http://www.xvt.com/docs/dscpp.html and http://www.xvt.com/docs/ dsc.html
Cross-platform development tools — simulated API approach	Open Interface Element	Neuron Data Mountain View, Calif., USA +1-415-528-3450	http://www.neurondata.com/ Products/oie.htm
GUI porting tools	Wind/U	Bristol Technology Ridgefield, Conn., USA +1-203-438-6969	http://www.bristol.com/Products/ windu.html
Application development tools	Galaxy	Visix Software Reston, Va., USA +1-703-758-8230	http://www.visix.com/products/ galaxy/
	RTworks	Talarian Corp. Mountain View, Calif., USA +1-415-965-8050	http://www.talarian.com/rtworks.html

particular API approach taken by the tool should match the requirements and operational concept of the system.

♦ *Support*. A tool's support includes documentation, training, and other materials provided by the vendor, as well as online technical help. A vendor's level of support is often correlated with a tool's maturity, reliability, and stability.

♦ *Cost*. Consider all costs related to obtaining and using a candidate tool. Costs often vary depending on the methods of procurement and licensing. Evaluate the initial investment costs, recurring operating costs such as maintenance, and training costs. Cost is also a relative criterion. Choosing a lower-cost tool that doesn't get the job done can lead to disaster.

Our checklist, shown in the boxes on pages 38 and 39, presents a number of subheadings under each criterion. The

questions presented for each section are neither exhaustive, nor are they intended to result in a numeric rating of a GUI tool. They do provide, however, a list of critical issues for a development team to consider when evaluating a candidate tool. They should also trigger the generation of more application-specific questions.

Application user interface development can benefit greatly from use of the many tools currently available. The categories and criteria described here are only suggested guidelines for choosing a tool. Your choice is rarely black and white; it will be affected by the specific requirements of your project. Select the tool that is not only the most efficient for the developers' use, but also contributes the most to creating a more effective user interface for the given application domain.

Because the area of user interface development is changing so rapidly, it is important to keep current with the latest vendors and available tools. As an example, on top of the normal pace of change in the business world, tools for Java, virtual reality, and home page creation continue to emerge.

The criteria presented here comprise just another tool to help you make better decisions. However, simply picking the most appropriate tool for a given application's development does not guarantee the effectiveness of the final product. Using the right tool enhances but does not replace good user interface design and development techniques. ◆

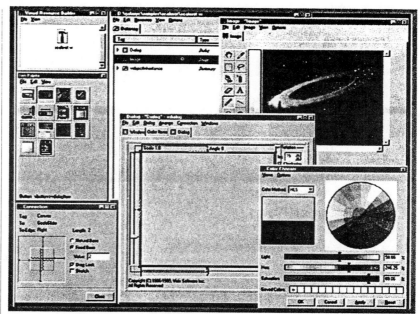

Figure 15. The Galaxy application environment features a comprehensive tool set for complete application development, including the capability to build GUIs. (Courtesy of Visix Software)

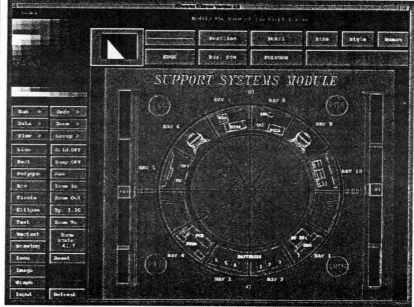

Figure 16. RTworks includes RThci, a dynamic graphical user interface builder. (Courtesy of Talarian Corp.)

GUI TOOL CHECKLIST

USABILITY

Install, License
♦ Is the tool provided on a variety of media?
♦ How easy is it to install? To license? To incorporate into the existing license manager scheme?

Learning Curve
♦ How much new product-specific information/functionality must the user learn?
♦ What is the required skill level of the user? Can nonprogrammers use it?
♦ How many different tools are provided?
♦ Does the tool provide help? Online? Context-sensitive?
♦ How extensive is vendor/second-party documentation?

Editing/Refinement of Displays
♦ Does the tool provide a WYSIWYG display editor? A graphical tool palette? Multiple methods for modifying objects? Ability to edit fonts, colors, text, and so on?

Performance
♦ What is its normal performance or speed?
♦ Does performance degrade with an increase in number of displays created? With the number of simultaneous users?

Error Recovery
♦ Does the tool warn users of errors? Provide recovery alternatives? Provide an Undo function?

Compilation Support
♦ Does the tool provide sample makefiles? Automatically generate makefiles? Require recompilation after every GUI change?

Mapping Functionality
♦ How easy is it to assign callbacks?
♦ Can callbacks be edited interactively with the tool? Without using the tool?

Code Maintenance
♦ How easy is it to modify code?
♦ Is generated code logically organized? Easy to read?

Tool Dependency
♦ Does execution of the interface require availability of any runtime libraries? Runtime licenses? Presence of the tool?

FUNCTIONALITY

Widgets
♦ Does the tool provide a standard widget library? A method to customize widgets? A method to integrate second-party widgets?

Code Generation
♦ Does the tool automatically generate code?
♦ What languages does it support?
♦ Is generated code readable? Scalable? Portable? Efficient?
♦ Does the code follow any standards? Can the user customize standards?
♦ Can code be regenerated after being modified?
♦ Does the performance of the code meet application requirements?

Languages, Standards, Platforms Supported
♦ Does the tool support multiple languages? Multiple design and development standards?
♦ Is it available on required platforms?

Application Integration
♦ Is the interface code clearly separated from the application code?
♦ Does the tool facilitate integration?
♦ How easy is it to integrate interface code with legacy application code? With output from other GUI tools?

Prototype Capability
♦ Can the user create prototypes quickly? Without compiling and executing code?
♦ Can the user switch from prototype to actual development easily?

Additional Features
♦ Does the tool provide needed plotting/graphing? Dynamic graphics? Hard-copy outputs? Database support? 3D graphics? Additional application

development support?
♦ Can context-sensitive help be incorporated into the developed interface?

FLEXIBILITY

Object-Oriented Programming
♦ Does the tool support OO design methodologies? OO programming languages?

Internationalization/Multilingual Support
♦ Does the tool support multiple (human) languages? Multiple languages within a single interface?
♦ Does the multilingual feature affect developer productivity? Interface performance? Product purchasing or support?

Internetworking
♦ Can the tool be integrated/networked with compilers? With version control systems? With debuggers? With communication packages? With database tools? With other GUI tools?

PORTABILITY

Multiplatform Support
♦ Is platform-specific code isolated?
♦ What API approach does the tool use?
♦ Does the tool take most of the responsibility for porting effort?

Tool Stability
♦ Does the vendor plan to continue multiplatform support?
♦ How stable are different platform-specific versions of the tool?
♦ How often are new versions released?

SUPPORT

Documentation
♦ What types of documentation exist?
♦ Is the documentation well written? Thorough? Well illustrated? User-oriented? Professionally prepared?

Examples/Demos

♦ Does the tool provide examples of code/displays? Thorough explanations of examples? Demos of display capabilities?

Training

♦ Is formal training available? Is it taught by the vendor or a third-party company? Is it customizable to the customer's needs?

♦ Where and how often is training offered?

Technical Support

♦ Is a technical-support hotline provided?

♦ Is support available online? Via the WWW?

♦ How knowledgeable and responsive are support staff?

♦ What days of the week is support available?

Vendor/Tool Stability

♦ Is the vendor well established? Is it the developer or a reseller? Reputable?

♦ Does the vendor provide other similar tools?

♦ How long has the tool been on the market?

♦ Who provides support?

♦ What is the current customer base?

♦ What is the current version?

♦ How frequently are new versions released?

COST

Nonrecurring Costs

♦ What is the purchase cost?

♦ Are discounts available?

Recurring Costs

♦ Are there yearly technical-support costs? Yearly upgrade or maintenance costs?

Licensing

♦ What license schemes are available?

♦ What are the license fees?

Training

♦ What does formal training cost?

♦ Is travel required for training?

ACKNOWLEDGMENTS

We thank Doris Y. Tamanaha, Alpha M. Doo, Gale R. Mathiasen, Tracy Catron, Nash Aragam, Steve Clement, and personnel from Hughes Training for their contributions. During the past three years, these individuals have conducted studies and written documentation regarding the selection of graphical user interface tools for specific applications.

REFERENCES

1. B. Myers, "User Interface Software Tools," http://www.cs.cmu.edu/afs/user/bam/www/toolnames.html.
2. B.A. Myers, "User Interface Software Tools," *ACM Trans. Computer-Human Interaction*, Vol. 2, No. 1, March 1995, pp. 65-103.
3. D. Hix and H.R. Hartson, *Developing User Interfaces: Ensuring Usability through Product and Process*, John Wiley & Sons, New York, 1993. See especially Chapter 11, "User Interface Development Tools."
4. T. Parker, "GUI Development Tools Roundup," *Unix Rev.*, Sept. 1995, pp. 65-71.
5. J.C. Armstrong Jr., "GUI Tools Mature," *Advanced Systems*, Mar. 1995.
6. J.C. Armstrong Jr., "1995 Editor's Choice Awards," *The X Journal*, May/June 1995, p. 78.
7. WebHCI, http://www.acm_org/sigchi/webhci.
8. HTML: http://www.yahoo.com/Computers_and_Internet/Information_and_Documentation/Data_Formats/HTML.
9. VR Bibliography: http://www.cms.dmu.ac.uk/~cph/VRbib.html.
10. Java Tool Reviews: http://www.andromeda.com/people/ddyer/java/Reviews.html.
11. Sam's Java Page: http://www.suba.com/~spullara.
12. HCI Virtual Library: http://www.usableweb.com/hcivl.

Laura A. Valaer is a software engineer at Hughes Information Technology Systems, where she has been designing and developing satellite ground station software for the last five years. Part of that work included user interface design and development. Her interests are in human-computer interaction and the design of user interfaces.

Valaer received a BS and an MS in computer science from the University of Denver.

Robert Babb is an associate professor of math and computer science at the University of Denver and chief scientist of the software tools company Seki Systems. Previously he was with the Oregon Graduate Institute and before that with Boeing Computer Services. He founded and coedits *Scientific Programming*, a journal devoted to bridging theory and practice for languages, compilers, tools, and environments to support scientific programming. His main interests are in software engineering and parallel processing.

Babb received a PhD in electrical engineering and computer science from the University of New Mexico. He is a member of the IEEE Computer Society and ACM.

Address questions about this article to Valaer at Hughes Information Technology Systems, 16800 E. CentreTech Parkway, Aurora, CO 80011; lvalaer@redwood.dn.hac.com; or to Babb at the University of Denver, Dept. of Mathematics and Computer Science, 2360 S. Gaylord St., Denver, CO 80208; babb@cs.du.edu.

Reprinted from IEEE Software,
Sept./Oct. 1998, pp. 60-69.

• • •

Given the rapid pace at which technology evolves, developers
need a means for segregating a company's core business
information from the technological specifics of the systems upon
which it resides, while at the same time allowing different
applications to exchange data across the enterprise. The author
asserts that Boca provides a solution to this challenge.

• • •

Business Object Component Architecture

Tom Digre, Data Access Technologies

lobal competition and the shift from commodity to short-life-cycle
or custom products have created an environment of continuous
change. To effectively compete, companies must accelerate changes
to their products and processes. Yet at the same time software's increasing complexity lengthens development time and adversely affects reliability, flexibility, and cost.

One strategy for meeting these challenges involves giving users the tools to directly change their processes, workflow, rules, policies, presentation, and other environmental aspects. Mechanisms for achieving these goals use the interrelated
concepts of components, model-based contracts, and end-user solution composition. In this context, components embody the semantics of a target problem domain, isolated from the complexities that underlie distributed object technology.

209

0740-7459/98/$10.00 © 1998 IEEE

In early 1996, the Object Management Group initiated a process to address some of the fundamental issues related to the success of enterprise component technology. These issues included development cycle time, maintenance and enhancement capability, and program complexity.[1] Two complementary aspects of component technology emerged from the OMG's process: an enterprise object interoperability framework built atop Corba technology, and a business object component architecture. Boca is an architectural abstraction that isolates enterprise domain semantics from specific technology bindings. As part of Boca, the component definition language provides a textual representation for enterprise domain contracts that conform to Boca.

I believe that Boca can provide the means for organizations to gain a competitive edge through the rapid deployment of new software across distributed, heterogeneous, and technically complex frameworks.

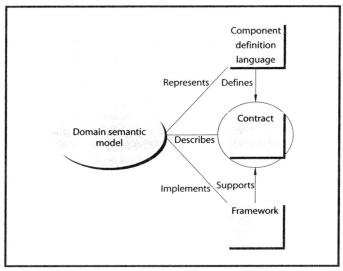

FIGURE 1. Key elements of Boca, the business object component architecture. The domain semantic model is Boca's driving element, enabling domain objects to be highly abstracted and yet retain the precision necessary for implementation and validation.

BOCA

Boca supports a range of technology implementations and many application domains, including manufacturing, finance, health care, electronic commerce, and transportation. It serves as an architectural template for defining concrete domain- and technology-specific architectures that contain several key technology elements, shown in Figure 1: a domain semantic model, a component definition language, a contract, and a framework.

The *domain semantic model* models the concepts associated with the targeted domain-specific architecture. This model lets developers specify the collective behavior for groups of domain objects at high levels of abstraction, yet these specifications retain sufficient precision to enable implementation and validation. The domain semantic model is technically a metamodel. It is derived from the Boca semantic metamodel, which embodies a set of base concepts that support distributed, persistent, transactionable enterprise objects. As formal extensions of the Boca semantic metamodel, domain-specific semantics from multiple domains can be combined into an integrated enterprise information system.

A *contract* is defined in terms of domain-specific concepts. The contract configures and structures domain concepts to describe aspects of the problem domain such as customers, orders, employees, hir-

ing, and invoicing. Business semantic contracts expose neither implementation details nor expected performance profiles. A contract enforces a strict separation of business semantics from their possible implementations. The set of contract instances is technically a model, an instantiation of the domain semantic model.

For the purposes of domain contract publication and contract distribution, the *component definition language* provides a common textual representation for defined contracts. Contracts can be rendered in a variety of alternative formats, including visualization forms to enhance end-user manipulation. The CDL's intent is to express in text the contract among a community of cooperating domain objects. There is an isomorphic relationship between the elements of the CDL grammar and the elements of the domain semantic model.

A *framework* provides an execution environment for implemented domain components. A domain framework will typically encapsulate common technology infrastructure elements, which enables component contracts to focus on domain-specific semantics. Business system requirements are transformed into domain contracts. Domain contracts are, in turn, instantiated as framework-specific component artifacts. These artifacts implement business solutions and support business processes. The framework's responsibility is to enforce the semantic contract across independently provisioned domain objects, the technical infrastructure, and domain object clients.

The functionality, portability, and performance characteristics of any specific enterprise framework will invariably evolve. The contract abstraction iso-

Boca's metamodel enables tight coupling across components' design-time and runtime aspects.

lates the domain specification from the technology implementation, preserving the integrity and interoperability of enterprise objects across an evolving technical infrastructure.

Components

There is a multidimensional perspective to software component technology.

♦ Component granularity ranges from integers, stacks, or arrays to large-scale application components.

♦ Technology targets range from GUI, database, or communication components to enterprise interoperability frameworks.

♦ Components may be derived from different development life-cycle phases, ranging from environment-specific implementation packages to reusable analysis and design models.

Even given this range of component technology perspectives, individual components are virtually useless. Components have value only within well-defined environmental contexts—frameworks—which support groups of cooperating components. Further, for independently developed components to cooperate, a contract specifying structural and behavioral constraints must be well understood and specified.

Frameworks typically provide a formal mechanism for defining an interface between cooperating objects, such as OMG's Interface Definition Language.[2] In conjunction with the full Corba specification, the interface definition encapsulates a layer of semantics fundamental to the supporting framework, such as the set of distribution transparencies incorporated into the Corba infrastructure.

An interface definition provides tremendous leverage in defining a contract, but is insufficient for frameworks that support semantic concepts beyond those provided by a messaging infrastructure. Higher-level semantic concepts are typically defined by framework-specific cookbooks, naming conventions, coding patterns, natural language specifications, or other techniques. Such definitions let fundamental enterprise domain concepts be expressed in the abstraction of a specific technology implementation. Without these abstractions, the original enterprise contract semantics become mired in the labyrinth of technology implementation artifacts associated with a framework.

A software component consists of multiple interrelated artifacts that support tight coupling across the development life cycle. The requirement to provide a group of independently developed components typically requires loose coupling (dynamic runtime binding) between components. On the other hand, maintaining the integrity of enterprise requirements within a complex and evolving implementation environment suggests the need for a tight coupling of artifacts across the development life cycle. Many frameworks, such as JavaBeans,[3] recognize that a component consists of multiple interrelated artifacts that support introspection, customization, stubs and skeletons for distribution transparencies, factories, helpers, serialization, documentation, and other framework-specific concepts. Some of these artifacts are used in the design and composition of other components, while other artifacts are intended for runtime.

Within Boca, the metamodel enables tight coupling across both the design-time and runtime aspects of components. The Boca metamodel provides a specification for a community of components at a well-defined level of abstraction. Runtime component artifacts that implement a Boca specification have introspective operations that enable navigation to relevant Boca metamodel elements. Thus, any Boca implementation includes access from domain object instances to the complete Boca semantic model, at the appropriate level of domain abstraction. This ensures interoperability at the semantic level, and enables, in some cases, interoperability between domain objects implemented in different framework technologies. Depending on the specific framework technology targets, other implementation artifacts generated from the Boca metamodel, such as source code, documentation, and editors, have corresponding traceability to original Boca specification elements.

Rapid problem solving in an evolving technology environment is best supported by component

contract definitions that use domain-specific abstractions. Domain contract stability in an environment of multiple evolving frameworks requires a framework- and technology-independent contract that focuses on domain semantics. The contract should be in terms of an abstract domain architecture. There should be a rigorously defined and automated mapping from analysis and design—using, for example, the Unified Modeling Language[4]—to the abstract domain architecture, and from the abstract domain architecture to concrete framework implementations. Appropriate domain abstractions enable automated transformation from a stable contract base to multiple technologies.

Frameworks

A *framework* provides services and facilities to support some set of semantic primitives for a community of cooperating components. These primitives are typically exposed from a technology viewpoint and related to domain semantics using framework-specific conventions.

Most frameworks are defined in terms of a small set of primitive concepts, such as object types and operations. Higher-level abstractions are often defined in terms of type and operation primitives. For example, an attribute is an abstraction for which a framework typically defines a Get and a Set operation. Based on framework-specific coding conventions, the Set operation may be required to check if any constraints are imposed on the value of the attribute prior to the change (including domain-specific contractual constraints), and notify any interested components when the value has changed.

Notification mechanisms associated with attribute changes may in turn require implementation of special event classes, listener classes, registration methods, and so on. While these technology aspects must be part of the implementation, specific details of the technology should not be included in the domain contract.

Another common framework semantic is the specification of structural relationships between components. Using framework-specific conventions, a single relationship concept in the Boca domain specification is typically mapped to many operations, depending upon combinations of cardinality, uniqueness, ordering, keys, mutability, and so on. Within each of these operations, the implementation must incorporate change-delete-

create notification mechanisms, as was done for attributes. Again, because this is a domain contract abstraction, these technology-specific operations and coding conventions should not be reflected in the domain contract.

Loose coupling between components is implemented using some form of framework-specific event model. Framework event models are generally oriented toward the event producer. The event producer must define the events, listener interfaces, adapters, registration, and other artifacts in conformance with the specific framework event model. Although an event-production orientation is appropriate for the technology-viewpoint framework, a domain contract focuses on event consumption—the need to specify what happens when an event fires. From the standpoint of a domain contract, most events are implicit—they reflect changes in the state of the system or common behavioral mechanics such as invoking an operation. Implicit events do not need to be declared in the domain contract, and the technology artifacts associated with implicit events should not be exposed in the domain contract.

Frameworks support a number of services and facilities, such as introspection, customization,

Most frameworks are defined by a small set of primitive concepts, such as object types.

attribute editing, object instance creation, collections of types, location of objects with identity, and redirection to adapters or delegated implementation classes. Most of these services require, by framework-specific convention, additional class implementations for each originally defined type. Frameworks that support distributed components also have stubs, skeletons, helpers, holders, and other classes associated with the underlying distributed messaging infrastructure. Frameworks have facilities and conventions for documentation, archiving, database binding, GUI clients, and so on. These technology artifacts should not be included in the domain contract.

Frameworks provide a simplifying technology abstraction above the layer of a messaging infrastructure. However, that technology abstraction is not sufficiently close to the domain abstraction to let end users provision solutions. Framework-defined services such as documentation and introspection—which are technology- and framework-specific—cannot convey to a user the original domain abstraction.

Productivity and ease of development are improved by reducing *surface area*.[5] This term refers to the number of things that must be understood and properly dealt with to successfully enable interoperability between domain application components. Several factors influence surface area:

♦ *Amount of visible information.* Surface area increases with the number of names that are exposed through the software component interface, including data element names, data types, and function names.

Components are expressed in terms of externally visible interfaces and semantics, not the implementation.

♦ *Sequence dependencies.* Surface area increases with each requirement that causes users to perform operations in a particular order.

♦ *Environment and responsibility scope dependencies.* Surface area increases whenever the software component user is responsible for managing life cycle, persistence, location, or environmental aspects of software components within a more global application context.

♦ *Technology dependencies.* Surface area increases with exposure to each technical domain and form of interface, such as middleware communications and data storage.

♦ *Concurrency.* Surface area increases when concurrency issues are exposed to the user.

CDL reduces surface area and complexity by providing a domain-oriented abstraction that enables the user to focus on the domain problem at hand. Supporting the CDL abstraction, and encapsulated by it, is a domain-specific profile of services and facilities implemented as a standardized composition, configuration, and specialization of a technology-viewpoint framework. The encapsulation of the framework reduces the surface area exposed to the user or developer because of environment, responsibility scope, technology, concurrency, and other factors not directly related to the business-problem domain.

Components cannot exist or function without frameworks. However, even the superficial requirements for implementing basic enterprise domain

semantics can be overwhelming. The key to overcoming cycle-time and integrity issues associated with framework-specific implementation barriers is to encapsulate implementation artifacts within a domain-specific contract.

Component definition language

The CDL provides a level of abstraction needed to express the semantics of domain components and to combine components. CDL and semantic definition are required to support the definition and standardization of common business objects, and domain-specific and enterprise-specific components. CDL supports contractual specifications for enterprise domain semantics, including constraints, rules, roles, policies, relationships, states, attributes, visibilities, dependencies, protocols, pre- and post-conditions, exceptions, and events. A contract written in CDL defines

♦ enterprise object interfaces,

♦ structural relationships between enterprise objects, and

♦ collective behavior for groups of related enterprise objects.

Application software is not written in CDL, which is a declarative language, but in a framework-specific language for which language bindings have been defined. CDL syntax and semantics have the following characteristics:

♦ The CDL grammar is a superset of OMG's Interface Definition Language with additional constructs to formally support semantic concepts.

♦ CDL obeys the same lexical rules and preprocessing features as OMG's IDL, although new keywords are introduced to support additional semantic concepts.

The language supports

♦ OMG's IDL syntax for constant, type, and operation declarations;

♦ syntax to represent information model concepts;

♦ expression syntax for constraint expressions, scripting, and declarative query; and

♦ additional constructs required to model business objects and domains.

The defined mapping from CDL concepts to framework-compliant implementations lets CDL be used as a mechanism for description and transfer of component contracts. Components are specified in terms of externally visible interfaces and semantics, not the implementation. This separation of contract from implementation allows a wide variety of implementation choices, both for the domain logic and for the supporting framework.

To achieve component interoperability, there must be a consistent, standardized mapping between the domain contract and any given target framework. Well-defined relationships help preserve the integrity, flexibility, maintainability, and longevity of CDL-based contracts across multiple, evolving, technical frameworks. The relationship between CDL and the proposed OMG Business Object Interoperability Framework has been defined. Relationships could also be defined for other open or proprietary frameworks.

CDL provides a higher-level and simplified programming model, encapsulating some of the functionality provided by a framework. Enterprise domain contracts written in CDL are independent of visualization technology, domain framework implementation, and data-store technology. Changes to technology implementation can occur without modification of the domain contracts, enabling those enterprise domain contracts to outlive the underlying technology.

The complementary relationship between contract specification and supporting frameworks makes enterprise domain components a reality. I expect that CDL will form the basis for specifications issued from many of the OMG domain task forces.

Development life cycle

As evidence of the progress being made toward providing adaptable software that functions smoothly across the life cycle, a proof-of-concept demonstration was held in June 1998 at the OMG Technical Committee meeting in Orlando, Fla. The demonstration showed the ability to automate generation of an implementation for a selected target framework from a technology-independent CDL specification. The CDL specification itself was produced from a Unified Modeling Language diagram.

COMPONENT COMPOSITION

Boca supports component composition at multiple layers of abstraction.

♦ At high levels of abstraction, the composition of nested types and subsystems yields increasingly coarser-grained components.

♦ At the lowest layer of abstraction, types—

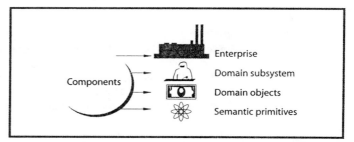

FIGURE 2. Component granularity can range from, at the highest level, coarse-grained components that represent an entire enterprise to, at the lowest level, semantic primitives.

including subsystems—are composed from semantic primitives. Semantic primitives are themselves extensible and composed of components.

Together, these abstractions influence components' required characteristics.

Granularity

Components exist at several levels of granularity, from coarse-grained components that represent an entire enterprise to fine-grained components that represent the semantic primitives of a single enterprise domain. Figure 2 shows one possible categorization of components.

Enterprise

At this level, application models are brought together and integrated to represent the enterprise. Enterprise applications that have been procured from external sources are integrated into the information system by systems integrators and advanced end users. Components at the enterprise level may represent entire divisions, plants, or enterprise-wide processes.

Genericity, the staged refinement of entire models,[6] is a key concept for component composition at the enterprise level. Genericity uses stepwise instantiation to go from aggregations of generic components, through increasing specialization of business domains, to enterprise, facility, and work area implementations. It is a controlled process that uses the principles of specialization, inheritance, relationships, and contexts to leverage reusable industrial models. Genericity is aligned with language specialization and domain-specific semantic specialization. Domain- and enterprise-specific abstractions are derived from, and isolate their domain semantics from, more generic semantic primitives.

Domain subsystem

The domain subsystem represents a particular area of concern such as payroll or document management. Domain subsystems are composed of integrated sets of domain objects for a particular purpose. Domain subsystems may also be composed of smaller domain subsystems. The following CDL example defines a subsystem to represent trucking that contains a `truck` entity, a `service_trucks` method, and a `location` entity.

```
subsystem trucking {
   entity truck {};
   void service_trucks ();
   entity location {};
};
```

Domain objects represent a particular process, entity, or other concept in the domain model.

Domain object

Domain objects represent a particular process, entity, or other concept found in the domain model, such as an ordering process or manufactured component. The Boca semantic metamodel defines several kinds of domain types, each of which represents a domain concept such as process or entity.

CDL lets domain object interfaces and behaviors be specified well enough so that one contract-compliant implementation can be substituted for another and the parts will still work together. The following CDL example defines a process named `MoveTruck`, within the `Truck` entity. `MoveTruck` represents moving a `Truck` to a new `Location` and has a set of move states such as `ready_to_move`, `moving`, and so on.

```
entity Truck {
   // Other truck stuff...

process MoveTruck {
   [is_read_only]
   relationship the_truck
     References Truck;

   relationship move_to
     References Location;
   state_set move {ready_to_move,
     moving, moved, move_aborted};
   };
};
```

Semantic primitives

Semantic primitives are the building blocks for domain objects. They include, for example, rules and the kinds of relationships between objects. These atomic-level components can be used to compose domain-specific components.

Semantic concepts

The Boca semantic model embodies several concepts.

♦ *Object models.* Derived from OMG Corba, these concepts include interface and type definitions, primitive data types, operations, exceptions, attributes, multiple inheritance, and modules.

♦ *Structural semantics.* Derived from the ODMG's Object Definition Language,[7] these concepts specify the relationship between types.

♦ *Side-effect free expressions.* These concepts specify invariants, pre- and postconditions, initialization, and various forms of constraints. Boca expressions are declarative, based on a subset of Java expression syntax and semantics, and are influenced by the OMG Object Constraint Language.

♦ *Parameterized semantics and types.* Each type, or semantic specification within a type, has a set of parameters. Parameters are used to configure each occurrence of a semantic primitive within a contract specification. For example, a postcondition is an operation parameter that obligates a community of objects to satisfy the specified condition upon the operation's successful completion.

♦ *Composable semantics.* In Boca, a type is specified as a composition of structural and behavioral semantic components. Each semantic primitive is itself a component. These semantic components are assembled and generated into framework-specific implementation artifacts. The exact nature of component assembly and generation is dictated by each domain's specific architecture.

♦ *Extensible semantic components.* The extensible Boca semantic metamodel is adaptable to multiple domains. Consequently, any number of semantic concepts can be applied to a domain architecture. The Boca semantic metamodel's base semantics include but are not limited to life-cycle partitioning, relationships, events, and applying behavioral abstractions.

Life cycle partitioning

A life-cycle partition defines a set of behavioral

and structural features associated with a system state. The partition explicitly relates behavioral and structural semantics with a state model.

In CDL, a `state_set` construct enumerates states. The CDL `during` construct defines features valid during a specified condition. The `during` construct is typically used in conjunction with an enumerated state to qualify nested states, conditional attributes, and protocols such as state-dependent operation sequences. The following CDL example shows that within the entity `ElectricDrill`, a state set named power has states `on` and `off`.

```
entity ElectricDrill {
  state_set power {on, off};

  during (power==on) withPower {
  state_set direction {forward,
    reverse};
    attribute float speed;
  };
};
```

During power on, a substate set `direction` has states `forward` and `reverse` and an attribute named `speed` is defined.

Relationships

A *relationship* is a structural feature that relates two types. In most cases relationships are declared to allow traversal between instances of the two types: given an instance of one type you can traverse the relationship to an instance or instances of the other type.

A traversal specification is prerequisite to defining the behavioral semantics for a community of cooperative objects. Relationships enable the specification of behavioral semantics across groups of objects and thus form an integral part of the domain contract.

Each kind of relationship implies a profile of interface and behavior characteristics. Relationship parameters include uniqueness constraints, cardinality, ordering, and aggregation characteristics such as copy-move-delete propagation. CDL assigns familiar names to common relationship profiles such as References, Aggregates, and IsPartOf. Extensibility mechanisms within CDL enable new profiles to be defined or default parameters for predefined profiles to be selectively overridden. The following CDL example defines a relationship `forOrder` using the `Aggregates` relation on `Part`. The `forOrder` relationship will be a many-to-one relation as speci-

fied in the `Aggregates` relation type.

```
entity Box {
  relationship forOrder Aggregates
    0..* Part inverse whenShipped;
};
entity Part {
  relationship whenShipped
    IsPartOf 0..1 Box inverse
    forOrder;
};
```

The inverse relation is called `whenShipped`, a feature of the `Part` type.

Applying behavioral abstractions

Boca's extensibility mechanism enables behavioral semantics to be defined as a semantic component and applied to type specifications. This mechanism allows domain-specific architectures to define, apply, and encapsulate technology implementation for new domain-specific semantics. Examples of predefined behavioral semantics include invariants, state transitions, and event-condition-action rules.

A semantic component serves as a template for applying and configuring behavioral abstractions to a community of objects. A semantic component instance is configured and applied to a type specification, using defined relationships for navigation

> **A semantic component serves as a template for applying and configuring behavioral abstractions to objects.**

to related objects. Applying behavioral-semantic-component specifications to a type shows how semantic components can be used to compose the semantics of a contract specification.

The following CDL example shows the application of an invariant rule named `small_balance` to the type `small_customer`. This rule requires that small customers must have a balance less than 10,000. This invariant should be enforced (scheduled) on any commit, including subcommits, as shown in the following CDL example.

```
entity small_customer {
  attribute[TD2] float balance;
  apply Invariant small_balance {
    guard = (balance < 10000);
    schedule = DO_AFTER_SUB_COMMIT;
  };
};
```

Focus

Events

Events specify observable changes in what may happen to an object. Attribute, relationship, and state changes, as well as object creation and destruction, are implicitly events and need not be declared with the event declaration. External events may be explicitly declared.

Events trigger actions, including interactions with other objects. The semantic contract focuses on the consumption of events, that is, what happens to the system as a result of an event.

Triggers specify rules and dependencies, which are forms of semantic component.

Triggers are used to specify rules and dependencies, which are forms of semantic component. When a rule containing a trigger specification is applied to a type, it declares that the type is interested in the identified event, which may originate from any related object in the community. In the following CDL example, `signal place_order` explicitly declares an external event. The `StateTransitionRule` is triggered upon occurrence of the `place_order` event from the same instance of `Order`; if the status `state` is `input` when trigger occurs, the status `state` is changed to `placed`.

```
entity Order
{
    state_set status { input,
        placed, shipped };
    signal place_order ();
    // Do state transition for
        placing an order
    apply StateTransitionRule
        order_being_placed {
        trigger = {place_order};
        source = input;
        target = placed;
    };
};
```

Required component characteristics

Components must be specialized, tailored, extended, and configured for use in specific vertical-application domains, enterprises, or even workgroups. Fundamental characteristics for composable enterprise components include the following.

♦ *Semantic inheritance.* Domain objects support the core object concept of multiple inheritance. All semantics defined for a component—business rules, properties, and so on—apply to all subtypes of that component.

♦ *Composition inheritance.* Component compositions, including entire business subsystems, may be subtyped and extended.

♦ *Structural and behavioral semantics specification.* In Boca, a subsystem is a type that may contain other types such as entity or subsystem. A Boca subsystem will include specification of structural and behavioral semantics related to a community of objects.

♦ *Subsystem specification inheritance.* A subsystem's specification can be subtyped by another subsystem specification. The subtyped specification inherits the entire base subsystem specification, including all the contained types and all structural and behavioral semantics.

♦ *Subsystem specification extensibility.* The subtyped subsystem specification can be extended by adding new types. Structural and behavioral semantics can be associated with those new types or with the new subsystem. The subtyped subsystem specification can also be extended by deriving and refining types inherited from the base subsystem specification.

♦ *Substitutability.* The unit of substitutability is defined by component. It must be possible to relocate or replace a component with another implementation of the component transparent to all clients. Enforcement of domain contract specifications helps ensure transparency across component substitutions.

♦ *Semantic composition.* Semantic primitives may be composed into contract definitions. Semantic primitives define the structure and behavior of an object within the context of a community of related objects.

♦ *Semantic extensibility.* Semantic primitives are themselves extensible components. Examples of semantic extensions include new component types, rules, processes, events, and adapters.

♦ *Configurability.* This characteristic manifests as component properties. Every component has properties that represent an externally accessible view of the type's abstract state. Properties are specified by the component designer and used to tailor an instance of a component or the type of a component, which consequently applies to all component instances. Properties are also used for design-time customization of a component and can be referenced in queries, policy constraints, or other user-specified semantic contracts to control component behavior. For example, a contract may state that a change in value, in conjunction with a gating condition, will trigger an event or action.

To date, the success of GUI components within relatively homogeneous, nondistributed, and narrowly focused frameworks has been achieved largely by using semantic visualization to abstract the underlying technical complexity. By analogy, providing enterprise solutions within distributed, heterogeneous, and technically complex frameworks can be achieved by extending this approach to define the appropriate business semantic abstractions. The goals of rapid delivery, end-user component assembly, and high-integrity implementations depend upon technology encapsulation and a tight coupling of component artifacts across the development life cycle, from enterprise requirements analysis through automated implementation within a target framework.

CDL lays the foundation for specifying and implementing interoperable business objects. It enables contracts to be specified in terms of domain semantic concepts, isolated from underlying technology concerns. ❖

REFERENCES

1. C. Casanave, cf/96-01-04: CF RFP4 (BOMSIG RFP), OMG public document, Jan. 1996, http://www.omg.org/cgi-bin/doclist.pl.
2. OMG, Corba 2.0/IIOP Specification, OMG formal/97-09-01, Sept. 1997, http://www.omg.org/corba/corbiiop.htm.
3. D. Brookshier, *JavaBeans Developer's Reference*, New Riders, Indianapolis, Ind., 1997.
4. OMG, UML Specification, OMG ad/97-08-xx, Sept. 1997, http://www.omg.org/library/schedule/Technology_Adoptions.htm#UML_Specification.
5. B.J. Cox, *Object Oriented Programming: An Evolutionary Approach*, Addison Wesley Longman, Reading, Mass., 1987.
6. Esprit Consortium Amice, *CIMOSA: Open System Architecture for CIM*, Springer-Verlag, London, 1993.
7. R.G.G. Cattell, *The Object Database Standard: ODMG-93*, Morgan Kaufmann, San Francisco, 1996.

About the Author

Tom Digre is vice president of product development for Data Access Technologies, where he supports the research and development of the NIST Advanced Technology Program "Business Object Component Specification, Generation and Assembly." Digre also makes ongoing contributions to many OMG activities related to business objects, metaobjects, object analysis and design, and Corba components.

Digre received a BS in electrical engineering and computer science from the University of California, Berkeley.

Address questions about this article to Digre at tomd@dataaccess.com.

FOCUS

69

Reprinted from IEEE Software,
January 1997, pp. 36-42.

Idioms and Patterns as Architectural Literature

JAMES O. COPLIEN, *Bell Laboratories*

If patterns are not about objects, and if they reach beyond software architecture, then what is a pattern? The author explores the relationships that might exist between objects, patterns, and architecture, then examines their implications for software developers.

Patterns have achieved the status of a must-have or must-do both in object-oriented circles and among software architects. Although a few foresighted software folks have had Christopher Alexander's works on their bookshelf for 15 years or more, only recently have I seen a table full of his books for sale at a software conference. Patterns are here with a vengeance, and most programmers will tell you that we have objects to thank for it.

There are strong parallels between Alexander's architecture patterns and our field's own object patterns. Alexander strove to use software for semiautomated urban design in his early work. He built tools intended to lower the cognitive load of design by exploring large design spaces for the architect.[1] Patterns were in part a reaction to the shortcomings of this approach.

Software design has traversed a similar history. We, too, went through an era when we were fascinated with CASE tools and the prospects of automating design. With or without CASE tools, early adopters of the object paradigm focused on the "find-the-objects" exercise, deferring or forever losing the system perspective of interactions between classes or between objects.

219

Though patterns are most valuable as a sound foundation for design literature, they are also important because they fill design gaps that objects handle poorly. Patterns build on no specific software paradigm, so they are unconstrained in describing the incredibly rich structures of our increasingly complex systems. For me, this is what most distinguishes patterns from other contemporary paradigms and methods. Alexander found that patterns helped him express design in terms of the relationships between the parts of a house and the rules to transform those relationships. That is a much different focus than a method that builds houses from predesigned modules.

UNVEILING STRUCTURE

So it is with software patterns. They are not just another way to capture legacy knowledge, for they rise above the component level to capture information about system-level relationships. Patterns have given us a vocabulary to talk about structures larger than modules, procedures, or objects—structures that outstrip the vocabularies of the proven object design methods that have served us for the past decade. Many of these structures aren't new; but even though some of them are decades old, they are seldom explicit. Patterns bring these structures to the everyday programmer.

This perspective is crucial to any operative definition of "architecture." Traditional architecture focuses on the parts of a system in isolation, each one defined in terms of its internal structure and external interfaces. Although these interface definitions capture the formal behavior of system parts, the overall system behavior is richer than the sum of its parts. Architecture captures and articulates the relationships as well as the parts.

Patterns—at least as Alexander posed them, and as many are practicing them in software—focus directly on whole-

ness. Although I don't believe the pattern discipline is following or should follow Alexander slavishly, analogies to many of his building architecture principles strike home. Consider this excerpt from *The Timeless Way of Building*[2]:

> Design is often thought of as a process of synthesis, a process of putting together things, a process of combination.
>
> *According to this view, a whole is created by putting together parts. The parts come first: and the form of the whole comes second.*
>
> But it is impossible to form anything which has the character of nature by adding preformed parts.
>
> *When parts are modular and made before the whole, by definition then, they are identical, and it is impossible for every part to be unique, according to its position in the whole.*

MISUSED AND MISUNDERSTOOD

Yet people have difficulty letting go of old ways. Pattern papers submitted to and occasionally published by software conferences and journals too often are CASE or object sheep in pattern clothing. The literature describes tools that automatically "instantiate patterns," by assembling preformed parts. Panels such as "Why will patterns fail" and "Patterns: Cult to Culture" are making the software conference scene. As with any new technique, patterns have tremendous potential for abuse and misinterpretation. In fact, this problem is not unique to patterns, but is symptomatic of much contemporary software literature: design, architecture, process, and programming are understood only as disconnected concerns. Today's programmer can better appreciate patterns by studying their history and the relationship between patterns, objects, and

architecture. Such a perspective can take us beyond objects and beyond paradigm to attack the central problems of contemporary software development. This article offers my perspective on pattern history, and a vision of where patterns can have their greatest value in the future.

> **Patterns give us a vocabulary to talk about structures larger than modules, procedures, or objects.**

Patterns: beyond objects. Their most important contemporary value is that they complement existing design methods, solving problems that are often beyond the reach of those methods. They help a large body of programmers gain competence, and sometimes excellence, in object-oriented programming and design, using microarchitectures such as those published in *Design Patterns*.[3] Patterns are also reaching to broader abstractions at the framework level, where the designer must often mix the object paradigm with other paradigms: *Patterns take us beyond objects.*

Patterns: beyond architecture. Patterns are just starting to make inroads into areas other than software design. Teaching, organization and process, and other areas have growing bodies of pattern literature. Structures, skills, and patterns of behavior from these domains are as important to a software product's success as are any of the software patterns: *Patterns take us beyond architecture.*

Patterns: toward a holistic approach. If we really take seriously the term "system" in "software system," we must consider facets of software development that

range from technological to humanistic. It isn't that we need to forge new relationships between these perspectives, but that we must recognize and manage the relationships that have been there,

Today's problems call for something that extends across objects and ties them together.

beneath the surface, all along. These considerations combined form a structure, an architecture, much as Alexander's urban planning patterns have both structural and human components. Alexander consciously brought all these components into his pattern languages. At this degree of integration, we can aspire to incorporate in our software the ideals of classic architecture we find expressed in Vitruvius's durability, utility, and aesthetics.[4] Approaching this threshold of integration truly puts objects, architecture, and patterns in their proper perspective: *Patterns return us to a more holistic view of architecture.*

BEYOND OBJECTS

Alexander's *A Pattern Language* has been around for almost 20 years, so why has its influence only taken root in the object paradigm? Partly this has to do with complexity: Software problems, and the solutions to address them, are becoming exponentially more complex. Although 20 years ago an individual programmer could comprehend nearly any software problem, most of today's problems are larger than one person. They call for something bigger than objects, something that extends across objects and ties them together into larger structures. Objects started people thinking abstractly, but patterns can

take us further than objects could.

Limited abstraction. Why are objects high on the complexity scale? It's because of their abstracting power. Under the procedural paradigm, we chunked hierarchies of procedures under some top-level procedure, using structured design techniques. The object paradigm supports hierarchies too—class hierarchies—but now we chunk several procedures at each level of the hierarchy. Also, the abstractions of the procedural paradigm were fairly concrete. We could look at a procedure call at compile time and tell where it would branch to at runtime. In the object paradigm, even the procedure names are just abstractions that might be bound to one of any number of functions at runtime. These are the properties that distinguish the object paradigm from its siblings. These complexities show up as relationships:

♦ each procedure to its associated data,

♦ procedure names to multiple procedures, and

♦ classes to their parent and sibling classes.

Complexity shows up in these relationships, and patterns thrive on capturing and articulating them.

Relationship focus. Before Alexander pioneered his pattern-based design approach, he used tools to arrange the objects of his domain—rooms, windows, walls—to fit a specification.[1] Alexander likely moved away from this approach and toward patterns because his tools-based approach focused on the objects in the final solution, rather than on the structure of the solution itself: the relationships between the objects. To study relationships is to study systems, and we find patterns in the structure of system relationships. Good and bad relationships are respectively the strength and downfall of all systems, regardless of type.

Even in the early days of the object

paradigm's popularity, the importance of focusing on relationships was recognized, if not widely subscribed to. My own *Advanced C++ Programming Styles and Idioms*[5] captured the practices of contemporary expert C++ programmers, who were the early creators and adopters of the language. These practices solved problems encountered by most inexpert C++ programmers as they struggled to master the language. By pointing out the idiomatic nuances of C++, *Advanced C++* supplemented the basic literature with the techniques necessary to exhibit competence, if not excellence. You can master a language only after its idioms become second nature. Most of the idioms in my book provided not only guidance in finding the right objects, but also captured interactions between objects.

In his 1995 *UNIX Review* article, Jim Waldo credits *Advanced C++* with being the foundational work behind software patterns.[6] That's certainly a C++ centered view, but idioms are one foundation of patterns in the object community. Most of the idioms in *Advanced C++* were design rules that helped programmers use C++ as an even more object-oriented programming language. Each OO language lacks features available in others, and many hold some of these features to be fundamental to OO programming. Multiple dispatch is one example, and one early idiom shows programmers the "right way" to fake multiple dispatch in C++. The idioms aren't in pattern form, but they provide a "solution to a problem in a context," which is Alexander's straightforward definition of a pattern.

If you view idioms as protopatterns then, yes, early patterns were very tightly tied to OO design. But even then, the patterns addressed object and class relationships for specific design problems. These problems were the ones left unaddressed by OO design methods and by fundamentals of the paradigm itself: multiple dispatch, reference counting and other memory manage-

ment schemes, brokering, type promotion, and dozens of others.

Such concerns sometimes reached beyond the object paradigm because, as is true of many idioms, they are low-level design considerations such as reference counting. But others, like multiple dispatch, needed patterns to map from the problem to the solution because they outstripped available methods. Most methods don't really explain the relationships between classes or between objects. The meaning of many relationships is left implicit, except for subtyping and containment, which obey well-defined conventions. Even today, few design methods deal coherently with multiple dispatch. Patterns underscore the meaning and the rationale behind such relationships.

This body of knowledge generalized and broadened over time as the object paradigm and its idioms and patterns matured and became better understood. *Design Patterns*[3] acknowledges these early idioms as one influence on its authors, though that book is organized around patterns while *Advanced C++* is organized around language features. Designers can apply the *Design Patterns* material to most programming languages; *Advanced C++* focuses on one language. I have explored the mapping between these two models in more detail.[7] Mastery of *Design Patterns'* patterns is perhaps the best measure of competency in the object paradigm, yet even the best methods rarely produce the structure captured by the design patterns. This is particularly true for patterns of dynamic behavior.

Beyond idioms. Idioms and, later, design patterns, armed early C++ adopters with training that took them beyond curious inquiry to serious applications. But time and again, technological soundness alone did not win the day. Process, organizational structure, politics, culture, personalities, and a host of other outlying factors figured

heavily in the success of new techniques and tools. I decided to focus on these areas as I moved from development into research, rising above the "details" of technology to address the fundamental problems of process.

Our studies of the organizational and process side of software development uncovered patterns there as well. Not only do sound software architectures exhibit the same, recurring patterns, but accomplished organizations likewise share patterns of organization and process. These patterns cannot be separated from the patterns of architecture. An OO project can succeed only if supported with the right patterns from the human side.

I wrote my first process pattern, Buffalo Mountain,[8] at the first Hillside workshop in August of 1993. Many authors have contributed to the body of organizational patterns since then, including Norm Kerth[9] and Bruce Whitenack.[10] At least one author has achieved the ultimate integration: in Steve Berczuk's pattern language,[11] process and architecture patterns work together.

This genre contains an abundance of earlier literature that did not bear the pattern label. Cultural anthropology has been studying patterns of relationship in organizations for the better part of a century, as have cultural observers dating back to Lao Tzu and beyond. Patterns provide an outlet for these time-honored worldviews to once again be fashionable, and objects have been one of the vehicles to usher patterns into the modern world.

Patterns of preservation. Patterns' biggest payoff may lie in capturing the great truths about to be lost to history, instead of focusing on pattern support for the best-funded buzzwords. At Bell Laboratories, we are mining the patterns of classic embedded systems to capture the core competencies of our businesses. Telecommunication system architectures have evolved over the

past 40 years to the point where they are among the most reliable systems in the world. Why? We can trace availability and fault tolerance to patterns, and we have extracted those patterns from the minds of long-standing experts. These patterns are a fundamental component of emerging systems that face equally stringent requirements. Of the 150 or so patterns we've gathered, none are really object-oriented.[12-14]

We have progressed a bit beyond our initial flirtations with patterns of OO programming and design into other design disciplines, and even into domains such as training and human enterprise organization. A wide variety of patterns lies beneath the code and practices of our recurring successes, waiting to be uncovered and woven into the emerging literature of good software practice. Patterns take us beyond objects into grander structures. Perhaps, they take us beyond software architecture itself.

> **A wide variety of patterns lies beneath the code and practices of our recurring successes.**

BEYOND SOFTWARE ARCHITECTURE

Alexander's patterns emphasize the human element of environmental design; in fact, this is the focus of his patterns. Buildings don't care about their architectures, people do. Alexander saw his patterns as a way to free us from all method and to uncover the good practices we all draw from deep cultural roots. Patterns are mostly about people, and much less about houses, software, or design methods.

The human focus has two major components: utilitarian and aesthetic. On one hand, Alexander's patterns eschew aesthetics for its own sake, deferring to basic human comforts. This is an eminently practical point of view. On the other hand, many human needs transcend physical world models and touch on issues of sociology, psychology, and other soft sciences far from the comfortable realm of tangible, physical architecture. Alexander takes us squarely into these fields with patterns such as Wings of Light and Structure Follows Social Spaces.[15]

Humanizing software. We face the same dilemma in software. In the age of "software factories" and repeatable software processes, modern software tries to distance itself from unreliable human beings. We try to capture and sometimes formalize software architecture. Most architecture documents still capture only application programming interfaces and data structures, missing the important nuances of relationships. Such documents still pretend that architecture can be divorced from downstream design and implementation concerns, an idea that runs counter to predominant empirical practice, particularly in successful development organizations.[8] Few architecture documents draw in issues of paradigm, process, expertise, organization, aesthetics, or even the obvious concern of long-term maintainability. Software is of, by, and for the people too, and few software development problems or solutions lack human overtones. To omit the human element is to miss the thrust of most interesting problems. Consider the pattern from Richard Gabriel, shown in the box on this page.

Right-brain patterns. Some of our biggest pattern successes have come not from patterns of software architecture and design, but from patterns of organization and process. Such patterns help organizations see beyond themselves and develop a vision of what is possible. The organizational patterns in Chapter 13 of the *Pattern Languages of Program Design*[8] helped the engineering organization of an established software company revitalize itself.[16]

The human aspect of patterns displaces most software engineers from their comfort zones. Few software engineers are schooled in experimental psychology or sociometric science; to them, these areas are mysterious black holes of nonsense. These are disciplines of the right brain, of emotion, and of the soul. They defy the left brain's attempts at quantification: for most of us, such qualities thrive unnamed. Bean counters can and do ascribe numbers to these properties: cyclomatic complexity and function points for "this feels complicated," for example. But such numbers are only shadowy projections of accomplished architects' intuition, and most metric systems don't know how to measure such intangibles. We are finding that patterns can and do help us, both in software architecture[12] and in (sometimes remarkable) organization changes.[16]

ARCHITECTURE RESTORED

We have followed patterns beyond

structure architecture into objects, beyond software architecture into organizations. Are patterns then intrinsically linked to "architecture," to this notion of the parts of a system and the relationships between them? And if so, what are the architectural principles of an organization?

I believe that patterns and architecture *are* linked, at least in any definition of architecture that goes beyond enumerating parts or interfaces. We've begun to realize that organizations have architecture; the phrase "process architecture" crept into the literature about a decade ago. In fact, "organizational architecture" is a refreshingly different perspective than the flowchart-like "development process."

Peter Sengé speaks of the patterns of organizational structure. These patterns can be characterized by a few system archetypes, each of which has a structure with opposing forces. It's not a purely Alexandrian formulation, but the similarity in patterns, structure, and forces is striking.[17]

Even Gabriel's Simply Understood Code pattern is curiously structural. It talks about system granularity from the human cognitive perspective—a crucial aspect of the system's abstraction structure. If that isn't architecture, what is?

A system needn't be something huge or something containing computer hardware. And we needn't limit ourselves to the most abstract meaningful view, either. A system comprises smaller systems, each of which obeys its own set of patterns. Handle/body pairs are a system; model-view-controller is a system; so are client-server pairs or a pair of half-objects with a protocol between them. Each of these has been the topic of at least one noteworthy pattern. In his seminal book on systems engineering, Arthur Hall related the following about systems in 1962, two years before Alexander's *Notes on Synthesis of Form* saw print.[1]

Of all the possible ways of defining the systems engineering function, the most significant and explicit is an operational one, which gives a description of the general pattern of work from formulation of a program of projects to completion of a specific project. For it is the pattern, more than anything else, which gives the function its essential structure and characteristics. Furthermore, there is more agreement about the pattern, and the detailed steps within it, than about any other aspect. Finally, and most important, experience shows that this mode of definition is the most useful to those who want to learn how to do systems engineering better.

Hall understood the scope of system engineering to be very broad. His book contains chapters on communication problems, value system objectives, the psychological theory of value, and the psychological aspects of synthesis. He recognized the limitations of an objective-based definition of system engineering because of the force of personal value judgments.[18] If patterns are about systems, they are about more than software, and certainly about more than objects.

If patterns are not about objects, and they reach beyond software architecture, then what is a pattern? Most of this article has worked to explain the relationships that might exist between objects, patterns, and architecture. But since objects and architecture have fueled the hype many ascribe to patterns, patterns might best be served by a definition distanced from these influences. Such a perspective should be important both to the educator planting seeds in the designer's mind, and to the practitioner seeking more pragmatic ends.

To me, patterns are a literature that goes beyond documentation. They capture an important structure, a central idea, a key technique long known to expert practitioners. It can be an architectural structure, a process practice, or a marketing strategy. What ties this body of literature together is that all patterns solve problems. Alexander[2] offers the following inspiration:

These patterns in our minds are, more or less, mental images of the patterns in the world: they are abstract representations of the very morphological rules which define the patterns in the world.

However, in one respect they are very different. The patterns in the world merely exist. But the same patterns in our minds are dynamic. They have force. They are generative. They tell us what to do; they tell us how we shall, or may, generate them; and they tell us too, that under certain circumstances, we must create them.

Each pattern is a rule which describes what you have to do to generate the entity which it defines.

System concerns and software architecture have too long received short shrift. And too many people who have taken a 16-hour design method course think they understand objects. Left unaddressed, these problems will seriously hurt our craft. If patterns produce literature that attacks these problems, then the alliances between patterns,

Patterns are a literature that goes beyond documentation.

objects, and architecture will have served us well. We shouldn't lose sight of the goals, however: to serve human needs, to restore dignity to programming, and to add Alexander's right-brain quality-without-a-name to our traditionally left-brain outlook on software development and project management. ◆

REFERENCES

1. C. Alexander, *Notes on Synthesis of Form*, Harvard Univ. Press, Cambridge, Mass., 1964.
2. C. Alexander, *The Timeless Way of Building*, Oxford Univ. Press, New York, 1979, p. 368.
3. E. Gamma et al., *Design Patterns: Elements of Reusable Object-Oriented Software*, Addison-Wesley, Reading, Mass., 1995.
4. Vitruvius, *The Ten Books of Architecture*, translated by Morris Morgan, Dover Publications, New York, 1960.
5. J.O. Coplien, *Advanced C++ Programming Styles and Idioms*, Addison-Wesley, Reading, Mass., 1992.
6. J. Waldo, "Minor Patterns," *UNIX Rev.*, Vol. 13, No. 4, 1995, pp. 79-82.
7. J. O. Coplien, "The Column Without A Name: Patterns and Idioms in Circles, Complex Ellipses, and Real Bridges," *C++ Report*, May 1995, pp. 54-59, 74.
8. J.O. Coplien, "A Development Process Generative Pattern Language," *Pattern Languages of Program Design*, J.O. Coplien and D.C. Schmidt, eds., Addison-Wesley, Reading Mass., 1995, pp. 218-220.
9. N. Kerth, "Caterpillar's Fate," *Pattern Languages of Program Design*, J.O. Coplien and D.C. Schmidt, eds., Addison-Wesley, Reading, Mass., 1995, pp. 293-320.
10. B. Whitenack, "RAPPeL: A Requirements Analysis Process Pattern Language for Object-Oriented Development," *Pattern Languages of Program Design*, J.O. Coplien and D.C. Schmidt, eds., Addison-Wesley, Reading, Mass., 1995, pp. 259-292.
11. S. Berczuk, "A Pattern Language for Ground Processing of Science Satellite Telemetry," excerpted in "The Column Without a Name: The Human Side of Patterns," *C++ Report*, Jan. 1996, p. 83.
12. K. Beck et al., "Industrial Experience with Design Patterns," *Proc. 10th Int'l Conf. Software Eng.*, IEEE Computer Soc. Press, Los Alamitos, Calif., 1996, pp. 103-114.
13. J.O. Coplien. "The Column Without a Name: Pattern Mining," *C++ Report*, Oct. 1995.
14. J. Vlissides et al., eds., *Pattern Languages of Program Design-2*, Addison-Wesley, Reading, Mass. 1996.
15. C. Alexander et al., *A Pattern Language*, Oxford Univ. Press, New York, 1977.
16. J.O. Coplien, "The Column Without a Name: The Human Side of Patterns," *C++ Report*, Jan. 1996, pp. 81-85.
17. P. Sengé, *The Fifth Discipline*, Doubleday, New York, 1990, Chapter 6.
18. A.D. Hall, *A Methodology for Systems Engineering*, Van Nostrand Reinholdt, Princeton, N.J., 1962, p. 11.

James O. Coplien is a principal investigator in the Software Production Research department at Bell Laboratories in Naperville, Illinois. He conducts research in software design patterns, empirical organizational modeling, multiparadigm design, and the object paradigm. Coplien received a BS in electrical and computer engineering and an MS in computer science from the University of Wisconsin at Madison.

Address questions about this article to Coplien at Bell Laboratories, ILL650 1G341, 1000 East Warrenville Rd., Naperville, IL 60566; cope@bell-labs.com.

Reprinted from IEEE Real-Time
Sys. Comp. 98, pp. 358-367.

A Development Framework for Ultra-Dependable Automotive Systems Based on a Time-Triggered Architecture

Bernd Hedenetz
Daimler-Benz Research, HPC T721, D-70546 Stuttgart, Germany
hedenetz@dbag.stg.daimlerbenz.com

Abstract

Today by-wire systems are well-known and utilised in the area of aircraft construction. In the last few years there has been an endeavour in the automotive industry to realise by-wire applications without mechanical or hydraulic backup systems in vehicles. The required electronic systems must be highly reliable and cost-effective due to the constraints of mass production.

A time-triggered architecture is a new approach that satisfies these requirements. The backbone of communication in this architecture is the fault-tolerant Time-Triggered Protocol (TTP), developed by the Vienna University of Technology and the Daimler-Benz Research. The TTP protocol has been designed due to the class C SAE [25] classification for safety critical control applications, like brake-by-wire or steer-by-wire.

For time-triggered architectures a new development process is required to handle the complexity of the systems, accelerate the development and increase the reliability. In this paper we present an approach for the development of distributed fault-tolerant systems based on TTP. The present approach is evaluated by a brake-by-wire case study.

1 Introduction

In the past few years there has been the tendency to increase the safety of vehicles by introducing intelligent assistance systems (e.g., ABS, Brake-Assistant (BA), Electronic Stability Program (ESP), etc.) that help the driver to cope with critical driving situations. These functions are characterised by the active control of the driving dynamics by distributed assistance systems, which therefore need a reliable communication network. The faults in the electronic components, which control these functions, are safety critical. However, the assistance functions deliver only an add-on service in accordance with a fail-safe strategy for the electronic components. If there is any doubt about the correct behavior of the

assistance system, it will be switched off. For by-wire systems without a mechanical backup a new dimension of safety requirements for automotive electronics is reached. After a fault the system has to be fail-operational until a safe state is reached.

For the fail-operational assumption we demand that after any arbitrary fault the system is fully operational. The effective use of the redundancy is important, in order to reduce the production costs for automotive by-wire systems. A major goal is to increase the reliability of the system by adding additional redundancy without increasing the complexity of the system. Therefore, new electronic architectures have to be developed.

Distributed time-triggered architectures (TTA) can be realised through the Time-Triggered Protocol (TTP) which guarantees a global time synchronisation over the whole system and an adequate message transmission.

In this paper we present an approach for the development of distributed fault-tolerant systems based on TTP. This paper is organised as follows: Section 2 gives an overview of the general architecture and elaborates on the time-triggered approach and the communication subsystem. Section 3 gives a short overview about the lifecycle of safety related automotive systems. In Section 4 the development framework for TTA systems is presented. In Section 5 the development approach is demonstrated at the example of a brake-by-wire case study. The paper is concluded in Section 6.

2 Time-Triggered Approach

The TT paradigm of a real-time system is based on a distinctive view of the world: the observer (the computer system) is not driven by the events that happen in its environment. The system decides through the progression of time when to look at the world. Therefore, it is impossible to overload a time-triggered observer.

A TT system takes a snapshot of the world, an observation, at recurring predetermined points in time determined by the current value of a synchronised local clock. This snapshot is disseminated within the computer system by the communication protocol to update the state variables that hold the observed values. The semantic of the periodic messages transported in a TT system is a state-message semantic, i.e., a new version of a message overwrites the previous version and messages are not consumed on reading. This semantic is well suited to handle the transport of the values of the state variables used in control applications. The state message semantic provides a predefined constant load on the communication system and eliminates the problem of dynamic buffer management [23].

2.1 Time-Triggered Protocol (TTP)

For the realisation of a distributed time-triggered architecture a communication network is necessary that provides the features mentioned above. This type of communication belongs mainly to class C of the SAE classification [25].

None of the commonly used in-vehicle communication systems (CAN, A-BUS, VAN, J1850-DLC, J1850-HBCC [26]) meet the requirements for safety related by-wire systems since they were not designed for this case [17]. They are all lacking in being deterministic, in synchronisation and fault tolerance characteristics.

These missing properties are the motivation for developing new approaches for in-vehicle communication systems. As a new start we examine the Time-Triggered Protocol developed by the University of Vienna and Daimler-Benz Research. TTP is especially designed for safety related applications and fulfills these requirements.

TTP is an integrated time-triggered protocol that provides:

- a membership service, i.e., every single node knows about the actual state of any other node of the distributed system
- a fault-tolerant clock synchronisation service (global time-base),
- mode change support,
- error detection with short latency,
- distributed redundancy management.

All these issues are supported implicitly by the protocol itself. A comprehensive description of the TTP protocol is given in [13,14,15]. The TTP protocol has been designed to tolerate any single physical fault in any one of its constituent parts (node, bus) without an impact on the operation of a properly configured cluster [15].

The overall TTP hardware architecture is characterized by both the TTP system architecture and the TTP node architecture as shown in Figure 1. A TTP real-time system consists of a host subsystem, which executes the real-time application and the communication subsystem

providing reliable real-time message transmission. The interface between these subsystems is realised by a dual ported RAM (DPRAM) called *Communication Network Interface (CNI)* [16]. The assembly of host and TTP-controller is called *Fail Silent Unit (FSU)*. Two FSUs form a single redundant *Fault-Tolerant Unit (FTU)*. The physical layer consists of two independent transmission channels.

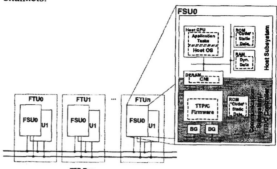

Figure 1: Architecture of a TTP-based fault-tolerant real-time system

2.2 Node Architecture

The overall aim of the node architecture is to fulfill the fail-silence assumption without developing special hardware for fault detection. We use software fault detection methods and low cost hardware mechanisms (such as watchdogs) and mechanisms provided by the CPU (bus error, address error, illegal op-code, privilege violation, division by zero,...). In [12] it is shown that a high degree of fault detection can be achieved by software fault detection mechanisms. We follow this approach for trying to fulfill the fail-silence assumption. Our architecture can be separated into three subsystems (see Figure 2):

- *Communication subsystem*: this part is responsible for the communication between distributed components.
- *Fault-tolerant subsystem*: this part contains safety critical and fault tolerance mechanisms. The safety related application is handled by this subsystem.
- *Application subsystem*: this part includes the safety related tasks, which build the application.

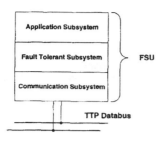

Figure 2: Subsystems of an FSU

2.3 Propagation of TTP

TTP is in discussion in the Brite-EuRam Project „Safety Related Fault Tolerant Systems in Vehicles" (acronym: „X-By-Wire") to be proposed as a European or International Standard [2].

In 1997 the Esprit Project „Time Triggered Architecture" (acronym TTA) has been started with the intention to develop a prototype TTP controller chip [9]. Other aims of the TTA project are the development of tools for the design of TTP systems and the formal verification of parts of the TTP protocol e.g. the clock synchronisation algorithm.

3 Lifecycle

The typical lifecycle for the development of safety related automotive systems consist of the following phases: *system specification*, *system design*, *design verification*, *implementation* and *integration* (see Figure 3). Several, more detailed descriptions of the lifecycle exist, for further study a large number of books [27] and standards are available [10,11]. All steps of the lifecycle have to be supported with tools to manage the complexity of the systems, accelerate the development process and increase the reliability. New tools have to be developed and common used tools have to be adapted to the requirements of TTA systems.

4 Development Process

For TTA systems a new development process is required which supports every phase of the lifecycle. Our aim is to devise a approach for designing complex distributed safety-related automotive systems using *commercial-off-the-shelf* tools to as high a degree as possible. Our approach based on verification of the system design by functional simulation, fault modeling in the models, functional test and fault injection in the real system architecture. Therefore we separate the development process in seven single steps (see Figure 3).

During the first step - *requirement specification* - we specify the functional requirements, the time constrains and the reliability requirements of the system. In the second step - *architectural design* - the structure of the communication network, communication relations between the nodes and the schedule of the application tasks are defined due to the specification. In the next step - *functional design* - we realise the application, e.g., a control loop for an anti blocking system (ABS), as a functional model. For the actual realization of this part we use the tool Statemate™ from i-Logix [7] and MATLAB®/Simulink™ from MathWorks [19]. In the following step - *functional simulation* - the functional models are verified through simulation and the reliability is examined by *fault modeling* into the functional models. In the step - *realisation and integration* - the real architecture is realised and integrated in a vehicle. Therefore we use the capability of automatic code generation of the tools. Additionally, we use monitoring tools to trace the system behavior. In the final step - *test and fault injection* - we execute test and fault injection experiments in the target system to verify the behavior of the real system with respect to the requirement specification.

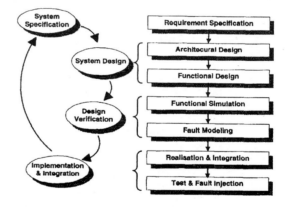

Figure 3: Overview about the development process

4.1 Requirement Specification

System specification is a very sensitive phase. The most faults that lead to critical failures are system-faults, and most design errors are not low-level implementation errors but errors committed at the system specification phase [18]. The description of the requirement specification has to include:

- Identification of the objects in the environment
- which produce or consume data flows.

- Definition of the input and output signals for these objects.
- Specification of the functional and time behavior of these objects.
- Specification of the reliability requirements.
- Definition of a fault hypothesis.

To verify the functional models and the system realisation we have to specify the system with a sufficient accuracy. The requirement specification is used to generate test pattern, fault pattern and environment models. Environment models are used as a reference for the functional simulation. Environment models can be described by:
- Statemate™ models,
- Input, output signals (stimulation and reaction),
- Differential equations, and
- C-code.

4.2 Architectural Design

The complexity of a system depends on the number and types of elements and relations and on the amount of their inner states. A method to handle complex systems is the decomposition into smaller subsystems. A common way is to partition the entire system into subsystems with high inner connectivity and few relations crossing the subsystem boundaries [1]. For the design of time triggered architectures we follow this approach; first we design the highest subsystem level, the communication nodes in a TTP communication system. This step is called *global design* and consists of all steps associated with the overall system architecture:
- A time-triggered system is partitioned into a set of components connected by the TTP bus.
- In respect with the reliability requirements, critical components can be replicated.
- The communication relations between the components are defined.
- In the last step, a bus schedule is determined that fulfills the communication requirements of the previous steps.

These steps are typically done by the system manufacturer. The structure is commonly determined by the function which the system has to fulfill. For example, in an automotive steer-by-wire system, redundancy is required for measurement of the steering wheel angle and control of the steering actuator. The redundant nodes have to be distributed that there is no common mode failure - e.g. intruding of water in the ECU - can cause a fatal failure.

4.3 Functional Design

After the global design, the *local design* contains all steps associated with the specification of a single component. The bus message scheduling specified in the global design defines the interface of each component in the value and time domain. The local design consists of the following steps:
- Definition of the software structure of the components.
- Description of the application tasks and their communication relations and time constraints.
- Adding of fault tolerant schemes, e.g. double execution and variable protection through cycle-redundancy checks (CRC).
- Finally, a task schedule which fulfills the functional requirements and time constraints is determined.

The single components in the automotive environment are typically developed by sub-suppliers.

4.4 Functional Simulation

Models of real-time systems have to support different views of a system. A system can be described by four different views:
- Structural view: represents the structure of the subsystems.
- Functional view: describes the functions and processes of the system, the input and output signals, and the information flows between the functions and processes.
- Behavior view: describes the time and dynamic behavior and the internal states of the components.
- Implementation view: represents the realisation of the system by source code.

For the actual realisation of the functional models we use the tools Statemate™ and MATLAB®/Simulink™. Statemate™ provides a hierarchical modeling approach for the specification and analysis of complex systems. The special feature of Statemate™ is that it puts emphasis on the dynamic verification of the specification. This tool provides facilities for the model execution, in interactive or batch mode, and to instrument the models in order to collect statistics during execution. The model can be either connected to a software environment model (software-in-the-loop) or to a target hardware environment (hardware-in-the-loop). The source code can be generated automatically from the functional specification.

The main benefit of this approach is that the system behavior can be examined from a very early design phase and changes can be made with minor effort.

Statemate[TM] uses three methods for system modeling, *module charts*, *activity charts*, and *statecharts* [5,6]. The module charts describe the structural view of the system while activity charts describe the functional view and are similar to conventional data flow diagrams. Activity charts illustrate the identified sub-functions and the information flows between them. Statecharts describe the behavioral view of the system. Through automatic code generation Statemate[TM] also supports the implementation of the system.

4.4.1 Modeling a TTA System

The Statemate[TM] approach is typically used for reactive systems. Time constraints are only an implicit part of the models. An important property in a TTA is the fulfillment of the time constrains. If the time boundaries are violated the system can not fulfill its duty. We solve this problem by building up a complete model of the TTA system in the Statemate[TM] developing environment. The time constraints of the system architecture are guaranteed by the model of the TTP communication system. The time constraints on the node subsystem are guaranteed by the model of the fault tolerant subsystem.

The *system architecture* is the highest modeling level. This level represents the structure of the system. Every node is also modeled in detail. *Node* represents the node structure and consists of the *fault tolerant subsystem*, the *communication subsystem* and the *application subsystem* (corresponding to Figure 2). The fault tolerant subsystem

builds the environment for the safety critical tasks, defined in the application subsystem. The communication subsystem handles the communication services provided by the TTP system (see Figure 4).

For the design of a new system the developer has to define the application dependable parts, the architectural structure of the TTP cluster and the application subsystem, corresponding to the global and local design in Section 4.2 and 4.3. The other parts of the model are available in a model library and can be reused.

4.4.2 Application Functional Specification

Applications on the top of a TTA consist usually of the parts; periodically reading sensor signals, calculation of new system states, and activation of actuators. The function of applications are usually described through statemachines and the control algorithms. The Statemate[TM] environment provide for the specification of statemachines the modeling concept of activity charts and statecharts. The control algorithms are developed with the help of MATLAB®/Simulink[TM] or MATRIX$_X$[TM] [28]. The control algorithms can be integrated in Statemate[TM] through C source code or in the case of MATRIX$_X$[TM] directly, due to a common interface.

4.4.3 Application Development Environment

For the developing of applications we use a *software-in-the-loop* simulation environment (see Figure 5). We

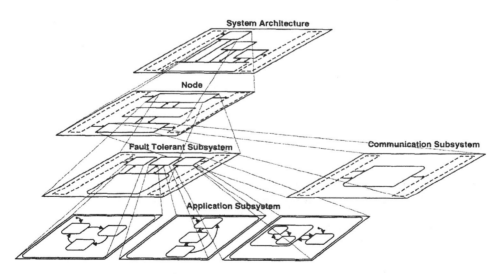

Figure 4: Functional model of a TTA

define a test environment out of the requirement specification, in which the functional model can be tested. We connect the functional model of the TTA system with the behavioral model of the vehicle. This method is called software-in-the-loop. To verify the functional model a set of test patterns have to be defined. The number of test patterns depend on the complexity of the system, the number of signals and the used test strategy. The environment model is realised by using MATLAB®/Simulink™.

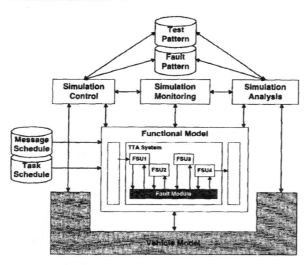

Figure 5: Overview of the simulation environment

The simulation environment consists of five components:

- The *vehicle model* is used as a test environment for the functional modeling. The vehicle model delivers the reactions of the environment to the functional model.
- The *simulation control* stimulates and controls the simulation. Additionally, the test pattern and the vehicle parameters are handled.
- The *simulation monitor* shows the current state of the simulation.
- The *simulation analysis* stores and analyses the reaction of the functional model to the different test and fault pattern.
- The *fault module* allows the fault injection into the functional model. Section 4.5 describes the fault module closer.

If any fault is detected during the simulation, the fault has to be localized and corrected. In addition to the verification of the functional models, faults and open issues in the requirement specification can be detected.

4.5 Fault Modeling

To examine the reliability of the functional specification we introduced a fault module in our simulation environment, which allows us formal analysis of the system behavior in the presence of faults. In our fault hypothesis we claimed to tolerate any single arbitrary fault. To validate this property we use the fault module. The fault module is an optional part of the functional model and is controlled by the simulation control. The behavior of the fault module corresponds to the behavior of the fault injection device (see Section 4.7). So the result between fault modeling and fault injection can be compared and the fault modeling can be verified. Our focuses of fault injection activities on the real system focus on the disturbance of the communication on the TTP transmission channel. Thus the fault injection module is realised for the transmission channels only.

4.6 Realisation and Integration

After finishing the global and local design and verification of the behavior through functional simulation and fault modeling, the complete system is integrated by connecting all components, by downloading and execution of the application software.

For the system integration the opportunity to monitor the global behavior by tracing the bus is important. Therefore we developed, together with an outhouse partner a monitoring tool, which allows us during run-time to monitor and trace the messages on the communication bus, without influencing the system. The inner state of the components like task states, variable values, etc. can be observed via local monitoring. Local monitoring should be applied very carefully, because it changes the behavior, especially the timing behavior of the components.

In industrial projects parts of the system are developed by different project teams or outhouse partners. For the component developer the whole system is typically not available. For the test of a single component a tool which simulates missing nodes is required. Therefore we realised a first prototype tool [3].

4.7 Test and Fault Injection

We have three intentions with the test and the fault injection experiments:

1. Verify the behavior of the TTP bus against the preliminary TTP specification, the TTP protocol is still under current investigation.
2. Verify the behavior of the simulation models for the nodes, the communication subsystem and the fault

module during the developing phase of the simulation environment.

3. Verify the behavior of the real system with respect to the system requirement specification.

4.7.1 Test

The definition of the test pattern is very important for the quality of the test. The aim is to reach as high as possible coverage of the test room with a minimum number of test patterns. The test method has to be understandable and reproducible, therefore, we used a functional test method.

Functional test methods examine the functional behavior and not the code itself. The program is considered as a *black box* [22]. The aim of the functional test is to test the specified requirements as completely as possible. The test specification can be described in a formal and informal way [4]. Formal methods nowadays are only accepted for a few applications in the industry. The most important functional test methods are *equivalent class, boundary test* [20], the *category-partition method* [21], and the *classification tree method* [4]. We generate our test pattern with the help of the classification tree method. It supports the combination of different input signals to generate test patterns. In the first step the relevant classifications are identified with the help of the requirement specification. In the next step the classifications are separated into mathematical disjunctive classes. The classifications and classes can be defined hierarchically and form a classification tree. The test patterns are generated by the combination of the non classifiable basic classes, from each single classification one class is used.

4.7.2 Fault Injection

Fault injection is a method for testing the fault-tolerance of a system with respect to the specified behavior. Fault injection is needed for two different purposes: to test the correct operation of the fault tolerance algorithms/mechanisms and to predict the dependability of the system in a realistic scenario where faults are expected to occur and have to be handled properly [12].

Our present fault injection techniques concentrate on disturbing the transmission channel. Therefore we use a fault injection hardware called *TTP-Stress*, which allows to disturb the communication channel of TTP. In a distributed fault-tolerant system the communication between the nodes is of utmost importance. Faults which are injected:

- Faults of the Physical Communication Layer: short cuts between transmission wires, short cuts to ground or power supply, loss of connections, faulty bus termination, etc.
- Loss of Frames: the switch off and reconfiguration of nodes can be simulated.
- Change of bits: the message contents can be changed.

The disturbances can be injected for a defined time interval, periodically or permanently. The start trigger is set manually through the user or via an external device, e.g., from a monitoring tool.

TTP supports different physical transmission layers. The currently implemented physical layer is in conformance with the ISO/DIS 11898 CAN [24] standard, i.e., differential transmission on a two-wire broadcast bus with one dominant state and one recessive state. The higher layers defined in the CAN specification (e.g. arbitration) do not apply for TTP.

5 Brake-by-wire Case Study

Automotive applications like brake- or steer-by-wire are typical examples for the use of a time-triggered architecture. We selected a *brake-by-wire* application, which we realised as a case study to evaluate the TTP protocol [8]. This application has several advantages:

- Realistic workload in a hard real-time application.
- Reuse for future realisations.
- Experiences on a real automotive example.

5.1 Requirement Specification

The requirement specification consists of the parts: specification of the system and definition of the test environment.

We realise the system specification in textual form with in-house used methods. So we do not have the opportunity to execute consistence checks in the description of the specification. Therefore we use the system model, which represents a detailed functional specification of the system.

5.2 Architectural System Design

Our fault tolerant architecture consists of a set of two redundant ECU's for the *Brake-by-Wire-Manager (BBW-Manager, BBWM)* and 4 single ECU's, one for each brake (see Figure 6). The ECU's are connected by two replicated busses. In this case study the brake ECU's are not designed redundant, in order to reduce costs, since the failure of a single brake is not considered to be as severe as the failure of the BBW-Manager.

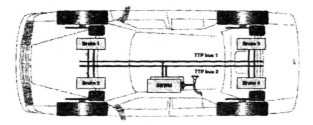

Figure 6: An Example for an TTA Architecture

The functional of the BBW-Manager is to read the sensor values of the brake pedal, the revolution counters of the wheels, the yaw-sensor, the acceleration sensors, and to calculate from these signals the brake force set points for the four brake actuators. The BBW-Manager also manages higher assistance functions like ABS, traction and driving dynamic control. The brake electronics get the brake force set points from the BBW-Manager.

The whole communication between the BBW-Manager, and the brake electronics is based on the fault tolerant TTP system.

In contrast to event triggered systems a TTP system is built upon a static message schedule. Figure 7 depicts the result of this phase, the static synchronous time division multiple access (TDMA) scheme and its constraint that each subsystem has to send exactly once in a TDMA cycle. The messages marked with 'I' are so called I-Frames, used for reintegration of rebooted nodes and do not transmit information for the application layer.

A TDMA slot has a length of about 1.2 msec. New brake force set points are sent every 7.2 msec, which is sufficient for an ABS control loop. The brake control ECU's send their status and the current brake force. These messages are not so time critical as the transmission of the brake force set points. The brake ECU's send their messages only once in a cluster cycle, each 12 TDMA slots. In the remaining slots the brake ECU's send I-Frames for the network management.

5.3 Functional Design

As one example of a component with fail-silent property we describe in this section the realisation of the BBW-Manager. The four brake ECU's are realised in a similar manner. The BBW-Manager has the functionality to calculate the four brake force set points. The brake force set points are safety related and have to be protected from transient and permanent faults. Figure 8 shows the schedule which is periodically executed on the BBW-Manager:

1. *Pedal signal measurement*, of the pedal signals from the pedal sensors.
2. *Pedal signal plausibility checks*, from the three pedal signals one valid value is calculated. This task is executed three times, to detect faults.
3. *Voter*, a voter task votes from the result of the three plausibility check tasks and starts an exception handling if a fault is detected.
4. *Brake force control*, the brake forces for the four actuators are calculated. This task is also executed three times.
5. *Voter*, a voter task votes from the result of the three brake force control tasks.
6. *TTP-communication*, the brake forces are send to the brakes via the TTP communication network.
7. *Diagnose*, a diagnose task is executed.
8. *Diagnose output*, the diagnose values are transmitted to an extern diagnose device.

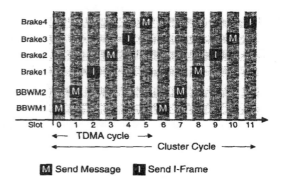

M Send Message   I Send I-Frame

Figure 7: Communication Matrix of the Brake-by-wire Case Study

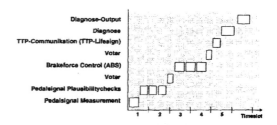

Figure 8: Local Task Schedule of the BBW-Manager

5.4 Functional Simulation

The system model represents the same structure of nodes as the real architecture. As an example we show the functional model of the system architecture (see Figure

234

9). We only present this part of the model, because the description of the whole model is beyond the scope of this paper.

The activity charts BBWM1_AC and BBWM2_AC represents the BBW-Manager nodes 1 and 2, similar the activity charts BRAKE_ACx the brake nodes. @ is part of the Statemate™ syntax and means that a more detailed description of the activity exists. The external activities SENSORS and ACTUATORS represent the source and sink for the input and output data flows. The external activities MEDL_COMPILER and TADL_COMPILER, the configuration of the communication and task schedule of the nodes.

For the functional simulation first we use the single step mode to verify the model being complete and consistent. After this, we define the test pattern and exercise the simulation in the batch mode. We instrument the simulation for control and collecting of statistics during execution.

5.5 Fault Modeling

The fault module is a optional part of the system model and is represented by the activity chart TTP_STRESS_AC. To compare the results between fault modeling and fault injection the fault model has the same function as the fault injection device (TTP-Stress). In the real system we use a broadcast bus, therefore TTP-Stress can be connected at an arbitrary point with the bus. In the system model every TTP message transmitted on the bus is piped through the fault module. For the verification of the fault module behavior we use the same setup in fault modeling and fault injection.

5.6 Realisation and Integration

For the realisation we use the capability of automatic code generation of Statemate™ and MATLAB®/Simulink™. By using automatic code generation we still have the problem that we use non validated code generators; this problem will be addressed in our future work. As target platforms we use a VxWorks [29] based system for the BBW-Manager and a controller platform without floating point unit for the brake ECU´s. Currently download and execution of automatic generated code is only possible for the BBW-Manager. The complexity of BBW-Manager is much higher than the Brake ECU´s.

For system integration we use bus monitoring and additionally every node sends its internal states via a diagnosis bus to an external monitoring device. So we have the capability of monitoring and logging of all important system states.

5.7 Test and Fault Injection

We use functional test for the verification of our implementation. To define the test pattern out of the

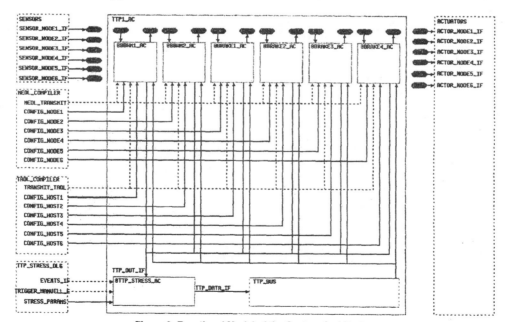

Figure 9: Functional Model of the System Architecture

requirement specification we use classifications trees [4].

The test pattern for the fault injection is separated into three groups; verification of the protocol behavior, verification of the fault, and verification of the system behavior under fault conditions.

The verification of the protocol behavior, depends on the protocol specification. We generate the fault pattern manually through examining the TTP specification. For the examination of the system behavior under fault conditions, we use the results of classification tree analysis.

6 Conclusion

In this paper we present a framework for the development of ultra-dependable automotive systems based on a time-triggered architecture. In the first part of the paper we introduce the time-triggered architecture and the time-triggered protocol. We showed that time-triggered architectures are well suited for safety critical automotive by-wire applications. In the second part we describe an approach is for the development of TTP based systems. Our approach based on verification of the system design by functional simulation, fault modeling, functional test and fault injection in the real system. At the end we gave a brief example of how this approach can be used in a brake-by-wire case study.

References

[1] C. Alexander, *Notes On The Synthesis of Form*, Harvard University Press, Cambridge, Massachusetts and London, England, 1964.

[2] E. Dilger, L.A. Johansson, H. Kopetz, M. Krug, P. Lidén, G. McCall, P. Mortara, B. Müller, U. Panizza, S. Poledna, A.V. Schedl, J. Söderberg, M. Strömber, T. Thurner: *Towards an Architecture for Safety Related Fault Tolerant Systems in Vehicles*, Proceedings of the ESREL'97 International Conference, 1997.

[3] Fleisch, Ringler Th. and Belschner, R., *Simulation of Application Software for a TTP Real-Time Subsystem*. Proc. of European Simulation Symposium, Istanbul, Turkey, June 1997.

[4] K. Grimm, M. Grochtmann, *Classification Trees for Partition Testing*, in Software Testing, Verification and Reliablility, Bd. 3, No. 2, pp. 63-82, 1993.

[5] D. Harel, *Statecharts: a visual formalism for complex systems*, Science of Computer Programming, vol. 8, no. 3, pp. 231-274,1987.

[6] D. Harel et al., *On the formal semantics of Statecharts*, in Proc. 2nd IEEE Symposium on Logic in Computer Science, IEEE Press, NY, USA, pp. 54-64, 1987.

[7] D. Harel et al., *Statemate™: a working environment for the development of complex reactive systems*, IEEE Trans. On Software Engineering, vol. SE-16, no. 4, pp. 403-414, 1990.

[8] B. Hedenetz, R. Belschner, *Brake-by-wire without Mechanical Backup by Using a TTP-Communication Network*, SAE International Congress 1998.

[9] G. Heiner, T. Thurner, *Time-Triggered Architecture for Safety-Related Distributed Real-Time Systems in Transportation Systems*, FTCS-28, June 1998.

[10] IEEE Std. 1074.1991, *IEEE Standard for Developing Software Lifecycle Processes*, The Institute of Electrical and Electronics Engineers, Inc., 1991.

[11] ISO/ICE 1508, *Functional safety: safety-related systems*, International Electrotechnical Commission, 1995.

[12] J. Karlsson, P. Folkesson, J. Arlat, Y. Crouzet, G. Leber, *Integration and Comparison of Three Physical Fault Injection Techniques*, Predictably Dependable Computing Systems, Springer Verlag 309-329, 1995.

[13] H. Kopetz, et. al., *A Prototype Implementation of a TTP/C Controller*, Proceedings SAE Congress 1997, Detroit, MI, USA, Febr. 1997. Society of Automotive Engineers, SAE Press. SAE Paper No. 970296.

[14] H. Kopetz, *Real-Time Systems - Design Principles for Distributed Real-Time Systems*, Kluwers Academic Publishers, 1997.

[15] H. Kopetz, G. Grünsteidl, *TTP - A Protocol for Fault-Tolerant Real-Time Systems*, IEEE Computer, pages 14-23, January 1994.

[16] A. Krüger, *Interface design for Time-Triggered Real-Time System Architectures*, doctor thesis, Institut für Technische Informatik, Vienna University of Technology, 1997.

[17] M. Krug, A. V. Schedl, *New Demands for Invehicle Networks*, Proceedings of the 23rd EUROMICRO Conference, pp. 601-606, 1997.

[18] N. Leveson, *Safeware - System safety and computers*, Addison-Wesley, Reading, MA, 1995.

[19] MathWorks, *MATLAB® - The Language of Technical Computing*, MathWorks Inc., MATLAB® 5.1, June 1997.

[20] G.J. Myers, *The Art of Software Testing*, Wiley-Interscience, Chichester, 1979.

[21] T.J. Ostrand, M.J. Balcer, *The Category-Partition Method for Specifying and Generating Functional Test*, in Communications of the ACM, Bd. 31, Nr. 6, Juni 1988.

[22] N. Parrington, M. Roper, *Softwaretest*; Mc Graw-Hill, Hamburg, 1990

[23] S. Poledna, *The Problem of Replica Determinism*, Fault-Tolerant Real-Time Systems, Kluwer Academic Publishers, 1996.

[24] SAE, *Control Area Network: an invehicle serial communication protocol*, SAE Information Report J1583, SAE Handbook, 1990.

[25] SAE, *Class C Application Requirement Considerations*, SAE Recommended Practice J2056/1, SAE, June 1993.

[26] SAE, *Survey of Known Protocols*, SAE Information Report J2056/2, SAE, April 1993.

[27] I. Sommerville, *Software Engineering*, Addison-Wesley Publishing Company, Wokingham, England, 3rd edition, 1989.

[28] URL: http://www.isi.com/products/matrixx/.

[29] URL: http://www.wrs.com/.

feature

Reprinted from IEEE Software,
January 1997, pp. 73-85.

Formal Methods: Promises and Problems

Successfully applying formal methods to software development promises to move us closer to a true engineering discipline. The authors offer suggestions for overcoming the problems that have hindered the use of formal methods thus far.

LUQI
Naval Postgraduate School

JOSEPH A. GOGUEN
University of California
at San Diego

Today's fast-moving technology demands ever quicker and more reliable ways to develop software systems that meet user needs. Although industry spends billions of dollars each year developing software, many software systems fail to satisfy their users. Moreover, many systems once thought adequate no longer are, while others are never finished or never used. The September 1994 issue of *Scientific American* gives some sobering examples and concludes that "despite 50 years of progress, the software industry remains years—perhaps decades—short of the mature engineering discipline needed to meet the demands of an information-age society."[1] Software development failures have reached staggering proportions: an estimated $81 billion was spent on canceled software projects in 1995 and an estimated $100 billion in 1996.[2]

Many computer scientists have suggested that formal methods can play a significant role in improving this situation. Although these methods have achieved impressive successes, they have also produced disappointments.

> **Requirements for large and complex systems are nearly always problematic initially and evolve throughout the life cycle.**

Formal methods do not yet effectively handle large and complex system development, although they can make a contribution. We know that requirements for large and complex systems are nearly always problematic initially and that they evolve continually throughout the life cycle. Thus, any method you use to implement requirements should be flexible and robust, so that it can easily accommodate the inevitable and often continuous stream of changes. We suggest that you can more effectively use formal methods by

♦ putting more emphasis on formal models and on domain-specific formal methods;

♦ using formal models as a basis for computer support of software evolution;

♦ using large-grain software composition methods, rather than small-grain statement-oriented programming methods; and

♦ taking better account of the system development context by tracing objects and relationships back to requirements.

FORMALIZATION

Webster's Dictionary defines *formal* as definite, orderly, and methodical; defines *method* as a regular, orderly, and definite procedure; and defines *model* as a preliminary representation that serves as a plan from which the final and usually larger object is to be constructed. Thus, to be formal does not necessarily require the use of formal logic, or even mathematics. But in computer science, the phrase "formal methods" has acquired a narrower meaning, referring specifically to the use of a formal notation to represent system models during program development. An even narrower sense refers to the formalization of a method for system development. Typically, you first write a specification in a formal notation, then refine it step by step into code. Correctness of the refinement steps guarantees that the code satisfies the specification. In some methods, developers can check correctness of the refinement steps using a theorem prover for the method's underlying formal logic, but other methods remain manual because it is difficult to automate the notation used. To better understand the issues and myths related to the practical usefulness of formal methods, consult "Seven More Myths of Formal Methods,"[3] and for an appraisal of their recent industrial applications, see "An International Survey of Industrial Applications of Formal Methods."[4]

Logical foundation. The prototypical formal notation is first-order logic. This notation has been extensively studied and has inference rule sets known to be sound and complete for a convenient class of models. Unfortunately, mechanical theorem provers for first-order logic can be difficult to work with.

More powerful logical systems can capture additional levels of meaning, but their theorem provers can be even harder to work with. For example, second-order logic can express security requirements for computer systems, but it does not have a sound and complete inference rule set.

Context. Experience shows that many of the most vexing problems in software development arise because any computer system is situated in a particular social context. Moreover, much of the information needed to design a system is embedded in the worlds of users and managers, and is extracted through interaction with these people. This information is informal and highly dependent on its social context for interpretation. On the other hand, we define the programming languages and other representations used to construct computer-based systems using formal syntactic and semantic rules. Both the formal, context-insensitive, and the informal, socially situated aspects of information are crucial for success. These two aspects have been called "the dry" and "the wet," and their reconciliation claimed to be the essence of requirements engineering.[5]

The dry and the wet. That we can make sense out of social life suggests it is somewhat orderly enough to be at least partly formalizable. But it is difficult to formalize domains that have many ad hoc special cases or contain much tacit knowledge or are subject to change. Formalization is more successful on narrow and orderly domains, such as sporting events, which have long traditions, regulating bodies, rule books, referees, and so on. For example, it would be more difficult to formalize a children's game than a regatta, and more difficult still to formalize human political behavior.

There are *degrees* of formalization, ranging from the very formal *dry* to the very informal *wet*. In the driest formalizations, the metalanguage is also formalized, and an object-level model is given as a formal theory in the metalanguage. In less fully formalized models, the metalanguage may be simply a natural language, or a somewhat stylized dialect. There can be rules at both the object and the meta levels. Rules at the object level are part of the model, while rules at the meta level define the language used for formalization. For a given application, it can be a serious error to formalize more than is appropriate to the particular situation.

Formalization is useful only to the extent that it helps meet concrete goals. For example, it would only make it harder to bake cookies if the recipe were expressed in a fully formalized language. There are many similar examples in requirements engineering. Good formalizations do not usually arise top-down from desires, but rather are based on extensive experience and intuition with the domain being formalized and the intended development process.

Formal methods generally address some large class of systems, such as information systems, or even all possible systems, whereas formal models are often tailored to a specific application domain. Experience suggests that using mechanically processable formal models in building and integrating tools can yield systems that increase automation and decrease inconsistency, and thus produce software faster, cheaper, and more reliably. For example, attribute grammars are a formally processable notation that can be useful in this way. Experience also suggests using an evolutionary development process that involves rapid prototyping, such as that supported by the computer-aided prototyping system (CAPS).[6] Such an approach contrasts with formal methods that call for mathematical rigor throughout the development process, usually by using a formal notation with a precise mathe-matical semantics in connection with a step-by-step refinement process. We believe it makes more sense to provide computer support for software evolution by formalizing the activities of the supporting tools rather than those of the software engineers.

In software engineering, you cannot validate results purely by proving theorems. On the contrary, you must measure the value of a contribution by its impact on practical software development and ultimately on customer satisfaction. But formalization still plays a fundamental role in software engineering, because you must have a formal (in the broad sense) model of a domain before you can design effective software for that domain. That is, problem formalization is an essential part of requirements capture.

In this respect, software engineering differs from other engineering disciplines. For example, in electrical engineering, the formalization of the problem domain is already done, and the practicing engineer need only apply it. The lack of such formalization makes software engineering more difficult than other engineering disciplines, which makes it less developed and less effectively practiced than its cousins.

Unfortunately, like many things in computer science, formal methods have been oversold. Formal methods, notations, and tools do not yet adequately support the development of large and complex systems. In general, practitioners consider formal methods useful for proving that programs satisfy certain mathematical properties, but such methods are also often considered too expensive to be practical. This view ignores evidence that appropriate and correctly used formal methods can reduce time to market, provide better documentation, improve communication, facilitate maintenance, and organize activities throughout the life cycle. Factors that influence the cost-effec-tiveness of formal methods include the consequences of software failure, the type of formal method to be applied, the availability of automated support for the formal method, and the skill level of available personnel.

SOFTWARE EVOLUTION

Traditionally, many in industry have viewed software evolution as occurring only after the completion of initial development. For example, L.J. Arthur defines software evolution as consisting of "the activities required to keep a software system operational and responsive after it is accepted and placed into production."[7] This is synonymous with maintenance, but avoids that word's negative connotations. According to Lawrence Bernstein (formerly of AT&T), evolution emphasizes the dynamic aspect of software development.[8]

Here, we consider software evolution to include all the activities that

> **The lack of formalization makes software engineering more difficult than other engineering disciplines.**

change a software system, as well as the relationships among those activities. In this case, evolution is not just another name for maintenance, because it occurs throughout the life cycle. Evolution encompasses activities ranging from adjusting requirements to updating working systems, including responses to requirements changes,

feature

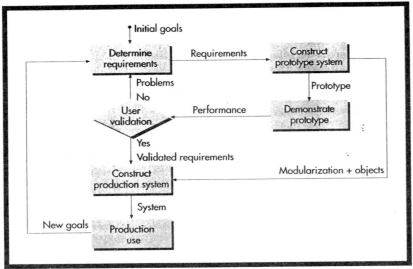

Figure 1. *An iterative prototyping life cycle. Once constructed, the prototype is demonstrated to check its actual behavior against its expected behavior. This helps identify problems and can lead to a redefinition of requirements.*

improvements to performance and clarity, bug repair, version and configuration control, documentation, testing, code generation, and the overall organization of the development process.

The term "evolution" focuses attention on change. Change is inevitable and unending during software development, because it is so difficult to get a system right before it has been tried by actual users under actual operating conditions. Not only do the code and design change, the requirements and the needs that drive the requirements change as well. This occurs partly because users and analysts get a better understanding of what they really need when they see the software operating, but also because the system context changes: laws and regulations change, the competition changes, workers' expectations and habits change, management structure changes, organizational goals change, and so on.

Flexibility through prototyping. Change

motivates the use of *iterative* life cycle processes, and in particular, *prototyping*: the process of quickly building and evaluating a series of concrete, executable models of selected aspects of a proposed system. In prototyping, evolution activities are interleaved with development, and continue even after delivery of the system's initial version.[6,9]

This contrasts with traditional life cycles, such as the waterfall model, which assume that requirements can be correctly determined at the beginning of a project. Generally, project staff develop an overall system architecture from the requirements, write specifications and code for individual components, then test and debug the system. Maintenance appears in or after the final phase of testing and debugging.

Figure 1 shows an iterative prototyping life cycle. The user and designer work together to define the requirements for the envisioned system. The designer constructs a prototype at the specification level. Demonstrations of

the prototype let the user evaluate the prototype's actual behavior against its expected behavior, identify problems, and work with the designer to redefine requirements. This process continues until the prototype successfully captures the critical aspects of the envisioned system. The designer then uses the validated requirements as a basis for the production software. In this way, software systems can be delivered incrementally and requirements analysis can continue throughout the system's lifetime. Incremental delivery gives users early experience with the software, leading to new goals, triggering further iterations, and extending the advantages of prototyping to the production environment.

Evolution and formal methods. Given the inevitability of change and iteration, formal methods should be more useful in supporting evolution than in their traditional role of verifying that code meets certain fixed requirements. Possible contributions to software evolution include computer-aided design completion, program transformation, dependency maintenance (among needs, requirements, design information, documentation, code, and so on), code generation (for certain limited purposes), and merging changes to programs. These contributions become even more valuable when many programmers work concurrently on a large and complex system.

The difficulties of software evolution often extend beyond the purely technical: Social, political, and cultural factors can be significant and in many projects will dominate development costs.

Nevertheless, formal model-based tools can help maintain a software development project's integrity in many ways, such as scheduling project tasks, monitoring deadlines, tracing reasons for objects and changes, and maintaining dependency relations

A HYPERGRAPH MODEL FOR SOFTWARE EVOLUTION

Because evolution plays a fundamental role in software development, we must understand it better, formalize key aspects, and build suitable tools based on the resulting formal models. This endeavor is still at an early stage. Here we briefly describe a formal model that helps develop tools to manage both the activities in a software development project and the products that those activities produce.

This model simplifies and clarifies previous CAPS models by incorporating some of their features into a more abstract mathematical structure. We intend that the software evolution data model presented here be easier to modify, extend, and understand than earlier models; this should also make it easier to implement. The model represents the evolution history and future plans for software development as a *hypergraph*. Hypergraphs generalize the usual notion of a directed graph by allowing *hyperedges*, which may have multiple output nodes and multiple input nodes. The following mathematical concepts are used in this software evolution model:

Definition 1. A (directed) hypergraph is a tuple (N,E,I,O) where

N is a set of *nodes*,

E is a set of *hyperedges* (sometimes simply called edges),

$I : E \to 2^N$ is a function giving the set of *inputs* of each hyperedge, and

$O : E \to 2^N$ is a function giving the set of *outputs* of each hyperedge.

A path p from a node n to a node n' is a sequence $e_1...e_k$ of $k>0$ edges and a sequence $n_1...n_{k+1}$ of nodes such that $n_i \in I(e_i)$ and $n_{i+1} \in O(e_i)$ for $i = 1,...,k$, where $n = n_1$ and $n' = n_{k+1}$. A hypergraph H is *acyclic* if there is no path from any node in H to itself.

A set N' of nodes is reachable from a set R of nodes if there is a path to each $n' \in N'$ from some $n \in R$. A hypergraph H is reachable from a set R of its nodes if its set N of nodes is reachable from R. A *root* of H is a node from which H is reachable. A *leaf* of H is a node from which no other node is reachable.

If $H = (N,E,I,O)$ is a hypergraph, then its opposite, denoted H^{op}, is the hypergraph (N,E,O,I). We say that H is core-achable from N' if H^{op} is reachable from N'. A hyperpath in a hypergraph $H = (N,E,I,O)$ from $D \subseteq N$ to $T \subseteq N$ is a minimal hypergraph contained in H, whose node set contains D and T, and that is reachable from D and coreachable from T; we call D and T the input and output sets of the hyperpath, respectively.

In the hypergraph software evolution data model each node represents a software component, which is an immutable version of a software object. Edges record dependencies among various versions of software objects in the system and represent the evolution steps (development activities that create the output objects of the edge). These software objects can be of many different kinds, including problem reports, change requests, reactions to prototype demonstrations, requirements, specifications, manuals, test data, design documents, and many other kinds of object besides program code. The dependencies represent the essence of the derivation history, as well as plans for future evolution.

Definition 2. An evolutionary hypergraph is a hypergraph $H = (N,E,I,O)$ together with functions $L_N : N \to C$ and $L_E : E \to A$ such that the following assumptions are satisfied:

N and E are disjoint subsets of a set U whose elements are called *unique identifiers*;

if $O(e) \cap O(e') \neq \varnothing$ then $e = e'$; we call this the *identifiability* condition;

H is acyclic; and

$A=\{s, d\} \cdot A$ (that is, each element of A has the form (S, a') or (d, a'), where $a' \in A'$.

An edge labeled "s" is called a step and one labeled "d" is called a decomposition.

The elements of N are identifiers for software components, the elements of E are identifiers for evolution steps, and I and O give the inputs and outputs of each evolution step. The function L_N labels each node with component attributes from the set C, including the corresponding version of the software object, and the function L_E labels each edge with step attributes from the set A, including the current status of the step. The notion of component used here includes components in the usual sense as well as systems built by combining subcomponents, test cases, bug reports, and other kinds of software objects. Decomposition edges include the part_of relation in earlier versions of this model.

The first condition says that the node and edge identifiers are distinct. The second says that the output sets of different evolution steps are disjoint; this implies that each step is uniquely identifiable by any component that it produces, so that the producing step can be considered an attribute of a component. The third condition implies that the process of software evolution never brings us back to a component we have already built; this simply means that we never reuse a unique identifier for a component. However, it is certainly possible that a later version of a component is equal to an earlier one, in the sense that $L(n) = L(n')$ where $n \neq n'$ and n' depends on n, in a sense made precise by the following:

A node n' depends on a node n if there is a path from n to n'. Similarly, a node n depends on a step s if there is a path to n involving s. A step s' depends on a step s if there is a path involving both s and s' with s earlier in the path than s'. We may say that a component c' depends on a component c if there is a path from n to n' such that $c = L(n)$ and $c' = L(n')$.

The model developed so far does not include the idea that some evolution steps may be composites of other, lower level steps. To model this, we introduce a hierarchical structure on the hyperedges in a hypergraph. This also has the advantage of permitting overviews of the evolution history at various levels of detail.

Definition 3. An *(edge) hierarchical hypergraph* is an acyclic graph with nodes labeled by hypergraphs, such that: the graph has just one leaf and one root; each of its edges corresponds to an edge expansion of a single hyperedge in its source hypergraph, the result of which is the hypergraph in its target; and the result of the composite expansions along

Continued on page 78

Continued from page 77

any two paths between the same two nodes are equal. A *hierarchical evolutionary hypergraph* is a hierarchical hypergraph whose nodes are labeled by evolutionary hypergraphs and whose edges are labeled by the step that is expanded.

The intuition behind this definition is that the root node hypergraph is the most abstract top-level view of the system's evolution history and structure, while the leaf node is the fully expanded form. The nodes of the root hypergraph are different versions of the entire software product, while the nodes of the leaf hypergraph include the versions of the atomic software objects that constitute the software product. All of the steps in the leaf hypergraph are atomic. An edge expansion in a hypergraph replaces a hyperedge by a hypergraph containing the original nodes; we leave this technically complex notion informal and illustrate it in the following example. We do not intend that the evolution data should be represented as described in the preceding definition; rather, we intend it as an abstract *model* against which efficient implementations can be tested.

The top level of Figure A (1) contains three versions of a software system, labeled P1.1, P1.2, and P2.2. Step s1 derives a new version P1.2 from P1.1, and step s2 derives another variant P2.2 from P1.1. This is a simple evolutionary hypergraph, which is just an ordinary graph. The lower level in Figure A (1) shows the expansion of the edge s2. The decomposition edges d1.1 and d2.2 show that A1.1 and B1.1 are parts of P1.1, and that A2.2, B1.1, and C2.1 are parts of P2.2. The substep s2.a2 derives A2.2 from A1.1, while the substep s2.c1 derives the new component C2.1 from nothing at all. In a more complete example, C2.1 might be derived from a new requirement.

These two descriptions of the system's history and structure correspond to the hypergraphs labeled H0 and H2 in Figure A (2); the edge from H0 to H2 represents the expansion of the evolution step s2. If we also expand the step s1, corresponding to the edge from H0 to H1, then we must also have a fourth hypergraph H12, containing both edge expansions. The complete evolutionary hypergraph has the diamond shape shown in Figure A (2), in which H0 is the root and H12 the leaf. This model can be improved and extended in many ways, such as by imposing more structure on the set U of unique identifiers to define the concepts of version and variant; we have already used such a structure informally in the example.

Our intention has been to abstract away as much detail as possible while still showing the basic concepts. For example, the decomposition of the abstract set A as {s,d} X A' introduces structure that conveys further information about evolution; by further decomposing A', even more information can be represented. For example, steps can have attributes and relationships to reflect management decisions, such as deadlines, priorities, and the designers involved.

The evolution control system,[1] based on an earlier version of this model, provides algorithms using the information in the graph to support several different kinds of automation. This support includes first approximations to the decomposition structure of a step derived from the decomposition structure of the current version of the affected components

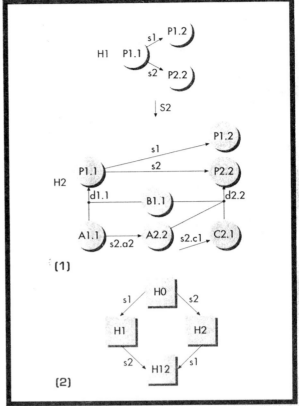

Figure A. *Hierarchical Evolutionary Hypergraph. The topmost part of (1) shows three versions of a software system; the bottom part of (1) shows the expansion of the edge s2. The complete evolutionary hypergraph appears in (2).*

and induced steps implied by dependencies between components. For example, if a requirement is modified then the program components derived from that requirement must also be modified.

The tool based on such models also has scheduling algorithms that provide estimated completion times for project activities and alerts when project deadlines are affected. The schedule is adjusted as more information becomes available, using the management policies recorded as attributes of steps to automatically assign new tasks to designers as they complete previous tasks. The system also uses the dependency information in project plans to deliver the proper versions of the components needed to carry out each step and to insert the versions of components produced by completed steps in the proper places in the graph. This automates check-in and check-out from the project database.

REFERENCE

1. S. Badr, *A Model and Algorithms for a Software Evolution Control System*, doctoral dissertation, Naval Postgraduate School, Monterey, Calif., 1993.

among versions, variations, and component decompositions. The hypergraph model described in the box on pages 77 and 78 is designed to support such activities.

The US Department of Defense issued MIL-STD-498 in 1994.[10] This standard has evolved into ISO/IEC 12207, which will be adopted as joint standard J-STD-016. These software development standards will have a profound effect on software evolution. They replace several previous standards that mandated the waterfall model, thus creating new opportunities by allowing considerably greater flexibility. But it also requires greater skill levels because it must be tailored to specific projects and organizations. Large and complex software development projects based on specially tailored standards will be difficult to manage without appropriate tool support, and it will be difficult to develop such tools without appropriate formal models. Contrary to typical assumptions in work on software processes, we believe that such models should focus on what the tools do rather than on what the personnel involved do.

SCALABILITY FOR APPLICATIONS

Our analysis of formal methods distinguishes between small-, large-, and huge-grain methods, referring to the size of the atomic parts used, rather than to the size of the system being developed. We reluctantly chose the word *huge* as the next step above *large*, because *large* is already in common use in certain communities; it would have been better if the three steps were instead called fine, medium, and coarse.

Small-grain methods. The classic formal methods fall into the small-grain category. These methods have a mathematical

basis at the level of individual statements and small programs, but rapidly hit a complexity barrier when programs get large. In particular, systems for reasoning with pre- and postconditions—such as Hoare axioms, weakest preconditions, predicate transformers, and transformational programming—all have small-size atomic units and fail to scale up because they do not provide structuring or encapsulation. In general, small-grain methods have great difficulty handling changes, and thus fit poorly into the life cycle. Transformational programming is less resistant to change than other small-grain methods, but has the problem that in general there is no bound to the number of transformations that may be needed; this restricts its use to relatively small and well-understood domains.

Large-grain methods. The most important techniques of large-grain programming involve module composition. The CAPS system[11] provides module composition for rapid prototyping, with a dataflow-like semantics that supports hard real-time constraints and with facilities for retrieving reusable software components from a repository. The project is also working on the foundations of software maintenance and developing techniques to support design evolution, requirements tracing, configuration management, and project management. One of these techniques, change merging, has the potential to aid in combining concurrent changes to the same base version of a prototype as well as updating multiple versions of a prototype with a common change.[12]

CAPS consists of an integrated tool set that helps you design, translate, and execute prototypes. These include an evolution control system based on a graph model for evolution, a change merge facility, automatic generators for schedule and control code, and automated retrievers for reusable components.

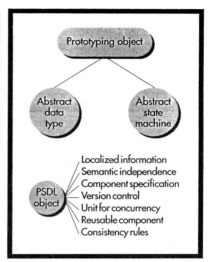

Figure 2. *Class structure and properties of PSDL objects. This prototype system description language provides a simple way of specifying software systems for prototypes and production software.*

The prototype system description language PSDL[11] provides a simple way to abstractly specify software systems for both prototypes and production software. A PSDL program consists of two kinds of objects, corresponding to abstract data types (PSDL types) and abstract state machines (PSDL operators) as shown in Figure 2. Their function is to localize the information for analyzing, executing, and reusing independent objects. They are also the basis for version control and are natural units of work in a distributed implementation.

When an executable Ada module is associated with each atomic PSDL object, CAPS can automatically generate "glue code" that composes these modules into a system having the structure described by the dataflow diagram. This code includes a generated schedule and tests for all the real-time constraints that have been declared; these components can be used to check the design assumptions on which the schedule is based. The system can then be compiled, executed, and tested. Error messages are produced during execution if constraints are violated.

Parameterized programming lets you express designs and system properties in a modular way.

Huge-grain methods. Huge-grain parts are much larger than small-grain statements and large-grain modules. Huge-grain parts may be systems themselves, typically commercial off-the-shelf systems. Developing systems using huge-grain parts is qualitatively different from working with small- and large-grain parts. In particular, correcting some errors in a huge-grain part may be impossible, in which case they must be accepted and worked around. For example, a network protocol such as TCP/IP may have been obtained from an external vendor, so the developers of the larger system do not have access to its source code. If the version being used has a bug, there is no choice but to find a way to avoid that bug. This is often possible because of the multiplicity of features provided in such parts. Specification and requirement methods for huge-grain systems must be robust, effective, easy to learn, and easy to incorporate into the life cycle.

Technology developed for large-grain system development can also be useful for the huge-grain case, since huge-grain parts can often be treated as modules. For example, PSDL's control constraints, such as execution guards and output guards, support adjustments to the behavior of huge-

grain parts without access to their source code. The wrapper concept is also relevant. Huge-grain methods are an important area for further research.

Parameterized programming. The object-oriented version of the *parameterized programming*[13] approach is another example of a large-grain method. It uses module expressions, theories, and views to compose systems from subsystems. It distinguishes among sorts for values, classes for objects, and modules for encapsulation. Parameterized programming lets you express designs and high-level system properties in a modular way, and lets you parameterize, compose, and reuse designs, specifications, and code as well.

In this approach, the main programming unit is the *module*, which lets you declare multiple classes together. Module composition features include summing, renaming, enhancing, modifying, parameterizing, instantiating, and importing. The *sum* of modules is a kind of parallel composition that takes account of sharing. *Renaming* lets you assign new names to the sorts, classes, attributes, and methods of modules; *enhancing* lets you add functionality to a module; and *modifying* lets you redefine some of its units.

Parameterized programming was first implemented in the OBJ language, and has also been implemented in the Functional Object-Oriented Programming System (FOOPS) and Eqlog languages. It has a rigorous semantics based on category theory. Much of the advantage of parameterized programming comes from the ability to parameterize modules using theories and views; for example, a higher-order capability can be provided in a purely first-order setting.

Parameterized programming supports *design* in the same framework as specification and coding. Designs are expressed as module expressions and

can be executed if specifications that have a suitable form are available. This gives a convenient form of prototyping. Alternatively, prototypes for the modules involved can be composed to give a system prototype by evaluating the module expression for the design. A novel feature of the approach is to distinguish between structuring, genericity, and compositionality in horizontal and vertical modes. *Vertical structure* relates to layers of abstraction, in which lower layers implement or support higher layers. *Horizontal structure* is concerned with module aggregation, enrichment, and specialization. Both kinds of structure can appear in module expressions and both are evaluated when a module expression is evaluated. The approach can also support relatively efficient prototyping through *built-in* modules, which can be composed just like other modules, and which offer a way to combine prototypes with efficient programs in a standard programming language. This is similar to the CAPS approach.

The module and type systems of parameterized programming are considerably more general than those of languages like Ada, Clu, and Modula-3, which provide only limited support for module composition. For example, interfaces in these languages can only express syntactic restrictions on actual arguments, cannot be horizontally structured, and cannot be reused. Lileanna[14] implements many ideas of parameterized programming for the Ada language, including horizontal and vertical composition, following the design of the LIL (library interconnection language) system.[13]

DOMAIN-SPECIFIC FORMAL METHODS

There is much more to formal methods than suggested by the themes dominant in the past, namely synthesis and correctness proofs for algorithms. Although both of these remain interesting topics for theoretical research, their direct impact on the practice of large-scale software development is limited.

Several recent, successful applications of formal methods seem to form a cluster suggesting a new paradigm for applying formal methods. These applications involve a tool having all or most of the following attributes:

♦ A narrow, well-defined, and well-understood problem domain is addressed, which may have an existing, successful library of program modules.

♦ There is a coherent user community interested in the problem domain; the users have a good understanding of the domain, good communication among themselves, a standard terminology, and access to financial resources.

♦ The tool has a graphical user interface that is intuitive to the user community, embodying that community's own language and conventions.

♦ The tool takes a large-grain approach: rather than synthesizing procedures out of statements, it synthesizes systems out of modules; it may use a library of components and synthesize code for putting them together.

♦ Inside the tool is a powerful engine that encapsulates formal methods concepts and/or algorithms: it may be a theorem prover or a code generator; users do not have to know how it works, or even that it is there.

We suggest the name *domain-specific formal methods* for this emerging paradigm, in recognition of the role played by the user community and their specific domain. Some systems that fall under this heading include

♦ Amphion, which combines programs for astronomy calculations,[15]

♦ CAPS for real-time programming,[8] and

♦ Panel for multimedia animation.[16]

This paradigm falls into the category of large-grain methods and can potentially be extended to huge-grain problems. The development of domain-specific formal methods should enable our discipline to replace the current practice of inventing new formal models with the more efficient practice of refining and recombining existing application models within supported domains.

This suggests a vision for the future that is less ambitious and more realistic than that of the past. It calls for using formal models and algorithms as a basis for creating computer tools to help solve practical problems that are more limited and well defined than in the past. This vision replaces the unrealistic artificial-intelligence goals of fully automatic software synthesis and verification with the recognition that human understanding and creativity must play an important role and that automated decision support can effectively enhance human capabilities. It also recognizes that requirements changes are a dominant aspect of practical software development that relies on automated tools to make software easier to change.

LIMITS AND PROBLEMS

Despite their many potential benefits, formal methods are not a panacea. We have identified nine specific problems with them[17]:

♦ Formal notation is alien to most practicing programmers, who have little training or skill in higher mathematics. Also, supporting tools are often insufficiently automated or lack user interfaces suitable for engineers.

♦ Formal methods papers and training often consider only toy examples taken from existing literature. Although it may be impossible to give a detailed treatment of a realistic example in a research paper or in the class-room, such examples must exist for a method to have credibility. Effective training in formal methods should treat parts of a realistic, nontrivial application.

♦ Many of the most popular formal methods do not scale up to practical-size problems. The gap between specifications and code is still great. Despite serious and long-term efforts in type theory, weakest preconditions, transformational programming, and so on, coding remains largely manual.

♦ Some advocates of formal methods dogmatically insist that everything must be proved to the highest possible degree of mathematical rigor. At the least, they argue, it must be machine-checked by a program that allows no errors or gaps, and it should be produced by a machine as well. However, mathematicians rarely achieve or even strive for such rigor; published proofs in mathematics are highly informal and often have small errors. Mathematicians never explicitly mention rules of inference from logic unless they are proving something *about* such rules. The highest levels of formality can be very expensive, and are only warranted

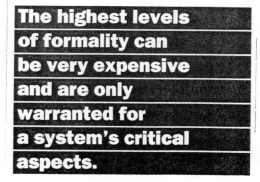

The highest levels of formality can be very expensive and are only warranted for a system's critical aspects.

for a system's critical aspects.

♦ Formal methods tend to be rigid and inflexible. In particular, it is difficult to adapt a formal proof of one statement to prove another, slightly different statement. Since requirements and specifications are constantly changing in the real world, such adaptations are frequently necessary. But classical formal methods have great difficulty in dealing with such changes; their proofs are a discontinuous function of how problems are formulated.

♦ Important aspects of practical software evolution are often ignored. In particular, it is difficult to integrate formal methods into existing software processes. A related difficulty is that when you use multiple methods together you may not be able to integrate their underlying models in a way that supports building a practical software development system to support the methods.

♦ Often vendors do not use the best technology or even understand software development very well; they tend to be interested in profits above all and to have little time for learning either new technologies or their benefits. They often use brute-force methods to speed up projects, forgetting that this can be a shortcut to disaster.

♦ Some formal methods have technical difficulties. A technical deficiency of many small-grain formal methods is that first-order logic is inadequate for expressing the weakest precondition of a loop, as noted in the late 1960s by the logician Erwin Engeler.[18] For example, the weakest precondition for a theorem prover for first-order logic with arithmetic cannot itself be expressed in first-order logic (the postcondition is that the input is a tautology). However, a second-order formulation is adequate, and has been used by us for some years in teaching and research, including the SPEC language used at the Naval Postgraduate School.[9,19]

♦ Finally, certain fundamental limitations are imposed because all formalizations are situated in a certain context. In particular, formalizations are *emergent* in that they are always constructed and interpreted in a context. Formalizations are *contingent* in that their construction and interpretation depend upon details of the context in which this construction or interpretation actually occurs; these details may include interpretations of prior events. Moreover, interpretations are subject to negotiations among interested parties. Formalizations are *open* in that they can always be revised in the light of further analyses. They are also *vague* in that their interpretation is only elaborated to the extent that it is practically useful to do so; the rest is left as tacit knowledge. Further discussion of these points may be found elsewhere,[5] including a general introduction to the social aspects of requirements engineering.

These limits imply that both human effort and context necessarily play a fundamental role whenever formalizations are created, interpreted, or updated. Furthermore, much of the context of that information may be social, such as goals, responsibilities, and needs associated with particular roles in an organization. These considerations are significant for designing tools to support software development. In particular, as an aid to future modifications it is highly desirable to make contextual information available along with specifications and code. The lack of such information is what makes redesign difficult and what motivates current research on reengineering. Clearly, it would be better if such information were systematically recorded in the first place.

LESSONS LEARNED

We have taken a broad view of formalization's role in the software development process and have considered the role of formal methods within that context. In particular, we found that you must understand software evolution to understand the promises and problems of formal methods, that evolution is inevitable and unending in software development, and that much of the pressure for change arises from the social context of system development. Since formal methods tend to be brittle or discontinuous—a small change in

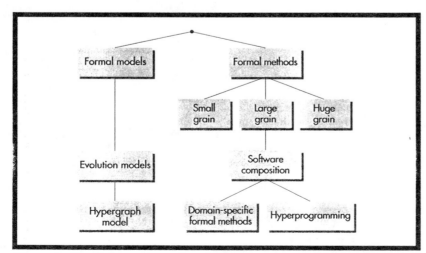

Figure 3. *Classification of some formal methods concepts. Any concept connected by a line to a higher concept is a subclass of that concept.*

HYPERREQUIREMENTS

The requirements phase of a large-system development project is the most error-prone, and requirements errors are also the most expensive to correct. Therefore improvements here will have the greatest economic leverage. Unfortunately, requirements are one of the least-explored areas of software engineering. There is lively debate about even the definition and scope of the term "requirements." Ian Sommerville defines requirements capture and analysis as "the process of establishing the services the system should provide and the constraints under which it must operate."[1] Al Davis suggests that requirements engineering is the analysis, documentation, and ongoing evolution of both user needs and the external behavior of the system to be built.[2] Goguen believes that requirements are properties that a system should have to succeed in its implementation environment.[3] These properties refer to the system's context of use and thus to social as well as technical factors.

Since many large software projects fail because of social, political, or cultural factors, we must take into account the social context of computer-based systems, in addition to the usual technical factors. Social context is especially important for requirements.

Traceability. We have undertaken several projects on improving the acquisition, traceability, accessibility, modularity, and reusability of the many objects that arise and are manipulated during software development, with a particular focus on the role of requirements.[3] One study administered a detailed two-stage questionnaire to software engineers at a large UK telecommunications firm. The questionnaire revealed that traceability was a major concern that consisted of several different problems that would best be treated in different ways.

Major distinctions appeared between the traceability of prerequirements specification and that of postrequirements specification and between forward and backward traceability. Analysis also showed that access to users was a common difficulty that prevented acquiring necessary information. Further investigation revealed certain policies and traditions that restrict communication within this firm, so that requirements engineers often could not discover what users really needed. One problem was an internal market that restricted communication between "vendors" and "clients" within the firm. Various political considerations also played an important role. Abolition of the internal market for requirements projects, and generally improving the openness of information, could potentially save enormous sums for firms like the one studied.

Tracing dependencies. Another aspect of the traceability problem is the difficulty of maintaining the huge mass of dependencies among the many objects produced by a large software system development effort. Often these objects are not adequately defined; for example, module boundaries may be incorrectly drawn or not even explicitly declared at all and interfaces may be poorly drawn or badly documented. Without using representations for the objects involved, formal models for the dependencies, and tool support for managing them, it is impossible to know what effect a change will have, and in particular, to know what other objects may have to be changed to maintain consistency.

To meet this challenge, the TOOR system (for Tracing Object-Oriented Requirements) was developed.[4] It is a flexible, user-configurable object-oriented system that supports,

♦ links among objects representing user-definable relationships,

♦ grounding decisions in the prior objects that justify them, and

♦ tracing dependencies.

Particular challenges include formalizing dependencies and developing methods for calculating dependencies and propagating the implications of changes. This approach, called *hyperrequirements*, builds on earlier work on *hyperprogramming*, and is intended to support, by linking related objects, both the social context of requirements decisions and their traceability. Parameterized programming will support reuse, and the generalized notion of relation will support links among design, coding, and maintenance. Other work at Oxford is exploring the use of novel methods from sociology such as ethnomethodology, and the use of situated abstract data types, a new concept that helps bridge the gap between computer technology and its social context.[3]

REFERENCES

1. I. Sommerville, *Software Engineering*, Addison-Wesley, Reading, Mass., 1989.
2. A. Davis, *Software Requirements: Analysis & Specification*, Prentice-Hall, Englewood Cliffs, N.J., 1990.
3. J. Goguen, "Requirements Engineering as the Reconciliation of Social and Technical Issues," *Requirements Engineering: Social and Technical Issues*, M. Jirotka and J. Goguen, eds., Academic Press, London, 1994, pp. 165–200.
4. F. Pinhero and J. Goguen, "An Object-Oriented Tool for Tracing Requirements," *IEEE Software*, Mar. 1996, pp. 52-64.

the domain can require a great deal of new work—automation is often vital for their practical application.

The construction, interpretation, and updating of formalism is always situated in a context, and under-

> **We need traceability to get better control of the software life cycle.**

standing that context can be important in capturing the requirements for large and complex systems. Some fundamental formalization limits arise in this way. Modularity and reuse can help with any approach to improving the quality and reducing the cost of software development. We need traceability to get better control of the software life cycle.

Figure 3 shows the relationships between some of the concepts we've described. A line indicates that the lower concept is a subclass of the higher one.

Building a brighter future. Whatever we learn about software development should be appropriately formalized, implemented, and put into computer science curricula so that future generations can do better than we have. Teaching a formal method while ignoring its use in real projects can have a highly negative impact. For example, students may be taught programming from formal specifications, but not that specifications come from requirements, and that requirements are always changing, often because of social, political, and cultural factors.

As a result, students are not prepared for the rapid change and polit-

ical problems found in real industrial work. Many students also feel that formal methods turn programming from a creative activity into a boring, formal exercise. We have seen cases in which students have left the discipline because teachers have failed to deal with these problems.

Students need to know how to deal with real programs that have thousands or even millions of lines of code. Most of the examples used in textbooks and the classroom are very small, however, and carefully crafted correctness proofs of simple algorithms give an entirely misleading impression of what real programming is like. Also, most of the techniques taught are small-grain and thus do not scale up to large and complex problems.

Reliable tools based on a formal model can let students do problems that would be impossible by hand. Teachers should also present methods and tools that work on large-grain units—modules—rather than on small-grain units—statements, functions, and procedures—because large-grain methods can scale up, whereas small-grain methods cannot. Suites of sample problems should be developed that systematically show how and when to apply formal methods, and how to combine them with informal approaches. This will require developing appropriate module collections, refining and extending existing formal methods and tools, developing more natural user interfaces, re-thinking process models, revising curricula, retraining teachers, and experimentally validating the resulting methods in practical situations.

If we fail to properly train the next generation of software developers, the problems that we see today will worsen as the size and complexity of systems continue to grow and

the dead weight of legacy code continues to mount.

There is no doubt that formal models and methods can be very useful in practical software development. It also seems clear that they are necessary for transforming software engineering into a discipline that is as well understood and well organized as other engineering disciplines, which rely on sound and well-tested mathematical models. The difficulty is that formalization itself plays a more basic role in software engineering than in other engineering disciplines. Because software is still actively expanding into completely new application domains, and because requirements capture is a process of formalization, software development requires the construction of new formal models for each new application, as well as using established formal models.

More emphasis should be placed on *context* in system development and on domain-specific formal methods. However, basic research in computational logic still provides the foundation for many practical applications of formal models and methods, and advances in this area will increase the amount of computer support that can be provided in practice. A short-term view of what technology needs should be avoided, as should overselling formal methods, either as a general field or as an approach to particular applications.

With these caveats, formal methods and formal models should play an increasingly important part in coming to grips with the ongoing crisis engendered by our escalating expectations about the size, complexity, and reliability of software systems. ◆

ACKNOWLEDGMENTS

The research reported in this article has been supported in part by the National Science Foundation under grant number CCR-9058453, the Army Research Office under grant number ARO-145-91, British Telecommunications plc, the European Community under ESPRIT-2 BRA Working Group 6071, IS-CORE (Information Systems COrrectness and REusability), Fujitsu Laboratories Ltd., and a contract under the management of the Information Technology Promotion Agency (IPA), Japan, as part of the Industrial Science and Technology Frontier program "New Models for Software Architectures," sponsored by the New Energy and Industrial Technology Development Organization. We thank Valdis Berzins and David Dampier for their valuable comments on a draft of this article. We also thank Shari Pfleeger for her inspiration and support.

REFERENCES

1. W. Gibbs, "Software's Chronic Crisis," *Scientific American*, Sept. 1994, pp. 86-95.
2. Chaos 97, tech. report, Standish Group Int'l, Dennis, Mass., to appear Jan. 1997 at http://www.standishgroup.com/chaos.html.
3. J. Bowen and M. Hinchley, "Seven More Myths of Formal Methods," *IEEE Software*, July 1995, pp. 34–41.
4. D. Craigen, S. Gerhart, and T. Ralston, "An International Survey of Industrial Applications of Formal Methods," tech. report TR GCR 93/626, US Nat'l Inst. of Standards and Technology, Washington, D.C., 1993.
5. J. Goguen, "Requirements Engineering as the Reconciliation of Social and Technical Issues," *Requirements Engineering: Social and Technical Issues*, M. Jirotka and J. Goguen, eds., Academic Press, London, 1994, pp. 165–200.
6. Luqi, "Software Evolution through Rapid Prototyping," *Computer*, May 1989, pp. 13–25.
7. L.J. Arthur, *Software Evolution: The Software Maintenance Challenge*, Wiley Interscience, New York, 1988.
8. L. Bernstein, "Importance of Software Prototyping," *J. Systems Integration Special Issue: Computer-Aided Prototyping*, Vol. 6, Nos. 1-2, Mar. 1996, pp. 9-14.
9. V. Berzins and Luqi, *Software Engineering with Abstractions*, Addison-Wesley, New York, 1990.
10. Software Development and Documentation, MIL-STD-498, US Dept. of Defense, Washington, D.C., 1994, http://www.itsi.disa.mil/cfs/std498.html.
11. Luqi, V. Berzins, and R. Yeh, "A Prototyping Language for Real-Time Software," *IEEE Trans. Software Eng.*, Vol. 14, No. 10, 1988, pp. 1409–1423.
12. V. Berzins, *Software Merging and Slicing*, IEEE Computer Soc. Press, Los Alamitos, Calif., 1995.
13. J. Goguen, "Principles of Parameterized Programming," *Software Reusability, Volume I: Concepts and Models*, T. Biggerstaff and A. Perlis, eds., Addison-Wesley, New York, 1989, pp. 159–225.
14. W. Tracz, "Parameterized Programming in LILEANNA," *Proc. 2nd Int'l Workshop Software Reuse*, IEEE Computer Soc. Press, Los Alamitos, Calif., Mar., 1993, pp. 66-78.
15. M. Stickel et al., "Deductive Composition of Astronomical Software from Subroutine Libraries," *Conf. Automated Deduction*, Vol. 12, Springer-Verlag, Heidelberg, Germany, 1994.
16. J. Schwartz and W. Snyder, "Design of Languages for Multimedia Presentations," *Proc. 1994 Monterey Workshop: Increasing Practical Impact of Formal Methods for Computer-Aided Software Development*, Naval Postgraduate School, Monterey, Calif., 1994, pp. 46-55.
17. Luqi and J. Goguen, "Some Suggestions for Progress in Software Analysis, Synthesis and Certification," *Proc. 6th Int'l Conf. Software Eng. and Knowledge Eng.*, Knowledge Systems Inst., Skokie, Ill., 1994, pp. 501–507.
18. E. Engeler, "Structure and Meaning of Elementary Programs," *Lecture Notes in Mathematics*, Vol. 188, Springer-Verlag, New York, 1971, pp. 89-101.
19. V. Berzins and Luqi, "An Introduction to the Specification Language Spec," *IEEE Software*, Mar. 1990, pp. 74-84.

Luqi is a professor of computer science at the Naval Postgraduate School, where she leads a team that is producing computer-aided prototyping tools in a distributed high-performance lab. This team also developed the CAPS rapid-prototyping system. Luqi has also worked on software R&D for the Science Academy of China, the Computer Center at the University of Minnesota, International Software Systems, and others.

Luqi received a PhD in computer science from the University of Minnesota. In addition to chairing or serving on the program committees of more than 40 conferences, she is or has been an associate editor for *IEEE Expert*, *IEEE Software*, the *Journal of Systems Integration*, and *Design and Process World*. She is a senior member of the IEEE.

Joseph Goguen is a professor in the Department of Computer Science and Engineering at the University of California at San Diego and director of the Program in Advanced Manufacturing. Previously, he was a professor at Oxford University, a senior staff scientist at SRI International, and a senior member of the Center for the Study of Language and Information at Stanford University.

Goguen received a BS in mathematics from Harvard University and an MS and a PhD in mathematics from the University of California at Berkeley. He is a member of the IEEE.

Address questions about this article to Luqi at NPS, Computer Science, Monterey, CA 93943; luqi@cs.nps.navy.mil; or to Goguen at Dept. of Computer Science and Engineering, University of California at San Diego, 9500 Gillman Drive, La Jolla, CA 92093-0114; goguen@cs.ucsd.edu.

CHAPTER 5
TESTING

The quality of a software product rests upon two main pillars. One is the inspection process, whereby several engineers look at each artifact (specification, design, code etc.) in detail. The other is the testing process, in which the product itself is exercised. Regardless of the effectiveness of their development process, most companies engage in testing: in many cases, they test intensively *because* the rest of their process is weak. Since inspection and testing are expensive, we need to understand the ways in which they complements each other.

In the papers that follow, Whittaker surveys the testing process and the problems that testers face. Yamaura decribes "how to design practical test cases", citing successes at Hitachi. Chen and Kao review the testing of classes, showing its effect on the reliability of object-oriented programs. Voas asserts that "true product certification…is almost never employed," and calls for "a new generation of certification methodologies." Laitenberger studies the relationship between code inspection and testing, exposing the fact that these activities are not complementary in the way they are often thought to be. Musa describes the emerging discipline of Software Reliability Engineering, which "combines the use of quantitative reliability objectives and operational profiles."

Reprinted from IEEE Software,
Jan./Feb. 2000, pp. 70-79.

What Is Software Testing? And Why Is It So Hard?

Software testing is arguably the least understood part of the development process. Through a four-phase approach, the author shows why eliminating bugs is tricky and why testing is a constant trade-off.

James A. Whittaker, *Florida Institute of Technology*

Virtually all developers know the frustration of having software bugs reported by users. When this happens, developers inevitably ask: How did those bugs escape testing? Countless hours doubtless went into the careful testing of hundreds or thousands of variables and code statements, so how could a bug have eluded such vigilance? The answer requires, first, a closer look at software testing within the context of development. Second, it requires an understanding of the role software testers and developers—two very different functions—play.

Assuming that the bugs users report occur in a software product that really is in error, the answer could be any of these:

- *The user executed untested code.* Because of time constraints, it's not uncommon for developers to release untested code—code in which users can stumble across bugs.
- *The order in which statements were executed in actual use differed from that during testing.* This order can determine whether software works or fails.
- *The user applied a combination of untested input values.* The possible input combinations that thousands of users can make across a given software interface are simply too numerous for testers to apply them all. Testers must make tough decisions about which inputs to test, and sometimes we make the wrong decisions.
- *The user's operating environment was never tested.* We might have known about the environment but had no time to test it. Perhaps we did not (or could not) replicate the user's combination of hardware, peripherals, operating system, and applications in our testing lab. For example, although companies that write networking software are unlikely to create a thousand-node network in their testing lab, users can—and do—create such networks.

Through an overview of the software testing problem and process, this article investigates the problems that testers face and identifies the technical issues that any solution must address. I also survey existing classes of solutions used in practice.

253

0740-7459/00/$10.00 © 2000 IEEE

Readers interested in further study will find the sidebar "Testing Resources" helpful.

Testers and the Testing Process

To plan and execute tests, software testers must consider the software and the function it computes, the inputs and how they can be combined, and the environment in which the software will eventually operate. This difficult, time-consuming process requires technical sophistication and proper planning. Testers must not only have good development skills—testing often requires a great deal of coding—but also be knowledgeable in formal languages, graph theory, and algorithms. Indeed, creative testers have brought many related computing disciplines to bear on testing problems, often with impressive results.

Even simple software presents testers with obstacles, as the sidebar "A Sample Software Testing Problem" shows. To get a clearer view of some of software testing's inherent difficulties, we can approach testing in four phases:

- Modeling the software's environment
- Selecting test scenarios
- Running and evaluating test scenarios
- Measuring testing progress

These phases offer testers a structure in which to group related problems that they must solve before moving on to the next phase.

Every software development organization tests its products, yet delivered software always contains residual defects of varying severity. Sometimes it's hard to imagine how a tester missed a particularly glaring fault. In too many organizations, testers are ill-equipped for the difficult task of testing ever-more-complex software products. Informal surveys of seminar audiences suggest that few of those who perform testing (either as a profession or as an adjunct to development or other roles) have been adequately trained in testing or have software testing books on their desks.

James Whittaker sheds some light on why testing today's software products is so challenging, and he identifies several solid approaches that all testers should be able to thoughtfully apply. The effective tester has a rich toolkit of fundamental testing techniques, understands how the product will be used in its operating environment, has a nose for where subtle bugs might lurk in the product, and employs a bag of tricks to flush them out. The methods described here can help testers provide a sensible answer to the question of what they really mean when they say they are done testing a software system.

—Karl Wiegers and Dave Card, Nuts & Bolts editors

Testing Resources

Literature on software testing has appeared since the beginning of computer science but the paper that defined the field and instigated much of today's research agenda is John Goodenough and Susan Gerhart's classic, "Toward a Theory of Test Data Selection" (*IEEE Trans. Software Eng.*, June 1975). That same year began the prolific research career of William Howden, whose papers and book chapters have helped shape the field (see www-cse.ucsd.edu/users/howden for a complete listing). A complete list of testing researchers along with links to their home pages can be found at Roland Untch's Storm site (www.mtsu.edu/~storm).

The seminal book on testing was Glenford Myers' *The Art of Software Testing* (John Wiley & Sons, 1979), which was the only testing book of note for years. Today, however, a search of amazon.com for "software testing" yields more than 100 matches. Among those books, a handful are considered contenders to succeed Myers'.

Brian Marick's *The Craft of Software Testing* (Prentice Hall, 1995) is my pick for a solid introduction to the subject and is full of good advice for handling tough testing problems. In addition, the author is active at posting updates to the appendices and interacting with his readers on his Web site (www.rstcorp.com/marick). Cem Kaner's *Testing Computer Software* (The Coriolis Group, 1993) is very popular among industry practitioners for its easy reading and good examples. The best-selling testing book is standard issue for new testers at many of the best software testing companies. Boris Beizer's *Black Box Testing* (John Wiley & Sons, 1995) is chock-full of examples and is perhaps the most methodical and prescriptive of the testing books. It also provides a good treatment of using graph techniques to test programs. Finally, I like Bill Hetzel's *The Complete Guide to Software Testing* (John Wiley & Sons, 1993) for its thoroughness. It is one of the few testing books that discusses testing process and life-cycle activity.

If you prefer finding free information on the Web, I suggest visiting the Storm site mentioned earlier and also highly recommend Bret Pettichord's software testing hotlist: an annotated list of links to some of the Web's best testing information (www.io.com/~wazmo/qa). Finally, you might consider participating in Danny Faught's discussion list (swtest-discuss@rsn.hp.com) or the newsgroup comp.software.testing.

254

A Sample Software Testing Problem

A small program displays a window with the current system time and date, which can be changed by typing new values into the edit fields as shown in Figure A. The program is terminated by the Alt-F4 keystroke sequence, and the Tab key moves between fields.

In deciding how to test this (or any) program, a software tester considers the environment in which the software operates; the source code that defines the software; and the interface between the software and its environment.

Environment

Software exists in an environment in which other entities (users) stimulate it with inputs. The software provides those users with output. This example program has two input sources, the obvious human user who supplies inputs from the set {*time*, *date*, Tab, Alt-F4}, and the operating system "user" that supplies memory for the program to run and supplies the current system time and date as an application service.

A diligent tester will consider the valid inputs from each of these sources as well as invalid and unexpected inputs. What if the human user types other Alt-sequences or keystrokes outside the acceptable input set? What if available memory is insufficient for the program to run? What if the system clock malfunctions? Testers must consider these possibilities, select the most important ones, and figure out how to simulate these conditions.

Testers next think about how users interact in ways that might cause the software to fail. What happens, for example, when some other program changes the time and date—does our application properly reflect this change? Today's multitasking operating systems demand that testers think through such scenarios.

Source code

The code for this application might have a While loop similar to the one in Figure B.

How many test cases does it take to fully cover, or exercise, the source code? To determine this, we evaluate each con-

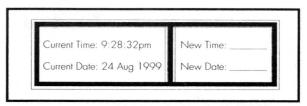

Figure A. Current system time and date, along with fields for entering new values.

dition to both true and false by means of a truth table. We thus execute not only each source statement, but we also cover each possible branch in the software. The truth table in Figure C documents each possible combination of conditions in the While loop, the three parts of the Case statement, and the nested If statements.

```
Input = GetInput()
While (Input ≠ Alt-F4) do
   Case (Input = Time)
      If ValidHour(Time.Hour) and ValidMin(Time.Minute) and
         ValidSec(Time.Second) and ValidAP(Time.AmPm)
      Then
         UpdateSystemTime(Time)
      Else
         DisplayError("Invalid Time.")
      Endif
   Case (Input = Date)
      If ValidDay(Date.Day) and ValidMnth(Date.Month) and
         ValidYear(Date.Year)
      Then
         UpdateSystemDate(Date)
      Else
         DisplayError("Invalid Date.")
      Endif
   Case (Input = Tab)
      If TabLocation = 1
      Then
         MoveCursor(2)
         TabLocation = 2
      Else
         MoveCursor(1)
         TabLocation = 1
      Endif
   Endcase
   Input = GetInput()
Enddo
```

Figure B. Sample source code demonstrating a While loop.

Phase I: Modeling the Software's Environment

A tester's task is to simulate interaction between software and its environment. Testers must identify and simulate the interfaces that a software system uses and enumerate the inputs that can cross each interface. This might be the most fundamental

These eight possible cases cover only statements and branches. When we consider how each complex condition in the If statements actually gets evaluated, we must add several more cases. Although there is only one way for these statements to

Possible cases	While	Case 1	If 1	Case 2	If 2	Case 3	If 3
1	F	–	–	–	–	–	–
2	T	T	T	–	–	–	–
3	T	T	F	–	–	–	–
4	T	F	–	T	T	–	–
5	T	F	–	T	F	–	–
6	T	F	–	F	–	T	T
7	T	F	–	F	–	T	F
8	T	F	–	F	–	F	–

Figure C. A truth table such as this helps keep track of all possible combinations of inputs.

evaluate true (that is, every condition must be true for the statement to be true), there is more than one way for the first two If statements to evaluate false. In fact, we'd find that there are $2^x - 1$ ways (where x is the number of conditions in the statement).

Using this logic, there are $2^4 - 1 = 15$ ways to execute the third test and $2^3 - 1 = 7$ ways to execute the fifth (each of these cases appears in bold, above), for a total of 28 test cases. Now, imagine how many test cases would be required to test a software system with a few hundred thousand lines of code and thousands of such complex conditions to evaluate. It's easy to see why software is commonly released with unexecuted source code.

In addition to covering the source code, testers also must think about missing code. The fact that the Case statement has no default case could present problems.

Interface

Besides testing the environment and the source code, we must also determine the values assigned to the specific data that crosses the interface from the environment to the software under test; for example, Time and Date. Variable input is difficult to test because many variable types can assume a wide range of possible values. How many different times are there in a day? The combinatorics aren't encouraging: 12 hours × 60 minutes × 60 seconds × 2 am/pm for a total of 86,400 different input values. That's just the valid values; invalid values like 29 o'clock must also be tested.

Next we must consider the possible legal and illegal values for the date field, and finally, decide on specific combinations of time and date to enter simultaneously—like midnight of the year 1999. This is enough to overwhelm even the biggest testing budget.

Finally, we must determine which inputs will be applied consecutively during testing. This is, perhaps, the most subtle and elusive aspect of testing. Obviously, the first input to be applied is the one that invokes the software. Next, we must choose to apply one of the other inputs, choose another to follow that, and so on until we exit the software. Much can happen during such sequencing. Will the software accept several consecutive Tab keys? Will it handle a change to the Time field only (leaving the Date field unchanged), the Date field only, and also changes to both? The only way to find out is to apply each of these cases separately.

How many cases are there? Since the While loop is unbounded, there is no upper limit. Testers have two ways to handle infinite input domains. First, we might isolate infinite input subsets into separate subdomains,[1] decomposing the problem into smaller problems.

Second, as in development, we can abstract; here, inputs into *events*. Rather than deal with specific physical inputs such as mouse clicks and keystrokes, testers create abstract events that encompass a number of physical input sequences. We did this in the example above by creating the inputs *Time* and *Date*. During analysis of the input domain, testers can use these abstractions to think through the problem. When the test scenario is actually implemented, testers can replace the abstraction with one of its possible physical instantiations. (I use "scenario" to mean simply "instructions about what things to test." A more precise term is "test case," which implies exact specification of initial conditions, inputs to apply, and expected outputs.)

Reference

1. E.J. Weyuker and T.J. Ostrand, "Theories of Program Testing and the Application of Revealing Subdomains," *IEEE Trans. Software Eng.*, Vol. 6, No. 3, May 1980, pp. 236–246.

issue that testers face, and it can be difficult, considering the various file formats, communication protocols, and third-party (application programming interfaces) available. Four common interfaces are as follows:

- *Human interfaces* include all common methods for people to communicate with software. Most prominent is the GUI but older designs like the command line interface and the menu-driven interface are still in use. Possible input mechanisms to consider are mouse clicks, keyboard events, and input from other devices. Testers then decide how to organize this data to understand how to assemble it into an effective test.

- *Software interfaces,* called APIs, are how software uses an operating system, database, or runtime library. The services these applications provide are modeled as test inputs. The challenge for testers is to check not only the expected but also the unexpected services. For example, all developers expect the operating system to save files for them. The service that they neglect is the operating system's informing them that the storage medium is full. Even error messages must be tested.

- *File system interfaces* exist whenever software reads or writes data to external files. Developers must write lots of error-checking code to determine if the file contains appropriate data and formatting. Thus, testers must build or generate files with content that is both legal and illegal, and files that contain a variety of text and formatting.

- *Communication interfaces* allow direct access to physical devices (such as device drivers, controllers, and other embedded systems) and require a communication protocol. To test such software, testers must be able to generate both valid and invalid protocol streams. Testers must assemble—and submit to the software under test—many different combinations of commands and data, in the proper packet format.

Next, testers must understand the user interaction that falls outside the control of the software under test, since the consequences can be serious if the software is not prepared. Examples of situations testers should address are as follows:

- Using the operating system, one user deletes a file that another user has open. What will happen the next time the software tries to access that file?
- A device gets rebooted in the middle of a stream of communication. Will the software realize this and react properly or just hang?
- Two software systems compete for duplicate services from an API. Will the API correctly service both?

Each application's unique environment can result in a significant number of user interactions to test.

Considerations

When an interface presents problems of infinite size or complexity, testers face two difficulties: They must carefully select values for any variable input, and they must decide how to sequence inputs. In selecting values, testers determine the values of individual variables and assign interesting value combinations when a program accepts multiple variables as input.

Testers most often use the *boundary value partitioning* technique[1] for selecting single values for variables at or around boundaries. For example, testing the minimum, maximum, and zero values for a signed integer is a commonly accepted idea as well as values surrounding each of these partitions—for example, 1 and –1 (which surround the zero boundary). The values between boundaries are treated as the same number; whether we use 16 or 16,000 makes no difference to the software under test.

A more complex issue is choosing values for multiple variables processed simultaneously that could potentially affect each other. Testers must consider the entire cross product of value combinations. For two integers, we consider both positive, both negative, one positive and one zero, and so forth.[2]

In deciding how to sequence inputs, testers have a sequence generation problem. Testers treat each physical input and abstract event as symbols in the alphabet of a formal language and define a model of that language. A model lets testers visualize the set of possible tests to see how each test fits the big picture. The most common model is a graph or state diagram, although many variations exist. Other popular models include regular expressions and grammars, tools from language theory. Less-used models are stochastic processes and genetic algorithms. The model is a representation that describes how input and event symbols are combined to make syntactically valid words and sentences.

These sentences are sequences of inputs that can be applied to the software under test. For example, consider the input `Filemenu. Open`, which invokes a file selection dialog box; `filename`, which represents the selection (with mouse clicks, perhaps) of an existing file, and `ClickOpen` and `ClickCancel`,

257

which represent button presses. The sequence `Filemenu.Open filename ClickOpen` is legal, as are many others. The sequence `ClickCancel Filemenu.Open` is impossible because the cancel button cannot be pressed until the dialog box has been invoked. The model of the formal language can make such a distinction between sequences.

Text editor example

We can represent legal uses of the file selection dialog in, for example, a text editor with the regular expression:

```
Filemenu.Open filename*   (ClickOpen |
ClickCancel)
```

in which the asterisk represents the Kleene closure operator indicating that the `filename` action can occur zero or more times. This expression indicates that the first input received is `Filemenu.Open` followed by zero or more selections of a filename (with a combination of mouse clicks and keyboard entries), then either the Open or Cancel button is pressed. This simple model represents every combination of inputs that can happen, whether they make sense or not.

To fully model the software environment for the entire text editor, we would need to represent sequences for the user interface and the operating system interface. Furthermore, we would need a description of legal and corrupt files to fully investigate file system interaction. Such a formidable task would require the liberal use of decomposition and abstraction.

Phase 2: Selecting Test Scenarios

Many domain models and variable partitions represent an infinite number of test scenarios, each of which costs time and money. Only a subset can be applied in any realistic software development schedule, so how does a smart tester choose? Is 17 a better integer than 34? How many times should a filename be selected before pressing the Open button?

These questions, which have many answers, are being actively researched. Testers, however, prefer an answer that relates to coverage of source code or its input domain. Testers strive for *coverage*: covering code statements (executing each source line at least once) and covering inputs (applying each externally generated event). These are the minimum criteria that testers use to judge the completeness of their work; therefore, the test set that many testers choose is the one that meets their coverage goals.

But if code and input coverage were sufficient, released products would have very few bugs. Concerning the code, it isn't individual code statements that interest testers but *execution paths*: sequences of code statements representing an execution of the software. Unfortunately, there are an infinite number of paths. Concerning the input domain, it isn't the individual inputs that interest testers but *input sequences* that, taken as a whole, represent scenarios to which the software must respond. There are an infinite number of these, too.

Testers sort through these infinite sets to arrive at the best possible *test data adequacy criteria*, which are meant to adequately and economically represent any of the infinite sets. "Best" and "adequately" are subjective; testers typically seek the set that will find the most bugs. (High and low bug counts, and their interpretation, are discussed later). Many users and quality assurance professionals are interested in having testers evaluate *typical use* scenarios—things that will occur most often in the field. Such testing ensures that the software works as specified and that the most frequently occurring bugs will have been detected.

For example, consider the text editor example again. To test typical use, we would focus on editing and formatting since that is what real users do most. However, to find bugs, a more likely place to look is in the harder-to-code features like figure drawing and table editing.

Execution path test criteria

Test data adequacy criteria concentrate on either execution path coverage or input sequence coverage but rarely both. The most common execution path selection criteria focus on paths that cover control structures. For example,

- Select a set of tests that cause each source statement to be executed at least once.
- Select a set of tests that cause each branching structure (If, Case, While, and so on) to be evaluated with each of its possible values.

However, control flow is only one aspect of the source code. What software actually

> "Best" and "adequately" are subjective; testers typically seek the set that will find the most bugs.

does is move data from one location to another. The *dataflow* family of test data adequacy criteria[3] describe coverage of this data. For example,

- Select a set of tests that cause each data structure to be initialized and then subsequently used.

Finally, *fault seeding*, which claims more attention from researchers than practitioners, is interesting.[1] In this method, errors are intentionally inserted (seeded) into the source code. Test scenarios are then designed to find those errors. Ideally, by finding seeded errors, the tester will also find real errors. Thus, a criterion like the following is possible:

- Select a set of tests that expose each of the seeded faults.

Input domain test criteria

Criteria for input domain coverage range from simple coverage of an interface to more complex statistical measurement.

- Select a set of tests that contain each physical input.
- Select a set of tests that cause each interface control (window, menu, button, and so on) to be stimulated.

The *discrimination* criterion[4] requires random selection of input sequences until they statistically represent the entire infinite input domain.

- Select a set of tests that have the same statistical properties as the entire input domain.
- Select a set of paths that are likely to be executed by a typical user.

Summary

Testing researchers are actively studying algorithms to select minimal test sets that satisfy criteria for execution paths and input domains. Most researchers would agree that it is prudent to use multiple criteria when making important release decisions. Experiments comparing test data adequacy criteria are needed, as are new criteria. However, for the present, testers should be aware which criteria are built into their methodology and understand the inherent limitations of these criteria when they report results.

We'll revisit test data adequacy criteria in the fourth phase, test measurement, because the criteria also serve as measures of test completeness.

Phase 3: Running and Evaluating Test Scenarios

Having identified suitable tests, testers convert them to executable form, often as code, so that the resulting test scenarios simulate typical user action. Because manually applying test scenarios is labor-intensive and error-prone, testers try to automate the test scenarios as much as possible. In many environments, automated application of inputs through code that simulates users is possible, and tools are available to help.

Complete automation requires simulation of each input source and output destination of the entire operational environment. Testers often include data-gathering code in the simulated environment as test hooks or asserts. This code provides information about internal variables, object properties, and so forth. These hooks are removed when the software is released, but during test scenario execution they provide valuable information that helps testers identify failures and isolate faults.

Scenario evaluation, the second part of this phase, is easily stated but difficult to do (much less automate). Evaluation involves the comparison of the software's actual output, resulting from test scenario execution, to its expected output as documented by a specification. The specification is assumed correct; deviations are failures.

In practice, this comparison is difficult to achieve. Theoretically, comparison (to determine equivalence) of two arbitrary, Turing-computable functions is unsolvable. Returning to the text editor example, if the output is supposed to be "highlight a misspelled word," how can we determine that each instance of misspelling has been detected? Such difficulty is the reason why the actual-versus-expected output comparison is usually performed by a human *oracle*: a tester who visually monitors screen output and painstakingly analyzes output data. (See the "Testing Terminology" sidebar for an explanation of other common testing terms).

259

Two approaches to evaluating your test

In dealing with the problems of test evaluation, researchers are pursuing two approaches: formalism, and embedded test code.

Formalism chiefly involves the hard work of formalizing the way specifications are written and the way that designs and code are derived from them.[5] Both object-oriented and structured development contain mechanisms for formally expressing specifications to simplify the task of comparing expected and actual behavior. Industry has typically shied away from formal methods; nonetheless, a good specification, even an informal one, is still extremely helpful. Without a specification, testers are likely to find only the most obvious bugs. Furthermore, the absence of a specification wastes significant time when testers report unspecified features as bugs.

There are essentially two types of embedded test code. The simplest type is test code that exposes certain internal data objects or states that make it easier for an external oracle to judge correctness. As implemented, such functionality is invisible to users. Testers can access test code results through, for example, a test API or a debugger.

A more complex type of embedded code features self-testing programs.[6] Sometimes this involves coding multiple solutions to the problem and having one solution check the other, or writing inverse routines that undo each operation. If an operation is performed and then undone, the resulting software state should be equivalent to its preoperational state. In this situation, the oracle is not perfect; there could be a bug in both operations where each bug masks the other.

Regression testing

After testers submit successfully reproduced failures to development, developers generally create a new version of the software (in which the bug has been supposedly removed). Testing progresses through subsequent software versions until one is determined to be fit for release. The question is, how much retesting (called *regression testing*) of version n is necessary using the tests that were run against version $n - 1$?

Any specific fix can (a) fix only the problem that was reported, (b) fail to fix the problem, (c) fix the problem but break something that was previously working, or (d) fail to fix the problem *and* break some-

Software testing is often equated to finding bugs. However, test scenarios that do not reveal failures are also informative, so I offer this definition:

Software testing is the process of executing a software system to determine whether it matches its specification and executes in its intended environment.

The fact that the system is being *executed* distinguishes testing from code reviews, in which uncompiled source code is read and analyzed statically (usually by developers). Testing, on the other hand, requires a running executable.

A specification is a crucial artifact to support testing. It defines correct behavior so that incorrect behavior is easier to identify. Incorrect behavior is a software *failure*. Failures are caused by *faults* in the source code, which are often referred to as *defects* or *bugs*. The *oracle* compares actual output with specified output to identify failures. Generally, the code developer diagnoses the causal fault.

Software can also fail by not satisfying environmental constraints that fall outside the specification. For example, if the code takes too much memory, executes too slowly, or if the product works on one operating system but not another, these are considered failures.

Software testing is classified according to the manner in which testers perform the first two phases of the testing process. The scope of the first phase, modeling the software's environment, determines whether the tester is doing *unit, integration,* or *system* testing.

Unit testing tests individual software components or a collection of components. Testers define the input domain for the units in question and ignore the rest of the system. Unit testing sometimes requires the construction of throwaway driver code and stubs and is often performed in a debugger.

Integration testing tests multiple components that have each received prior and separate unit testing. In general, the focus is on the subset of the domain that represents communication between the components.

System testing tests a collection of components that constitutes a deliverable product. Usually, the entire domain must be considered to satisfy the criteria for a system test.

The second phase of testing, test selection, determines what *type* of testing is being done. There are two main types:

Functional testing requires the selection of test scenarios without regard to source code structure. Thus, test selection methods and test data adequacy criteria, described in the main text, must be based on attributes of the specification or operational environment and not on attributes of the code or data structures. Functional testing is also called *specification-based testing, behavioral testing,* and *black-box testing.*

Structural testing requires that inputs be based solely on the structure of the source code or its data structures. Structural testing is also called *code-based testing* and *white-box testing.*

thing else. Given these possibilities, it would seem prudent to rerun every test from version $n - 1$ on version n before testing anything new, although such a practice is generally cost-prohibitive.[7] Moreover, new software versions often feature extensive new functionality, in addition to the bug fixes, so the regression tests would take time away from testing new code. To save resources, then, testers work closely with developers to prioritize and minimize regression tests.

Another drawback to regression testing is that these tests can (temporarily) alter the purpose of the test data adequacy criteria selected in the earlier test selection phase. When performing regression tests, testers seek only to show the absence of a fault and to force the application to exhibit specific behavior. The outcome is that the test data adequacy criteria, which until now guided test selection, are ignored. Instead, testers must ensure that a reliable fix to the code has been made.

Related concerns

Ideally, developers will write code with testing in mind. If the code will be hard to test and verify, then it should be rewritten to make it more testable. Likewise, a testing methodology should be judged by its contribution to solving automation and oracle problems. Too many methodologies provide little guidance in either area.

Another concern for testers while running and verifying tests is the coordination of debugging activity with developers. As failures are identified by testers and diagnosed by developers, two issues arise: failure reproduction and test scenario re-execution.

Failure reproduction is not the no-brainer it might seem. The obvious answer is, of course, to simply rerun the offending test and observe the errant behavior again, although rerunning a test does not guarantee that the exact same conditions will be created. Scenario re-execution requires that we know the exact state of the operating system and any companion software—for example, client–server applications would require reproduction of the conditions surrounding both the client and the server. Additionally, we must know the state of test automation, peripheral devices, and any other background application running locally or over the network that could affect the application being tested. It is no wonder that one of the most commonly heard phrases in a testing lab is, "Well, it was behaving differently before...."

Phase 4: Measuring Testing Progress

Suppose I am a tester and one day my manager comes to me and asks, "What's the status of your testing?" Testers are often asked this question but are not well equipped to answer it. The reason is that the state of the practice in test measurement is to count things. We count the number of inputs we've applied, the percentage of code we've covered, and the number of times we've invoked the application. We count the number of times we've terminated the application successfully, the number of failures we found, and so on. Interpreting such counts is difficult—is finding lots of failures good news or bad? The answer could be either. A high bug count could mean that testing was thorough and very few bugs remain. Or, it could mean that the software simply has lots of bugs and, even though many have been exposed, lots of them remain.

Since counting measures yield very little insight about the progress of testing, many testers augment this data by answering questions designed to ascertain structural and functional testing completeness. For example, to check for structural completeness, testers might ask these questions:

- Have I tested for common programming errors?[8]
- Have I exercised all of the source code?[1]
- Have I forced all the internal data to be initialized and used?[3]
- Have I found all seeded errors?[1]

To check for functional completeness, testers might ask these questions:

- Have I thought through the ways in which the software can fail and selected tests that show it doesn't?[9]
- Have I applied all the inputs?[1]
- Have I completely explored the state space of the software?[4]
- Have I run all the scenarios that I expect a user to execute?[10]

These questions—essentially, test data adequacy criteria—are helpful to testers; however, determining when to stop testing, determining when a product is ready to release, is more complex. Testers want quantitative measures of the number of bugs left in the software and of the probability that any of these bugs will be discovered in the field. If testers can achieve such a measure, they know to stop testing. We can approach the quantitative problem structurally and functionally.

Testability

From a structural standpoint, Jeffrey Voas has proposed *testability*[11] as a way to determine an application's testing complexi-

261

ty. The idea that the number of lines of code determines the software's testing difficulty is obsolete; the issue is much murkier. This is where testability comes into play. If a product has high testability, it is easy to test and, consequently, easier to find bugs in. We can then monitor testing and observe that because bugs are fewer, it is unlikely that many undiscovered ones exist. Low testability would require many more tests to draw the same conclusions; we would expect that bugs are harder to find. Testability is a compelling concept but in its infancy; no data on its predictive ability has yet been published.

Reliability models

How long will the software run before it fails? How expensive will the software be to maintain? It is certainly better to find this out while you still have the software in your testing lab.

From a functional standpoint, *reliability models*[10]—mathematical models of test scenarios and failure data that attempt to predict future failure patterns based on past data—are well established. These models thus attempt to predict how software will behave in the field based on how it behaved during testing. To accomplish this, most reliability models require the specification of an *operational profile*, a description of how users are expected to apply inputs. To compute the probability of failure, these models make some assumptions about the underlying probability distribution that governs failure occurrences. Researchers and practitioners alike have expressed skepticism that such profiles can be accurately assembled. Furthermore, the assumptions made by common reliability models have not been theoretically or experimentally verified except in specific application domains. Nevertheless, successful case studies have shown these models to be credible.

they tell you about the quality of your software. Ignoring them might be the most expensive mistake you ever make.

Testing researchers likewise face challenges. Software companies are anxious to fund good research ideas, but the demand for more practical, less academic work is strong. The time to tie academic research to real industry products is now. We'll all come out winners. 🐧

References

1. G.J. Myers, *The Art of Software Testing,* John Wiley & Sons, New York, 1976.
2. T.J. Ostrand and M.J. Balcer, "The Category-Partition Technique for Specifying and Generating Functional Tests," *Comm. ACM,* Vol. 31, No. 6, June 1988, pp. 676–686.
3. S. Rapps and E.J. Weyuker, "Selecting Software Test Data Using Dataflow Information," *IEEE Trans. Software Eng.,* Vol. 11, No. 4, Apr. 1985, pp. 367–375.
4. J.A. Whittaker and M.G. Thomason, "A Markov Chain Model for Statistical Software Testing," *IEEE Trans. Software Eng.,* Vol. 20, No. 10, Oct. 1994, pp. 812–824.
5. D.K. Peters and D.L. Parnas, "Using Test Oracles Generated from Program Documentation," *IEEE Trans. Software Eng.,* Vol. 24, No. 3, Mar. 1998, pp. 161–173.
6. D. Knuth, "Literate Programming," *The Computer J.,* Vol. 27, No. 2, May 1984, pp. 97–111.
7. G. Rothermel and M.J. Harrold, "A Safe, Efficient Algorithm for Regression Test Selection," *Proc. IEEE Software Maintenance Conf.,* IEEE Computer Soc. Press, Los Alamitos, Calif., 1993, pp. 358–367.
8. B. Beizer, *Software Testing Techniques,* Van Nostrand Reinhold, New York, 1990.
9. J.B. Goodenough and S.L. Gerhart, "Toward a Theory of Test Data Selection," *IEEE Trans. Software Eng.,* Vol. 2, No. 2, June 1975, pp. 156–173.
10. J.D. Musa, "Software Reliability Engineered Testing," *Computer,* Vol. 29, No. 11, Nov. 1996, pp. 61–68.
11. J.M. Voas, "PIE: A Dynamic Failure-Based Technique," *IEEE Trans. Software Eng.,* Vol. 18, No. 8, Aug. 1992, pp. 717–727.

Software companies face serious challenges in testing their products, and these challenges are growing bigger as software grows more complex. The first and most important thing to be done is to recognize the complex nature of testing and take it seriously. My advice: Hire the smartest people you can find, help them get the tools and training they need to learn their craft, and listen to them when

About the Author

James A. Whittaker is an associate professor of computer science at the Florida Institute of Technology, Melbourne, and chair of the software engineering program. He is the founder and codirector of the Center for Software Engineering Research, an industry-sponsored university research lab dedicated to advancing software engineering theory and practice. His research interests are in software engineering, particularly testing and coding. He stays as far away from software process as possible. He holds a PhD in computer science from the University of Tennessee and is a member of the ACM and the IEEE Computer Society. Contact him at Florida Tech, Computer Science Dept., 150 West University Blvd., Melbourne, FL 32901; jw@cs.fit.edu.

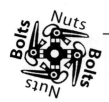

Reprinted from IEEE Software,
Nov./Dec. 1998, pp. 30-36.

Programmers can build high-quality tests by
following certain basic steps, outlined here. The
author also discusses the cost, time, and personnel
resources required for debugging and testing.

HOW TO DESIGN
PRACTICAL
TEST CASES

Tsuneo Yamaura, Hitachi Software Engineering

t Hitachi Software, our software has attained such high quality that only
0.02 percent of all bugs in a software program emerge at the user's site.[1]
If a typical project—10 engineers working for 12 months to develop
100,000 lines of code—contains 1,000 bugs, at most one will surface at
the user's site. We do not use sophisticated tools or state-of-the-art methodology—
we simply test programs and fix the bugs detected.

Our secret is that we document all test cases before we start debugging and testing. The written test cases provide significant advantages, and all our quality assurance activities start from this point.

Figure 1 shows the percentage of defects detected at each stage in a 1990 Hitachi software development project. (More recent data, still being collected, will not show drastic changes.) Of all the bugs detected since the project's inception, only 0.02 percent came out at the customer's site. Such high quality could never have been attained if we had not employed written test cases.

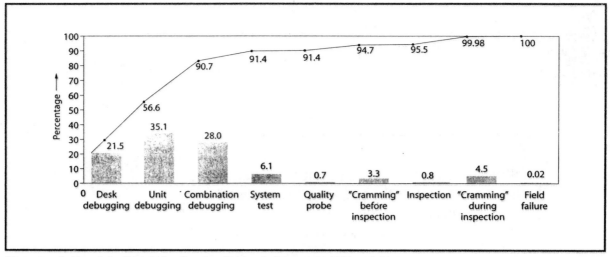

FIGURE 1. Bug detection during the development phases of a 1990 project.

DOCUMENTING TEST CASES

Documented test cases can benefit your development process in several key ways:

♦ Designing test cases gives you a chance to analyze the specification from a different angle.

♦ You can repeat the same test cases.

♦ Somebody else can execute the test cases for you.

♦ You can easily validate the quality of the test cases.

♦ You can estimate the quality of the target software early on.

A new viewpoint

Test cases provide another rendition of the functional specification. Designing the test cases will give you pause: "Aha, I didn't consider such and such conditions. Was that specification really correct?" The bugs revealed in this way would be harder to detect and would require enormous time and money to fix later, such as in the system integration phase. Roughly speaking, you can catch 10 percent of a system's bugs when you are designing the test cases—a significant advantage.

Repeating test scenarios

You can easily reiterate the same test cases if everything is documented. Reusing test cases lets you reproduce bugs, which helps ensure that detected bugs are fixed properly.

Passing the test along

If you specify the test conditions, input data set, and expected outcome, you can ask somebody else to execute the test—which can prove particularly valuable on a project running late. Adding programmers to a project that is behind schedule frequently causes more delays because the project engineers must spare precious time to educate the new personnel. If the test cases are properly documented, however, the new staff can run the test cases as written.

Validating test case quality

You must, of course, test the test cases to ensure that they visit all the features implemented in the software. Check whether they are well-balanced among normal, abnormal, and boundary cases, and evaluate their overall sufficiency. Ad lib or random testing will never suffice—if you do not document the test cases clearly, you cannot precisely measure their quality metrics and success.

Estimating software quality

If the test cases are properly developed, you can easily estimate the quality of the target software in the midst of debugging by applying the fish-in-the-pond analogy: If you detect four bugs after executing 100 test cases out of 1,000, common sense says the software will carry about 40 bugs altogether. State-of-the-art software reliability theory is not that simple, but this quick and easy estimation gives you a rough idea of the software's quality.

SCHEDULE, COST, AND PERSONNEL

You see how useful it is to document the test cases. There is no free lunch, however—you must invest time, money, and personnel to enjoy the advantages. The question is how much you will need.

Here is a rough idea, with some statistical data.

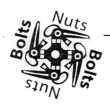

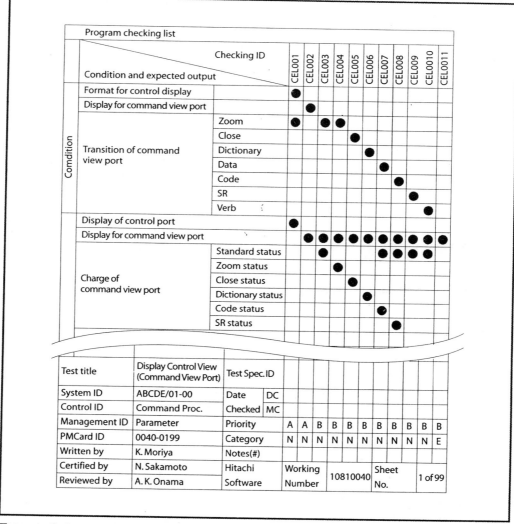

FIGURE 2. A matrix-based test sheet.

Assume that an average 12-month project with 10 engineers develops C-based software with 100,000 lines of code. An average project might apportion 12 months among the following phases:

♦ requirement specification: two months
♦ designing: three months
♦ coding: two months
♦ debugging: three months
♦ testing (handled by the quality assurance team): two months

At Hitachi Software, when the project completes debugging, the product is sent to the QA department where testers spend approximately two months evaluating whether the software is shippable. Since the testers must be unbiased and understand the customer's requirements, they never reuse the programmers' test suites; they redesign all the test items from scratch.

The test-case density—"how many test cases do we need?"—is one of the most critical engineering issues in testing. Too few test cases will leave easy bugs undetected, and too many will run short of time.

Our 30-year empirical study based on trial and error found that the proper test case density converges on the standard of one test case per 10 to 15

LOC. This means that a product with 100,000 LOC needs approximately 10,000 test cases—1,000 per programmer. Of 1,000 test cases, approximately 100 will be checked in the code inspection phase, and all of them will be checked in the machine debugging phase (which means that the first 100 cases for code inspection overlap with the machine debugging). Based on our study, these figures do not look unrealistic. An average programmer takes two weeks to execute 100 test cases in the code inspection phase (10 cases per day), and two months to execute 1,000 test cases in the machine debugging phase (25 cases per day). Ten programmers will take two weeks to design the test cases (assuming 100 test cases a day per programmer), or 3.8 percent of the entire project.

STEPS FOR DEBUGGING AND TESTING

Systematic testing follows six core procedures:
1. Design a set of test cases.
2. Check the test cases.
3. Do code inspection based on the test cases.
4. Do machine debugging based on the test cases.
5. Collect quality-related data during debugging.
6. Analyze the data during debugging.

Designing test cases

There is only one rule in designing test cases: cover all the features, but do not make too many test cases. We use a matrix-based test sheet to visit all the necessary functions, and apply equivalent partitioning and boundary analysis to eliminate redundant test cases. When needed, we use other test methods based on a state transition model, decision table, or dataflow model.

Figure 2 illustrates the matrix-based test sheet we employ. The first step is to itemize all the conditions, then consider all the possible combinations. This step will reveal considerable defects, because designing the test cases in this manner means redesigning the software based on another method, namely the decision table.

Note that all the test cases in Figure 1 have the corresponding expected outputs, without which you cannot reveal bugs while designing the test cases. You also need to indicate if the test case checks a normal, abnormal, or boundary case; this is essential to evaluate the quality of the test cases.

And you must specify the testing priority, which shows the testing order.

In the early 1970s, we employed natural language to describe the stepwise conditioning of the test cases. For example:

♦ *When the person in the form is 65 years or older:*
♦ *When the person's annual income is $10,000 or less:*
♦ *When the person lives in area A-1: ...* (the nesting of the conditions goes deeper)

Since this approach frequently caused us to overlook various combinations of the conditions (or holes in the test items), we migrated to matrix-based test design in the mid-1970s.

Equivalent partitioning,[2] a well-known testing technique, uses a single value to represent the same domain. Suppose, for example, an admission fee varies by age, such that there is no fee for age 6 or under, a $5 fee for 12 years old or younger, $8 for 18 years or under, and $10 for 19 and above. The test cases you pick up from each domain can be "age 2" for the domain of $0 \le age \le 6$, "age 10" for $6 < age \le 12$, "age 14" for $12 < age \le 18$, and "age 43" for $18 < age$. Picking up "age 43" and "age 50" is redundant unless each represents a different domain in terms of the white-box testing.

Boundary analysis[2] is another well-known testing technique whose core idea is that bugs tend to exist on the borders of domains. Thus, in the admission fee example above, you need to test the ages of –1, 0, 6, 7, 12, 13, 18, and 19.

We extracted the following test case design criteria (or lessons) based on our empirical study.

♦ As I mentioned earlier, our optimized, pragmatic density of the test cases is one per 10 to 15 LOC. A language processor generally needs more test cases (approximately one test case per eight to 12 LOC) than a batch program, and an online program requires more (one per five to 10 LOC) than a language processor.

♦ From the viewpoint of white-box testing, the number of IF statements serves as a better index than the LOC because it relates directly to the number of executable paths in the program. The most error-prone structure in software is a loop. For white-box testing, you should test the iteration of 0, 1, 2, average number, max – 1, max, and max + 1.

♦ The basic and normal cases must constitute less than 60 percent of the test case set, with the boundary and limitation cases at least 10 percent, the error cases 15 percent, and the environmental test cases (whether the program runs on different

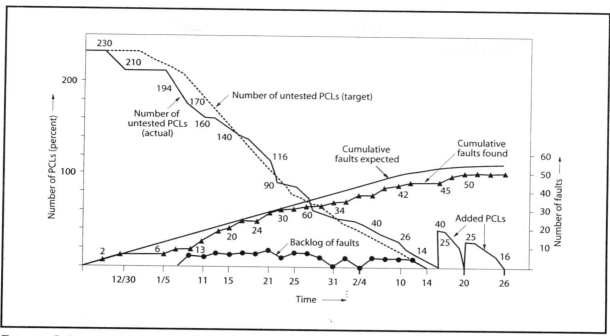

FIGURE 3. An example of test execution and bug detection.

operating systems, and performance requirements) 15 percent.

♦ As a finishing touch, we run a 48-hour continuous-operation test. All you have to provide is a test suite that unlimitedly reiterates the same basic functions. This test reveals many bugs related to a memory leakage, deadlock, and connection time-out.

Several tips can help you design successful and effective test cases:

♦ Do not design too many test cases, in particular for syntax testing. If you consider the error combinations of half a dozen parameters, you will easily end up with thousands of test cases, which may take several months to execute. The reality is, somebody—most likely you—must run the test. Design it so it can be completed within the planned period.

♦ Refer to previous projects that developed similar software. If they have test suites, by all means get them—you may not be able to reuse them, but they will give you insight.

♦ Indicate which test cases you will execute in the code inspection phase, and which in machine checking. It is advisable to use approximately 10 percent of test cases for code inspection; this can help you start tracing the software's main streets.

♦ A software engineer tends to make too many test cases for the features that he or she understands well and too few for unfamiliar functions. Compare the number of test cases with the LOC or number of IFs to reveal such an anomaly.

Checking test case quality

Test cases, of course, must be tested. When your test case design is complete, evaluate its properness and correctness based on

♦ whether the test cases cover all features;

♦ the balance between normal, abnormal, boundary, and environment test cases;

♦ the balance between code inspection (for checking hard-to-provide conditions and for enabling the detection of bugs that can be easily and effectively fixed) and machine execution (which eats up testing time);

♦ the balance between black-box and white-box testing; and

♦ the balance between functional tests and performance tests.

Code inspection

Our empirical study indicates that 21.5 percent of all bugs are detected in this phase. Of this number, I roughly estimate that code inspection reveals half, and test case designing reveals the rest. I recommend assigning 25 to 33 percent of the debugging time to check 10 percent of the test cases as code inspection.

Record the defects detected during this phase. This will tell you what bugs are left unfixed, where and of what type the bugs will tend to be, what module carries more defects, and so on. When you execute a test case successfully, put the completed date on the test case sheet.

267

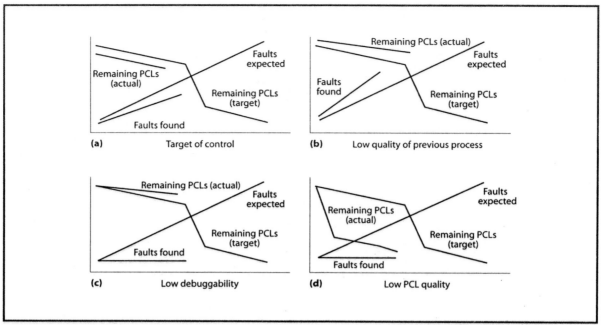

FIGURE 4. Diagnostics of test progress.

Machine debugging

This step is simple—just run a test case on the actual machine (or simulator) and keep a record of the result: passed or failed. When a test case reveals a defect, fill out a bug report to record information such as who revealed what, when, the symptom of the bug, and the test case ID. Without such information, you may end up thinking you have already fixed the bug—until it resurfaces.

Before starting machine debugging, implement the test cases as a test suite if possible. A test suite is a program that automatically runs test cases and compares the actual outputs with the expected ones to determine "pass" or "fail." This provides many advantages. Although the test suite implementation takes time (the test suite engine is small—more than 95 percent of the work goes to providing execution commands and defining the expected results), you save enormous time once it is built by letting your computer debug the programs while you are away. Stupid but costly typing errors can be completely eliminated, and you can use the test suite as a functional degradation checker in the final stage of software development when you have to make the scheduled shipment date but the program still needs modification and bug fixing.

You must remember one important thing when implementing the test suite: make sure it reinitializes all data when it goes on to the next test case. If a test case cannot be executed because a bug in the previous case terminates the test suite, the early bug may overshadow the consequent bugs, and these will not be revealed unless the early bug is completely fixed.

Collect data for quality analysis

To maximize the usefulness of the documented test cases, keep a record of all defects detected: their symptoms, seriousness, who caught them and when, the ID of the test case that caught them, the modules where they reside, and when they are fixed.

Also, project managers should collect the daily record of the number of test cases successfully executed and the number of bugs detected and fixed. They can plot this daily information and draw up a target plan to run further test cases, as illustrated in Figure 3.

Analyze the data

A diagram like that in Figure 3 offers useful information for controlling software quality and the expected shipment date. How should you interpret this data?

First, analyze the differences between the target number and the actual number of successfully executed test cases, and the target and actual number of detected bugs. This will help you pinpoint the problem in the early stage of debugging. Figure 4 illustrates four such diagrams. Figure 4a shows a target of control. Figure 4b shows that many bugs have been caught even though few test cases have been executed. This likely results from previous processes, such as module designing, not being properly com-

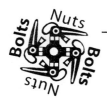

pleted or tested. In a very serious case, you should suspend debugging to revisit the previous process. Figure 4c indicates that the programmers cannot run the test cases as planned, hence very few bugs have been caught. This occurs when programmers are not able to debug a program. In such a case, ask an expert to oversee the programmers until they become familiar with debugging. Figure 4d indicates two possibilities: the test cases do not adequately reveal bugs, or the software does not carry many bugs. The former, of course, is much more likely than the latter, and the remedy is to create more effective test cases.

Second, if you catch 10 bugs for 10 days in a row, it is unlikely that today's are the last 10 you'll see. Bug occurrence never stops suddenly but diminishes gradually. From the bug accumulative curve, you can estimate when the curve goes flat, or the date you should attain the quality goal. We use the Gompertz Curve or the Logistic Curve for more accurate estimation, but intuitive observation alone can be a powerful tool.

Third, statistical data from bug reports can show you, for example, what the most common errors are, or what modules are error-prone. This kind of software metric "during the fact" works as a quality control parameter.

Finally, you can analyze what kind of defects your programmers tend to make—bug characteristics such as memory leakage, keeping a file unclosed, and so forth—and seek out errors that follow that pattern. This may be a project manager's task, but it also may reveal the presence of more complicated organizational and cultural issues.[3,4]

What might happen if a project does not employ the documented test cases or the QA approach based on the written test cases? Of 1,000 bugs, suppose only five percent of the bugs revealed during code inspection (215 bugs based upon the bug distribution in Figure 1) and machine debugging (631 bugs) are left undetected (43 bugs), and emerge at the end of the development life cycle, or—even worse—at the customer's site. Our data indicates that detecting and fixing each such defect requires two to three days. This means you will need an additional 86 to 130 days to raise the product quality to the desired level for shipment. We spend two weeks documenting the test cases and another two weeks executing the (written) test cases in the debugging phase—four weeks that may save four to six months. This alone justifies the usefulness of test case documentation. ❖

REFERENCES

1. A. Onoma and T. Yamaura, "Practical Steps Toward Quality Development," *IEEE Software*, Sept. 1995, pp. 68-77.
2. G.J. Myers, *The Art of Software Testing*, John Wiley & Sons, New York, 1979.
3. T. Yamaura, "Standing Naked in the Snow," *American Programmer*, Vol. 5, No. 1, 1992, pp. 2-9.
4. T. Yamaura, "Why Johnny Can't Test," *IEEE Software*, Mar./Apr. 1998, pp. 113-115.

About the Author

Tsuneo Yamaura is a senior engineer at Hitachi Software Engineering. His research interests include testing methodologies, software metrics, development paradigms, software modeling, and CASE.

Yamaura received a BS in electrical engineering from Himeji Institute of Technology and was a visiting scholar at the University of California, Berkeley. He is a member of the IEEE Computer Society and ACM.

Address questions about this article to Yamaura at Hitachi Software Engineering, 6-81 Onoe-cho, Naka-ku, Yokohama, 244 Japan; e-mail yamaur_t@soft.hitachi.co.jp.

269

Reprinted from IEEE ISSRE 97,
pp. 275-282.

Effect of Class Testing on the Reliability of Object-Oriented Programs

Mei-Hwa Chen
SUNY at Albany
Albany, NY 12222
mhc@cs.albany.edu

Howard M. Kao
GE Fanuc Automation NA, Inc.
Albany, NY 12203
kao_h@alb005.dnet.ge.com

Abstract

Although object-oriented programming has been increasingly adopted for software development and many approaches for testing object-oriented programs have been proposed, the issue of reliability of object-oriented programs has not been explored. The objective of this study was to investigate the effectiveness of class testing from the perspective of reliability. The experiments in this study involved testing and measuring the reliability of a C++ program and a Java program. We introduced a class testing technique that exploits the function dependence relationship to reduce testing effort in subclass testing and in testing polymorphism without degrading the reliability of object-oriented programs. In subclass testing the impact of function dependence class testing on reliability was compared with two other techniques: exhaustive class testing, which flattens every class and tests every function in the class; and minimal class testing which tests only new and re-defined functions. The results show that function dependence class testing preserves the same level of program reliability as does exhaustive class testing, while the effort is significant reduced. In polymorphism testing we conducted an experiment to observe the relationship between the binding coverage and the reliability of the program. The results suggest that testing possible bindings is necessary, and using the function dependence relationship to determine which bindings to cover in testing is sufficient.

Keywords: *Software reliability, object-oriented testing.*

1 Introduction

Software reliability is defined as the probability of successful operation of a given program within a specified time interval in a specified environment [9]. Reliability engineering on traditional software has been well researched over the past two decades. To date, object-oriented programming has been widely adopted in software development; however, the

issue of reliability of object-oriented programs has not been explored. Object-oriented features such as encapsulation, inheritance and polymorphism facilitate software reuse, but they also introduce problems that expose the inadequacy of traditional testing techniques when they are applied in the object-oriented paradigm.

Research on object-oriented testing has emerged in the 90's, with the strength of each testing method varying in different aspects. However, from the reliability point of view it has never been addressed. In this paper we present a case study that investigated the impact of object-oriented testing on the reliability of object-oriented programs. The emphasis of this study was placed on the class level which, we believe, is the stage that is influenced most by object-oriented features. We addressed two issues in class testing: subclass testing and polymorphism testing which stem from the nature of the inheritance feature. In subclass testing, should we re-test inherited functions that have been thoroughly tested in the parent class? Perry and Kaiser [10] suggested that retesting inherited functions is necessary if there exist interactions between new instance variables and functions and the inherited instance variables and functions. Harrold, McGregor and Fitzpatrick [4] further developed the incremental testing algorithm for class testing, in which only new functions, re-defined functions and "affected" inherited functions are tested. An inherited function is considered "affected" if the function accesses a data member as a new or redefined function does, or if it is invoked by a new or redefined function. They claim that their algorithm may significantly reduce the effort required in subclass testing. The other issue concerns testing polymorphism, which is rarely discussed. In polymorphic substitution, an object may be bound to the parent class or one of its subclasses in the run time. Should we exercise all the possible bindings during testing? McDaniel and McGregor [6] adopted a *Robust Testing* method to reduce the testing effort required by the combination of polymorphism and object-state. This method relies heavily on the program specification to generate the orthogonal array for test case selection.

To address the above issues, we defined the function dependence relationship on classes and developed a class testing technique that exploits the function dependence relationship to determine which inherited functions need to be re-tested in the subclasses and how many polymorphic substitutions need to be exercised in order to minimize test efforts without degrading program reliability. The function dependence relationship defined in this paper takes both direct and indirect dependence relationships into account. To aid the test automation, we generated function dependence graph to display both intra- and inter-class function dependence relationship. The function dependence graph lists only the functions that need to be tested in the class and suggests which dynamic bindings need to be exercised. From the results of the experiments that we conducted on subclass and polymorphism testing, we conclude that using function dependence class testing technique in class level testing is necessary and sufficient to ensure program reliability while the test efforts are significant reduced.

This paper is organized as follows: in the next section we examine the implications of object-oriented features on testing. Section 3 describes the function dependence relationship and the class testing technique that utilizes the function dependency relationship is presented in Section 4. The experiments conducted to support our arguments are also presented in Section 4. Section 5 gives an overview of existing approaches for testing object-oriented programs and we conclude our study in Section 6.

2 The Pitfalls

In this section we use two examples to illustrate the problems that may be introduced by the nature of inheritance.

1. The inheritance problem: a subclass may re-define its inherited functions and other functions may or may not be affected by the re-defined functions. When this subclass is tested, which functions need to be re-tested?

   The following pseudo-code example shows the fault introduced by the inheritance feature of an object-oriented program.

```
Class foo {
    int local_var;
    .
    .
    .
    int f1() { return 1; }
    int f2() { return 1/f1(); }
}


Class foo_child :: Public foo {
```

```
// child class of foo
    int f1() { return 0; }
}
```

In the parent class foo, f2 always returns 1 since f1 returns 1. While in the subclass foo_child, f1 has been modified, so, when f2 is invoked in the subclass foo_child, it will fail since f1 returns 0 in the new environment. Thus, even though f2 is inherited from the parent class, it still needs to be re-tested when we test the subclass foo_child.

2. The polymorphism problem: an object may be bound to different classes during the run time. Is it necessary to test all the possible bindings?

   Assume class P1 is the parent class of C11 and C12, class P2 is the parent class of C21 and C22. f1 is defined in all these classes. Now the question is, how many test cases should we generate for the following code?

```
// beginning of function foo
.
.
P1  p;
P2  c;
.
.
.
return (c.f1()/p1.f1());
// end of function foo
```

In the runtime, the object p can be an instance of P1, C11 or C12, while the object c can be an instance of P2, C21 or C22. If the f1 function in C2 returns 0 under some environment, then the function foo will fail. It is likely that if we only test a set of a randomly selected combination, we might miss the fault. This example demonstrates that it is necessary to have a method to sufficiently test the "relevant" polymorphic substitutions.

3 Function Dependence Relationship

A class defines the data relevant to an object of that class and a set of the operations that may be performed on that data. Class data are referred to as instance variables or data members, and class functions are called methods or member functions. Before we define the function dependence relationship, we first describe the relationship between functions and variables.

- A function *uses* a variable means that the value of the variable is referenced in a computation expression or used to decide a predicate.

- A function *defines* a variable means that the value of the variable is assigned when the function is invoked.

- A variable x *uses* a variable y means the value of x is obtained from the value of y and others. x is affected when the value of y is changed.

The Function dependence relationship is defined as follows: For each function f_1, if there exists a variable x that is defined in f_1 and used in function f_2 then f_1 and f_2 have a data dependency relationship. Therefore, $f1$ depends on $f2$ if and only if one of the following conditions holds:

1. $f1$ uses a variable x that is defined in $f2$,

2. $f1$ calls $f2$ and uses the return value of $f2$,

3. $f1$ is called by $f2$ and uses a parameter p that is defined in $f2$.

4. $f1$ uses a variable x and x uses a variable y which is defined in $f2$.

The following example explains the function dependence relationship, where JetEngine is a subclass of Engine and the function InjectGas is redefined in JetEngine. The function UpdateTemperature depends on InjectGas (condition 1) and ShowTemperature depends on UpdateTemperature (condition 1) and InjectGas (condition 4).

```
Class Engine {
private:
    boolean status;
    //started, stopped
    float   internal_temperature;
    // engine temperature
    float   external_temperature;
    // engine temperature

Public:
    Engine() ;
    ~Engine();
    StartEngine() { status = started; }
    StopEngine(); { status = stopped; }
    InjectGas();
    // this gas injection action will
```

```
    // increase the temperature
    ShowTemperature();
    UpdateTemperature();
}


Engine :: Engine() {
    status = stopped;
    internal_temperature = 0;
    external_temperature = 0;
}

Engine :: InjectGas() {
    internal_temperature += 100;
}

Engine :: UpdateTemperature() {
external_temperature =
internal_temperature / 100;
}

Engine :: ShowTemperature( ) {
    if (external_temperature <= 20)
        c.out << "Normal temperature"
        << external_temperature;
 else if (external_temperature >= 21) &&
    // fault-- the correct code is
    // external_temperature >= 20
        (external_temperature <= 40))
        c.out << "Middle temperature"
        << external_temperature;
        else
        c.out << "High temperature"
        << external_temperature;
}


Class JetEngine :: Engine {
Public :
    JetEngine(){};
    ~JetEngine(){};
    InjectGas();
}

JetEngine :: InjectGas () {
    internal_temperature += 99.99;
}
```

While Engine is tested, the fault will not be triggered, since the internal temperature is always an integer. But in Jet Engine, the internal temperature is not an integer; the fault will cause a failure under the following scenario.

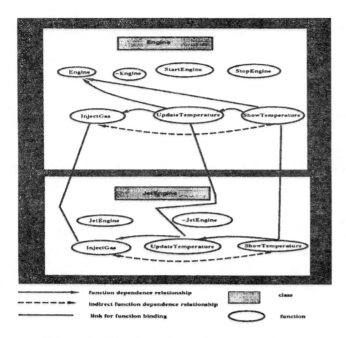

Figure 1. Function dependence graphs for `Engine` **class and** `JetEngine` **class.**

For example, in JetEngine, the application calls Inject-Gas() 21 times; the value of the internal temperature will be 2099.979. So when the ShowTemperature() gets invoked, instead of printing out *Middle temperature 20.99979* it will print out *High temperature 20.99979*.

Function dependence Graph

To facilitate class testing using the function dependence relationship, we generate a function dependence graph for each class. A node in the function dependence graph represents a function which needs to be tested in the current scope and the inter-class links suggest which bindings need to be tested in the polymorphic substitutions. Figure 1 shows the function dependence graphs for the class `Engine` and subclass `JetEngine`. Where an inherited function that depends on new or re-defined functions directly or indirectly is presented by a node in the function dependence graph. (Indirect dependence means that an inherited function does not depend on new or redefined functions, but depends on some inherited functions that depend on new or re-defined functions recursively, i.e., in one or more steps.) These inherited nodes are linked with the nodes in the parent classes that represent the same functions. These links are used to direct bindings for testing in light of polymorphic substitution.

4 Class Testing

Many studies have been done on class testing, with the proposed definitions and techniques varying in each work. The class testing used in this work involves intra-class and inter-class testing. In intra-class testing, each function appearing in the function dependence graph of the class under test is tested by a functional testing technique. The testing starts from the node that has highest fan-in and lowest fan-out, i.e., the function which has the most dependents and depends on the fewest functions, then traverses this dependence path and tests the functions on the path. The advantages of this approach are the following: (1) every function that needs to be tested is displayed in the function dependence graph; therefore, when subclasses are tested, the functions needing to be tested can be automatically and systematically determined; (2) the testing order proposed here can reduce the number of test drivers and stubs; (3) in inter-class testing, each function that needs to be re-tested in the subclasses is linked with the parent class; therefore, when testing dynamic bindings, we can just follow these links and test the functions on these links only.

The experiments conducted using this approach are described in the next two sections.

4.1 Subclass Testing

4.1.1 Objective

This experiment was designed to observe the impact of class level testing, especially in subclass testing, on the fault detectability and the reliability of object-oriented programs. It made use of existing Visual C++ (Microsoft) class hierarchies to observe its effect on testing.

4.1.2 Description

We used one of the Visual C++ (Microsoft) application programs, CheckBook, which defines nine classes that consist of 76 new, re-defined or virtual functions and approximately 2000 lines of code in total. The classes we tested are part of the Microsoft Foundation Classes, a library class, and some application level classes. They are CScrollView, CRowView, CBookView, CFixLenRecDoc and CCheck-Doc where the CRowView is the subclass of CScrollView, CBookView is the subclass of CRowView. CCheckDoc is a subclass of CFixLenRecDoc. The class testing techniques we used are described as follows:

Exhaustive class testing: in each class every function, including new, re-defined and inherited functions, is tested.

Function dependence class testing: in the subclasses new and re-defined functions are tested; inherited functions that depend on functions which need to be tested are tested.

Minimal class testing: only new and re-defined functions are tested in the subclasses.

4.1.3 Experimental setup

`step 1 -- fault insertion:`

Sixty-two various types of faults were evenly inserted into the classes. The types of faults we inserted consist of "missing statement", "missing initialization", "using prefix increment operator for postfix increment operator", "boundary value fault", "replacing == with =", and other faults which are easily made by programmers.

`step 2 -- class testing:`

Testing the faulty version classes using the three testing techniques described above. After testing and debugging, three versions of the original program are obtained, denoted P_e, P_d and P_m with respect to the testing methods exhaustive, function dependence and minimal testing.

`step 3 -- specification testing:`

Testing the four programs P, P_e, P_d and P_m. Test cases are generated according to the program specification. All the faults that are responsible for any failures are removed.

`step 4 -- reliability measurement:`

Repeat step 3, but faults are not corrected. The reliability of the programs is computed as the number of successes against the total number of executions. This step is repeated until the reliability reaches the 95% confidence interval.

4.1.4 Data Analysis

Figure 2 shows the relationship between the number of remaining faults in the program and the number of test cases applied. Results obtained from the exhaustive class testing and the function dependence class testing are similar: 38 out of 62 inserted faults were revealed at the end of class testing. However, the exhaustive class testing required 98 test cases and the function dependence class testing used only 58 test cases to detect the 38 faults. The minimal class testing took 49 test cases to detect 33 faults. After 203 test cases were executed in specification testing, there were two, two, three and nine faults remaining in the programs, respectively. Figure. 3 shows the reliability of the programs on the completion of 113th, 155th and 203th test run, respectively. The reliability measures are 0.854944, 0.854944, 0.791013 and 0.645292 after 113 tests; 0.905624, 0.905624, 0.887541 and 0.751962 after 155 tests; and 0.980844, 0.980844, 0.975519 and 0.947944 after specification testing.

From this experiment we observed that 41% of the test efforts were reduced in functional dependence testing and the same reliability measure was achieved as that obtained from exhaustive testing.

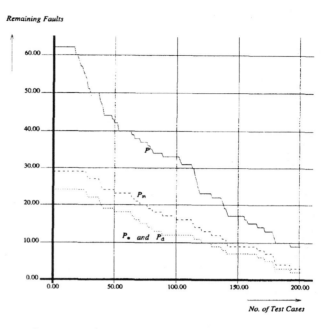

Figure 2. Number of remaining faults vs. number of test cases applied.

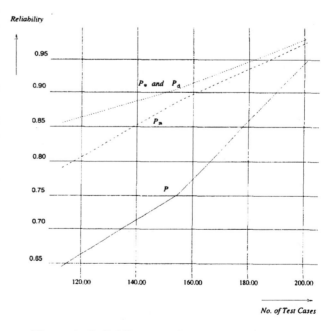

Figure 3. Reliability measures vs. number of test cases applied.

275

4.2 Testing Polymorphism (Dynamic Binding)

4.2.1 Objective

To observe the effect of polymorphic substitution on the reliability of object-oriented programs, we conducted an experiment that covered different numbers of bindings in testing and observed the reliability of the resulting programs. The objective was to show that using the function dependence relationship to decide which bindings to test is necessary and sufficient.

4.2.2 Description

This experiment was conducted on a Java program, ImageMap. ImageMap consists of 15 classes which have 102 new, re-defined or virtual functions and approximately 2400 lines of code. The class we selected to test the dynamic bindings is ImageMapArea which has nine directly inherited subclasses: AniArea, ClickArea, DelaydSoundArea, HighlightArea, HrefButtonArea, LinkArea, NameArea, SoundArea and TickerArea, In the run time an instance of ImageMapArea can be bound to ImageMapArea or one of the subclasses; therefore, there are ten possible bindings. Among them, only six bindings are required to test according to the function dependence relationship.

4.2.3 Experimental Setup

```
step 1 -- fault insertion
```
Twelve faults were inserted into the ten classes; the types of faults are similar to those described in the previous experiment.
```
step 2 -- testing and reliability
measurement
```
We measured the reliability of ten versions of the program. The version number indicates the number of different bindings that were tested and corrected in testing, i.e., version 1 is the program in which we only tested the binding to the parent class; version i means we tested i different bindings in testing and all the bindings are suggested by the function dependence class testing technique, where i ranges from two to six. The versions from seven to ten are the programs that were tested with bindings to the functions suggested by the function dependence class testing technique and others. The process of testing and reliability is the same as in the previous experiment.

4.2.4 Data analysis

Figure 4 depicts the relationship between coverage of bindings and the reliability of the programs. From version one to six, the reliability of the programs increased almost linearly, which shows that the reliability of the program

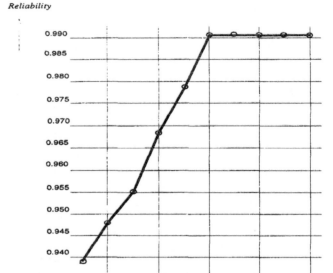

Reliability

Figure 4. Relationship between binding coverage and reliability.

directly proportional to the number of necessary bindings tested. The second half of the figure shows that from version seven to ten, the reliability remains the same, which indicates that it is not necessary to test the bindings to the functions that do not have any function dependence relationship with other functions that need to be tested in the subclasses. Therefore, we conclude that, in this experiment, function dependence class testing is necessary and sufficient in testing polymorphism.

5 Related Work

A number of testing techniques have been proposed in the literature. For class testing, Frankl and Doong [1] proposed a strategy based on formal specification of the class under test. They emphasized the interaction of operations and proposed that two equivalent sequences of messages $S1$ and $S2$ should put objects of the class under test into equivalent states. The equivalence of the sequences is based on the algebraic specification of the class. To facilitate their research, they built a testing system ASTOOT to test Eiffel programs. In their experiments, they investigated the relationships among fault detectability and length of sequence, range of parameters and relative frequency of various operations and suggested that a large range of parameters and long sequences is likely to have higher fault detectablity.

This approach is good at locating methods that expose the error; however, if the formal specification is unavailable, all the possible combinations of the method invocation order should be considered. An exhaustive testing of all possible sequences is not feasible under schedule and budget constraints.

Smith and Robson [11] modeled a testing process as a search for the order of routines with various parameters that yield errors. They presented a framework for object-oriented testing, FOOT, which provides test strategies that guide the testing process by supporting functions that return the next combination of member functions to test.

The state-based approach proposed by Turner and Robson [12] tests the interactions within a class by observing the changes that occur in the values of the data members. A class is modeled as a state machine, and a result of method invocations is a transition. A 100% state coverage can be achieved by testing all the features of an object with all the possible states, where a state is defined as a particular combination of values of all of the data-members of an object. Kung et. al. [2, 5] used a reverse engineering approach to define object states, which gives a systematic way to partition varies states of objects.

From the experience of testing an object-oriented system, Murphy, Townsend and Wong [8] presented the importance of class testing. They reported the results of testing TRACS, a system for monitoring telecommunication networks, which showed evidence that by adding class testing, fewer defects were found in the system level test. They developed an automatic class and cluster level testing tool, ACE, which supports the specification and execution of class testing script. With their methodology and the ACE tool, more than 50% of the total development time was saved.

For test data adequacy, Perry and Kaiser [10] postulated that inherited methods must be retested in most contexts of subclass, even though the parent classes of the subclass have been thoroughly tested. Harrold et al. presented an incremental algorithm which uses test histories from parent classes to design the test suites for the subclass. They claim that flattening subclass testing is not necessary; only new attributes or affected inherited attributes need to be tested.

Harrold and Rothermel [3] described a method which applies data flow testing to object-oriented programs. The strength of dataflow testing has been well studied. In addition to revealing errors that may not be uncovered by black-box testing, data flow information can be used to determine which sequences of methods should be executed to test a class. This resolves the problem of selecting execution sequences in a specification-based approach.

6 Conclusions

We have addressed the two most discussed issues in object-oriented testing. To apply object-oriented programming to large scale system development, we need to resolve these two issues in order to produce reliable software under limited resources. Our approach suggests that using the function dependence relationship in class testing can improve program reliability without exhaustive testing of all the functions in the subclass or all the bindings in polymorphic substitution.

The differences between our work and other approaches are the following. (1) We have considered the impact of testing technique on program reliability, our approach not only reduces test effort but also ensures program reliability. (2) The function dependence graph provides necessary and sufficient information, since it resides on the function level, a simple display can be easily traced.

We are currently developing a tool for automating class testing. The tool generates a function dependence graph for each class and provides a list of functions and the order of testing.

7 Acknowledges

We thank the anonymous reviewers and Dr. Dechang Gu for their valuable comments and suggestions. We thank the students in the Advanced Software Engineering Spring'96 class for their efforts in conducting experiments for this work.

References

[1] R. Doong and P. Frankl. The astoot approach to testing object-oriented programs. *ACM Transaction on Software Engineering and Methodology*, April 1994.

[2] J. Gao, D. Kung, P. Hsia, Y. Toyoshima, and C. Chen. Object state testing for object-oriented programs. In *Proceedings of the 19th Annual International Computer Software & Applicaitons Conference*, 1995.

[3] M. Harrold and G. Rothermel. Performing data flow testing on class. In *ACM SIGSOFT symposium on the Foundations of Software Engineering*, Dec. 1994.

[4] M. J. Harrold, J. D. McGregor, and K. J. Fitzpatrick. Incremental testing of object-oriented class structures. In *Proceedings of the 14th International Conference on Software Engineering*, 1992.

[5] D. Kung, N. Suchak, J. Gao, P. Hsia, and Y. Toyoshima. On object state testing. In *Proceedings of the 17th Annual International Computer Software & Applicaitons Conference*, 1993.

[6] R. McDaniel and J. D. McGregor. Testing the polymorphic interactions between classes. Technical Report 94-103, Clemson University, 1994.

[7] B. Meyer. *Object-Oriented Software Construction*. Prentice Hall, New York, 1988.

[8] G. Murphy, P. Townsend, and P. Wong. Experiences with cluster and class testing. *Communication of ACM*, Sep 1994.

[9] J. D. Musa, A. Iannino, and K. Okumoto. *Software Reliability: Measurement, Prediction, Application*. McGraw-Hill, New York, 1987.

[10] D. Perry and G. Kaiser. Adequate testing and object-oriented programming. *Journal of Object-Oriented Programming*, Jan. 1990.

[11] M. Smith and D. Robson. A framework for testing object-oriented programs. *Journal of Object-Oriented Programming*, Jun 1992.

[12] C. D. Turner and D. J. Robson. The state-based testing of object-oriented programs. In *Proceedings of the Conference on Software Maintenance*, pages 302–310, 1993.

Reprinted from IEEE
COMPSAC 98, pp. 99-104.

Certifying High Assurance Software

Jeffrey Voas
Reliable Software Technologies Corporation
jmvoas@rstcorp.com

Abstract

*Software certification processes have become so
intertwined with development processes that true
product certification, which should demonstrate
that the software will behave appropriately, is almost never employed. This deficiency calls for a
new generation of certification methodologies.*

1 Introduction

This paper presents a methodology for measuring
whether software *will do what we want*. If the software will, it deserves to be labeled as being of high
quality (or *high assurance*). The methodology we
will provide is applicable to all types of software,
covering the spectrum from safety-critical control
software to games.

When software does not do what we want, it is
because the software exhibits undesirable behaviors. Note that there are several levels at which undesirable behaviors can be defined. First, there is
the Utopian set of behaviors, that for *any* set of circumstances, define precisely what we want the software to do. You should think of Utopian software
behaviors as absolute universal truths concerning
what is "good" behavior versus "bad" behavior (for
all circumstances that the software could ever find
itself in).

Secondly, the *specification* also defines "good"
versus "bad" behaviors, but it is possible that
the specified behaviors are erroneous and conflict
with the Utopian behaviors. Specification behaviors are usually what we think about when we
discuss whether the software is *correct*, but cor-

rect software can still lead to serious system-level
problems.[1] If a program *always* exhibits Utopian
behaviors, then there cannot be system-level problems, and thus the software *is* of high assurance
even if the program violates the behaviors defined
as correct in the specification. So preferably software that needs to be of high assurance will satisfy the Utopian definitions for "goodness" instead
of the specified definitions if those definitions disagree.

A Utopian software behavior is defined as a
three-tuple: (the software input, the desired software output or range of acceptable software output
values, and the state of the system or environment
at the time when this input is executed). For a fixed
software input, many different system states might
be possible, and hence there could be ranges of output values that could be acceptable depending on
the specific state of the system. Or for a fixed software input, there might be only one unique system
state, but there might be a range of acceptable output values or possibly only one specific output that
could be tolerated. Unfortunately, software specifications usually only consider two parts of the
Utopian three-tuple: (the software input, the correct software output or a range of acceptable output
values).

2 The High-Assurance Pipeline

We are now ready to walk the reader through our
high assurance certification model. Before unveil-

---

[1]Here, system refers to the entity that the software is embedded in, and not just the software inside of the system.

ing the model, we will first discuss the initial processes that must be performed before certification begins. In our model, certification is a function of the information produced from the first pipe (See Figure 1). Certification processes will be independent of the processes in the second pipe, but certainly the results of certification will not be.

2.1 Pipe 1: Requirements and Specifications

Defining correct requirements is not sufficient for high assurance. It is also necessary to define outputs that we do not want the software to produce. It is too simplistic to say that everything outside the set that defines what is desired defines the set of "undesired" behaviors. There may be software behaviors that the software could exhibit that are not ideal, but can be tolerated by the system, and do not impact negatively on the assurance afforded by the software. Since defect-free software is, in general, an oxymoron, it is prudent to succumb to certain problems while concentrating effort on thwarting those problems that are totally unacceptable.

We are now ready to illustrate the benefit of considering the Utopian perspective on quality. Figure 2(A) shows two spaces: A is the space of desirable (correct) software output behaviors given the inputs, and B is the space of undesirable (incorrect) behaviors. Here, the definition for the quality of the software ignores the state of the system that the software operates in, and instead determines software quality as if the software were a stand-alone entity. Most existing quality assessment processes make this mistake.

To address the deficiency of ignoring system state, Figure 2(B) illustrates four different classes of software behavior: C, D, E, and F. Class E represents those behaviors that are incorrect with respect to the specification but have no negative affect on the system as a whole. They are simply nuisances. Class D is the reverse, where the behaviors are correct with respect to the requirements, but from the Utopian perspective on "goodness" are anything but good. F represents those behaviors

that were not good according to specification and the Utopian perspective, and C represents those behaviors that were good according to specification and the Utopian perspective.

Thus in Figure 2(B), space $(C \cup D)$ is equal to the previous A space in Figure 2(A). And the previous space B from Figure 2(A) is now equal to $(E \cup F)$. In Figure 2(B), $(C \cup E)$ defines all Utopian behaviors, whereas $(D \cup F)$ represents those behaviors that must be shown are not possible before high assurance certificates are granted.

Note the implicit partitioning of *failure severities* between Figure 2(A) and Figure 2(B). *Failures* defined in B appear as *successes* in E because their impact to the system was inconsequential and could be tolerated. Thus once system state is taken into account, outputs defined as failures may find themselves redefined as successes or *vice versa*.

Certifying high assurance, then, requires a convincing argument that the behaviors in $(D \cup F)$ cannot occur. Thus for high assurance certification, it is necessary that the first pipe define C, D, E, and F.

2.2 Pipe 2: Design for High Assurance

The second pipe builds software. The second pipe contains a cornucopia of processes for transforming the software requirements into code. This pipe contains processes such as CASE tools, compilers, debuggers, design paradigms (*e.g.*, Bertrand Meyer's *Design-by-Contract*, *defensive programming*, etc.). Because this pipe contains the more creative and enjoyable tasks associated with software engineering, this pipe usually receives more attention than the other two.

2.3 Pipe 3: Certification Through Stress

This section is devoted to three *assurance* processes that determine how often behaviors in $(D \cup F)$ manifest themselves. These processes will decide whether to grant high assurance certification without regards for what occurred in the first two pipes, with one exception being that we need the first pipe to define the sets shown in Figure 2(B).

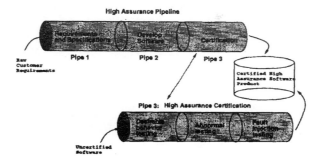

Figure 1: The high-assurance certification pipe

The goal here is simple: justifiable high assurance certification based on demonstrated software behavior. For this, the three processes are:

1. **Desirable behavior testing**: Demonstration that under *operational* scenarios, the software performs only those behaviors contained in (**C** ∪ **E**).

2. **Abnormal testing**: Demonstration that under *abnormal* scenarios, the software performs only those behaviors contained in (**C** ∪ **E**).

3. **Fault injection**: Demonstration that failures of any subsystem, whether hardware, OTS software, or components of the software under analysis, cannot convince the software to behave in a manner that contradicts those behaviors contained in (**C** ∪ **E**).

2.3.1 Desirable behavior testing

The first process is "desirable behavior testing." *Desirable behavior testing* (DBT) checks to see if the software exhibits behaviors in (**D** ∪ **F**), and if so, counts those as software failures. Output behaviors in (**C** ∪ **E**) are counted as successes. In comparison, *reliability testing* seeks to ensure that the software performs correctly according to the correct behaviors defined in the requirements.[2]

---

[2]Reliability testing would deem output behaviors shown in **E** as failures, whereas DBT would deem them as successes.

Existing certification standards usually recommend that some level of reliability testing be performed [1]. But DBT is slightly different than traditional reliability testing: all behaviors defined in Figure 2(B) are defined with respect to the system, and not simply based on (input, output) pairs as illustrated in Figure 2(B).

Desirable behavior testing is performed with the software executing with inputs selected at random from an "operational profile." An *operational profile* describes the probability that each input will be selected when the software is deployed [5].) DBT provides an analysis of how well-behaved the code is when it is executing in operational modes. So for example, if an input value of '100' to the software is likely according to the operational profile, DBT would force the software to receive a '100' with appropriate system states.

As an example of the value of considering the system state when selecting test cases, consider the Ariane 5 rocket disaster [2]. In this failure, software was reused from the Ariane 4 rocket and embedded into the different system environment of the Ariane 5. The software was reliable in the Ariane 4 environment (thus the software exhibited behaviors consistent with those in (**C** ∪ **E**)). The software failed, however, when put into the Ariane 5 environment, because (**C** ∪ **E**) was different for Ariane 5 than for Ariane 4. Some of those members from Ariane 4's (**C** ∪ **E**) now found themselves in Ariane 5's (**D** ∪ **F**).

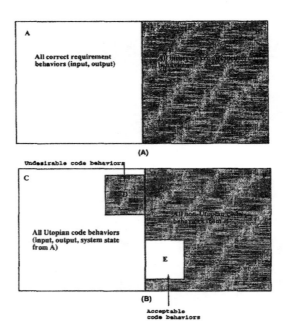

Figure 2: (A) Requirement behaviors based on inputs and outputs, (B) Code behaviors based on inputs, outputs, and system state.

2.3.2 Abnormal testing

After DBT is performed, the second process is *abnormal testing*. Abnormal testing employs infrequent and rare test cases. (DBT employed the more likely test cases.) Rare test cases have low likelihoods of being selected according to the operational profile, but they are still possible candidates for execution after the software is released. Like desirable behavior testing, abnormal testing watches to see that all outputs from the software are members of $(\mathbf{C} \cup \mathbf{E})$. Abnormal testing keeps a count of how many outputs are not.

DBT provides valuable insights into how successful the earlier processes were in developing well-behaved code under usual operating inputs. Abnormal testing provides insights into how successful the earlier processes were at developing well-behaved code under unusual circumstances.

Abnormal testing is conceptually similar to procedures such as *stress* testing. Stress testing checks a system's ability to cope with unusually heavy workloads, whereas here we are simplying talking about testing the software using infrequent inputs. Abnormal testing employs the best information available concerning the operational profile, inverts the profile (as defined in [4]), and then performs the same processes as DBT. This provides an analysis of how well-behaved the code is when it is executing in the more unlikely input modes. So for example, if an input value of '1' is unlikely according to the operational profile, abnormal testing would force the software to receive a '1' with appropriate system states (defined in Figure 2(B)) and observe if the outputs produced are in $(\mathbf{C} \cup \mathbf{E})$.

One alternate approach to test case selection than the method used by abnormal testing is to skew the operational profile such that greater weight is given to (input, system states) pairs for which failure occurring would result in grievous consequences. In certain cases, this testing approach will be identical to what we just defined as being abnormal testing, but more often, this variant on abnormal testing will allow us to employ test inputs that exercise the software's more critical functions. This approach can be used at the same time when abnormal testing is performed. This process may rarely be feasible in practice, however, because the functions needed for skewing the profile may not be known.

2.3.3 Fault injection

After abnormal testing is completed, the third certification process is fault injection. *Fault injection* employs the same procedures already described in Sections 2.3.1 and 2.3.2 but adds a twist: it uses specific rules to mangle the internal states that the software creates during execution and observes whether the software still produces outputs consistent with $(C \cup E)$ (given the input values and system states used during each program execution). So in essence, while a program executes under operational and abnormal inputs, fault injection corrupts the software's internal states and observes whether the software still behaves in a Utopian manner. If so, the software is fault-tolerant and has good recoverability.

The difference between fault injection and the previous two testing processes is that those processes are essentially testing techniques that use a modified definition for what is a successful output that includes system state. In contrast, fault injection tests the tolerance of the software to various types of subsystem failures, including failures of the software's components, external hardware components, and human user errors, meanwhile still observing whether the outputs are consistent with $(C \cup E)$.

Note that there will be situations where it is acceptable if the software does not behave in a manner consistent with $(C \cup E)$ after fault injection is applied. Specifically, the situation where it can be shown that the mangled internal states created during fault injection were such that there were no circumstances by which those mangled states could manifest themselves in "real-life." For each observed behavior that is not in $(C \cup E)$, if we can

mitigate the possibility of it ever occurring naturally, then we ignore the fact that an undesirable behavior was observed, i.e., we will not hold this fact against the software when we decide whether certification is warranted.

Of the three processes in the certification pipe, software fault injection is the most intensive and most expensive to perform. It is also the one that is the most likely to ferret out hidden behaviors that are outside of $(C \cup E)$.

3 Summary

Each component of our certification pipeline has been applied to actual control software systems (including aviation, medical, and nuclear). For brevity, these results will not be reprinted here; they are discussed in detail in Chapter 7 of [3]. But we will say that our belief that software must be stressed prior to certification appears to be gaining momentum, particularly among those who act in a regulatory capacity.

As evidence that the demand for software product certification is on the rise, consider the recent formation of the Software Testing Assurance Corporation. This organization, on behalf of United States insurance firms, has received the right to be the exclusive source for testing, verification and insurability endorsement for Y2000 software risks. The goal of this organization is to be the global organization that will be dedicated to testing and insuring the quality of information systems against failures that have adverse financial consequences. Their current Y2000 certification standard is product-oriented, and it requires that certain levels of code testing and analysis be accurately applied.

Our perspective that software certification must be product-oriented differs with many of our peers. We believe that software certification should be independent of how the software was developed. We contend that if an accurate operational profile cannot be found, high assurance certification should not be granted. Further, we contend that high assurance certification should not be granted if attempts were not made to define the undesirable behavior space with respect to system state. We accept that this behavior space can never be fully defined, and in some cases will be incorrectly defined, leading to improper certification decisions. But it is time that this space start receiving attention early in the software life-cycle. The more we practice defining it, the better we will get at defining it.

Acknowledgements

Jeffrey Voas has been partially supported by DARPA Contracts F30602-95-C-0282 and F30602-97-C-0322, National Institute of Standards and Technology Advanced Technology Program Cooperative Agreement Number 70NANB5H1160, US Army Contract DAAL01-98-C-0014, and the Air Force Research Laboratory under US Air Force Contract F30602-97-C-0117. THE OPINIONS AND VIEWPOINTS PRESENTED ARE THE AUTHOR'S PERSONAL ONES AND THEY DO NOT NECESSARILY REFLECT THOSE OF THESE AGENCIES.

References

[1] D. R. WALLACE, L. M. IPPOLITO AND D. R. KUHN. High Integrity Software Standards and Guidelines. US Department of Commerce, NIST, September 1992. Report 500-204.

[2] Prof. J. L. LIONS. Ariane 5 flight 501 failure: Report of the inquiry board. Paris, July 19, 1996, available at http://www.cnes.fr/actualites/news/rapport_501.html.

[3] J. VOAS AND G. McGRAW. *Software Fault Injection: Inoculating Programs Against Errors.* John Wiley and Sons, New York, 1998.

[4] J. VOAS, F. CHARRON, AND K. MILLER. Investigating Rare-Event Failure Tolerance: Reductions in Uncertainty. In *Proc. of IEEE High-Assurance Systems Engineering Workshop*, Niagara-on-the-Lake, Canada, October 1996.

[5] J. D. MUSA. Operational Profiles in Software Reliability Engineering. *IEEE Software*, 10(2), March 1993.

Reprinted from IEEE ISSRE 98,
pp. 237-246.

Studying the Effects of Code Inspection *and* Structural Testing on Software Quality

Oliver Laitenberger

Fraunhofer Institute for Experimental Software Engineering
Sauerwiesen 6 D-67661 Kaiserslautern-Siegelbach
+49 (0)6301 707251
laiten@iese.fhg.de

Abstract

This paper contributes a controlled experiment to characterize the effects of code inspection and structural testing on software quality. Twenty subjects performed sequentially code inspection and structural testing using different coverage values as test criteria on a C-code module.

The results of this experiment show that inspection significantly outperforms the defect detection effectiveness of structural testing. Furthermore, the experimental results indicate little evidence to support the hypothesis that structural testing detects different defects, that is, defects of a particular class, that were missed by inspection and vice versa. These findings suggest that inspection and structural testing do not complement each other well. Since 39 percent (on average) of the defects were not detected at all, it might be more valuable to apply inspection together with other testing techniques, such as boundary value analysis, to achieve a better defect coverage.

We are aware that a single experiment has many limitations and, often, does not provide conclusive evidence. Hence, we consider this experiment a starting point and encourage other researchers to investigate the optimal mix of defect detection techniques.

1. Introduction

Numerous examples of system failures, such as billing errors or large scale disruptions of telephone services, show that despite much effort, high quality software artifacts often remain an elusive goal. The reason for failures are defects introduced into software artifacts during development and maintenance. In this work, we regard a defect as an anomaly in a software artifact [14] that must be detected and repaired in order for the software product to be correct, i.e., uncorrected defects lead to a system failure during software testing or operation. Given that software quality is becoming an increasingly important success criterion in the software industry [21], it is crucial for companies to detect and remove defects before the software is delivered to customers.

The most common techniques for detecting defects in software artifacts are inspection and testing. However, both, inspection and testing, require a significant commitment of resources [7], [20], [27]. Hence, previous work in the form of controlled experiments compared the effectiveness of inspection and testing when applied independently of each other, i.e., the subjects of these experiments applied either inspection or testing on a software artifact but not both. However, as pointed out in [26], there is little clear, consistent evidence that one defect detection technique is more effective than another when applied in isolation. It is hypothesized that each defect detection technique has its own merits, e.g., by catching different classes of defects. Therefore, it is often suggested that inspection and testing should be applied in combination rather than in isolation [3], [4], [19], [20], [26]. Few controlled empirical studies investigate this approach in more detail. Hence, its merits are rather unclear, that is, what percentage of defects are detected by inspection, what percentage of defects are detected by testing, and what percentage of defects are not detected at all when applying the defect detection techniques in sequence.

To tackle these questions, we describe in this paper a controlled experiment to study the effects of inspection **and** testing on software quality when applied in combination, i.e., in sequence. We adopted this sequence because it is recommended for use in industry. Twenty subjects performed code inspection and structural testing using different coverage values as test criteria on a C-code module in which we introduced some defects. The experiment provided us with reliable data on the defect detection effectiveness of inspection and structural testing, how both defect detection techniques together contribute to software quality, and whether defects of a particular defect class are more easily detected by structural testing than by inspection and vice versa.

The remainder of this paper is structured as follows: Section 2 summarizes related work. Section 3 describes the defect detection techniques applied in the controlled experiment. Section 4 provides a description of the experiment. Section 5 presents the analysis and the experimental results. Section 6 concludes the paper.

2. Related Work

This work is built upon a number of controlled experiments in which subjects applied either inspection or testing to a software artifact, but not both. The first one was performed by Hetzel [11] more than two decades ago. He compared code reading, functional testing, and a variation of structural testing. Code reading can be regarded as the defect detection step of an inspection. His main finding was that functional testing and the variation of structural testing were equally effective, with code reading appearing inferior.

This work was extended by Myers [19] who compared team-based, code "walkthroughs/inspections" with variations of functional and structural testing. Myers found the three techniques to be of similar effectiveness. However, the "walkthrough/inspection" method had a higher labour cost than the other methods. Furthermore, the ability to detect certain classes of defects varied from technique to technique. Myers also investigated theoretical combinations of defect detection techniques. He found that individual subjects detected on average 33% of the defects while pairs of subjects applying the same or different techniques detected on average 50%.

In the 1980's Basili and Selby performed some experiments to compare functional testing using equivalence partitioning and boundary value analysis, structural testing using 100% statement coverage, and code reading by stepwise abstraction [3]. In their experiments, Basili and Selby found some evidence that code reading detected more defects. They concluded, however, that each technique had some merit and the effectiveness of the individual technique depended on the software type. Apart from investigating individual techniques in isolation, Basili and Selby also looked at all six possible pairwise combinations of the three techniques across hypothetical teams of two. He found that, on average, the combinations detected 67.5% of the defects in comparison with an average of 49.8% of individual techniques.

Kamsties and Lott [16] have replicated the Basili/Selby experiment twice. They found no statistically significant difference regarding the effectiveness of the three techniques in either of the replications. However, they did find that functional testing is the most cost-effective technique. Most recently, Wood et al. [26] performed a replication of the Kamsties/Lott experiment. They also found no significant difference regarding the effectiveness of the various defect detection techniques. They report that the effectiveness of the techniques depend on the nature of the programs and more specifically the nature of the defects in those programs. Furthermore, they theoretically combined the results of subjects and found that the best results are obtained by combining all defect detection techniques.

Looking at this review of controlled experiments, one may draw two conclusions: First, there is little consensus on which defect detection technique is the most effective when applied independently of each other. Second, the fraction of defects the subjects detected by applying either of the defect detection techniques ranges between 30 and 58 percent. Table 1 presents the concrete percentages, that is, the defects found of the total number of defects present. It remains, however, unclear whether one defect detection technique help detect defects that cannot be detected by using another one and vice versa. Moreover, this finding suggests that it is not possible within reasonable effort margins to detect all defects in a software artifact with a single defect detection technique. Therefore, several defect detection techniques must be applied to achieve the goal of high quality software. However, since each defect detection technique is effort consuming, it is crucial to determine the optimal combination of defect detection techniques. This work makes one step into this direction.

Authors	Average Percentage of defects found by subjects applying		
	Inspection (Code Reading)	Functional Testing	Structural Testing
Hetzel [11]	37.3	47.7	46.7
Myers [19]	30.0	36.0	38.0
Basili & Selby [3]	54.1	54.6	41.2
Kamsties & Lott [16] (1. Replication)	40.0	37.0	36.0
Kamsties & Lott [16] (2. Replication)	50.3	53.4	33.5
Wood et al. [26]	43.41	55.05	57.87

Table 1: Average percentage of detected defects in previous experiments

3. Defect Detection Techniques

This section outlines the defect detection techniques the subjects of the controlled experiment applied.

3.1 Software Inspection

Software inspections were first introduced at IBM by Fagan in the early 1970s [8]. They can be used to tackle software quality problems because they allow the detection and removal of defects after each phase of the software development process. In the context of this work we only consider code inspection. Code inspection participants usually follow a well-defined inspection process consisting of three steps: Defect detection, defect collection, and defect correction. While the defect correction step is performed by the author of the inspected code module, the defect detection and defect collection steps can either be performed by inspectors individually or in a group meeting. Fagan [8] reports that group meetings provide a synergy effect, i.e. that most of the defects are actually found in a group meeting. However, recent experimental results show that the synergy effect of inspection meetings is rather low [22]. Therefore, we share the viewpoint argued in [25] that defect detection is rather an individual than a group activity and that the major benefit of an inspection meeting is to collect the defects individually detected. Hence, the subjects of the experiment followed this three step inspection process:

1. Defect Detection
   Subjects individually scrutinized a code module for potential defects. They documented all potential defects they have found on a defect report form.

2. Defect Collection
   As some of the potential defects suggested by a subject might prove not to be real defects, two subjects performed an inspection meeting. The goal of the inspection meeting was to decide upon which of the potential defects were real ones. In addition, new defects might be detected during the inspection meeting. However, defect detection was not the primary goal of the inspection meeting. All real defects were documented on a meeting report form.

3. Defect Correction
   Since we knew the existing defects in the code module, we corrected the ones documented on the meeting report form before the subjects applied structural testing.

3.2 Structural Testing

Testing activities within the software development and maintenance process validate system functionality while identifying remaining defects. Hence, testing is most often used to reveal the presence (and not the absence) of defects. Although functional testing, such as boundary value analysis, at first sight appears more complementary to inspection, we had two reasons for choosing structural testing as testing technique. First, Wood et. al. [26] found that the worst mix of defect detection techniques is code reading and functional testing when theoretically combining individual results. Second, while inspection is a static analysis, structural testing is its dynamic counterpart. Hence, we assumed that both defect detection techniques complement each other well, i.e., that defects missed by inspection are detected by structural testing.

Structural testing requires a knowledge of the implementation details [4]. It is concerned with the degree to which test cases cover the logic (source code) of the program. More precisely, structural testing was performed as follows: Subjects received the printed source code. They tried to construct test cases that achieve 100% coverage of all branches, multiple conditions, loops, and relational operators. The coverage criteria were defined as follows [18], [20]:

- *Branch coverage:* Complete branch coverage requires that every branch be exercised at least once in both the true and false directions.

- *Loop coverage:* Complete loop coverage requires that a loop condition be executed once, several times and also should be skipped (without ever entering the loop) in some test condition.

- *Multi-condition coverage:* This has a stronger requirement than branch coverage. It checks for all parts of a logical expression being used. That is, each of the logical expression components must evaluate to TRUE in some test, and to FALSE in some other test. Multi-condition coverage is a stronger requirement than branch coverage.

- *Relational coverage:* This checks for tests that probe common mistakes regarding relational operators. A likely mistake could be using ">" when ">=" is intended.

To instrument the code module with test cases, we reused a test suite from a previous experiment [16] that let the subjects of the experiment use the Generic Coverage Tool [18] (GCT), which is publicly available. Subjects ran their test cases, analyzed the associated coverage values, and were required to develop additional test cases until they reach 100% coverage of the criteria given above, or believed that they could not achieve better coverage. After executing the code module with test cases, the subjects handed in the testing results, received a copy of the specification in exchange and began to observe failures in the output by comparing the testing results with the specification. Finally, the subjects isolated the defects in the code module that caused an observed failure and documented the defects on a defect report form. They finished the experiment by handing in the list of isolated defects.

3.3 Notation for the Defect Detection Process

The major difference between related and our work is that in our case subjects applied both inspection and structural testing to one code module. In previous experiments, subjects applied inspection and structural testing to different code modules. To ease discussion, we formalize the defect detection processes and define the notation as depicted in Figure 1.

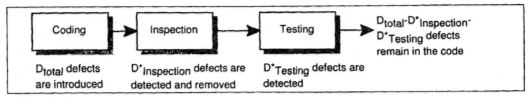

Figure 1: Defect Detection Process

- Let D_{total} denote the total number of defects seeded into the code module.
- By carrying out inspection $DInd_{Inspection}$ defects were detected by each subject while reading the code individually.

    Two subjects were randomly assigned to an inspection team. They performed an inspection meeting and reported $DTeam_{Inspection}$ defects on the meeting report form.

    For each inspection team, we corrected the detected defects ensuring that throughout the correction no new defects were introduced. Hence, $D_{total} - DTeam_{Inspection}$ defects remained to be detected by each subject in testing.

- Let $DInd_{Testing}$ denote the number of defects a subject detected in testing. We pooled the individual testing results of subjects who previously participated in an inspection team. This approach allows us to perform a valid comparison between inspection team results and testing team results. Let $DTeam_{Testing}$ denote the number of defects detected by a testing team.

    Hence, we assume $N = D_{total} - DTeam_{Inspection} - DTeam_{Testing}$ defects remain in the code module after inspection and structural testing. In Figure 1 we use * to denote either team or individual.

4. Description of the Experiment

The main goal of our experiment was to determine how each single defect detection technique and both techniques together contribute to software quality. Hence, we first investigate the percentage of defects detected by inspection and the percentage of defects detected by structural testing. Then, we discuss the effectiveness of both techniques when applied in combination and whether structural testing focuses on defects of a particular class that were missed by inspection and vice versa.

4.1 Variables

In this experiment, we manipulate one independent variable: defect detection technique for individuals and teams.

We defined the dependent variables as follows:

1. The *individual defect detection effectiveness*

$$\text{Individual inspection effectiveness} = \frac{DInd_{Inspection}}{D_{Total}}$$

$$\text{Individual testing effectiveness} = \frac{DInd_{Testing}}{D_{Total} - DInd_{Inspection}}$$

2. The *team defect detection effectiveness*

    For an inspection, we randomly assigned two subjects to one inspection team. In the case of testing, we pooled the test results of the two subjects to allow a valid comparison.

$$\text{Team inspection effectiveness} = \frac{DTeam_{Inspection}}{D_{Total}}$$

$$\text{Team testing effectiveness} = \frac{DTeam_{Testing}}{D_{Total} - DTeam_{Inspection}}$$

Our effectiveness measures are consistent with the "Review yield"; a measure proposed by Humphrey [12] that refers to the percentage of defects in the code module at the time of the defect detection activity that were found by that defect detection activity.

We emphasize that for the individual analysis we take into account the results of the defect detection (code reading) step and the structural testing results of each individual subject. For the team analysis, we consider the inspection meeting results of an inspection team and pool the testing results of the two subjects that participated in an inspection team for the testing team results.

We also measured the effort for each step of the defect detection process. However, since individuals and teams had a fixed time limit, the effort differences are marginal and we do not report efficiency values (i.e, effectiveness related to effort) here.

4.2 Hypotheses

We base the hypotheses of this experiment on the assumption that inspection and structural testing complement each others well in their defect detection capabilities. To study this, we first investigate whether there is a significant difference in the defect detection effectiveness of both techniques. Then we investigate the combination and whether the two defect detection techniques focus on different defects. If a defect detection technique A outperforms defect detection technique B and the two defect detection techniques do not focus on defects of different defect classes, it is debatable whether it is justified to spend much effort for defect detection technique B.

To investigate this in more detail, we state the following hypotheses:

1. Hypothesis regarding individual defect detection effectiveness:

H_{01} : Subjects applying code reading within the defect detection step of an inspection are equally effective in detecting defects as subjects applying structural testing.

H_{A1} :Subjects applying code reading within the defect detection step of an inspection are not equally effective in detecting defects as subjects applying structural testing.

2. Hypothesis regarding team detection effectiveness:

H_{02} : Teams applying inspection are equally effective in detecting defects as teams applying structural testing.

H_{A2} :Teams applying inspection are not equally effective in detecting defects as teams applying structural testing.

3. Hypothesis regarding the combination:

H_{03} : Teams applying inspection and structural testing detect all the defects in the code.

H_{A3} :Teams applying inspection and structural testing do not detect all the defects in the code.

4. Hypothesis regarding defect classes:

H_{04} : Inspection and structural testing focus on defects of different defect classes.

H_{A4} :Inspection and structural testing focus on the same defect classes.

4.3 Subjects

The subjects of the experiment were graduate students of the Computer Science Department at the University of Kaiserslautern, Germany. Twenty students participated in the experiment. All students had their *"Vordiplom"*, an initial set of exams which students have to pass after at least two years of study and which includes theoretical, practical and technical computer science, mathematics, and an elective class. Before performing the experiment, we captured the knowledge of each student with the help of a questionnaire. The questionnaire asked a student about her/his proficiency with the programming language C as well as with inspecting and testing computer programs. The subjects reported an average knowledge of C Programming language (0..4, (0 = no knowledge, 4 = C specialist), minimum 1, median 3, maximum 4), and an average knowledge in programming experience in (0..4, (0

= no knowledge, 4 = Programmer), minimum 1, median 3, maximum 4). Few subjects reported experience in performing inspection, while most of them reported some experience on testing computer programs.

4.4 The Code Module

The code module used in this experiment is implemented in C and allows one to calculate some basic statistical measures, such as the mean, mode, or standard deviation of a given set of data values. It consists of a main body realizing a selection mechanism of which statistic to calculate and ten functions to perform the statistical calculations. We extracted the following information about the code module using the Metrics toolkit available from [17]:

Total Line of Code	407
Noncommented Lines of Code	262
Lines of Comments	62
Blank Lines	83
Number of Functions	10
Number of Exec. Statements	132
Number of Decl. Statements	43

Table 2: Characterization of the C-Code module

The subjects had approximately two hours for defect detection in inspection, 1 hour for defect collection in an inspection meeting, and two hours for structural testing. Hence, they had to review and test about 200 LOC per hour. This inspection rate is consistent with findings in other environments [2], [9], [10], [13].

We injected 13 defects into the code module resulting in an overall defect density of 13 defects in 262 NCLC. This defect density is consistent with defect densities reported for example in [8]. The defects were the ones we made while developing the program and some additional ones. 11 defects lead to failure of the system, such as to a wrong calculation. 2 defects were only cosmetic in nature, i.e., they do not result in a failure, but are visible on screen while executing the program and may confuse the user of the program, e.g., instead of printing "Calculation of the standard error of the mean" the program prints "Calculation of the standard mean". We ensured that each defect lead to maximal one failure during testing. Moreover, we ensured that the defects cannot be detected by a compiler, i.e., a compiler (in our case: GCC - the GNU project C and C++ Compiler) does not report a single defect message. We did not make assumptions about the defect detection probability of each defect. We classified the defects according to the following defect classification scheme: Initialization, computation, control, data, cosmetic.

4.5 Data Collection

We collected defect and effort data throughout the detection step of an inspection, the collection step of an inspection, and the structural testing step. Defect data include the location of a defect, the classification of a defect, and the description of a defect. Effort data are the effort a subject required in a particular step. At the end we distributed a debriefing questionnaire to capture some additional information on the experiment.

4.6 Running the experiment

We ran the experiment in a classroom setting over 5 consecutive days. Figure 2 depicts the sequence of activities.

Day	Activity
day 1	Training in inspection
day 2	Training in structural testing
day 3	Performing the defect detection step of an inspection (code reading)
day 4	Performing the defect collection step of an inspection (inspection meeting)
	Correction of defects
day 5	Structural testing

Figure 2: Running the Experiment

On day 1 and day 2, all subjects received training in inspection and structural testing. Training was necessary to make the subjects familiar with (1) the ideas behind inspection and structural testing and how the defect detection techniques work (2) the material, e.g., forms, used in the experiment (3) the testing tool GCT used in the experiment. Part of the training involved inspection and structural testing on an example exercise. Moreover, the training offered the subjects the possibility to ask questions about each technique. Each training session lasted around 2 hours. On day 3, each subject individually read the code module and documented all potential defects found. On day 4, we randomly assigned two subjects to an inspection team and the inspection team performed the inspection meeting. Afterwards, we corrected the detected defects found by each inspection team. On day 5, the subjects individually tested the corrected versions of the code module and filled out a debriefing questionnaire before leaving.

Throughout the experiment, we urged the subjects not to exchange information about detected defects nor to take any material (i.e. the source code) with them. Hence we consider plagiarism not an issue. Considering the design of this experiment, one can argue that the sequence of defect detection activities can make a difference in the results and that we rather should have used a counterbalanced design [24], i.e., one subject or team follows one sequence of experimental conditions while another subject or team follows a different one. However, some reasons prevented us from choosing this experimental design approach. First, practitioners usually do not apply structural testing before code inspection. At least, we did not find any literature in which this sequence was recommended. Second, we assume that all the defects we inserted in the code module have the same probability of being detected by either inspection or testing. Hence, the sequence has little influence on the defect detection effectiveness.

5. Experimental Analysis and Results

5.1 Analysis Methods

We investigated hypothesis 1 and 2 by means of statistical tests. Since we want to compare inspection effectiveness with testing effectiveness for individuals and teams, we apply a matched-pair t-test [1] [23] for the individual analysis and the Wilcoxon matched pair test for the team analysis. Both tests require an adequate alpha-level to be set up. Based on power analysis [6], we stick to an alpha level of $\alpha = 0.1$. For hypothesis 3 and 4 we made some qualitative analysis.

5.2 Analysis of Individual Results

Table 3 present the summary descriptive statistics of defect detection effectiveness for individuals. The mean values show that inspection effectiveness outperforms structural testing effectiveness.

We performed a Shapiro-Wilks W test to check whether the data are normally distributed. The test result confirmed that the normality assumption is valid for our data. Table 4 shows the results of the matched pair t-test. Based on this test, we can reject H_{01}. The effectiveness values achieve statistical significance regarding the chosen alpha level of $\alpha = 0.1$. The significant result is attributable to a high effect size between inspection and structural testing results.

	Number of Subjects	Mean Value	Std dev.
Individual Inspection Effectiveness	20	0.38	0.1747
Individual Testing Effectiveness	20	0.09	0.1339

Table 3: Summary descriptive statistics for individual results

	Valid N	t	df	p
Effectiveness	20	6.35	19	0.000004

Table 4: Results for individual inspection vs. individual testing effectiveness

This result, however, is not what we expected - we hypothesized no difference in defect detection effectiveness when inspection and structural testing are applied in combination, i.e., that most of the defects not detected by inspection are detected by structural testing. Regarding defect detection effectiveness, the mean value of 0.38 for inspection is broadly in line with the effectiveness range (0.30-0.54) found in related work. On the other hand the value of 0.09 for structural testing is far below the effectiveness range (0.34-0.55) that was found previously. We remind the reader that for calculating the effectiveness value of structural testing, we divided the number of defects found by a subject applying structural testing by the number of defects that remained in the code module after inspection.

We found several possible explanations for this result. First, subjects did not have enough time to isolate defects based on the failures they detected. This can be compensated for by considering in the analysis failures instead of isolated defects. Following this approach, we could not observe a significant increase in the effectiveness values of structural testing. Hence, we can rule out this explanation. The fact that results are only slightly better for structural testing when considering failures also rules out a second explanation: After detecting a failure, a subject could not isolate the defect causing this failure. Debriefing of our subjects revealed that this happened, but it did not have a significant impact on the results. However, this shows an important benefit inspection has over structural testing: Once a defect is detected in inspection, its location in the code module is obvious. Structural testing, on the other hand, allows subjects rapidly detect a failure. But it involves considerable effort for locating the defect in the code module leading to the failure. A third explanation is that subjects did not recognize a failure in the testing results and consider the program as correct. We believe this happened only in exceptional cases. Fourth, subjects did not test the code module in an adequate manner, i.e., the subjects did not create enough test-cases, the coverage values were low, or both. However, this was not the case as Table 5 reveals. Apart from loop coverage, all other coverage values can be considered high, i.e., they adequately cover the code module. For loop-coverage, one must consider that it is often impossible to execute a loop zero times, i.e., if a loop has 1 as initial value it can not be executed 0 times. Hence, the loop coverage value is, on average, lower than other coverage values.

	Mean	Std. dev.
Binary Coverage	92.35	17.11
Loop Coverage	60.10	14.84
Multiple Condition Coverage	88.75	18.98
Relational Coverage	87.26	17.83
Number of test cases	24.65	5.57

Table 5: Summary descriptive statistics for coverage values and test cases

The final explanation is that prior software inspection hinders the effectiveness of structural testing since in both cases subjects analyze the structure of a code module either statically in inspection or dynamically in structural testing. The data suggest that one static analysis technique is satisfactory for defect detection. Regarding our discussion, we consider this explanation the most probable one for our data.

Based on these findings, we can conclude that structural testing after performing software inspection is only worth the effort if it focuses on different classes of defects. If not, it might be more valuable to replace structural testing with another testing approach, such as, boundary value analysis.

5.3 Analysis of Team Results

Table 6 presents a summary of the descriptive statistics of defect detection effectiveness for teams. The results of this analysis are similar to the results of the individual analysis, that is, team inspection effectiveness is higher than team testing effectiveness.

	Number of teams	Mean Value	Std dev.
Team Inspection Effectiveness	10	0.52	0.11
Team Testing Effectiveness	10	0.17	0.16

Table 6: Summary descriptive statistics for team results

On average, inspection teams detect 52% of the defects. Of the remaining 48% of defects, only 17% are detected on average by structural testing teams. Table 7 shows the results of the Wilcoxon matched-pair test. The test results reveal that we can reject our null hypothesis H_{02} and conclude that there is a significant difference in defect detection effectiveness between inspection teams and structural testing teams.

	Valid N	t	z	p
Effectiveness	10	0.00	2.80	0.010

Table 7: Results for inspection team vs. testing team effectiveness

In this case, we cannot compare our results with the results of previous experiments since no real inspection meetings were performed previously.

5.4 Analysis of the Combination of Inspection and Structural Testing

The message regarding the individual and team analysis is that inspection outperforms structural testing for defect detection effectiveness. Two questions remain to be answered: First, what percentage of defects remain in the code module after inspecting and testing it? Second, do inspection and structural testing focus on the detection of defects of different defect classes? Both questions are captured by hypothesis H_{03} and hypothesis H_{04}

Figure 3 presents an overview of the percentage of defects found by inspection, testing and remaining after both defect detection activities. It shows that on average 39 percent of the defects still remain in the code module after structural testing. In fact, the effect of structural testing on software quality was low. However, structural testing may be still considered worthwhile if it focus on defects of a particular defect class that were missed by inspection.

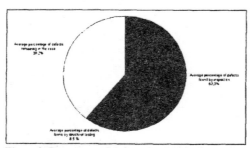

Figure 3: Percentage of defects detected by inspection, detected by testing, and remaining

Figure 4 shows how often each defect was detected by an inspection team and by a structural testing team and to which class a defect belongs (Cont = Control flow defect, Cosm = Cosmetic defect, Init = Initialization Defect, Data = Data defect).

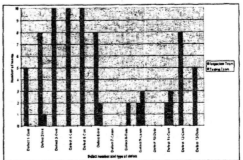

Figure 4: Defects detected by teams

It is important to note that if a defect is detected by an inspection team, it cannot be detected any longer by the same testing team because it has been corrected. Hence, defects 3, 4, and 5 cannot be detected by testing because each team has found it throughout inspection. However, we cannot state that inspection focus on calculation defects since subjects applying structural testing would detect them as well if applied first. Apart from the fact that testing teams did not find many defects, we found no clear pattern that structural testing detects defects of different defect classes than testing or vice versa. Defect 8 is a data defect that was only detected by testing. However, defect 13 is also a data defect that was only detected by inspection. Moreover, defects 7 and 10 were not detected at all. While defect 7 belongs to the class cosmetic, this is not the case for defect 10. Defect 10 causes a failure if one of the input parameters will be beyond the range of a valid integer value. We were surprised that none of the subjects detected this defect while testing the code module and enforces our suggestion that another testing approach, such as boundary value analysis, might be more valuable if code modules are previously inspected.

Regarding our finding that inspection is more effective and efficient than testing in detecting defects and the fact that both defect detection techniques do not particularly focus on different defect classes lead us to the conclusion that in our experiment inspection and structural testing do not complement each others well when applied in sequence

5.5 Limitations

It is the nature of experimentation that in many controlled experiments assumptions are made that later on restrict the validity of the results. Here, we provide a list of assumptions we were aware of, but had no hope of overcoming while designing and running this experiment. However, we believe that they are helpful for other researchers who plan to perform such an experiment.

1. We are assuming that each defect has the same probability of being detected by applying a particular defect

detection technique. This assumption is made in many experiments on defect detection techniques performed so far [3], [22].

2. Each defect in the code module leads to exactly one failure. This assumption is necessary to make a valid comparison between inspection and structural testing. In practice, there might be the case in which a particular failure is caused by several different defects or a particular defect causes several failures.

3. Each defect belongs to one particular defect class and we used only a limited set of defect classes. Moreover, we did not apply techniques such as orthogonal defect classification [5], which help distinguish the nature of the defects.

4. In our experiment inspection and testing are performed by the same subject. Hence, some subjects may be faster than usual in isolating defects from detected failures throughout the structural testing step because they know the code module already from inspection.

5. We only check the sequence inspection- structural testing and not the sequence structural testing-inspection. We did not counterbalance our experimental design. Further investigations might consider the order in which the defect detection techniques are applied. However, we have no reports from practitioners who have applied structural testing first and then, in a second step, performed inspection.

Despite these assumptions, we believe that our experiment provides insight into the effectiveness of inspection and structural testing when applied in sequence. In addition to these assumptions, we identified the following threats to validity. Threats to validity are factors that may influence the dependent variable in addition to the setting of the independent variables [15]. We distinguish between internal validity and external validity.

5.5.1 Internal Validity

Threats to internal validity are unknown factors that may influence the results without our knowledge [15]. We identified the following possible threats to internal validity:

History. During the experiment, there was time in between the sessions in which subjects could exchange information about defects. We told the subjects not to discuss the defects with others nor do anything else which could influence the results in an attempt to control this threat to validity.

Maturation. A maturation effect is caused by processes within the subjects that may change their behaviour. Examples are learning, fatigue effects, or loss of motivation. To avoid a learning effect, we performed training on inspection and structural testing before we conducted the experiment. Each session only lasted about two hours to avoid fatigue effects. There may be a maturation effect from one day of the experiment to the other, causing the

subjects to loose motivation and therefore performance. Although we did not observe a loss in motivation while performing the experiment, we could not control it. To address this issue, a change in the design of the experiment would be necessary, i.e., using a control group consisting of subjects that perform inspection or structural testing twice. A control group might be considered in the experimental design of a replication.

Selection. Selection effects are caused by variations in human performance, e. g., programming language skills. We controlled this threat by capturing the experience of our subjects and assigning subjects randomly to teams.

5.5.2 External Validity

Threats to external validity are problems that prevent generalizing the results of the experiment [15]. We identified the following possible threats:

Representative subjects. The subjects are not representative of professional software engineers. Our experiment was conducted with graduate students of computer science who had on average little experience with inspection and testing. The lack of experience may limit the external validity of our results.

Code Module. The size of the C-code module is small in comparison with the size of systems in industry. However, the effort available for inspecting and testing a code module of this size is comparable with the effort reported from industry.

6. Conclusion

This paper investigated the effects of combining software inspection and structural testing on software quality. In contrast to the claim, that each technique has its own merits and, therefore, should be applied in combination, the results of a controlled experiment with students as subjects showed little empirical evidence that this claim is justified. In the experiment, software inspection and structural testing did not complement each other well, that is, defects subjects missed in inspection were often not detected by subjects applying structural testing. In fact prior inspection even hinders the effectiveness of structural testing. Hence, it is necessary to allocate more effort for structural testing to increase its effectiveness, to replace structural testing with another testing approach, such as boundary value analysis, or to use structural testing for reliability certification and not for defect detection. This result is supported by our finding that inspection outperforms structural testing with respect to effectiveness and that both defect detection techniques do not focus on the detection of defects of different defect classes. However, whether other testing approaches, such as boundary value analysis, are really more complementary to inspection than structural testing is in need of further experimentation.

We consider this experiment as only one step in the determination of the optimal mix of defect detection techniques. Additional research as well as replication of this experiment are required to develop a better understanding of defect detection techniques and make further progress in this direction.

References

[1] Arthur Aron and Elaine N. Aron. *Statistics for Psychology*. Prentice Hall, first edition, 1994.

[2] Jack Barnard and Art Price. Managing code inspection information. *IEEE Software*, 11(2):59–69, March 1994.

[3] Victor R. Basili and Richard W. Selby. Comparing the effectiveness of software testing techniques. *IEEE Transactions on Software Engineering*, 13(12):1278–1296, December 1987.

[4] Boris Beizer. *Software Testing Techniques*. International Thomson Publishing Inc., 2nd edition, 1990.

[5] Ram Chillarege, Inderpal S. Bhandari, Jarir K. Chaar, Michael J. Halliday, Diane S. Moebus, Bonnie K. Ray, and Man-Yuen Wong. Orthogonal defect classification – a concept for in-process measurements. *IEEE Transactions on Software Engineering*, 18(11):943–956, November 1992.

[6] Jacob Cohen. A power primer. *Psychological Bulletin*, 112:155–159, 1992.

[7] Tom DeMarco. *Controlling Software Projects*. Yourdon Press, N.Y., 1982.

[8] M. E. Fagan. Design and code inspections to reduce errors in program development. *IBM Systems Journal*, 15(3):182–211, 1976.

[9] Michael E. Fagan. Advances in software inspections. *IEEE Transactions on Software Engineering*, 12(7):744–751, July 1986.

[10] Tom Gilb and Dorothy Graham. *Software Inspection*. Addison-Wesley Publishing Company, 1993.

[11] William C. Hetzel. *An Experimental Analysis of Program Verification Methods*. PhD thesis, University of North Carolina at Chapel Hill, 1976.

[12] Watts H. Humphrey. *A Discipline for Software Engineering*. Addison-Wesley, 1995.

[13] Watts S. Humphrey. *Managing the Software Process*. Addison Wesley, Reading, Massachusetts, 1989.

[14] Institute of Electrical and Electronics Engineers. *IEEE Standards Collection – Software Engineering – 1994 Edition*, 1994.

[15] Charles M. Judd, Eliot R. Smith, and Louise H. Kidder. *Research Methods in Social Relations*. Holt, Rinehart and Winston, sixth edition, 1991.

[16] Erik Kamsties and Christopher M. Lott. An empirical evaluation of three defect-detection techniques. In W. Schäfer and P. Botella, editors, *Proceedings of the Fifth European Software Engineering Conference*, pages 362–383. Lecture Notes in Computer Science Nr. 989, Springer–Verlag, September 1995.

[17] Paul Long. Metre 2.3 - a rule-based software metrics tool for standard C. http://www.cs.umd.edu/users/cml/cmetrics.

[18] Brian Marick. *The Craft of Software Testing*. Prentice Hall, 1994.

[19] Glenford J. Myers. A controlled experiment in program testing and code walkthroughs / inspections. *Communications of the ACM*, 21(9):760–768, September 1978.

[20] Glenford J. Myers. *The Art of Software Testing*. John Wiley & Sons, New York, 1979.

[21] Leon Osterweil. Strategic direction in software quality. *ACM Computing Surveys*, 28(4):738–750, December 1996.

[22] Adam A. Porter, Harvey P. Siy, Carol A. Toman, and Lawrence G. Votta. An experiment to assess the cost-benefits of code inspections in large scale software development. *IEEE Transactions on Software Engineering*, 23(6):329–346, June 1997.

[23] Richard J. Shavelson. *Statistical Reasoning for the Behavioral Sciences*. Allyn and Bacon, second edition, 1988.

[24] Paul E. Spector. *Research Designs*. Number 07-023 in Quantitative Applications in the Social Sciences. Sage University Papers, 1995.

[25] Lawrence G. Votta. Does every inspection need a meeting? *ACM Software Eng. Notes*, 18(5):107–114, December 1993.

[26] Murray Wood, Marc Roper, Andrew Brooks, and James Miller, Comparing and Combining Software Defect Detection Techniques: A Replicated Empirical Study, in *Proceedings of the 6th European Software Engineering Conference*, pp. 262-277, 1997.

[27] Edward Yourdon. *Death March*. Prentice Hall, 1997.

Reprinted from IEEE ISSRE 97, pp. 3-12.

Introduction to Software Reliability Engineering and Testing

John D. Musa
Software Reliability Engineering and Testing Courses

Abstract

Software testing often results in delays to market and high cost without assuring product reliability. Software reliability engineering can be applied to carefully engineer testing to overcome these weaknesses [1]. This application is often referred to as software-reliability-engineered testing . This book presents several case studies illustrating the application of software reliability engineering to testing. In this introduction we will take a quick overview of the field, so that you can better understand the terms used and procedures discussed in the case studies.

The testing of software systems is subject to strong conflicting forces. A system must function sufficiently reliably for its application, but it must also reach the market at the same time as its competitors (preferably before) and at a competitive cost. Some systems may be less market-driven than others, but balancing reliability, time of delivery, and cost is always important. One of the most effective ways to do this is to engineer the test process through quantitative planning and tracking. Unfortunately, most software testing is not engineered, and the resulting product may not be as reliable as it should be, and/or it may be too late or too expensive.

Software reliability engineering combines the use of quantitative reliability objectives and operational profiles (profiles of system use) [2]. The operational profiles guide developers in testing more realistically, which makes it possible to track the reliability actually being achieved.

AT&T has been a major user of SRE. Hence in this article, I describe SRE in the context of an actual project at AT&T, which I call Fone Follower. I selected this example because of its simplicity; it in no way implies that SRE is limited to telecommunications systems. SRE is based on the AT&T *Best Current Practice of Software Reliability Engineering*, approved in May 1991. Qualification as an AT&T best current practice requires use on typically eight to 10 projects with documented large benefit/cost ratios, as well as a probing review by two boards of high-level managers. Some 70 project managers also reviewed this particular practice. Standards for approval as a best current practice are high; only five of 30 proposed best current practices were approved in 1991.

1. Software reliability engineering: a rapidly growing discipline

Software reliability engineering is maturing to the extent that standards bodies and publishers are undertaking activities to promote it. An AIAA standard for software reliability engineering was approved in 1993, for example, and IEEE standards are under development. McGraw-Hill and the IEEE Computer Society Press recently recognized the rapid maturing of the field, publishing a handbook on the topic [3]. The IEEE Computer Society's Technical Committee on Software Reliability Engineering has grown in the six years since its founding from around 40 people to more than 1,000, an annual growth rate of about 70 percent. It publishes a newsletter, sponsors the annual International Symposium on Software Reliability Engineering (ISSRE), and engages in numerous other activities, including standards.

Growth of the software reliability engineering research community is about 35 percent per year, as judged by the number of papers submitted to ISSRE. There is also an active software reliability engineering bulletin board on the Internet.

The growth of software reliability engineering is not unfounded. Those incorporating it into their development practices are enjoying significant improvement. In AT&T's Operations Technology Center of the Network Computing Services Division, software reliability engineering is part of the standard software development process, which is currently undergoing ISO certification. This organization, which has the highest percentage use of software reliability engineering in AT&T, was the primary software development organization for the AT&T business unit that won the Malcolm Baldrige National

Quality Award in 1994. In addition, four of the first five software winners of the AT&T Bell Laboratories President's Quality Award used software reliability engineering.

AT&T's International Definity project illustrates the benefits that result from applying software reliability engineering along with related technologies. In comparison with a previous release that did not use these technologies, reliability increased by a factor of 10. Customer satisfaction with the product increased correspondingly—sales increased by a factor of 10. Moreover both the system test interval and system test costs decreased by a factor of two, the total project development time decreased by 30 percent, and maintenance costs decreased by a factor of 10.

These successes are not limited to AT&T. Alcatel, Bellcore, CNES (France), ENEA (Italy), Ericsson Telecom, Hewlett Packard, Hitachi, IBM, Jet Propulsion Laboratory, Lockheed-Martin, Microsoft, Mitre, Nortel Technology, Tandem Computers, and various government agencies and universities—just to name a few users—have also employed software reliability engineering profitably.

As benefits like this become more widely publicized, software reliability engineering can be expected to grow even more. Many areas that are as yet untouched might benefit greatly from this discipline. In object-oriented technology, for example, there seems to be potential in applying software reliability engineering to certify object libraries. Although object-oriented concepts have made better modularization possible, the promise and benefits of reuse are not being fully realized because developers (and probably rightly so) strongly resist using objects whose reliability they cannot vouch for.

2. Process overview

The standard definition for *software reliability* [4] is the probability of execution without failure for some specified interval, called the *mission time*. This definition is compatible with that used for hardware reliability, though the failure mechanisms may differ. In fact, SRE is generally compatible with hardware reliability technology and practice. This is important because no system is purely software; all systems mix software and hardware components. A "software system" is really a "software-based system."

2.1 Application scope

You can apply SRE to any software system and for most kinds of testing. For example, you can apply it to feature, load, performance, regression, certification, or acceptance testing. SRE should be applied over the entire software life cycle, including all releases, with particular focus on the phases from subsystem test to delivery. Testers are the prime movers in implementing SRE, but system engineers, architects, and users are also involved.

2.2 Testing types

There are two types of testing using SRE: *development testing*, in which you find and remove faults, and *certification testing*, in which you either accept or reject the software. In many cases, the two types of testing are applied sequentially. Development testing precedes certification testing, which in turn serves as a rehearsal for customer acceptance testing.

During development testing, you estimate and track *failure intensity*, which is the failures per unit execution time, say, six failures per 1,000 execution hours. Execution time is the actual time used by a processor in executing a program's instructions. Failure intensity is an alternative way of expressing software reliability. Testers use failure intensity information to determine any corrective actions that might need to be taken and to guide release. The release decisions include release from system test to beta test and release from beta test to general availability. Development testing typically comprises feature, load, and regression testing. It is generally used for software developed in your own organization.

Certification testing, on the other hand, does not involve debugging. There is no attempt to "resolve" failures you identify. Certification testing typically comprises only load testing. It is generally used for software you acquire, including off-the-shelf or packaged software, reusable software, and software developed by an organization other than your own.

2.3 Application steps

SRE has seven major steps. The first two steps consist of decision-making and form the basis for the five core application steps. The decision-making steps generally take only a few hours. The core steps are spread over the life cycle of the release. Figure 1 shows the core steps along with the development life-cycle stages in which they typically occur. The core steps are virtually identical for the two types of testing, except for the first and last steps. I describe the core steps in more detail later in the context of the Fone Follower project.

- *Determine which associated systems require separate testing*. In addition to the testing of the entire system, testers may need to test major system variations. The system may have different hardware configurations, for example, or it may work with different communication protocols in different countries. You should test any major components of unknown reliability. You can also profitably test smaller components you expect to reuse extensively. If the system interacts strongly with other software systems, you may want to test a supersystem that represents these systems functioning together.

- *Decide which type(s) of testing are needed for each system to be tested.* Development testing is appropriate only for systems that you code at least in part, for example.

- *Define "necessary" reliability.* This step consists of defining failure in terms of severity classes, setting failure intensity objectives for the developed software, and engineering the reliability strategies you will employ. It does not include engineering reliability strategies for software that involves only certification testing. Although this step is performed primarily by system engineers and architects, it affects testers also.

- *Develop operational profiles.* An *operation* is a major task the system performs. Some examples of operations are a command activated by a user, the processing of a transaction sent from another system, a response to an event occurring in an external system, and a routine housekeeping task activated by your own system controller. An *operational profile* is simply the set of operations and their probabilities of occurrence.

- *Prepare for testing.* This step includes preparing test cases, test procedures, and any automated tools you decide to use.

- *Execute tests.* This step entails conducting testing and then identifying failures, determining when they occurred, and establishing the severity of their impact.

- *Interpret failure data.* The interpretation of failure data is different for development testing and certification testing. In development testing, the goal is to track progress and compare present failure intensities with their objectives. In certification testing, the goal is to determine if a software component or system should be accepted or rejected, with limits on the risks taken in making that decision. For development testing, failure data is generally interpreted at fixed intervals. For certification testing, interpretation is done after each failure

The SRE process follows a spiral model, in a manner analogous to the software development process. Iteration occurs frequently. Figure 1 represents an "unwound coil" of this model. "Execute tests" and "interpret failure data" occur simultaneously and are closely linked, with the relative emphasis on interpretation increasing with time.

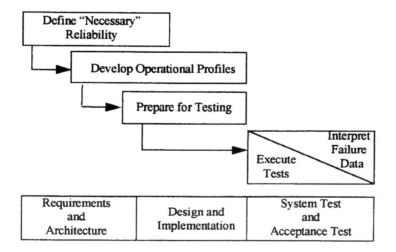

Figure 1. The core application steps of applying software reliability engineering to testing and the corresponding development life-cycle stages.

Testers define necessary reliability and develop operational profiles in partnership with system engineers and architects. I and my AT&T colleagues originally thought that these activities should be assigned solely to system engineers. However, this did not work well in practice. Testers depend on these activities and are hence more strongly motivated than system engineers to ensure their successful completion.

We solved the problem by making testers part of the system engineering and architecture team. This approach also had unexpected side benefits. Testers had much more contact with users, which was very valuable in knowing what system behavior would be unacceptable and how unacceptable it would be, and in understanding how users would employ the product. The result was more realistic testing. System engineers and architects obtained a greater appreciation of testing and of where requirements and design needed to be made less ambiguous and more precise so that test-case and test-procedure design could procced. System testers made valuable contributions to architecture reviews, often pointing out important capabilities that were missing.

2.4 Fone Follower

Fone Follower is a system that lets telephone calls "follow" users anywhere in the world (even to cellular phones). Users dial into a voice-response system and enter the telephone numbers at which they plan to be at various times. Most of these entries are made between 7 am and 9 am each day. Calls that would normally be routed to a user's telephone are then sent to Fone Follower, which forwards them in accordance with the program entered. If there is no response to a voice call and the user has pager service, the system pages. If there is still no response or if the user doesn't have pager service, the system forwards calls to the user's voice mail.

Fone Follower was designed to use a vendor-supplied operating system. We did not know the reliability of the operating system. Fone Follower does not interact substantially with other systems in the telecommunication network. I have changed certain information about Fone Follower to keep the explanation simple and to protect proprietary data.

3. Applying SRE

For Fone Follower, the decisions were to apply development testing to the product and certification testing to the operating system.

3.1 Define "necessary" reliability

As I described earlier, this step consists of three parts.

3.1.1 Define failure in terms of severity classes. A *failure* is the departure of program behavior during execution from user requirements; it is a user-oriented concept. A *fault* is the defect in the program that causes the failure when executed; it is a developer-oriented concept. Thus, when you define failures you are implicitly expressing users' negative requirements for program behavior. The definition process itself consists of outlining these negative requirements in a system-specific fashion for each severity class.

A *severity class* is a set of failures that affect users to the same degree. The severity is often related to the criticality of the operation that fails. Common classification criteria include impacts on human life, cost, and operations. In general, classes are widely separated in impact because you can't estimate impact with high accuracy.

We used operational impact as the criterion for establishing the following severity classes in Fone Follower:

- *Class 1.* Failure prevents calls from being forwarded.
- *Class 2.* Failure prevents phone number entry.
- *Class 3.* Failure makes system administration more difficult although it remains possible through alternate means: for example, you can't add or delete users from a graphical user interface but you can still accomplish this with text-based commands.
- *Class 4.* Failure affects an operation that is deferrable, such as preventive maintenance.

3.1.2 Set failure intensity objectives. These failure intensity objectives are for the developed software of each system. Setting failure intensity objectives for the developed software of a system has several steps:

1. Establish the *system* failure intensity objective, which you derive from an analysis of specific user needs, existing system reliability and the degree to which users are satisfied with it, and the capabilities of competing systems.
2. Determine and sum the failure intensity of the acquired hardware and software components (these will often be certified at acceptance of delivery).
3. Subtract the total acquired failure intensity from the system failure intensity objective in clock hours. This gives you the failure intensity objective for the developed software.

4. Convert the results into a failure intensity objective for the developed software per unit of execution time.

3.1.3 Engineer reliability strategies.

There are three principal reliability strategies: fault prevention, fault removal, and fault tolerance. *Fault prevention* uses requirements, design, and coding technologies and processes, as well as requirements and design reviews, to reduce the number of faults introduced in the first place. *Fault removal* uses code inspection and development testing to remove faults in the code once it is written. *Fault tolerance* reduces the number of failures that occur by detecting and countering deviations in program execution that may lead to failures.

Engineering these reliability strategies means finding the right balance among them to achieve the failure intensity objective in the required time and at minimum cost. In addition to achieving balance, system engineers/architects focus effort on operations that are most frequently executed and/or most critical.

In later product releases, system engineers/architects obtain and use information on the actual failure intensities of components in relation to their failure intensity objectives to determine which components a project should target in its reliability-improvement efforts. System and field engineers evaluate field failures in terms of their frequency and severity. They then assign priorities to the project's responses to the failures. System engineers/architects attempt to determine how the development process could be cost-effectively improved to avoid the most important field failures. Studying *triggers* or the conditions that tend to expose faults may suggest ways of improving the fault removal process.

3.2 Develop operational profiles

You must first determine the operational modes. An *operational mode* is a distinct pattern of system use and/or environment that needs separate testing because it is likely to stimulate different failures. Factors that may yield different operational modes include day of the week or time of the day (prime hours vs. off hours), time of the year (year-end processing for accounting systems), traffic levels, user profile, user experience, system maturity, and reduced system capability. Division into operational modes is based on engineering judgment: more operational modes can increase the realism of test but they can also increase the effort and cost of selecting test cases and performing system test.

We selected three operational modes for Fone Follower:

- *Peak hours.* Heavy incoming calls and entries (of phone numbers) traffic, no administration or audit functions permitted.
- *Prime hours.* Average incoming calls and entries traffic, administration functions permitted but audit functions limited.
- *Off hours.* Low incoming calls and entries traffic, low administration traffic, extensive audit traffic.

You will need to develop two kinds of operational profiles, system (across all operational modes) and operational mode. The system profile is used to select the test cases to prepare. The operational profile for each operational mode is used to select operations for execution when that mode is tested.

Fone Follower expected an average of 100,000 operations per clock hour over all operational modes. Table 1 shows a segment of its operational profile and how we obtained it from the occurrence rates of individual operations. This is a tabular representation. You can also represent the operational profile graphically as a network of nodes and branches. The tabular representation is generally better for systems whose operations have few (often one) attributes. The graphical representation is generally better for systems whose operations have multiple attributes, such as telecommunications switching systems. The operations of Fone Follower had few attributes, so we chose the tabular representation.

Operation	Operations/clock hour	Probability
Process voice call, no pager, answered	18,000	0.18
Process voice call, no pager, not answered	17,000	0.17
Process voice call, pager, answered	17,000	0.17
Process fax call	15,000	0.15
•		
•		
•		
Total	100,000	1.00

Table 1. Part of an operational profile in tabular form.

For the sake of illustration, Figure 2 shows part of a graphical representation of a telecommunications switching system. The nodes represent attributes of an operation; the branches, attribute values. An operation is represented by a path through the network. The occurrence probabilities of attribute values can be conditional on the previous path to that point.

Regardless of which representation you choose, the procedure to develop an operational profile is similar. Here is the procedure for the tabular representation (with the variations for the graphical representation in parentheses):

- *Identify the initiators of operations.* System users are most commonly the initiators of operations, but initiators can also be external systems and the system's controller. To identify the users, you first determine the expected customer types on the basis of information such as the system business case and marketing data for related systems. You can then analyze the customer types for the expected user types or sets of users who will tend to use the system in the same way. User types are often highly correlated with job roles.
- *List the operations (attributes and attribute values) each initiator produces.* The system requirements are

perhaps the most useful source of information for this task. Other sources include work-process flow diagrams for various job roles, draft user manuals, prototypes, and previous versions of the system. Direct discussions with "typical" expected users are usually highly enlightening and highly recommended. Bear in mind that an operation is actually a logical rather than a physical concept, in that it can be executed over several machines in noncontiguous time segments.

- *Determine the occurrence rate per clock hour of the operations (attribute values).* Many people using SRE for the first time expect this task to be very difficult; our experience generally indicates it is much less difficult than expected. Frequently, field data already exists for previous versions of the same or similar systems. If not, you can often collect it. If the operations are event driven, you can often simulate the environment that determines event frequency. Finally, even if there is no direct data, there is usually some related information that lets you make reasonable estimates.
- *Determine the occurrence probabilities.* To do this, you divide the occurrence rates for each operation (attribute value) by total operation (attribute) occurrence rates.

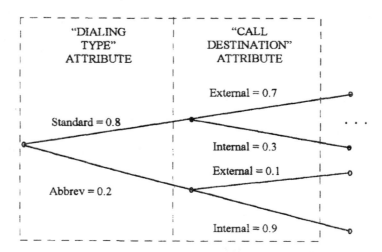

Figure 2. Graphical representation of an operational profile for a telecommunications switching system. The graphical representation is better than the tabular representation (Table 1) when there are multiple attributes.

3.3 Prepare for testing

The activities in this step consist of specifying the test cases and test procedures and preparing any automated tools you decide to use. For these activities, it is worth noting some important definitions.

A *run* is a specific instance of an operation and is characterized by that operation and a complete set of values of its input variables. *Input variables* are variables that exist external to the run and influence it. In Fone Follower, for example, a run for the connect call operation is specified by seven input variables: call type (for example, fax), dialing type (standard or abbreviated), destination, billing type, operational mode, database state, and resource state.

The first four input variables are *direct* because they control processing in a known, designed way. The last three are *indirect* because although they influence processing, it is not in any predictable way. For example, if an operational mode has heavy traffic, it may change processing because of resource conflicts. A different database state, due to, say, increasing data corruption with time, may also change processing as a result of its different values.

A run differs from a *test case*. In a test case, you provide the values of only direct input variables. A test case becomes a run when you also specify the values of indirect input variables. This has implications for testing productivity because, by changing the indirect input variables, testers can use a moderate number (perhaps hundreds) of test cases to generate a very large number of different runs.

3.3.1 Specify test cases. The first activity is to estimate the number of test cases you can cost-effectively prepare, on the basis of the effort needed for each. You can then select test cases in two steps.

1. Make sure that each critical operation is assigned at least one test case. "Critical" in this context means that an operation adds considerable extra value when it executes successfully, or results in an extreme impact when it fails. "Value" and "impact" refer to safety with respect to human life, cost, or operations. Then select the operations in accordance with their occurrence probabilities, using the system operational profile, modified appropriately for any critical operations. For Fone Follower, the occurrence probability of the process fax call operation was 0.15 (Table 1), so 15 percent of the test cases were from the connect call operation.

2. Complete the selection of the test case by choosing levels for all direct input variables. First, list the levels for each direct input variable, as we have done in Table 2 for the process fax call operation. A *level* is a value or a range of values of an input variable for which failure behavior is expected to be the same because of processing similarities. For example, in Table 2, a value of the input variable "Destination" would be a specific phone number. "Local calling area" would be a level of that input variable because the system would probably behave in the same way for all local phone numbers. You need select only one value within a level for a test case. In some cases, a level has only one value, such as "fax" in "call type." The next activity is to randomly choose a level for each direct input variable. The choice should be made with equal probability from the set of levels. For the process fax call operation, a possible random selection of levels is "Local calling area, per call, abbreviated, with screening, originator not on screenlist." The operation and the set of direct input variables selected specify a test case.

3.3.2 Define test procedure. A test procedure is the specification of the set of runs and environment associated with an operational mode. You generally specify the set of runs statistically by providing values of operation occurrence rates. When executed, the test procedure will select test cases at random times from the prepared set, following these occurrence rates.

Call type	Destination	Billing type	Dialing type	Screening	Originator
Fax	Local calling area	Flat rate	Standard	Yes	On screenlist
Voice	Within area code	Per call	Abbreviated	No	Not on screenlist
Data-modem	Outside area code	Per call discount			
Data-ISDN	International				
	Wireless				

Table 2. Levels of the four direct input variables for the connect call operation of Fone Follower.

In feature testing, test runs are executed essentially independently of each other. Interactions are controlled by such measures as frequent reinitialization of the database. In load testing, large numbers of test runs are executed in the context of an operational mode, driven by a test procedure. Load testing stimulates failures that can occur as a result of interactions among runs, both directly and through the slowly corrupting database. In regression testing, feature test runs are repeated after each build to see if any changes made to the system have spawned faults that cause failures.

3.3.3 Prepare automated tools. You can apply SRE without test automation, but test-management and failure-identification tools usually make the process faster and more efficient. You should also provide for recording operations executed so that you can collect use data for comparing the test operational profile with the profile expected in the field. Actually, operation recording should be more than a feature of the test platform; it should be an integral part of the system itself. You can then collect extensive field data, both to evaluate the current system and to provide a base for engineering future systems.

3.4 Execute tests

During this step, you begin with feature testing and follow that with load testing. Regression testing is typically done after each build that involves significant change. In load testing, you execute each operational mode separately. For Fone Follower, this means we tested the peak hours, prime hours, and off hours operational modes. You should allocate test time among the operational modes in the same proportions that they are expected to have in the field.

Test execution involves identifying failures, determining when they occurred, and establishing the severity of their impact. To identify failures, first look for deviations of program behavior. Determine which ones affect the user; only those that do are failures. Generic tools can detect many types of deviations, including interprocess communication failures, illegal memory references, and deviant return code values. You can also manually insert assertions in the code to detect programmer-defined deviations. You will probably require at least some manual inspection of test results to identify failures not amenable to automatic detection and to sort out deviations that are true failures—unless you can demonstrate that the ratio of failures to deviations is essentially constant. In that case, you can use deviation data in place of failure data, adjusting by the known ratio. You must also consider many special circumstances such

as cascaded failures, repeated failures, and failures that will deliberately not be resolved [2,4].

You should determine the time of failure occurrence or number of failures per time period in execution time. If execution time is not readily available, you can use one of many possible approximations [1,4]. You will need a special approach to handle failure data if testing is done on multiple machines [4].

3.5 Interpret failure data

The interpretation of failure data depends on whether you are doing development or certification testing.

3.5.1 Development testing. The first activity is to consider trends (in feature, load, and regression testing) by estimating and plotting the failure intensity over all severity classes and across all operational modes against calendar (ordinary) time. Figure 3 shows a failure intensity trend very similar to what we obtained for Fone Follower. The center plot (black) represents the most likely estimate; the other two plots (gray) represent the upper and lower 95-percent confidence bounds.

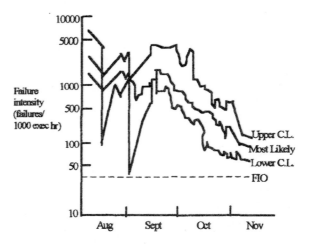

Figure 3. Example of a failure intensity trend. The center line shows the most likely estimate; the outer lines represent the upper and lower 95-percent confidence bounds.

Comparison with the overall failure intensity objective helps you identify "at risk" schedules or reliabilities and lets you take appropriate and timely corrective actions. Long, large upswings in failure intensity commonly indicate that either the system has evolved or the test operational profile has changed. System evolution can be an indication of poor change control. A change in the test operational profile may indicate poorly planned test execution. In either case, corrective actions are necessary if you are to have a dependable test.

The next activity is to guide release decisions. Estimate the system failure intensity and compare it with the objective. Release decisions include component test to system test, system test to beta test, or beta test to general availability.

You can estimate failure intensity from failure times or the number of failures per time period, using reliability-estimation programs based on software reliability models and statistical inference, such as CASRE (Computer-Aided Software Reliability Estimation) [3].

3.5.2 Certification testing.
Certification testing uses a reliability demonstration chart [1] such as that in Figure 4. Fone Follower applied a similar chart to certifying its operating system. To normalize failure times, you multiply them by the appropriate failure intensity objective. You can then plot each failure on the chart and label it with its severity class. Depending on the region in which it falls, you may accept or reject the software being tested or continue testing. In Figure 4, the testing resulted in three failures, which occurred consecutively in time. Each of the first two indicates that testers should continue testing. The third falls in the accept region, indicating that sufficient data has finally been collected to demonstrate that the software can be accepted at the risk levels for which the chart was constructed.

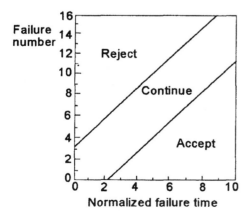

Figure 4. Reliability demonstration chart similar to that produced in the Fone Follower project.

You can build reliability demonstration charts for different levels of consumer risk (the risk of accepting a bad program) and supplier risk (the risk of rejecting a good program)[1].

4. Deployment

Practitioners have generally found SRE unique in offering a standard proven way to engineer and manage testing in a way that lets them increase their confidence in the reliability of the software-based system they delivered. They have also appreciated the decrease in time to market and increase in testing efficiency. Given these reactions, I expect the use of SRE to continue growing at a rapid rate.

This growth gives rise to the important issue of how to effectively deploy SRE. I and my colleagues have tried several approaches and have found marked differences in their effectiveness.

- *Consultant does all.* Hiring a consultant to do everything is the most expensive and probably the worst approach; true commitment of development projects is often lacking and company personnel do not gain skills in SRE.
- *Self-teaching.* This is only slightly better than having a consultant do everything. The main drawback is that project personnel have no one to answer their questions or give them feedback on what they are doing. Consequently, there is a high risk that they are not applying SRE correctly.
- *Course without a workshop.* Participants acquire knowledge, but they don't get the opportunity to try what they have learned or to receive feedback.
- *Course with a workshop.* This approach is probably the most cost-effective one. It teaches participants the necessary skills, allows them to try out what they've learned and to get feedback, and to ask questions. The course with the workshop is most effective when done on site, with work groups organized by projects. Each project team brings its requirements specification and architecture documents. Each should leave with the initial outline of a plan for applying SRE to their project.
- *Custom or group jump starts.* Jump starts also teach participants the necessary skills, allow them to try out what they've learned and get feedback, and ask questions—but they cost considerably more than a course with a workshop. In a jump start, a consultant participates in projects over a substantial period of time to answer questions and review the work of the projects. The custom jump start, which is dedicated to one project, is more expensive than the group jump start, in which consulting resources are shared.

Jump starts are very nice for projects that can afford them, but they aren't essential. You can choose the course with a workshop and supplement it with access to a consultant for questions without the investment in time that project participation involves. The principal high cost element is the time the consultant must spend to learn and follow the project. Organizations can avoid this cost by selecting a project representative to work with the consultant. The project representative attends the course with a workshop along with the project team. The representative then translates project issues into questions that relate to SRE practices and poses them to the consultant.

Those interested in learning more about software reliability engineering have many opportunities for participation. To join the IEEE Computer Society Technical Committee on Software Reliability Engineering (membership is free), you may contact the web site http://www.tcse.org/tcseform.html. To subscribe to the software reliability engineering bulletin board on the Internet, contact vishwa@hac2arpa.hac.com; to post items on the bulletin board, contact sw-rel@igate1.hac.com. There is a Software Reliability Engineering site on the Worldwide Web [5]. It provides an overview of the topic, an article for managers, a list of articles published by practitioners who have used SRE, the "Question of the Month" with answer, information on courses, and other material.

John D. Musa teaches courses and consults in software reliability engineering and testing. He has been involved in software reliability engineering since 1973 and is generally recognized as one of the creators of that field. Recently, he was Technical Manager of Software Reliability Engineering at AT&T Bell Laboratories, Murray Hill. He organized and led the transfer of software reliability engineering into practice within AT&T, spearheading the effort that defined it as a "best current practice." Musa has also been actively involved in research to advance the theory and practice of software reliability engineering. He has published more than 90 articles and papers, given more than 175 major presentations, and made several videos. He is principal author of Software Reliability: Measurement, Prediction, Application *(McGraw-Hill, 1987).*

Musa received an MS in electrical engineering from Dartmouth College. He is listed in Who's Who in America *and* American Men and Women of Science. *He is a fellow of the IEEE and the IEEE Computer and Reliability Societies and a member of the ACM and ACM Sigsoft. Contact Musa at 39 Hamilton Rd., Morristown, NJ 07960; j.musa@ieee.org.*

This article is adapted from an article that appeared in the November 1996 *Computer*, copyright IEEE 1996.

Acknowledgments
I am most grateful for the careful review and helpful experience-based comments of Willa Ehrlich, Susie Hill, Steve Meyer, and Ray Sandfoss of AT&T.

References

1. J. Musa, *More Reliable, Faster, Cheaper Testing through Software Reliability Engineering* , McGraw-Hill, New York, to be published

2. J. Musa, "Operational Profiles in Software Reliability Engineering," *IEEE Software*, Mar. 1993, pp. 14-32.

3. *Handbook of Software Reliability Engineering*, M. Lyu, ed., McGraw-Hill, New York, and IEEE CS Press, Los Alamitos, Calif., 1996 (includes CD/ROM with CASRE and other reliability-estimation programs).

4. J. Musa, A. Iannino, and K. Okumoto, *Software Reliability: Measurement, Prediction, Application*, McGraw-Hill, New York, 1987.

5. Software Reliability Engineering web site, http://members.aol.com/JohnDMusa/

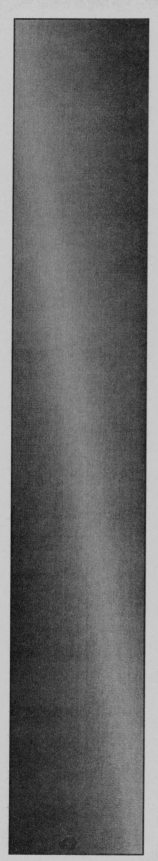

CHAPTER 6
MAINTENANCE

As many as 70 cents of every dollar spent on software development are consumed by maintenance. Maintenance consists of repairs and enhancements. "Repair" is the process of correcting defects. "Enhancement" is the process of improving on the product. Any activity that consumes 70% of a budget is bound to draw attention, and so cost control is a major maintenance issue. Tools and automation can reduce the burden, and case studies can provide valuable insights.

In the papers that follow, Kilpi treats the version control process separately from configuration management, providing a way in which tools for each of these purposes can be compared. He makes specific tool recommendations. Dumke and Winkler discuss the use of computer-assisted software measurement and evaluation tools for maintenance. Schneidewind discusses a method for evaluating the effectiveness of maintenance efforts, using data from NASA's Space Shuttle flight software. His process measures the influence on product reliability of maintenance actions and testing. Rugaber and White discuss the restoration of a legacy telephone system, contributing an interesting case study in maintenance.

Reprinted from IEEE
EUROMICRO 97, pp. 33-41.

New Challenges for Version Control and Configuration Management: a Framework and Evaluation

Tapani Kilpi
Department of Information Processing Science, the University of Oulu
Linnanmaa 90570 Oulu, FINLAND
email: tapani@rieska.oulu.fi
fax: +358 8 553 1890

Abstract

Software production of today lays high demands on the capabilities of software product management (SPM) process. SPM is defined as a process basing strongly on the well-known approaches of version control (VC) and configuration management (CM). The improvement of SPM demands well designed and implemented VC- and CM-processes on bottom. For this reason a selection of a suitable VC/CM-tool is an important part of the SPM improvement process. It is necessary to be able to specify the right tool selection criteria for each specific case.

1. Introduction

Software industry is developing strongly towards becoming a product business. This lays increasing demands for the development of software product management process and its tool support in the companies. Software product management (SPM) is defined as a process consisting of version control (VC), configuration management (CM), product management (PM) and total product management (TPM). Each of these sub-processes manages an archive containing product related information. Version control manages and keeps track of the *configuration items* which are any documents created during a software development process, and which are found necessary to be placed under configuration control: requirements documents, data flow diagrams, design documents, source code, test results etc. Configuration management controls *configuration data*, i.eg. which components belong to a certain product, and also means of building the product. Product management controls *delivery data*, i.eg. what exact combination of product components and to which environment have been delivered to some specific customer. Finally, total product management controls *customer data* and *bug records*. This covers all customer contact and feedback data as well as the

identified bugs. In an ideal situation both of these can also be tracked back to the source code level.

The problems companies have with SPM can normally be classified into two main-groups: process-related and tool-related problems. In this paper a real world example of SPM analysis and improvement plan is presented. The ideas presented here base on the findings of TPM-Project (Towards Total Product Management in Technopolis Oulu) that is run by three companies each having an objective of improving the maturity of software product management. This paper describes the selection of VC/CM-tool for the TPM-companies. The VC/CM-tool selection was found to be of primary meaning as the first actual development step after the analysis of SPM maturity in TPM companies. This can also be derived from the definition of SPM that presents VC and CM as the core of SPM. In TPM the first step of SPM improvement plan consisted of the definition of the VC/CM-processes model and the implementation of them. The selection of suitable VC/CM-tool for the needs of TPM-companies was an essential part of this. This paper describes the VC/CM-tool selection process, the ideas behind the framework used for the selection and also the result of the selection.

2. Problems explored in software product management

The ideas presented in this paper base on the findings in TPM project (Towards Total Product Management in Technopolis Oulu). The objective of the project is to define and implement an ideal and at the same time a realistic software product management (SPM) model for three companies participating the project [6, Kilpi 1996.] Software product management is defined to consist of the following sub-processes: version control (VC), configuration management (CM), product management (PM) and total product management (TPM) [1, Auer

1996]. The sub-processes form together a hierarchy that is illustrated with the necessary data storages in figure 1.

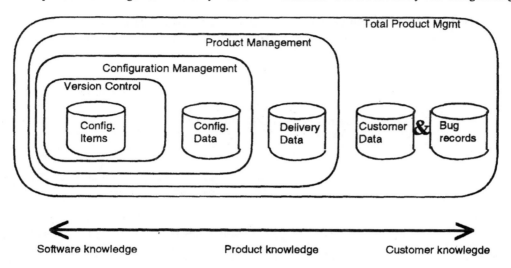

Figure 1. Software Product Management [1, Auer 1996].

The original status of SPM processes in the TPM companies were evaluated and analysed by using Pr²imer method [7, Pr²imer 1996] developed by VTT Electronics of Finland. The question series of Trillium method [8, Trillium 1994] were used in combination with Pr²imer for the evaluation part. Because the aim of the project was to define a common model for all the three companies, also the problems were analysed together. The problems of SPM found during the analysis phase are presented in table 1.

	Problems
Configuration Items	• version control is missing from source codes and other documents • tools and 3rd party components are not version controlled • reusable components are neither identified nor used
Product Data	• the decision of new product revisions is not documented • source codes are not completely module tested, nor have they any quality metrics • changes are neither tracked nor verified
Delivery Data	• traceability from specifications to source code does not exist • delivery and order processes are not documented • the identification of all deliveries (serial number) is not fully seamless • the delivery database is not complete in all deliveries • testing procedures are not integrated to the delivery process
Customer Data	• a lot of time is spent to solve customers' problems in their attempts to use the products in different environments • all customer data is not saved (for example customer environment data) • customer reports are neither formally documented nor analysed • service requests are not fully handled and tracked • minor bug fixes are not informed to all customers
Change Request Data	• change requests are neither formally documented nor analysed for process improvement

Table 1. The problems of Software Product Management Processes in TPM-companies

The three TPM-companies are all quite small-sized, and locate in Technopolis Oulu. **QPR** (Oy Quality Production & Research Ltd) specialises in developing, manufacturing and marketing of software tools on business management area. At the moment there are about 30 employees in QPR. The technical environment of QPR is based on a Novell network. The workstations are PC-based, using Windows95 and WindowsNT. The main tools in development are Borland Delphi and Visual Basic. **Modera** (Modera Point Oy) specialises in systems developed for waterworks, peat suppliers and telecommunications. The current number of employees is 10. The technical environment of Modera is based on a Novell network. The workstations are PC-based, using Windows. Internet-addresses are provided for almost all employees. **Prosoft** (Prosoft Oy) has specialised in developing, manufacturing and marketing the testing tools for embedded software. The number of employees is 5. The technical environment of Prosoft is based on TCP/IP

network with Sun server. The workstations are PC-based using Windows95, WindowsNT and OS/2. Internet-addresses are provided for almost all employees.

3. Software product process in the TPM-companies

In the next phase of TPM-project a model of software product process was defined for managing the software change process in the TPM-companies efficiently. This was found necessary in order to define the objectives of the project on a detailed level. The redefined process model is to remove as many as possible of the problems found in the original status analysis of the companies. In software industry the requirement for changing products is caused by the needs of the market and the customers. The task of a software company is to satisfy the needs of their customers, and to be able to correspond to the changing demands in the market.

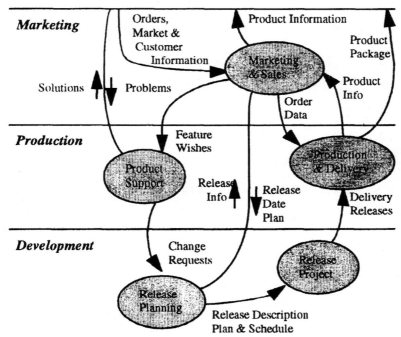

Market & Customers

Figure 2. Software Product Management Process in TPM-Companies

The function of a company is modelled with three activity areas in the TPM-process model, which are: the *Development*, the *Production*, and the *Marketing*

activities. The three activities complete each other, and have been designed to work together and to complete each other in order to reach the company objectives. The

Marketing activity collects and analyses the market and the customer information, as well as informs the market and the customers of the products and the new releases of them. The *Production* activity provides the support facilities for the customers' problems, and takes care of handling the orders and the deliveries. The *Development* activity manages the product change process by analysing all the feedback and the development ideas collected, and by planning the release projects. The general level TPM-process model is illustrated in figure 2.

The model consists of five main processes: the *Marketing & Sales*, the *Product Support*, the *Production & Delivery*, the *Release Planning*, and the *Release Project*. The *Marketing & Sales* process collects the Market Information and the Customer Feedback, and produces Feature Wishes basing on the results of the information and the feedback analysis. The Feature Wishes are then passed to the *Product Support* process where they are classified and saved together with the Customer Problem data in the Change Request format in the Change Request database. Solutions to the customers' problems are normally provided by the *Product Support* process, and sent to the customers, and the unsolved ones are saved as Change Requests. The general level Product Strategy is defined as a part of the *Marketing & Sales* process, and the Release Date Plan basing on the Strategy is delivered to the *Release Planning* process. The *Release Planning* process starts to plan a new release basing on the Release Date Schedule by analysing all the collected Change Requests.

As a result of the *Release Planning* process detailed Release Description, Plan, and Schedule are delivered to the *Release Project* process for starting the development work. The *Release Planning* process also sends Release Info of the next release to the *Marketing & Sales* process. The *Release Project* process produces a new release of a product corresponding to the Release Requirements. The accepted new Releases are delivered then as delivery Releases to the *Production & Delivery* process for archiving and managing deliveries. The deliveries base on the Customer Orders that are passed to the *Production & Delivery* process normally through the *Marketing & Sales* process. In a delivery a customer gets a Product Package containing all the product components, the manuals, the examples, etc. The *Production & Delivery* process also sends Product Information to the use of the *Marketing & Sales* process.

A successful implementation of the process model presented in this section lays high demands for VC/CM process supporting it like presented in section 1. Along

with the traditional VC/CM needs the supporting system should also be capable of saving customer, delivery and bug information. The customer interaction and bug information are in most cases related to some specific versions of a product. An analysis of the feedback collected is not possible if the former product versions and their building environments can not be regenerated. All the former deliveries made should be able to be rebuilt in their original form in a company. The VC/CM system should support along with this also saving of all the delivery-, bug- and customer related data possibly needed for development and production processes.

4. Criteria for VC/CM-tool selection

After defining the problems (section 2) and the SPM process model (section 3) it became obvious that the tool support of SPM needed to be renewed in the TPM companies. In the first place this meant a selection of a suitable VC/CM-tool and a definition of a selection criteria for it. On the one hand the criteria had to be tool oriented and on the other hand SPM process oriented. In outlining the demands for a VC/CM-tool the CM-services model [4, Dart 1992] and the CM requirements [2, 3, Dart 1990, 1991] were applicated.

The services model ties together process model and user roles. It does this through the definition of services independent of user role and process. The user picks and tailors the services to suit a particular role for a particular process. Figure 3. gives an indication how the services model was used in TPM. The services selected are made out of various mechanisms that have been customised and integrated together to meet certain policies. The role used is the VC/CM-needs of the TPM-companies. These needs can straightly be led from the SPM problems presented in section 2. To analyse the needs from the point of view of tools the functionality of VC/CM-systems needs to be defined and understood first. Dart (1992) [4] has defined the CM functionality areas as follows:

- **Components:** identifies, classifies, stores and accesses the components that make up the product.
- **Structure:** represents the architecture of the product.
- **Construction:** supports the construction of the products and their artefacts.
- **Auditing:** keeps an audit trail of the product and its processes.
- **Accounting:** gathers statistics about the product and the process.
- **Controlling:** controls how and when changes are made.

- **Process:** supports the management of how the product evolves.

- **Team:** enables a project team to develop and maintain a family.

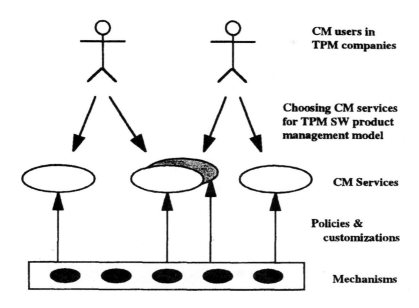

Figure 3. Applicating the CM Services Model for TPM needs [4, Dart 1992].

The demands towards the tools were outlined by analysing the practical VC/CM-experiences of the companies through the functionality areas. As a result of this a set of CM services required was defined. The set of services is strongly tool oriented because it is meant to be applicated straightly for tool evaluation. The services are called here the tool evaluation criteria, and they are presented in table 2.

CM services for TPM needs / tool view	
Components	1. creation of a new project 2. creation of a new file 3. making project specific variants of components
Structure	4. taking a commonly usable component into use in a project 5. using 3rd party components (libraries)
Construction	6. handling files through using menus (VC++) 7. version management of development tools
Auditing	8. listing the revision history of a single file 9. listing the revision history of the whole project 10. listing the revision history of the whole project between two releases of the project
Accounting	11. listing which files are locked in a project
Controlling	12. parallel use of the same files by more than one developer 13. locking of file revisions against further changes (before 'promotion')
Process	14. definition of a 'promotion' hierarchy (draft, proposal, accepted, published, obsolete) 15. automation of actions when 'promoting'
Team	16. defining different 'roles' in the development process

Table 2. CM services for software product management model of the TPM project

In defining the CM-services the TPM project group found several SPM service needs in TPM companies which are outside VC and CM. These needs had to be left out of the set of services because the primary goal was to select a VC/CM-tool. Including the outside features to the criteria might have interfered the results of the tool evaluation. However, the necessary product management features will be implemented later during TPM project to the SPM support system of the companies. Some additional tool support will be needed for the SPM features, which had also to be noticed on a general level in the tool selection. The general level knowledge concerning this was collected mainly through benchmarking in other companies.

5. Evaluating the long list of VC/CM tools

The CM-services defined in the previous section were applied as selection criteria for VC/CM-tool selection in the TPM-project.

The long list	Notes
1. Aide-De-Camp	- requires UNIX server - change set model as a primary CM-model
2. CCC/Harvest	- requires UNIX server - change set model as a primary CM-model
3. CCC/Manager	+ quite good functionality for TPM needs - interferse with the way a developer would normally work
4. ClearCase	+ second best functionality for TPM needs - requires windows NT or UNIX server - Windows client /Attache) only a subset
5. CMZ	- poor functionality for TPM needs - a bit academic to be an industrial strength tool
6. Continuus/CM	+ the best functionality for TPM needs - requires UNIX server - the most expensive
7. ExcoConf	+ covers much of the functionality required by TPM + good overall impression - no clear picture of the capabilities (project concept?) - product literature hard to understand
8. MKS Source Integrity	+ cheap - no version tree, slow reports, file based
9. PVCS	+ large installed base + TPM-companies' earlier experiences of PVCS + offers a large area of functionality for TPM needs - expensive because of a lot of separate add-on tools - GUI just a recent feature - file oriented - slow - standard report format is not very good
10. RCE-Revision Control Engine	- no project concept, no support for process management - poor functionality for TPM needs
11. VCS-UX	- long transaction model as a primary CM-model - the model feels a bit "strange" - product literature hard to understand
12. Visual Source Safe	+ cheap - no support for process management - strange branching - poor functionality for TPM needs

Table 3. The tools of TPM "Long List" and notes made of them

The use of the criteria demands installation and test use of all the tools that are to be tested. Because the selection of the VC/CM tools on the market is numerous at the moment, it was not possible to test all the tools in TPM. A pre-evaluation was found necessary in order to find a set of four tools for the final selection where the selected tools were to be examined in detail. The pre-evaluation was based on the literature, brochures, benchmarking, interviewing, internet and the experiences of the TPM companies. Preliminary filtering was done by using platform availability and pricing as criteria. Through this method a "Long List" of twelve tools was gathered: Aide-De-Camp, CCC/Harvest, CCC/Manager, ClearCase, CMZ, Continuus/CM, ExcoConf, MKS Source Integrity, PVCS, RCE-Revision Control Engine, VCS-UX and Visual Source Safe.

The twelve tools were examined closer in order to reduce the number of the final candidates. The selection criteria used for this phase was:

- availability of the tool on platforms used by the TPM companies
- functionality required by the TPM project objectives
- pricing
- the CM-model behind the tool

In estimation of the CM-model the four CM-models [5, Feiler, 1991] were applied as a base. The four models could be characterised as follows. The *checkout/checkin model* offers version management of individual components. The *composition model* focuses on improving the construction of system configurations through selection of alternative versions. *The long transaction model* emphasises the evolution of systems as a series of configuration versions and the co-ordination of concurrent team activity. The *change set model* promotes a view of configuration management focused on logical changes. Typically one or two of the models are supported by a CM system/tool. Each of the tools selected to the long list were then examined on a general level. The notes made each of them are presented in table 3.

Four tools were selected to the "Short List" of TPM through analysing the notes presented in table 3. Up to the improvement plan these tools were to be installed for trial use in the TPM companies, and evaluated through experimenting there. The tools selected to the Short List are: ClearCase, ExcoConf, PVCS and SourceSafe.

6. Evaluating the short list of VC/CM tools

Each tool of the TPM short list except ClearCase was evaluated up to the detailed testing plan. The results of the evaluations of ExcoConf, PVCS and Visual SourceSafe are presented in table 4 where the support provided for each of the CM services used as the criteria in the tool selection are marked with one, two or three stars (one star is the lowest support and three stars the highest). The results base on the test use done in TPM companies, as well as the criteria defined for TPM tool evaluation in section 4.

The evaluation of ClearCase VC/CM tool was prevented because some serious problems were encountered in installation and configuration of the tool. The relatively hard platform demands of ClearCase were complied, but problems were encountered with the network configuration. The Attache part of the ClearCase suite was not able to authenticate users, probably because it was incompatible with the domain controller which was running OS/2 Lan Server Program 3.0. ClearCase tool was initially developed and targeted for the UNIX platform, and probably for this reason the administrative demands of it appear to be relatively complicated in relation to other types of platforms.

Considering the experiences having with ClearCase at this point of the project, and also because of the lack of experienced system administration resources in the TPM companies, it was decided to abandon further investigation of this tool in the TPM project. In addition to the criteria based on the evaluation of table 4 the test use of the three tools produced also a general level comments of each of the tools. These descriptions give an overview of the tools and their suitability for TPM-project needs. The descriptions are as follows:

ExcoConf implements a hierarchical folder structure, where directories are stored as folders which can contain documents and other folders. ExcoConf can manage entire directory trees. Each document or folder can exist in either of the two states: 'released' or 'work'. The released versions of the documents are stored under the folder's 'release' directory, and the 'work' versions are stored in 'work' directories. For multiple users, it is possible to specifically lock files so that all users can not access all files. The file saving system of ExcoConf uses a lot of disk space. ExcoConf supports branching, but it relies on third-party merge and branch tools (a user must provide his own merge and branch). Also, there is no special make tool; only a pre-processor to process the make files so that logical file names can be used instead of physical ones. ExcoConf is available on VMS, UNIX and Windows 3.1, and the Windows 3.1 version runs also under NT and Windows 95. ExcoConf is fairly easy to install and maintain. The graphical user interface is a bit awkward. It supports file drag-and-drop and file associations, but it must be kept open practically all the time, and it takes a lot of room in a display.

CM service	ExcoConf	PVCS	Visual Source Safe
1. creation of a new project	* *	*	* * *
2. creation of a new file	* *	* *	* *
3. making project specific variants of components	*	*	* *
4. taking a commonly usable component into use in a project	* *	* *	* * *
5. using 3rd party components (libraries)	*	*	*
6. handling files through using menus (VC++)	*	* * *	* *
7. version management of development tools	*	*	*
8. listing the revision history of a single file	*	* * *	* * *
9. listing the revision history of the whole project	*	* *	* * *
10. listing the revision history of the whole project between two releases	*	* *	* *
11. listing which files are locked in a project	*	* *	* *
12. parallel use of the same files by more than one developer	*	* * *	* *
13. locking of file revisions against further changes (before 'promotion')	*	* * *	*
14. definition of a 'promotion' hierarchy (draft, proposal, accepted, published, obsolete)	*	* * *	*
15. automation of actions when 'promoting'	*	* *	*
16. defining different 'roles' in the development process	*	* * *	*

Table 4. The results of the TPM tool evaluation

PVCS implements a hierarchical folder structure, where directories are stored as folders. A problem with PVCS folder structure is that it is just a one level hierarchy, and the creation of a hierarchy of more than one level has to be done by manual creation and linking of working directories. PVCS does not support a creation of separate personal working directories for different members of a project team. This can only be managed by creating different projects for different users, but this causes a mix up with varying settings and policies of the users. PVCS contains facilities for branching but only one revision can be in a given promotion status at a time. Problems occur with this when bug fixes are done to a recent release and features belonging to the next release have already been added to the "newest" version. The new features are not wanted to deliver to the customer, only the bug fixes. The merging facilities of PVCS worked inaccurately in the TPM test use. Automatic merge did not work at all and the manual one was very complex to use.

Visual SourceSafe proved to be the most easy-to-use of the VC/CM tools of TPM short list. The GUI is well designed, the project view logical and loading time of a project is fast. A major shortage of Visual SourceSafe is that it does not contain a promotion hierarchy feature. Another disadvantage of VSS is that it does not provide the user with a proper diagrammatic view of the revision history of a file. The multiple check-out feature which enables many users to check out the same file affected quite useful in the test use. VSS does not revision files like other VC/CM tools do, instead it assigns version numbers to each revision of a file. This might cause confusions in normal use.

7. Conclusion

The conclusion of the TPM evaluation team was to recommend the selection of PVCS VC/CM-tool for supporting the SPM-processes in the TPM companies. PVCS collected the highest number of stars in the tool evaluation, illustrated in table 4 in section 6. Considering this result as well as the verbal statements of the TPM evaluation team of each of the tools, the TPM project group found the following reasons for making the selection. *ClearCase* was not recommended because of the difficulties in setting it up and getting it into working condition in the platforms of TPM companies. The price of ClearCase and its purchase and maintenance costs were also found to be high. The relatively high expertise required to support the tool was also found unsatisfactory by the TPM project group. *ExcoConf* was not recommended because the VC-model it uses was experienced to be unfamiliar to the TPM team, intermediate versions of source files are not stored by it, it requires a lot of disk space for the archives and there are inconsistencies and bugs in the user interface. *Visual SourceSafe* was not recommended because the functional limitations discovered in it were found to be fatal. Although many problems were found with the *PVCS* tool as well, it was recommended to be selected for TPM because it carries a large installed base of tools and it also has large coverage of functionality required by the TPM companies.

On a general level the remarks made in the TPM project by this far have showed that the development of version control and configuration management processes have to be regarded as a part of developing the whole product management process in a company. In the next phase the TPM project will concentrate on adding product management facilities on top of the already implemented VC/CM-processes. In practice this means design and implementation of customer interaction and bug data management features to the processes. The long term objective of TPM companies is to raise the standard of their software product management to a level that covers also the marketing processes. This lays high demands, for example, on the release planning and scheduling of the products.

The concepts of release project, release planning and release approval need to be defined and formalised, and as the most important part, they need to be implemented to software product management processes of the companies.

On this stage of improvement the software product management reaches a state where it is a part of business process of a company. However, the most important finding of the TPM project by far is the old truth: there is no such thing as a perfect process. That is why the software product management process improvement will be added as a regular and steady part to the business processes of the TPM companies.

References

[1] Auer, A. 1996. Seminar Presentation Material of the Final Presentation of LEIVO-project 14.2.1996 in Helsinki. Organised by VTT Electronics.

[2] Dart, S. 1990. Spectrum of Functionality in Configuration Management Systems. Technical Report. CMU/SEI-90-TR-11. ESD-90-TR-212.

[3] Dart, S. 1991. Concepts in Configuration Management Systems. Proceedings of the 3rd International Workshop on Software Configuration Management, June 1991, pp. 1 - 18.

[4] Dart, S. 1992. The Past, Present, and Future of Configuration Management. Technical Report. CMU/SEI-92-TR-8. ESC-TR-92--8.

[5] Feiler, P. H. 1991. Configuration Management Models in Commercial Environments. Technical Report. CMU/SEI-91-TR-7. ESD-9-TR-7.

[6] Kilpi, T. 1996. Evaluating the Maturity of Software Product Management: A Case Study in Three Companies. Proceedings of the Ninth Australian Software Engineering Conference ASWEC '96 July 14 to July 18, 1996. IREE Society.

[7] Pr^{2}imer. 1996. http://www.ele.vtt.fi/projects/primer/primer.htm. VTT Electronics/Technical Research Centre of Finland.

[8] Trillium. 1994. Trillium: Model for Telecom Product Development & Support Process Capability. Bell/Canada. Release 3.0. December. 118p.

Reprinted from IEEE
EUROMICRO 97, pp. 74-81.

CAME Tools for an Efficient Software Maintenance

Reiner R. Dumke   Achim S. Winkler
University of Magdeburg, Faculty of Computer Science
Postfach 4120, D-39016 Magdeburg, Germany
email: {dumke, winkler}@irb.cs.uni-magdeburg.de

Abstract

This paper describes the role of the metrics tools as Computer Assisted Software Measurement and Evaluation (CAME) tools in the software life cycle, especially in the maintenance phase. The most CAME tools are designed for code analysis and measurement. They are predestined to be applied to the implementation and maintenance development phases. But, more and more tools are developed for the earlier phases of software development to estimate the effort, complexity, and size of the software that will be created. This paper will provide an overview of the present situation on the area of the CAME tools and discuss their efficient use in the software maintenance.

1 Introduction

CAME tools are tools for modelling and determinating the metrics of software development components referring to the process, the product and the resource. Presently, the CAME tool area also includes the tools for model-based software components analysis, metrics application, presentation of measurement results, statistical analysis and evaluation. In general, we can establish CAME tools for classification, for component measurement, for process or product measurement and evaluation, as well as for training in software measurement. The application of CAME tools is based on the given measurement framework (see [2], [3], [4], [7], [12], [13], [17], [18], [19], [20], [24], [25], [28] and [29]). The integration of CAME tools in the tool supports in the software engineering cycle is given in the Figure 1. On the other hand CAME tools can be classified according to the degree of integration in software development environments such as integrated forms, external coupling forms and stand-alone metrics tools.

Fig. 1   The general CAME tool integration

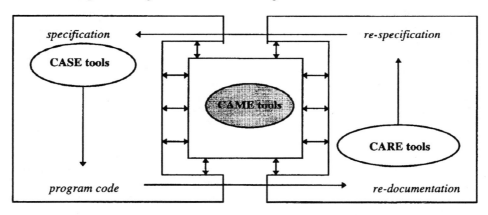

The existing CAME tools in the Software Measurement Laboratory at the University of Magdeburg are given in the following table ([8], [11], [26], [27]). The market Tools can be obtained at the University of Magdeburg (ftp.cs.uni-magdeburg.de in /pub/metrik). The languages given in the brackets are the versions of these tools applied at our University. In general, these tools support more languages.

Tab. 1 CAME tools applied at the University of Magdeburg

Process Measurement and Evaluation:
* SynQuest *(Bootstrap)* **Switzerland**
* NEXTRA *(gen. classification)***USA**
* Ami Tool *(GQM, CMM)* **France**
* SPQR/20 *(Jones Experience, Function Points)* **USA**
* SOFT-ORG *(general organizational model)* **Germany**
* SQUID M-Base *(COQUAMO) U.K.*

Product Measurement and Evaluation:
* Requirement Analysis and Specification:
  * PDM* *(HTML Text)* **Magdeburg**
  * RMS *(Documentation)* **Germany**
  * Function Point Workbench **Australia**
  * FPTOOL (Demo) **Germany**
  * CHECKPOINT (Demo) *USA*
  * SOFT-CALC *(Function Point, Data Point, Object Point)* **Germany**
  * SVS* *(McCall Model)* **Magdeburg**
  * OOM* *(OOA/OOD Models of Coad/Yourdon)* **Magdeburg**
  * COSMOS *(Lotos) Netherlands*
* Software Design:
  * MOOD (Demo, *C++*) **Portugal**
  * DEMETER (Demo) *USA*
  * SmallCritic (Demo, *Smalltalk*) **Germa-ny**
* Program Evaluation:
  * MCOMP* *(Modula Subset)* **Magdeburg**
  * CodeCheck *(C, C++) USA*
  * SOFT-AUDITOR *(Cobol)* **Germany**
  * QUALIGRAPH (Demo) **Hungary**
  * MPP* *(C++)* **Magdeburg**
  * OOMetric (Demo) *USA*
  * QUALMS *(Fortran, Pascal, C) U.K.*
  * ProVista *(C)* **Germany**
  * DATRIX *(C)* **Canada**
  * LOGISCOPE *(C, C++) USA*
  * COSMOS *(C) Netherlands*
  * PMTool* *(C++)* **Magdeburg**

---

* PC-METRIC *(Fortran, C, Pascal) USA*
* PMT* *(Prolog)* **Magdeburg**
* MJAVA* *(Java)* **Magdeburg**
* Software Test:
  * IDAS-TESTDAT *(C)* **Germany**
  * LDRA Testbed *(C++) U.K.*
  * STW-METRIC *(C++) USA*
* Software Maintenance:
  * Smalltalk Measure* **Magdeburg**

Resource Measurement and Evaluation:
* Productivity:
  * SPQR/20 *USA*
  * and the other above
* Performance:
  * Foundation Manager *USA*
  * SunNet Manager *USA*

Measurement Presentation and Statistical Analysis:
* SOFT-MESS **Germany**
* EXCEL *USA*
* SPSS *USA*

Software Measurement Training:
* METKIT *U.K.*
* MIS **Germany**

The CAME tools should be embedded in a software measurement framework which includes the software process characteristics and their assessment and controlling. In general, we can distinguish two kinds of frameworks: the *informal* and the *formal*. *Informal approaches* of software measurement frameworks consist of the general components of textual descriptions/questions, rules and 'laws', experience notices, and standards. Examples of these measurement frameworks are ([1], [10], [12], [13], [17], [28]) the *ISO 9000-3 standard,* the *Capability Maturity Model* (CMM) (SEI in Pittsburgh), the *Goal Question Metric* paradigm (GQM) (University of Maryland), the *Software Quality Metrics* report (FAA Technical Center, New Jersey), the *TickIT approach* (UK), the *BOOTSTRAP quality standard* (ESI, European Esprit project), the *Software Measurement Guidebook* (NASA), the *Trillium standard* (Bell Canada), the *AQAP* and the *DOD STD 2167A* (USA military area), the European *SPICE project* etc. The situation in the informal approaches can be characterized by a 'break' in the measurement methodology between the measurement goals and the (selected) metrics. *Formal approaches* for the software measurement frameworks can be divided in *algebraic* approaches, axiomatic approaches, functional approaches, and rule-based approaches ([8], [12], [13], [25], [29]) and we can establish the situation no independence of the development paradigm, only a few practicable results or few empirical evaluations, and only a few empirical evaluation. The underlying rules in software (quality) measurement frameworks are for example in the NASA Guidebook [24]: establishing a *measurement program* (including the definition of the goals, the responsibilities and selecting the measures),

core measures (especially the costs, errors, process characteristics, project dynamics, and project characteristics), operation of the measurement program (with the use of metrics tools, storage the measurement values etc.), analysis, application, and feedback (as goal of the (software process or product) improvement). A general idea of measurement frameworks is shown in the Figure 2 in a simplified form.

Fig. 2 Measurement Frameworks

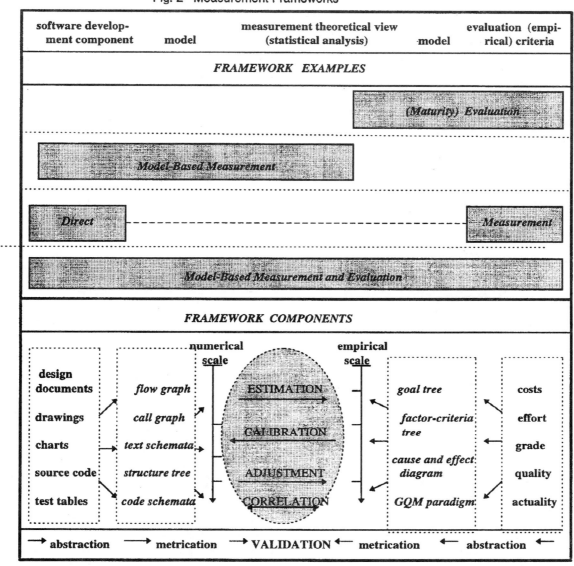

Examples of the different measurement strategies and frameworks are the Bang metric for the Structured Analysis development method as model-based measurement and the Capability Maturity Model as evaluation. The quantifiable aspects of the software process, the software product and the used resources is shown in the Table 2 (the full metrics hierarchy see [7]).

Tab. 2   An overview of software metrics

PROCESS METRICS	PRODUCT METRICS	RESOURCES METRICS

Maturity Metrics
- organization metrics
- resources, personnel and
  training metrics
- technology management metrics
- documented standards metrics
- process metrics
- data management and analysis
Management Metrics
- milestone metrics
- risks metrics
- workflow metrics
- controlling metrics
- management data base metrics
Life Cycle Metrics
- problem definition metrics
- requirement analysis and
  specification metrics
- design metrics
- implementation metrics
- maintenance metrics
	Size Metrics
	- elements counting
	- development size metrics
	- size of components metrics
	Architecture Metrics
	- components metrics
	- architecture characteristics
	- architecture standards metrics
	Structure Metrics
	- component characteristics
	- structure characteristics
	- psychological rules metrics
	Quality Metrics
	- functionality metrics
	- reliability metrics
	- usability metrics
	- efficiency metrics
	- maintainability metrics
	- portability metrics
	Complexity Metrics
	- computational complexity metrics
	- psychological complexity metrics
		Personal Metrics
		- programmer experience metrics
		- communication level metrics
		- productivity metrics
		- team structure metrics
		Software Metrics
		- performance metrics
		- paradigm metrics
		- replacement metrics
		Hardware Metrics
		  performance metrics
		- reliability metrics
		- availability metrics

2 The current situation of CAME tools

In the following, we present some examples of CAME tools with the different possibilities of model based presentation, metrics execution, component evaluation, and measurement education (see [6], [8], [15], [16], [21], and [29]). The following two diagrams characterize the current situation in short, concise, and very simplified form [6].

Fig. 3   CAME tool situation

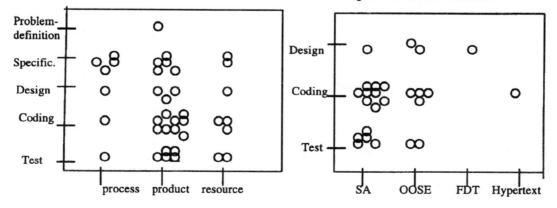

The left diagram describes the CAME tool situation in the software development phases for the process, product and resource evaluation, wheras, the diagram on the right side describes the relations to the different programming/development paradigms (SA - Structured Analysis, OOSE - object-oriented, and FDT - formal description techniques). Figure 4 describes the situation of selected CAME tools corresponding to the different measurement aspects of flexibility and openness. The

flexibility is necessary to manage the software development complexity in the company, and it allows to define new metrics in the tool or to change the empirical evaluation criteria. Openness is required to use any components of the CAME tool for the applied measurement framework, such as the modelling part, the metrics execution part or the statistical analysis and the presentation.

Fig. 4   Flexibility and openness of CAME tools

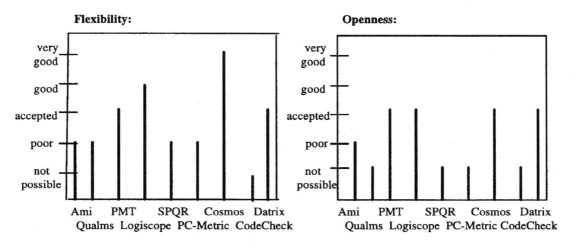

Obviously, a lack of openess of the analyzed tools can be observed. Figure 5 shows how useful the evaluation of the selected CAME tools is.

Fig. 5   Validity and stability of the CAME tools

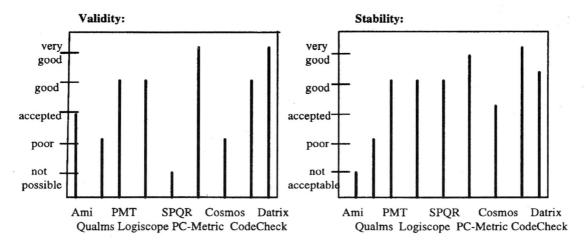

The usefulness is divided in validity and stability of the tool application. The validity is the characterization of the correctness of the metrics values and the reconstructability of the results. The stability corresponds to the reliability of the tool at run-time. You can see in *http://irb.cs.uni-magdeburg.de/se/metrics_eng.html* a short description of these tools in the World-Wide Web in our Measurement Laboratory Interface. In the next section we will describe an efficient use of the CAME tools, especially in the maintenance phase.

3 Problems of an efficient use of CAME tools in the software maintenance

We can establish the situation in the software measurement strategies as more and more consensus about the measurement areas (as process, product and resources) and the empirical goals for the evaluation and the assessment. But the goal must be a measurement-based controlling cycle. CAME tools are mostly directed to special areas of the measurement phases. The following table gives a brief idea of this situation.

Tab. 3   CAME Tools in the measurement phases

CAME Tool	Measurement Definition & Scheduling →	Modelling →	Measurement →	Data Analysis (Presentation) →	Evaluation
AMI	■				
ATHENA		■	■		
Battlemap		■	■		
CodeCheck		■			
COSMOS		■	■	■	
DATRIX		■	■		■
FP Workbench				■	■
LDRA			■		
LOGISCOPE		■	■	■	
MCOMP			■		
OOM			■		
OOMetric			■	■	
PC-METRIC		■	■		■
ProVista			■	■	■
Qualigraph			■	■	
QUALMS			■	■	
Smalltalk M.			■		■
SPQR/20		■	■	■	■
SynQuest	■				

Some general CAME tool application problems and the necessity of standardization of the interfaces between the modelling, measurement, data analysis, and evaluation are described in the following:

- in *modelling*: the visualization of the software development components (especially standardization of flow graphs, call graphs, diagrams etc.) including modern visualization facilities;
- in *measurement*: modification of the IEEE standard to a standard measurement input and a standard measurement output and the extension with metrics definitions in a ''workflow'' manner;
- in *data analysis*: classification and standardization of the measurement output for the use of the existing statistical methods;
- in *evaluation*: the application of the experience in "classical" software develop-ment methodologies in new development paradigms.

The standardization must be considered the high dynamic in the software measurement process and the measurement objects itself.

Other criteria for an efficient use of CAME tools are given in the following points.

- The efficiency of CAME tool application depends on the "well-definedness" of the software process or product themselves.
- CAME tools require in general a good structuring of the measurement area or components: this can be also established as a (first) improvement aspect.
- The main problem in the application of CAME tools is to establish a really measure-ment-controlled cycle, like in the controlling engineering.

For the use of different CAME tools it is necessary to implement a measurement data base. The following Figure 6 presents the JAVA interface of our measurement data base that is based on Oracle. You are invited to participate in some measurement analysis for predefined experiments in these Internet facilities (for the http address see above).

Fig. 6 The architecture of the measurement data base

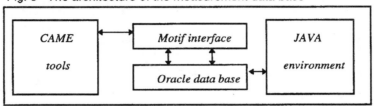

It is a prototype of a company-wide measurement data base to install software measurement-based control cycles. Especially for the maintenance phase we consider the application aspects of the CAME tools in the following manner.

Tab. 4 Forward and backward CAME tool application

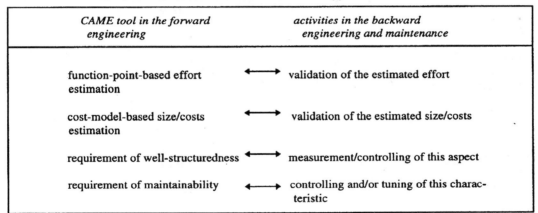

CAME tool in the forward engineering	activities in the backward engineering and maintenance
function-point-based effort estimation	validation of the estimated effort
cost-model-based size/costs estimation	validation of the estimated size/costs
requirement of well-structuredness	measurement/controlling of this aspect
requirement of maintainability	controlling and/or tuning of this charac-teristic

The above table demonstrate the relations between the development forms and the necessity of an *integrated use of CAME tools* with the applied CASE and CARE tools.

4 Conclusions

This paper has summarized the current situation and the problems of the efficiency of use of the CAME tools. One of the goals was also to present an overview of the present situation of the software measurement. In order to use CAME tools efficiently, some rules should be kept in mind:

- The present CAME tools are no suitable means of complex software evaluation. They are mostly based on existing assessment methodologies such as the Function Point method. The applied metrics must be algorithmic.
- The selection of a software metric tool should be influenced by the following considerations:
  - The tool should be designed specifically for the respective software/hardware platform.

- The philosophy of the CAME tool should be applied consequently. The tool-specific conception of modelling, presentation and metrics evaluation should not be violated.
- Both hardware and software platforms are subject to a highly dynamic development process.
- Specific parameters of the software development environment should be known to ensure correct and complete input information for the CAME tool. A profound analysis of the empirical aspects such as effort and costs is an imperative precondition for the proper use of any selected CAME tool (*for the right use of the right metrics tool*).

Further investigations are directed on the measurement and evaluation of the CAME tools themselves to improve the different parts of the software development in a quantitative manner. The current situation of the CAME tools prefers the start in the code evaluation in the implementation or in the maintenance phase for reengineering. But, it is only an assessment to involve the other aspects of the process and product measurement and improvement.

5 References

[1] Ami (application of metrics in industry) - *a quantitative approach to software management.* Handbook, CSSR, London, 1993

[2] Arnold , R.S.: *Software Reengineering.* IEEE Computer Society Press, 1994

[3] Arthur , L.J.: *Improving Software Quality - An Insider's Guide to TQM.* John Wiley & Sons, 1993

[4] Basili, V.R.; Selby, R.W.; Hutchens, D.H.: *Experimentation in Software Engineering.* IEEE Transactions on Software Engineering, 12(1986)7, pp. 733-743

[5] Boehm , B.W.: *Software Risk Management.* IEEE Computer Society Press, 1989

[6] Dumke, R.: *CAME Tools - Lessons Learned.* Proc. of the Fourth International Symposium on Assessment of Software Tools, May 22-24, Toronto, 1996, pp. 113-114

[7] Dumke, R.; Foltin, E.; Koeppe, R.; Winkler, A.: *Measurement-Based Object-Oriented Software Development of the Software Project "Software Measurement Laboratory".* Preprint Nr. 6, 1996, University of Magdeburg (40 p.)

[8] Dumke, R.; Foltin, E.; Koeppe, R.; Winkler, A.: *Softwarequalität durch Meßtools.* Vieweg Publ., 1996

[9] Dumke, R.; Pinkert,K.: *Measurement and Evaluation of LINUX Components with the COSMOS Measure-ment Tool.* SMLAB Report, 002/96

[10] Dumke, R.; Winkler, A.: *Object-Oriented Software Measurement in an OOSE Paradigm.* Proc. of the Spring IFPUG'96, February 7-9, Rome, Italy, 1996

[11] Dumke, R.; Winkler, A.; Zbrog, F.: *Metrics in the Hypertext and Hypermedia Software Development. (German)* Research Reports in Computer Science 1995-25, Technical University of Berlin, 1995, pp.121-127

[12] Ebert, C.; Dumke, R.: *Software-Metriken in der Praxis.* Springer Publ., 1996

[13] Fenton , N.: *Software Metrics - a rigorous approach.* Chapman & Hall, 1991

[14] Fix, A.: *Conception and Implementation of a Measurement Data Base for Distributed Use.* Diploma Thesis, University of Magdeburg, July 1996

[15] Grigoleit, H.: *CAME Tools - An Overview.* in: http://irb.cs.uni-magdeburg.de/se/metrics_eng.html

[16] Heckendorff, R.: *The Smalltalk Measure Browser.* Study, University of Magdeburg, June 1996

[17] Henderson-Sellers, B.: *Object-Oriented Metrics - Measures of Complexity.* Prentice Hall Inc., 1996

[18] Jones , C.: *Assessment and Control of Software Risks.* Yourdon Press, 1994

[19] Kan, S.H.: *Metrics and Models in Software Quality Engineering.* Addison-Wesley Publ., 1995

[20] Kitchenham, B.: *Software Metrics.* Blackwell Publ., Cambridge, Mass., 1996

[21] Kompf, G.: *Conception and Implementation of a Prolog Measurement and Evaluation Tool.(German)* Diploma Thesis, University of Magdeburg, July 1996

[22] Lorenz, M.; Kidd, J.: *Object-Oriented Software Metrics.* Prentice Hall Inc., 1994

[23] Lubahn, D.: *The Conception and Implementation of an C++ Measurement Tool.(German)* Diploma Thesis, University of Magdeburg, March 1996

[24] NASA: *Software Measurement Guidebook,* Maryland 1995

[25] Oman, P.; Pfleeger, S.L.: *Applying Software Metrics.* IEEE Computer Society Press, 1997

[26] Prange, J.: *Conception and Implementation of a HTML document metrics tool. (German)* Study, University of Magdeburg, January 1996

[27] Rudolph, T.: *Implementation of a JAVA metrics tool. (German)* Study, University of Magdeburg, August 1996

[28] Software Productivity Consortium: *The Software Measurement Guidebook.* Thomson Computer Press, 1995

[29] Zuse, H.: *A Framework of Software Measurement.* to be published

Reprinted from IEEE Software,
July/Aug.. 1998, pp. 34-42.

Drawing on extensive data from the NASA Space Shuttle's
flight software, the author proposes a method for evaluating
the effectiveness of legacy software maintenance efforts.

How To Evaluate Legacy System Maintenance

Norman F. Schneidewind, Naval Postgraduate School

With software, we deal with a moving target. According to Manny Lehman, large programs are never completed, they just continue to evolve.[1] Therefore, programs must be adaptable to change and the resultant change process must be planned and controlled. Maintenance must be performed continuously and the stability of the maintenance process—defined as increasing functionality with decreasing failures, over time—affects the product's reliability.

Thus, when I and my colleagues analyzed the stability of the NASA Space Shuttle flight software maintenance process, we knew that the reliability of the software must be a priority. Further, we knew we must also consider the efficiency of the test effort, which forms part of the process and is a determinate of reliability.

We integrated these factors into a unified approach, which let us measure over time the influence of maintenance actions and test effort on the software's reliability. We sought to answer this question: Can various reliability and test metrics be used to measure maintenance process stability? Our research looked for relationships among maintenance actions, reliability, and test effort, as represented by, respectively, the number of code changes per KLOC, various reliability metrics (such as total failures, remaining failures, and time to next failure), and total test time.

THE STABILITY CONCEPT

To gain insight into the maintenance process's interaction with product metrics like reliability, we analyzed two types of metrics trends: across releases and within a release.[2] It was important to note whether an increasing or decreasing trend was favorable. For example, an increasing trend in time to next failure and a decreasing trend in failures per KLOC would be favorable. Conversely, a decreasing trend in time to next failure and an increasing trend in failures per KLOC would be unfavorable.

A favorable trend indicates maintenance stability only if the functionality of the software has increased with time across releases and within releases. I impose this condition because otherwise favorable trends could be the result of decreasing functionality rather than maintenance stability. Increasing functionality is the norm in software projects because, over time, users demand enhancements.

Although looking for a trend on a graph is useful, it is not a precise way of measuring stability, particularly if the graph has peaks and valleys and the measurements are made at discrete points. Therefore, we compute a *change metric* as follows:

1. Note the change in a metric from one release to the next (release j to release $j + 1$, for example).

2. If the change is in the desirable direction (failures/KLOC decrease, for example), treat the change as positive. If the change is in the undesirable direction, treat the change as negative.

3. If the change is an increase, divide it by the value of the metric in release $j + 1$. If the change is a decrease, divide it by the value of the metric in release j.

4. Average the values obtained in Step 3, taking into account the positive or negative sign. This is the change metric. The CM's numeric value, between −1 and 1, indicates the degree of process stability or

Stability should be evaluated with respect to a set of metrics, not a single metric.

instability with respect to the particular metric evaluated: a positive value indicates stability, a negative value indicates instability. Stability should be evaluated with respect to a set of metrics, not a single metric. You can obtain an overall stability metric by averaging the CM values across releases.

SAMPLE APPLICATION

We used the Shuttle application to illustrate these concepts because it is a large legacy project that has been evolving with increasing functionality since 1983.[3] We define, measure, and demonstrate both long-term metrics—those computed across a chronological sequence of releases—and short-term metrics—those computed within a single release. Across releases, we analyzed

♦ mean time to failure (MTTF),
♦ total failures normalized by the number of changes per KLOC,
♦ total test time normalized by the number of changes per KLOC,
♦ remaining failures normalized by the number of changes per KLOC, and
♦ time to next failure.

Within a given release, we analyzed
♦ total test time versus the number of remaining failures and
♦ the failure rate versus total test time.

The following examples show relationships drawn from predicted and actual metrics.

We used data collected from the developer of the NASA Space Shuttle's flight software covering the period 1983–1997, as shown in Table 1. Here A, ..., Q denote the shuttle's *operational increments*. An OI is defined as a software system comprised of modules and configured from a series of builds to meet Shuttle mission functional requirements.[4] For each OI, the table shows the release date by the contractor to NASA, total number of post-delivery failures, and failure severity, decreasing in severity from 1 to 4.

TABLE 1
CHARACTERISTICS OF MAINTAINED SOFTWARE ACROSS SHUTTLE RELEASES

Operational Increment	Release Date	Launch Date	Mission Duration (Days)	Reliability Prediction Date	Total Post Delivery Failures	Failure Severity	KLOC Change	Total Test Time (Days)	MTTF (Days)	Total Failures/ KLOC	Total Test Time/ KLOC
A	1/9/83	No Flights		9/12/85	6	One 2 / Five 3s	8.0	1078	179.7	0.750	134.8
B	12/12/83	30/8/84	6	14/8/84	10	Two 2s / Eight 3s	11.4	4096	409.6	0.877	359.3
C	8/6/84	12/4/85	7	17/1/85	10	Two 2s / Seven 3s / One 4	5.9	4060	406.0	1.695	688.1
D	5/10/84	26/11/85	7	22/10/85	12	Five 2s / Seven 3s	12.2	2307	192.3	0.984	189.1
E	15/2/85	12/1/86	6	11/5/89	5	One 2N / Four 3s	8.8	1873	374.6	0.568	212.8
F	17/12/85				2	Two 3s	6.6	412	206.0	0.300	62.4
G	5/6/87				3	One 1 / Two 3s	6.3	3077	1025.7	0.476	488.4
H	13/10/88				3	Two 1N's / One 3	7.0	540	180.0	0.429	77.1
I	29/6/89				3	Three 3s	12.1	2632	877.3	0.248	217.5
J	18/6/90	2/8/91	9	19/7/91	7	Seven 3s	29.4	515	73.6	0.238	17.5
K	2/5/91				1	One 1	21.3	182			8.5
L	15/6/92				3	One 1N / One 2 / One 3	34.4	1337	445.7	0.087	38.9
M	15/7/93				1	One 3	24.0	386			16.1
N	13/7/94				1	One 3	10.4	121			11.6
O	18/10/95	19/11/96	18	26/9/96	5	One 2 / Four 3s	15.3	344	68.8	0.327	22.5
P	16/7/96				3	One 3 / Two 3s	7.3	272	90.0	0.411	37.3
Q	5/3/97				1	One 3	11.0	75			6.8

We also show the source code changes and additions (in KLOC) and the time used to test each OI. Because the flight software runs around the clock, in simulation, test, or flight, "total test time" refers to continuous execution time from the time of release. For the seven OIs with a sufficient sample size—that is, A, B, C, D, E, J, and O had enough post-delivery failures to predict software reliability—the table shows the OI letter in bold and the launch date, mission duration, and the date when the reliability prediction was made.

Fortunately for the safety of the crew and mission, there have been few post-delivery failures. Unfortunately, from the standpoint of prediction, this leaves us with a sparse set of observed failures from which to estimate reliability model parameters. Nevertheless, predictions were made prior to launch date for OIs with as few as five failures spanning many months of maintenance and testing. In the case of OI E, the prediction was made after launch because we had no prelaunch failures to use in the prediction model.

Because of the scarcity of failure data, we also made predictions using all severity levels of failure data. Doing so proved beneficial when making reliability risk assessments using the number of remaining failures. For example, rather than specifying that the number of predicted remaining failures must not exceed one severity-1 failure, the criterion

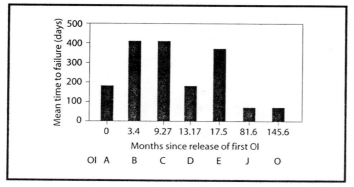

FIGURE 1. Mean time to failure, plotted against operational increment (OI) release time, based on historical data for the NASA Space Shuttle.

could specify that the prediction not exceed one failure of any type—a more conservative criterion.[4]

KEY RELATIONSHIPS

We want our maintenance effort to result in increasing software reliability over a sequence of releases. By presenting a graph to management of this relationship over time, accompanied by CM calculations, we can show whether the reliability aspect of long-term maintenance has been successful.

To measure reliability, I used both predicted and actual metrics values. I used predictions to estimate reliability before the software was deployed. Favorable predictions give you confidence that it is safe to deploy the software; unfavorable predictions may prompt you to delay deployment and perform additional inspection and testing.

Predictions also help you to assess whether the maintenance process improves reliability. If the predictions indicate that reliability is not improving, you will be able to use this information to improve your maintenance process. In addition to making predictions, you must collect and analyze historical reliability data, which shows in retrospect whether your maintenance actions increased reliability. Also, you do not want the test effort to be disproportionate to the amount of code you change or to the reliability you achieve as a result of maintenance.

We want mean time to failure (MTTF), computed as total test time divided by the total number of failures during testing, to show an increasing trend across releases, indicating increasing reliability. Similarly, we want the total number of failures and faults, normalized by the number of code changes per KLOC, to show a decreasing trend across releases, indicating that reliability is increasing with respect to code changes. Figures 1 and 2 plot actual historical data for MTTF and total failures per KLOC, respectively, against OI release time. This is the number of months elapsed since the OI's release, using 0 as the release time of OI A. The CM value for MTTF is –0.060, indicating slight instability, and 0.087 for normalized total failures, indicating marginal stability. These plots and CMs help us assess whether our maintenance process exhibits long-term stability.

We want the normalized total test time per KLOC to show a decreasing trend across releases, indicating that test effort is decreasing with respect to code changes. To assess whether this was achieved, we plotted total test time per KLOC across releases, as

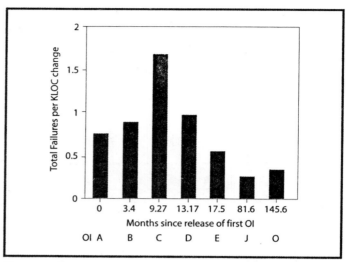

FIGURE 2. Failures per thousand lines of code (KLOC), plotted against operational increment release time, based on historical data for the NASA Space Shuttle.

shown in Figure 3, and then computed the CM value for this plot. The CM was 0.116, indicating stability with respect to test effort efficiency.

RELIABILITY PREDICTIONS

So far, our analysis has used only actual data. Now we include both actual data and predictions for those seven OIs for which we could make predictions. Using the Schneidewind Model[4-8] and the SMERFS (Statistical Modeling and Estimation of Reliability Functions for Software) reliability tool,[9] we show prediction equations using 30-day time intervals and make predictions for OI A, B, C, D, E, J, and O. Other models are also available.[5,9]

Total failures

To predict failures over the life of the software, expressed as total failures in the range [1,∞], we use

$$F(\infty) = \alpha/\beta + X_{s-1} \qquad (1)$$

where
  ♦ α is the initial failure rate,
  ♦ β is the rate of change of the failure rate,
  ♦ s is the starting time interval for using failure counts to compute parameters α and β, and
  ♦ X_{s-1} is the observed failure count in the range $[1, s-1]$.

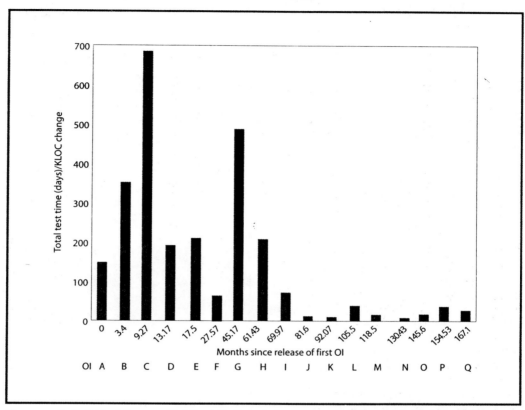

FIGURE 3. Total test time per KLOC, plotted against operational increment (OI) release time, based on historical data for the NASA Space Shuttle.

TABLE 2 RELIABILITY OF MAINTAINED SOFTWARE: PREDICTIONS VERSUS ACTUALS						
	Total Failures		**Remaining Failures**		**Time to Next Failure**	
Operational Increment	**Predicted**	**Actual**	**Predicted**	**Actual**	**Predicted (Intervals*)**	**Actual (Intervals*)**
A	6.44	6	1.44	1	19.70	8.26
B	9.78	10	3.78	4	3.49	1.43
C	6.85	10	1.85	5	2.03	5.83
D	14.60	12	8.60	6	6.54	4.77
E	6.04	5	2.04	1	19.27	10.90
J	13.32	7	7.32	1	2.57	3.97
O	5.02	5	0	0	No Failure	No Failure

*Interval length is 30 days.

Table 2 shows the predicted and actual total failures (using values from Table 1 for the selected OIs), while Table 3 shows total and remaining failures normalized by number of changes per KLOC.

We want predicted normalized total failures to show a decreasing trend across releases. The CM value for this data is .115, indicating stability with respect to this metric.

TABLE 3					
TOTAL & REMAINING FAILURES NORMALIZED BY MAINTENANCE CHANGE TO CODE					
		Normalized Total Failures		**Normalized Remaining Failures**	
Operational Increment	**KLOC Change**	**Predicted**	**Actual**	**Predicted**	**Actual**
A	8.0	0.805	0.750	0.180	0.125
B	11.4	0.857	0.877	0.332	0.351
C	5.9	1.161	1.695	0.314	0.847
D	12.2	1.197	0.984	0.705	0.492
E	8.8	0.686	0.568	0.232	0.114
J	29.4	0.453	0.238	0.249	0.034
O	15.3	0.328	0.327	0	0

Remaining failures

To predict remaining failures $r(t)$ at time t, we use[5-7]

$$r(t) = F(\infty) - X_t \qquad (2)$$

This is the predicted total failures over the life of the software, minus the observed failure count at time t.

We approximate actual remaining failures at time t by subtracting the observed failure count at time t from the observed total failure count at time T, where T is much longer than t. We want $r(t)$ and the actual remaining failures, normalized by the number of changes per KLOC, to show decreasing trends across releases. Figure 4 shows predicted and actual values plotted for the seven OIs. The CM values for these plots are 0.107 and 0.277, respectively, indicating stability with respect to remaining failures.

Time to next failure

We predict the time for the next F_t failures to occur by computing[4,5,7]

$$T_F(t) = \log[\alpha/(\alpha - \beta(X_{s,t} + F_t))] /\beta - (t - s + 1) \qquad (3)$$

where

t is the current time interval,

$X_{s,t}$ is the observed failure count in the range $[s, t]$, and

F_t is the specified number of failures to occur after interval t.

Table 2 shows the predicted and actual times to the next failure. We want $T_F(t)$ to show an increasing trend across releases. Figure 5 shows predicted and actual values plotted for six OIs (OI O had no failures). The CM values for these plots are –0.152 and –0.065, respectively, indicating slight instability with respect to time to next failure.

We use the predicted values of total failures, remaining failures, and time to next failure as indicators of the risk of future software operation: is the

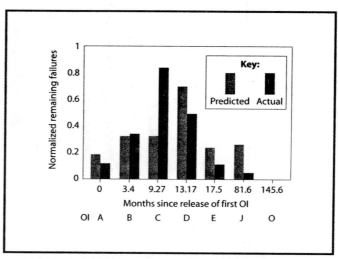

FIGURE 4. Reliability of maintained software, predicted and actual values of remaining failures, plotted for the Space Shuttle's seven operational increments.

predicted future reliability of the software an acceptable risk? If unacceptable, improving the maintained product or the maintenance process may be called for. We use the actual values to measure the software's reliability, and the risk of deploying it, that result from maintenance actions.

LONG-TERM RESULTS

Table 4 summarizes the change metric values. Overall, the average CM values indicate marginal stability. You can use this table as a template for constructing a similar one for your applications. Negative results could be caused by greater software functionality and complexity across releases, a maintenance process that needs to be improved, or a combination of these causes. Regardless of the cause, if the majority of the table's results and the

Focus

Metric	Actual	Predicted
TABLE 4		
CHANGE METRIC SUMMARY		
Mean Time to Failure	−0.060	
Total Test Time per KLOC	0.116	
Total Failures per KLOC	0.087	0.115
Remaining Failures per KLOC	0.277	0.107
Time to Next Failure	−0.065	−0.152
Average	**0.071**	

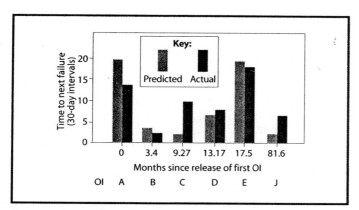

FIGURE 5. Reliability of maintained software, predicted and actual values for time to next failure, plotted across six operational increments for the Space Shuttle.

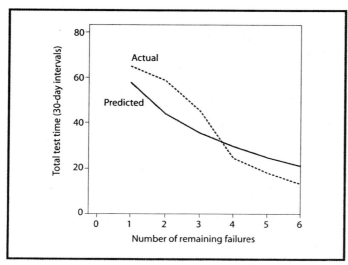

FIGURE 6. Predicted and actual values for total maintenance test time to achieve remaining failures, plotted for the Space Shuttle's operational increment D.

average CM were negative, management would know to investigate the cause.

SHORT-TERM RESULTS

In addition to the long-term maintenance criteria we've established, we want the maintenance effort to result in increasing reliability *within* each release or OI. Also, we want the test effort to be efficient in finding residual faults for a given OI. In the analysis that follows we use predictions and actual data for a selected OI, D, to illustrate the process.

Total test time

We use Equation 4[5,7] to predict the total test time required to achieve a specified number of remaining failures, $r(t_t)$, at time t_t:

$$t_t = \log[\alpha/(\beta[r(t_t)])]/\beta + (s - 1) \qquad (4)$$

Table 5 shows predicted and actual total test times for five OIs. In Figure 6, Equation 4 is plotted against the given number of remaining failures for OI D. The two plots have similar shapes and show the typical asymptotic characteristic of reliability (such as remaining failures versus total test time). The plots indicate the possibility of big gains in reliability in the early part of testing; eventually the gains become marginal as testing continues. Predicted values can be used to gauge how much maintenance test effort would be required to achieve desired reliability goals and whether the predicted amount of total test time is technically and economically feasible. Actual values can be used to judge whether the maintenance test effort has been efficient in relation to the reliability achieved.

To judge whether your predictions have sufficient accuracy, compute the average relative error using the formula ((actual – predicted)/actual). Our predictions for total failures, remaining failures, time

R	Operational Increment Total Test Time (30-Day Intervals) Required to Achieve R Remaining Failures									
	OI A		OI B		OI C		OI D		OI J	
	Predicted	Actual	Predicted	Actual	Predicted	Actual	Predicted	Actual	Predicted	Actual
1	34.15	27.67	17.00	87.53	40.22	43.80	58.08	65.03	48.76	13.20
2			11.58	10.37	31.57	27.07	43.56	58.27		
3			8.41	9.63	26.51	16.93	35.06	45.17		
4			6.15	8.20	22.93	13.93	29.04	23.70		
5					20.14	7.43	24.36	17.50		
6							20.54	12.73		

TABLE 5
TOTAL TEST TIME: PREDICTIONS VERSUS ACTUALS

A blank entry means that there were no more remaining failures for the operational increment.

to next failure, and total test time have averaged a 22 percent error rate.

Failure rate

We should expect an initial period of instability after each release of an OI, reflected in an increasing failure rate (1/MTTF) as personnel learn how to maintain the new software. After this period, we want the failure rate to decrease over the OI's total test time, indicating increasing reliability.

Figure 7 shows the failure rate for OI D, computed from a listing of its complete failure history, plotted against total test time since its release. As total test time increases, the failure rate asymptotically approaches zero, demonstrating short-term stability. You can use such plots to assess whether your maintenance process shows short-term stability, reflected by increases in reliability as changes are made to the code.

The type of results shown in Figures 6 and 7 indicate whether the maintenance process is stable in the short term. You don't need to compute CM for these metrics because they are continuous functions and not discrete values, as was the case with long-term analysis. In addition, the curves have obviously decreasing trends, which indicate stability. If you obtain contrary results, you should investigate if such results are caused by the growing functionality and complexity of the OI as it is being maintained, a maintenance process that needs to be improved, or a combination of these causes.

Based on both predictive and retrospective use of maintenance, reliability, and test metrics, I conclude that it is feasible to measure the stability of a maintenance process for legacy systems. Further, these factors can be integrated into a unified approach for assessing the impact of the maintenance process on the reliability and risk of deploying the software.

Any organization can apply this approach because the methods are not domain-specific. The

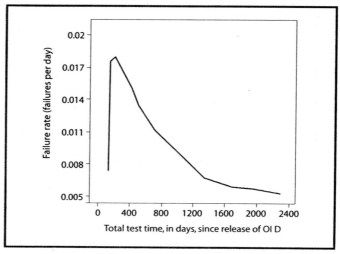

FIGURE 7. Failure rate of Space Shuttle operational increment D, plotted against total test time since the increment's release date.

next step in this research will be an attempt to quantify the functionality introduced in each release—a formidable challenge. ❖

ACKNOWLEDGMENTS

Support for this project was provided by William Farr of the Naval Surface Warfare Center and Ted Keller, Patti Thornton, and Julie Barnard of Lockheed-Martin. I also acknowledge the reviewers' helpful comments and suggestions.

REFERENCES

1. M.M. Lehman, "Programs, Life Cycles, and Laws of Software Evolution," *Proc. IEEE,* Vol. 68, No. 9, Sept. 1980, pp. 1060-1076.
2. N.F. Schneidewind, "Measuring and Evaluating Maintenance Process Using Reliability, Risk, and Test Metrics," *Proc. Int'l Conf. Software Maintenance,* IEEE Comp. Soc. Press, Los Alamitos, Calif., 1997, pp. 232-239.
3. C. Billings et al., "Journey to a Mature Software Process," *IBM Systems J.,* Vol. 33, No. 1, 1994, pp. 46-61.
4. N.F. Schneidewind, "Reliability Modeling for Safety Critical

Software," *IEEE Trans. Reliability*, Vol. 46, No.1, Mar. 1997, pp.88-98.

5. "Recommended Practice for Software Reliability," R-013-1992, Am. Nat'l Standards Inst./Am. Inst. of Aeronautics and Astronautics, Washington, DC, 1993.

6. T. Keller, N.F. Schneidewind, and P.A. Thornton, "Predictions for Increasing Confidence in the Reliability of the Space Shuttle Flight Software," *Proc. AIAA Computing in Aerospace 10*, Am. Nat'l Standards Inst./Am. Inst. of Aeronautics and Astronautics, Washington, DC, 1995, pp. 1-8.

7. N.F. Schneidewind, "Software Reliability Model with Optimal Selection of Failure Data," *IEEE Trans. Software Eng.*, Vol. 19, No. 11, Nov. 1993, pp. 1095-1104.

8. N.F. Schneidewind and T.W. Keller, "Application of Reliability Models to the Space Shuttle," *IEEE Software*, July 1992, pp. 28-33.

9. W.H. Farr and O.D. Smith, *Statistical Modeling and Estimation of Reliability Functions for Software (SMERFS) Users Guide*, NAVSWC TR-84-373, Revision 3, Naval Surface Weapons Center, Dahlgren, Va., revised Sept. 1993.

About the Author

Norman F. Schneidewind is professor of Information Sciences and director of the Software Metrics Research Center at the Naval Postgraduate School. He is the developer of the Schneidewind software reliability model used by NASA to assist prediction of the Space Shuttle software's reliability. Previously, Schneidewind held several technical management positions in the computer industry, where he directed IT projects in both the public and private sectors.

Schneidewind received a BSEE from the University of California Berkeley, an MSEE and MSCS from San Jose State University, and an MSOR and PhD with a major in operations research from the University of Southern California. He is a Life Fellow of IEEE.

Address questions about this article to Schneidewind at Code IS/Ss, Naval Postgraduate School, Monterey, CA 93943; nschneid@nps.navy.mil.

333

FOCUS

Reprinted from IEEE Software,
July/Aug. 1998, pp. 28-33.

• • •

Legacy software systems represent a significant investment of time and resources, and provide important services. The restoration of this legacy telephony system generated some lessons of widespread interest to all developers.

• • •

Restoring a Legacy: Lessons Learned

Spencer Rugaber, Georgia Institute of Technology

Jim White, Nortel

n 1508, Pope Julius II commissioned Michelangelo Buonarroti to paint the ceiling of the Cappella Sistina (Sistine Chapel) in Rome. Michelangelo labored for five years—lying on his back much of that time—to complete the task. In 1538, Pope Paul III called him back to add an enhancement, the Last Judgment, over the altar; this took seven more years. Michelangelo's work on the Sistine Chapel is a legacy—a gift from the past that would be impossible to recreate and warrants preserving. In 1965, the Holy See commissioned a team of scientists, historians, and artists to restore the paintings. Though the restoration decision stirred controversy, work proceeded over the next 30 years. Although no software system compares to Michelangelo's masterpieces, the restoration process offers striking parallels to software reengineering.

Software systems can also be legacies—though in this context "legacy" often connotes a burden rather than a gift from the past. The RT-1000 telephony system was originally built by a team of about 70 developers over five years, and cost millions of dollars. In its current incarnation, it produces millions of dollars of revenue, provides service to thousands of users, and would be prohibitively expensive to recreate. Hence the decision was made to restore and enhance it instead.

335

Over the last four years, the RT-1000 development team has worked to improve quality and add features, turning a neglected system into a high-quality software product. With one eye looking back at the legacy of Michelangelo's work, we can learn something by examining the factors that enhanced the RT-1000 restoration process as well as those that hindered it.

SYSTEM DESCRIPTION

RT-1000 is a telephony software system for automated call distribution. An ACD system employs software features that distribute incoming telephone calls to a designated set of agent positions. An agent might handle service requests, accept sales orders, or supply information to callers. If all agents are busy, the calls are queued according to their priority and order of arrival. When an agent becomes available, the system presents the call that has been waiting the longest.

ACD features allow a supervisor to monitor the quality of service provided to incoming callers. Status displays indicate how well different queues or individual agents are performing and where potential problems may exist. Detailed management reports highlight service factors such as average waiting times and the number of abandoned calls. To match fluctuations in call traffic, ACD supervisors can fine-tune employee schedules or even reconfigure an entire call center in real time.

Load management capabilities allow a customer's ACD administrator to monitor and manage call load and configuration. Management information system capabilities let customers generate real-time displays and statistical reports on the performance of a group of agents. A typical customer for an ACD is a telephone company that uses it to handle customer service requests for a whole state, and a typical installation includes 5,000 agents and 150 supervisors.

Figure 1 shows how the legacy RT-1000 system was configured before restoration commenced.

Initial status

Michelangelo's Sistine Chapel paintings cover more than 9,000 square feet. Previous restorations, including efforts to censor parts of the nude figures, left doubts as to the original conception. And centuries of soot from candles burned in the chapel had done an unknown amount of damage.

The RT-1000 has somewhat similar (if less dra-

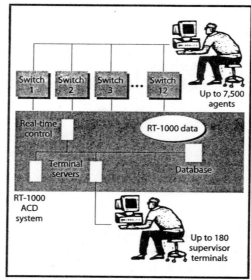

FIGURE 1. The original RT-1000 system configuration locked customers into outdated hardware, allowed no local area network connectivity, and provided no data transfer protocols to support data archiving.

matic) history. It was developed by a third-party software vendor in the late 1980s and acquired by Nortel in 1990. For the next three years Nortel enhanced and maintained it before outsourcing it to another vendor to be systematically rewritten. This effort failed and the system was returned to Nortel in mid-1994. By this time, the original design team had been disbanded and scattered, and the product's six customer organizations were quite unhappy.

RT-1000 was assigned to Nortel's Atlanta Technology Park laboratory. No staff members there had any experience with ACD software, and, due to another project's cancellation, staff morale was quite low.

Technical difficulties

RT-1000 is a complex system. Several things made it difficult to deal with:

♦ it was very large,

♦ it had a small user base,

♦ it comprised third-party software and hardware components,

♦ it lacked formal software process and version control,

♦ it lacked documentation, and

♦ it was not Y2K compliant.

SISTINE FACTS

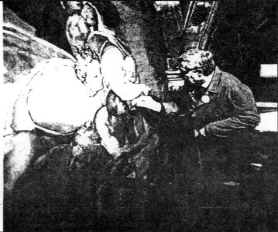

To learn more about the Sistine Chapel restoration, read "An Account of the Restoration" and other selections in *The Sistine Chapel: A Glorious Restoration* (C. Pietrangeli et al., eds., Harry N. Abrams Publishers, New York, 1994). On the Web, take a virtual tour of the chapel and view restoration efforts at http://www.christusrex.org/www1/sisteen/0-Tour.html.

Size

The system constitutes about 500,000 lines of code that implement a long list of powerful and interrelated features. The system is written in multiple programming languages including Fortran (for the computational components), C (for the real-time part), an SQL-like fourth-generation language (for the MIS), and various Unix scripting languages (for system configuration). The system combines multiple architectural styles including real-time (managing up to 50 concurrent processes), MIS, computational, and an event-driven graphical user interface.

Moreover, the RT-1000 must satisfy a long list of difficult, nonfunctional requirements such as data integrity, real-time response, distributed processing, reliability, information security, usability, performance under load, and openness to customer and third-party extensions.

User base

The small user base meant that field trials could be conducted with at most two customers prior to general delivery. And the widely varying ways in which customers use the system presented further difficulties. For example, some customers use the workforce management feature as a key part of their business, while others do not use it at all. This makes field trials problematic in terms of guaranteeing that features are exercised from a true user perspective prior to making the software generally available.

Moreover, when the system was first moved to Atlanta, no one knew exactly how customers used the system. One customer used third-party (custom-designed) software to postprocess reporting data. When the RT-1000 team modified a standard report (to add an extra column for additional precision, as other customers requested), the downstream software could no longer process the report. The customer based its payroll processing on the downstream software output and was therefore highly sensitive to this change, yet the design team often has no knowledge of these off-board systems.

Another customer contracted with a third-party company for display of RT-1000 data on LED-based wallboards in remote offices. When a new screen sequence created a problem with the wallboard display, the wallboard company contacted the development team requesting information, to the complete surprise of the RT-1000 team.

Third-party components

The RT-1000's third-party components were out of date and no longer supported by their vendors. For example, the system included an out-of-date operating system with no vendor support and no means of controlling changes to the field-deployed versions. A commercial vendor's database management system was also out of date. The hardware platform could no longer support customer demands. Customer terminal software was proprietary and failed to conform to the emerging Windows-based industry standard. Finally, the distributed-component interconnectivity mechanism required upgrading the local area network.

337

Other issues

Software process was nonexistent, as was version control. Product testing was not formalized. And over 300 outstanding customer service requests existed. Little if any documentation of the software architecture existed, and the code itself contained virtually no comments. And, of course, RT-1000 faced a serious Year 2000 exposure.

RESTORATION STRATEGY AND LESSONS LEARNED

During the first two years, the development team sought to determine its contractual exposures (the classes of deliverables Nortel still owed to its customers), and to categorize its CSRs (the classes of known problems in the system). Armed with this knowledge, we focused on making improvements with the biggest payoff.

For example, we gave priority to a single additional feature that responded to three contractual issues and also addressed several CSRs. Similarly, the two largest classes of CSRs accounted for over half the reported system issues, so we focused on these. As designers incrementally developed expertise in these areas, they were able to address issues with increasing speed. As the major classes were exhausted, repair efforts branched out into other areas.

Restoring the paintings in the Sistine Chapel was also a massive undertaking. The Last Judgment alone required more than a year of preparation, both in a laboratory and experimenting on the painting itself. The restorers had to contend with technical issues that varied across the surface of the painting, and had to develop an elaborate cleaning process including a bath of distilled water and chemical mixtures, sometimes filtered through layers of paper and sometimes applied with sponges. Restoration involved not only cleaning the painting but removing retouchings added over the centuries. Finally, the restorers had to design an entirely new environment for the Chapel, including filtered air and a tailored microclimate.

Likewise, restoring a software system involves far more than updating lines of code. In a sense, it requires constructing a whole new development environment—while continuing to support customers and develop new features.

Current status

Over the past three years, the RT-1000 team has restored the system to address many of the problems mentioned:

♦ We reduced CSRs from 300 to less than 15.

♦ We placed all RT-1000 software into a standard Nortel version-control library and instituted an automated, reproducible load-building process.

♦ We automated over 80 percent of the original 900 test cases, reducing load regression times from around 90 staff-weeks to under five. We introduced formal capacity testing using simulation software to parallel field conditions of up to 200 users (rather than rounding up 10 people on a weekend to stress-test the system manually, as was formerly the case).

♦ We negotiated software maintenance and support contracts with the OS and hardware vendors to guarantee that all OS software for delivered systems can come only from the development team, thus ensuring more standard configurations.

♦ We upgraded system hardware and the accompanying OS and developed a long-term hardware migration plan.

♦ We obtained ISO-9001 certification for the development process.

♦ We improved customer relationships by encouraging regular customer visits to the Atlanta lab.

♦ We upgraded the database management system to its latest release.

> ## In a sense, restoring a software system requires constructing a whole new development environment.

♦ We published the architecture and opened it up to customer and third-party enhancements.

♦ We added significant new functionality.

The restoration has enabled a much more open and flexible architecture, as Figure 2 shows.

Tools

At the start of the project, we researched commercial, source-browsing software to support the code-understanding process. Eventually, we purchased the most sophisticated commercially available tool. Although it provided powerful analysis and browsing capabilities, it could not deal with multiple processes: different processes contained subprograms with the same name, and the tool confused these. Moreover, soon after delivery, the providing company went bankrupt. We have yet to find

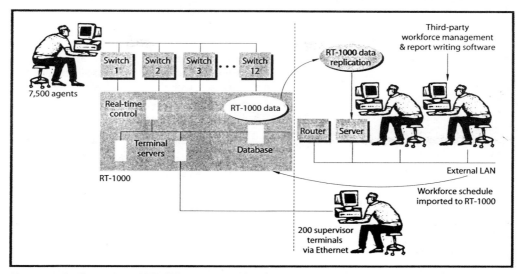

FIGURE 2. The restored RT-1000 system configuration opened up the system to new hardware, allowed the export of results to third-party report writers, supported the import of customer workforce-management schedules, and provided off-board data replication.

a tool addressing the name collision problem.

We also sought tools to support Fortran-to-C conversion. Approximately half of the original RT-1000 code was written in Fortran, but we felt that C would enhance system performance and be easier to maintain. We used a freeware toolset to support the conversion effort and, while the trial was technically a success, the resulting C code was so convoluted that it was impossible to maintain or modify. As an alternative, we increased the use of configuration scripts (makefiles), which allowed C and Fortran code to coexist in compiled modules. This gave designers a choice of languages for working on any given feature or problem.

We are now using an automated Web-based metrics tool that evaluates the quality of software systems by measuring complexity and maintainability using standard statistical techniques. This tool will help us periodically assess code releases as they are developed and assure customers that quality is being incorporated throughout the entire development life cycle. The tool will also permit more informed decisions on software architecture modifications by bringing attention to areas that need to be overhauled or eliminated.

Verification

Restoration has greatly improved product verification. In place of marginally documented single-line descriptions, we now have fully described test cases. We have also added a number of our own test cases (both for systemic tests and to test features we have added). We have automated a large part of the test suite so as to easily compare new versions of the

code with past runs to detect GUI or data errors. Finally, we have added true capacity testing to our suite, and can now emulate an entire complement of supervisors rather than being limited to the number of physical PCs we could connect to the system in the same way customers do.

With a product as complex and flexible as the RT-1000, however, the task of verification is daunting. The more we learn about rigorous testing, the more we realize we need to learn.

The Web

At the start of the RT-1000 effort, we knew the development team would have to learn a lot about the system. But how could this knowledge be effectively shared? We created an internal hypertext of Web pages to address this issue, and have found the Web to be a real ally in managing this project. We began to use the Web as an information repository and retrieval system, and aligning it with our ISO-9001 processes and goals has made adherence to the standard easy. Also, we added tools to automatically keep updated problem lists for easy reference and historical tracking.

Project transfer

Transferring a project of this size across geographic and managerial boundaries took longer than expected. The first three months included physical transfer and setup of the hardware and software as well as staff training. Interfaces to other groups, such as verification, field support, and product management had to be reestablished. Technical responsibility for the software components had to be par-

339

titioned and a software maintenance infrastructure built. It took at least a year to gain full productivity.

We found that when the restoration project originates from the outside and differs radically from the original one it replaces, it may cause large staff turnover. In our case, more than half the original staff either left the company or transferred internally. In such a case, it would be better to leave the project at its original geographic location and hire new staff. This would add some complications but reduce others and, in the end, probably be simpler and less costly than moving the project.

Also, higher management needs to offer extra support to a project such as this to reassure those assigned to it that the corporation deems it a worthwhile effort. A lack of corporate support to back up the organizational decisions can further delay and complicate the project.

Organization

The most important problem we had to overcome was the lack of a single point of managerial control. At first, every element of the team (design, verification, technical assistance, and product management) reported upwards through different management structures. But when a disagreement developed, we could not resolve it quickly. The only practical solution was to have reporting lines converge at a managerial level closer to the working-level groups; otherwise, a very high-level manager would have had to administer petty details.

CSRs

Customer service requests had been piling up within Nortel prior to the project being farmed out to the third-party company, at which time the customers were told that "the rewrite will fix everything!" During the rewrite period, problem reports continued to come in, but there was no longer a design group within Nortel tasked with addressing them. When the rewrite failed to materialize, customers demanded action on their backlog of problems, which had now grown appreciable.

We took a phased approach to solving the CSRs. We initiated weekly meetings with senior managers (design, product line management, and testing) to discuss one customer's list that, week to week, we pared down. Also, we made efforts across the board to solve some issues independently. Managers worked to classify the large pool of issues by affected areas (database, reports, workforce management, real-time, and so forth). We targeted the area with the highest customer interest and the most problems for software overhaul via features, which addressed some of the CSRs as well. We also removed the CSR list's duplicate and "non-issue" elements via reviews.

During the subsequent release, we addressed the next most important set of issues with a feature enhancement. We tackled the next most troublesome list once we had reduced the first; within 18 months, we had radically shortened it.

Restoration of the Sistine Chapel painting took over 30 years of painstaking effort. The result enables us to fully appreciate one of the most glorious human artistic endeavors. Legacy software restoration can likewise entail a massive commitment of resources by management and software developers. In both cases, the effort requires careful planning, a well-thought-out process, deep technical understanding, and a great deal of patience. In the case of RT-1000, about 20 developers labored over three years to restore the system to full functionality. The resulting increase in customer satisfaction and product revenue has made the effort worthwhile. ❖

About the Authors

Spencer Rugaber is a senior research scientist in the College of Computing at the Georgia Institute of Technology. His research interests include software engineering, specifically software evolution and program comprehension. He is currently Principal Investigator in several research projects funded by the National Science Foundation, the Defense Advanced Research Projects Agency, and private industry.

Rugaber received a PhD in computer science from Yale University. He is vice chair of the IEEE Committee on Reverse Engineering and past program co-chair of the Workshop on Program Comprehension.

Jim White has worked at Nortel in Atlanta for more than nine years. His project experience has included developing switching access products and MIS systems, working on both design and management. Prior to joining Nortel, he worked on F-16 flight simulators at General Dynamics.

White received a BSEE and an MSEE from the Georgia Institute of Technology.

Address questions about this article to Rugaber at the College of Computing, Georgia Institute of Technology, Atlanta, GA 30332; spencer@cc.gatech.edu. White may be reached at Nortel, 5555 Windward Parkway, Alpharetta, Georgia, 30004; jwhite@nortel.ca.